1-2-73

Comparative
Economic Systems

COMPARATIVE ECONOMIC SYSTEMS

JOHN E. ELLIOTT

University of Southern California

with the collaboration of

ROBERT W. CAMPBELL

Indiana University

PRENTICE-HALL, INC.

Englewood Cliffs, New Jersey

ISBN: 0–13–153379–7

Library of Congress Catalog Card Number: 72-4528

10 9 8 7 6 5 4 3 2 1

Printed in the United States of America

Prentice-Hall International, Inc., London
Prentice-Hall of Australia, Pty. Ltd., Sydney
Prentice-Hall of Canada, Ltd., Toronto
Prentice-Hall of India Private Limited, New Delhi
Prentice-Hall of Japan, Inc., Tokyo

Selections from Douglas Jay, *Socialism in the New Society*, by permission of the author's agent, Harold Ober Associates Inc. Selections from *Politics, Economics and Welfare* by Robert Dahl and Charles E. Lindblom, copyright 1953 by Harper & Row, Publishers, Inc.; and selections from *Capitalism, Socialism, and Democracy*, 3rd edition, by Joseph A. Schumpeter, copyright 1942, 1947 by Joseph A. Schumpeter, copyright 1950 by Harper & Row, Publishers, Inc., reprinted by permission of the publishers. Selections reprinted by permission of Schocken Books Inc. from *The Conservative Enemy* by C.A.R. Crosland, copyright © 1962 by C.A.R. Crosland. Selections from *The General Theory of Employment, Interest, and Money* by John Maynard Keynes by permission of the publishers, Harcourt Brace Jovanovich, Inc. Selections from Lange, Oskar and Fred M. Taylor, *On the Economic Theory of Socialism*, Benjamin Lippincott, editor, University of Minnesota Press, Mpls., © 1938 University of Minnesota; also available in hardcover from August M. Kelley Publishers (1970) and in paperback from McGraw-Hill Book Company (1964). Selection from Herbert Spencer, *Social Statics*, courtesy of Appleton-Century-Crofts. Selection by Adolph A. Berle, Jr. and Gardiner C. Means reproduced by permission from *The Modern Corporations and Private Property*, published and copyrighted 1932 by Commerce Clearing House, Inc., Chicago, Illinois 60646. Selections reprinted by permission of the publisher, from Marvin E. Rozen: *Comparative Economic Planning* (Lexington, Mass.: D.C. Heath and Company, 1967). Selection from *The Method of Freedom* by Walter Lipman by permission of the Macmillan Company and George Allen & Unwin Ltd. Selections from *Selected Correspondence* by Karl Marx and Frederick Engels, copyright © 1968; from *Imperialism: Highest Stage of Capitalism* by V.I. Lenin, copyright; from *Economic Theory of Socialism* by Maurice Dobb, copyright © 1955; from *Selected Works*, Vols. I and II, by Karl Marx, copyright © 1932; from *Soviet Economic Development* by Maurice Dobb, copyright © 1966; from *State and Revolution* by V.I. Lenin, copyright © 1932; from *The Communist Manifesto* by Karl Marx and Frederick Engels, copyright © 1948; reprinted by permission of International Publishers Co., Inc. Selections from *An Essay on Marxian Economics* by Joan Robinson by permission of St. Martin's Press and Macmillan London and Basingstoke. Selection from *The Great Transformation* by Karl Polanyi by permission of Holt, Rinehart and Winston, Inc. Selections from William Ebenstein, *Today's Isms: Communism, Fascism, Capitalism, Socialism*, 5th ed., © 1967; reprinted by permission of Prentice-Hall, Inc. Selections from *The General Theory of Employment Interest and Money* by John Maynard Keynes by permission of Macmillan London and Basingstoke. Selections reprinted by permission of Quadrangle Books from *Road to Reaction* by Herman Finer, copyright © 1945, 1963 by Herman Finer. Selection from *European Socialism*, Vol. II, by Carl Landauer, originally published by the University of California Press; reprinted by permission of the Regents of the University of California. Selections reprinted by permission of the owners, the President and Fellows of Harvard College, from *Essays of J.A. Schumpeter*, edited by Richard V. Clemence, Addison Wesley, Cambridge, Mass., 1951. Selections copyright © 1941 by James Burnham, reprinted from *The Managerial Revolution* by James Burnham, by permission of the John Day Company, Inc., publisher. Selections from *The Life of John Maynard Keynes* by Roy Harrod, and from *The Nature and Significance of Economic Science* by Lionel Robbins, by permission of Macmillan London and Basingstoke. Selections from *The Political Economy of Growth* by Paul Baran, copyright © 1957 by Monthly Review, Inc., reprinted by permission of Monthly Review Press. Selections from *The Theory of Capitalist Development* by Paul Sweezy, copyright © 1942 by Paul M. Sweezy; reprinted by permission of Monthly Review Press. Selections from *Economic Policy: Principles and Design* by Jan Tinbergen by permission of North-Holland Publishing Company, Amsterdam. Selections from *The Road to Serfdom* by Friedrich A. von Hayek, copyright © 1944; from *Individualism and Economic Order* by Friedrich A. von Hayek, copyright © 1948; from *Economic Policy for a Free Society* by Henry Simons, copyright © 1948; from *Adam Smith and Laissez-Faire* by Jacob Viner, copyright © 1927; from *The Economic Theory of Socialism: A Suggestion for Consideration* by Jan Drewnowski, copyright © 1961; from *Economic and Social Policy in a Democratic Society* by Frank Knight, copyright © 1950; reprinted by permission of the University of Chicago Press. Selection from *Freedom Under Planning* by Barbara Wooton, from *An Expenditure Tax* by C. F. Nicholas Kaldor, from *Role of the Economist as Official Advisor* by W. A. Johr and H. W. Singer, from *Principles of Private and Public Planning* by Wilhelm Keilhau, from *Principles of Economic Planning* by Arthur Lewis and from *Planning and the Price Mechanism* by James E. Meade, reprinted by permission of George Allen & Unwin Ltd. Figure 3.1 adapted from Richard Stone, "Models of the National Economy for Planning Purposes," in *Mathematics in the Social Sciences and Other Essays* (Cambridge, Mass.: M.I.T. Press, 1966), p. 69.

Contents

4 Competitive Market Capitalism 61

THE BASIC CHARACTER OF COMPETITIVE MARKET CAPITALISM. Units of Economic Decision and their Market Interdependence. Competitive Market Capitalism as a Planning System. CAPITALISM'S SOLUTION TO ITS ECONOMIC PROBLEMS. The Allocation of Resources. The Distribution of Income. Economic Stabilization and Full Employment. Economic Growth. THE CLASSIC CRITIQUE OF MONOPOLY. Monopoly and Resource Allocation. Monopoly and Income Distribution. Other Criticisms of Monopoly. Criticism of Monopoly versus Criticism of Capitalism. THE MAJOR CRITICISMS OF CAPITALISM. Critique of Capitalism at Less Than Its (Purely-Perfectly Competitive) Best. Critique of Capitalism at Its Best. A CONCLUDING NOTE. SUMMARY OF CHAPTER 4.

4 Appendix: Capitalism, Classical Liberalism, and Conservatism 98

Laissez-Faire: The Rejection of the State in Economic Life. From Classical Liberalism to Laissez-Faire Conservatism. Limited Government: The Role of the State in Economic life.

5 The Marxian Critique of Capitalist Industrialization 107

INTRODUCTION. Marxian Economics. General Features of Marxian Economic Theory. The Marxian Conception of Capitalism. DEFINITIONS AND TERMINOLOGY. Capital, Output, and Income. The Marxian Ratios. THE MARXIAN THEORY OF RESOURCE ALLOCATION, VALUE, AND PRICE. The De-Emphasis of Allocation in Marxian Economics. The Labor Theory of Value. THE MARXIAN THEORY OF CAPITALIST INDUSTRIALIZATION. The Distribution of Income: Mobilization of the Economic Surplus. Economic Growth: Investment of the Economic Surplus. Economic Instability. SUMMARY OF CHAPTER 5.

5 Appendix: The Marxian Theory of Capitalist Development and Transformation 134

THE MARXIAN THEORY OF HISTORY AND SOCIAL CLASSES. The Marxian Vision of Historical Development. Social Classes and Class Struggles. CAPITALIST DEVELOPMENT AND TRANSFORMATION. Increasing Severity of the Economic Cycle. Increasing Concentration and Centralization of Capital. Increasing Size, Concentration, Organization, Misery, and Antagonism of Workers. Increasing Capitalist Imperialism and Colonial Exploitation. Increasing State Oppression and Improbability of Genuine Social Reform. THE END OF CAPITALISM: MARX'S APOCALYPTIC VISION.

6 The Schumpeterian Theory of Capitalist Development 152

WHAT IS SCHUMPETERIAN CAPITALISM? ALLOCATIONAL AND DISTRIBUTIONAL PROCESSES OF THE STATIC AND STATIONARY CIRCUALR FLOW. SOURCES OF CAPITALIST

ECONOMIC DEVELOPMENT. The Concept of Economic Development. Innovation. Financing of Innovations. The Entrepreneur. ECONOMIC FLUCTUATIONS. The First Approximation: A Two-Phase Cycle. The Second Approximation: Secondary Waves and a Four-Phase Cycle. Third Approximation: Different and Simultaneous Cycles. ECONOMIC GROWTH. CAPITALISM'S PAST PERFORMANCE AND FUTURE PROSPECTS. The Record of the Past. The Promise of the Future. The Plausibility of the Extrapolation. Can Capitalism Survive? CONCLUSIONS: AFTER CAPITALISM, WHAT? SUMMARY OF CHAPTER 6.

WHAT IS KEYNESIAN CAPITALISM? THE KEYNESIAN CRITIQUE OF TRADITIONAL ECONOMIC THEORY. Allocation and Distribution Under Conditions of Full Employment Equilibrium. The Macroeconomics of Full Employment-Stability. TOOLS AND CONCEPTS OF KEYNESIAN ECONOMIC THEORY. The Scope of Keynesian Analysis. Keynesian Models of Aggregate Demand. KEYNESIAN ANALYSIS OF THE MAJOR PROBLEMS OF CAPITALISM. Unemployment. Inflation. Cyclical Fluctuations. Long-Run Problems and Prospects. GOVERNMENT ECONOMIC POLICY. Institutional Complementarity: The Agenda of Government. Goals of Economic Policy. The Instruments of Government Economic Policy. The Basic Strategy of Macroeconomic Policy. KEYNESIAN SOCIAL PHILOSOPHY, CAPITALISM, AND SOCIALISM. The Keynesian Position. Uses to Which Keynesian Policies Might Be Applied. SUMMARY OF CHAPTER 7. SELECTED READINGS FOR PART II.

A BASIC DUALITY IN THE MARXIAN VISION OF INDUSTRIALIZATION AND ECONOMIC DEVELOPMENT. Utopian Socialism and Crude Communism. THE TRANSITION FROM CAPITALISM TO SOCIALISM. When? Where? How? THE MARXIAN CONCEPTION OF SOCIALISM. THE ECONOMICS OF SOCIALISM IN THE MARXIAN VISION. Allocation of Resources. Distribution of Income. Economic Growth and Full Employment Stability. PURE OR IDEAL COMMUNISM: THE MARXIAN VISION OF THE PERFECT SOCIETY. Division of Labor and Distribution of Income in Affluent Communism. The Transformation of Man. CONCLUDING NOTE. SUMMARY OF CHAPTER 8.

INTRODUCTION. The Basic Character of the Neo-Austrian Critique. The Political Framework of the Neo-Austrian Critique of Socialism. Goals of Economic Planning. The Structure of Socialist Economic Organization. RATIONAL ECONOMIC CALCULATION, THE PRICE SYSTEM, AND SOCIALISM. The Necessity of Economic Calculation. The Necessity of a Competitive Price System. The Incompatibility

Goals: Critique of Consumer Sovereignty and Defense of Centralized Goal-Setting. Analysis of Conditions and Formulation of Plans. Execution of Plans and Techniques of Social Control. CENTRALIZED SOCIALISM AND OTHER MAJOR ECONOMIC GOALS. Economic Growth. Full-Employment Stability. Equity and Equality in the Distribution of Income. SUMMARY AND CONCLUSIONS TO CHAPTER 11. SOURCES CITED IN PART III.

WHAT IS MANAGED CAPITALISM? Introduction. Managed Capitalism: Theory, Practice, Movement. Structure and Organization of Managed Capitalism: Synopsis. LEVEL OF ECONOMIC DEVELOPMENT AND RESOURCE BASE: THE TECHNOLOGICAL AND ECONOMIC REVOLUTIONS. OWNERSHIP AND CONTROL OF INDUSTRY: THE CORPORATE AND MANAGERIAL REVOLUTIONS. Corporate Dominance: The Corporate Revolution. Separation of Stock Ownership and Managerial Control in the Large-Scale Corporation: The Managerial Revolution. Government Ownership and Control. THE LOCUS AND ORGANIZATION OF ECONOMIC POWER: THE ORGANIZATIONAL REVOLUTION. Corporate Power. The Organizational Revolution. Government as Manager. THE NEW BLEND OF SOCIAL PROCESSES. FROM ECONOMIC MOTIVATIONS TO SOCIAL GOALS: INCOME DISTRIBUTION AND THE WELFARE STATE. Economic Motives and Social Goals. Income Distribution. SUMMARY AND CONCLUSION: OLD AND NEW ELEMENTS.

VARIETIES OF PRICE SYSTEMS. Monopolistic Competition. Oligopoly. COUNTERVAILING AND SUPPLEMENTARY FACTORS IN MARKET CONTROL. Competition from the Entry of New Firms. Competition in Product Quality and Sales Promotion (Non-Price Competition). Competition as a Dynamic Process. Price System Controls over Business Firms. NON-MARKET PROCESSES: BUREAUCRACY, BARGAINING, AND DEMOCRACY. Bureaucracy. Bargaining. Democracy. MANAGED CAPITALISM AND SOCIAL GOALS. Efficiency in the Allocation of Resources. Managed Capitalism and Other Social Goals. SUMMARY TO CHAPTER 13.

WHAT IS DEMOCRATIC SOCIALISM? ENDS AND MEANS. Introduction. Democratic Socialist Goals and the Structure of Democratic Socialist Economic Organization. THE DEMOCRATIC SOCIALIST CRITIQUE. The Democratic Socialist Critique of Competitive Market, Laissez-Faire Capitalism. The Democratic Socialist Critique of Marxism. The Democratic Socialist Critique of Modified, Managed Capitalism. RECENT DEMOCRATIC SOCIALIST PROGRAMS AND PROPOSALS. Allocation of Resources. Distribution of Income and Wealth. Economic Stabilization and Growth. FROM MANAGED CAPITALISM TO DEMOCRATIC SOCIALISM? Social Ownership. Economic

Planning. Industrial Democracy and Worker Control of Industry. CONCLUSIONS. SUMMARY OF CHAPTER 14. SOURCES CITED IN PART IV.

Alternative Outline

Preface

Interest in the study of comparative economic systems has expanded significantly in the last several years. Most departments of economics offer at least one course in the area and many offer several. The establishment of specialized scholarly associations and the energy and space devoted to comparative economics at scholarly conferences and in professional journals demonstrate the heightened interest of the economics profession. Investigations of congressional committees, an outpouring of books and monographs, and feature articles in newspapers and magazines testify both to the subject's contemporary relevance and to public interest in it.

Contemporary economic systems have been characterized by diversity and dynamic change. Diversity in forms of economic organization heightens our interest in two major ways. First, it broadens our perspective and helps to offset a natural tendency toward parochialism. Second, a comparative study of economic organization sharpens our understanding of the functioning of our own economy. Recent change in economic organization—whether in the post-Stalinist economic reforms of the Communist countries, the establishment of institutions and agencies for accelerating economic development in newly emergent less developed nations, or the further evolution and modification of the character of economic life in the developed, democratic Western nations—has also been profound, and undoubtedly helps explain expanded interest in the subject.

This book is intended as a core text, primarily for upper division undergraduate courses in comparative economic systems. Its major focus is on theories of economic systems, both the classic systems of capitalism and socialism and their contemporary variants: managed capitalism, democratic socialism, and Stalinist and revisionist Communism. No previous study in economics beyond basic economic principles is presumed. To provide a bridge between the economic principles course and the study of economic systems and, at the same time, to enhance the comparability of different theories of economic organization, a common framework is used, emphasizing how economic systems do or might resolve such problems as resource allocation, income distribution, economic stability and employment, and economic growth.

The coverage is purposefully not comprehensive. Many teachers will wish to supplement the text with additional readings, to enable an examination of systems not incorporated in any major way (e.g., fascism, guild socialism, feudalism) or to provide further illustrative materials or applications of theories to actual economies. Suggestions for supplementary readings are given at the end of each major section.

The concentration upon classic and contemporary theories of economic systems reflects the character of and changes in the economics curriculum, the needs and backgrounds of students typically enrolling in this course, the availability of supplementary literature, and the importance of theoretical concepts and ideas in the light of rapid institutional change.

The economics curriculum at many colleges and universities has changed substantially over the last two decades. Rapid and bewildering change and diversity in actual economic systems, combined with a tremendous expansion of applied and descriptive studies of particular national economies, has made the traditional attempt at comprehensive coverage of economic systems in one course increasingly difficult. At the same time, the expansion of specialized courses in Soviet-type economies, has diminished the need for an omnibus theoretical-and-descriptive text. The literature of economic systems is also conductive to theoretical focus in a core text. Supplementary readings about particular economies in practice are readily available, often in inexpensive paperbacks.

A sharper theoretical focus in also indicated by student needs and backgrounds. Many undergraduate students enrolling in comparative economic systems courses major in areas other than economics, and consequently have had little, if any, prior study in economic theory. For this reason, economic theory is developed a bit more fully here than would be true if the comparative systems course were populated largely by economics majors. (Some of the more technically theoretical discussions may be omitted without disrupting basic continuity.) Similarly, theories of capitalism, Marxism, and socialism are explored reasonably fully because undergraduate courses in the history of economic thought are rapidly vanishing, and even economics majors often lack needed background in this area.

While challenging the relevance and requiring the reassessment of older theories of comparative economic organization—especially the traditional dichotomy between capitalism and socialism—rapid change in the specific forms of economic systems also increases the need for theoretical analysis, to provide a framework which makes sense out of the bewildering array of economic systems and relates them to basic ideas about the functioning of the economic order.

After an introductory section on the nature and problems of economic systems and the process of economic planning, this book reviews and compares the major classic theories of capitalism and socialism. For each, four major alternative theories are examined and compared: (1) the classic exposition and rationale of the system; (2) the challenge presented by the most prominent critical theory of the system; and (3) and (4) two prominent twentieth-century theories of the system.

For capitalism (which is the subject of Part II of this book), (1) the classic exposition and rationale of the system is represented by the theory and philosophy of the competitive market system, (2) the challenge is provided by the Marxian analysis and critique of capitalist industrialization, and (3) and (4) are illustrated by the theories of capitalism formulated by John Maynard Keynes and Joseph A. Schumpeter.

For socialism (examined in Part III of this text), (1) the classic exposition and rationale is represented by the Marxist-Leninist vision(s) of the ideally functioning socialist and communist economies; (2) the challenge is provided by the critical theories of socialism of such economists as Friedrich A. Hayek; while (3) and (4) are illustrated by the theories of decentralized, market socialism (Oskar Lange and others) and by the Western, neo-Marxist theories of centralized, authoritarian socialism (Maurice Dobb, Paul Baran, and Paul Sweezy).

Parts IV and V of the book examine contemporary economic systems, and their associated economic theories, social philosophies, and programs for economic reform. Part IV is devoted to systems "between and beyond" capitalism and socialism, notably managed capitalism and democratic socialism, while Part V examines Stalinist, revisionist, and Yugoslav Communism. In contrast to the earlier comparison of capitalism and socialism, these last two parts of the text are relatively more empirical and applied in approach. Still, the focus is essentially theoretical, and examples are offered from experience primarily to illustrate basic theoretical ideas rather than to describe in detail particular institutions and practices.

Capitalism, socialism, communism, and their contemporary variants, are not merely systems of economic organization. They are "ways of life." Accordingly, throughout the book, theories of economic systems are placed in a broader setting by reference to social goals and criteria for the evaluation of economic performance, the relations between economic and political systems, and philosophies and strategies for economic reform.* Objectivity is extremely difficult to achieve in the study of a subject as controversial as comparative economic systems, but an endeavor has been made to avoid the twin evils of masking implicit social value judgments in the form of explanatory hypotheses, on the on the one hand, and the sterile and artificial practice of avoiding contamination with the social and political implications of economics on the other.

The book is written so as to permit alternative organization of chapters, if desired. For example, some teachers may wish to treat Marxism as a unit and consequently to assign Chapter 8 on the classical Marxian vision of socialism and communism in conjunction with Chapter 5 on the Marxian

---

*At one point in the preparation of the manuscript, the social philosophies associated with the major theories of economic systems were expected to play an even larger role than in fact has turned out to be the case. However, the volume of materials on these matters became unmanageable and it was decided to prepare a separate book, *Competing Economic Philosophies in Contemporary American Capitalism: Essays and Readings* (Goodyear Publishing Co.: Pacific Palisades, Calif., 1974). This book provides readings, with extensive editorial commentary, on major "economic philosophies," with special emphasis upon classical liberalism and contemporary neo-liberalism (Hayek, Friedman), Marx and contemporary neo-Marxism (Baran and Sweezy), liberal and conservative wings of Keynesianism (Hansen, Wallich), socialism and the New Left, and the writings of Schumpeter and Galbraith.

analysis of capitalism. The chapter on Keynes provides a bridge between the section on capitalism and that on contemporary "managed capitalism" and can be assigned as easily with the latter as with the former. Similarly, Chapter 11 on Western neo-Marxist theories of centralized socialism can be read to good advantage in conjunction with Chapter 15 on Stalinist Communism. Even more extensive realignments of topics can be made, as is illustrated in the Alternative Outline.

The author wishes to acknowledge his debt and gratitude to many people who have helped in the preparation of this book. A special debt is owed to Professor Robert W. Campbell, who had primary responsibility for the chapters on Contemporary Communism. Sincere appreciation is extended to Professors Alan A. Brown, Andrzej Brzeski, John M. Montias, and Charles E. Lindblom, who have read various portions of the manuscript and offered helpful suggestions concerning content and organization.

The author wishes to express his appreciation to the various members of the editorial and production staff at Prentice-Hall, especially to Joan Lee for her helpfulness and patience. Sincere thanks also go to Terry Sherf for her excellent copyediting, Barbara Ingle for the preparation of the index, and Rachel Bingham for the typing of the final draft.

Special thanks go to Dave Roberts, doctoral candidate at the University of Southern California, for his invaluable assistance in the final stages of putting the book into publication.

Special thanks are also due to the several colleagues and numerous students at the University of Southern California and elsewhere who have graciously submitted to the inconveniences of using prepublication versions of the manuscript in their classes and who thereby served invaluably as sounding boards in the book's preparation.

As is customary, the author has by no means invariably taken the good advice of others and acknowledges his responsibility for errors and shortcomings.

Comparative
Economic Systems

Introduction

This introductory section describes the nature and problems of economic systems in general, identifies some prominent criteria for defining and comparing economic systems, and defines the concept and describes the major dimensions of economic planning.

Economic systems have certain problems in common. They differ both in the emphasis each system places on various economic problems and in the ways each endeavors to resolve them. The systematic endeavor to resolve economic problems, regardless of the particular institutions involved, requires some strategy and methodology for economic planning.

The chapters in Part I provide a framework for answering questions such as

1. What is an economic system?
2. What are the central and recurring problems of any economic system?
3. What are the different approaches to the study of economic systems? What is the role of the study of economic systems within the discipline of economics?
4. What are the major criteria for identifying, defining, and comparing economic systems?
5. What are the major characteristics, similarities, and differences between the classic theories of capitalism and socialism?
6. What major developments in the twentieth century have reduced the applicability of the classic debate over capitalism versus socialism and have stimulated the emergence of contemporary theories of economic systems?
7. Why is economic planning a strategic ingredient in any economic system?
8. What are the major dimensions in economic planning as a dynamic process?

Economic Systems: What's It All About?

ECONOMIC SYSTEMS

Economic systems and planning is one of the most fundamental subjects in modern economics because the problems and issues of man's economic existence are as old as mankind itself. Man's recurring preoccupation with these problems is projected even in his search for his origins. Adam and Eve, prior to eating the forbidden fruit, are portrayed as living the ideal life, having no economic system nor planning, and no economic problems. All their wants and needs were satisfied from a superabundant supply of resources, a bounty from heaven. The products which they consumed all were "free goods," that is, goods which were not scarce and whose acquisition did not require human effort. In this idyllic state, the problems of organization and coordination of economic life in some systematic, planful way did not exist.

But with their ejection from the Garden of Eden, Adam and Eve were thrown into a world of economic necessity, in which, as in all social relationships, they faced the recurrent, unending problems of "making a living," of meeting the central fact that resources are scarce in relation to the uses to which they can be put, and thus, that procedures for "economizing" in their uses must be established. This central economic problem is not unique nor peculiar to any one time,

place, culture, or economic system. It is found universally in all economic systems—socialist, capitalist, fascist, anarchist, cooperativist—and it is the foremost common feature among all systems.

INDIVIDUAL AND SOCIAL ECONOMY

The problem of economizing has its individual aspects, of course. Even a hermit or a Robinson Crusoe, as writers have been fond of observing, has his economic problems. The most interesting and compelling aspects of economizing from the standpoint of human welfare, however, are those of *social* economy, that is, those connected in some direct, significant way with the actions, plans, programs, institutions, and aspirations of man in society. Whereas individual economy has two central problems—that of *calculating* the advantages and disadvantages of alternative courses of action, and *allocating* resources in particular directions to satisfy the alternatives chosen—social economy faces the additional problem of *coordinating* the actions and decisions of thousands or millions of individuals or groups in the entire society, of creating some sort of economic order or organization for society. As used herein, the word *economy* will denote *social economy* unless otherwise indicated.

Any economy faces a number of central economic problems or issues, all interrelated and stemming primarily from the fundamental necessity of establishing methods and procedures to administer society's scarce resources to satisfy human wants. Each of these problems may appear compelling or important in some particular time or place. Different economic systems will attempt to meet them in varying ways, with varying degrees of success. But they recur and remain in any economy. These basic issues may be classified under the following headings: (1) allocation of resources, (2) distribution of income, (3) stability in the overall level of economic activity, (4) rate of economic growth.

Resource Allocation

Because resources (human, natural, and capital or man-made) are limited, whereas the uses to which these resources can be put are generally many or even unlimited, all economic systems must establish techniques or methods to select which uses or combinations of uses are most urgent, and to obtain and administer resources so as to most closely satisfy wants. The first problem is one of choice, the second, of allocation.

Economic choice is a function of scarcity. Were resources not scarce in relation to human desires, all wants could be met, and economic choices would not be necessary. Man would, in these conditions, be living in a pre- or post-economic paradise. The existence of scarcity, however, raises a number of necessary, continuing choices, such as guns versus butter, necessities versus luxuries, work versus leisure, consumption versus saving, and present versus future. Incidentally, the reduction of scarcity through the increase in the quantity and quality of resources does not necessarily simplify the problem of choice, since the increase in

resources may be more than matched by an increase in the volume and variety of human wants. "The Emperor Charlemagne," wrote David McCord Wright, "lived in a flea-haunted, stinking kennel which scarcely the poorest slum-dweller would touch today."[1] The bathtub in the nineteenth century was a luxury; today, it is commonplace. Has the problem of choice become more simple and less important because we have more bathtubs?

Choice-making is difficult and complex. It raises, for example, such questions as: Who is to have the responsibility and authority for making basic economic choices, and what "weights" should be attached to each person's wants? Is decision-making power to be shared equally among all members of society, or do (or should) some persons or groups have greater influence than others? How should we determine the proportion of total output to go into consumption goods to satisfy current desires versus investment goods to raise the capacity to satisfy future wants? To what extent are choices "independently" arrived at? To what degree are they interdependent with and influenced by social institutions, the state of economic development, the pattern of income distribution, or mass advertising and propaganda? How are choices to be communicated to other members of society? Through the ballot box? Through consumer demand ("dollar ballots")? Or by some alternative technique?

A set of choices, complex as it is, is only part of the problem. If choices are to be made effective, resources must be allocated. Land, labor, capital, and entrepreneurship must be obtained, organized, and directed toward production. On many occasions, the proportions of these resources or factors of production are variable rather than fixed; that is, a given level of output may be produced with varying combinations of inputs. The construction of a highway, for example,

---

[1] David McCord Wright, *Democracy and Progress* (New York: The Macmillan Company, 1948), p. 13.

may be labor-intensive, using a good deal of human labor power, or capital-intensive, relying heavily on labor-saving machinery. A desk-top may be made from wood, plastic, glass, or aluminum. Thus, the decision to construct a highway or to produce 100 desk-tops per day requires another set of decisions about what resources should be used, and in what quantities and combinations, to produce specific quantities of particular products and services. The question of *what* is to be produced necessarily is followed by the question of *how*. Because resources are scarce, every economic system requires some means to economize in their use, that is, some way to "get the most" out of a given body of resources and to apply them in those specific directions which correspond most closely to the satisfaction of human wants.

Income Distribution

The employment of resources results in the production of output, that is, a flow of products and services ("economic goods") over a period of time. It simultaneously creates income, since *real income* consists, by definition, of this same flow of goods. A person's *money income* (for example, wages, rents, interest payments, profits) represents in essence a "claim" against national output, and the totality of these claims during any past period of time (abstracting from foreign trade) must be equal by definition to total output. This necessary identity of output and income is a characteristic common to all economic systems.

Total output, or income, must be distributed somehow among the members of society. In other words, every economy must determine "for whom" products and services are to be produced. Should income be distributed according to "contribution to production"? Or, should people be rewarded according to "need"? How can productive contribution or need be measured? Should income be distributed more equally? Or less equally? Should the share of national income

going to wages be greater? Or is it too large already?

Few topics in the history of economic systems have aroused hotter debate than those centering around income distribution. Perhaps this is because income is so close to our personal well-being, both directly, in terms of its capacity to satisfy our wants, and indirectly, through its impact upon power, prestige, and status in society. Perhaps it stems from the realization that if a larger per cent of a *given* national economic pie accrues to one person or group in society, some other person or persons necessarily must receive less. At any rate, the distribution of income is an issue which faces every economic system. Conversely, one of the prominent differences among competing economic systems lies in the particular techniques and methods of distributing or redistributing income, as well as the actual patterns of equality and inequality.

Economic Stability

No contemporary economy seems able to escape the fluctuations upward and downward in the overall level of activity we call "economic instability." The nature, causes, severity, and regularity of these fluctuations differ considerably in different countries, and, indeed, in the same country at different times. Unemployment, for example, comes in a much different form in a poor or under-developed economy than in a highly developed one. Unemployment is typically "open" in the latter; that is, the unemployed are out of work and seeking jobs. Unemployment in the former is sometimes "disguised"; for example, agricultural workers are being used so ineffectively that, were they moved to industry, agricultural output would not fall, or, at least, would not fall greatly. Their net contribution to agricultural production is low, perhaps zero. Similarly, inflation (defined as "a period of generally rising prices") suppressed by governmental price, wage, and rent controls has different characteristics and raises different problems from "open" price inflation, where prices are permitted to rise. Still, no contemporary economic system remains perfectly stable. The level of aggregate economic activity at any time and its fluctuations over the passage of time are matters of concern for any social economy.

One important aspect of "aggregate economics" in the last 25 or 30 years has been the compilation and development in various countries of statistical data on such variables as output, employment, money, and prices. These data should be used with care, since they are full of pitfalls for the unwary. Still, they afford us valuable information both for comparing national economic performances in different countries and for preparing economic plans.

These various aggregate economic indicators not only provide a measure of national economic performance and "well-being," but also reveal certain relationships important to any economy. For example, any aggregate figure, such as output, may be viewed or measured in various ways. One way would be to summate the value added to total output of different industries—manufacturing, agriculture, services, or retailing. Another would be to add expenditures on output, in the forms of consumption, investment, government purchases, and net foreign investment. A third method would be to find the total of all income claims against the output, such as wages, rents, interest, and profits. Though the components of these three calculations would be different, the totals, except for minor discrepancies, would be equal because, by definition, they refer to the same thing.

Another revealing set of relationships is provided by the famous "equation of exchange," $MV = PT$, where M stands for the quantity of money, V its velocity of circulation or rate of turnover in any period of time, P the average or general price level, and T the total transactions or physical volume of trade. MV, on the left-hand side of this "identity equation," or identity, measures total money purchases, whereas PT measures the total money value of sales. Since total sales, by definition, are equal to total purchases, MV must equal PT. This identity, and the logical relationships implied by it, are applicable to any economic system, or, at least, to any economy which uses money in the process of exchange. Several logical relationships emerge easily from an examination of this equation: If MV rises (falls), or if either M or V rises (falls), while the other remains constant, either P or T or both must rise (fall). If PT rises (falls), or if either rises (falls), while the other remains constant, either M or V or both must rise (fall). If MV rises (falls) and T rises (falls) more vigorously, P must necessarily fall (rise).

A final example in economic stability involves aggregate supply and demand. Every economic system has supplies of resources potentially or actually employed in the productive processes. Every system also has demands for resources to meet various wants or to attain alternative planning targets. If aggregate demand falls short of potential aggregate supply, the result is a failure to fully utilize society's resources, which will mean that actual output will fall short of its potential. If aggregate demand for resources exceeds aggregate supply, at full employment utilization of resources, some demands cannot be met, resulting in a number of possible pressures in the economic system, for example, rising prices. Overly ambitious central planners, as well as overly exuberant consumers and investors, may all encounter this problem.

Economic Growth

Economic growth, defined as a sustained upward movement in the aggregate level of output (or output per person), is a matter of vital concern for most contemporary economic systems, while its existence (or lack of it), is an important issue for any economy. Soviet Russian leaders, for example, are concerned with the prospects and possibilities of "catching up with the West" in overall output. The industrially advanced Western democracies are interested in economic growth both to maintain their collective industrial and economic edge in the cold war, and to continue to expand their domestic living standards, and to meet the pressing public needs of an urban society. The emerging economically underdeveloped and largely politically uncommitted nations of Africa, South and Central America, and the Near and Far East similarly are concerned with this issue.

In part, the issues of economic growth overlap those of resource allocation. Growth and development for a national economy require decisions regarding: (1) the rate of capital formation or overall division of output into consumption versus investment goods; (2) the apportionment of investible funds among alternative firms, industries, or projects; (3) the geographic location of industry. All of these decisions, crucial to economic growth, involve the allocation of society's scarce resources.

Yet, economic growth goes beyond the notion of resource allocation for at least two reasons: (1) the essence of economic growth lies in the progressive augmentation of the quantity and quality of society's resources (and in the accompanying increase and alteration in the uses or ends toward which resources can be allocated), not in the administration of a *given* body of resources among *constant*, unchanging ends; (2) some of the most important causes, characteristics, and results of growth are qualitative, having to do with alterations in the basic institutional and ideological structure of society and its fundamental "ways of thinking and doing," not simply with the making of economic decisions within a more or less constant social, economic, and political environment.

Not all economic systems experience or have experienced economic growth as we have defined the term. Moreover, economic growth, as a goal or objective of economic policy, is not shared by all societies and cultures. Indeed, a continued and sustained expansion in income or output per capita and the idea that such an expansion is both possible and desirable for the large masses of society is historically unique to a very small geographic and temporal segment of human civilization, specifically, to a small number of countries in Western Europe and the Western hemisphere, and Australasia, in modern times.

Still, every economic system has some long-run pattern of economic change, even if it is a downward one. Even more important, though economic systems may experience different growth rates, may have different degrees of interest in economic growth, and may attempt to encourage or discourage long-run expansion in a variety of ways, all economies, to grow, must draw upon some combination of: (1) human, natural, and capital resources; (2) technology, or the application of human knowledge to production: (3) institutions, or ways of organizing human activity; and (4) motivations, or ways of thinking about economic organization and development. The nature, quantity, and quality of these four factors are the major sources of economic growth and the basic determinants of long-run economic change in any social economy.

A Graphical Illustration

A simple graphical illustration of these basic economic problems is seen in Fig. 1.1. The problem of *resource allocation* can be illustrated as follows: The employment of a given quantity and quality of scarce human, natural, and capital resources, under given technological conditions, might yield a potential maximum output of, say, 2,000,000 hats or 4,000,000 shirts, or some combination of the two. Suppose that all resources were employed in the production of hats only. Hat production would be OH_2 and shirt

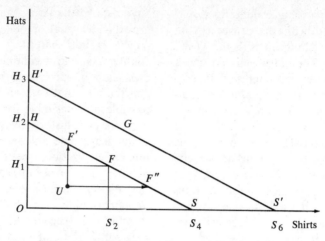

Fig. 1.1. Central issues in economic systems

production would be zero. Now suppose that consumers (or central planners) desire some shirts as well as hats. To accomplish this, under the assumed conditions, it would be necessary to decrease production of hats, to, say, 1,000,000, thereby releasing resources which might be reallocated to the production of 2,000,000 shirts. Hat production would fall to OH_1 and shirt production would rise from zero to OS_2. In Fig. 1.1 this would be illustrated by a movement from point H to point F along line HS. The same idea would hold in reverse. Commencing at point S, where shirt production is 4,000,000 and hat production is zero, a decrease in the production of shirts to OS_2 would release resources which could be reallocated to the production of OH_1 hats. This would be illustrated in Fig. 1.1 by a movement from point S to F. Line HS thus illustrates a *production possibility frontier*: It shows all the potential combinations of hats and shirts which might be produced from the employment of a given quantity and quality of resources under given technological conditions.[2]

This diagram also may be used to illustrate other major economic problems. If wages and profits were substituted for hats and shirts, respectively, the line HS would illustrate alternative patterns of *income distribution*. If we recognize the possibility of *unemployment* of resources (such as labor), the whole region lying below line HS becomes economically relevant. Point U, for example, illustrates one possible combination of hat and shirt production when the labor force is less than fully employed. Under conditions of *full employment*, an increase in hat production requires a decrease in the production of shirts, as illustrated by a movement along line HS. But the creation of unemployment results in a level of production lower than the potential full-employment output and is illustrated by a movement to a point below HS, as, for example, point U. A shift from unemployment to full employment, by

---

[2] HS is depicted as a straight line in Fig. 1.1 for purposes of simplicity and brevity. As a straight line, it shows a *constant* ratio in the transformation of H to S (or S to H). This implies that the ratio of the costs of producing hats to the costs or producing shirts remains constant regardless of the shift of resources from one to the other, that is, that resources are equally adaptable to producing hats or shirts. A more realistic illustration is provided by the concave-shaped production possibility curve shown in Fig. 1.2. Resources used in the production of hats may not be equally adaptable in the production of shirts and vice versa. Thus, the shift of resources from hat to shirt production plausibly will be accompanied by increase in costs. Equal decrements in the production of hats (I, G, F, E) are accompanied by *decreasing* increments of shirts (R, T, U, V). The same is true in reverse as we move up the curve.

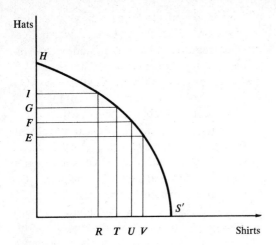

Fig. 1.2. A production possibility curve with increasing costs

contrast, is illustrated by a shift to the full employment production possibility frontier, for example, from point U to any point on line HS. Under these conditions, it is possible, through the employment of formerly unemployed resources, to expand the production of one commodity without decreasing the production of any other. This is illustrated by a movement from point U to any point between F' and F''.

Economic growth also may be illustrated in the diagram. Line HS represents potential full employment output possibilities only under conditions of given quantities and qualities of resources and given technology. An expansion in the quantity of labor, land, capital, or entrepreneurship, or an improvement in the quality of resources or technology, changes these underlying conditions and increases potential full employment output, as illustrated by an upward and outward shift in the production possibility curve from HS to $H'S'$. Under these conditions, point F no longer represents full employment. A failure to realize the growth potentials illustrated by the outward shift from HS to $H'S'$ would transform point F from a position on a full employment production possibility curve to a situation of unemployment and below-potential production.

WHAT IS AN ECONOMIC SYSTEM?

Problems linked to resource allocation, income distribution, economic stability, and economic growth cannot be resolved by the waving of a magic wand. They are human problems, requiring human decisions and solutions. An economic system, in essence, is a set of relations among decision-makers and between decision-makers and economic variables. It consists of the sum of ideas, goals, methods, and institutions used in society to resolve these economic issues in some more or less organized or "systematic" way.

The central feature of an economic system is the planning and making of economic decisions. The concept and general process of economic planning are given extended treatment in Chapter 3. The resolution of economic problems in society requires difficult choices and decisions. The wisdom and success of these decisions depend in part upon systematic planning. Planning, in turn, requires organization, four prominent aspects of which are summarized in the following.

First, every economic system must have a method or set of techniques to establish social *goals* or priorities, in terms of which decisions can be made and resources allocated. Goals often are multiple and not consistent with one another. Thus, choices must be made and priorities established regarding the four problems previously cited and all the complex sub-problems involved in relation to them.

The organization of economic activity also requires methods or procedures for *analysis*, that is, processes for comparing the gains and costs, the advantages and disadvantages of alternative goals and programs.

Economic decisions may be made through a variety of social *institutions*: governments, labor unions, business firms, agricultural associations, families, banks, and cooperatives. These institutions are of central importance because they largely determine the location and degree of concentration of economic power, or the capacity to make and enforce economic decisions.

In order to execute plans and programs, and thus, to translate into practical action the decisions of persons and organizations exercising economic power, methods must be available to enforce decisions and to *control* economic actions, that is, to encourage or reward desired actions and to discourage or penalize undesired actions.

THREE APPROACHES TO THE STUDY OF ECONOMIC SYSTEMS

The study of comparative economic systems may be approached in at least three related, yet very different, ways. These are from the standpoints of: (1) theoretical economic systems, (2) actual economic systems, and (3) economic systems as movements for social change or reform. We shall be concerned primarily with the first of these three approaches, with emphasis upon underlying theoretical analysis. We will also be concerned with the second and third approaches, particularly as they relate to the first.

A theoretical economic system is a body of ideas or concepts about the organization and direction of economic activity, such as capitalism, socialism, and communism. Some theoretical economic systems are descriptive; that is, they are alleged to correspond to some degree to an actual set of economic arrangements. Many, however, are not descriptive; that is, they refer to how an economy would be organized *if* it were characterized by the institutional features of the theoretical model. Theoretical economic systems also may be classified as explanatory or normative. An *explanatory* theory purports to offer an analytical apparatus to explain how an economy does (or would) operate. A *normative* theory attempts to evaluate how an economy *should* be organized. Explanatory theories

of economic systems require close attention to questions of logic and fact. Normative theories require, in addition, judgments of value, that is, judgments about what is socially desirable or undesirable. Needless to say, the same body of ideas (for example, the classic theory of competitive market capitalism) may serve all theoretical purposes.

Actual economic systems are those which exist or have existed in practice, such as the Swedish, English, ancient Athenian or sixteenth-century Spanish economies. Actual economic systems rarely correspond precisely to theoretical models. Most are "impure" or "mixed," that is, they contain elements found in more than one theory. Most economic systems in practice, for example, contain an *interblending* of the institutional characteristics associated with classic or pure capitalism and classic or pure socialism; they are "socio-capitalist." Of course, there are degrees of capitalism and socialism, and a particular economy may lie closer to one pole than the other. Still, the student of economic systems should be cautious of identifying theory and practice too readily and loosely.

Movements for social and economic change or reform consist of parties, platforms, and programs propagated and carried on by social groups prior to their acquisition of economic and political power, or prior to their full-scale establishment in practice. Examples of these are the socialist movement in England during the nineteenth century or the pronouncements and activities of American communists. Soviet Russian communism, in one sense, falls into this third category. The Russian communists have acquired political and economic power, but they have not established, nor do they claim to have established, classic or pure communism. Thus, it is misleading to classify the Russian economy as "communist." Yet they claim to be working toward and for the eventual establishment of this goal in Russia and throughout the world. Thus, it is relevant to speak of a communist political and economic movement.

A proper, balanced knowledge of comparative economic systems requires an understanding of explanatory theoretical models, philosophies or value judgments about how economic systems could or should be organized, descriptive information about the operations of particular economies in practice, and movements for economic reform. Many unproductive and emotional debates could be avoided in discussion of economic systems if we learned to recognize the natures of, and the differences among, theories, facts, ideals, and movements.

SOME MAJOR DIFFERENCES AMONG ECONOMIC SYSTEMS

Economic systems differ in at least two basic ways: (1) in the economic problems faced and the degrees of emphasis placed on specific economic issues; and (2) in the methods, techniques, and institutions used to meet similar or different problems. As an illustration of the first difference, compare the heavy, primary emphasis placed on intense, rapid industrialization in Soviet Russia during roughly the last half century (and the accompanying de-emphasis upon income distribution and equality) with the "cradle-to-grave" social security system and steeply progressive income tax rates in England's postwar "welfare state." Clearly, economic growth has been of compelling and foremost importance to Russia's political leaders and planners, whereas the promotion of lesser inequality and insecurity in income distribution has engaged the attention of the English in recent years.

Even if the problems and goals of economic life were the same in all economic systems, wide disagreements and differences could and probably would exist as to the most effective and appropriate means, techniques, and institutions to resolve these problems or to attain these goals. Industriali-

zation and economic growth, for example, are prominent objectives of economic planning and policy in both Communist China and India. But wide differences of opinion exist as to *how* to foster these goals. The Communist Chinese industrialization program, based upon the Soviet Russian model, with some interesting variations of its own, has been committed to intense, rapid development of heavy industry and a system of highly centralized, nearly comprehensive governmental economic planning, whereas Indian economic development is proceeding under a less intense program, involving a mixture of heavy and light industry, capital investment and current consumption, government plans and private business decisions.

Disagreements about goals and programs exist within, as well as among, economic systems. A number of prominent American economists, for example, are convinced that recession and unemployment are the most compelling aspects of economic instability. Others are equally concerned with the dangers of inflation. Among those who believe that recession is the greater of the two problems, disagreements exist over the extent to which our public policies should be directed toward attaining full employment. Even if people do agree on a goal in this area of economic stabilization (for example "full employment"), there is apt to be disagreement over how best to attain it (for example, through monetary measures, tax and expenditure changes, foreign trade policies, or other methods).

Moreover, we should not think of methods and institutions *solely* in an instrumental sense, that is, from the standpoint of their effectiveness in attaining goals or solving problems; these ways and means of organizing and directing economic activity acquire an independent significance in different economic systems, quite apart from the problems toward which allegedly they are directed. One example is private versus public ownership. In both the United Kingdom and the United States, transportation, gas, water, electricity, communications, and banking are considered industries "affected with a public interest," and which, accordingly, cannot be left alone to pursue private profit on an individualistic basis. However, Americans are more disposed to the idea of private ownership than Englishmen. In England, all of the aforementioned industries, with the exception of inland truck transportation, are government owned. In the United States, *ownership* is private but is supplemented by public *regulation* through semi-independent regulatory commissions, such as the Federal Power Commission and the Interstate Commerce Commission.

COMPARATIVE ECONOMIC
SYSTEMS AND THE DISCIPLINE
OF ECONOMICS

Comparative economic systems often is thought to be a "part" of or an applied field within the discipline of economics, in the sense that labor economics, public finance and fiscal policy, and economics of development are specialized sub-fields within the discipline. But this is misleading for two reasons. First, it would be more accurate to think of comparative economic systems as an *approach to*, rather than a "part" of, the discipline of economics. The unifying theme of the study of comparative economic systems is the use of the comparative approach or methodology. Because this methodology may be applied to the study of topics pertinent to *any* sub-field within economics (for example, a comparative analysis of systems of taxation or labor unions in different countries), or to economics as a whole (for example, a comparative analysis of the theories of socialism or the overall performances of selected national economies), comparative economic systems cannot be isolated from the general principles of the discipline or from any of its branches. When the study of comparative economic systems takes the form of comparisons of general

theories or systems of thought about the overall organization and functioning of the total "economic system," it is more appropriately described as an approach to, rather than a separable subdivision of, the discipline.

Second, comparative economic systems is not solely a matter of econnomics, at least not as a scientific discipline. In part, this stems from the fact that the study of comparative economic systems includes criteria for the evaluation of the effectiveness of the economic system and judgments about the goodness of economic performance. These criteria and judgments, found implicitly in most theories and philosophies of economic systems and in most strategies for economic change and reform, transcend scientific economic analysis and involve more fundamental moral and political dimensions of human action and social institutions.

Comparative economic systems also goes beyond economics as traditionally conceived, by virtue of its central substantive concern. Economics, at least as customarily conceived and taught in Western societies, is concerned with analysis of the determination of the values or magnitudes (or changes therein) of selected economic variables, such as investment, saving, national income, prices, quantities, and employment within an institutional, motivational, and technological framework, which is "given" in that it is regarded as being determined by forces beyond the scope of economic analysis. In contrast, comparative economic systems is concerned with the comparative specification of alternative institutional-motivational-technological frameworks, and with the comparative explanation and evaluation of their impact upon economic processes and performance. Thus, comparative economic systems regards as variables, or at least as topics to be carefully identified and compared, social, political, psychological, and technological factors given within economics in general. Thus, comparative economic systems incorporates an approach to the subject of economics which is broader than the traditional one.

Finally, comparative economic systems transcends the traditional boundaries of the discipline of economics by virtue of its comparative methodology and concern for alternative systems. As a systematic social scientific discipline, economics emerged and developed coterminously with the emergence and development of competitive market capitalism as an economic system in the western world. In the minds of many economists, economics became essentially a study of one major type of economic system: market capitalism. But comparative economic systems, by its very nature, is concerned with various systems of economic organization, including, but not limited to, coordination through markets, and thus, even when restricted to the study of processes for economizing (allocation, distribution, stability, full employment, and growth) it is broader in scope than the traditional analysis of market forces.

SUMMARY OF CHAPTER 1

1. The fundamental basis of, and central problems for, all economic systems is the *scarcity of resources* relative to the uses to which resources may be put.

2. The most interesting and compelling problems of economizing are those involved in *social economy*, involving the task of *coordination* of actions and decisions, as well as calculation and allocation.

3. Four central issues of social economy are: the *allocation* of resources; the *distribution* of income; *stability or instability* in the overall level of economic activity and *full employment* or *unemployment* of resources; and the rate of economic *growth*.

4. An *economic system* consists of the ideas, goals, methods, and institutions used in society to resolve economizing problems, such as these, in some "systematic" way.

5. The central feature of any economic system is planning and making economic decisions. This requires systematic economic planning and organization which, in turn, have four prominent dimensions: the determination of social *goals*; the *analysis* of the benefits and costs of alternative methods to obtain goals; the determination of the *institutional framework* for the exercise of *economic power* in the selection and execution of economic decisions; the *execution* of plans and policies and the control of economic action.

6. Economic systems may be studied in three related but distinguishable ways: as *theoretical* economic systems; as *actual* economic systems; as *movements* for economic change or reform. The primary emphasis in this book is on classic and contemporary theories of economic systems and associated philosophies and strategies for economic reform.

7. Economic systems differ in two basic ways: in the *problems* faced and goals formulated and in the *methods and institutions* used to solve problems and attain goals.

8. Comparative economic systems is more appropriately described as an *approach* to or methodology for the study of economics than as a separable part or branch of the discipline. By virtue of its subject matter and methodology, comparative economic systems is broader than economics. It deals, in part, with value judgments or criteria for evaluating the performance of economic systems and with social, political, and other institutional factors important in identifying and comparing different systems of economic organization.

2

Economic Systems:

Basic Concepts and Definitions

This chapter identifies several prominent criteria that are useful in defining and comparing economic systems. It also defines the major types of economic systems examined in later chapters. This classification does not in itself provide theories or explanations of how economic systems behave. But it will help to clarify the subject with whose behavior we are concerned and the use of terms.

Just as industrial markets may be characterized by certain features, such as the number of buyers and sellers or the nature of the product, which constitute their basic institutional structure (as, for example, in competition, monopoly, or oligopoly), so economic systems also may be structured or organized in various ways in terms of central features. It would be convenient if we could offer simple definitions of words such as "capitalism" and "socialism" in terms of two or three major characteristics. Unfortunately, the practical realities of economic systems are too complex and dynamic for such an approach. They are dynamic because both the theories and practices of economic systems, as well as the programs and ideologies of movements for economic reform, are subject to change, though the same terms

may continue to be used in the altered system. (Despite profound changes in the structure of the American economy since 1865, for example, it continues to be called "capitalist.") We may begin, however, by listing and identifying briefly eight prominent characteristics in terms of which economic systems traditionally have been defined, classified, and compared.

Level of Economic Development

Economic historians have suggested a number of classifications of economic systems in terms of historical stages. Using a monetary criterion, for example, some have been impressed by the movements from barter to monetary to credit economies. Others, emphasizing geography, have classified economies on the basis of development from local to regional to national and international scope. Karl Marx, whose contribution to the analysis of economic systems is examined in Chapters 5 and 8, conceived of a historical progression from feudal to capitalist, from there to socialist, and finally, to a communist economy. W. W. Rostow presented a historical model consisting of five major stages: the traditional economy (most ancient and medieval economies and many underdeveloped economies today); the transitional economy; the "take-off" into industrialization and sustained economic development; the drive to industrial maturity; and the mature economy.

Until recently, however, most of the writing and debate about comparative economic systems has centered upon a small number of highly developed economies in Western Europe, North America, and Australasia. When it is remembered that more than two-thirds of the world's population live in economies that are characterized as underdeveloped, the validity of this approach becomes suspect. At any rate, one important criterion for classifying economic systems is the level, as well as the patterns, of economic growth and development. It should be noted especially that: (1) economic systems with diverse institutional structures may still exhibit similar levels and/or patterns of economic development. The United States, the United Kingdom, Soviet Russia today, and Nazi Germany between 1933 and 1945 are all examples of industrially developed nations with modern technology. Contemporary India and Communist China are both underdeveloped-but-developing economies, with quite different institutional and political characteristics; (2) economic systems at similar levels or stages of economic development face similar problems and encounter pressures which partly transcend their institutional differences. American college students should not be surprised, for example, to discover that the problems and processes of such modern, industrialized economies as those of the U.S.A. and the U.S.S.R. are more similar than they thought.

Resource Base

Another major way to classify economic systems is in terms of factors of production or "resource base." A traditional terminology divides the factors or means of production into: (1) human resources (labor), defined as mental and/or manual human effort, from unskilled through semi-skilled and skilled,

to managerial, professional, and "entrepreneurial" forms;[1] (2) natural resources (land) and nature provided goods, such as mineral deposits, land, water, and climate; and (3) capital resources (capital), defined as material goods such as dams, power plants, buildings, machinery, tools, and industrial raw materials, created through the joint application of human and natural resources, and employed indirectly in a roundabout, time-consuming manner to produce goods which may be used, in turn, to satisfy human wants.

Excluding all other possible criteria, we thus may identify three major kinds of economic systems as (1) laboristic, (2) naturalistic (or, better, landistic), and (3) capitalistic, each defined in terms of heavy reliance in the productive process upon one of the three central factors of production. Using this terminology, nearly all pre-modern and many contemporary economies would be classified as "landistic" or as a mixture of laboristic and landistic. A small but highly important number of contemporary economic systems, including such diverse examples as the United States, England, West Germany, and Soviet Russia, might be termed, by contrast, "capitalistic." Yet the limitation of this approach immediately is clear. The institutions, organization, and operation of these four countries differ in a number of important ways. Soviet Russia and the United States both may use "capitalistic methods of production" and, in this sense, are similar. But this hardly justifies classifying them as two forms of similar phenomenon.

Ownership and Control of the Means of Production

Production may be organized in a variety of ways. Economic systems which are capital-

---

[1] Entrepreneurship is often cited as a separate factor, the central productive function of which is the making of basic policy decisions, thus coordinating and organizing other means of production, including other kinds of labor.

istic in terms of our second criterion often display quite different patterns in the ownership and control of man-made and natural resources. For our purposes, three prominent types of industrial organization may be distinguished as (1) public, (2) private, and (3) cooperative.

PUBLIC ENTERPRISE

A *public* enterprise exists when legal title to property (ownership) and managerial operation (control) are held by a governmental body rather than by private citizens or groups of them. Distinctions usually are drawn between a public enterprise in the strict sense, where a governmental body produces and sells products and services (for example, the T.V.A.), and a public service, where governmentally-provided products and services are financed wholly or largely out of taxation or general governmental revenues (for example, national defense or education). Public enterprises may be subject to tight administrative control (as, for example, in the production activities operated by the United States Department of Agriculture), or they may be permitted a high degree of administrative discretion (as, for example, the T.V.A., which is organized as a semi-independent "government corporation", with fairly wide powers over price, output, and personnel policies).

Governments often own *and* manage enterprises. Sometimes, however, these two functions are separated, and hybrid or mixed forms of enterprise develop. The railroad industry in the United States during World War I, for example, was under private ownership, but publicly operated. The legal title to atomic power in the United States is held by the federal government, but the development and production of atomic facilities, weapons, and research is handled largely on a contract basis with private enterprises. Moreover, government agencies may control and regulate production (as in American public utilities) even when *both* ownership

and day-to-day management are in private hands. Indeed, it is possible (as in Nazi Germany during the late 1930s) that enterprise is enmeshed in such a system of government controls and regulations that it remains "private" in name only.

PRIVATE ENTERPRISE

Private enterprise in its broad sense refers to any productive activity not owned and managed by government. In its more usual sense, the term denotes profit-seeking business firms, excluding non-profit organizations and activities, and cooperatives. Private enterprise in this sense operates in a variety of legal forms. But in terms of economic analysis, two major types are of special significance: (1) enterprises where ownership and management are fused, as in individual proprietorships, partnerships, small-scale and family corporations, and corporations where the majority of stock is owned by a small number of people; (2) enterprises where ownership and management are separated. This occurs typically in large-scale corporations, where legal ownership resides in the hands of a large number of small and dispersed stockholders, who individually (and, often, collectively) exert little influence over the actual running of the business, while the power to make basic policy decisions is held by a few large stockholders, the board of directors, top level executives, or some combination of these three.[2]

---

[2]The classic reference on the subject of separation of ownership and management in large-scale corporations is a study made in the early 1930s by the lawyer-economist team, Adolph A. Berle and Gardner Means, *The Modern Corporation and Private Property* (New York: Commerce Clearing House, 1932). On the basis of an investigation of the 200 largest nonfinancial corporations in the United States, they estimated that only 11 percent were controlled by people owning half or more of the stock, while 44 percent were controlled by managerial groups owning insignificant amounts of stock. Reproduced by permission from *The Modern Corporations and Private Property*, published and copyrighted 1932 by Commerce Clearing House, Inc., Chicago, Illinois 60646.

COOPERATIVE ENTERPRISE

Cooperative enterprise is a voluntary association of individuals in economic activity for mutual benefit. The range of cooperative activity is very broad, being found in manufacturing, retailing, credit, and agriculture, to name a few areas. Cooperatives differ from public enterprises in that they operate on the basis of voluntary association of private citizens. Like public and non-individual private enterprises, however, they are collective in nature, involving as they do joint entrepreneurship. The organizational structure of cooperatives differs from that of private business firms in many ways. Members of cooperatives are not hired employees, profit-seeking entrepreneurs, nor corporate stockholders. Three central organizational principles of the "classic consumer's cooperative," for example, are: (1) open membership or freedom of entry into the organization; (2) the practice of "one person, one vote," rather than one share of stock, one vote; and (3) the sharing of benefits on the basis of members' consumer expenditures at the cooperative store, not in terms of profits or dividend payments. The cooperative form of industrial organization is, in a sense, a "middle way" between private and public ownership and operation. Like public enterprise, it is socialized; yet, like private enterprise, it is non-governmental. Thus, "socialized industry" does not and need not require dominant government ownership and production, as the experiences of the Scandinavian countries attest.

The organization of production in many contemporary economies is mixed, that is, it includes examples of public, private, and cooperative forms of enterprise, as well as a variety of mixtures of them. Often, one or two of the forms predominate. The American economy, for example, is predominantly private-enterprise-corporate in structure. It is private in the sense that the vast majority of property and output is held by and accounted for by non-governmental and non-coopera-

tive enterprise. It is corporate in the sense that the corporation is the dominant American economic institution and that most of the major and fundamental economic decisions (the what, where, how, and how much of production) are made by corporate executives. Soviet Russia, by contrast, is a public enterprise economy, in that most industrial property is governmentally owned, and all but an insignificant portion of the national output is produced in government plants or directed and controlled by government agencies. A number of contemporary societies, however, are dominated by neither private nor public enterprise. In Denmark, Sweden, Norway, New Zealand, and Israel, cooperatives are highly significant, not only in retailing and agriculture, but in wholesaling, manufacturing, housing, and medical care.

Locus of Economic Power

Economies also may be distinguished in terms of the location of the power and responsibility to make basic economic decisions. A classic distinction in economic analysis is between individualistic economy, where the power to make economic decisions is dispersed among large numbers of individuals, and governmental-collectivist economy, where this power is vested in the national or central government and is used to formulate and execute economic programs of an overall or collectivist nature, concerning the economy as a whole. Today, we should recognize a third category, namely, the organizational economy, where economic power is exerted primarily neither by individuals nor by governments, but by a variety of collective organizations including governments.

INDIVIDUALS

In a purely individualistic economy, individuals (or individual units of economic decision, such as households, owners of productive resources, and business firms) would be free to select their own goals and formulate their own decisions and courses of action. Households would be free to allocate their scarce resources, temporally and spatially, among alternative firms and industries, and allocate their scarce incomes between consumption and saving, and among a variety of products and services, in terms of their appraisal of their own satisfactions and desires. Business firms would be free to buy those quantities and combinations of resources and to produce and sell those levels and combinations of products and services which, in the light of given market conditions, seemed most advantageous to them.

ORGANIZATIONS

In an organizational economy, goals would be established and decisions made by groups or organizations of individuals, such as corporations, labor unions, farm organizations, cooperatives, or professional associations, which might exhibit varying degrees of democratic control by the individual members over the leaders. The leaders of these organizations then could attempt to pursue group aims through such methods as bargaining with the leaders of other organizations (as, for example, in labor-management relations) or through pressure-group politics.

GOVERNMENTS

In a dominantly governmental economy, the power to state and formulate goals would be delegated to a governmental body or bodies. The organization of goal scheduling could be highly centralized, decentralized, or a combination of the two. It could be subject to a small or large degree of democratic control by the citizenry through such mechanisms as voting, which, in turn, could be organized in a variety of ways. Most postwar legislation has been preceded by "declarations of purpose," which amount to government statements of policy goals. "In the United States, the United Kingdom, Canada, Australia, and in other countries,

governments have declared their intention to maintain full employment without inflation, to provide greater economic security, to improve the income distribution, to accelerate the rate of economic expansion, and to improve the allocation of resources."[3]

In many societies, decisions are made not by individuals, groups, or governments, but by a combination of all three. The United States is a striking example of this dispersed organization of economic decision-making. Workers, businessmen, farmers, consumers, and bankers all have a considerable degree of freedom to determine their own goals and make their own decisions. But these compete, and sometimes conflict, with the decisions and objectives of labor unions, corporations, farm groups, and other organizations. In the area of public government, decision-making also is divided among varied sources, including political parties, pressure groups, congressional committees, the chief executive, regulatory commissions, and government corporations.

Motivational Systems

Economic systems also have been classified in terms of the systems of motivations which actually and/or presumably guide the making of economic decisions, especially in regard to incentives for production, and for reacting to changes in economic variables. Most studies of comparative economic systems place strong emphasis upon market-oriented versus non-market-oriented motivations, and particularly upon the role of the profit motive. In an economic system characterized by heavy reliance upon market-oriented motivations, the primary incentive to contribute to production would be the prospect of the acquisition of desired economic goods through market exchange. Further, both the calculation and pursuit of these

[3]Benjamin Higgins, *What Do Economists Know?* (Melbourne, Australia: Melbourne University Press, 1951), p. 63.

prospects would receive vigorous social sanction. In such a system, people would regard highly those goods and activities which claim a high market valuation.

It is an interesting reflection upon human nature (and our attitudes toward it) to note that market-oriented motivations and their social sanction, far from being a universal characteristic of all economic systems in history, have, as a general phenomenon, a very restricted geographical and temporal application. In the majority of pre-modern societies, the open pursuit of market or money-oriented personal gain was (at least, for the bulk of the population) either impossible (as, for example, in slave economies) or regarded with distaste. Even in modern cultures, the impact of market motivations is tempered and supplemented by such extra- or non-market aspirations as power, status, friendship, and good will.

In general, any unit of economic decision motivated by a desire for market or monetary gain can be said to be a "profit-seeker." But in economic analysis, the term *profit motive* is used in a narrower sense, being restricted to persons "who are in a position to make profit as a distinctive type of economic return, that is, to individuals who are business enterprisers and assume ultimate responsibility for the conduct of business enterprises."[4] The profit motive, then, refers to the desire by enterprisers to obtain or increase the residual or difference between expected total revenues of business and expected total costs (including both contractual expenses for the purchase of natural, labor, and capital resources, and a "normal profit" on the enterpriser's own non-entrepreneurial productive resources).

The profit motive is a somewhat broader concept, however, than that of "profit maximization," which implies not simply a desire for profit, but for the largest spread

[4]Ralph H. Blodgett, *Comparative Economic Systems* (New York: Macmillan Company, 1948), p. 33.

between expected revenues and expected costs. It is possible to say quite a bit about comparative economic systems simply in terms of the loose and broad notion of profit and profit-seeking. But more precise models of economic decision-making typically have been based on the more exacting assumption of profit maximization and the marginal calculus which this implies.

It should be emphasized that market-oriented motivations are distinguishable from the "market system" as a social process for coordinating economic decisions, though historically and analytically there have been and are close connections between them. It is difficult to conceive a "market system" in the absence of market-oriented economic motivations. Market-oriented motivations, however, may be found in a variety of economic systems. It is possible, for example, for the political leaders of a collectivistic governmental economic system to encourage incentives to produce and to entice the geographical and occupational movement of labor through systems of monetary and wage differentials. This is common practice, for example, in the U.S.S.R.

The Organization of Economic Power:
Centralization versus
Decentralization

Related to but distinguishable from the locus of economic power is the question of its organization. A purely individualistic economy also would be highly decentralized: the power to make economic decisions would be dispersed among a large number of decentralized, individual households and businesses. An organizational economy, by concentrating the power to make economic decisions in the hands of a small number of large collectivistic organizations, would also be accompanied by a higher degree of centralization. A purely governmental economy, by eliminating all nongovernmental organizations, would be characterized by still greater centralization in economic decision-making.

It should be emphasized, however, that any organization, private or public, may exhibit varying degrees of centralization in the decision-making process. Some large-scale private organizations, such as General Motors, may have a greater degree of central control over their economic decisions than some small-scale governmental organizations, such as the Peoria Fire Department. At the level of governmental administration, the centralization-decentralization issue has two major facets: first, the degree of localization versus centralization of decision-making among different levels of government, or the extent of local autonomy versus centralized control (for example, the relative roles of local, state, and federal governments in the United States); second, the degree of separation versus concentration of powers at each level of government, or the extent to which one agency or institution is supreme versus the extent of checks and balances involved in a "division of powers" among the different branches of government. These two criteria provide four possibilities: (1) separation of powers and decentralization or localization (for example, despite increased federal controls, the United States); (2) concentration of powers and decentralization (for example, Switzerland); (3) concentration of powers and centralization (for example, France); and (4) separation, yet centralization (for example, Costa Rica).

As we will explore later in detail, centralization versus decentralization in the organization of economic power plays an important role in the various classic and contemporary theories of capitalism and socialism. The classical and neo-classical model of competitive capitalism envisaged highly decentralized agencies and processes of decision-making. The Marxian and Schumpetarian models of industrialization in economically developing capitalist economies incorporate the vision of increasing centralization of economic power by and within large-scale capitalist enterprises. In the theories of the centralized socialists, basic production decisions are made by a central planning board (CPB) for the entire national economy [see Chapter 11]. In one prominent theory of decentralized socialism [see Chapter 10], the central planners function primarily as a price-fixing agency, altering prices in an attempt to promote market balance between supplies and demands, but leaving a large amount of latitude and discretion to government-employed industrial managers, as well as to individual consumers and workers. This distinction also has been phrased as that of authoritarian versus liberal socialism, the former substituting the authority of the CPB for market-expressed preferences, and the latter permitting a wide range of freedom of consumer and occupational choice.

Social Processes for Economic Coordination

The actions of units of economic decision, such as households, businesses, and governments, are mutually interdependent. Thus, all economies must contain social processes to coordinate their actions, to bring mutually interrelated decisions into equlibrium. Changes in tastes, techniques of production, or methods of social organization will have repercussions throughout the economy and will require readjustments to keep the different parts in balance. In part, economic coordination is a problem of social knowledge: Methods and techniques must exist for the calculation, communication, and analysis of the benefits and costs of alternatives. In part, economic coordination is a problem of social control: the attainment of goals and the coordination of the different parts of a complex, intricate modern economy require means or techniques for controlling the actions and responses of the various economic units. In a revealing study of economic organization, Robert A. Dahl and Charles E. Lindblom distinguish among four central methods or processes for the coordination of national economic activity: (1) the market or price system; (2) bureaucracy; (3) democracy; and (4) bargaining. (The more familiar terms *bureaucracy* and *democracy* will be used here synonymously with what Dahl and Lindblom call "hierarchy" and "polyarchy.")

THE MARKET SYSTEM

The *market system* should not be confused with the term "market." In economic analysis, a market is not merely a physical or geographical location where buying and selling take place. It is, rather, an entire set of exchange relations among units of economic decision. The "meeting of minds" of buyers and sellers establishes prices or ratios in terms of which products and services are exchanged for money. A system of prices or price system is, first, a set of relationships between the prices and quantities of all goods and resources bought on all markets in the entire economy. Second, a "market system" is an even broader concept than a market. In the view of its adherents, and some of its critics, as well, the fascinating thing about the market system is that, without conscious scheme or central direction, it serves as a social process for controlling economic actions, and thus, for coordinating and balancing national economic decisions. In a market system, "prices guide plans," "plans do not guide prices." Yet, it is a system where the plans of perhaps countless individuals are balanced with each other "as if by an invisible hand." How the price system does this, and how well it functions, will constitute a major part of our later analysis.

One point may be noted briefly here. The operation of a price system depends largely upon the market power of the various units of economic decision. In a purely competitive price system, each buyer and seller is a price-taker; that is, though market prices are established through the collective actions of all participants, each individual regards price as a given datum, beyond his individual manipulation and control. In non-purely competitive price systems, which are the more typical form in practice, buyers and/or sellers are price-makers; that is, individually and/or in cooperative action with others, they exert a significant degree of control over quantity, price, and other key market variables.

BUREAUCRACY

In a bureaucratic system, economic plans and decisions are made in relation to the "budget," not to the market. Bureaucracies typically are "hierarchically structured," that is, power and responsibilities pass from the top down through the organization. Since, in a pure bureaucracy, members cannot take their cues as to production decisions from the market, they take them from a set of budgetary directives, administered from below, but formulated from above. As a system for coordinating national economic activity, bureaucracy thus is, in essence, a social process whereby those in positions of power and responsibility control those under them, often through planned directives, quantified, evaluated, and communicated in terms of a budgeted itemization of revenue and cost.

In real life, the analysis of market and bureaucratic systems is complicated by the fact that both may and do exist together and are often intertwined. It is possible, for example, to have a price-directed bureaucracy, where private or public officials take their budgetary cues from market conditions, or a bureaucracy-directed price system, where prices are established by the leaders of bureaucratic organizations. An example of the former is the decentralized socialist model of Polish economist Oskar Lange; the latter is exemplified by U.S. government price and wage control during World War II. It also should be noted that bureaucracy is not restricted to government agencies or public enterprises, but plays an important role in all of the large-scale organizations in modern industrial societies, including corporations, labor unions, and farm groups.

Indeed, we may expect that economies like the United States, though price or market-directed, will become even more bureaucratized as these large, bureaucratically-structured organizations play greater roles in the coordination of the national economy.

DEMOCRACY

In democracy, large numbers of general citizens are able to exert significant degrees of influence on the actions of political leaders. Democracy need not be "pure" to be "workable." In all modern societies, there are those who rule and those who are ruled, and the former have means of influencing and manipulating the latter. The essence of imperfect or workable democracy is not that the general citizenry makes all or even most of the important political decisions. It is, rather, that means and mechanisms exist and are used, whereby the preferences of large numbers of people are communicated to and exert significant influence upon people who are in a position to make basic policy decisions. Democracy, like the market system, does not preclude the possibility of economic planning. Rather, it insists that the citizenry has some means to communicate its goals to the planners, and that the actions of the planners be subject to more or less continous scrutiny, criticism, and possible rejection by the voters through the technique of the ballot box and through organized political pressure of pressure groups.

Democracy has at least three connections with economic coordination: (1) democracy is "itself a process for economizing. The American federal budget, for example, has become a decisive influence on stability, size, and distribution of incomes, investment and innovation not only in the United States but all over the world." (2) It "is one of the major processes for shaping and changing the methods of economizing in the rest of society; thus the shift from laissez-faire to welfare state was brought about largely" via the democratic process. (3) Democracy "is a means for controlling" bureaucracy, and bureau-cracy "is an important economizing process." [1 : 276–77]

BARGAINING

In a bargaining system, policy-makers (often leaders of large-scale bureaucratic organizations) mutually or reciprocally control one another. Bargaining appears to be prominent especially in American politics and economics. Indeed, one contemporary economist, John Kenneth Galbraith, believes that organized blocs of economic power on one side of the market (for example, large firms as sellers of consumer goods) encourage the development of "countervailing power" on the other side of the market (for example, chain stores and mail order houses). [3] Of course, bargaining may take place around traditional market variables, such as wages and hours, in collective bargaining. A certain amount of bargaining also takes place in the customary "higgling" or horse-trading of the marketplace. But bargaining is not merely an appendage to the analysis of market behavior. It is a distinct social process. Partly for this reason, traditional economic analysis cannot give a theoretically "determinate" explanation of bargaining. Because A's actions are largely influenced by his expectations of B's reactions, and vice versa, almost "anything can happen." The outcome in a bargaining situation depends heavily on the relative strength and skill of the bargainers. Bargaining among organized economic groups is one important method of social control, and thus, for coordinating and perhaps "balancing the power" of these groups. As we will see later, it also limits any economic coordination which extends beyond the interests of particular groups to those of the national economy.

DISTRIBUTION OF INCOME AND WEALTH

A final criterion—to some interpretors, the most important one—is the distribution of income and wealth. Kelso and Adler argue that, though capitalistic in its methods of production, the American economy is laboristic in its distribution of income since some two-thirds of the national income is in the form of wages and salaries. The United States would be capitalistic in its distribution, they contend, only if most of the income went to owners of capital.[5] To many imbued with the aims of socialism and democratic social reform, a central distinction among economic systems lies in the degree of inequality in income, property, and/or opportunity. Thus, we might distinguish between equalitarian and inequalitarian economies. Or we might classify on the basis of how people obtain their incomes—for example, through market rewards for their contributions to production, or through various welfare state redistributive measures more oriented toward need. In Marxian economic theory [see Chapter 5], a central criterion for classifying economic systems is the distribution of ownership of man-made and nature-provided capital. In Marxian economics, the problem of capitalism, for example, is not merely that some people own and others do not own the means or instruments of production, but also that those who are owners are few in number, while those who are not are many.

THE MAJOR TYPES OF ECONOMIC SYSTEMS

With the preceding criteria in mind, it is possible to define more clearly and concisely the major kinds of economic systems to be studied herein. Rather than attempting an encyclopaedic description of all or most of the economies which exist in history, we will restrict ourselves to examining a selected number of basic classic and contemporary types.

Capitalism Versus Socialism

Traditionally, at least during the period falling between the latter eighteenth and the

[5]Robert Kelso and Mortimer Adler, *The Capitalist Manifesto* (New York: Random House, 1958), p. 8.

early twentieth century, attention was focused on two major types of economic systems, which we shall call *capitalism* and *socialism*.

Classic or competitive market capitalism is a theoretical economic system, that is, a model of how an economy would be organized and operated *if* it were characterized by the institutional and motivational features of the theory. No economy in practice today corresponds precisely to this model. (Historians also debate over the degree of its historical applicability.) Despite this lack of realism, the model of pure capitalism is very useful: (1) During the nineteenth century, the organization and practices of a number of economies, including those of England, Western Europe, and the United States, roughly approximated the characteristics of the model. (2) Several economies today, notably that of the United States, have strong remnants of capitalist institutions in their organizational structure, despite their significant differences from pure capitalism. (3) This classic model is a significant part of our intellectual heritage, having influenced both technical economic analysis and popular thinking about the workings of our economic system. (4) It also has been used as a "welfare norm" by providing a set of normative criteria in terms of which actual, impure systems can be appraised. (5) A good deal of attention and intellectual effort have been given to the analysis of ideal models of socialism. A fair appraisal requires an understanding of capitalism in its classic competitive form. (6) The classic model of capitalism provides a simple analytical framework to help us comprehend the more complex problems of impure or mixed systems.

The central characteristics of classic or competitive market capitalism are summarized in Table 2-1.

The major theories of capitalism reviewed and compared in Part II represent modifications of and variations on the preceding theme. We shall explore four main classic theoretical analyses of capitalism: (1) pure or classic competitive market capitalism, (2)

Table 2-1.

MAJOR CHARACTERISTICS OF CLASSIC CAPITALISM AND CLASSIC SOCIALISM

Criteria	Capitalism	Socialism
1. Level of Economic Development	Developed or developing economy, with an advanced or advancing technology	Developed economy, with a high per capita income and an advanced technology
2. Resource Base	Heavy reliance upon capital and capitalistic methods of production	Heavy reliance upon capital and capitalistic methods of production
3. Ownership-Control of the Means of Production	Predominantly private and individual ownership and control of business enterprise	Predominantly social ownership and control of business enterprise. (Some socialists place greater reliance upon governmental, others upon voluntary cooperative, forms of ownership.)
4. Locus of Economic Power	Relatively large role for individual units (households and businesses) and accompanying small role for large-scale organizations, especially government	Relatively large role for social and governmental organizations in economic decision-making
5. Motivational System	Market-oriented motivations with particular emphasis upon the profit motive	Elimination or sharp reduction of the role of the profit motive coupled with supplementation and modification of market by non-market motivations
6. Organization of Economic Power	Decentralization of economic decisions and wide areas of discretion for freedom of individual choice	Greater centralization of economic decisions than under capitalism (the extent and details being a major point at issue in centralized versus decentralized forms of socialism)
7. Social Processes for Economic Coordination	Primary reliance upon a competitive price/market system	Overall system of public economic planning for the entire national economy coupled with "democratization" or worker control over industry (the character and relative emphasis between the two being a major point of dispute among socialists)
8. Distribution of Income	Distribution according to market-determined contributions to production, with the possibility of considerable inequality in income and property	Elimination or sharp reduction of income from natural and capital resources, and of inequality in income

the Marxian critique of capitalist industrialization, (3) the Schumpeterian analysis and vision of the future prospects for "old-style" free enterprise capitalism, (4) the Keynesian critique of laissez-faire capitalism. (Recent contributions to the analysis of democratic, managed, or socially reformed capitalism are examined in Part IV.) In all of these classic cases except the Marxian critique, the theories and theorists are sympathetic to or defenders of capitalism. It also should be noted that, in the main, they were concerned with *essentially* the same system, rather than with different capitalisms. This is not entirely true, as we will discover in later chapters. Recent Keynesian and post-Keynesian reformulations of capitalism incorporate significant modifications of the classic model. There are subtle differences in the classic, Marxian, and Schumpeterian definitions and conceptions of capitalism. However, essentially it is true, and certainly more true than in the case of theories of socialism.

Classic socialism also is a theoretical economic system. Though emerging primarily as a movement of social protest against modern capitalism and capitalist industrialization, socialism also has included a vision and model of what, in socialist thinking, a more ideally organized economic system would or will be like if and when capitalism is displaced. For numerous reasons, the classic socialist model is less rigorous than its capitalist counterpart(s): for one thing, some socialists, notably Marx, have been more concerned with the economic analysis and critique of capitalism and its impending collapse than with the organization and operation of a socialist economy. Second, other socialists, such as the Fabians, have been more concerned with the gradual *movement toward* socialism through the democratic social reform of capitalism than with the economic analysis of socialism. Third, students of socialism often have different socialisms in mind (for example, decentralized versus centralized forms).

Keeping these variations in mind, and remembering that no definition will please everyone, the reader will find the major characteristics of classic socialism designated in Table 2-1.

The major theories of socialism reviewed and compared herein are modifications of and variations on this theme. We shall compare four major classic theories of socialism: (1) the classical Marxist vision of ideally functioning socialist and communist economic societies; (2) the neo-Austrian critique of the economic theory of socialism; (3) decentralized, liberal, or market socialism; and (4) centralized, authoritarian, or hierarchical socialism. (Recent contributions to the analysis of democratic, modified, or socially reformed socialism are examined in Part IV, and to socialism in the context of contemporary communism, in Part V.) As in our comparative review of the major theories of capitalism, all of the classic theories explored in Part III except the neo-Austrian critique are sympathetic toward socialism and provide intellectual rationales for it. It should be noted, however, that though united in their criticism of the theory and practice of capitalism, these various socialist theories diverge in their conceptions of what socialism "really is" or ought to be. They are less convergent than in the case of the major theories of capitalism.

Common Features of Capitalism and Socialism

It should be noted that classic capitalism and classic socialism are not exact opposites. They share the problems of industrialization associated with a developed and/or developing society and a capitalistic resource base. They differ most clearly in terms of the ownership and control of the means of production, the locus of economic power, the motivational system, social pressures for economic coordination, and the distribution of income and wealth. Socialists are not of one voice regarding the specific forms of ownership and the extent of centralization versus decentralization in the organization of economic power; they are not as clear about the details of methods for economic coordination and public planning and the specific motivations to replace or supplement those of the market-oriented gain as they are about other criteria. Further, in the case of centralized socialism, even the traditional assumptions of a developed economy and a capitalistic resource base are dropped, and socialism is conceived as an *alternative* to capitalist industrialization in underdeveloped economies. Finally, recent formulations of democratic socialism bring socialist theory into a sort of rapproachment with democratic, managed capitalism.

Beyond matters of definition, capitalism and socialism share an intellectual heritage and a historical setting. First, of course, is their *geographic and temporal proximity*. Socialism, like capitalism, is an essentially modern and western phenomenon—"as modern as industrial capitalism and as western as the idea that all men are created equal."[6] [9: 91] As a definite, serious movement of economic protest and social reform, distinguished from vague and general opposition to poverty, inequality, and oppression, socialism dates from the latter eighteenth and early nineteenth centuries. As a critical analysis of the nature, development, and prospects for capitalism, socialist economic thought developed more or less coterminously with nineteenth century economic thought in Western society. Systematic economic analysis of socialism as a distinct form of economic organization, as contrasted to earlier "visionary utopias," is as recent as the early mid-twentieth century. Second, like classical liberalism and the classical analysis of the competitive market capitalist system, socialism was a forward-looking movement of economic and social *reform*. Of course, the reforms envisaged by socialists in the eighteenth and nineteenth centuries were much more radical than those of classical liberalism. But socialists shared with classical liberals the optimistic belief of the Enlightenment that human knowledge could be applied successfully to the elimination of the irrational traditions and the "dead hand of the past". Society, they felt, could be reorganized on a scientific and rational basis to promote the common welfare better.[7]

Third, both capitalism *and* nineteenth- and twentieth-century conceptions of socialism are primarily *economic* systems; that is, they are systems in which the economic component plays or would play a central role. This helps to distinguish both capitalism and socialism from, say, fascism, in which political, racial, nationalist, and mythical elements are predominant and economics is secondary to these non-economic elements and aspirations. This does not mean that the non-economic features of capitalism and socialism are of small concern to defenders, critics, or participants debating these systems. Defenders of capitalism, for example, often have argued that the market principle, and its corollary of limited government, are more conductive to the promotion of individual freedom and self-reliance than alternative forms of economic organization. Socialist critics of capitalism, on the other hand, often have drawn upon religious and ethical teachings in their denunciations of capitalism and have alleged that perhaps the most important prospective gains from the establishment of socialism will or would be non-economic in nature, such as the promotion of justice, equality, and cooperation.

---

[6]Emphasis on this point, says Paul Sweezy, a prominent contemporary American neo-Marxist and centralized socialist, should help to dispel two common "misconceptions about the origin and nature of socialism: (1) that socialism is as old as recorded history, that every age has its socialists. . . . (2) that socialism is in some sense alien to the traditions of the Western world of which the United States is a part." [9: 91]

[7]Overton H. Taylor, *A History of Economic Thought* (New York: The McGraw-Hill Book Company, 1960), p. 274.

Yet both capitalists and socialists agree the core of both systems lies in the type of economic organization involved and the alleged non-economic benefits accrue from the manner in which economic problems are organized and resolved. "Every socialist wishes to revolutionize society," argued Joseph A. Schumpeter, "from the economic angle and all the blessings he expects are to come through a change in economic institutions." [8 : 169]

Fourth, both capitalism and the socialist movement historically had a familial association with anarchism and a distinct *anti-state* bias. This bias, of course, is implicit in the classical, liberal model of an automatic, spontaneously self-adjusting and self-regulating economy. Many nineteenth century socialists, including the Marxists, though desirous of sharp shifts in the economic organization of society, did not, in the main, regard the state as the vehicle for making these changes and were as anti-statist as any supporter of classical liberalism. Indeed, the vision of the future socialist economy often was accompanied in the nieteenth and early twentieth centuries by the anarchistic ideal of the disappearance of the state, that is, of coercive governmental control over individuals and the utilization of the state as a coercive instrument by the rich and propertied classes. Calvin Hoover stated this point succinctly: [5 : 17]

> The record is overwhelmingly clear that the early revolutionary socialist opponents of capitalism feared and hated not only the capitalist state, but any state, just as did the anarchists. The experience of the classes to which the revolutionary opponents of capitalism could appeal had always been with government as an instrument of repression, whether in feudal or in capitalistic times. It was quite logical, therefore, that Marx in appealing to the masses should advocate not an increased role for the state, but, instead, a total "withering away of the state."

Fifth, socialism as a movement of economic protest and social reform developed and spread initially in the context of Western constitutional *democracy*. Socialist movements have had their greatest successes historically in countries with strong democratic traditions, such as Sweden, Great Britain, and New Zealand. Political democracy thus is an important historical link between capitalism and the socialist movement, and is the bond between what sometimes is called "democratic capitalism," and "democratic socialism," or, to use the expression common in continental Europe, "social democracy." Political democracy has been, in fact, an important vehicle and source of pressure for the social reform and modification of capitalism, and the political successes of socialists in the twentieth century may be explained at least in part by the support of democratic institutions by socialism's opponents. Classical liberalism and socialism had a common historical base in the democratic struggle against aristocratic privilege in the late eighteenth-early nineteenth century. Consequently, socialism has often been infused with democratic ideals. Social democrats, or democratic socialists as they came to be called in England, have emphasized an evolutionary and peaceful route to socialism. Moreover, they have extended democracy's boundaries to include the economy, as well as government, and have sought to make the economic as well as the political system more responsive to the "will of the people." Also, in practice, "socialist governments" in Great Britain and continental Europe have shown great respect and support for constitutional liberties and democratic institutions.

Sixth, socialists typically have presumed that socialism would be a *post-capitalist* system, that is, that it would emerge in industrially advanced capitalist economies, or even that industrially advanced capitalism is a prerequisite to the establishment of socialism. The economics of this presumption is twofold: first, even those socialists who were highly critical of capitalism were greatly impressed by its production and productivity. There are few laudatory statements in the literature of capitalism to match the "hymn of praise" of capitalism (and capitalists) in the *Communist Manifesto* (see Chapter 5). Second, socialism is, among other things, "about equality." But an equalitarian distribution of income presumes as a prerequisite something to distribute. Capitalism, in at least one socialist view, has the "historic function" of developing the economic base of society to the point where it is affluent enough to make it feasible to commence serious consideration of the promotion of greater income equality.

Seventh, classical liberalism and socialism share "the underlying assumption that the *right to property ultimately rests on work, effort, and industry, rather than on formal law, custom, or birth.*" Socialism "inherits from capitalism one basic goal: to *preserve the unity of work and ownership.*"[8] The classic capitalist rationale of private ownership of property goes back at least in part to John Locke's *Second Treatise on Government* (1690) which contended that natural resources are provided to men in common, but that, since "every man has a property in his own person" which "nobody has any right to but himself," whatever man "removes out of the state that nature has provided . . . he has mixed his labor with . . . and thereby makes it his property."[9] The specific form in which Locke presented this idea (the mixture of individual labor with common land) is less important than the fact that, in his time, work and ownership did tend to coincide; the owners of businesses and farms tended generally to manage and/or work in those enterprises. Thus, even when modified by Locke to recognize inheritance and monetary accumulation, the basic and ultimate theme of the unity of work and ownership and the philosophical justification of private property acquisition through work had some empirical

---

[8]William Ebenstein, *Today's "Isms"* (Englewood Cliffs, N. J.: Prentice-Hall, Inc., 1967), pp. 213, 214.

[9]John Locke, *Second Treatise on Government* (New York: Liberal Arts Press, 1932), p. 17.

applicability. In the process of capitalist industrialization, however, as both socialist and non-socialist students of capitalism often have observed, work and production became increasingly collectivized and the relation between managerial control and ownership became more tenuous. As Marx used, in modified form, the classical labor theory of value for his own purposes, so socialists, too, generally have been quick to argue that (1) as private ownership became increasingly separated from management and work, the classical Lockean rationale for *private* property becomes less valid; and (2) as work and production become increasingly collectivized, the classical Lockean ideal of the unity of work and ownership would seem to require some form of social or collective ownership and/or control of industry.

Marxism, Socialism, and Communism

The classic "battle of the '-isms' " includes references to Marxism and communism as well as to capitalism and socialism. Marxism is not an economic system in the sense of capitalism and socialism. However, Marxism is an economic theory-philosophy and a movement for economic change with references to and relevance for both capitalism and socialism. As a contribution to the analysis-philosophy of theoretical economic systems, Marxism may be divided into two major parts: one, by far the larger part, a critical analysis of capitalism; two, a vision of an ideally functioning post-capitalist system. The former will be treated in Chapter 5 and its Appendix as one of the major theories of capitalism, and the latter, in Chapter 8 as part of the literature and vision of socialism. The former consists predominantly, though not exclusively, of the "economic theories of Karl Marx." In economic analysis, as contrasted to socialist ideology or political action, no post-Marxian Marxist has matched the master in terms of analytical skill or scholarly insight. Marx's analysis still provides a provocative, powerful, and penetrating critique of capitalist industrialization, and of old-style, competitive capitalism as an economic system. In the case of socialism, however, our treatment in Part III will incorporate a discussion of the writings and contributions of a variety of post-Marxian Marxists, including the Russian "revolutionary Marxist" Lenin and, especially, the "Western neo-Marxists" Maurice Dobb, Paul Sweezy, and Paul Baran.

MARXISM AND COMMUNISM

For several reasons, communism (in contrast to Communism)[10] will not be examined at length herein. First, communism as an economic system is essentially a vision of a future society, not a description of a real economy. Of course, elements of communist thought and organization may be discovered at various points in history, from Plato and the Old Testament to the Israeli Kibbutz and contemporary religious sects. None of these, however, constitute either the conception or the practical operation of communism as a comprehensive system for the organization of entire economies. It is also true that people who have called themselves "Communists" largely for tactical reasons have organized parties and movements, waged wars and revolutions, and operated governments, all of which may be termed, in this one sense, "Communist."

---

[10]Communism (with a capital *C*), as a specific term, refers to the theory or movement of "Communists" or to the economic organization of "Communist" countries; communism (with a lower-case *c*), as a generic term, refers to a system of economic organization which, in the Marxian vision, is to succeed socialism in the process of historical development. The relation between Communism and communism, like that between Marxism and Communism, is tenuous at best. The Marxian vision of communism, as a post-socialist economic system, is described in Chapter 8. Varieties of twentieth-century Communism are discussed in Part V. To simplify the presentation, however, the lower case will be used also where the general tenor of the exposition or the use of a qualifying adjective (for example, Stalinist communism) makes the meaning clear without the need for a capital letter.

But a communist economic society, as conceived by Thomas More in the sixteenth century, Marx in the nineteenth, and Lenin in the twentieth, does not exist in practice, and is unlikely to exist in the near future. The Russians are the first to acknowledge this. Though calling themselves "Communist" (that is, true socialists as distinguished, in their view, from the pseudo-socialists or social democrats), they refer repeatedly to the working Soviet economy as socialist, not communist. This reference, incidentally, does not constitute acceptance of Soviet terminology. We will re-examine this issue in Chapter 15.

Second, though socialists in the Marxist-Leninist tradition do have a vision of the future communist society and a broad philosophy of history purporting to depict the progression from the "lower" or first stage of socialism to the "higher" or second stage of full communism, their philosophical vision has not been supplemented by detailed economic analysis.[11] In terms of the criteria used in our definitions of capitalism and socialism, however, it is possible to suggest the central features of a communist economy: a highly developed economy, with an equally advanced technology; exceptionally heavy reliance upon capital and capitalistic methods of production; communal ownership, not only of the instruments of production, but of consumers goods as well; a relatively large role for communal and governmental action, combined, however, with a "withering away of the state" as an instrument of oppression; the transformation of human attitudes toward work, income, and wealth; and the distribution of income according to need, rather than according to productive contribution. But this hardly consitutes systematic analysis, particularly in regard to the details of social processes for economic coordination and the

---

[11]For a sample of what does exist, see Karl Marx, "A Critique of the Gotha Program," in Robert Freedman (ed.) *Marx on Economics* (New York: Harcourt, Brace & World, Inc., 1961) and V. I. Lenin, *State and Revolution* (New York: International Publishers, 1932), Chapter V.

specific degrees and forms of centralization versus decentralization. Indeed, both Marx and Lenin were persistent in their refusals to consider as proper the detailed analysis of a future system of economic organization which had no timetable and which could become clear only as the "historical process" unfolded.

Third, it is not altogether clear that pure communism would be an economic system, at least as economics is traditionally conceived. To permit the citizens of a communist society to contribute to production free from monetary inducement or bureaucratic ruling, and at the same time to allow them to acquire goods from public storehouses to the full extent of their estimated "needs" would seem to require an extremely simple and restricted set of human wants, a super-abundance of resources, or both. Any of these would require the absence or sharp reduction of the economic problem of scarcity as we know it now. We should not discount the possibility, especially for a very small number of "affluent" societies, such as the United States. However, it seems clear that no country now run by "Communist governments" is ripe for the transition and that the problems of a society of supreme affluence would require a quite different body of analysis than that provided by contemporary economics.

MARXISM AND SOCIALISM

The relations between Marxism and socialism are subtle and complex. But the heart of the relation can be described by three observations. First, the Marxian analysis of socialism (and of the transition from capitalism to socialism) was more a speculative vision than a rigorous theoretical model. This lack of clarity has permitted a variety of Marxist or semi-Marxist interpretations of socialism more or less within the framework of the Marxian vision.

Second, Marxism embodies and incorporates socialism, but socialism does not or need not incorporate or be based on Marxism. Socialism as a system, theory, or movement thus may come in Marxian or non-Marxian forms.

Third, the Marxian vision of socialism was a corollary to the Marxian critique of capitalism. In terms of the dynamics of historical development, Marxism emerged in the context of nineteenth century capitalist industrialization. Other conditions and circumstances have encouraged the emergence of other views on the appropriate route to and form of socialism. With the process of successful and continued capitalist industrialization in the West, post-Marxian "social democracy," or *democratic socialism*, as it came to be called, essentially "outgrew" its Marxian phase, even when profoundly influenced by the Marxian critique of old-style capitalism and vision of a post-capitalist socialist economy.

By contrast, circumstances in the Communist countries have encouraged subtle re-interpretations of the Marxian heritage. Classical Marxism was essentially "about" industrialization, that is, about the dynamism and creativity, tensions and contradictions involved in the transformation from the agrarian to the industrial way of life. In this sense, every industrializing society has or may have its "Marxian phase," and industrialization under socialism has been characterized by many features similar to those of Marxian capitalism, albeit in modified institutional form.

In sum, "democratic socialism" in the Western countries has become more and more a theory, philosophy, and movement for the democratic economic reform of industrialized capitalism, while "socialism" in the Communist countries has been, until recently, a theoretical rationale and strategy for the industrialization process.

Beyond Capitalism Versus
Socialism : Contemporary
Economic Systems

It has become increasingly clear that contemporary economic systems no longer correspond with any precision (if, indeed, they ever did) to the classic models of pure capitalism and/or pure socialism. Indeed, there is a good deal of healthy controversy these days as to whether even the issues posed by the classic debate (private versus public enterprise, individualism versus collectivism, price systems versus government coordination) are really the most central and important ones for late-twentieth-century economic affairs.

SOCIO-CAPITALISM

This controversy is supported by several prominent reasons. First, Great Britain, most of Western Europe, Scandinavia, the United States, Canada, Australia, and New Zealand have departed significantly from their earlier, more capitalist economic structure and have incorporated certain elements traditionally associated with the theoretical outlook of socialism. But none has established, even approximately, the old-style conception of pure or classic socialism. And all have incorporated certain dimensions and elements (for example, bargaining among corporations, labor unions, farm organizations, and governments) not prominent either in old-style capitalism *or* socialism. The economies of these countries cannot properly be called capitalist or socialist in any pure sense. They share two major economic traits: capitalistic methods of production and a high level of economic development; they also share two political characteristics: the ideals and mechanisms of democratic governments and individual freedoms. However, in terms of other criteria, they involve a mixture or *interblending* of the elements of capitalism *and* socialism, plus some new elements. Because of the joint emphasis on democracy and the mixture of characteristics from the two classic economic systems, we might refer to these countries as "mixed" economies or "socio-capitalist democracies."

The economic theory and social philosophy of socio-capitalism is in its infancy. Ideas about the system have lagged behind techno-logical and institutional changes in the twentieth century in the developed, democratic Western nations. But the last few decades have produced increasing literature on socio-capitalism. It has emerged from two directions: first, as an extension of the theory of capitalism, in theories and strategies of managed, socially reformed capitalism; second, as a reformulation of old-style socialism, in recent contributions to the theory and social philosophy of democratic socialism. These contemporary theories and strategies of managed capitalism and democratic socialism are described in Part IV.

TOTALITARIANISM

Second, after 1917, totalitarian control over economic life was established in a number of countries, including Russia and Germany between World Wars I and II and, after World War II, in China and East Europe. The two major forms of twentieth-century totalitarianism in practice have been Nazi fascism and Stalinist communism. The initial tendency, especially by their protagonists, was to sharply contrast the two systems and identify them as variants of the classic debate over capitalism versus socialism. More recently, with the insight of historical perspective, interesting comparisons have been drawn between them, and elements of totalitarianism have been identified which transcend the classic debate.

Contrasts between Stalinist Communism and Nazi Fascism: Totalitarianism as a Variant of Capitalism and Socialism. Clearly, a number of contrasts may be drawn between Stalinist communism and Nazi fascism, for they are far from identical. In terms of origin, Nazi fascism emerged in an industrially advanced capitalist economy and in a society which had experienced democratic institutions. It drew the support of industrialists, disenchanted lower-middle classes, and the military, and acquired power more or less within the existing constitutional framework, rather than by overthrow of the existing government. By contrast, Communism has generally emerged by war or violent revolution in relatively underdeveloped economies which have had little experience with democracy, and has drawn political support from workers and peasants.

Contrasts may also be drawn between alleged aims and aspirations, the character and content of official ideology, and the nature of selected institutions. The ostensible aim of Stalinist communism was to "build socialism in one country" so as to prepare the way for a "withering away of the state" and a transition to ideal communism. This aspiration was supported by an official and rather laboriously developed anti-capitalist ideology and by a thoroughgoing dismantling or circumventing of capitalist institutions. By contrast, Nazi leaders openly and proudly proclaimed both their territorial ambitions and the dictatorial and totalitarian character of their system; lacking a clear anti-capitalist ideology and emerging in a capitalist environment, they were willing to retain at least the shell of selected capitalist institutions in modified forms, as long as they could be used to attain the aims of the political leadership.

Elements of both capitalism and socialism may be discerned in Stalinist communism and Nazi fascism. Stalinist communism was, in part, a system for creating, distributing, and investing surpluses of income for the purpose of industrialization and economic development. In this, it might be described as a variant of Marxian capitalism, for actually it performed the investment/industrialization functions ascribed by Marx to capitalism. At the same time, because of such properties as public ownership and control of the means of production and overall government economic planning, it can be described in part as that variant of Marxian socialism which emerged as a socialist substitute for capitalism in certain economically underdeveloped countries and which was characterized by comprehensive and central government

guidance, direction, and control of the industrialization process.

Like Stalinist communism, Nazi fascism contained dimensions associated with both capitalism and socialism. As a movement, the Nazi form of fascism had a left-wing anti-capitalist faction and appealed to a public in which popular political movements generally had been socialist. As a system for using and employing economic resources, Nazi fascism involved comprehensive collective/government control. These "socialist" elements were interwoven with nationalist dimensions to form the incongruously titled "national socialism," the main ingredients of which were: (1) the view that society should be cooperative rather than strife-torn; (2) the conception of the nation as the basic unit of society; (3) the idea that all interests and classes must be coordinated in the promotion of national aims.

It is also possible to discern "capitalist" dimensions in Nazi fascism. Nazi opposition to communism, proposals for the control of labor and labor unions, and enticement of support from large industrialists, coupled with the absence of a clear anti-capitalist ideology and the Nazi system's evolution from an industrialized capitalist environment, gave Nazi fascism a distinctly capitalist flavor as a movement for economic reform. In addition, Nazi fascism retained at least superficial resemblance to certain selected capitalist institutions, most notably private ownership of the means of production, inequalities in income distribution, and maintenance of private profits for capitalist industrialists. The fact that Nazi leaders were primarily interested in political and governmental processes rather than economic issues, and were willing to use whatever institutions seemed applicable to attain their aims, resulted in greater continuity with the past than under Stalinist communism. Nazi ambitions for territorial expansion and preparation for and conduct of war, supplemented by support from and rewards to some cooperative large German industrialists, gave credence to the Marxist and official Soviet view of Nazi fascism as a form of imperialist-monopoly capitalism.

Totalitarianism as a Link between Communism and Fascism

A comparison of the salient features of Stalinist communism and Nazi fascism (Table 2-2) indicates that it is misleading to regard them simply as twentieth-century versions of the classic debate of capitalism versus socialism for at least two resons. First, both depart significantly from the classic models of capitalism and socialism. Stalinist communism was a system for capital accumulation and industrialization, but one with radically different motivational and institutional structures and processes than any classic model of capitalist economic organization. At the same time, Stalinist communism in practice all but abandoned through postponement several prominent aspects of nineteenth- and twentieth-century visions of socialism, including equality in income, wealth, and economic power, worker control over industry and the means of production, and, in the non-communist view, democracy.

Similarly, it is misleading to identify Nazi fascism with either capitalism or socialism. The totalitarian, anti-democratic, and anti-egalitarian dimensions of the Nazi system, combined with the (albeit superficial) retention of selected capitalist institutions, belie the name of national socialism. At the same time, the envelopment of nominally private capitalist entrepreneurs in a comprehensive system of hierarchically structured, centralized, governmental controls, the substitution of collective goals and hierarchically determined resource and budgetary allocations for market exchange processes, and the establishment of government determination of income differences and profit rates (through government control of wages, prices, and investment policies) demonstrates

Table 2-2.

MAJOR FEATURES OF STALINIST COMMUNISM AND NAZI FASCISM

Criteria	Stalinist Communism	Nazi Fascism
1. Level of economic development	Underdeveloped, in process of development	Developed
2. Resource base	Landistic, in process of transformation to capitalistic	Capitalistic
3. Ownership and control of the means of production	Government ownership and control	Private ownership with government control
4. Locus of economic power	Government	Government
5. Motivational system	Social goals (official ideology): revolutionary transformation of society	Social goals (official ideology): creation of a new order
6. Organization of economic power	Centralized	Centralized
7. Social processes	Hierarchy	Hierarchy
8. Distribution of income and wealth	Government-determined contributions to social goals; inequality	Government-determined contributions to social goals; inequality

the dominance of an essentially non-capitalist economic system within a facade of nominally capitalist institutions. Even "monopoly capitalism" fails to describe accurately the structure or behavior of Nazi fascism, for monopoly is characterized by the existence of autonomous (though monopolistic) business firms and processes of exchange. By contrast, Nazi fascism substituted centralized, governmental coordination and control for decisions by private monopoly capitalists, and budgetary and resource allocations for market exchange.

Second, whatever their differences, Stalinist communism and Nazi fascism contained striking and fundamental similarities. In both systems, the locus and organization of economic power was that of a centralized government; the basic motivational dynamism came from the political leadership, and the basic social process for making and coordinating economic decisions was government hierarchy. Both systems were characterized by large-scale inequalities in income, power, and status, though the recipients of the benefits and rewards from the systems were different. Both systems maintained an effective apparatus of government control over the means of production, though the forms of ownership were different. Both were characterized by the emasculation or elimination of private economic power and economic interest groups, such as private corporations and labor unions. Both systems restricted consumption and promoted high levels of investment, though for different purposes (state construction and war preparation in Nazi fascism, general industrialization in Stalinist communism).

In sum, totalitarianism is a link between Communism and Nazi fascism. Both Stalinist communism and Nazi fascism shared the fundamental similarity of a comprehensivity of government direction and control extended to the total economic system (the identifying property of totalitarianism for the study of comparative economic systems) and the incorporation of all nominally independent and autonomous organizations within the apparatus of the party and/or government bureaucracy. If Stalinist communism is described as the application of totalitarian methods of political control to the process of fostering industrialization in an underdeveloped economy, Nazi fascism may be described as the application of totalitarianism to the control and direction of an industrialized and developed economy.[12]

Contemporary Communism

Third, contemporary communism may not correspond to Marx's vision of an ideally functioning communist (or, indeed, socialist) economic society. But it is also true that the theory and practice of contemporary communism, like that of capitalism and socialism, are in the process of change and modification. Though evolving and developing from a totalitarian past, and retaining many features of its earlier Stalinist system of economic and political organization, contemporary communism clearly is in a stage of transition—and experimentation.

For one thing, communist monolithism is cracking, if not disintegrating, and in the process may be giving birth, painfully and with much internal disputation and recrimination, to different communisms—of which the Yugoslav case is perhaps the most prominent, but not the sole, example.

_____

[12]For several reasons, no separate or specialized examination of Nazi fascism will be made herein. First, fascism is largely defunct as an economic system in practice. Second, Stalinist communism will provide us with examples of a comprehensively and centrally planned and directed economy. Third, Nazi fascism was only secondarily an economic system, and its leaders and ideologists made no significant contribution to the debate over economic systems. It is possible to describe the economies of particular countries which at particular times have been called fascistic. We can also examine economic analyses of these countries by non-fascistic economists. But fascism had no systematically developed economic theory or allied social philosophy in the sense that do capitalism, socialism, and even contemporary communism.

In addition, certain elements of economic organization traditionally associated with decentralized socialism or "capitalism," such as greater decentralization in decision-making and greater reliance upon markets, are being incorporated into the communist economies. This has been accompanied by active, interesting discussions and debates by communist economists. These contemporary theories and strategies of communist economic organization and planning, including the Yugoslav variation, are examined in Part V.

G 1731526

Alternative Routes to Economic Development

Most discussions of comparative economic systems presume a highly developed economy with capitalistic methods of production and an advanced technology. But one of the most important types of economy in the twentieth century is the underdeveloped economy. The governments of many underdeveloped countries in Asia, Africa, the Middle East, and South and Central America are actively concerned with fostering a take-off from the "vicious circle of poverty" into sustained economic growth. What systems of economic organization are being used and will be used to promote this development? One thing is certain: few underdeveloped economies are following, or are likely to follow, the classic model of competitive market capitalism. In most cases, governmental and international organizations are playing prominent roles. The major alternative paths appear to be Communist development, as in China, or development within the framework of mixed economy or socio-capitalist democracy, as in India, with interesting variations in between (for example, Yugoslavia and Egypt).

A CONCLUDING NOTE ON TERMINOLOGY

The complexity, variety, and dynamic changes in the theory and practice of economic systems and movements for economic reform in the twentieth century have complicated immensely the uses and applications of terms. Prior to World War I, capitalism, in various forms, was dominant in the theory and practice of Western societies, and Western societies were dominant in world affairs. In this context, capitalism was a convenient, if imprecise, term for the theory and practice of the existing economic order and for strategies and movements for relatively mild economic reform; socialism was a convenient, if vague, term for various theories, strategies, and movements which envisaged substantial change in the existing economic order, though differing from one another in numerous ways.

Between World Wars I and II, the emergence of totalitarian governments, the coming to power of labor parties and "socialist governments" in some Western European countries, and the trend toward greater government involvement in economic affairs muddied the terminological waters considerably. The standard practice, until recently, was to use a four-fold typology, consisting of communism, socialism, capitalism, and fascism, with such empirical illustrations or counterparts as Soviet Russia, Great Britain, the United States, and Nazi Germany, respectively. The terms were used more or less indiscriminately to refer to theories, actual systems, and/or movements for economic reform.

This typology never was entirely satisfactory, consistent, or acceptable. The terminological distinction between communism and socialism was tempered by the fact that Communism, in strategy, theory, and practice, was far removed from the classical Marxian vision of communism, and both differed from, yet incorporated some traits traditionally associated with, classical visions and theories of socialism. Western democratic socialism, in turn, was evolving in theory and practice from the base of Western capitalism and contained or retained many features of democratic economic reform found in modified, democratic capitalism. Capitalism was clearly in dynamic transition and was incorporating some features traditionally associated with socialism. It never was clear to what extent fascism constituted a variation of capitalism, of socialism, or, simply, of totalitarianism.

These problems of typology and terminology were reduced only mildly and deceptively by endeavors to extract the "pure" economic system from the governmental-political system, as, for example, in distinctions among democratic capitalism, democratic socialism, totalitarian or authoritarian capitalism or fascism, totalitarian or authoritarian socialism or communism, partly because similarities and differences still remain to be identified and explained regardless of modifications in terminology, partly because it is an open question as to whether the nineteenth-century concepts of capitalism and socialism may be placed meaningfully in juxtaposition with the twentieth-century concept of totalitarianism, but largely because a major, compelling feature of all twentieth-century economic systems has been the growth in economic role and impact of government and politics and their increasing interdependence with economic life.

The period since World War II has been characterized by a healthy and growing recognition of the variety and complexity of economic systems and the limitations of the traditional terminology. The evaluation and revision of Communism has blunted somewhat the traditional distinction between Communism and Western democratic socialism; the rapprochement between Western European socialism and modified, managed capitalism has blurred any remaining distinctions between capitalism and democratic socialism; and the "emergence" of the underdeveloped (but developing) "third world" has added to the complexity and terminological difficulties.

Some of this complexity and growing obsolescence of traditional terminology is conveyed in Figs. 2.1 and 2.2. Figure 2.1 depicts movements and strategies for economic reform which have appeared in the twentieth century as partial offshoots of capitalism and socialism. The socialist movement is divisible into Marxist and non-Marxist branches, each with added offshoots and subdivisions, including such marked variations as Stalinist communism and contemporary democratic socialism. Capitalism is depicted as experiencing both democratic and non-democratic responses to the problems of the twentieth century, each with further variations and subdivisions. In this complicated mélange, where is "socialism"? Where is "capitalism"?

Figure 2.2 provides a roughhewn indication of the relative position of several variations of capitalism and socialism in theory and/or in practice, ranging from non-existent "pure capitalism," characterized by the absence or near-absence of government or other collective institutions in economic decision-making, to "pure socialism," characterized by comprehensive, centralized government control and determination of all or nearly all economic decisions. Again, where is capitalism or socialism in such an array?

The future may produce a more comprehensive, consistent, and satisfactory system of terminology. In the meantime, perhaps the simplest, most direct way to avoid the "tyranny of words" is to identify and compare carefully each theory, strategy, or actual system in terms of selected criteria, without worrying about the particular "-ism" used to describe it.

SUMMARY OF CHAPTER 2

1. Economic systems may be classified in terms of such criteria as:

    a. the level of economic development—for example, underdeveloped, developing, developed

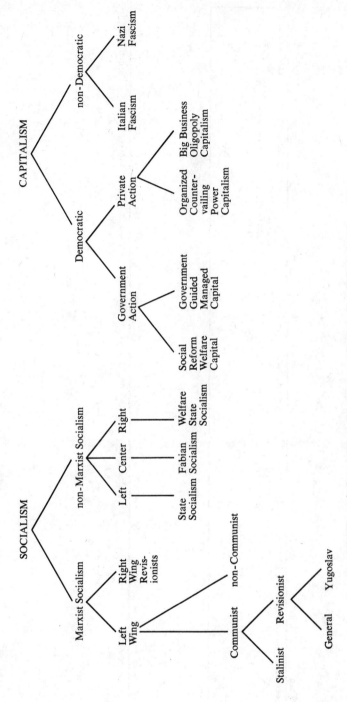

Fig. 2.1. Twentieth-century movements and strategies for economic reform

37

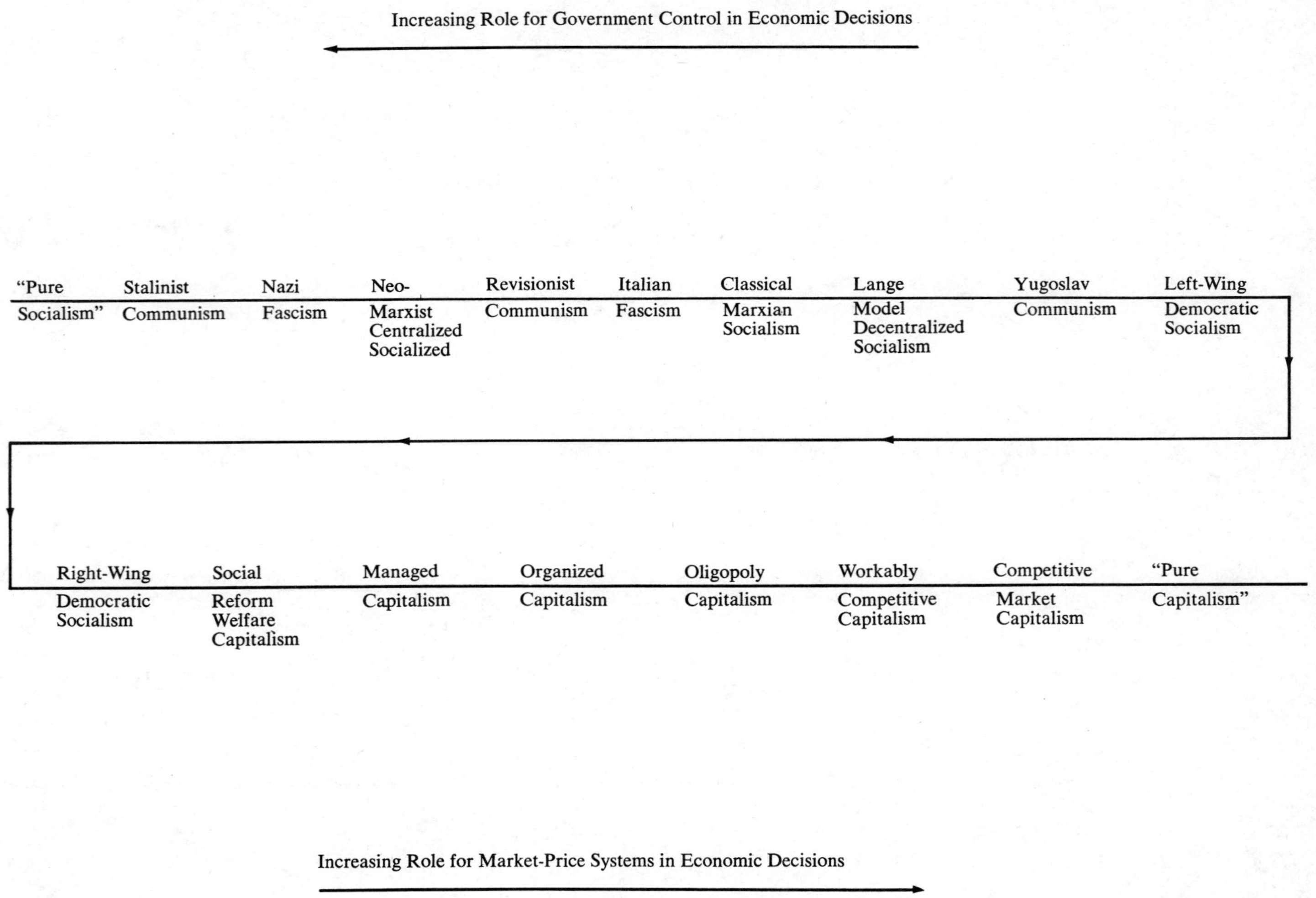

Increasing Role for Government Control in Economic Decisions →

| "Pure Socialism" | Stalinist Communism | Nazi Fascism | Neo-Marxist Centralized Socialized | Revisionist Communism | Italian Fascism | Classical Marxian Socialism | Lange Model Decentralized Socialism | Yugoslav Communism | Left-Wing Democratic Socialism |

| Right-Wing Democratic Socialism | Social Reform Welfare Capitalism | Managed Capitalism | Organized Capitalism | Oligopoly Capitalism | Workably Competitive Capitalism | Competitive Market Capitalism | "Pure Capitalism" |

Increasing Role for Market-Price Systems in Economic Decisions →

Fig. 2.2. Variations in economic systems in theory and practice between pure capitalism and pure socialism

b. the resource base—for example, landistic, laboristic, capitalistic

c. ownership and control of the means of production—for example, public, private, cooperative

d. locus of economic power—for example, individuals, private organizations, government

e. motivational system—for example, profit motive, pursuit of social goals

f. organization of economic power—for example, centralization, decentralization

g. social processes for economic coordination—for example, market system, bureaucracy, democracy, bargaining

h. basis of distribution of income and wealth—for example, productivity, need

2. The major classic theories of economic systems are those of *capitalism* and *socialism*. Most classic theories of capitalism emphasize the following characteristics:

a. developed or developing economy with an advanced or advancing technology

b. capitalistic resource base

c. private and individual ownership and control

d. economic individualism

e. market-oriented motivations

f. decentralized in the organization of economic power

g. competitive price or market system

h. inequality in income distribution, based upon market-determined contributions to production

3. The classic definition of socialism would emphasize the following characteristics:

a. developed economy with an advanced technology

b. capitalistic resource base

c. social or public ownership and control

d. social and public organizations as the locus of economic power

e. reduction of market relative to non-market-oriented motivations

f. greater centralization in the organization of economic power than under capitalism

g. overall system of national economic planning, coupled with greater worker control of industry than under capitalism

h. greater equality in the distribution of income and sharp reductions in income from capital and land

4. In the classic definitions, capitalism and socalism are different but not opposite. Beyond matters of definition, capitalism and socialism, in theory and practice, and as movements for economic reform, share an intellectual heritage and historical setting. Both systems generally:

a. are modern and Western phenomena

b. have been movements for economic reform

c. are primarily economic systems

d. share (in some versions) an anti-state bias

e. are associated with the spread of Western democracy

f. conceive of socialism as a successor to capitalism in economically developed societies

g. incorporate the underlying premise of the unity of work and ownership

5. Marxism is an economic theory and a movement for economic change, rather than an actual economic system. Classical Marxism was primarily a critique of the theory and practice of capitalism, and only secondarily a vision of an ideally functioning post-capitalist economic system or systems. As conceived by Marx, capitalism would be succeeded by socialism, and socialism, in turn, would be followed by the "higher" stage of communism.

6. Contemporary theories of economic systems recognize and emphasize divergences from the traditional, classic debate of capitalism versus socialism. These include: the emergence of a number of economic systems in practice, with associated theories and strategies for economic reform, between and beyond capitalism and socialism;

the emergence of totalitarianism in the twentieth century and its impact upon economic systems; the evolution and modification of contemporary communism; the emergence of a "third world" of underdeveloped economic systems for whom the choice of an economic system has become imperative for the promotion of economic development.

3

The Concept and Process
of Economic Planning[1]

THE CONCEPT OF ECONOMIC PLANNING

As the discerning reader may have discovered, the concept and process of "economic planning" was not included in our initial list of eight definitional criteria. Nor have we used such popular but misleading alternatives as "planned" versus "unplanned" economies as bases for distinguishing among capitalism, socialism, and other economic systems.

Economic planning is a very important and useful term, but much maligned and misused. Discussions of it are often fraught with emotional predilections. To planners, the term connotes a rational way to solve society's problems; to anti-planners, it implies comprehensive controls and regimentation. Part of the confusion in the attempt to define this central and controversial term arises

from a failure to distinguish between economic planning as a *general* concept and the *specific* types and forms of planning in particular times, places, and circumstances, or, in biological terms, between planning as a genus and its various specie. This chapter will emphasize the general concept and process of economic planning as applied to *any* economic system. In later chapters, we will examine the ways in which economic systems differ and thus the different structural forms which *particular* types of economic planning may take.

In its general form, *planning* means exactly what the dictionary and common usage say: an attempt to apply reason and foresight to the ordering of human affairs and the attainment of human goals. Just as a policy is a program for action, a plan is a program for *future* action. Planning is the dynamic process of preparing and executing these programs, drawing upon knowledge of the past, analysis of the present, and forecasts of future developments. Economic planning consists of the formulation and execution of policy programs in relation to goals, processes, techniques, institutions, and issues in which economic aspects, perhaps roughly and arbitrarily defined, play a significant role. Of course, an economic plan may be selected and executed, in which case it becomes operative policy, or, it may never get beyond the

---

[1] Portions of this chapter draw upon the author's article, "Economic Planning Reconsidered". [2: 55–76] For a concise and lucid treatment of definitional problems in the concept of economic planning, see also Myrdal [6], especially Chapter 1. For a spirited defense of the terminological restriction of "economic planning" to *particular* types of *government* activity, namely those which, by "centralizing the management" of resource allocation, attempt to consider social costs and benefits "irrelevant to the calculations" of "private, decentralized decision-makers," see Gerald Sirkin, *The Visible Hand: The Fundamentals of Economic Planning* (New York: McGraw-Hill Book Company, 1968), p. 45.

"blueprint planning" stage. Conversely, a policy may be based upon a considerable degree of prior planning, or, like Topsy, it may "just grow."

It should be noted that planning in this general sense is entirely neutral regarding specific types and forms of economic organization. It can occur under capitalism or socialism, in industry or government, in democracies or dictatorships, in developed or underdeveloped economies, in war or in peace. It can be centralized or decentralized; public or private; long run or short run; regional, national, or international; inspired or misguided. It can use or abuse the price system, enhance or decrease individual freedom, promote or deteriorate economic welfare. Economic planning is not one particular type of policy, but *any* policy from a specific point of view. In the words of Jan Tinbergen, known for his work in both the theory of economic policy and the practical problems of economic planning, "The general use of the word 'planning' has nothing to do with the type of policy involved. Planning in our sense can be applied to any type of policy, including, of course, the type of policy sometimes called 'planning'."[2]

The Scandinavian economists have been particularly prominent in the development of this general conception of economic planning. As one of them contends:[3]

> Every economy implies a plan. Economy consists in a totality of planned efforts to realize certain purposes. Planning is essential in every activity of economic character. The theory of economic planning does not deal with some special forms of human societies, but with a certain important part of every economy. It belongs to the general theory of economics.

"Plan or no plan?" thus is a highly misleading question. Every economy since

Adam and Eve has had some system or set of techniques for organizing and directing the making of economic decisions to attain social goals and satisfy human wants, that is, some type of economic planning. The leading issues rather are questions like these: Who is to plan? Toward what goals should planning be directed? How much planning is needed? What types of planning should be used? What methods of techniques should be used to enforce the plans in practice? Who is to plan the planners? [10]

IDEAL REALITY AND ACTUAL REALITY

In its broadest sense, the methodology of economic planning contains a confrontation of two conceptions of reality: ideal reality (Ri) and actual reality (Ra); it also embodies attempts to resolve the dilemma posed by this confrontation. In terms of economic systems, Ri is a conception of how the economy *ought* to be organized, how it should or would behave if it corresponded to certain specified "ideal" structural and/or behavioral criteria. It is emphasized that the specification of the content of Ri requires economic, political, and general moral value judgments which transcend scientific economic analysis.[4] Ra is a conception of how the

---

[2] Jan Tinbergen, *Economic Policy: Principles and Design* (Amsterdam, Holland: North-Holland, 1956), p. 10.

[3] Wilhelm Keilhau, *Principles of Private and Public Planning* (London, England: Allen and Unwin, 1951), pp. 16–17.

[4] Generally speaking, these value judgments or welfare criteria may refer to underlying goals of economic organization, to means and institutions used in society to attain goals, or both. A purely "structural test" would evaluate an economic system in terms of its correspondence to specified means or institutions *per se* without inquiring into the performance of the system. A purely behavioral or "performance test" would look to the *results* of the system and would regard the specific instruments for achieving goals as secondary. Many contributors to debates of capitalism versus socialism combine these two criteria of ideal reality. Most defenders of socialism, for example, regard a socialist economy as desirable *in itself*. To socialists, notes Schumpeter [cf. 8: 190–91], socialist bread "may well taste sweeter . . . than capitalist bread simply because it is socialist bread, and it would do so even if they found mice in it." Beyond this, socialists also contend that a socialist economy is

economy *does* (did, will, would, and/or might) behave and/or how an economy is organized. The specification of *Ra* clearly requires judgments of logic and fact in contrast to the value judgments indispensable to the specification of *Ri*.

A comparison of *Ri* and *Ra*, or, more accurately, of expectations about *Ra* in relation to *Ri*, is likely to reveal a divergence. Reality rarely corresponds to our conceptions of what it ought to be. *Ra* falls short of *Ri*. Broadly speaking, we may attempt to resolve this in one (or both) of two major ways: first, by taking *Ra* as given and modifying *Ri* to correspond to *Ra*; second, and a more typically Western solution, by taking *Ri* as given, and modifying *Ra* to bring it into closer correspondence with *Ri*.

It is possible and useful to distinguish comparative economic philosophies in terms of the divergence between their conceptions of *Ri* and *Ra* and of the magnitude and rapidity of change in *Ra* to realize *Ri*. A *reactionary* economic philosophy would specify a *large* gap between *Ri* and *Ra* and propose a *rapid*, *large-scale* change in *Ra* to bring it into closer correspondence with *Ri*, when *Ri* was defined in terms of a conception of an earlier and "better" *Ra*. A *conservative* economic philosophy would identify a *small* gap between *Ri* and *Ra* and would support and/or accept only *relatively small* and *gradual* enough changes in *Ra* to maintain intact as much as possible, for as long as possible, the "best" in the heritage and traditions of the past. A *liberal* economic philosophy would identify a *larger*, though less than "comprehensive," gap between *Ri* and *Ra*, would be less concerned with the "dead hand of the past," and would propose calculated risks and pragmatic experiments in the direction of *larger*, *more rapid* changes in *Ra*. A *revolutionary* economic philosophy would specify a

---

likely to behave in a manner more closely correspondent to their conceptions of "good" performance than a capitalist economy does or would. The same interblending of structure and performance tests is found in the literature of capitalism.

comprehensive gap between *Ri* and *Ra*, unsolvable except through an *immediate*, *large-scale* transformation of *Ra* to a completely new and different form of economic society.

As might be expected, the various theories of capitalism and socialism considered herein are scattered along the continuum, most roughly classifiable as liberal and/or conservative. Needless to say, the "liberal" (or even the revolutionary) of today may become the "conservative" of tomorrow. The classical liberalism embodied in the theory and philosophy of competitive capitalism often is cited, at least in the popular newspaper discussions and public debate, as "conservative". Further, the "liberal" or "conservative" in one society (for example, Soviet Russia) might be classified as a revolutionist in the context of a different society, such as the United States.

THE PROCESS OF ECONOMIC PLANNING: GOALS, ANALYSIS, AND SOCIAL CONTROL

As a general process, economic planning thus involves three main facets or elements: (1) the establishment of goals or objectives; (2) analysis both of the existing situation and of alternative polity measures which might bring *Ra* into closer correspondence with *Ri*; (3) the selection and execution of programs of action which, in turn, require procedures for social control.

Determination of Goals

It is misleading to presume that economic planners always begin with a clear statement of goals prior to analysis, policy selection, and execution. It is also misleading to regard planning in a strictly instrumental sense, that is, as a set of neutral methods or techniques applicable to the attainment of any objectives. Planning activity is purposive. It is difficult to think of planning in any specific sense except as related to purposes or goals. Planning for war and defense, for example, is one thing; planning for "social welfare" is another. One convenient and useful way to classify various types of economic planning is in terms of goals, such as distributional planning, developmental planning, and so on. Certainly, it is impossible to evaluate an economic plan unless one has a clear set of value judgments about desired aims to serve as criteria for appraisal. It is also clear that some of the prominent differences between economic systems and the role of economic planning in those systems stem from alternative conceptions of the goals which economic planning should serve.

A comparison of the theories and practices of economic systems reveals a large number of possible and actual goals of economic planning. In this book, we shall concentrate on five: (1) an efficient allocation of resources; (2) an equitable distribution of income; (3) stabilization of the overall level of prices at high levels of employment and income; (4) economic growth; (5) economic and political freedoms and democracy. Each of these has had its champion(s) in the history of economic thought. Some appear more significant in particular countries at particular times. But each has an important contribution to make to individual and social welfare.

More detailed analyses of these goals are presented in later chapters, but a number of general observations should be made here. First, economic goals are often multiple rather than monistic. Their multiplicity may be glossed over through the use of comprehensive terms such as "public interest" and "general welfare," but an economic planner hardly can pursue such vague generalities as these, regardless of their relevance for some analytical purposes. It is reasonable to say that general economic welfare is enhanced through the pursuit of some balance among these five goals, but equally apparent are the complexities of the relationships among them.

Second, goals are not generally in perfect harmony, but are often in conflict. Too rapid a pursuit of economic growth, for example, may heighten instability. Overzealous stabilization policies may reduce the flexibility needed for growth. The distribution of income regarded as just and equitable in a democratic society may not be perfectly compatible with the incentives necessary for an efficient allocation of resources. Resolution of these conflicts requires difficult choices and sacrifices. It may not be possible to achieve optimum efficiency, equity, stability, growth, freedom, and democracy all at the same time.

Third, these are not simple, clear-cut goals, but vague and imprecise. This is due, in part, to terminology. The Russians claim to be "democratic," but they have quite a different conception of the term than that used in the West. It is also, in part, a matter of conflicting value judgments. A good deal of agreement exists as to the desirability of an equitable distribution of income. But who is to determine what is fair, and what criteria should be used? Furthermore, several of the goals, notably freedom, democracy, and equity, are essentially qualitative, not quantitative, notions. Even growth and stability, though subject to greater quantification than the others, are not at all precise. *How* full, for example, is "full" employment?

Fourth, choices among these goals typically are not made on an all-or-nothing basis, for example, growth *or* stability, but on marginal grounds, such as, how much inflation are we willing to endure to maintain full employment? How far are we willing to restrict some freedoms in order to enhance others?

Fifth, goals are not isolated from the means employed to attain them. For one thing, we rarely know in advance what goals we regard as desirable. They are discovered as we make choices among various means or measures. Thus, the means chosen today can affect the ends selected tomorrow. Moreover, what is a goal for one person or group may appear as a means for another. One of the most difficult conflicts to resolve in economic planning arises when a group identifies as a basic end what is really only one of a possible number of means, as, for example, when farm groups identify equity in general with "parity price supports" in particular.

One of the most controversial issues in economic planning is this: Who is to determine what goals are important? Whose goals are to guide economic policy? This issue is closely related to that of the locus of power to make economic decisions, discussed in Chapter 2. It is also related to the political organization of society. In totalitarian societies, the power to formulate goals is concentrated in the hands of a small number of men at the top of the party or government hierarchy—ultimately, in the hands of one man. Because the power and freedom to formulate goals and decisions in a democratic society are shared among varied individuals and groups, no magic formula, whether it be the "general will," "majority rule," or "consumers' sovereignty," can transform disagreements over goals into harmony. We all have notions about what constitutes a "social welfare function" for the economic system in which we live; that is, we have the idea that the economic welfare of society is a function of such things as efficiency, equity, growth, stability, and freedom. But we disagree about the specific aims of particular plans and about the question of whose goals are most important. This does not mean a discussion of these goals is irrelevant, but it does mean that, in a democratic society, no one person or body is solely responsible for their establishment, and no clear, unequivocal statement of the general or national welfare exists.

Any economy must have some set of techniques for the formulation and communication of goals and decisions. One device is to delegate this responsibility to another person or persons. This is quite common, for example, in large-scale private and public organizations, such as labor unions, corporations, and governments. Another prominent and obvious device is that of voting, which consists essentially of formulating goals by counting in some way the expressed prefer-

ences of the participating voters. Allied to, but distinguished from, political voting, are the "dollar ballots" of the marketplace. Here, preferences are revealed by market prices, determined by market demands (given market supplies), which, in turn, are weighted by the expenditures of the different demanders. As we shall see later, the various theories of economic systems diverge on the question of the relative rationality of these alternative procedures for formulating goals as well as upon the issues of the distribution of power to formulate them and of the content of the goals themselves.

Analysis of Conditions and Formulation of Plans

Suppose a national consensus existed on the goals of economic planning, that the different goals are consistent or compatible with each other, that they are known in advance, and that they are clearly stated in terms of specific, quantitative targets. Assume the means chosen to attain the ends are in themselves entirely neutral in their impact upon economic welfare and may be evaluated solely in terms of their impact upon goals. Assume further that an adequately large, honest, and efficient body of private and public administrators exist to execute plans in practice once they have been selected, and that policy-makers charged with the selection of plans have complete faith in the impartiality and expertise of their scientific economic advisers. Under these conditions, only one planning problem remains: in the light of the existing or expected economic situation, what policy measures or combination of measures can "best" attain the specified ends?[5]

---

[5] This is essentially the approach of Jan Tinbergen in his various works on the methodology of economic policy. According to Jan Tinbergen in *Economic Policy: Principles and Design* (Amsterdam, Holland: North-Holland, 1956), pp. 8–9, the "logic of finding the best economic policy, that is, of finding the extent to which certain means should be used to achieve certain aims, is, in a sense, an inversion of the logic

Obviously, these conditions are more rigorous than those typically found in practice. First, goals generally are not "given" to impartial scientific analysts; as already noted, the goals, the criteria for determining "maximum economic welfare," are many, complex, interrelated, often inconsistent, and certainly controversial. Second, the relevant conditions for evaluating alternative economic plans often transcend economics, partaking of social, political, military, and other gains and costs. A policy with distinct economic advantages, for example, freedom of international trade, may be overruled by policy-makers because of other, non-economic considerations, which are rarely given full and adequate treatment by a purely economic analysis. Indeed, the *knowledge relevant* for making and revising economic plans may transcend scientific analysis. Friedrich Hayek, a major contributor to contemporary debates over comparative economic systems, has repeatedly emphasized the importance for economic planning of the essentially non-scientific knowledge of the "particular circumstances of time and place," known only to the "man on the spot," and by its nature not susceptible to statistical compilation, averaging, and aggregation. [4: 33–56, 77–91][6] Third, the analysis of

---

to which the economist is accustomed. The task of economic analysis is to consider the data (including the means of economic policy) as given or known, and the economic phenomena and variables (including the aims of economic policy) as unknown. The problem of economic policy considers the aims as given and the means as unknown, or at least partly unknown." In other words, given the goals and alternatives, and the methods of executing plans, the essential problem for scientific analysis is: What measures can most effectively attain these goals?

[6]Making wise policy decisions, writes English political philosopher A. D. Lindsay, "requires more than anything else an understanding of the common life; and that wisdom is not given by expert knowledge but by a practical experience of life. If the defect of the expert is his one-sidedness, the merit of the practical man of common sense judgment will be his all-around experience." *The Modern Democratic State* (New York: Oxford University Press, Inc., 1947), p. 279.

economic conditions and programs, no matter how precise and refined, provides neither the imagination, will, power, nor organization necessary to select and execute a particular plan. These things transcend economic analysis and involve the nourishment and understanding of the practical arts of administration, execution, and control. To have its greatest impact, a plan must be executed. The execution of plans is more than an intellectual problem and thus requires more than calculation and economic analysis. It is a problem in human organization, coordination, and control as well.

Still, recognizing these limitations of scientific economic analysis in the study of comparative economic systems and national planning should not blind us to at least three major contributions which it may make to this second facet of planning: economic measurement; economic forecasting; and economic analysis of alternative planning measures.

Economic Measurement

Because many economic policies evolve from the present or expected divergence between actual and desired conditions, that is, between Ra and Ri, it is necessary to understand, in measurable and quantitative form, the actual state of affairs. A planner is in no position to revise his plans *ex post* and determine where he wants to go *ex ante* unless he has a reasonably clear picture of where he has been and where he is. This requires economic measurement.

Economic measurement requires some unit of measurement, a standard or common denominator for compiling and comparing the sizes or values of economic variables. Different measures have been suggested at various times, such as physical units (for example, tons of steel, bushels of wheat), labor units (such as the Marxian notion of an hour's labor by an average, unskilled worker), and utility units (the famous "util" of utility). But because all these have limitations which restrict their applicability and relevance, economists generally use money as their unit of account. Cost, revenue, profit, output, income, saving, investment and other economic variables are expressed in terms of money.

No system of economic measurement is perfect, and monetary measurement is no exception. One limitation stems from fluctuations in the value of purchasing power of money. As prices rise and fall, the quantities that may be purchased with a single monetary unit (such as the dollar or pound) fall and rise; the two, by definition, vary inversely with one another. For this reason, economic statisticians insist on correcting money values (for example, national income) by price indices to determine their real or adjusted values.

A second and more significant limitation is that such important human values as cooperation, equity, and freedom cannot be brought precisely into the nexus of the "measuring rod of money" or any other quantitative standard. These values are essentially "non-marketable." We cannot excuse ourselves from studying them on this account; their importance to economic systems and planning is too great. We must recognize, however, that our study in these areas will be essentially qualitative and ordinal, rather than quantitative and cardinal.

In the area of private economic measurement, the monetary unit is used to measure two central economic variables: cost and revenue. Of course, not all costs involve cash outlays. Depreciation allowances and a normal return on the owner's own productive resources, for example, do not generally involve monetary expenditures. Further, the total costs of a private enterprise may include human sacrifices and penalties not always calculated by the accountants of that business, such as environmental pollution. Economists use the term "social costs" to refer to this phenomenon. The revenues, too, of private enterprise may be "social" as well as private, as, for example, when the installation of a flood control device by one farmer benefits other farmers. Clearly, social costs and revenues are not as susceptible to precise monetary measurement as are private outlays and receipts.

The monetary unit is also used in a number of social or national accounting systems, including national income statistics and input-output tables. As noted in Chapter 1, national income statistics provide three approaches to the monetary valuation of income or output, classified in terms of industrial origin, to productive resource owners, and types of purchasers. The second approach is important for distributive planning, while the third has special relevance for economic stabilization. In all three approaches, the measures do not simply stand on their own, but also may be used for making comparisons, which may be classified as those of structure, time, and space. Structural comparisons relate aggregate figures with component parts, for example, government spending as a percentage of gross national product, wages as a percentage of national income, or agricultural and manufacturing output as percentages of total output. These comparisons enable planners to more closely identify trouble-spots in the economy and to quantify the changing structure of economic activity. Time comparisons are of considerable importance in a variety of ways: in comparing prosperity and depression, in measuring rates of economic growth, and in studying trends in income distribution. National income data also may be used to compare economic performance, or aspects of it, in different regions and nations. The Marshall Plan in the early post-war period and various programs for economic assistance to underdeveloped countries have been based partly on these international comparisons.

Economic Forecasting

The preparation, selection, and execution of plans is time-consuming. Between the initial recognition of an economic problem and the actual impact on the economy of a program designed to resolve it several months or a year or more may pass. Therefore, the divergence between an actual and desired state of affairs cannot be determined simply by comparing present goals and conditions. By the time the program is executed, both the aims of economic planning and actual conditions may have changed. Planning requires a forecast of the divergence or lack of divergence between expected goals and expected economic conditions.

To isolate analytically the effects of planned policy programs, this initial forecast would be based on the assumption that there are no changes in these programs, that is, that plans are not revised. Government stabilization planners, for example, might appropriately make projections concerning population, productivity, and labor force trends, and then forecast total private spending and employment on the assumption that the overall levels of govenment spending and taxing will remain the same. This initial forecast must answer two questions: First, what changes will probably occur in the exogenous data not controlled by the planners, such as population, weather, and technology? Second, what will be the most likely impact of these changes upon endogenous economic variables (such as prices, outputs, incomes, employment) which planners hope to control?

From the standpoint of an economic planner looking forward at the beginning of a "planning period," the future may be divided into two distinct parts: "In the first instance we have all those happenings which are going to take place independently of our own will. We choose to refer to this immense totality as the *conjunctural future*. . . . But secondly, we have before us a limited number of events which must or may be influenced by our personal resolutions. We will call it the *affectable future*."[7] The former represents

the field of pure forecasting, the latter, a mixture of forecasting and control.

In the unusual case where the goals and the expected situation coincide exactly, the initial forecast would be adequate. It would not be necessary for plans to be revised, and the need for the appraisal of policy measures would not be great. In the more typical case, however, expectations would reveal a lack of correspondence between aims and reality. This requires a second and different forecast, which may be approached in one of two ways: First, if the planner begins with a specific policy measure, he must ask, "What will be the impact upon the economy of a change in this measure, and to what degree does this impact harmonize with the desired goal?" For example, if government purchases were to rise by $10 billion, what would be the effect upon the gross national product and the employment of labor, and how close would this bring the economy to a full utilization of its resources? Second, if the planner begins with a clear statement of a desired goal, he must ask: What changes in policy measures will be required, that is, how will plans have to be revised to maximize or most closely attain the goals in some future planning period? In either case, a forecast is required of the expected effects of different economic programs, that is, the expected efficiencies of alternative measures. This appraisal requires, in turn, economic analysis.

Economic Model-Building

The impact on the national economy of changes in policies depends on how people react to these changes. Economic analysis is concerned with just this question: How do people go about altering their plans, that is, responding to economic changes, including changes in the plans and programs of others? Economic analysis is based on the assumption that it is possible to discover and describe (at least approximately) the essential features of these actions and responses in terms of a relatively small number of central economic

---

[7]Wilhelm Keilhau, *Principles of Private and Public Planning* (London, England: Allen and Unwin, 1951), p. 48.

relations or equations. Some of these economic relationships are identities, as, for example, in $MV \equiv PT$, mentioned in Chapter 1, or $Y \equiv C + I$ (national income is identical with consumption plus investment), familiar to students of national income analysis. Others are "behavioral" or "functional" equations, as, for example, the equation $C = f(Y)$ (consumption is some function of the level of national income) or $Qd_1 = f(P_1)$ (quantity demanded of commodity one is some function of its price). Identities are tautological or definitional. What is on one side of the three lines $\equiv$ is identical with what is on the other. These tautologies are interesting and important because they indicate certain necessary, logical relationships which must exist, and thus, which help to insert greater order and system into our thinking about complex problems. Behavioral equations are more ambitious. They purport to indicate how the value of one economic variable (say, quantity demanded) is dependent upon or influenced by another variable (say, price) so that a change in one may be expected to bring a change in the other.

The decisions, responses, actions, and relations of people, which constitute an economy, are very complex. For this reason, it is helpful to begin with a simplified picture or "model" of the economic process, gradually inserting greater specifics, complexities, and refinements into the analysis to bring the model closer to reality. Any judgment as to the potential efficiency of an economic program in attaining a specific goal requires some conception of the economic process, that is, some model of how the different parts of economic life are intermeshed, and thus, how people can be expected to respond under given conditions to changes in particular economic variables by policy-makers.

Just as there are many types of planning problems, there are numerous kinds of economic models. Some are very restricted in scope, while others are more ambitious. Some are microeconomic, having to do with the

actions and decisions of individual economic units (for example, households and firms) and how they interrelate. Others are macroeconomic, concerned with the overall level of economic activity and its broad components (such as consumption and investment). Some are static models, focusing on economic actions in one time period or in one or comparative positions of "equilibrium." Others, like economic growth and fluctuation theories, are dynamic, based on intertemporal relations among economic variables (as, for example, in the expenditure lag equation $Ct = fYt - 1$, where consumption this year is held to be determined by the level of *last* year's national income). Many are expressed in literary form. Some employ algebra, geometry, or calculus. But all have in common three functions in the science of economic planning. First, they may help to specify and clarify the policy measures or techniques to attain goals. Second, they may be used to compare the effects upon goal attainment (and thus advantages and disadvantages) of any one policy measure. Third, they may be used to compare the effects of alternative measures. Ideally, such an analysis would yield a clear and quantitative forecast of the impacts of actual and potential policy changes on the economy, and thus, a means of appraising the gains and costs of attaining specified goals through specified policies.

Selecting and Executing Economic Programs

SELECTING ECONOMIC PROGRAMS

Planning is an art as well as a science. Policy-makers cannot and do not select a particular economic plan or program from a number of alternatives simply in terms of their respective anticipated net gains as determined by economic analysis. First, policy-makers generally are not professional economic analysts; that is, economic programs are generally selected by non-economists. *Their* criteria for appraising gains and costs may differ from those of their professional economic advisers (if, indeed, they employ them). "The advocates of controls," wrote Arthur Smithies, "usually avoid the crucial question whether the controllers will be greatly interested in the economists' welfare criteria. Experience with controlled systems seems to indicate that controllers have criteria of their own."[8]

Second, economic programs are not always selected on the basis of economic calculation and analysis of marginal gains and costs. They require, and are based on, will, courage, intuition, daring, and what the late Joseph Schumpeter called "vision". Great innovations and daring changes, Schumpeter argued, rarely result from careful, systematic appraisal of the net advantages of alternatives. Indeed, to systematic planners, the programs and proposals of an innovator may appear romantic, disorganized, or unsound. Most policy-makers do have at least a touch of this romantic and visionary spirit. Without economic calculations, wrote Kenneth Boulding, "man has no sense; without heroic and romantic visions, he has no meaning."[9]

Third, most economic plans, if executed, result in real or imagined costs to someone. The economic measure or change that makes *everyone* better off is the exception, not the rule. Theoretical welfare economics provides a sensible solution to this problem. If it is possible (say, through a system of government taxes and subsidies) to fully "compensate" the losers from the gains of the gainers, still leaving the gainers with something left over, then no one would really be worse off and someone might be better off. For example, it is conceivable that the removal of the American tariff on tuna packed in soybean oil would enable the importation of Japanese tuna at substantially lower

prices than those prevailing. In this way, an excise tax could be levied upon the sale of tuna, the proceeds of which could be used to compensate American tuna fishermen for their losses originating from competition with Japanese producers. The obstacles to such a policy are not so much economic as they are political and administrative. Most changes in economic policy (like economic changes in general) are *not*, in fact, accompanied by the compensation of losers.

Fourth, economic plans are effective when they are supported by the people which they affect. No farm program in the United States, for example, has a great chance of adoption unless it has the understanding and backing of a majority of politically active farmers and farm organizations. This means that the efficacy of any economic plan or program "cannot be assessed purely in terms of that program itself. It must instead be evaluated in terms of its impact on the existing structure and of internal modifications necessitated in order to gain its acceptance."[10]

Fifth, the selection of economic programs is complicated by opposition which precludes certain kinds of policy measures. For example, the late Henry Simons was firmly convinced that economic efficiency is best promoted either by competitive private *or* public enterprise. Where possible, he contended, competition should prevail. Where competition could not or would not work, government, he maintained, should produce the product or service in question. The halfway house in-between of government regulation of private industry through regulatory commissions, Simons argued, combined the worst features of both systems and the advantages of neither.[11] But Simons' plan for free competitive enterprise, whatever

[8]Arthur Smithies, "Economic Welfare and Policy", *Economics and Public Policy* (Washington, D.C.: The Brookings Institution, 1954), p. 20.

[9]Kenneth E. Boulding, *The Skills of the Economist* (Cleveland: Howard Allen, 1958), p. 183.

[10]Clark C. Bloom, "Is a Consistent Government Economic Policy Possible?" Dudley Ward (ed.), *Goals of Economic Life* (New York: Harper & Row, Publishers, 1953), p. 246.

[11]Henry Simons, *Economic Policy for a Free Society* (Chicago: University of Chicago Press, 1948), pp. 40–77.

its merits in terms of economic analysis, has had little effect on American public policy. Though political support for government regulation is reasonably large, support for government ownership and production is small.

Sixth, planners may feel that economic conditions are undesirable and that revisions in plans must be made, yet lack confidence in the validity of their measurements, forecasts, or analyses. In these cases, incremental, piecemeal, and "trial-and-error" changes may be preferable to comprehensive, conclusive ones. The major advantage of the former kind of planning is not its scientific validity, but its flexibility and reversibility. If our best-guess hunches, formulated in an uncertain and dynamic world, turn out to be wrong, the mistakes can be corrected. For the "economic optimum," trial-and-error planning substitutes the more easily attained "less undesirable."

Seventh, the extent, complexity, and sophistication of economic plans are limited by the costs of administration and the capacity of administrative personnel and organization to carry them out. Minor changes in economic organization, though advantageous, may yield too low a gain to justify the administrative costs involved in making them. Less ambitious (and less advantageous) plans may be preferable to more scientifically correct measures because of the lack of an adequate number of skilled and honest administrators.

EXECUTING ECONOMIC PLANS

Once an economic plan has been selected, the next step is to execute it. The effective execution of plans requires many factors, including administrative personnel, methods to measure plan fulfillment, methods of communication, procedures for anticipating and preventing problems which arise in administering plans and for revising programs in the light of unexpected changes in economic and non-economic conditions, and methods to control the responses of people and thus enforce plans. Methods for social control require special emphasis here.

The popular conception of control is one of directing or commanding the execution of some order. Control here is used in a much broader and more comprehensive way. It is defined as any method by which one person or group influences, in direct, significant way, the actions of any other person or group. A is "controlled" by B when A's actions are a function of (that is, are dependent upon) B's actions. Viewed in this way, it is clear that the "necessity for social control of economic processes is not peculiar to our present economic system. Control, usually social control, is a necessary function in any economic system."[12] Indeed, economic systems differ largely in terms of what combinations of methods and techniques are used to execute economic plans and thus control economic actions and responses.

Controls come in a variety of forms. First, they may be unilateral (where A controls B, but B does not reciprocate) or non-unilateral, for example, bilateral and multilateral, (where A controls B, B controls A; or both A and B control, and are controlled by, C). Very few control relations are purely unilateral. In societies where the power and responsibility to make economic decisions and to formulate and execute economic plans is divided among a large number of independent units, the execution of plans makes some form of reciprocal control imperative. Consumers control producers through the direction of consumption expenditures. Producers control consumers through sales promotional activities. Labor unions control business firms. Business, in turn, controls workers. Government controls agriculture, but farm groups reciprocate by exerting significant influence on the selection and administration of farm policies. General Motors controls Ford and Chrysler, while Ford and Chrysler control General Motors.

---

[12]Lester U. Chandler, *A Preface to Economics* (New York: Harper & Row, Publishers, 1947), p. 148.

Second, controls may be "conscious" (intended, visible) or "unconscious" (unintended, invisible). In conscious control, A actively and awarely attempts to influence B's actions. The controls over B under these conditions are likely to be visible, in the form of laws, decrees, enforcement agencies, and public statements. In unintended control, A controls B, though A may not intend to nor be aware of the impact of his actions, and though B may never "see" the control nor "feel" the connection between the revisions of his plans and A's actions. Adam Smith's famous "invisible hand" is a prime example of "unconscious" control. Under the atomistically competitive market system conceived by Smith, no one individual is large or powerful enough to exert significant control over the responses of others, and thus, over market conditions. But the summation of individual choices exerts a collective control over market variables, such as demand and price, and, in turn, both induces and compels responses from producers. Each individual producer feels he is "freely" and "automatically" forming and executing his own plans; but, in competition with other like-minded producers, he is led as if by an "invisible hand" to respond to the economic conditions of a social process beyond his individual manipulation and control.

Of course, one may object to the purposes or results of such a social control process or insist that conscious controls, in a number of important instances, may be preferable to, or more effective than, unconscious controls. But it is misleading to draw from these assertions the inference that multilateral control of individual plans embodied in the competitive price system must be "uncontrolled" and "unplanned" simply because it is "unconscious." Planning requires execution; execution requires controls. But controls just as easily may be unintended or unconscious as intended and conscious.

Third, the conscious attempt to manipulate economic activity may proceed by compulsion or by inducement. A may compel B to act or not to act in a particular way either through prohibition or command. Prohibition is negative; individuals are forbidden to engage in particular activities, for example, to employ children under fourteen, to pay less than a minimum wage, or to charge more than a maximum price. Command is positive: A orders B to report for induction, to arrive at work at 9:00 A.M., or to purchase a quantity of government bonds. Compulsion is effective as a method of control only if these controlled realize they will be subject to a penalty determined by the controller if they fail to respond as expected. Few planners, even in totalitarian societies, can control the execution of their plans through a *pure* or simple command and prohibition system. Furthermore, compulsion is an expensive, cumbersome, and frustrating method of control. If the only means of controlling a response is through fear or penalty for noncompliance, there is little incentive for doing more than the bare minimum necessary to avoid the penalties. Even this requires costly administrative machinery to supervise and enforce. For these and other reasons, command and prohibition nearly always are supplemented by inducement.

Inducement differs from compulsion by consciously manipulating and promising rewards as well as punishments. Examples of it are legion: any seller or buyer with some degree of monopoly power is in a position to control or influence prices, wages, or rents, which, in turn, can induce desired economic responses. The quantitative monetary policies of the Federal Reserve System illustrate economic planning by inducement. The buying and selling of government securities by monetary authorities can influence bond prices and interest rates, which, in turn, have some influence on lending, borrowing, and spending. Collective bargaining, where labor unions consciously attempt to manipulate management and management intentionally tries to control labor, is another example. Sales promotional activities and savings bond drives are still others. It is important to note, as a final observation, that economic planning through inducement does not eliminate the market, but generally works through it, whereas planning by compulsion often supersedes market forces.

Fourth, the controls embodied in the execution of economic plans may be specific (direct) or general (indirect). Specific controls affect directly some particular part, sector, or aspect of economic activity, such as controls over prices, wages, rents, interest rates, public utility services of particular firms or industries, location of specific firms, or priority systems for the allocation of strategic raw materials. General controls affect the overall level of economic activity, and thus, exert their impact on the economy indirectly by influencing overall levels of saving, consumption, investment, and employment. The two most prominent types of general or indirect controls are those of monetary and fiscal policy. Monetary policy may be specific and direct, as when controls are exerted over particular kinds of credit, such as down payments on houses or consumer credit. Monetary controls may also be general or indirect, as in the case of manipulation by a central bank of the rediscount or reserve rates for private commercial banks. Fiscal policy,

too, may be directed in specific ways. An example would be establishing or removing a sales tax on a particular product. But probably the greatest impact on the economy is in the manipulation of the overall levels of government spending, taxing, and borrowing. Monetary and fiscal policies affect the macroeconomic strategy of governments, whereas specific controls generally are concerned with the planning of particular production or price decisions.

Synopsis of the Economic
Planning Process

A synopsis of the process of economic planning is seen in Fig. 3.1. Reading from left to right, the coordination of economic theories with factual data yields models of economic analysis for the purpose of making decisions. The coordination of objectives or goals with economic models yields policies designed to attain objectives. The formulation of a policy or policies for goal-oriented future action, combined with methods or techniques for control and, thereby, execution, constitutes a plan. The interaction of plans and events, many of which are beyond the control of any plan, yields experiences.

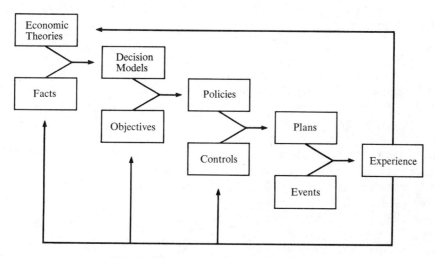

Fig. 3.1. The process of economic planning

In the light of experiences, successes or failures are evaluated and plans are revised, as illustrated by the feedback lines from experience to the other parts of the diagram. Economic theories are reformulated. New facts emerge. As a result, new decision models are constructed. Old objectives may be modified or abandoned and new goals or targets added. As a result, policies designed to achieve objectives in the light of decision models also are reformulated. New policy directives, combined with modified or reformulated methods or techniques of control, yield a new plan, which is tested in the light of events to yield new experiences.

Two key points emerge from this synopsis: First, economic planning is a dynamic and continuing process involving the constant interaction of thought and action, with periodic revision or reformulation in the light of experience; second, the dimensions of economic planning are far broader than a "plan" itself, and involve theoretical analysis, factual investigation and measurement, model-building and applications, goals or objectives, the design of policies, the development and application of methods or techniques of social control, and the interpretation of events often beyond the prediction or control of planners.

ECONOMIC PLANNING AND THEORIES OF ECONOMIC SYSTEMS

In this chapter, we have made a general survey of the processes of economic planning as they apply to any economic system. It should be noted, however, that planning is of many types and forms. This has been intimated in the preceding discussion of the planning process, especially in the role of controls in executing plans. Later chapters contain comparisons of the role of economic planning in the major classic and contemporary theories, philosophies, and strategies of economic systems. Thus, though economic planning does not explicitly appear as one of our criteria for comparing economic systems (as in the traditional and misleading dichotomy of "planned" versus "unplanned" economies), still it emerges as an important and useful focal point in the study of economic systems. The following summarizes the role of economic planning in the various major theories of economic systems.

Capitalism

Though economic planning is a central dimension of any economic system, the concept does not play a major explicit role in the prominent classic theories of capitalism. In the classic vision, the "invisible hand" was typically regarded as unconscious, undirected, and therefore, "unplanned." This unfortunate semantic tangle encouraged the development of a dichotomy of "planned" versus "unplanned" economy to supplement that of socialism versus capitalism.

Until recently, major twentieth-century theories of capitalism have generally continued the planned-unplanned economy dichotomy. The Schumpeterian theory of capitalism, for example, profoundly affected by both Marx and the classic nineteenth-century theory and philosophy of competitive market capitalism, viewed planning not as a dimension of any economic system or a possible vehicle for the reform of capitalism, but as more or less associated with socialist forms of economy.

Though Keynes did not develop an explicit or complete theory of economic planning, the Keynesian theory of capitalism generally is associated with a shift toward the idea of a distinctly capitalist form of central government policy and planning and, thereby, away from the identification of planning in general with some particular form of economic system.

Marxism

Marx was primarily an economic analyst rather than a planner. As many critics have noted, the concept of planning incorporates a voluntaristic element difficult to combine with deterministic "laws of social development." As has also been observed, the bulk of Marx's writings were concerned with capitalism and capitalist industrialization, which were typically labeled by Marx and Engels as "unplanned." "Economic planning" was expected to emerge in the post-capitalist economic systems of socialism and communism. As a consequence of the association of economic planning with socialism and emphasis upon the problems of capitalist industrialization, the concept never was clearly identified, much less subjected to careful analysis, in the Marxian literature prior to 1917.

Socialism

Economic planning has been a strategic dimension in most twentieth-century theories of socialism. Indeed, until recently, most economic theories of socialism, friendly or critical, accepted or extended the classic dichotomy of planned socialism versus unplanned capitalism. The major substantive contribution to the theory of socialist planning in the West prior to World War II, from the perspective of comparative economic systems, was the distinction between centralized and decentralized forms of economic planning in a socialist economy. In the economic theory of decentralized socialism, central planning essentially takes the form of the regulation of prices of investment and producer goods and interest rates, the formulation and supervision of rules for the conduct of plant and industry managers, and the provision of collective goods and services. In the theories of centralized socialism formulated by Western neo-Marxist socialists, economic planning is conceived as being much more comprehensive and centralized. (Indeed, centralized socialists tend to denigrate the kind of economic planning examined by decentralized socialists, calling it mere "price-fixing.") It consists of the planful

determination of input-and-output targets and requirements more or less throughout the entire economic system.

Communism

Economic planning is a central ingredient in the various major twentieth-century theories of communism. In Stalinist communism, plans for industrialization and economic development are the linchpin of economic organization, and an understanding of the goals, strategies, and techniques of economic planning is a prime factor in understanding the theory and practice of the economic system. The distinctive trait of economic planning under Stalinist communism is its pervasive and comprehensive character. In both theory and practice, annual and five-year plans have served as the central organizing principles of the Soviet Russian economy.

In the theories and strategies of revisionist communism, economic planning has been associated primarily with institutional and other reforms. Revisionist communism has been essentially concerned with a reform of the planning system. In some instances, for example, through greater use of computers and improvements in economic measurement and analysis, planning reforms point toward greater centralization of the economic system. In others, however, most notably in Yugoslavia, the thrust of communist reforms definitely is in the direction of greater decentralization. Since economic planning under communism has been so fundamental and pervasive a part of the economic system, decentralization of the process of economic planning can hardly avoid being associated with or even causing greater decentralization of the institutional structure of the economic system.

Socio-Capitalism

Economic planning also plays a strategic role in the theory and practice of the various forms of contemporary socio-capitalism. In contrast to communist planning, at least of the Stalinist variety, central or government planning in the West is not comprehensive nor pervasive in scope. It consists instead of the planful coordination of public policies, ranging from macroeconomic strategies designed to promote full employment, price stability, and economic growth to microeconomic measures designed to protect, support, regulate, control, or bring into "balance" various sectors of the economic system. Generally speaking, central planning in practice in the United States and Western Europe has not risen from ideological commitment to a particular form of economic organization, but from the premium placed on planful coordination of public policies in modern industrialized societies and/or from other economic and political pressures. Theories of economic planning in socio-capitalist economies have been accommodated in this context by focusing upon goals, issues, strategies, and techniques of public policy.

Similarly, in most instances, the theory and practice of economic planning in non-communist, underdeveloped economies has been pragmatic rather than ideological, and partialistic and incremental rather than comprehensive. The origins of central planning were quite different in underdeveloped and developed countries. Central planning has emerged *ex post*, so to speak, in the developed countries, as an attempt to coordinate public policies which emerged in the process of industrialization. It has come into being more or less *ex ante* in the underdeveloped-but-developing countries, a self-conscious endeavor to initiate industrialization and economic development. Partly as a result of this, ideological acceptance and recognition of central economic planning has lagged behind the reality of the planning process in the West—especially in the United States, where opposition to "economic planning" is heightened by its association with Marxism and communism. In contrast, the reality of economic planning has lagged significantly behind planning aspirations in non-communist underdeveloped societies, where planning

theory often consists of economic decision models (typically imported by economists from developed countries) which bear little resemblance to practical realities because of the lack or underdevelopment of a structure of institutions and policies to exercise social control and thereby execute economic plans.

SUMMARY OF CHAPTER 3

1. In the general sense of formulating and executing policy programs designed to realize goals, planning exists in every economic system.

2. Economic planning, and philosophies and strategies for economic reform, contain a confrontation between an ideal concept of what reality ought to be and an analysis of what reality is.

3. The process of economic planning includes three central dimensions: (a) establishment of goals or objectives; (b) analysis of existing and prospective conditions and of alternative policies to more closely realize goals; (c) selection and execution of programs and implementation of methods for social control.

4. The major goals relevant to a study of comparative economic systems are: (a) an efficient allocation of resources; (b) an equitable distribution of income; (c) full employment and general price-level stability; (d) economic growth; (e) economic and political freedoms and democracy. These goals are multiple, complex and imprecise, often in conflict, often pursued on marginal grounds, and interdependent with the means to attain them.

5. Though scientific economic analysis has practical limitations, it offers three major contributions to economic planning: (a) measurement; (b) forecasting; (c) formulation and utilization of models of analysis.

6. Because economic planning is an art as well as a science, plans or programs are not always or even generally selected on the

basis of their analytically-determined economic advantage.

7. The execution of economic plans requires methods of social control. Social control has a variety of forms, including: (a) unilateral or non-unilateral; (b) conscious or unconscious; (c) compulsive or induced; (d) specific-direct or general-indirect.

8. Though general economic planning exists in all societies, its specific form varies widely in different systems. For this reason, though economic planning as a generic concept is not a criterion for distinguishing economic systems, its specific, concrete forms and manifestations are very important in comparing and contrasting economic systems.

SOURCES CITED IN PART I

1. DAHL, ROBERT A. and CHARLES E. LINDBLOM, *Politics, Economics and Welfare* (New York: Harper & Row, Publishers, 1953).

2. ELLIOTT, JOHN E., "Economic Planning Reconsidered," *Quarterly Journal of Economics,* February 1958, pp. 55–76.

3. GALBRAITH, JOHN K., *American Capitalism: The Theory of Countervailing Power* (Boston: Houghton Mifflin Company, 1956).

4. HAYEK, FRIEDRICH A., *Individualism and Economic Order* (Chicago: University of Chicago Press, 1948).

5. HOOVER, CALVIN, *The Economy, Liberty and the State* (New York: Twentieth Century Fund, 1959).

6. MYRDAL, GUNNAR, *Beyond the Welfare State* (New Haven, Connecticut: Yale University Press, 1960).

7. ROSTOW, W. W., *The Stages of Economic Growth: A Non-Communist Manifesto* (New York: Cambridge University Press, 1960).

8. SCHUMPETER, JOSEPH A., *Capitalism, Socialism and Democracy* (New York: Harper & Row, Publishers, 1950).

9. SWEEZY, PAUL, *Socialism* (New York: McGraw-Hill Book Company, 1949).

10. TINBERGEN, JAN, *Central Planning* (New Haven, Connecticut: Yale University Press, 1964).

CAPITALISM

This section compares analytically four major classic theories of capitalism. The first—competitive market capitalism, together with the associated social philosophy of classic liberalism—provides the classic exposition and rationale of capitalism as an economic system.

The second—the Marxian critique of capitalist industrialization—provides, by contrast, the single most important critical theory of capitalism. It was Karl Marx who first clearly and explicitly introduced the concept of capitalism as an *economic system*, and the Marxian economic theory and accompanying social philosophy, despite its defects, is the most penetrating, provocative, and powerful critique of old-style capitalism to emerge in the nineteenth century.

The Schumpeterian and Keynesian analyses are the most important general theories of capitalism advanced in the early twentieth century. They are also the last of the major theories of old-style capitalism. The Schumpeterian vision of capitalist industrialization and transformation, as noted, was profoundly influenced both by Marx and by nineteenth-century theories of competitive market capitalism. Schumpeter reached essentially Marxian conclusions on non-Marxian bases and predicted the eventual demise of old-style capitalism, either by gradual disintegration into a "mixed" or "laboristic capitalism" or by an "outright leap" into socialism.

The Keynesian contribution was both the last of the major theories of old-style capitalism and the first of the contemporary theories of managed capitalism. As a theory of competitive market capitalism, Keynes' analysis, like that of Marx, provided a critique of capitalism's tendency toward depression and unemployment. As a social philosophy of "managed capitalism," the Keynesian theory represented an attempt to "save" the capitalist system. To some, Keynes' prescriptions seemed radical; to others, particularly in retrospect, they seem quite conservative. In any event, the Keynesian analysis marks a turning point in the theory of capitalism from the classic concept of the "invisible hand" to the contemporary analysis and emphasis upon social and public control.

Competitive Market
Capitalism

This chapter provides an exposition of the most famous of the various blueprints of capitalism, namely, the theory of competitive market capitalism and the social philosophy associated with this theory. It begins with an examination of how economic decisions would be planned and coordinated and basic economic problems resolved in an economy characterized by the assumptions of competitive market capitalism.[1] Following this is a brief exposition of the classic critique of monopoly and a review of the major criticisms of capitalism. The Appendix examines the implications of the classic theory of competitive capitalism for social philosophy, public policy, and economic reform.

The competitive capitalist model does not describe precisely any specific present-day economic system, such as that of the United States. But it does correspond roughly to some economies of the past, particularly those of England, much of Western Europe,

and the United States during most of the nineteenth century; and its fundamental organizing principles still play an important, though smaller, role in economies such as that of the United States.

THE BASIC CHARACTER OF
COMPETITIVE MARKET
CAPITALISM

Units of Economic Decision and
their Market Interdependence ✔

The simplest model of competitive market capitalism contains two major decision-making units, whose actions are interconnected and coordinated through two central processes of market exchange: (1) *business firms*, which buy resources from households and transform resource inputs into outputs of products and services which they sell to households; (2) *households*, which own and sell resources to firms and purchase outputs from them.[2]

---

[1] No attempt will be made here to trace the historical development of economic ideas on this subject, to distinguish among the various versions of theoretical capitalism, such as "classical" and "neo-classical," or to compare the contributions of various economists. Our purpose is, rather, to survey the most fundamental and continuing ideas about how competitive market capitalism in theory would go about solving its economic problems, and how such a system, according to its various defenders, could solve those problems in an efficient, effective manner.

[2] These are not the sole units of economic decision. Even an "old -style," laissez-faire capitalism would delegate a number of important functions to government, such as national defense, internal law and order, public works, and education. How far this list can be extended without altering substantially the structure of either the theory or practice of capitalism is open to debate. The point here is not that government plays

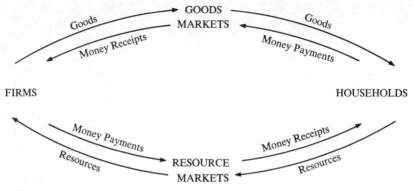

Fig. 4.1. The circular flow

The actions of these two units are interconnected by two basic types of market or exchange relations, illustrated by the familiar circular flow diagram in Fig. 4.1. In the *goods market* (in the top half of the figure), firms are sellers or suppliers, and consumers are buyers or demanders of a flow of final products and services. Consumption expenditures flow from consumers to firms in exchange for a corresponding flow of consumption products and services from firms to consumers. A second type of exchange, the *resource market*, is illustrated in the bottom half of the figure. Here, firms are shown as buyers or demanders, and households, as resource owners, are shown as sellers or suppliers. A stream of productive services flows from resource owners to businesses in exchange for a corresponding flow of money income payments to resource owners. From the standpoint of consumers, their expenditures represent consumption purchases. Firms view them as sales receipts or revenues. In similar fashion, the income payments received by resource owners are regarded as costs of production by firms.

The two kinds of market relations, as well as the two basic units of economic decision, are interdependent. The demand for productive services is derived from the demand for final products, in the sense that firms produce not for the intrinsic joy or satisfaction of producing, but for the purpose of selling (at a profit) to consumers. A supply of productive services, in turn, is required to create the output. Consumers are *able* as well as willing to purchase final products because they have money incomes, which represent a claim against the output of commodities and services. Consumers obtain their incomes through the sale or loan of their productive services to firms, who, in turn, organize and coordinate factors of production to create outputs from these inputs.

The classic blueprint of competitive market capitalism rests upon both motivational and institutional assumptions. The motivational assumption is that both firms and households desire to maximize their economic well-being through market exchange. Business firms are assumed to pursue profit maximization; for households, the equivalent motivation is the maximizing of utility or satisfaction. For both, the motivational assumption implies trying to buy at the lowest possible price (given quality) and to sell at the highest possible price.

The institutional assumption is that of competitive markets, more precisely, (in contemporary formulations) pure and perfect competition. The conditions of *pure* competi-

---

no role, but that its economic role, though important, is small relative to that of the private sector of the economy and is limited to certain "collective" and normally "non-marketable" functions. The implications of the classic model of competitive market capitalism for public policy and the role of government are examined in the Appendix to this chapter.

tion essentially are two: (1) a large number of small households and firms, none of which is large enough relative to the others and/or to the market as a whole to exert significant control over the quantity and, thus, the price of any good or resource; (2) homogeneity within groupings or categories so that no buyer or seller has control over prices through differentiating what he has to buy or sell in the sellers' or buyers' minds.

For pure competition to be characterized by conditions of *market perfection*, two additional qualities are required: (1) perfect knowledge of market conditions (specifically, prices and price differences); and (2) mobility and freedom in the movement of households and firms from the purchase, production, or sale of one good and/or resource to another.[3]

Competitive Market Capitalism as a Planning System

As an economic system, perhaps the essence of competitive market capitalism is the absence of a central economic plan or planner(s). The power and responsibility to make economic decisions and to form and execute economic plans is dispersed instead among many individuals. This does not mean that a capitalist economy is "unplanned" or characterized by anarchy and chaos. But it does mean that no one man or small group of men are in a position to establish goals for

---

[3]It is doubtful that the intellectual giants of economic individualism—men like Adam Smith, David Ricardo, John Stuart Mill, and Alfred Marshall—had very precise concepts of competition and monopoly in mind in their theories of capitalism. Nor is it clear that capitalism's philosophical rationale requires complete *purity* or *perfection* of competition. However, the institutional basis for economic coordination and control in capitalism is some form of competition among economic units, and if competition is to be "workable", it must involve: (1) a relatively large number of buyers and sellers; (2) a high degree of substitutability among products, services, and productive services; (3) a reasonable amount of market knowledge among buyers and sellers; and (4) reasonable freedom or mobility in the movement of resources.

society. It also means that the knowledge necessary to appraise alternative plans or programs is dispersed rather than concentrated, and that the execution of plans requires some process other than centralized coordination to bring individual plans into balance.

At the same time, though lacking a central plan, the competitive price system provides market capitalism with social processes for planning and coordinating economic decisions. In sum, competitive market capitalism has processes for establishing goals, analyzing conditions and plans, and selecting and executing plans and social control.

ESTABLISHMENT OF GOALS

A central feature of competitive market capitalism is economic individualism. Individual households and firms are free to formulate goals and make decisions in the effort to maximize economic advantage. However, the goals of the consumer are "ultimately" and "basically" the most compelling and directive. Firms are free to produce what they wish. But, if production is to be profitable, it must correspond to market demand. Entrepreneurs are "free" to produce bibles on the heads of pins—but who wants to buy them? Workers have the freedom of occupational choice—but the worker who chooses to become a blacksmith's apprentice in an industrial society may find his economic opportunities sorely limited. The consumer, in other words, has a freedom of choice among *existing* commodities; but more important, his choices also affect significantly the composition of future output. "Consumption," wrote Adam Smith, "is the sole end and purpose of production." Insofar as this is true, consumers are not merely passive spending and consuming units in the economy. Their goals also exert a directive influence over the choices of firms and resource owners. They are, in short, "sovereign" as well as free.

Competitive market capitalism is a price-

or market-directed economy. Individual goals are communicated to other units in society in market or monetary form, that is, in the form of a price or market exchange ratio. A seller says, "If you will give $1, I will give you a pound of ground round." A buyer says to a seller, "If you will work for me, I will pay you $2 an hour." As demands and supplies of business firms, consumers, and resource owners move up and down, prices (which are the ratios at which money, goods, or productive services change hands) also change. These changes in prices, in turn, function as a communications system. They express alternations in the goals or desires of other individual units in the economy. Any individual seeks to maximize his economic advantage in terms of given market prices. But his actions and attempts to attain his goals, in conjunction with similar actions by other individuals, may alter prices or exchange ratios, which thus express and communicate his goals to others.

✓ANALYSIS OF CONDITIONS AND PLANS

The analysis of divergence between goals and actuality, and the evaluation of alternative plans designed to achieve goals requires knowledge about gains and costs. Since many economic changes involve alterations at the margin of one's plans, it is also necessary to know (or estimate) marginal gain (MG) and marginal cost (MC), that is, the gains and costs of enlarging or contracting the quantity of one's purchases or sales by marginal or incremental units.

One of the major advantages of a price system is that it contains a method for quantifying and comparing marginal values of heterogeneous and diverse phenomena. The method, of course, is monetary measurement. Using money as a common denominator, it is possible to determine and compare market or exchange values of such qualitatively diverse items as, say, apples and oranges. If the market price of apples is five cents and that of oranges six cents, six apples and five oranges both will have an exchange value of 30 cents. Thus, exchange values of alternatives may be added and compared.

This leads us to the fundamental "*rule of maximization,*" which may be stated as the equality of *marginal gain and marginal cost.* As long as the marginal gain of any economic action exceeds its marginal cost, net additions may be made to total economic advantage through the continuation or extension of that action. If marginal cost exceeds marginal gain, however, it would be economical to decrease the activity in question, since the drop in gain would be more than offset by a larger drop in cost. Only when $MG = MC$ have all opportunities for increased economic advantage been exhausted. This central principle will be illustrated by examples from the economic decisions of business firms, resource owners, and consumers in later pages.

THE EXECUTION AND CONTROL OF PLANS ✓

Monetary measurement and exchange ratios or prices thus provide a basis for the analysis and comparison of alternative plans by economic units under capitalism. But if plans are to be executed, more is required than means of calculation. Methods must exist to put plans into practice. If capitalism is to qualify as an economic "system," it must contain some social process to control or direct economic plans in some systematic way. Otherwise, capitalism would be anarchy; and anarchy, whatever its joys, does not provide a systematic solution to society's economic problems.

Capitalism is an *atomistic* economy. It has neither master plan nor planner, neither central economic coordinator nor controller. Yet the plans of its atomic units are coordinated by an intricate series of rewards and punishments, and guided by a process of social control. The social process is the price system, and in the classic model, this process rests upon two bases: economic gain and competition.

The motivational underpinnings of social control under competitive market capitalism are not love, friendship, nor kindness, but the private pursuit of economic gain through market exchange by its constituent units (firms, consumers, resource owners). "It is not from the benevolence of the butcher, the brewer, or the baker that we expect our dinner," wrote Adam Smith, one of the classical architects of the philosophy of economic individualism, "but from their regard to their own interests. We address ourselves, not to their humanity, but to their self-love, and never talk to them of our own necessities but of their advantages." [24: 14]

The goals of households and firms are individual, not social, in nature. Economic units under capitalism seek their own welfare. Indeed, taken by themselves, and undirected by any counteracting institutional force, the unbridled pursuit of selfish, private interests may conflict not only with other private interests, but with the broader and more general interests of the society or community as a whole. In the absence of institutional barriers, for example, capitalist sellers are delighted in increasing profits at the expense of the consumer. "People of the same trade seldom meet together," wrote Smith, "but that the conversation ends in a conspiracy against the public, or in some contrivance to raise prices." [24: 128]

One important justification for capitalism, say its defenders, lies in the idea that the individual pursuit of selfish private interests, under specified institutional conditions, will result in greater welfare for society and its individual members. Although the individual "intends only his own gain," he is "led by an invisible hand to promote an end which was no part of his intention." Indeed, by "pursuing his own interest he frequently promotes that of the society more effectually than when he really intends to promote it." [24: 423]

The "invisible hand" should not be misconstrued as some mystical force or magic wand which mysteriously equates private and social gain. It is, rather, a shorthand expression for a very concrete (yet not immediately obvious) social process or institution for economic coordination and control, namely *competition*. The existence of competition among capitalism's economic units *compels* them to adjust their plans and actions to those of other units in a socially beneficial way. If one buyer or seller attempts to deviate from the collective pattern of the market, competitive market pressure forces him back into line. The rewards of economic gain may be countered by the punishments of economic loss under competitive conditions.

The practical impact for social control of market perfection is that individuals know how to maximize their economic gain and are free and mobile enough to attempt it. The knowledge assumption does not require omniscience. But it does require that the knowledge of the circumstances of time and place which buyers and sellers need to know generally is known and is not concentrated or withheld. The mobility assumption implies, first, the *freedom* to move resources from place to place and the absence of legal or other institutional barriers to the entry of firms or resource owners into new fields or occupations. It also implies a *willingness* to uproot one's resources and reallocate them from areas of the economy where monetary returns are low to areas where they are high, and a willingness to accept the consequences and conditions of mobility. Tariffs, agricultural price supports, and the closed shop, for example, are all inconsistent with the freedom and mobility of resources required under competitive market capitalism.

The practical impact for social control of large numbers of buyers and sellers and product and resource homogeneity is the absence or near absence of monopolistic elements in the economy. Price is an effective guide to economic decisions in the classic model only if it is a "given parameter," beyond the control of any buyer or seller, but subject to change as a result of the collective alterations in the demands and supplies of all buyers and sellers. Prices are established through the interaction of market supply and demand. Individual buyers and sellers respond to prices and price changes, but do not (individually) control them. Yet, given these assumptions, individual actions are guided and thus coordinated and controlled by these same prices. And because power is diffused widely among large numbers of buyers and sellers, the control process is reciprocal.

Buyers control sellers essentially through the threat of substitution. If a firm diverges from market price, its customers will shift their purchases to one of its competitors. Firms, in turn, as demanders of productive services, can substitute one employee for another, one resource for another. Resource owners control firms, on the other hand, through the potential and/or actual movement of their resources to other firms. Firms even have a means of controlling consumers, for if consumers as a group attempt to purchase more of a commodity at a given price than firms are willing and able to supply, the scarce commodity will be rationed among consumers through an increase in price. As long as market demands and market supplies are out of balance anywhere in the economy, their "disequilibrium" will cause changes in prices, which, in turn, will tend to induce actions and responses conducive to the elimination of the imbalance. These concepts will become clearer as we consider how capitalism, under ideal competitive conditions, could resolve the problems of allocation, distribution, stabilization, and growth.

CAPITALISM'S SOLUTION TO ITS ECONOMIC PROBLEMS

The Allocation of Resources

The classic model of how competitive market capitalism allocates society's resources to correspond to the economic choices of individual consumers may be divided into two main parts: first, an exposition on the behavior of the system; second, an evaluation of the impact of the system on the promotion of the conditions of *allocational efficiency*.

BEHAVIOR OF THE SYSTEM

The following discussion of the behavior of the competitive price system as an allocational process distinguishes between circumstances in which underlying conditions, such as technology, tastes, and incomes of consumers, do not change, and those in which they do change.

Allocation of Resources under Given Underlying Conditions. Given these underlying conditions, owners of productive services will offer for sale, rent, or loan, and business firms will offer to buy, specific quantities of productive services at specific rates of exchange (wages, rents, interest rates). Firms will, in turn, offer to sell, and other firms (and ultimately consumers) will offer to buy, specific quantities of products and services at specific prices. These prices and quantities of products, services, and productive services will be in balance or "equilibrium" throughout the economic system only if: (1) market demand = market supply in each particular market (the condition of market equilibrium); (2) each individual firm, consumer, and resource owner, given the prices determined by market supply and market demand, has exhausted all opportunities for improving his economic position, that is, has reached a "maximization position" (the condition of individual equilibrium). If market demand and supply are not equal for any particular good, or if any individual buyer or seller, given market prices, has not reached a position of maximization, various changes will take place which tend to restore or establish equilibrium.

On goods markets, the price system operates as a process for allocating products and services to consumers. At a price of, say, $1000, market demand for new Chevrolets may exceed market supply. If the price of $1000 were continued, sellers would be swamped by prospective buyers. Competition among buyers for the scarce and low-priced automobile would tend to force its price up. This would have two equilibrating results: (1) buyers would decrease the quantity of automobiles demanded, and (2) the quantity of automobiles which the sellers would be willing and able to supply would increase. Thus, rising quantities supplied and falling quantities demanded would tend to equalize supply and demand. Conversely, at a price of, say, $4000, market supply would perhaps exceed market demand. Were this price continued, dealers would accumulate large numbers of unsold automobiles. Competition among sellers in this event would force the price down, which, in turn, would encourage: (1) an increase in the quantity demanded, and (2) a decrease in the quantity supplied. Only when market demand = market supply at, say, $2500, would there be no further tendency for the price to change.

The same basic principle applies to resource markets. If the demand for electrical engineers in New York City, for example, exceeded the supply, competition among firms would raise their wage rates. If the supply exceeded the demand, however, competition among engineers would tend to lower the wage rates. Equilibrium would occur in this particular labor (or land, or capital) market only if market demand were equal to market supply.

Given prices of products and productive services, each firm, consumer, and resource owner adjusts purchases or sales so as to achieve the most favorable economic position. Each firm will select that combination of productive services which minimizes total unit costs, will purchase additional quantities of any productive service to the point where the value of its marginal product equals its wage (or rent, or interest rate), and will select that combination of products, output level, and plant size which maximizes its profits. Each consumer will attempt to balance, at the margin, the extra satisfaction from each product with its price, and thus, the ratio of marginal utility to price in

all directions. Each resource owner will seek to balance income and other satisfactions from the sale of productive services at the margin with the extra cost or dissatisfaction of providing these services.

If all markets and all individual buyers and sellers were in balance, and if underlying conditions did not change so as to disturb the equilibrium, there clearly would be no reason for change. Since market demand = market supply, the markets would be "cleared" of all excess supplies and/or demands, and there would be no reason for market price or supplies and demands to change. Since, given market prices, individuals would have exhausted all opportunities for further economic gain, firms would have no incentive to expand or contract inputs of productive services or outputs of products; consumers would not desire to increase or decrease their consumption (or saving) or their purchases of any commodity or service; and resource owners would have no reason to alter the supply or allocation of their productive services.

These basic principles are illustrated graphically in Figs. 4.2 and 4.3. Fig. 4.2 depicts a goods market in which households are demanders and firms are suppliers, while Fig. 4.3 shows a resource market in which the market roles of the two units are reversed. Given market price at Pe, each firm in Fig. 4.2a would adjust the quantity of the good supplied until it had maximized its profits. The positively sloped ss or MC curve by an individual firm represents the hypothesis that increases (decreases) in price will entice a firm to increase (decrease) the quantity supplied and is based on the premise that marginal cost of production varies directly with the quantity of output produced. At Oqe, the marginal cost of production is just balanced by the price.

Similarly, given market price at Pe, each household in Fig. 4.2c would adjust the quantity of the good demanded until it had maximized its advantage through market exchange. The negatively sloped demand

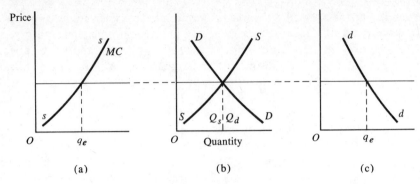

Fig. 4.2. Goods market: (a) individual firm, (b) market supply and demand of all individual firms and households, and (c) individual household

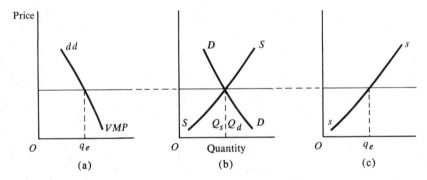

Fig. 4.3. Resource market: (a) individual firm, (b) market supply and demand of all individual firms and households, and (c) individual household

curve for an individual household illustrates the hypothesis that increases (decreases) in price will tend to entice a consumer to decrease (increase) quantity demanded, and is based on the premise that the marginal utility derived from a commodity varies inversely with its quantity. At Oqe, the additional marginal utility to the consumer is just balanced by the price that the consumer pays for the commodity.

While individual firms and households are price-takers and regard price as determined by impersonal market forces of demand and supply beyond their control, the market price is determined by the collective results of those individual decisions. Thus, in Fig. 4.2b, the market demand curve DD is the horizontal summation of the SS or marginal cost curves of all individual firms. Equilibrium price and quantity occurs where $OQd = OQs$. Only at this price are

demand and supply mutually consistent. At any other price, competitive market forces would tend to restore equilibrium by pushing the price toward Pe. At higher prices, the excess of market supply above market demand would tend to push prices down; at lower prices, the excess of market demand above market supply would tend to push prices up.

On the resource market, the roles of the economic units are reversed, but the logic is similar. The negatively sloped dd curve for a resource (such as labor) by an individual firm in Fig. 4.3a represents the hypothesis that decreases (increases) in price will entice a firm to increase (decrease) quantities demanded and is based on the premise that the value of the marginal product (marginal physical product of the resource times the price of the commodity) of a resource varies inversely with the quantity employed because of the operation of diminishing returns. At

Oqe, the price or marginal cost of the resource is just balanced by the value of the marginal product.

Similarly, the positively sloped *ss* curve of a resource (such as labor) by an individual household in Fig. 4.3c represents the hypothesis that increases (decreases) in price will entice a household to increase (decrease) quantities supplied and is based on the premise that the marginal disutility of a resource varies directly with the quantity employed. At *Oqe*, the price or wage of the resource is just balanced by the marginal disutility to the household.

As on the goods market, while individual firms and households are price-takers and regard price as determined by impersonal market forces of demand and supply beyond their control, the market price is determined by the collective impact of those individual decisions. Thus, in Fig. 4.3b, the market demand curve *DD* is the horizontal summation of the *dd*, or value of marginal product, curves of all individual firms, while the market supply curve *SS* is the horizontal summation of all individual household suppliers. Equilibrium price and quantity are determined where $OQd = OQs$. Any price other than *OPe* would be accompanied by a divergence between them and a resulting adjustment toward equilibrium price as a result of the competitive market process.

Allocation of Resources under Changing Conditions. The preceding discussion assumed that underlying conditions of demand and supply (for households, tastes, incomes, prices of other commodities, number of demanders; for firms, technology, resource prices, number of suppliers) are given. These underlying conditions determine the height or position of the given demand and supply curves. Were any of these conditions to change, the height or position of the demand and/or supply curve would change. These changes can and typically do disrupt previous market equilibria, and thus, previous positions of individual maximization. These

disequilibrating changes cause changes in prices which, in turn, encourage adjustments in quantities demanded and/or supplied. Assuming no further change in underlying conditions,[4] this leads to new equilibria and new maximization positions, with accompanying new patterns in the allocation of resources. Thus, the competitive price system in the classic model of market capitalism is not simply an identification of the logical conditions of general economic equilibrium. It is also a social process for facilitating and adapting to dynamic economic change. For example, suppose the market demand for television sets shifted up, while the market demand for radios shifted down. If Fig. 4.2b represents the TV market, the market demand curve *DD* would shift up and out to the right: the output quantity demanded at every price would be higher. (A similar diagram for radios would show a downward shift in the market demand curve.)

In the absence of simultaneous or immediate shifts in market supply, prices would presumably change: up for TVs, and down for radios. This would in turn alter price-cost ratios and, thus, profits. Existing TV makers in Fig. 4.2a would increase production up their positively sloped marginal cost or *ss* curves until marginal cost was again equal to the higher price. Existing radio makers would contract production until their marginal costs were again equal to the lower price. Demand for and employment of resources would rise in the TV industry and fall in the radio industry, with resource movements enticed by higher (lower) resource prices in TV (radio) production.

In the long run, the lure of profits in TV manufacture and the existence of losses in

---

[4]"Stability conditions", illustrated by "normal" shapes for demand and supply curves, are also assumed. Under "unstable conditions," illustrated, for example, by a positively sloped demand curve and a negatively sloped supply curve, divergence between demand and supply causes further divergence from equilibrium values rather than convergence toward equilibrium.

radio manufacture would encourage an entry of new firms into the former and an exit of old firms from the latter. The market supply curve for TVs in Fig. 4.2b would shift up and over to the right, while a similar diagram would show a downward shift in the market supply curve for radios.

As firms entered the TV industry and market supply increased, the competitive lowering of prices would cut back the excess of price over average cost, that is, lower profit margins. As some firms left radio manufacture, the ones that remained would find that decreases in the market supply of radios improved their position and that their losses had begun to fall because radio prices had begun to rise toward their former level as the market supply of radios decreased.

The logical terminus of the process would be reached when economic profits were eliminated in TV production and economic losses eliminated in radio production. As long as economic profits existed in the TV industry and economic losses in the radio industry, resources would be shifted from the latter to the former. This shifting or reallocation of resources, however, would activate counteracting forces, which, if un-interrupted, would tend to lead to the elimination of the economic profits and losses which caused the shifts. A new position of long-run equilibrium is reached. Once again, market supply = market demand in both TV and radio production, and all economic units, including enterpreneurs, have adjusted their purchases and sales to place themselves in the most advantageous position. In comparison with the starting point, though, TV demand and supply is higher and radio demand and supply lower.

After all adjustments have been made, the position of a representative individual firm in either TV or radio production would resemble that depicted in Fig. 4.4. Equilibrium output is Oq_e, where MC = price and profits are maximized. Because any excess of revenue over costs encourages the entry of new firms (which shifts market supply up

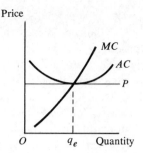

Fig. 4.4. Long-run equilibrium

and lowers price), and any excess of costs above revenue encourages the exit of old firms (which shifts market supply down and raises price), average cost also equals price; the price line is tangent to average cost at its minimum point; and the representative firm just breaks even, incurring neither pure economic profits (above the "normal profits" for the owner's own resources included in the concept of costs) nor losses.

EVALUATION OF ALLOCATIONAL EFFICIENCY

The major (marginal) conditions for static allocational efficiency may be identified as follows:

1. *Optimum Allocation of Goods Among Households*
   This condition requires an equality of marginal utility ratios between any two goods, x and y, for any two consumers, *1* and *2*.
   $$\left(\frac{MUx}{MUy}\right)_1 = \left(\frac{MUx}{MUy}\right)_2$$

2. *Optimum Specialization in the Production of Goods by Firms*
   This condition requires an equality of marginal cost ratios in the production of any two goods, x and y, by any two firms, *A* and *B*.
   $$\left(\frac{MCx}{MCy}\right)_A = \left(\frac{MCx}{MCy}\right)_B$$

3. *Optimum Allocation of Resources Among Firms in the Production of Goods by Firms*
   This condition requires an equality of the marginal physical product of any resource

a in the production of any good *x* by any two firms, *A* and *B*.

$$(MPPa^x)A = (MPPa^x)B$$

4. *Optimum Combinations of Resources in the Production of Goods by Firms*
This condition requires an equality of marginal productivity ratios of any two resources, *a* and *b*, in the production of any commodity, *x*, by any two firms, *A* and *B*.

$$\left(\frac{MPPa^x}{MPPb^x}\right)A = \left(\frac{MPPa^x}{MPPb^x}\right)B$$

5. *Optimum Composition in the Production of Goods by Firms*
This condition requires an equality of marginal cost ratios in the production of any two goods, *x* and *y*, by any firm, *A*, and marginal utility ratios of these two goods by any household, *I*.

$$\left(\frac{MUx}{MUy}\right)_1 = \left(\frac{MCx}{MCy}\right)_A$$

6. *Optimum Degree of Employment of Resources*
This condition requires an equality of the ratio between the marginal disutility of any resource, *a*, and the marginal utility of any good, *x*, by any household, *I*, and the marginal physical product of resource *a* in the production of good *x* by any firm, *A*.

$$\left(\frac{MDUa}{MUx}\right)_1 = (MPPa^x)_A$$

Under purely and perfectly competitive market capitalism, these various conditions of static allocational efficiency would tend to be met automatically through choices of individual firms and households in the process of purchase and/or sale.

1. Because, under purely competitive conditions, price ratios are given and beyond the control of individual households, the first condition would tend to be met automatically by consumer choices. In individual equilibrium, marginal utility ratios for any two goods are equal to price ratios between these goods for any two households. Because price ratios are common to both households, marginal utility ratios are also equal:

$$\left(\frac{MUx}{MUy}\right)_1 = \frac{Px}{Py} = \left(\frac{MUx}{MUy}\right)_2$$

2. Similarly, given price ratios beyond the control of individual firms, the second condition would also tend to be met, through the pursuit of profit maximization. In individual equilibrium, marginal cost ratios for any two goods are equal to price ratios between these goods for any two firms. Because price ratios are common to both firms, marginal cost ratios are also equal.

$$\left(\frac{MCx}{MCy}\right)_A = \frac{Px}{Py} = \left(\frac{MCx}{MCy}\right)_B$$

3. Given the ratio of the price of any good to that of any resource used in its production, the pursuit of profit maximization also tends to fulfill the third condition. In individual equilibrium, the value of the marginal product of any resource in the production of any good by any individual firm equals the price of the resource. This may be summarized alternatively as $(MPPa^x) \cdot Px = Pa$ or $MPPa^x = Pa/Px$. Because the price ratio Pa/Px is common to all firms, marginal physical product ratios are also equal:

$$(MPPa^x)A = \frac{Pa}{Px} = (MPPa^x)B$$

4. The fourth condition is also met automatically by the profit maximization choices of individual firms. In individual equilibrium, marginal physical product ratios for each firm will equal resource price ratios. Because resource price ratios are identical for all firms, marginal physical product ratios are also equal:

$$\left(\frac{MPPa^x}{MPPb^x}\right)^A = \frac{Pa}{Pb} = \left(\frac{MPPa^x}{MPPb^x}\right)^B$$

5. The fifth condition is automatically met with the attainment of the first two. In

individual equilibrium, marginal utility ratios between any two goods for any household equal price ratios for those goods, and marginal cost ratios between any two goods for any firm also equal price ratios. Again, with identical price ratios facing both households and firms, marginal utility ratios will equal marginal cost ratios:

$$\left(\frac{MUx}{MUy}\right)_1 = \frac{Px}{Py} = \left(\frac{MCx}{MCy}\right)_A$$

6. The sixth condition is also met through the separate pursuit of economic advantage by households and firms facing identical market prices. Any individual firm will maximize profits in the employment of a resource, as already noted, when its marginal physical product equals the ratio of the price of the resource to the price of any good produced with that resource. Independently, but by a similar principle, any individual household will maximize satisfaction when the ratio of the marginal disutility from the employment of a resource to the marginal utility from the real income enjoyed from a particular good equals the same ratio between resource input and output prices. Because the ratio of resource to output prices is identical for both firms and households, the marginal physical product of firms is brought into equality in equilibrium with marginal disutility/marginal utility ratio:

$$\left(\frac{MDUa}{MUx}\right)_1 = \frac{Pa}{Px} = (MPPa^x)A$$

In sum, in an integrated, efficiently working competitive price system, marginal utility ratios tend to be brought into equality with marginal cost ratios, and marginal disutility ratios tend to be brought into equality with marginal product ratios in all directions of consumption and/or production. Each firm, by producing up to the point where $MC = P$ for each good has served, as if by an "invisible hand," an end which was not part of its

intention; that is, by maximizing profits, each firm has also produced that quantity and composition of output that consumers want. If prices accurately reflect consumer preferences and marginal costs accurately reflect the costs of opportunities foregone in the process of production, an equality of marginal cost and price maximizes consumer welfare as well as business profits. Similarly, the preferences of households as resource suppliers (through marginal disutility) are brought into consistency with marginal productivity as well as marginal utility. If the six preceding conditions are met, no alternative pattern of resource allocation, at the margin, would yield as great a level or more desired a composition of output, and thus, none would promote consumer welfare as efficiently.

The Distribution of Income

THE CONTRIBUTIVE CRITERION FOR INCOME DISTRIBUTION

One of the most important single ideas in the classic theory of capitalism is that, given the assumptions and conditions of the model, resource owners tend to receive through market exchange with business firms money incomes, and thus claims against real output, corresponding to the contribution of their labor and property to marketable production.

How this would occur may be understood by assuming the opposite: that, under competition and with given underlying demand-supply conditions, some factor or factors is receiving a price (wage, rent, interest payment) for the marginal unit of its productive service, which is less or more than the market value of the marginal product obtained from the application to production of that marginal unit (VMP). Clearly, the continuation of such a situation would be inconsistent with both the assumption of competition *and* the "rule of maximization" discussed earlier, that is, the institutional and motivational foundations of the model.

This inconsistency exists from the standpoints of both resource owners and business firms. If resource owners discover they are receiving less than the *VMP* of their productive services in any sector of the economy, their desire to economize would encourage them to reallocate their supplies away from this low toward a higher wage, rent, or interest sector. This action would decrease the supply of productive services in the low-paying sector, which, in turn, would tend to raise the price of that productive service up toward its *VMP*. If business firms discover the price of any resource is lower than its *VMP*, their desire to economize in the use of that factor would entice them to increase their purchase of it. As they do so, the *VMP* of that particular resource will tend to fall, for two reasons: first, because of the "law of diminishing returns" (or, better, the law of eventually diminishing marginal product), which explains that the addition of a variable factor of production to the production process, assuming given conditions of technology and given amounts of other "fixed" factors, will eventually result in diminishing marginal physical product; second, because of the "law of demand," which maintains that if, given underlying conditions, buyers are to be enticed to purchase more of a commodity, its price (and thus, the marginal revenue from its sale) must fall. The logical terminus of this process of substitution would be where the *VMP* had been pushed down to its price, that is, where the resource owner was receiving a money income equal to his productive contribution.

Conversely, a price for a resource which exceeds the market value of its marginal product would clearly be conducive to two counteracting and equilibrating forces: first, resource owners would tend to reallocate the supplies of their productive services toward this high-paying area, and this increase in supply would tend to lower the price of the resource; second, firms would decrease their purchases of the expensive resource, which would tend to raise its

VMP. The logical terminus of this process, both for resource owners and for firms, would be a position of equality between monetary reward and market-productive contribution.

A divergence of monetary reward and productive contribution also would be inconsistent with the assumption of competitive resource markets. If the wage, for example, is above the *VMP*, it is competition among workers which drives it down. If the wage is below the *VMP*, it is the competition of business firms which drives it up.

The same basic ideas apply to changing underlying conditions. To revert to the TV-radio example: an increase (decrease) in the demand for and price of TVs (radios) indicates to business firms and resource owners that the *VMPs* of resources are rising in the TV industry and falling in the radio industry. This enables and encourages TV firms to increase their derived demands for productive factors, and thus, resource prices. This, in turn, encourages a movement of resources from radio to TV manufacture which continues until profits have been pushed down to normal and until a condition of equality again exists between the marginal costs of inputs and the market value of their marginal products.

In sum, resource pricing is an integral part of the competitive pricing process in market capitalism, and income distribution is intimately linked with the allocation of resources. The same processes which promote a tendency toward static allocational efficiency simultaneously will establish a pattern of income distribution consistent with an efficient pattern of resource allocation. Whether such a resulting pattern of income distribution is regarded as *equitable*, however, depends also upon value judgments about accompanying patterns of equality/inequality in income among individuals and families. This, in turn, depends upon a whole series of factors in addition to resource pricing, including property ownership, educational opportunities, government policies, and other factors.

In several important ways, the distributional process described in preceding paragraphs is more conducive to greater income equality than inequality. First, the competitive process that lowers prices toward average costs and a normal profit and raises wages toward the value of the marginal product of labor is, in part, a redistributive mechanism: It redistributes income from the smaller number of business firms to the general body of consumers and workers in the form of lower prices and/or higher wages.[5]

Second, the economic freedoms of the capitalist economy, especially those of entry, widen opportunities for economic gain, including profit, by opening areas of production and exchange closed to persons and groups under slave and feudal economies.

Third, the allocation of resources away from low toward high profit, wage, rent, and interest firms, industries, and areas of the economy tends to promote an equalization in rates of profit and other types of income, including wages for labor of given grades and skills (such as in the TV-radio example). Indeed, perfect equilibrium in the allocation of resources between two industries would require the elimination of such income inequalities. As long as profit rates or the prices of factors are higher in industry X than Y, it will benefit entrepreneurs and resource owners to reallocate their resources from Y to X. But their efforts to do so increase the supply, and thus, decrease prices

of factors in Y, promoting a tendency toward equalization.

Fourth, if capitalism is conducive to economic growth, the process of growth may, in turn, promote greater equality in numerous ways:

1. Through increased production of consumer goods, which "increases the purchasing power of the wage dollar more than that of any other dollar" and which, thus, "progressively raises the standard of life of the masses." [8:68]

2. Through expansion in the stock of capital per worker, which increases capital's relative abundance and labor's relative scarcity, and which, under certain circumstances, may be accompanied by an increase in the percentage of national income going to wages and salaries and a decrease in the percentage going to nonlabor incomes, which, if sellers of labor services tend to be in lower or middle-income brackets, will tend to promote greater equality in income.

3. Through the relatively greater expansion of skilled, technical, and professional jobs as compared to unskilled labor, which, in a free and mobile economy (a) permits upward movements in income via social mobility (the son of a janitor in a growing economy, for example, can become an engineer); and (b) decreases the relative supply of unskilled labor, thus pushing up its price in the manner already described.

4. Through expansion in the aggregate level of output, which provides the economic basis for legislation and philanthropy to raise and make more secure the income and employment positions of people in lower-income brackets.

At the same time, however, it is highly unlikely that competitive market capitalism, if established, would be free of *all* differences in income. Argues Friedrich Hayek, one of its prominent expositors and defenders, the workings of the competitive price system are

---

[5]We can state the matter differently by saying that, since competition is a central assumption in the classic model of capitalism, monopoly and monopsony profits (that is, profits obtained through restriction of outputs and inputs below competitive levels to raise prices to consumers above marginal cost or to lower resource prices below their *VMPs*) are logically inconsistent with the allocational and distributional processes of the system. This does not mean that "capitalist" economic systems in practice have no monopoly or monopsony profits. It means, however, that such profits are deviations from the logic of the classic model and presumably would be absent or insignificant in purely competitive capitalism.

"incompatible with a full satisfaction of our views of distributive justice." [4:22] In this view, inequality is part of the price we pay for individual freedom and competitive efficiency. First, people and jobs are not the same. Less pleasant, riskier, and less favorably located jobs may command higher monetary rewards than more pleasant, safer, and desirably located positions. These wage inequalities "compensate" the worker for the undesirable non-monetary features of the job. Further, if people are different, and make differing contributions to production, then personal incomes will differ. (It should be noted that income differentials as a result of personal or job differences are not necessarily unique to capitalism, but might be found in other systems as well.)

Second, incomes in an economic system relying upon the marketplace will be strongly influenced by relative scarcities of various goods and resources. Products, services, and productive resources scarce in relation to the demands for them will tend to command higher prices than if they were abundant. Those that are abundant in relation to demand will tend to receive lower prices than if they were more scarce. This response of the competitive price system to scarcity-demand relations is inherent in capitalism, and necessary for the allocational and distributional processes previously described. However, such a pricing process may provide high incomes for owners of scarce goods and resources, and low incomes for owners of more abundant goods and resources. Entrepreneurs fortunate enough to be producing in industries characterized by rising consumer demand may reap very large profits prior to their "long-run" elimination through the entry of new firms. Championship prize fighters, major-league ball players, motion picture stars, and "name" singers may earn exceptionally high incomes relative to those of unskilled and semi-skilled workers, who may have little opportunity or capacity to compete with such people. Fortunate owners of land in growing urban and industrial areas may reap large gains through rising land values denied to less fortunate non-owners.

Third, the distribution of income in any economic system, including capitalism, also is heavily influenced by the social institutions of that system. Two social institutions of great importance for income distribution in capitalism are: (1) the private ownership of land and capital resources; (2) inheritance of the ownership of land and capital resources. Because of these two institutions, capitalism permits, fosters, substantial inequality in the distribution of income. However, it is possible that the right of inheritance could be more severely restricted than has been done in economies called "capitalist" without destroying or even significantly modifying the operations of the competitive price system. Many people save, invest, and engage in entrepreneurial activities with little, if any, thought or plan for willing their holdings to any specific person upon their deaths. The necessity of unrestricted inheritance as a motivational basis for an effectively operative price system has probably been exaggerated. In relation to the institution of ownership, it is important to note that it is the *inequality in the distribution of ownership* in land and industrial capital which fosters income inequality, *not necessarily private ownership* per se. It is possible to conceive of a "purer" capitalism with a much wider diffusion of ownership among individuals than has been the case historically in capitalist economies, a diffusion which would not necessarily be incompatible with the workings of the competitive market as an allocational and distributive process.

Still, unless inheritance is completely abolished and the ownership of land and capital resources is perfectly equal, their impact is probably to encourage inequality in income. Inequality may be considerable in a capitalist economy simply because of wage and salary differentials. If, in addition, some people own property used in production, their ownership enables them to claim an income in resource markets in the forms of rents, interests or profits above what they could obtain through the sale of their labor services. The institution of inheritance can perpetuate the resulting inequality by permitting the rich man's progeny to obtain incomes in addition to those from their own labor or accumulations of property. Indeed, inheritance may increase inequality in income by enabling the rich man's son to obtain the education, skills, and financial head start often denied to children from low-income families.

Economic Stabilization and Full Employment

Of equal importance to the productivity theory of income distribution in the classic model of competitive market capitalism is the idea that, given the assumptions and conditions of the model, the economy tends toward a stable aggregate equilibrium of national income under full employment conditions. As in the case of allocation and distribution, this process is more or less automatic and spontaneous. The classic model of the role of competitive market processes in the promotion of aggregate equilibrium at full employment has three major dimensions: the labor market; the saving-investment market; the money market.

THE LABOR MARKET

In the classic model of competitive market capitalism, labor market equilibrium *must* be accompanied by full employment. This follows from the definition of full utilization of a resource at that rate of employment which is desired by resource owners. If Fig. 4.3b is illustrative of the labor market in general, then *any* point along the market supply curve *SS* could be a full employment position. (Full employment is not defined in terms of an absolute number of people, because the number of people willing and able to be employed would vary at different wage levels.) A movement along curve *SS*

represents not a change from unemployment toward full employment, but, instead, varying levels of full employment labor supply, where the size of the labor force depends directly upon the real wage or price of labor.[6]

Which of the many possible full employment positions turns out to be full employment *equilibrium*, given the position of market supply, depends upon market demand. Thus, in Fig. 4.3b, the equilibrium position occurs at that real wage-employment combination where market demand equals market supply. This is an equilibrium position because only here are market demand and supply consistent with each other. Any other position would involve disequilibrium and a tendency to move toward the point of equality between market demand and market supply. Thus, equilibrium in the labor market entails and requires full employment. In equilibrium, all workers willing and able to work at the going real wage can secure employment.

The existence of unemployment in the classic competitive model is indicative of an imbalance between demand and supply. If workers willing and able to work at going wage rates cannot find employment, clearly the supply of labor exceeds the demand for it. But equally clearly, an excess of supply over demand means that wages in these sectors are above equilibrium levels. Under these conditions, competition among workers will tend to lower wages.[7] Workers who find themselves involuntarily unemployed can resolve the problem by accepting lower money wage rates. But decreases in wages

---

[6] In the classic model, neither employees nor employers are supposed to be affected by a "money illusion." Both are concerned with the real wage level, that is, money wage levels divided by money price levels or W/P. For the individual firm, this is implied in the maximization condition, as already noted: By simple algebraic manipulation, $MPPL \cdot P = W$ may be transformed into $MPP = W/P$.

[7] This assumes that wage cuts are accompanied by smaller cuts in prices, so that money wage level cuts are accompanied by lower real wage levels.

will tend to restore full employment by two equilibrating tendencies: first, an increase in the quantity of labor demanded by business firms; second, a decrease in the quantity of labor supplied. The ultimate long-run equilibrium thus is characterized by an equality between demand for and supply of labor in the various labor markets. But such equality, if attained, means the absence of involuntary unemployment of labor.

As in the basic model of resource allocation, the competitive pricing system serves to absorb shifts in market demand and/or supply caused by changes in underlying conditions. Suppose, for example, that the market supply curve in Fig. 4.3b were to shift up and out to the right because of a general increase in the labor force at all real wage levels. At the former equilibrium real wage, supply now would exceed demand. Wages would fall, tending to restore full employment equilibrium (at a higher level of employment). Conversely, suppose that the market demand curve were to shift downward. Once again, former real wage levels could not be sustained. The newly created excess supply would push wages down, which, as in the first example, would also tend to restore full employment equilibrium (at a lower level of employment).

THE SAVING-INVESTMENT MARKET

The second dimension of classic macroeconomics in the theory of competitive market capitalism is that of saving and investment. Full employment output must be sold to someone if aggregate demand is to be sufficient to sustain full employment supply of goods. Abstracting from government and foreign trade, final output may be sold to consumers in the form of such consumer goods as automobiles, food, or airline tickets, or to investors in the form of machinery, buildings, or accumulation of inventories. If investment, one of these two major components of aggregate demand, is insufficient to match the saving occurring out of a fully employed output, the demand for goods in the aggregate will be insufficient to match supply.

As in the model of the labor market, the classic blueprint of competitive market capitalism provides a process for promoting equilibrium in a manner consistent with full employment production. Built into the workings of the competitive price system are some more or less "automatic stabilizers," as well as automatic allocators and distributors. One of the most important of these stabilizers is the rate(s) of interest, which intertwines and coordinates saving and investment in the market(s) for investment funds. If the desires to save and invest *temporarily* should diverge and the economy thus should temporarily depart from its normal long-run position or path of stable aggregate equilibrium, such divergence would cause changes in the rate of interest, which, in turn, would cause changes in saving and investment so as to restore a position of equilibrium.

Suppose, for example, that at full employment, firms desire to invest $125,000,000,000, while savers want to save only $100,000,000,000. This excess demand for investment funds over and above the willingness and ability of savers to provide them will tend to force interest rates up, just as the excess of any demand over supply will tend to raise the price of the item being exchanged. This will result in an increase in the quantity of saving, since savers are presumed to be responsive to changes in interest rates, and a decrease in investment, since firms are presumed to operate on the same "law of demand" applicable to market relations in general.

If, on the other hand, firms desire to invest only $75,000,000,000 when savers wish to save $100,000,000,000, the excess supply of savings over the demand for them will tend to force the price of savings, or interest rates, down. Decreases in interest rates will bring (as in the case of excess investment demand, but in reverse) two counteracting tendencies: (1) a decrease in the quantity of saving; (2) an increase in the quantity of investment funds demanded. In both cases, the ultimate resting place is the point at which saving and investment are again brought into equality. The essential point of this theory is that, though saving and investment may change and/or temporarily diverge from one another, such changes and divergences do not activate repercussive changes in the overall levels of output, income, or employment. Interest rates, an integral part of the price system, operate as a sort of shock absorber. It is instability in the interest rates which reestablishes stable equilibrium in the economy, that equilibrium having been disturbed.

These saving and investment factors are illustrated in Fig. 4.5, which depicts saving as a positive and investment as an inverse function of the rate of interest. Because savers earn nothing for maintaining their savings in idle cash balances and because they prefer some return to nothing, they will desire to purchase financial assets (such as corporate bonds) with their savings. And under the assumption that savers prefer a higher to a lower rate of return, the saving function will slope up to the right. Because of diminishing marginal productivity of capital, the investment demand for savings will vary inversely with the rate of interest. An equilibrium rate of interest will exist when $S = I$ at i_e. If $i > i_e$, $S > I$, and the interest rate will decrease until $S = I$ at i_e.

The reverse would occur were the rate of interest to lie below i_e.

Note that curve SS represents varying levels of saving out of a given level of full employment output or income. A movement along curve SS shows a change in saving as a result of an alteration in the rate of interest (given income), *not* in the level of national income. Thus, *any* point along curve SS represents a position of full employment saving, and equilibrium in the saving-investment market requires and entails full employment, as well as an equality of investment and saving. What the full employment level of saving will be depends upon the positions of the saving and investment curves.

The positions of the saving and investment curves depend upon the values of the other variables (for example, tastes, income, technology) compounded in the "other things remaining equal" assumption. An increase in either income or the propensity to save out of income, for example, would be accompanied by an upward and outward shift in the saving function in Fig. 4.5. As long as the interest rate mechanism functions effectively, this creates no problem. The increase in saving lowers the interest rate; this causes an increase in investment, and a new equilibrium is established where $S = I$ and both are at higher levels. Similarly, a downward shift in the investment curve is counteracted by a decrease in the interest rate, and thus, an accompanying decrease in saving until equilibrium is restored, with both saving and investment equal at lower levels. Thus, divergences between and changes in desired saving and desired investment bring changes in the allocation of resources between the consumption and investment goods industries and in the disposal of national income between consumption and saving, but *not* in the overall level of national income or employment.

These ideas may be stated differently by saying that aggregate demand tends toward equality with aggregate supply. The aggregate supply constitutes the basic "real" conditions

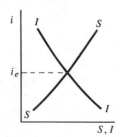

Fig. 4.5. (*Left*) Saving and investment

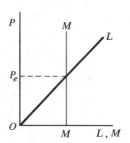

Fig. 4.6. (*Right*) Demand for money, supply of money, and equilibrium

of production, as determined by the quantity and quality of capital, natural, and human resources, technology, and the institutions and motivations of society. It is the employment of resources, under given technological, institutional, and motivational conditions, which creates the flow of products and services that we call "aggregate supply." Aggregate demand, on the other hand, is represented by the expenditure of money income upon these products and services, including investment and consumption goods.

Aggregate supply depends upon aggregate demand, since business firms would not be willing and able to supply an aggregate collection of goods to buyers unless they expected to receive an incoming flow of consumption and investment expenditures large enough to induce them to produce and supply. Aggregate demand, on the other hand, depends upon aggregate supply, since resource owners are able to make monetary expenditures (and thus, present a claim against real output) because of their incoming flows of money incomes, obtained from the sale of their productive services to business firms.

Thus, stable equilibrium requires a balance or equality between the underlying "real" conditions of production and the "monetary" conditions of expenditures—between aggregate supply and aggregate demand. A basic assumption of the classic model of capitalism is that the supply of output, by creating a money income equal to the monetary value of output, creates thereby the ability and the willingness to purchase the output. Though buyers may *temporarily* choose to not exercise this ability, with a resultant *temporary* gap between aggregate supply and aggregate demand, they will as a general rule choose to do so, and, as noted, any temporary divergence will activate countervailing movements in interest rates, which, in turn, will lead to a reestablishment of equilibrium and equality between investment and full employment saving. In short, supply tends to create its own demand at full employment.

THE MONEY MARKET

The third dimension of the classic model of economic stabilization and full employment in competitive market capitalism is that of the money market. Monetary equilibrium at full employment requires equality between the demand for and supply of money. An excess supply of money at full employment may generate inflation, while an excessive demand to hold money or an inadequate supply of money may disrupt the balance between potential full employment supply of goods and aggregate demand.

As in the labor and saving-investment markets, the classic capitalist blueprint contains a process on the money market for sustaining or promoting monetary equilibrium in a manner consistent with full employment production. Full-employment equilibrium, in the labor market, rests on flexibility of wages, and, in the saving-investment market, on flexibility of interest rates. The process of sustaining or promoting equality between the supply of and demand for money at full employment depends upon flexibility of prices.

The Barter Economy. In the simplest case, that of a barter economy, money raises no problems for the exchange process because it exists solely as a unit of account, not as a medium of exchange. In other words, there is a unit of account, but no circulating "money." Suppliers of goods expect goods in exchange, and thus are simultaneously demanders of goods. Because goods are bought with goods, demanders automatically are suppliers. Though demands for particular goods may exceed supplies, it is logically impossible for aggregate supply and demand to diverge because circulating money is nonexistent; thus, it cannot be excessive or insufficient in relation to money.

Money as a Medium of Exchange. In a more complex and realistic case, money functions also as a medium of exchange, but not as a store of value. Immediately upon its receipt from the sale of goods, money is spent. The receipt of money thus is transformed immediately into a demand for goods. The demand for goods (supply of money) thus is equal to the supply of goods, and the demand for money (that is, the demand to hold money) is zero.

A Transactionary Demand for Money. In a still more complex and realistic case, the demand for or desire to hold money or to have "liquidity" exceeds zero, but all money held is of an "active" or "transactionary" sort, that is, it is intended to be used shortly for economic transactions. Money thus serves as a store of value as well as a medium of exchange, but only for short periods of time, so that, for all practicable purposes, the medium of exchange function is dominant.

In such an economy, the demand to hold money for future transactions could be said to depend upon the monetary value of transactions and other "underlying determinants," such as the earning and payments habits of businesses and households and the degree of vertical integration of industry. Supposing that these underlying determinants are given, the magnitude of money demanded may be designated as varying directly with the level of money income, as illustrated by line OL in Fig. 4.6. Because money income equals real output or income times the general price level ($Ym = Yr \cdot P$), a change in either can cause changes in the demand for money. In a full-employment economy, where real output is given at the full-employment level, changes in money income and transactions would represent changes in the price level.

The price level at full employment would then be determined by the interaction of the demand for money function and the supply or stock of money (coin, paper currency, demand deposits), which, at this juncture, is assumed to be given and independent of the level of transactions, as illustrated by line MM in Fig. 4.6. Monetary equilibrium occurs at price level OPe, where the demand for money equals the given supply or stock of money. If, temporarily, the supply of and demand for money diverged, price flexibility under the assumed conditions would tend to restore equilibrium. If, for example, the price level were higher than OPe, the demand for money would exceed the supply of money and, if the two alternatives are money and goods, people would try to get money by selling goods. Thus, an excess of the demand for money over the supply of money exerts deflationary pressures: the price level falls. As the price level falls, the quantity of money demanded would decrease until, in equilibrium at price level OPe, the demand for goods would equal the supply of goods because the demand for money equals the supply of money. The reverse would occur if the price level were initially lower than OPe.

As in the labor market and saving-investment market cases, monetary equilibrium or equality between the supply of and demand for money simultaneously requires and entails full employment utilization of resources. It requires full employment because the transactionary demand for money function rests upon the assumption of a given, full-employment income determined by the full employment of labor, given the productivity of labor. It entails full employment because *if* unemployment existed, characterized by an excess of the labor supply over labor demand, the money wage level would fall, as described earlier, and employment would tend to rise. But higher employment generates a larger output of goods which, in the absence of an increase in the supply of money and/or a downward shift in the demand for money function, would require a lower price level. (Given these factors, the equilibrium level of monetary demand would remain constant. To sell a larger real output with a given level of monetary expenditures requires a lower price level.) A decrease in the price level would decrease the quantity of money required for transactionary purposes and thus, increase the demand for goods. This would continue until the price level was low enough so that the demand for money again equalled the supply of money at full employment.[8]

As long as prices are flexible in competitive markets, the price system functions as an automatic stabilizer or shock absorber to maintain full employment in the event of shifts in either or both the stock of money and the demand for money function. For example, as long as prices are flexible in a downward direction, a decrease in the supply of money or an upward shift in the demand to hold money rather than to buy goods is no cause for alarm. Either development transforms the monetary equilibrium of Fig. 4.6 into one of disequilibrium with an excess of the demand for money over the supply of money at the former equilibrium price level OPe. In effect, the demand for goods falls short of supply at full employment. Under competitive conditions, prices would tend to fall. But as the price level falls, the magnitude of transactionary demands for money also falls down along line OL (or a higher OL', not depicted, in the case of an upward shift in the demand for money function) until monetary equilibrium is restored at a lower price level. Price deflation thus functions as an automatic stabilizer to prevent depression in output and employment. No real variables (such as output, employment, real wages, saving, investment, or the rate of interest) are affected.[9]

As long as the transactionary demand for money function is reasonably stable at full employment, the only major source of prospective short-run monetary instability in a competitive capitalist economy would be a shift in the supply of money. For example, an upward shift in the supply of money (up and out to the right for line MM in Fig. 4.6) would create an excess of the supply of money over the demand for money at the old equilibrium price level OPe. This would mean an excess of the demand for goods over supply because people would be trying to get rid of their excess money by buying goods. The excess of aggregate demand over aggregate supply and the supply of money over the demand for it would tend to push the price level up; that is, $P = fM$, given L and given the physical quantity of output at full employment. An increase in the price level would be accompanied by an increase in the quantity of money demanded for transactionary purposes until equilibrium is restored at a higher price level, where D once again equals S because $L = M$. This monetary development, as before, however, has not altered the magnitude of any real phenomena in the economy: real wage levels, employment, real output, the allocation of resources between consumption and investment, and the disposal of income between consumption and saving remain unaffected.

This does not mean that the supply of money is economically irrelevant. A prudent government in a competitive capitalist economy will refrain from excessively overburdening the absorptive capacity of the price

---

[8] As already noted, the decrease in the price level would have to be smaller than that in the money wage level to enable a decrease in the real wage level. This is possible in the classic theory because the decrease in the price level decreases the quantity of money demanded.

[9] It would seem that a decrease in P would be accompanied by an increase in W/P, given W. However, an increase in W/P pushes real wages up and above labor market equilibrium, where the excess of the supply of labor over the demand for it would tend to push money wage levels down until, in the new equilibrium, *both* W and P are lower, but W/P levels are the

---

same as they were prior to the decrease in the supply of or increase in the demand for money. Conversely, an increase in the price level, caused by an increase in the supply of and/or decrease in the demand for money, would bring a decrease in W/P on the labor market. The resulting excess of demand over supply of labor would tend to push W up, so that in the new equilibrium, both W and P would be higher, but the initial real wage level would be retained.

system by avoiding, if possible, large-scale increases or decreases in the supply of money, to avoid extreme inflation or deflation. The competitive pricing system, according to the classic theory of market capitalism, has built within it automatic processes for adjusting to and absorbing changes in demands for and/or supplies of money to prevent depressions and unemployment and/or to restore full employment if the economy were to temporarily depart from its normal equilibrium position.

An Asset or Speculative Demand for Money. The demand for money is divided into two main parts: one, a transactionary demand, varying directly with the price level; two, a "speculative" or "asset" demand, varying inversely with the rate of interest.[10] In the case of a speculative demand, money serves as a store of value against an uncertain future, and people would like to hold on to money for a more or less extended period of time. The magnitude of the speculative or asset demand for money depends upon relations among the actual rate of interest, a "normal" rate of interest, and expectations about future interest rates. If the actual interest rate is significantly above "normal," and many people speculate that it will soon go down, they will wish to transform their idle money into financial assets while interest rates on these assets are high. Thus, the quantity of speculative money demanded is low. If the interest rate is significantly below "normal" and it is generally expected that it will soon go up, people will desire to hold on to money and to part with it later at a more favorable rate of return. Thus the quantity of money demanded for speculative purposes is high.

The existence of a speculative demand for money significantly complicates, but does not invalidate, the classic reasoning about competitive market capitalism. Any change

in saving and/or investment will bring changes in the rate of interest, as before. But now, changes in the rate of interest will cause changes in the speculative demand for money, which, given the supply of money and the transactionary demand for money, will cause changes in the price level. Price level changes will involve changes in the real wage in the opposite direction, unless offset by changes in money wage levels. Thus, an upward shift in the saving function or a downward shift in the investment function will be accompanied by a decrease in the rate of interest. But a lower interest rate will be accompanied by a higher quantity of money demanded for speculative purposes. This means there will be a smaller portion of the given money supply to satisfy transactionary demands. Thus, the money supply minus the speculative demand for money will decrease, and, given the transactionary demand for money, the equilibrium price level will fall. A decrease in the price level is the same as an increase in the real wage level, which, in the absence of countervailing forces, creates an excess of supply of labor over demand for labor, that is, unemployment in the labor market. But an excess of supply over demand in the labor market pushes money wages down proportionately with the decrease in the price level, and thus, full employment real wage levels are restored and full employment maintained. Therefore, the interest rate cannot *by itself* absorb shifts in S and/or I; greater pressure is exerted on the wage-price mechanism to maintain full employment-stability, and the absence of wage-price flexibility may be accompanied by unemployment. However, as long as wages and prices are freely flexible on competitive markets, an automatic and spontaneous social process exists to maintain full employment-stability, and the speculative demand for money, like the supply of and the transactionary demand for money, has effects only upon the *monetary* variables (price levels, money wage levels) and not upon the *real* variables (W/P, N, Yr, S, I, i).

---

[10]The speculative demand for money is described more fully as part of the Keynesian theory of capitalism in Chapter 7.

The Wealth Effect. A variation developed recently on the role of money in sustaining or promoting full employment under competitive capitalism is the concept of the wealth or "real balance" effect. This approach focuses directly on the aggregate demand for goods by suggesting that the level of desired consumption and/or investment expenditures in the economy depends upon the *real value* of money and monetary assets or wealth, even when their *nominal monetary value* is fixed. For example, as the price level decreases, the nominal money value of $1,000,000 United States government bonds remains fixed, but the real value, that is, the goods that may be purchased with these bonds were they redeemed, rises. Thus, price deflation makes bondholders feel richer and increases their propensities to consume and/or invest. Conceivably, there is *some* degree of wage-price deflation that should be sufficient to eliminate *any* possible or actual excess of full employment supply above demand through an upward shift in consumption plus investment. Most contemporary economists believe that though this may be true as a general logical proposition, the degree of price deflation required and/or the length of time needed to yield significantly large "wealth effects" may be so great as to make reliance upon the theory impractical. It is, however, an interesting, provocative addition to the classic idea of the automatically adjusting competitive market capitalist economy.

Economic Growth

The final major component in the classic model of competitive market capitalism is the idea that, built into the internal workings of the capitalist system are social processes which automatically and spontaneously generate and stimulate economic growth—consistent, however, with individual economic choices regarding saving versus consumption and work versus leisure.

CAPITALIST MOTIVATIONS AND INSTITUTIONS AS A STIMULUS TO ECONOMIC GROWTH

According to the classic model, the institutional and motivational structure of capitalist economies contributes to economic growth in at least four important and interdependent ways:

Incentives. In capitalism, individual motivation and economic growth coalesce. It is advantageous to individuals not only to attempt to maximize their economic gain at any one point or period of time, but to augment economic gain over the passage of time—for example, by working longer, harder, or better, saving and investing, and discovering and applying new methods or resources to production. These devices simultaneously increase individual income and/or profit and contribute to economic growth in society. There is no greater and simpler incentive to increased production and productivity than the harnessing of individual aspirations and desires. Capitalism, according to its classic supporters, has a built-in mechanism for accomplishing this without the need for expensive, time-consuming centralized systems of persuasion, manipulation, coercion, and enforcement.

Competition. The pursuit of private economic self interests by individual consumers, resource owners, and business firms promotes the social objective of economic growth because such private interests are channeled and controlled by the social process of the competitive price system. Indeed, competition compels business firms to act in such a way as to promote economic growth. Consider a capitalist firm tending toward "long-run equilibrium" by the allocational process previously described. In a competitive market, the existence of "above-normal" profits in any short-run situation eventually will attract the entry of new firms, an increase in market supply, and a decrease in market price. As the price falls toward the minimum point of the long-run average cost curve, as illustrated in Fig. 4.4, the annihilation of economic profits becomes imminent. What would you do if you were a businessman under these circumstances? Unless you were rather uneconomical, you would attempt to shift your demand curve up (perhaps by introducing a new and better product) and/or your cost curve down. And, since the rivalry of your competitors is ever-present, even though atomistically diffused, you might keep up these profit-*and* growth-oriented activities more or less continuously, rather than waiting for the long-run tendency toward equilibrium.

Specialization and Exchange. "The greatest improvement in the productive powers of labour," wrote Adam Smith in 1776, "and the greater part of the skill, dexterity and judgment with which it is any where directed, or applied, seem to have been the effects of the division of labour." [24: 3] Though specialization and division of labor are not unique to capitalist economies, the wide opportunities under capitalism for individuals to follow their economic inclinations insures that the institution will be widespread. Specialization is not, of course, an unmitigated blessing: the overly-specialized worker, noted Smith, loses the habit of exerting himself in creative and inventive thought "and generally becomes as stupid and ignorant as it is possible for a human creature to become . . . . His dexterity at his own particular trade seems . . . to be acquired at the expense of his intellectual, social, and martial virtues." [24: 734–35] However, specialization does contribute to a tremendous increase in productivity in at least three ways: first, by the increase in worker "dexterity"; second, by saving time "commonly lost in passing from one sort of work to another"; and third, by encouraging the invention of new and improved machinery. [24: 8]

Moreover, specialization requires exchange, and indeed, is limited "by the extent of the market." But the expansion of exchange, encouraged by division of labor, rebounds, in turn, upon the organization of production by enabling an extension of specialization. Latter nineteenth-century economists often favored freedom of international trade on the grounds of prospective maximization of satisfaction of wants. Adam Smith and the early nineteenth-century classical economists who followed him support free trade on the presumption that specialization of countries in lines of production in which they had an economic advantage would contribute vigorously to economic growth.

Profits-Investment-Technology. The dynamics of the capitalist growth process involves interaction of profits, investment, and technology. Given economic institutions and motivations, the rate of growth in potential output (equal to the rate of growth in actual output under the assumption that supply creates its own demand at full employment) depends upon the rate of growth in resources and technology. Technology, in turn, depends upon and is embodied in investment. Thus, if technological improvements are to be made, saving and capital accumulation often must increase. Given the institutional structure of a capitalist economy, investment depends upon profits. Profits, in turn, depend upon technology. Technological improvements, by decreasing costs, raise profits for further investment. Consider, for example, an increase in profits. Under static conditions, pure economic profits tend to be eliminated by capitalism's competitive allocational process. Under dynamic conditions, however, profits are allocated to capital investment. But investment does more than add to the existing stock of capital goods. It may also embody new technological improvements and innovations which both raise output and, by decreasing costs, raise profits, which, in turn, provide the basis for further output- and profit-generating investment.

In sum, according to its classic expositors, capitalism combines an *institutional* system for generating, mobilizing, and distributing

economic surpluses to capitalist entrepreneurs, a *motivational* system which encourages allocation of economic surpluses to
productive investments embodying new cost-
reducing technologies, and a *technological*
system in which investments are embodied,
and which, by reducing costs, operates as an
automatic feedback mechanism to create
more economic surpluses in a form suitable
for further investment.

THE CAPITALIST GROWTH PROCESS AND
INDIVIDUAL ECONOMIC CHOICE

A centrally and comprehensively planned
economy may be characterized by a higher
rate of economic growth than a market-
directed competitive capitalist economy
because of the central planners' allocation
of a higher proportion of national income
to saving and investment and the enforcement
of a larger labor force and/or longer working
hours than would be voluntarily forthcoming
under conditions of free choice. The United
States, for example, could probably approximately double its growth rate were the length
of the work week or the percent of gross
national product going into investment
doubled.

In the classic theory of competitive market
capitalism, the rate of economic growth is
not determined by a central plan, but instead
emerges from and is consistent with individual
market choices of consumers, resource
owners, and business firms. Whether the
rate of economic growth is to be 3, 4, or 5
percent per year, for example, is not a question of "national purpose" or public debate,
but the collective result of the private market
decisions of large numbers of individual
units in the economic system, each seeking
its own economic advantage. Two prominent
examples are work versus leisure and saving
versus consumption.

Work Versus Leisure. If individuals wish
to move into the labor force, and if workers
in the labor force wish to increase their
working hours, they will attempt to do so.
The results of this increase in the supply of
labor will be a decrease in wages, an increase
in employment, and an increase in output—
that is, other things being equal, a higher
level of economic performance and a higher
rate of economic growth. There may be
limits to this, of course: workers could not
work 24 hours a day even if they wanted to;
the length of the work week, in any short
period of time, may be customarily or
habitually set at a certain figure or range.
The point is that individuals are free, in
competitive market capitalism, to move into
or out of the labor force and increase or
decrease their working hours. The rate of
economic growth is influenced significantly
by these individual decisions.

Saving Versus Consumption. The proportion of society's resources to be allocated to
the production of capital rather than consumption goods also is affected by individual
market choices. On the supply side, people
generally prefer to consume in the present
rather than in the future. If they are to
increase the percentage saved out of a given
income, they must, in the classic theory, be
enticed to do so. The interest rate serves this
enticement function in a capitalist economy.
As the interest rate rises, the "price" of current
consumption increases, and the willingness
and ability to save (that is, to postpone
consumption into the future) also rises.

On the demand side, capital is productive
of output, though according to the law of
diminishing returns, at a decreasing marginal
rate. If net investment is to increase, funds
over and above current consumption and
depreciation must be obtained by business
firms, either from internal (profit) or external
(personal saving) sources. Because capital
is productive, business firms are willing to
pay for these funds—that is, an interest rate
can be paid. As investment increases, however, the marginal productivity of capital
declines, and the interest rate that firms are
willing and able to pay thus also declines.

In other words, the demand for funds to purchase capital goods varies inversely with the rate of interest, as illustrated by the negatively sloped curve of investment in Fig. 4.5.

The total number of possible investments, however, is larger than the total of funds forthcoming from savers. Somehow, scarce savings must be allocated among alternative investment projects so that more, rather than less, productive projects are selected and, so that, in the aggregate, total investment is brought into equality with total saving. Both of these functions are also performed by interest rates. Given the rate of interest, individual business firms within any sector of the economy will find it profitable to continue to invest up to, but no farther than, the point where the expected rate of return on the investment equals the rate of interest. As to the allocation of capital resources among different sectors of the economy, business will expand investment in the areas with the greatest gaps between profit rates and interest rates. The movement of capital to high net profit areas tends to lead to an equalization of profit rates throughout the economy as well as an equalization, for any individual firm, of the rate of profit with the rate of interest. For the economy, the rate of interest serves to equalize the demand for and supply of saving, and thus, to bring saving and investment into equilibrium as illustrated by equilibrium interest rate i_e and equilibrium saving and investment in Fig. 4.5.

Suppose this position of equilibrium is disrupted by a rise in the investment demand curve, say, as a result of technological improvements. The upward shift in investment demand will cause the interest rate to rise. As it does so, saving will also rise, establishing a new equilibrium position where saving and investment are higher. Suppose, now, an upward shift occurs in the supply of saving curve. The increase in saving will deflate the interest rate, which will encourage an expansion of investment to a new equilibrium where, again, both saving and investment are higher. In both cases, economic growth is encouraged by expanded saving and investment, but the expansion is consistent with the market preferences of individual consumers and investors. Their choices are coordinated and brought into balance by the interest rate, which simultaneously serves to "ration" scarce savings among alternative investment projects so that, consistent with the maximization of profit, savings are allocated to the areas of highest productivity, and thus, the greatest contribution to economic growth.

In sum, the classic capitalist analysis of economic growth contains two central assertions: First, given work-leisure and saving-consumption ratios and choices, the combination of favorable motivational-institutional-technological conditions generates a "dynamic efficiency" which stimulates economic growth, presumably at a faster pace than under monopoly capitalism or a centrally planned economic system. Second, the rate of growth, given this dynamic motivational-institutional-technological framework, depends upon market coordination of free individual choices regarding work versus leisure and saving versus consumption.

THE CLASSIC CRITIQUE OF MONOPOLY

The classic exposition and defense of the competitive price system as a process for resolving resource allocation, income distribution, full employment-stability, and economic growth problems in socially beneficial ways is one side of a coin; the classic critique of monopoly is the other. Whether viewed by Adam Smith in the eighteenth, John Stuart Mill in the nineteenth, or Frederick A. Hayek in the twentieth century, orthodox economic theory has not been a defense of capitalism or private enterprise per se, but a defense of the competitive price system within the institutional framework of private enterprise. This has two implications:

First, were it possible to utilize or simulate a competitive price system within the framework of public enterprise and a socialist economy, then orthodox economic theory, somewhat ironically, might be used in the exposition and defense of socialism. This is precisely what some socialists have insisted. Second, the central tradition in economic theory, regarded as a defense of private enterprise and business interests, provides a powerful indictment of private enterprise economies if and when they become monopolistic.

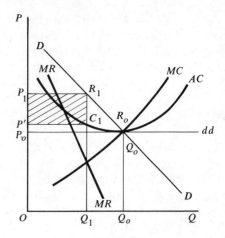

Fig. 4.7. Monopoly

Monopoly and Resource Allocation

The first criticism of monopoly power is that it leads to an inefficient allocation of resources. This may be expressed by saying that under pure competition, where price is given and beyond the control of individual firms, and where, therefore, price = marginal revenue (MR) sellers, seeking profit maximization ($MC = MR$), extend output to the point where $MC = P$. Under monopoly, where sellers have the power to affect price by restricting supply, and where, therefore, $P > MR$, the profit maximization position ($MC = MR$) must entail an output below the point where $MC = P$, and P must exceed MC.[11] Assuming market demand and

cost conditions are identical for firms in both cases, the quantity will be lower and the price higher in monopoly than in competition.

This may be seen in Fig. 4.7. In long-run, purely and perfectly competitive equilibrium, price is OP_o, and quantity is OQ_o, at the intersection of the market demand curve and the market supply curve (equal to the sum of the MC curves of all individual firms in the industry). Because of the entry (or exit) of firms in response to pure profits (losses), the price line (equal to demand as seen by each individual firm, dd) is tangent to the average cost (AC) curve at its minimum point. Average cost is thus minimized at Q_oC_o, and, because average revenue is Q_oR_o where $R_o = C_o$, pure economic profits are zero.

Given the same market demand and industry cost conditions, a monopolist would produce output OQ_1 (where MC = the negatively sloped MR). The average revenue (AR) from this quantity of output is Q_1R_1, a point on the demand or AR curve directly above Q_1. Price (equal to AR) is OP_1. In addition, in this case, it is also true that Q_1C_1, although as low as it can be for output OQ_1, is higher than that of each competitive

---

[11]In pure competition, price, and thus, MR, remains given for individual firms as output expands and/or contracts. For example, if $P = \$5$ per unit, an individual seller might sell, alternatively, 1 though 5 units yielding total revenues of 5, 10, 15, 20, and 25 dollars respectively. MR, equal to $\Delta TR/\Delta Q$, would remain at $\$5$, equal to the given price, as in Fig. 4.2a. In monopoly, the seller faces a negatively sloped demand curve. In *pure* monopoly, where a seller has no rivals selling a close substitute, the market demand curve *is* the demand curve for the product of the individual firm. Thus, price and quantity are inversely related. For example, quantity of output sold may be at 1, 2, 3, 4, and 5 respectively if price is $\$5, 4, 3, 2,$ and 1 respectively. TR in this case would be 5, 8, 9, 8, and 5. AR (equal to TR/Q) or P would be $\$5, 4, 3, 2,$ and 1 respectively. MR would be $\$3, 1, -1,$ and -3 respectively, as quantity changed from 1 to 2, 2 to 3,

and so on. If the demand or AR curve is negatively sloped, as in the monopoly case, the MR curve lies below and diverges from it.

firm because the AC associated with the lower output is at a higher point on the U-shaped AC curve. As long as the demand curve lies above the AC curve at this point, a gap of AR over AC (of R_1C_1) exists, which constitutes average pure economic profits. (Total pure economic profit equals this gap multiplied by the quantity of output, OQ_1, and is shown by the shaded area $P_1R_1C_1P'$.) In sum, given identical market demand and industry cost conditions, a monopolist will produce a lower output at a higher price and generally a higher cost than a purely competitive seller. If AC lies below AR at this point, the monopolist will also be able to obtain pure economic profits.

The profit maximization output in monopoly need not entail an output lower than minimum AC. If the demand, or AR, curve is just at that height which makes the MR curve intersect the MC curve at the minimum point of the AC curve, profit maximization output for the monopolist is also cost minimization output. Indeed, if the AR curve is higher than this, the profit maximization output will be higher than that associated with minimum AC (thus entailing higher average costs). However, in both cases, price will lie above AC (because AR lies above MR), pure economic profits will exceed zero, and output, though equal to or higher than OQ_1, is lower than that which would have been produced (at the higher demand and higher price) under competitive conditions.

Similarly, profit maximization output for the monopolist need not involve pure economic profits. If demand is lower, AR may be sufficient to cover AC when $MC = MR$. But the same basic indictment may be levied against the monopolist: output is lower, cost is higher, and price is higher than under competitive conditions.

Must or will monopolistic sellers always behave in these socially unbeneficial ways? Of course not. Monopolists may choose not to behave like monopolists, or, more accurately, not to fully exploit their monopoly oppor-

tunities for profit maximization. Second, they may be regulated by some collective or public body, as are public utilities. Third, they may fear potential competition if they push their monopolistic advantages too vigorously. Fouth, their cost conditions may be different from those of competitive sellers. Because of economies of large-scale production, the monopolist's AC curve may slope more vigorously and farther than in the competitive case, permitting him to maximize profits, yet be more efficient.

To most defenders of the competitive model, these arguments are not impressive. The first depends on the good will and social conscience of the monopolist rather than the more certain institutional pressures of competition. The second, at best, is an argument for the regulation of monopoly, not for unregulated monopoly. The third may temper the monopolist's exploitation of his power, but surely would not be as powerful a constraining force as competition itself. The fourth confuses two different points: economies of large-scale production, which is a function of absolute size; and monopoly power, which is a function of size in relation to the market. Monopoly does not guarantee large-scale economies. Large size does not necessarily require monopoly.

Monopoly and Income Distribution

The second criticism of monopoly is that, in contrast to competition, it generates inequality in the distribution of income by redistributing income from consumers and resource owners to the owners of monopoly businesses.

Monopoly does not guarantee pure economic profits. Indeed, it does not guarantee even "normal profits." If demand for the output of a monopoly lies everywhere below AC, the best the monopolist can do is minimize losses. But if demand lies initially above AC, the absence of close substitutes and the maintenance of barriers against the entry of new firms may permit the retention of pure economic profits even in the long run as "monopoly profits."

The corollary to monopoly power in selling is monopsony power in buying. Just as a monopolist has the power to restrict the quantity of what he sells in order to sell it at a higher price, so the monopsonist has the power to restrict the quantity of what he buys in order to buy it at a lower price. Under purely competitive conditions in the purchase of resources, where resource prices (P) are given and beyond the control of individual firms, and where, therefore, the average resource cost (ARC) or price of the resource equals marginal resource cost (MRC), buyers, seeking profit maximization (where marginal revenue product, MRP, equals marginal resource cost), extend the purchases of inputs to the point where MRP = the price of the resource. Under monopsony, where buyers have the power to affect price by controlling resource purchases, and where, therefore, $MRC > ARC$ or resource price, the profit maximization position must entail an input purchase below the point where MRP = the price of the resource and P must therefore lie below MRP. Resource owners, in short, receive incomes below their marginal revenue products (and incidentally below the value of their marginal products), constituting a kind of "monopsonistic exploitation."[12]

---

[12]In pure competition, resource price, and thus, MRC remain given for individual firms as purchases of inputs expand or contract. For example, if the wage rate is $5 per hour, a competitive firm might hire, alternatively, one through five units of labor, yielding total resource costs per hour of $5 through $25. $ARC(TRC/Q)$ would be equal to Pr at each quantity of labor: ($5/1 = 5$, $10/2 = 5$, and so on.) MRC ($\Delta TRC/\Delta Q$) would also remain at $5 per hour and thus would equal resource price. ($5/1 = 5$ as TRC increases from 5 to 10, 10 to 15, and so on.) In monopsony, the buyer faces a positively sloped supply or ARC curve. (Indeed, in pure monopsony, the market supply curve *is* the supply curve faced by the individual firm.) Thus, price and quantity are positively related. For example, the quantity of labor purchased might be one through five, if the wage rate were $5

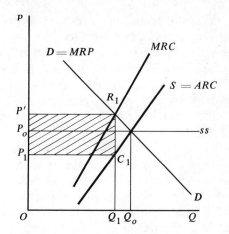

Fig. 4.8. Monopsony

This may be seen in Fig. 4.8. In competitive equilibrium, P is OP_o, and quantity is OQ_o, at the intersection of the market demand curve (equal to the sum of the MRP curves of all individual firms in an industry) and the market supply curve (equal to the supply curve faced by the monopsonist). The price line (equal to the supply curve as seen by each individual competitive firm, ss) is parallel to the horizontal axis at the height determined by the intersection of market demand and supply.

Given the same market demand and cost conditions, a monopsonist would restrict the employment of a resource input to OQ_1, directly below the profit maximizing intersection of MRC and MRP at R_1. But the resource price, that is, the price which the monopsonist must pay to obtain quantity OQ_1, is shown at C_1 as a point on the ARC curve directly above OQ_1. $ARC = Q_1C_1$, and the resource price is P_1. Because $MRC > ARC$ when $MRP = MRC$, the resource price and the employment of the resource will be lower under monopsony than under

---

through $9 per hour. TRC in this case would be $5, $12, $21, $32, and $45, respectively. ARC would be $5 through $9, respectively. ($5/1 = 5$, $12/2 = $6, and so on.) MRC would be $7, $9, $11, and $18, respectively, as the quantity of labor purchased changed from 1 to 2, 2 to 3, and so on. If the supply or ARC curve is positively sloped, the MRC curve lies above and diverges from it.

pure competition. In addition, because resource prices are lower for the monopsonist, his AC curve is lower than for competitive sellers who are not monopsonists in the purchase of resource inputs. Thus, the monopsonist receives a pure "monopsony profit," equal to the difference between MRP (equal to MRC) and resource price (equal to ARC) multiplied by the quantity of the resource purchased. This is shown as the shaded area $P'R_1C_1P_1$ in Fig. 4.8.

What if the monopsonist is also a monopolist? What if firms possessing monopsony power in the purchase of inputs also have monopoly power in the sale of output? Then, the MR will lie below P, and MRP will lie below VMP. The price of the resource will lie below VMP for two reasons: First, because MRP exceeds Pr (monopsony); second, because VMP exceeds MRP (monopoly). As noted, the former entails "monopsonistic exploitation" of resource owners and will be characterized by "monopsony profits." The latter is another way of expressing "monopolistic exploitation" of consumers and may or may not be accompanied by "monopoly profits."[13]

Monopoly transforms the price system from a social process by which society controls its business sector to one in which individuals or groups rig the market in their favor and thereby control society. It promotes an inefficient allocation of resources, exploitation of consumers, and/or an inequitable distribution of income and exploitation of resource owners.

In addition, the classic indictment of monopoly includes four supplementary criticisms: First, monopoly obstructs the operation of the competitive price system as an automatic stabilizer. The flexibility of prices in competitive sectors of the economy, according to traditional economic theory, helps maintain output and employment during periods of falling demand. But monopolists typically respond to falling demand by restricting output and employment instead of cutting prices, thereby generating decreases in income and consumer demand. "By stabilizing price, the monopolist unstabilizes the whole economy."[14]

Second, the monopolist *may* contribute to economic progress, but "no threat of competition compels him to do so."[15] The monopolist *may* engage in research and invention leading to innovations, but he will be loath to do so if the latter require scrapping existing plants and equipment. Monopoly *may* be accompanied by economies of large-scale production, but it also may be

---

[13]Because $VMP = P \times MPP$ and $MRP = MR \times MPP$, to say that VMP exceeds MRP is equivalent to saying that P exceeds MR. If a monopolistic seller purchases resource inputs under purely competitive conditions, its MRC equals its resource price, and thus, its resource price equals MRP when $MRP = MRC$ under profit maximization conditions. But because of monopoly power as a seller, the resource price still lies below VMP. This gap of VMP above resource price, however, has nothing to do with restriction or control of the resource market or exploitation of resource owners. It is explained by the excess of price above MR (and thus, VMP over MRP). If $AR = AC$ (that is, if monopoly profits are zero), total revenue is exhausted by total costs, that is, by payments to resource owners according to their marginal revenue products plus normal profits. But the employment of resources and the production of output is less than what it would be under pure competition, where employment would be pushed to the point where MRC (and thus resource price) equalled VMP and output to the point where MC equalled price. The excess of P over MC, and thus, VMP

over MRC because of the divergence of VMP and MRP represent an exploitation of consumers, a failure to employ resources and produce output according to consumer preferences revealed through prices established in market exchange.

[14]Clair Wilcox, "Competition and Monopoly in the American Economy," Monograph No. 21, Temporary National Economic Committee, *Investigation of Concentration of Economic Power*, 76th Congress, 3rd Session (Washington, D.C.: U.S. Government Printing Office, 1940), p. 17.

[15]Ibid., p. 16.

accompanied by diseconomies stemming from security-conscious "bureaucratic organizations of officials"[16] more concerned with maintaining their jobs and the industrial status quo than with inaugurating risky new ventures.

Third, monopoly is incompatible with free enterprise. The establishment and maintenance of a monopoly position requires ejecting existing competitors and/or preventing entry of new competitors. Either conceivably may be accomplished through superior economic efficiency. But either also may be accomplished through tactics and devices, including government protection, which have little or nothing to do with economic efficiency and which restrict the freedom and opportunity of businessmen to compete.

Fourth, the concept of private economic power is incompatible with political democracy: "The enemy of democracy is monopoly in all its forms, and political liberty can survive only within an effective competitive system. If concentrated power is tolerated, giant pressure groups will ultimately gain control of the government or the government will institute direct regulation of organized pressure groups. In either event, free enterprise will then have to make way for collectivism, and democracy will be superseded by some form of authoritarianism."[17]

Criticism of Monopoly Versus Criticism of Capitalism

It should be emphasized, however, that criticism of monopoly is not, or not necessarily, criticism of capitalism as an economic

16Daniel Hamberg, "Size of Firm, Monopoly, and Economic Growth," *Employment, Growth and Price Levels*, Hearings Before the Joint Economic Committee, Part 7 (Washington, D.C.: U.S. Government Printing Office, 1959), pp. 2337–53.

17Walter Adams, "Public Policy in a Free Enterprise Economy," *The Structure of American Industry* (New York: The Macmillan Company, Publishers, 1954), p. 520.

system. This would be so only if capitalism were or would become essentially monopolistic. This is the prognostication of Marx and some post-Marxian socialists. But it was not the view of the great contributors to the classic theory of competitive market capitalism, nor is it the view of most contemporary expositors of the theory and philosophy of socially reformed-managed capitalism. The classic view, as modified and amplified by contemporary contributors, essentially is threefold: (1) Capitalist economies are competitive or, at least, incorporate competitive and monopolistic elements; (2) There is no clear evidence that capitalist economies like the United States are becoming more monopolistic. Indeed, certain tendencies associated with industrialization (such as technological advances, new products, urbanization, increased sources of alternative supply, higher living standards, and greater "discretionary income") are generating more, instead of less, competition. (3) The propensity to monopolize can be (and, to a limited but significant extent, has been) controlled and restricted by anti-monopoly actions and policies of government.

In sum, a criticism of monopoly is not necessarily a criticism of capitalism. Indeed, in the classic theory of competitive market capitalism, the reverse is true: By maintaining competition and restricting-preventing monopoly, we maintain the conditions for the effective functioning of the competitive price system and, thereby, for the socially beneficial resolution of society's economic problems within the context of a capitalist economy. From this vantage point, criticism of monopoly and the private concentration of economic power is not criticism of the capitalist economic system, but, rather, a criticism of certain imperfections which may prevent it from functioning at top form.

THE MAJOR CRITICISMS OF CAPITALISM

Many theories of economic systems have been indirectly, if not directly, extensions and/or critiques of the theory of competitive market capitalism and the accompanying social philosophy of classical liberalism (or its aberration, *laissez-faire* conservatism). Thus, much of the critical evaluation of capitalism is to be found in the writings of other theories. It will be useful to assemble systematically the major criticisms that have been levied against capitalism as an economic system.

These criticisms have been of two sorts: first, a critique of capitalism at less than its (purely-perfectly competitive) best—this by comparisons of the simplicity, automaticity, and beneficial performance of pure and perfect competition with the problems, tensions, and failures of actual capitalist economies; second, a critique of capitalism at its (purely-perfectly competitive) best— this, by citing alleged inadequacies and/or inaccuracies of the basic competitive model and/or the classical liberal philosophy accompanying it.

Critique of Capitalism at Less Than Its (Purely-Perfectly Competitive) Best

Many critics of capitalism have pointed out the divergence between the classic blueprint of the smoothly functioning purely and perfectly competitive price system and the functioning of capitalist economies in practice. Actual economic systems have not been characterized, in fact, by the conditions of pure and perfect competition. In many markets in capitalist reality, the number of sellers is few, not many. Products are rarely homogeneous. Knowledge of market conditions by firms and households is imperfect and uncertain. Resources are only imperfectly mobile, and impediments, both natural and contrived, block or reduce freedom of entry in many instances. As a result, prices are rarely given and beyond the control of buyers or sellers, and the classic model of competitive market capitalism, based on the assumption of given prices, often departs from reality.

As a result of monopoly and market imperfections, capitalism in practice cannot and does not contain the simplicity, automaticity, and socially beneficial performance of the idealized models of the competitive price system. Instead, as described earlier, it may be characterized by varying degrees of allocational inefficiencies and distributional inequalities, by failure to automatically function at or move toward full utilization of resources, especially labor, and by rates of growth often considered insufficient by its political leaders and citizenry alike.

To this indictment, defenders and sympathetic critics have responded in four ways: First, no system works at its best. To demonstrate that actual capitalist economies are less than purely-perfectly competitive merely indicates that these economies are real, working societies and not idealized theoretical models. The real questions are the criteria used for evaluation and the degree of imperfection or extent of success. Criteria for evaluation of capitalism may include dimensions (for example, consumer sovereignty) lacking or neglected in other economic systems. The extent of imperfection in capitalist reality should be compared with that of other actual economic systems.

Second, as noted, a critique of monopoly and market imperfections is not necessarily one "in principle" of capitalism as an economic system. Many classic expositors-defenders of competitive market capitalism are as critical of monopoly as some socialist critics and propose that market power and imperfections may be reduced, if not eliminated, by vigorous government anti-monopoly policy. (Note, however, the paradox: to establish and/or sustain the preconditions for an effectively working free enterprise system, it is necessary to restrain the freedom of monopoly enterprisers by government action and depart from a policy of laissez-faire, perhaps even from the less exacting policy of limited government.)

Third, pure and perfect competition, though useful in developing models of economic analysis, may be too exacting and demanding a standard for public policy. Many benefits of competitive market capitalism may be forthcoming in an impure and imperfect, but "workable" competition. The decentralized processes of market exchange envisaged in the classic theory of competitive capitalism may have their greatest advantages in the economical utilization and communication of information rather than in the attainment of idealized but unrealistic "marginal conditions" of optimum resource allocation.[18]

Fourth, there may be circumstances (for example, local telephone companies) where monopoly, if subject to careful and special public supervision and regulation, may be preferable to pure competition. Insofar as such instances are efficiently regulated to prevent exploitative uses of monopoly power, the absence of pure-perfect competition is not an indicator of failure or inefficiency.

Critique of Capitalism at Its Best

Even at its "best," however, under pure and perfect competition, capitalism would still experience problems and be characterized by defects, argue its critics.

---

[18]Some defenders of competitive market capitalism would prefer to have it both ways. In his more technical writings, for example, Friedrich Hayek insists that pure-perfect competition is an excessively and unrealistically demanding standard for evaluation of capitalist economic systems, and that the *real* advantages of economic individualism and decentralized market processes lie in their utilization of the qualitatively heterogeneous knowledge of "particular circumstances of time and place" that, by definition, are absent from pure and perfect competition. At the same time, in *The Road to Serfdom* [35], Hayek suggests that in capitalist economies, prices are given and beyond the control of business firms, which would seem to rest on the assumption of pure competition.

ECONOMIC INSTABILITY AND UNEMPLOYMENT

Though competitive markets *may* function as social processes to promote full utilization of resources, they *need not necessarily* do so; and even if they do so, the magnitude of required wage-price level changes, and/or the length of time necessary to make price system adjustments, may be larger or longer than is politically acceptable in a democratic society. The view that capitalism, even under ideally competitive conditions, can and/or will tend to generate economic instability and will not necessarily or automatically function at full employment of resources is common to nearly all contemporary theories of capitalism and varieties of socialist criticism.

AN INSUFFICIENT RATE OF ECONOMIC GROWTH

Even at its competitve best, the rate of economic growth under market capitalism may be regarded as insufficient. First, as already observed, capitalist growth depends on individual choices of households and firms between consumption and saving, work and leisure. If households are consumption- and leisure-oriented, the rate of economic growth may well be lower under competitive market capitalism than under monopoly capitalism or centrally planned socialism, where consumer and worker sovereignty do not act as such impediments to centralized decisions on saving, investment, and the labor force. Government actions designed to raise growth rates, incidentally, need not be undemocratic, for citizens may approve conscious government measures to raise the rate of economic growth that would not be voluntarily forthcoming from their market choices as consumers. Indeed, insofar as investment is embodied in new technologies which increase productivity, the present generation of consumers may be better off as well.

Second, decentralized market choices under competitive conditions have their greatest applicability in making relatively small and gradual adjustments. They are or may be less efficient in making the large-scale, rapid adjustments often required to foster industrialization and economic development, especially in the early stages in underdeveloped economies. Just as mercantilism, a period characterized by relatively large participation of centralized government in the economic arena, *preceded* the emergence of market capitalism in the West and helped lay the foundations or preconditions for economic development, so political leaderships in the underdeveloped non-Western areas of the world may be expected to refrain from exclusive or heavy reliance on competitive market processes in fostering the economic development of their countries.

Third, a corollary to the two preceding points is a defense of monopoly or oligopoly power, or other forms of "market imperfection" in the dynamics of development. The defense of tariff protection, for example, as a vehicle for the support of "infant industries" has a long history. A contemporary variation on this theme, developed pointedly by Joseph Schumpeter (see Chapter 6) is that temporary monopoly may provide both the motivation and economic capacity (in the form of monopoly profits) for innovative investment conducive to greater dynamic efficiency and, thereby, a higher growth rate than pure-perfect competition, with its tendency toward the elimination of pure economic profits.

AN INEQUITABLE DISTRIBUTION OF INCOME

Explored in the discussion of income distribution have been reasons for expecting substantial inequalities in income and wealth under competitive market capitalism. Even if capitalism were characterized in practice by pure and perfect competition, resulting inequalities in the distribution of income might well offend our democratic sensitivity, humanitarian impulses, or feelings of social justice and community. In addition, capitalist inequalities of income, even if based solely on

differences in the values of marginal products, may threaten social cohesion, stability and political order. An inequalitarian distributional pattern also rebounds on the question of efficiency in resource allocation under conditions of consumer sovereignty, for nothing in competitive market processes prevents unequal income distributions from affecting consumer choice through the "plural voting" of the affluent. An "efficient" allocation of resources, though politically unacceptable, thus may be consistent with a pattern of production which provides filet mignon for pampered puppies before providing needed minimum levels of food, clothing, housing, or medical care for a substantial portion of the population.

AN INEFFICIENT ALLOCATION OF RESOURCES

We have noted two classic criticisms of the competitive price system as a choice and allocational process in connection with other problems: First, the required magnitude and speed of a particular change may be greater than that which is readily capable of being absorbed by the price system, or, even if capable of this absorption, may involve a change too great or rapid to be politically acceptable; second, pure competition may not always yield optimum economic results. Another illustration of the first criticism and an expansion of the second may clarify their applicability to issues of resource allocation.

Inadequacy of Monetary Rewards. Illustrating the first limitation of the competitive price system is the situation in which monetary rewards operating through the price system are insufficient to yield desired allocations. During a major war, for example, conscription of soldiers is substituted for monetary inducement precisely because of the inadequacy of monetary rewards relative to non-monetary dangers.

Increasing Returns and/or Economies of Large-Scale Production. The central point to the second criticism is that, if the size of market demand is relatively small, then, in the event of increasing returns to variable proportions in the short run and/or economies of large-scale production in the long run, the number of firms which can be sustained by the market at high output levels may be much smaller than consistent with the conditions of pure competition. Pure competition would break down in this case and be replaced by oligopoly or monopoly, with lower costs of production for any level of output, but with attendant failures to satisfy the various "marginal conditions" of optimum resource allocation.

Allocation of Resources Between Collective (Non-Marketable) and Private (Marketable) Goods. The competitive price system is a social process for allocating resources among the production of marketable goods within the private sector of the economy. But many important goods, such as national defense, a judicial system, or a sanitation program, are not sufficiently marketable. First, these goods yield general benefits to an entire region or nation. Second, their high cost may be prohibitive to one or a small number of consumers. Third, since benefits accrue to all independently of contribution, it is implausible to expect voluntary contribution (as a general rule or in sufficient magnitude) or voluntary conveyance of individual preferences to government authorities for purposes of tax assessment. If such collective, indivisible, and essentially non-marketable wants are considered important, some social process other than the competitive price system (such as government provision financed through general taxation) will be necessary.

Marketable Merit Wants: Critique of Consumer Sovereignty. Collective wants are non-marketable and must be provided by some process other than the price system. By contrast, "merit wants"[19] refer to goods

[19]Richard A. Musgrave, *The Theory of Public Finance* (New York: McGraw-Hill Book Company, 1959), p. 13.

partially, if not entirely, marketable to consumers, but whose production and distribution is regulated or influenced in part by public action designed to encourage (or discourage) particular allocations of income and resources because of the merit (or demerit) of the goods in question. For example, the collective provision of a public educational system, free medical services, or subsidized housing to low-income groups may be considered meritorious. The opposite may be applied to the purchase and sale of dangerous drugs. Strictly and narrowly conceived, the concept of merit wants involves a critique of consumer sovereignty as a basis for choice, rather than a criticism of the competitive price system as a process for resource allocation, given consumer preferences. If the range of choices over which merit wants are applied, however, is relatively small, consumer sovereignty may still be regarded as the general rule to which strategic but limited exception is taken.

External Effects: Divergences Between Private and Social Costs and Benefits. It was suggested earlier that, given a general value judgment in favor of consumer sovereignty, an efficient pattern of resource allocation would require an equality between marginal cost and marginal utility (and marginal disutility and marginal productivity) ratios, and that, under purely competitive conditions, where price ratios are given and beyond the control of individual households and firms, this requirement would tend to be met as follows:

$$\frac{MCx}{MCy} = \frac{Px}{Py} = \frac{MUx}{MUy}$$

and

$$\frac{MDUa^x}{MDUb^x} = \frac{Pa}{Pb} = \frac{MPPa^x}{MPPb^x}$$

But these formulae implicitly assume an equality between marginal *private and social* costs, productivities, utilities, and disutilities. If private and social utilities and costs (and disutilities and productivities) diverge, then competitive market capitalism, even at its best, will not entail an optimum pattern of resource allocation.

Critics have identified numerous illustrations and areas of divergence between private and social valuations. Automobile producers, for example, do not calculate the social cost of smog, traffic congestion, carnage on the highways, and unwed motherhood which has accompanied the production of automobiles. As a result, automobile production, even under purely competitive conditions, would tend to be carried *beyond* levels justifiable in terms of optimum resource allocation. Similarly, private firms may engage in activities (such as planting trees to provide a windbreak by one farm) which benefit others. In the absence of methods for bringing such external benefits into private cost calculations, the level of such activities, even under pure-perfect competition, is likely to be *lower* than optimum.

Similar illustrations apply to consumption and/or resource provision. For example, the holder of raucous 2 A.M. parties may create disutilities for his next-door neighbors not included (nor considered) in his own private calculations. As a result, the length of the party will predictably extend beyond the point of equality between the ratios of marginal *social* utilities and market prices even under purely and perfectly competitive conditions.

In all of these instances, a strong case can be made, even under ideally competitive conditions, for some form of collective action, ranging from taxes or subsidies designed to discourage and/or encourage production, consumption, or resource provision, to various forms of direct controls (such as zoning laws or regulations prohibiting the sale of alcoholic beverages to minors).

A CONCLUDING NOTE

We have already considered the responses of defenders and sympathetic critics to the critique of capitalism at less than its purely-perfectly competitive best. Noted here are responses to the second major area of criticism.

Defenders of the capitalist system would contend that: First, any economic system, *even at its best*, will have problems and difficulties because even the "best" of systems are less than perfect. To demonstrate that pure-perfect competition is not all milk and honey does not necessarily prove the wisdom or desirability of a radical alteration in the economic system, for other systems, even at their best, may or do experience defects or limitations.

Second, even if *all* the criticisms are valid, the net result may be a strong case for the modification or reform of capitalism through supplementary and complementary governmental and collective action, rather than the elimination of the price system by the substitution of a comprehensive system of socialist planning.

Socialists, naturally, dissent and argue that the conflicts, defects, and limitations of competitive market capitalism are so serious, and the needed reforms or modifications so comprehensive, that nothing short of a transformation to a new and different (socialist) economic system will do. Probably the most powerful and influential illustration of this point of view in the development of socialist thought is found in the Marxian critique of capitalist industrialization, in Chapter 5.

SUMMARY OF CHAPTER 4

1. The basic characteristic of competitive market capitalism is a system for making and coordinating economic decisions. The two major units for decision-making in a capitalist economy are business firms and households. Their plans and decisions are coordinated through processes of exchange on goods and resource markets.

2. The unifying theme of the theory of competitive market capitalism is that, built

into the internal workings of the price system under competitive conditions, are decentralized social processes which automatically and spontaneously resolve society's economic problems of resource allocation, income distribution, full employment-stability, and economic growth, in socially beneficial ways. According to the classic theory, under competitive conditions:

a. resources tend to be allocated in an optimum manner to create maximum output and patterns of production most closely correspondent to consumer preferences;

b. income tends to be distributed according to the values of market-determined marginal productivity;

c. the aggregate level of economic activity tends to stabilize at a full-employment utilization of resources;

d. the system tends to promote a dynamic efficiency and rate of growth consistent with individual choices regarding saving versus consumption and work versus leisure.

3. The corollary to the classic defense of the competitive price system as capitalism's central and unifying social process is a classic indictment of monopoly. Monopoly is held to promote inefficient patterns of resource allocation and an inequitable distribution of income, to interfere with the price flexibility needed to contribute to the automatic attainment of full employment, and to reduce dynamic efficiency and/or promote rates of economic growth inconsistent with individual preferences.

4. The major criticisms of capitalism are, first, that it does not generally function at its (purely-perfectly competitive) best; and, second, that even at its (purely-perfectly competitive) best, capitalism still has defects or limitations in attaining efficiency, equity, growth, and full employment-stability. The classic responses to these criticisms are that any economic system has problems in theory or in practice which may be rectified or reduced by modifications or reforms far short of a comprehensive transformation of the economic system.

4

Appendix:

Capitalism, Classical Liberalism,

and Conservatism

Capitalism is more than a set of economic relations and the theory of competitive market capitalism more than a technical analysis of allocation, distribution, stability, and growth. Capitalism is also a philosophy or "way of life"—a body of ideas and practices incorporating economic relations and issues as central and strategic components, but, at the same time, transcending them. The economic model of built-in automatism or self-regulation, plus a conception of the state and its role in society, and general philosophical and psychological assumptions about man, his aspirations and capabilities yield a social philosophy of capitalism, a body of ideas concerning public policy, social reform, and the role of government and private enterprise that has come to be known as "classical liberalism."

Classical liberalism, suggests Girvetz, is that "philosophy of life inseparably identified with capitalism." [13: 15] It is important not only in its own right, as a systematic body of ideas incorporating yet supplementing and complementing the economic theory of capitalism, but also in terms of its influence upon social thought and practice: "Emerging as the radical philosophy of the eighteenth century and becoming the pervasive con-

servative philosophy of the middle and late nineteenth century, classical liberalism is still important. Knowledge and understanding of classical liberalism are indispensable to a firm grasp of the contemporary economic philosophies. They are after all either adaptations or hostile reactions."[1]

Laissez-faire: The Rejection of the
State in Economic Life

THE DOMINANT THEME

The social and political corollary to the economic theory of the built-in automatism or self-regulatory character of the competitive price or market system is that of laissez-faire, which holds that society will be organized in such a way as to permit the economy to function on the basis of its automatic self-regulatory processes, that is, that social, cultural, religious, and governmental controls will not be permitted to intervene or interfere with either the free economic choices of individuals or the functioning of the market system. "A market economy," wrote Karl Polanyi, "is an economic system controlled,

---

[1]Donald S. Watson, *Economic Policy* (Boston: Houghton Mifflin Company, 1960), p. 47.

regulated and directed by markets alone; order in the production and distribution of goods is entrusted to this self-regulating mechanism."[2]

The most important component of the *laissez-faire* philosophy is the concept of the limited or minimum state. According to this view government should be limited to a minimum role in economic life. Wrote Adam Smith in 1776:

> The sovereign is completely discharged from a duty, in the attempting to perform which he must always be exposed to innumerable delusions, and for the proper performance of which no human wisdom or knowledge could ever be sufficient: the duty of superintending the industry of private people, and of directing it towards the employment most suitable to the interest of the society. [24: 651]

In a similar vein, J.S. Mill later stated the case for limited government and *laissez faire* as the general rule:

> In all the more advanced communities, the great majority of things are worse done by the intervention of government, than the individuals most interested in the matter would do them, or cause them to be done, if left to themselves . . . . The preceding are the principal reasons, of a general character, in favor of restricting to the narrowest compass the intervention of a public authority in the business community: and few will dispute the more than sufficiency of these reasons to throw, in every instance, the burden of making out a strong case, not on those who resist, but on those who recommend, government interference. *Laissez-faire*, in short, should be the general practice: every departure from it, unless required by some great good, is a certain evil.[3]

---

[2]Karl Polanyi, *The Great Transformation* (New York: Farrar, Straus & Giroux, Inc., 1944), pp. 68.

[3]John Stuart Mill, *Principles of Political Economy* (London: Longman's, Green & Company, 1926), p. 950.

THE CLASSICAL CASE FOR LAISSEZ-FAIRE

The classical liberal case for *laissez-faire* is, first of all, an economic one. If, built into the internal workings of the competitive price or market system, is a set of social processes which more or less automatically coordinate economic decisions and resolve economic problems in a socially beneficial way, then why bother with other forms of social, especially governmental, coordination and control? Why bother with conscious governmental direction and guidance of the national economy if the economy has its own principles of self-regulation, spontaneously built into its internal structure and functioning?

But the classical liberal case for *laissez-faire* is also political. Classical economic liberalism incorporates a rejection of the state as well as a defense of the competitive price system. The classical liberal critique of government action in the economy rests partly on the idea that the knowledge needed to make economic decisions is not known (or knowable) to one man or a small number of men, but, instead, is dispersed among large numbers of men. Even at its best, government cannot have the knowledge to make rational decisions for an entire economy. But, in addition, government is not necessarily or generally at its best:

> Whatever the merits of the universal proposition that the state is inherently oppressive, corrupt, and inefficient, these titles did aptly fit most government in the eighteenth and much of the nineteenth century, even after the more tyrannical regimes had been ousted. England's parliamentary government was notoriously unrepresentative when it was not downright despotic. The middle classes, not to mention the masses, were virtually excluded from participation or control until 1832. . . . In short, government intervention in economic life *was* arbitrary and repressive, and such intervention was rarely in the interest of the classes excluded from participation in government. [13 : 67]

The classical liberal case for *laissez-faire* rests, lastly, upon general philosophical and psychological assumptions. Though several nineteenth-century contributors to the theory and philosophy of liberal, competitive capitalism expressed qualifications and reservations, the dominant pattern of thought includes the following assumptions: Man, as utilitarian philosopher Jeremy Bentham suggested in the early nineteenth century, (1) is an egoist, interested in the promotion of his own interest, specifically, the maximization of his economic gain through market exchange; yet (2) is rational and dedicated to the calculation of gains and costs of alternative courses of action. These behavioral traits are rooted in "human nature." The implication of these assumptions for public policy and the role of government in the economy is that consumers, businesses, investors, and workers know their own interests and are prepared to and do act on the basis of them in a manner superior to that which could be provided by any external collective agent, such as government. (3) Social behavior and social relations between men operate according to "laws" essentially similar to those of nature which (4) are generally socially beneficial and, in any event, are immutable. According to Herbert Spencer, mid-nineteenth century English social and political philosopher who carried classical liberalism to extreme positions beyond those of Adam Smith, Jeremy Bentham, and John Stuart Mill, proponents of government control and social reform, endeavor (unsuccessfully) "to supersede the great laws of nature," the "principles that show themselves alike in the self-adjustment of planetary perturbations, and in the healing of a scratched finger—in the balancing of social systems, and in the increased sensitiveness of a blind man's ear—in the adaptation of prices to produce and in the acclimatization of a plant."[4]

---

[4]Herbert Spencer, *Social Statics* (New York: Appleton-Century, 1868), Chapter XXII, Sect. 8.

COMPETITIVE MARKET SYSTEM HISTORICALLY ATYPICAL

The concept and practice of a regulatory mechanism built into the internal working of the economic system and its socio-political corollary *laissez-faire* is atypical rather than typical in the historical development of economic systems. It was never established completely in the Western industrializing economies even during the "liberal interlude" [6: 19–20] of the nineteenth century. There were always reservations and exceptions for government intervention in economic life in the United States, on the continent of Europe, and even in Great Britain. But however we interpret the role of *laissez-faire* in the nineteenth century, the general principle is that *laissez-faire* has not been the rule. More typically, economy has been submerged in and controlled by society.

In pre-market, pre-capitalist economies, economic activity was bound with and inseparable from its broader social, political, cultural, and religious context. Such otherwise diverse forms of economic organization as that of ancient Greece, medieval feudalism, and early-modern mercantilism shared two common characteristics: (1) the absence of the power and freedom to make economic decisions solely or even primarily in terms of the individual pursuit of economic gain and the social and religious sanction of such a motivational and decision-making pattern for large numbers of people; (2) the absence of a market system as an autonomous self-regulatory mechanism for coordinating economic decisions free from social and governmental control. Economic decisions, to a much greater extent than in market capitalism, were made in terms of non-economic criteria—for example, ethical, religious, and political—and were coordinated and controlled more by government, church, society, and custom than by the marketplace.

In both the Greek polis and the medieval manorial system, for example, large portions of the population were excluded from the process of decision making. The very existence of slavery in classical times and serfdom in the medieval age precluded the existence of a free labor market. Land, in both antiquity and the early Middle Ages, was the fundamental basis of economic and political power and was not an integral part of a market exchange process between landlords and farmer-capitalists. The surplus of income above consumption was typically small. What economic surpluses that did exist were distributed mainly to church, state, and a landed aristocracy, and were allocated primarily to the construction of castles and churches and the conduct of wars rather than to productive investment in industry. Loans, when made, went more for consumption than investment purposes. Consequently, money and capital markets were not dominant processes in economic life. Although commerce and trade was by no means absent, markets did not widely penetrate society at large as a process for coordinating and integrating economic life. Agriculture was the dominant sector of the economy. Agricultural production was typically conducted by more or less self-sufficient households or manors. Its essential properties were the physical ones of transforming inputs into outputs rather than the social processes embodied in the continuous circular flow of the market purchase of inputs to be transformed into exchangeable outputs.

Moreover, pervading classical and medieval thought were ethical considerations largely absent from the market capitalist world of Adam Smith and J. S. Mill. Plato and Aristotle extolled the virtues of cultivated leisure, citizenship, and the contemplative life. In the Middle Ages, the church criticized the taking of interest as unchristian as well as unproductive. St. Thomas Aquinas, a prominent thirteenth-century schoolman, contended that prices should be "just" and that gain from trade was consistent with a good Christian life only if directed to some noble purpose, for example, support of the church

or alleviation of poverty. Thus, the pursuit of economic gain through market exchange lacked the social and religious sanction that it came to receive in modern times. In short, economic life was largely submerged in its social, political, and religious context and subject to non-economic controls of church, state, and tradition. The ideas of a *self*-regulated market system, with rules for social coordination built into its internal functioning, and the political corollary of *laissez-faire*, were largely absent from ancient and medieval life and thought.

In these respects, the economic life of the 'mercantilist era' of the late Middle Ages and early modern times was characterized by transition. From the thirteenth century onwards, society assumed a more secular character and this was both result and cause of the growth of commerce and the capitalist spirit. The consolidation of political power by absolutist monarchs in nation states contributed to economic development and the growth of markets in a number of ways: (1) the introduction of national currencies and national systems of weights and measures, (2) the reduction of barriers to *intra*national trade, (3) government encouragement of exploration, colonization, and exports, (4) government protection of life and property, (5) government construction of roads and other transportation and communications facilities. Moreover, the national monarchs discovered that their interests often coalesced with those of the merchant capitalist. The monarchy therefore deliberately fostered production, commerce, and export, and merchants and businessmen, in turn, often lent their support to the monarchy.

Still, the key element in economic thought and policy during these transitional centuries between feudalism and capitalism was less the market principle than the pursuit of the power and wealth of the nation state through government regulation of the internal and external affairs of the economy. Classical liberals, notably Adam Smith, criticized the 'mercantile system' in several ways.

First, mercantilism involved the *power state*; that is, the key criterion for any economic policy or prospective change in economic organization was: How does it promote the power and wealth of the nation state, especially as embodied in the national monarch? This does not necessarily imply that private interests must be trampled. But it does require that conflicts between private and national interests be resolved in favor of the latter and that private actions be channeled and directed by governmental action toward the pursuit of national aims. The social philosophy of market capitalism implied by contrast the concept of the *general welfare state*—not in the now-popular sense of "social welfare" legislation, but in the broader view of: How does this policy promote the wealth and welfare of private individuals? This does not necessarily require a weak state. (Defense may well take precedence over opulence.) But it does involve a substitution of the welfare of individuals for the power of the state as the dominant theme in economic organization and policy.

Second, mercantilism was characterized by government guidance and regulation of the national economy toward the pursuit of collective goals, whereas classical liberalism presumed individuals are better equipped to make their own judgments. This rests in part on the classic theory of the automatic regulatory mechanism of the marketplace. It also rests on the often short-sighted and restrictive policies of venal and corrupt monarchs and government officials.[5] The corollary to this is the idea of the *limited state*, that is, that governmental authority should be restricted to certain clearly prescribed duties and responsibilities, leaving large areas for individual freedom of choice.

Third, mercantilism involved a variety of

---

[5] The greater reliance upon the state in the economic development of Germany in the latter nineteenth century than in England in the early nineteenth century rested in part on the prior development of a reasonably efficient German system of public administration.

governmental restrictions and controls over the movement of goods and resources, especially restrictions over imports, and the accompanying attempt to promote a "favorable" balance of trade (balance of payments, in contemporary terms) by an excess of all export over all import items. Classical economic liberalism, in contrast, included as a key element freedom of trade and mobility of resources. Adam Smith's great work, *The Wealth of Nations*, is in part a polemic against the vestiges of feudal and mercantilistic control over economic life. "All systems either of preference or of restraint, therefore, being . . . completely taken away, the obvious and simple system of natural liberty establishes itself of its own accord. Every man, as long as he does not violate the laws of justice, is left perfectly free to pursue his own interest his own way, and to bring both his industry and capital into competition with those of any other man, or order of men." [24: 651]

From Classical Liberalism to Laissez-Faire Conservatism

Classical liberalism, as the social philosophy most closely and clearly associated with the theory of competitive market capitalism, should be distinguished both from *classical conservatism*, represented by such figures as Edmund Burke (1729–1797) and contemporary Russell Kirk, and from *laissez-faire conservatism* which, as a modified and Americanized version of classical liberalism, became the dominant social philosophy associated with capitalist industrialization in the United States from the post-Civil War to the depression of the 1930s. [21: 128–62]

CLASSICAL CONSERVATISM

In the context of the late eighteenth and early nineteenth centuries, classical liberalism represented a liberal-radical philosophy of social reform. By contrast, classical conservatism "from Burke to Kirk" [21: 20] represented an intuitive preference for gradual and incremental change to maintain intact for as long as possible the best in the constitutional but aristocratic heritage of the past.

Classical conservatism gives qualified support to market processes, but not as an agency for economic efficiency and growth; instead, it views the market as an institution that contributes to individual freedoms, property, and social pluralism.

Similarly, classical conservatism gives qualified approval to the modern state. The classical conservative maintains governments should be limited and representative, not for the classical liberal reasons of government inefficiency or incapacity, but because of the corrupting influence of power on those who govern. At the same time, the wisely-governed state will avoid the "tyranny of the democratic majority" and maintain controls over the rule of the undifferentiated majority.

As characterized by classical conservatives, man is neither purely rational, economic, nor individualistic. He is equal in the sight of God and before the law, but sharply unequal in talents, abilities, and capacity for leadership, and has considerable capacity for evil as well as good.

The classical conservative view of the market and government, combined with these philosophical-psychological assumptions, yields a social philosophy of private and public action not dissimilar to, yet distinguishable from, that of classical liberalism. A vigorous, healthy private sector is espoused by classical conservatism, but primarily because of its contributions to self-reliance, social pluralism, and a balance of power between governors and the governed, and as a defense against the potential tyranny of the democratic and/or collectivist state. The role of public action should be small, so as to offset the corrupting impact of the concentration of power (not merely limited in function, as in the classical liberal view, to promote an effective division of labor between private and public sectors).

However, lacking the classical liberal's faith in the efficacy of market processes and emphasizing tradition, the classical con-servative is on occasion willing to support a larger role for government than classical liberals, if necessary to maintain social and political order, stability, and security. Social security measures, for example, have never given classical conservatives the qualms they have given to classical liberals. In early nineteenth-century England, the main proponents of factory legislation and other measures to protect the economic security of workers were from the Tory Party, representative of traditional, aristocratic, and conservative interests. In the United States, during and after the period of the New Deal, a somewhat similar function was performed by conservative Senator Robert A. Taft.

LAISSEZ-FAIRE CONSERVATISM

The social philosophy most closely associated with the development of American capitalism in the late nineteenth and early twentieth century was neither classical liberalism nor conservatism, but a popularized American offshoot of the former, incorporating selected dimensions of the latter, which we shall call "laissez-faire conservatism." This American social philosophy "rose to prominence between 1865 and 1885, to ascendency between 1885 and 1920, to domination—to virtual identification with the 'American way'—in the 1920s." [21: 131] It provided the rhetoric and substance for the conservative defense of the *status quo* against the social and economic reforms of the New Deal and has continued to play a rear-guard function of reaction against the extension of liberal social reform since 1945.

Laissez-faire conservatism shares with classical liberalism the concept of the socially beneficial built-in automaticity of market processes, the critique of short-sighted, inefficient, and ineffectual government, the motivational assumption of the "economic man," the defense of economic individualism, and the support of the principle of limited government. But it modifies classical liberalism in important ways.

Some of the major differences between

Table 4-1.

SOME MAJOR DIFFERENCES BETWEEN CLASSICAL
LIBERALISM AND LAISSEZ-FAIRE CONSERVATISM

	Classical Liberalism	Laissez-Faire Conservatism
1. Time	Late 18th/early 19th centuries	Late 19th/early 20th centuries
2. Place	Primarily England	Primarily the United States
3. Leading contributors	Adam Smith, Bentham, J. S. Mill (typically intellectuals and scholars)	William Graham Sumner (often businessmen and their spokesmen)
4. Conception of society	Mechanism	Organism—"survival of the fittest"
5. Central unifying principle	Competitive price system as an automatic social process	Property rights of dynamic and progressive private enterprise
6. Interpretation of free enterprise	Freedom to compete	Freedom from government interference
7. Attitude toward business	Mean, rapacious with a tendency to conspire and monopolize if not checked or countervailed by competition	Central decision-makers; guardians and trustees, with responsibility to rule because of an aristocracy of demonstrated ability and talent
8. Corollary for public policy	Limited government, with a division of labor between private and public sectors	Small government, with a *laissez-faire* policy toward the economy, but pro-business legislation and administration

classical liberalism and laissez-faire conservatism are listed in Table 4-1. In addition to differences in time and place, laissez-faire conservatism is a variation of classical liberalism in several prominent ways: Whereas classical liberalism was primarily the product of intellectuals, laissez-faire conservatism is more a popular ideology, promulgated by businessmen and their spokesmen, the church, and the press. In the form of "social Darwinism," laissez-faire conservatism may be characterized as an amalgam of a popular rendition of classical economics and of the ideas of Charles Darwin and Herbert Spencer. To the view of society as a mechanism held together by the automaticity of the competitive price system, laissez-faire conservatism added the view of society as an organism which, through the process of

'survival of the fittest,' weeds out the inefficient. The central unifying principle in social Darwinism is less the marketplace than the inalienable property rights of the successful captains of industry.

For Adam Smith, as noted, the hero of the piece is the impersonal social process of the marketplace. A major social function of competition is to keep the rapacious and monopolizing tendencies of businessmen in check. But for laissez-faire conservatives such as William Graham Sumner (1840–1910), the businessman becomes the hero. In Andrew Carnegie's *The Gospel of Wealth*, the businessman is admonished to use his accumulated wealth virtuously for the benefit of mankind, thereby functioning as the guardian of civilization.

In another subtle shift of emphasis, free

enterprise, in laissez-faire conservatism, came increasingly to be interpreted primarily as freedom *from* government interference and only secondarily as freedom *to* enter competition. The corollary of limited government was transformed into an extreme version of laissez-faire, with the exception of government support of business (for example, tariffs, land grants to railroads). In sum, while classical liberalism in England was a liberalizing social philosophy of economic reform, laissez-faire conservatism in the United States became increasingly a defense of the status quo and an identification of the "American way of life" with an aristocracy of wealth and a monistic dominance by business interests, which one contemporary author calls "the Great Train Robbery of American Intellectual History." [21:128]

Limited Government: The Role of the State in Economic Life

Classical liberalism does not imply anarchism, for limited government is neither small nor zero government. The establishment of competitive market capitalism may require preconditions which, in turn, require government action—either in relinquishing some of its controls over economic life or in restricting or preventing private monopoly. In his balanced and thorough review of Adam Smith's views on laissez-faire, Jacob Viner lists free occupational choice, free trade in land, and internal and external free trade as four reforms requiring this kind of negative government action.[6]

But in addition to establishing preconditions for competitive market capitalism, government has selected and limited *positive* functions to perform in economic society. For both reasons, government is not strictly an "external agent" apart from the "natural

order" of things, but is part of that natural order. What are government's positive economic functions in a liberal society? According to Adam Smith, government has three main functions in a "system of natural liberty": ". . . first, the duty of protecting the society from the violence and invasion of other independent societies; secondly, the duty of protecting, as far as possible, every member of the society from the injustice or oppression of every other member of it, or the duty of establishing an exact administration of justice; and thirdly, the duty of erecting and maintaining certain public works and certain public institutions, which it can never be for the interest of any individual, . . . because the profit could never repay the expense to any individual or small number of individuals, though it may frequently do much more than repay it to a great society." [24:651]

Other contributors to classical liberalism (such as Bentham and J. S. Mill) added other specific functions, services, and reforms of and by government.[7] Government does exist, and should perform important economic functions. Its role is essentially complementary to and supportive of the private sector.

It is sometimes suggested that the essence of the laissez-faire prescription of classical liberalism is that government's role in economic life should be absolutely or relatively *small*. This is not accurate. Government could be restricted to the provision of the three central Smithian functions (law and

---

[6]Jacob Viner, "Adam Smith and Laissez-Faire," *Journal of Political Economy* (April 1927). Reprinted in Joseph J. Spengler and William Allen, *Essays in Economic Thought* (Chicago: Rand McNally and Company, 1969), pp. 315–16.

[7]Girvetz [13:91–101] systematically identifies the functions of the liberal state, as gleaned from the writings of classical liberalism, as: (1) the preservation of both internal and external order; (2) the enforcement of contracts; (3) the promotion of exchange (through, for example, the provision and regulation of the medium of exchange and the physical means of exchange in the form of transportation and communication facilities); (4) the maintenance of freedom of competition; (5) the "meliorative function" (for example, protection of or provision of assistance to the young and the disabled, the conservation of natural resources, the provision of public works and institutions, such as schools or museums).

order, national defense, public works and institutions) and still be quite large, both absolutely and relative to the private sector.

It has also been suggested that classical liberalism is a defense of private enterprise, perhaps merely an ideological rationalization of the economic interests of businessmen. This, too, is not accurate. It is true that classical liberalism included a defense of capitalism as an economic system, of the competitive price or market system as a regulatory process, and of the economic functions of capital and private capitalists-entrepreneurs. It is also true that businessmen, and their ideological supporters, from the Manchester School in the nineteenth century to the National Association of Manufacturers in the twentieth, have discovered in classical liberalism a ready-made economic ideology suitable, with modifications, for the defense of their class interests. Recalling Adam Smith's famous strictures on the mean, rapacious, selfish, conspiratorial, and monopolizing tendencies of businessmen, free private enterprise is equated with neither goodness nor godliness in classical liberalism. The hero is not the businessman, but the market principle; and the theme is not the glory of private enterprise, but the notion that the competitive price or market system operates as a social process to organize, channel, and control the selfish interests and free choices of large numbers of individual decision-markers, including capitalist-entrepreneurs, to resolve society's economic problems more or less beneficially. Further, the classical liberal views the division of labor between government and private enterprise as essentially an empirical matter; it depends on concrete circumstances of time and place, especially the efficiency of systems of public administration. "The modern advocate of laissez-faire who objects to government participation in business on the ground that it is an encroachment upon a field reserved by nature for private enterprise cannot find support for this argument in *The Wealth of Nations*."[8]

What are the criteria for government participation in economic life, and how far can government intervene in a capitalist economy without transforming it to a new collectivist economic system? The classical liberals, for whom laissez-faire was the rule and government action the exception, and for whom exceptions and qualifications were to be made on the basis of empirical, commonsense judgments of the particular circumstances of time and place, did not clearly answer this question. It is, however, a question of major concern for today's neo-liberals, who find inspiration in the economic individualism of classical liberalism, but who want to bring it up to date in light of contemporary conditions.

---

[8] Jacob Viner, "Adam Smith and Laissez-Faire," *Journal of Political Economy*, (April 1927), reprinted in Joseph J. Spengler and William Allen, *Essays in Economic Thought* (Chicago: Rand McNally and Company, 1969), pp. 324–25.

The Marxian Critique
of Capitalist Industrialization

INTRODUCTION

One of the anomalies of comparative economic thought, resolvable on closer examination, is that Marxian socialism was essentially an analysis of capitalism. At first glance, this may seem paradoxical, considering the common association of Marxism with socialism and the popular identification of Marx as a founding father of contemporary communism. This chapter describes the Marxian analysis and critical evaluation of the process of capitalist industrialization. Chapter 8 examines Marxist-Leninist vision(s) of the ideally functioning socialist and communist economic societies. Later we will see how Marxian economics, initially formulated in the nineteenth century in relation to then current problems of capitalism and capitalist industrialization has affected and been modified by twentieth-century theories and social philosophies of economic systems and strategies for economic reform.

Marxian Economics

Marx and Marxism involve many dimensions other than economics. But whatever else Marx was—philosopher, sociologist, historian, journalist, revolutionist, prophet— he was an economist. Whatever else Marxism was (or is), it was (and is) fundamentally and significantly a body of economic ideas. At the same time, Marxian economics is part of a broader scheme of thought, extending to history, sociology, and politics. Because comparative economics is concerned, in part, with the institutional structure of economies and their development, transformation, or reform, reference will also be made to these broader dimensions.

The economics of Marxism can be examined as (1) an actual economic system, (2) a movement for economic reform, and/or (3) a theoretical economic system. Our examination will be on the third of these approaches. Marxism is *not* an actual economic system in the sense that are the Soviet Russian, the Communist Chinese, or the American economies. Marxism was and is *partly* a revolutionary movement for economic change. Marx—and his collaborator and financial supporter Friedrich Engels— helped establish, and were in other ways closely associated with, a number of anticapitalist organizations in the mid-nineteenth century. Marx was intimately concerned with the development and success of these organizations, their tactics and programs.

But it is not with Marxism as (and certainly not with Marx as a leader of) a revolutionary movement for economic change that we are here primarily concerned. "Had Marx produced nothing more . . . than a revolutionary labor movement, he would not loom today as so important a figure in the world. Marx was only one of a dozen revolutionaries and by no means the most successful . . ."[1] Many Marxists (and non-Marxists) have been much more successful in the practical arts and tactics of revolution and/or reform than Marx, but no post-Marxian Marxist has ever matched the intellectual brilliance and performance of the master. Though the proverbial "man on the street" may regard Marx primarily as a "bomb-throwing revolutionist," and Marxism as a sort of "revolutionist's handbook" guiding contemporary international communism, we are concerned here instead with Marx, the penetrating, provocative analyst of economic organization, and with Marxism as a theoretical economic system.

General Features of Marxian Economic Theory

Certain general features of Marxian economic theory should be noted. First, Marxian economics is essentially, though not exclusively, the *economics of Karl Marx*. Where relevant, we will distinguish between classical Marxian and contemporary neo-Marxian analyses of comparative economic systems. But the most important single contributor to Marxian economic theory was Marx. "Marxian economics" thus may be regarded as interchangeable with "the economics of Karl Marx."

Second, despite the common, but highly misleading, phrase "Marxian socialism," Marxian economic theory is essentially an analysis and critique of capitalism as an economic system—its origins, characteristics, problems, and prospects—and only secondarily, in a relatively minor way, is concerned with the organization and behavior of

prospective post-capitalist economic systems, that is, socialism and communism.

Third, the Marxian theory of capitalism is both an analysis of the behavior and prospects of *capitalism* as an economic system and a model of the process of capitalist *industrialization* and economic development. These two elements are intertwined for, in the classic Marxian view, capitalism is the route to industrialization in underdeveloped and developing economies. Industrialization via capital accumulation is capitalism's "historic function."[2]

Fourth, emphasis on industrialization and economic development places Marxian economic theory primarily, though not exclusively, in economic *dynamics* rather than economic statics. The purpose of his analysis, emphasized Marx, was "to lay bare the economic law of motion of modern society . . ." [16: I, 14] rather than to examine the characteristics of economic equilibrium under static resource, technological, and institutional conditions. Marxian dynamics contains both "quantitative" and "qualitative" elements. Quantitatively speaking, capitalism grows—and fluctuates. Under given technological and institutional conditions, the magnitudes of economic variables change, grow, oscillate. But in the process of industrialization, capitalism also alters its qualitative structure—it *develops* as well as grows—to be transformed eventually into a new, different post-capitalist system of economic organization.

Fifth, the theory of competitive market capitalism was concerned basically with how capitalism works and resolves its economic problems. Marx was concerned with how capitalism fails to work—with its "contra-

---

[1] Robert Heilbroner, *The Worldly Philosophers* (New York: Simon and Schuster, Inc., 1967), p. 140.

[2] This view is subject to possible criticism on at least two grounds: one, the neo- and post-Marxian view that there may be or are alternative routes to industrialization other than capitalism; two the anti- and non-Marxian view that many problems which Marx associated with capitalism as an economic system may be only the growing pains of any modern industrializing society.

dictions" and with how the latter, inherent in the system and unresolvable through social reform, eventually will lead to capitalism's demise.

Marx's analysis of capitalism is also a critical evaluation and assessment. Though most contemporary Western economists disagree with much of Marxian economic theory, many agree it provides an important critical analysis of capitalism, perhaps the most powerful and provocative critique of the process of capitalist industrialization to emerge in the nineteenth century. Certainly it has had tremendous influence on post-Marxian theories of economic systems.

The Marxian Conception of Capitalism

Marx had not one, but two or more conceptions of capitalism: one was a competitive, decentralized form, prevalent in the earlier stages of capitalist industrialization; another, a more monopolistic, centralized form, which Marx felt was emerging and would emerge more fully in later stages of capitalist industrialization. The latter conception, though underdeveloped and nebulously formulated, played a central role in the Marxian theory of economic development and in Marx's prognostications about the future of capitalism, and will be examined in the Appendix. The first, the more rigorously developed concept, is examined here in depth.

From the standpoint of economic rhetoric, there are two major reasons for Marx's emphasis on *competitive* capitalism: First, if capitalism at its best, that is, under purely competitive conditions, has problems and contradictions, they would presumably be greater were capitalism to function at its worst, that is, under monopolistic conditions. Second, if capitalism's problems stem solely from the imperfections of monopoly, a traditional and non-Marxian solution would be at least conceivable: Reduce monopoly power (through a vigorous anti-trust program, for example). By contrast, if capitalism's problems arise not from monopoly but from the structure of the system itself, then, in the Marxian view, the only solution is the elimination of capitalism as an economic system and the establishment of a new and different system.

The Marxian concept of capitalism (see Table 5-1) is quite similar to and overlaps that of competitive market capitalism. However, special Marxian emphases and modifications should be noted, for they play an important role in Marxian economic theory. Already cited have been Marxian emphasis upon (1) a developing economy with an advancing technology, and (2) capital, capitalistic methods of production, and capital accumulation as central ingredients of capitalism. Given these two elements, the most important characteristic of capitalism in the Marxian view is (3) private ownership of the means of production. As in the classic conception of pure capitalism, the dominant form of business organization is the individual proprietorship. Thus, the Marxian capitalist is simultaneously owner, money-capital provider, entrepreneur, and (possibly) manager of the enterprise. But it is the *ownership* which gives him the basis for control. Another Marxian emphasis: Only a relatively small portion of the population owns the instruments of production. The large majority of the population work for those who own industrial property. Thus, even under the purest of competitive conditions, capitalists have monopoly as a *class* over the ownership and control of business enterprises.

This concentration of the ownership of the means of production in the hands of a relative few is the key to understanding the Marxian emphases in the remaining criteria: (4) Between units of economic decision, the locus of economic power, in the Marxian view, is in business firms, controlled by their capitalist owners. Power, in short, is a function of property ownership. What of consumer power via the dollar-ballots of the marketplace? In the Marxian view, consumption is a function of income, and personal

Table 5-1.

MARXIAN CAPITALISM

1. Level of economic development	Developing economy with an advancing technology
2. Resource base	Heavy reliance on capital and capitalistic methods of production
3. Ownership-control of the means of production	Predominantly private ownership and control of business enterprise
4. Locus of economic power	Relatively large role for individual units (households and businesses) and small role for large-scale organizations, including governments. Capitalists dominate power structure through ownership of means of production
5. Motivational system	Market-oriented motivations, with particular emphasis on profit and capital accumulation motives
6. Organization of economic power	Decentralization of economic decisions and wide areas of discretion for freedom of individual economic choice within the limitations of the objective conditions of ownership and production
7. Social processes for coordination	Primary reliance on the essentially anarchic competitive price or market system, supplemented by hierarchy within business units and political democracy in government (controlled by capitalists as a social class)
8. Distribution of income and wealth	Division of society into owners (capitalists) and non-owners (workers). Accompanying division of income into surplus (profit, rent, interest) and market-determined wages

income depends on how national income is distributed. But this distribution is affected significantly by the division of society into owners versus non-owners of industrial property. The locus of economic power is in the processes of production, not consumption.

(5) The motivational system, too, is affected by private ownership and its distribution. All units of economic decision seek to promote their own economic gain. But workers, lacking control over the productive process, are concerned primarily with use values, with their satisfactions as consumers. Capitalists, on the other hand, through their ownership and control of business, are more concerned with exchange values, profit from production, and capital accumulation.

(6) The organization of economic power also is profoundly affected in the Marxian view, by the conditions of property ownership. Property-owners, according to Marx,

have much economic freedom; non-owners have little. The worker under capitalism is free to contract with any capitalist-employer he wishes. Yet, because he is *free from* ownership of the means of production, he is, in effect, a "wage-slave," since, to obtain income, he must relinquish his power over his own labor to an owner-capitalist. His "freedom" requires a "choice" between working for a capitalist or not working. In Marx's words, the worker is a "free labourer, free in the double sense, that as a free man he can dispose of his labor-power as his own commodity, and that on the other hand he has no other commodity for sale, is short of everything necessary for the realisation of his labour-power." [16: I, 186–88] Capitalists, on the other hand, as owners of industrial capital, are free from the necessity of working for someone else, and can freely utilize the power from their institutional class monopoly to make and maximize money profits through the use of other men's labor.

The sphere of the free labor contract, wrote Marx in *Capital* [16: I, 195–96] is ". . . a very Eden of the innate rights of man. There alone rule Freedom, Equality, Property and Bentham. Freedom, because both buyer and seller of . . . labour-power are constrained only by their own free will. They contract as free agents, and the agreement they come to, is but the form in which they give legal expression to their common will. Equality, because each enters into relation with the other, as with a simple owner of commodities, and they exchange equivalent for equivalent. Property, because each disposes only of what is his own. And Bentham, because each looks only to himself. The only force that brings them together and puts them in relation with each other, is the selfishness, the gain and the private interests of each. . . ."

Marx added "On leaving this sphere . . . we think we can perceive a change in the physiognomy of our dramatis personae. He, who before was the money owner, now strides in front as capitalist; the possessor of labour-power follows as his labourer. The one with an air of importance, smirking, intent on business; the other, timid and holding back, like one who is bringing his own hide to market and has nothing to expect but—a hiding."

(7) As in the classic model, the Marxian concept relies heavily on a competitive price system as a social process for economic coordination. Though capitalists as a class have a monopoly over industrial property, they function in an economic society characterized by large numbers of other capitalists with whom they are in competition. The market forces of supply and demand, in the Marxian view, are beyond the control of any individual producer, and competitive market prices, determined by the interaction of market supply and market demand, are given parameters to which individual capitalists must adjust as best they can. This sounds very classical, as, indeed, it is. It is important to note, however, two special Marxian twists. First, the competitive price system, even at its purest and best, functions imperfectly as a social coordinative process. Specifically, it cannot prevent recurrent periodic crises and depressions. Second, though the price system is the dominant social process for coordinating production decisions, however imperfectly, and "anarchically," for the entire economy, the internal organization of business firms is hierarchical. "Modern industry," argued Marx and Engels in 1848 in *The Communist Manifesto* [19: 16.], ". . . has converted the little workshop of the patriarchal master into the great factory of the industrial capitalist. Masses of labourers, crowded into the factory, are organized like soldiers. As privates of the industrial army they are placed under the command of a perfect hierarchy of officers and sergeants. Not only are they slaves of the bourgeois class, and of the bourgeois state; they are daily and hourly enslaved by the machine, by the over-looker, and, above all, by the individual bourgeois manufacturer himself."

(8) Property ownership is the Marxian key to the distribution of income. The division of society into nonowner-workers and owner-capitalists is the basis for the division of output into wages and non-wage ("surplus") income. The ownership of industrial capital, says Marx, gives a relatively small group of men the economic power to exploit another larger group of men, that is, to obtain income by taking a portion of the results of other men's labor. The ownership of property, then, is not an economic function. (This is *not* the same, incidentally, as saying the *capital* has no economic function or makes no contribution to production.) It is essentially a basis for exploitation and oppression. Thus a division of society between owners and non-owners is also a division between exploiters and exploited, between oppressors and oppressed.

DEFINITIONS AND TERMINOLOGY

The Marxian analysis of capitalism is formulated in terms of its own definitions and terminology, an understanding of which is prerequisite to understanding the analysis.

The first sentence of the first Chapter, Volume I, of *Capital* states: "The wealth of those societies in which the capitalist mode of production prevails, presents itself as 'an immense accumulation of commodities,' its unit being a single commodity." [16: I, 44] Marxian economic theory essentially is a study of *commodities*, that is, physical, tangible, objects which satisfy human *wants* and are produced through the application of human and non-human "*capital*" resources in the *social* process of production. This conception excludes services (including those of exchange and merchandising), goods provided directly by nature "without human assistance, such as land, wind, water . . . ," [16: I, 227] and the direct satisfaction of human wants through the application of individual labor as, for example, in a do-it-yourself project.

Capital, Output, and Income

Marx divided the flow of the national product or total output of commodities into two major parts: the "means of production" (investment goods) in "department I" and the "means of consumption" (consumption goods) in "department II." The former are consumed in the production of commodities; the latter, directly by capitalists and workers. The output of commodities in both departments results from the employment of the economy's resources or "social capital." In each "department," the social capital is divisible into two parts: "variable capital" (labor), the value of which "is equal to the value of the social labor-power" (or capacity to engage in labor), and "constant capital," that is, the "means of production," which are

subdivided into *fixed* capital (plant and equipment) and *circulating* capital (intermediate products and raw materials). Marx maintained that, despite its contributions to the productivity of labor, "constant capital" merely passes on *its* value (measured in units of "socially necessary labor-time") into the output of commodities, whereas labor or "variable capital" has the special and unique quality of undergoing in the process of production an alteration of value. It both reproduces the equivalent of its own value and produces an excess, a surplus-value. [16: I, 232–33] The value of raw materials passes directly into the commodity, whereas the value of plant and equipment is gradually transferred to commodities over their respective lifetimes through wear and tear or depreciation. Thus, constant capital may be considered as a stock (C) existing at a given moment in time or as a flow of capital inputs (raw materials and depreciation) over a period of time (c).

These ideas can be translated into the circular flow models of contemporary national income accounting. Excluding government and foreign trade sectors of the economy, the sales receipts of businesses are divisible into expenditures upon consumption plus investment, which is equal to the value of output produced in the two sectors of the national economy. Output is created by a flow of input of human and non-human capital. The total cost to business firms of the gross output is equal to the cost of raw materials and depreciation plus the cost of labor. Because variable capital (labor) has the unique quality of creating an output the value of which exceeds its cost, the value of gross output (w) exceeds its cost ($c + v$), leaving a residual or surplus (s). Thus, gross output in each department equals $c + v + s$ and output net of raw materials and depreciation is composed of $v + s$. Output also is equal to the income ($v + s$) and non-income (c) claims against it. Because one man's expenditures are another man's income, v, which appears as an expense or cost to capitalists, is identical with the wage income of workers, and net output $(v + s)$ is equal to the net income available for distribution to workers and capitalists.[3] In an uninterrupted circular flow, income is disposed of in expenditures for investment and consumption goods. In a stationary economy, gross investment equals depreciation and raw materials, net investment is zero, and the capital stock remains constant. In a growing economy, gross investment exceeds depreciation and raw materials, net investment is positive, and the capital stock increases. Consumption expenditures are divided into commodities "required for the maintenance of the laboring class" and luxuries, "which are consumed only by the capitalist class, being purchased only with the surplus-value, which never falls to the share of the laborer." [16: II, 466, 467]

The Marxian Ratios

In addition to definitions of the components of capital expenditures, output, and income, the Marxian terminology employs three central ratios: s/v, the rate of surplus value or "rate of exploitation"; C/v, the ratio of capital to labor or "organic composition of capital"; and $s/C + v$, the rate of profit.

(1) If net national income is composed of s and v, then s/v symbolizes the proportions of income going to these two major income components. If national income is 100 percent, and the ratio of s to v is 1:1, then 50 percent would go to capitalists and 50 percent to labor. An increase of s/v to 2:1 would indicate the distribution had changed to 66 2/3 percent versus 33 1/3 percent. The higher the ratio of s to v, the greater the rate of "exploitation" of labor, and the greater the rate of creation of surplus (or profit) per worker.

(2) The "organic composition of capital," C/v, is the ratio of constant to variable capital, that is, capital stock per worker. An increase in C/v could occur in a variety of ways. Marx emphasized the case where the absolute size of both C and v increase, but where C increases more than v.

(3) The rate of profit, $s/C + v$, is the ratio of surplus to total investment in both constant and variable capital. Whereas s/v is profit per worker, $s/C + v$ is profit per unit of capital plus labor. The prudent capitalist is more interested in $s/C + v$, which signifies the rate of profit on total investment, than in s/v, the more restricted concept of rate of profit on labor costs. As in the case of s/v, $s/C + v$ varies directly with s, other factors remaining equal. But absolute levels of profit (s) should be distinguished from the rate of profit $(s/C + v)$ because one can remain constant or move in the opposite direction when the other changes. Indeed, Marx repeatedly emphasized the possibility, which he considered likely, of a decrease in the rate of profits accompanied by an increase in the absolute level or "mass" of profits [16: III, 253–58].

The determinants of $s/C + v$ are anything that affect s, C, or v. The magnitude of $s/C + v$ thus may be derived from the first two ratios. Anything that increases (decreases) s/v will tend to increase (decrease) $s/C + v$, whereas an increase (decrease) in C/v will tend to decrease (increase) $s/C + v$. Thus, $s/C + v$ varies directly with s/v and inversely with C/v. If both s/v and C/v are rising, the magnitude of $s/C + v$ will depend on the respective rates of change in the first two ratios. A simple way of expressing this is to

[3]Portions of this surplus may be siphoned off to pay interest to money lenders and rents to landlords, leaving a net surplus or profit for the industrial capitalist. However, Marx's major concern was not with how different types of capitalists divide the economic surplus, but with the generation of the surplus and its relation to capital and labor. Thus, Marx's classificatory schema, though consistent with the idea of income = wages + interest + rent + profit, is generally presented in the simpler, more restricted form of income = wages + surplus.

divide both the numerator and denominator of $s/C + v$ by the quantity v. This does not change the value of the ratio, but helps to express this value in terms of the other two ratios. Thus:

$$\frac{s}{C + v} = \frac{s/v}{(C + v)/v} = \frac{s/v}{(C/v) + (v/v)}$$
$$= \frac{s/v}{(C/v) + 1}$$

From the preceding version of this ratio, it should be clear that: (1) if s/v increases (decreases) and C/v remains constant, then $s/C + v$ will increase (decrease); (2) if C/v increases (decreases) and s/v remains constant, then $s/C + v$ will decrease (increase); and (3) if s/v increases (decreases) and C/v decreases (increases), then the two changes will exert the same effect on $s/C + v$, and $s/C + v$ will increase (decrease). It is not so obvious what will happen if s/v and C/v both increase (decrease), for then the two changes will exert opposite effects on $s/C + v$. We are tempted to say, for example, that if C/v increases faster than s/v, then $s/C + v = (s/v)/(C/v + 1)$ surely will fall. Unfortunately, this is not necessarily true, because the "1" in the denominator complicates things mathematically. For our purposes, it is best to be content with the qualitative statement: (4) if s/v and C/v both increase (decrease), then $s/C + v$ will increase (decrease) if the change in s/v is "large enough" to offset the change in C/v. [For a slightly different and more complex formulation, see 25: 67–68, 102.]

It should be noted that the C in C/v and $s/C + v$ is different from the c in $c + v + s$. The former is the stock of capital existing at any given moment in time, while the latter is the flow of depreciation and raw material costs during any given time period. To avoid confusion, regard C/v as capital per employed member of the labor force and $s/C + v$ as *the rate of profit* in terms of capital stock plus employed labor. These ratios, defined in this way, play a major role in Marx's economic theories, particularly the labor theory of value.

THE MARXIAN THEORY OF RESOURCE ALLOCATION, VALUE, AND PRICE

To facilitate comparison with the classic model of competitive market capitalism, the following discussion of Marxian economic theory will consider the same four issues: allocation; distribution; growth; economic stability and full employment. The first is intimately related to Marx's theory of value and price. The last three comprise Marx's theory of capitalist industrialization and will be examined separately.

The De-Emphasis of Allocation in Marxian Economics

Marx's economic analysis is both more and less than a model of resource allocation as traditionally conceived. It is less than this because, as noted previously, Marx was more concerned with a critique of capitalism's problems than with a detailed study of the allocational mechanisms of the "invisible hand." It is more than this because allocation for Marx was really a prelude to, or part of, the larger issues of distribution, growth, and instability. The concept of an efficient allocation of scarce resources in terms of relative prices and relations between costs and consumer demands is, at best, a minor and underdeveloped theme in Marxian economics.

Scattered throughout Marx's three-volume *Capital* are references to an allocational mechanism operative in a capitalist economy, similar to the one described in the last chapter and based on some of the same institutional and motivational assumptions or conditions: specialization, exchange, competition, free contract, private enterprise, the profit motive, and so on. There is, however, one striking difference: Consistent with his underlying interpretation of social classes, Marx applied this allocational mechanism and these institutional and motivational assumptions primarily to the capitalist, who, in the mid-nineteenth century, was also the owner and manager of business firms.

The capitalist seeks to maximize profits in a process symbolized by the letters M-C-M', where M = money, utilized to purchase labor power; C = commodities produced via the allocation of labor resources; M' = the sales revenues of the businesses; and where M' exceeds M. Competition among capitalists encourages them to reallocate resources from low to high profit areas, with the consequent equalization of rates of profit throughout the economy. The worker, however, though a "free" economic agent, has little market power and control, because of his lack of property. The consumer's purchases are a function of family incomes, which also, in turn, are dependent on the distribution of income, which, in turn, is structured by the division of society into the propertied, exploiting versus the propertyless, oppressed classes. Thus, Marx's allocational mechanism is essentially a model of the economic activities of the business firm, owned and controlled by the capitalist.

The Labor Theory of Value

VALUE, EXCHANGE VALUE, USE VALUE, AND PRICE

A central issue in Marxian economic theory is the use and "exploitation" of human resources (labor) in the production of commodities. The "value" of commodities thus is a major theme. The value of a commodity, said Marx, is determined by the "socially necessary labor time" embodied in its production. Other things remaining equal, the larger (smaller) the magnitude of labor-time embodied, the higher (lower) the "value"; and the relative values of any pair of commodities (value of commodity one/value of commodity two) will be proportional to the relative labor-times embodied in their production (L_1/L_2).

One of the confusing aspects of this idea for contemporary students of economic systems is that, in Marx's analysis, "value" is related to but not identical with "use value," "exchange value," and/or "price." Marx argued that, to possess value, a commodity must have the capacity to satisfy human wants, that is, utility or use value. Use value is a prerequisite to value in general and exchange value in particular. But Marx was clearly more interested in exchange value than use value. Use value is a property of a commodity itself and involves a relation between men and commodities. Exchange value requires the creation of "social use values," and involves a social relation between men and men, not a subjective relation between men and things. The terms on which commodities are exchanged with one another (their exchange values) are determined by, but are not the same as, the underlying value of the commodities. The value of a commodity is something embodied or "congealed" in it, and "intrinsic" to it. Value is "the common substance that manifests itself in the exchange value of commodities . . . ." [16: I, 45] Exchange values may temporarily (though not permanently) deviate from underlying values, as determined by the quantity of socially necessary labor-time embodied in commodities. However, even if exchange values bore no systematic relation to value in this underlying and "intrinsic" sense, it is "value" with which Marx was primarily concerned.

For many twentieth-century economists, value theory is simply an historical backdrop to the contemporary theory of market prices, and much of the criticism of the labor theory of value is due to its inability to adequately and accurately explain market prices. For Marx, however, value and price are on two fundamentally different levels of abstraction, and the connections between them are neither clear nor consistent.

At one point in his analysis, Marx suggested that market prices tend, with minor deviations, to correspond to their values, and that a price "is the money-name of the labour realised in a commodity." But he argued that price is a "more or less accidental exchange-ratio between" money and a particular commodity, and that the "value of a commodity is expressed in its price before it goes into circulation, and is therefore a precedent condition of circulation, not its result." [16: I, 114, 175–76] In other words, prices tend to correspond to values, but if they do not, it is not significant, because value is the much more fundamental and important issue. At a later, more sophisticated stage in his analysis (16: III), Marx argued that particular prices will not generally correspond to particular values, but that some commodities will sell at prices above and others below their values so that, *on the average*, values are "converted" into prices. [16: III, 181–86, 230–31.] In effect, Marx abandoned at this point the labor theory of value as a vehicle for explaining relative or particular market prices.

SIMPLIFYING ASSUMPTIONS

If the "labor theory of value" is to be an operationally testable hypothesis, it must contain clear links to real world phenomena, such as relative market prices. To help provide these links, and thereby give plausibility to the labor theory of value, Marx made a number of simplifying assumptions. These assumptions pertain to the quality of labor, technology, market demand and equilibrium, and the character of competition.

First, different qualities of labor are resolvable into "unskilled average labor." Skilled labor is simply a "multiple" of unskilled labor. This reduction of different types of labor to a common standard of unskilled labor proceeds by "a social process that goes on behind the back of the producers," [16: I, 52, 220–21] that is, the social process of market exchange. (On this point, incidentally, Marx is open to possible criticism of circular reasoning. He wanted to show that the value of a commodity is determined by the labor-time embodied in it and not simply by the "superficial" market phenomena of supply and demand. But the establishment of the standard unit to measure

labor-time via the reduction of skilled to average unskilled labor is based on this very market exchange process.)

Second, the phrase "socially necessary labor-time" assumes a given technique. "The labor-time socially necessary is that required to produce an article under the normal conditions of production, and with the average degree of skill and intensity." [16: I, 46] A doubling of the incidence of featherbedding, for example, does not double the value of a commodity. The introduction of a new technique or machine changes the labor-time "socially necessary". If the introduction of a power loom, for example, doubles output per man-hour, workers who continue to use hand looms find that their "social labor" and, therefore, contribution to value, is cut in half.

Third, a commodity cannot have value unless there is a demand for it, and exchange values will adequately reflect their "values" as determined by embodied labor-time only if market supply equals market demand. If supply exceeds demand for a particular commodity, this demonstrates the quantity of labor-time embodied in its production is more than that which is "socially necessary," and its average value or price must fall. "In order that a commodity may be sold at its market value, that is to say, in proportion to the necessary social labor contained in it, the total quantity of social labor devoted to the total mass of this kind of commodities must correspond to the quantity of the social demand for them, meaning the solvent social demand. . . ." [16: III, 226–27]

Fourth, labor-time values will correspond to market prices only under purely and perfectly competitive market conditions; that is, Marx assumed competition among large numbers of producers of "identical commodities" and an allocational mechanism which transfers resources from low to high profit areas, leading to industry and market equilibrium. As "far as selling is concerned, there must be no accidental or artificial monopoly which may enable either of the contracting sides to sell commodities above their value or compel others to sell below value." [16: I, 209]

SPECIAL ASSUMPTIONS AND CONDITIONS OF DEMAND AND SUPPLY

In addition to these simplifying assumptions, Marx posited a number of special assumptions and conditions of demand and supply, the purpose of which was to rule out any role for demand and supply other than embodied labor-time in the creation of value.

For market demand to play no role and for supply or cost factors (notably embodied labor-time) to play an exclusive role in determining market prices, it is necessary (though Marx did not specify it) for firms to produce under *constant cost* conditions: Average cost must equal marginal cost for each firm producing a particular commodity, and the level of average cost must be the same for all firms. If this were true, then a shift in market *demand* would be accompanied by a change in *quantity* demanded and supplied, but by no change in price. By contrast, an upward shift in cost caused by an increase in the "socially necessary labor time" required to produce a commodity is accompanied by an increase in price.

If, however, firms produce under conditions of *increasing cost*, then changes in the scale of output for an industry in the long run will shift costs for individual firms, and the long-run supply for an industry will be positively sloped instead of horizontal. Under these conditions, upward or downward shifts in market demand will be accompanied by increases or decreases in market price, not merely changes in quantity demanded and supplied. Further, even under long constant-cost conditions for an industry, individual firms may experience rising (falling) costs in the short run with expansions (contractions) in output because of varying returns to variable factors of production. In this event, shifts in market demand will affect prices as well as quantities demanded and supplied.

On the supply side, Marx endeavored to rule out factors other than embodied labor-time in the creation of value. Natural resources were disposed of by definition: Because value is created by labor-time, natural resources "without human assistance" contribute no "value" to commodities. Capital gave Marx greater difficulty, and his treatment of the subject was ambiguous. A major theme in Volume I of *Capital* is that a capital good embodies past or "dead" labor and passes *its* value into the product—its value being determined by the past labor-time that went into its production. The value of raw materials passes directly into the commodity, whereas the value of plant and equipment gradually is transferred to commodities over their respective lifetimes through wear and tear. In short, capital itself has no *net* productivity, no contribution to value other than the past labor-time embodied in it.

The major criticism of this view is that, if capital or land are scarce relative to their uses in the production of commodities, they will fetch a price in competitive market exchange, just as labor will, depending upon the relation between market supply and market demand. And since all capital goods at any moment in time have been produced through the joint collaboration of past capital, natural and human resources, the attempt to explain the value of capital exclusively in terms of past embodied labor is futile.

A variation of this Marxian view is the suggestion that capital *is* productive, but that, in the long run, competition pushes the prices of capital goods toward the values of their marginal products. If this were so, then capital goods would be productive of value as a separate factor of production, without reference to past embodied labor, but not productive of profit or surplus value. Even this modified, semi-Marxian interpretation, however, is not consistent with all Marx wrote on the subject, for at several points, he suggested that capital, *by increasing the productivity of labor*, can increase the level and rate of surplus value (*s* and *s/v*).[4] Clearly, this is cumbersome and confusing. Marx would have been on firmer ground had he argued that capital is "immensely productive," but that *owning* capital or property "is not productive . . . without erecting a special analytical apparatus in order to make the point." [20: 18–19]

Despite assertions to the contrary throughout his works, Marx tended to confuse his critique of *capitalism* as an economic system with a critique of *capitalists* as unproductive exploiters of labor, and his critique of the latter with a denial that *capital* is productive. But a critique of capitalism, as Marx stated, may acknowledge the important and productive social functions of capitalists; and a critique of capitalists as recipients of essentially "unearned" income may coexist with a recognition of the strategic importance of capital as a productive and scarce resource. Presumably, a rationally organized socialist economic system would utilize (and economize in the utilization of) scarce capital resources and, indeed, the services of "capitalists," employed by public enterprises and/or central planning boards and charged with making decisions (subject, perhaps, to consumer and/or citizen control via marketplace and/or ballot box) regarding the mobilization, allocation, and utilization of capital. A recognition of the productivity of capital is not a defense of private-enterprise capitalists and their receipt of private profits; a recognition of the productive functions of "capitalists" is not necessarily a defense of an economic system of private-enterprise capitalism.

---

[4]Indeed, Marx suggested that surplus is created by *both* capital and labor: "Surplus value . . . arises equally out of the fixed and circulating components of the invested capital. The total capital serves substantially as the creator of values, the instruments of labour as well as the materials of production and labor. . . . Surplus value arises simultaneously from all portions of invested capital." [16: III, 48].

THE MARXIAN RATIOS AND THE
CONVERSION OF VALUES INTO PRICES

The labor theory of value and the relation between labor-time values and market prices may be stated in terms of the three Marxian ratios: s/v, C/v, $s/C + v$. First, if the labor theory of value is to provide an explanation of market prices, then prices must equal labor-time values, and relative prices must equal ratios of labor-time values. This, in turn, requires that the rate of surplus value or profit per dollar invested in workers (s/v) must be equalized for all firms ($s_1/v_1 = s_2/v_2$). Were this not so, the higher (or lower) profit per worker would have to be explained by some factor other than labor-time, for example, by differences in the organic composition of capital (C/v) or in relative demands for different products.

Second, competitive equilibrium conditions are characterized by an equalization in the rate of profit for different firms, both within particular industries and throughout the economic system. This results from the exit of firms from below-average profit areas (thus reducing supply and raising prices) and the entry of firms into above-average profit areas (thus raising supply and decreasing prices).

Third, the labor theory of value accurately explains relative market prices or exchange values under the conditions of competitive equilibrium in the Marxian analysis only if the organic composition of capital, or ratio of capital to labor, is everywhere the same. The reasons for this are as follows: $s/C + v$ may be restated as $(s/v)/(C/v + 1)$. If s/v (the numerator) is to be equalized among firms, when $(s/v)/(c/v + 1)$ (the ratio of the numerator to the denominator) is equalized, then C/v (in the denominator) must also be the same. If C/v were not equalized when $s/C + v$ was equalized through the competitive allocational process, then s/v would be different for different firms and industries, labor-time values would not correspond to price ratios, and prices would not correspond to the "socially necessary labor-time" embodied in commodities.

Marx illustrated the labor theory of value and the process of "conversion" of values into market prices in terms of these ratios in a numerical example, reproduced in Tables 5.2 and 5.3. In Table 5.2, five firms in five different industries are assumed to be characterized by different organic compositions of capital but a common rate of surplus value (100 percent) and, therefore, different rates of profit. With common rates of exploitation, high (low) rates of profit will be associated with low (high) organic compositions of capital. The average rate of profit for all firms (shown in the bottom line in Table 5.2) is the ratio of the average surplus value to the average $C + v$. Because not all capital stock is depreciated in any particular year, the

value of each commodity equals $c + v + s$ rather than $C + v + s$. Assuming, for purposes of illustration, that depreciation of "used-up" C is as shown in the fifth column, then the value of commodities $(c + v + s)$ is shown in the sixth column and the "cost price" (value minus surplus value) is shown in the last column.

This illustration is consistent with the labor theory of value. Firms with lower organic compositions of capital (and thus, higher ratios of labor to capital) will generate larger surpluses and higher-valued products. The ratios of costs of labor and of surplus values are equalized for any pair of firms (for example, $v_2/v_1 = s_2/s_1$ or 30/20 = 30/20); phrased alternatively, the ratios of surplus value to investment in variable capital are everywhere equalized $(s_2/v_2 = s_1/v_1 = 100$ percent). But the example in Table 5.2,

Table 5-2.

Capitals		Rate of Surplus Value: s/v	Surplus Value s	Rate of Profit: $s/(c + v)$	Used-up c	Value of Commodities: Used-up $c + v$ $+ s$	Cost Price: Used-up $c + v$
I.	$80c + 20v$	100%	20	20%	50	90	70
II.	$70c + 30v$	100	30	30	51	111	81
III.	$60c + 40v$	100	40	40	51	131	91
IV.	$85c + 15v$	100	15	15	40	70	55
V.	$95c + 5v$	100	5	5	10	20	15
Total	$390c + 110v$		110	110%			
Average	$78c + 22v$		22	22%			

Table 5-3.

Capitals	Surplus Value	Value of Commodities	Cost-Price of Commodities	Price of Commodities	Rate of Profit	Deviation of Prices from Value
I. $80c + 20v$	20	90	70	92	22%	+2
II. $70c + 30v$	30	111	81	103	22	−8
III. $60c + 40v$	40	131	91	113	22	−18
IV. $85c + 15v$	15	70	55	77	22	+7
V. $95c + 5v$	5	20	15	37	22	+17

though consistent with the labor theory of value, is inconsistent with the assumption of competition. Under competitive conditions, argued Marx, firms will withdraw from areas with lower than average profit rates (I, IV, V) and enter fields with higher than average profit rates (II, III). The resulting shifts in supply relative to demand will cause changes in prices relative to costs: Prices will fall in formerly high profit industries and rise in formerly low profit industries, yielding, in the long-run competitive equilibrium, an equalization of the rate of profit.

The equalization of the rate of profit and its impact on the relation between prices and values are illustrated in Table 5.3. When competition has done its work and all firms are receiving the same average rate of profit (22 percent), the price of each commodity will equal the "cost price" $(c + v)$ plus an average surplus value of 22. Prices will deviate from labor-time values, lying above them in industries (I, IV, V) with higher than average organic compositions of capital from which firms have exited, and lying below them in industries (II, III) with lower than average organic compositions of capital into which firms have entered. Profits per worker (s/v) will also diverge in different firms, varying directly with the organic composition of capital: Firms with high (low) investment in capital per worker will receive a larger (smaller) profit per worker. In short, ratios of labor-time values will *not* correspond to price ratios, and prices will correspond to quantities of socially necessary labor-time "only in this vague and meaningless form." [16: III, 203] The labor theory of value, by Marx's conclusion, does not provide an accurate theory of relative market prices.

THE ROLE AND IMPORTANCE OF THE
LABOR THEORY OF VALUE IN MARXIAN
ECONOMICS

If Marx's value theory is not a price theory, then what is it? And, what is the role of the labor theory of value in Marx's economic analysis? There are two points to

emphasize in answer to this question: First, Marx wanted to "pierce beneath" the "superficial" market phenomena of the exchange of commodities to the underlying social relations of production. But we have made a "fetish" of commodities, as if *things* rather than human effort create value. To avoid this, we must "get behind" the mysterious secret of commodities to the social processes of capitalist versus worker. The labor theory of value is Marx's vehicle for doing this.[5]

_____

[5] Marx's position on this issue is summarized by contemporary American neo-Marxist economist Paul Sweezy: "Insofar as the problems which are posed for solution are concerned with the behavior of the disparate elements of the economic system (prices of individual commodities, profits of particular capitalists, the combination of productive factors in the individual firm), there seems to be no doubt that value calculation is of little assistance. Orthodox economists have been working intensively on problems of this sort for the last half century and more. They have developed a kind of price theory which is more useful in this sphere than anything to be found in Marx or his followers." But, Sweezy notes: "The entire social output is the product of human labor. Under capitalist conditions, a part of this social output is appropriated by that group in the community which owns the means of production. This is not an ethical judgment, but a method of describing the really basic economic relation between social groups ... value calculation makes it possible to look beneath the surface phenomena of money and commodities to the underlying relations between people and classes." On the other hand, price calculation "mystifies the underlying social relations of capitalist production. Since profit is calculated as a return on total capital, the idea inevitably arises that capital as such is in some way 'productive.' Things appear to be endowed with an independent power of their own. From the point of view of value calculation it is easy to recognize this as a flagrant form of commodity fetishism. From the point of view of price calculation it appears to be natural and inevitable." [25: 129] In short, as a *micro*economic theory of the determination of the prices of individual commodities and their interrelationships, Marx's labor theory of value leaves much to be desired. But as a *macro*economic theory of the social and exploitative relations between workers and capitalists, it offers important insights. There is something to this point of view, even when (as in Sweezy) it is overstated. However, most non-Marxian economists would argue there are better ways of analyzing the problem of economic power and

Second, the labor theory of value is Marx's basis for his exploitation theory of income distribution. If value is determined by labor-time, then to pay workers less than the full value of the commodity is exploitation. The contentions that capital has no net productivity and that workers are exploited are two sides of the same coin.

One final question: What are the relations (and how important are they) between the labor theory of value and the other elements of Marxian economic theory? There are two points of view on this: One, generally held by partisan Marxists and anti-Marxists, is that the labor theory of value is Marx's basic premise, a sort of intellectual structure on which a superstructure of ideas rests. Another point of view, expressed by Joan Robinson, is that "no point of substance in Marx's argument depends upon the labor theory of value . . ." and that "none of the important ideas which he expresses in terms of the concept of value *cannot* be better expressed without it." [20: 22, 20] Though the labor theory of value is now, in Schumpeter's words, "dead and buried" [8: 25], Marxian ideas about economic power, capitalist growth and development, and economic instability are not. A good deal of what Marx had to say on these issues can be separated from his value theory and appraised independently of it.

THE MARXIAN THEORY OF CAPITALIST INDUSTRIALIZATION

The Marxian theory of capitalist industrialization has three central dimensions: the mobilization of an economic surplus; the investment of the economic surplus; and a critique of the defects and "contradictions" of the industrialization process. The first of these provided the basis for Marx's theory of income distribution, the second, for his theory of economic growth, and the third,

---

social classes than the powerful and provocative, yet tenuous and roundabout, labor theory of value.

for his theory of crises and cyclical economic fluctuations.

The Distribution of Income: Mobilization of the Economic Surplus

THE PIVOTAL POSITION OF INCOME DISTRIBUTION

Income distribution occupies a pivotal position in the Marxian analysis of Capitalism. It is interwoven with allocation, growth, and stability. Its link with allocation is clear. Consumption is a function of income. Income, for the working-class segment of the population, is received in the form of money wages. Wages are obtained by non-property-owning workers through the sale of their labor-power to property-owning capitalists. The allocation of human resources in the process of production creates a valuable output of commodities which constitutes the real income of the economy, the sale of which by capitalists provides the revenues with which inputs may be purchased, thus completing the circular flow in which allocation and distribution are interconnected.

The Marxian distributional process also is clearly related to economic growth. Like most economists from Adam Smith to the present, Marx regarded investment as a key determinant of the rate of economic growth, and a sharp reallocation of resources from the production of consumption to the accumulation of capital goods as an important causal factor in rapid industrialization. The allocation of a portion of society's scarce resources to investment rather than consumption requires a social process to generate a "surplus" of income over and above consumption, and to allocate this surplus to investment projects. In Marx's analysis, the generation of this surplus is rooted in a system of production and distribution which creates a gap between the value of national output and the wages paid to workers for their labor-power, this gap existing in the form of a surplus income appropriated by property-owning capitalists on the basis of their economic power rather than productive contribution, and allocated by them, in the main, to investment.

Problems associated with income distribution, says Marx, are the major source of "crises," depressions, and oscillations in economic growth that we today call *cyclical fluctuations.* Marx identified two major sources or types of instability in a developing capitalist economy: first, crises in the process of production associated with decreases in the rate of profit; second, crises caused by problems associated with "realizing" on the market-place, through sales to consumers at prices corresponding to values, the surpluses "created" in the process of production. Clearly, Marx's theory of income distribution is a necessary underpinning to his analysis of economic instability.

Thus, the application of labor, under given technological conditions and in combination with capital goods, creates a total output the value of which exceeds both the value of the capital goods used in the process of production and the value of the workers' labor-power, represented by the wage costs of the capitalists and the wage income of the worker. This excess constitutes a surplus, created by the variable component of total capital—labor—but actually received by the capitalists. Because capitalists have not contributed to the value of the product by virtue of their ownership of the means of production, their generation and receipt of a labor-created economic surplus constitutes an exploitation of the workers. Thus, Marx substitutes an exploitation theory for the productivity theory associated with the classic model of competitive capitalism.

THE MARXIAN THEORY OF WAGES

Marx's theory of wages lies more in the area of *macro-*, than *micro*-economics, and is more concerned with the division of national income into wage versus non-wage (surplus) income than with principles governing individual wage-rates and how they differ. As a corollary, Marxian wage theory is more concerned with the macroeconomic class relations between capitalists and workers than with the microeconomic relations between one specific capitalist and one specific worker or between capitalists and workers in one specific labor market.

In the classic theory of competitive market capitalism, competition on markets for productive resources compels employers, seeking their own interests, to pay incomes to resource owners (including workers) equal to the value of the marginal product (*VMP*) of each resource. But the absence of competition on either markets for goods (monopoly power) or resources (monopsony power) enables employers to pay resource owners less than their *VMP* and thus engage in monopolistic or monopsonistic "exploitation." The exploitation theory of wages is not unique to Marx.

The Marxian concept of distributional exploitation, however, though it includes monopoly and/or monopsony cases, especially under mature, monopoly-capitalism, radically differs from the classic theory in two ways: (1) In the classic theory business firms may exploit *any* resource owner, since any resource may contribute to the value of the output and yet conceivably be paid an income below *VMP*. In the Marxian analysis, since only labor contributes to the value of output, *only labor* can be exploited. (2) The orthodox explanation of exploitation requires the assumption of monopoly power by one firm in relation to others. The Marxian analysis insists exploitation can and will occur independently of monopoly power by any one capitalist, that is, in an economy characterized by pure competition on all product and resource markets.

Under purely competitive conditions, in both the classic and Marxian analyses, no one capitalist is able to pay a wage below the going market level. If he did, his workers would desert him and go to work for his compettitors. But capitalists *as a class*, in the Marxian schema, are able to keep the general level of wages below the value of national output (equal to the total of the sales receipts of all business firms) because of their monopolization *as a class* of the instruments of production. The worker under capitalism, according to Marx, is "free" in a "double sense": (1) "as a free man he can dispose of his labor-power as his own commodity"; (2) "he has no other commodity for sale, is short of everything necessary for the realisation of his labor-power." [16: I, 187–88]

By itself, this line of reasoning is neither complete nor convincing. It is true the worker needs the capitalist, and that in an industrializing capitalist economy, he can obtain an income only through the sale of his capacity to labor to a capitalist-employer. Yet, it is also true that capitalists require human resources in order to produce and create surplus value. In a regime of pure competition, something besides property ownership is required to explain the distribution of national income.

In Marxian capitalism, market wages must be consistent with two major requirements: First, they cannot go below "subsistence," for if they did, workers would be unable to produce and reproduce more workers, that is, the industrial labor force could not be maintained continuously; second, market wages must lie below the value of total output. Were wages to equal net national product (*NNP*), no surplus income would be available for additional capital accumulation and net investment, and, assuming wage income went entirely into consumption, the dynamics of capitalism would dissipate. Thus, wages must lie below *NNP* and at or above subsistence.

What the worker sells to the capitalist is his power or capacity to labor. It is in one special sense a commodity. What the capitalist receives from this exchange is the possibility of the application of labor-power to the process of production, thus transforming labor-power into labor. In Marx's analysis, wages tend to move toward a low level of "subsistence," and a subsistence wage, by definition, is equal to the *value of the labor-power* of the worker, that is, to the socially necessary labor time embodied in those quantities of commodities that would just enable the worker to subsist, to maintain and reproduce his labor-power. The "value of labor-power is determined ... by the labor time necessary for the production, and consequently also the reproduction, of this special article ... in other words, the value of labor-power is the value of the means of subsistence necessary for the maintenance of the laborer." [16: I, 189–90][6]

Subsistence, however, is more of a lower limit than a continuous actuality. Within the limits determined by subsistence and the *NNP*, market wages tend to vary directly with the demand for and inversely with the supply of labor. During periods of prosperity, for example, demand for labor may exceed supply, and wages may rise considerably above subsistence, thus threatening surplus and the continuity of investment. During periods of deep depression, demand for labor may drop sharply and workers even may be willing temporarily to accept wages below subsistence.

With a given technology and a constant capital-labor ratio, the demand for labor, and thus, wages, varies directly with the accumulation of capital, or volume of net investment. Thus, disregarding automation, labor-saving inventions, and the substitution of capital for labor, an increase in investment

---

[6]One of the major difficulties in a subsistence theory of wages lies in the definition of subsistence. For Marx, the concept did not mean simply brute self-survival, but also included provisions for wife and children, education and training. Indeed, at one point [16: I, 190], Marx suggested the subsistence level depends on the conditions, "the degree of civilisation of a country," and "the habits and degree of comfort in which the class of free laborers has been formed," and thus contains "a historical and moral element." At best, this is an unclear, ambiguous definition of subsistence. It seems to imply, in part, that subsistence is determined by the historical level of real wages, rather than the other way around.

stimulates the demand for labor and wages. This is typical in an expanding economy, especially "... under special stimulus to enrichment, such as the opening of new markets, or of new spheres for the outlay of capital in consequences of newly developed social wants. ..." Under these conditions, "the scale of accumulating capital may exceed the increase of labor-power or of the number of laborers; the demand for laborers may exceed the supply, and therefore, wages may rise." [16: I, 672]

If this is the case, however, what is to prevent wages in an expanding economy from being bid up in competitive labor markets to the full value of the national product? Or, conversely, what keeps wages at a low enough ("subsistence") level to permit continued accumulation of saving and investment, and thus, continuity of the capitalist system? The answer, says Marx, comes from the *supply* of labor.

In a full-employment economy, the major factors affecting the supply of labor are the size of the population and the percentage of it that constitutes the labor force. Other things being equal (specifically, demand for labor, technology, and the quality of workers), an increase in the size of the population and/or of the percentage of it in the labor force would depress wages. One classic theory of capitalism, the early nineteenth century Malthusian-Ricardian analysis, developed the following subsistence theory of wages based upon changes in population: Increases in saving provide a basis for an expansion in net investment or accumulation in the stock of capital. Rising capital stock increases the demand for labor, and, thereby, increases wages. Higher wages encourage a larger population and, thereby, an increase in the supply of labor, which depresses wages toward the subsistence level.

Marx would agree with the general contours of this causative chain except for the dimension of population growth. Marx wanted an economic, not biological, interpretation of wages. Further, an increase in

population will affect the labor force only after an extended time lag (say, 16 years) and thus cannot explain short-run, cyclical shifts in wages. The Marxian solution was to drop the assumption of full employment and to insert the possible existence of and fluctuations in the volume of unemployment—what Marx called the "industrial reserve army" or "reserve army of unemployed."

As the economy approaches full employment an expansion of investment will push demand for labor above supply, and wages will rise. During periods of unemployment and depression, the surplus workers, coupled with the low demand for labor, depress wages. At any time, capitalists may substitute capital for labor or introduce new technology that decreases the ratio of labor to capital, "setting free" some of the workers and creating technological unemployment. This may take "the more striking form of the repulsion of laborers already employed, or the less evident but not less real form of the more difficult absorption of the additional laboring population through the usual channels." [16: I, 691]

The process of economic growth, characterized by increased investment, increased demand for labor, and increased wages, cannot continue uninterrupted for three reasons: (1) increased wages induce the substitution of capital for labor; (2) increased wages lead to lower profit margins, which slows the rate of capital accumulation and thus decreases the demand for labor; (3) increased wages induce the introduction of labor-saving inventions. These factors create unemployment and lower wages. In addition, (4) the mechanization involved in the new technology destroys old skills and decreases the demand for skilled labor, thus generating further unemployment and reducing wages of formerly skilled workers toward the subsistence level of unskilled workers; and (5) during depressions, smaller capitalists sell out to larger ones, then join the ranks of the workers, thus swelling the industrial reserve army of unemployed and decreasing wages. [19 : 16–17] In short, "the general movements of wages are exclusively regulated by the expansion and contraction of the industrial reserve army, and these again correspond to the periodic changes of the industrial cycle. They are, therefore, not determined by the variations of the absolute number of the working population, but by the varying proportions in which the working class is divided into active and reserve army. . . ." [16 : I, 699]

THE MARXIAN THEORY OF SURPLUS

As noted, Marx's concept of surplus (or surplus value) is the difference between net national income and wages. Because wages cannot stay below subsistence for long, a surplus can exist only if national income lies above (subsistence) wages, only if the value of the output exceeds the value of the labor-power (when workers receive wages corresponding to the value of the labor-power). The generation of surplus requires social processes (1) to push wages down toward or to subsistence and/or (2) to push national income above subsistence. The process for the former is fluctuations in the volume of unemployment—the "industrial reserve army," as already described.

Marx rejected a number of possible explanations of the latter: (1) surplus through monopolistic and/or monopsonistic exploitation of buyers and/or sellers is ruled out by the assumption of competition; (2) surplus is not possible through exchange because (a) commodities tend to exchange at their values; (b) if commodities did not exchange at their labor-time values, a capitalist who gained surplus value as a seller (buyer) would lose it as a buyer (seller); (3) capital goods pass their value on to commodities, but do not create surplus value. (If a capitalist buys a machine for $10,000, for example, then its contribution to the value of the output will be $10,000. If it is more, competition among buyers will tend to elevate its price to its value. If it is less, competition among sellers will tend to depress its price to its value.)

Marx's explanation depends instead on a distinction between *labor* and *labor-power* under capitalistic conditions of production. What the worker sells is his labor-power. What the capitalist obtains through the exchange of wages for labor-power is the *use* of labor-power, that is, labor for the length of the working day (determined by capitalists, not workers nor the marketplace) and the right to the revenue from the sale of the output of labor. Wages, equal (in the limiting case) to "the value of labor-power, and the value which that labor-power creates in the labor process, are two entirely different magnitudes . . ." [16 : I, 215–16] and it is the ratio of this differential surplus to $C + v$ that the capitalist seeks to maximize.

Suppose, for example, that wages are $4 a day (the lower *limit* would be a subsistence wage equal to the value of the labor-power), that it takes six hours to produce an output which can be sold for $6, and that the value of the raw materials, plant, and equipment going into the output is $2 per six hours. The business would just break even, and net revenue (gross revenue of $6 − $2 for constant capital) would be just sufficient to cover wages. It would be a foolish capitalist who would permit his workers to go home after a six-hour day under these conditions. More typical would be a working day of, say, twelve hours. Gross revenue in this case would be $12, $v + c$ would be $8 ($4 + $4), and net revenue or surplus would be $4 per day.

Marx divided the working day into (1) the "necessary labor time" required to produce output equal to subsistence, and (2) the "surplus labor time" beyond that necessary for such production. In the limiting case, wages tend to equal the output of necessary labor, and the entire output produced by surplus labor time goes to the capitalist in the form of surplus income. The essence of this case is that in "a day's work the laborer produces more than a day's means of subsistence." [25 : 61–62] In the expanding economy case, wages go above subsistence, thus eating into the output of surplus labor. This is kept in check, however, by increases in unemployment in the manner previously described.

In conclusion, (1) Marx's analysis was an exploitation, not a productivity, theory of income distribution. Ownership of capital, in Marx's judgment, was not a contribution to production. Ownership enables capitalists to exploit workers by taking from them a portion of the output they have produced. (2) The generation of surplus does not depend on imperfections or impurities of competition or on dishonest or grasping employers. It is rooted in the nature of capitalistic methods of production and the social relations between workers and capitalists. Therefore, its elimination cannot be achieved simply by removing institutional and psychological imperfections, but through a fundamental ("revolutionary") transformation to a new and different system of economic organization.

THE DISTRIBUTION OF INCOME AND THE MARXIAN RATIOS

The Marxian theory of income distribution is closely related to Marx's three strategic ratios: s/v, C/v, and $s/C + v$. The ratio of s to v is, as noted, a measure of the division of national income between capitalists and workers. It is also identical with the ratio of surplus labor-time to necessary labor-time. The ratio of six hours surplus to six hours necessary labor-time, for example, is the same as that of $6 surplus to $6 wages, that is, 100 percent. The size of s/v thus varies (1) directly with the length of the working day and (2) inversely with necessary labor-time, or the portion of the total working day necessary to produce the worker's subsistence. Anything that can increase the length of the working day or decrease the necessary labor-time (and thus increase the surplus labor-time) can raise s/v.

One important technique for accomplishing these objectives is the introduction and application of machinery. Capital, according to Marx, though not productive of any net increase in value over and above the value of the labor-time embodied in it, can raise the productivity of labor and/or the s/v in at least four ways: (1) by increasing labor productivity, thus cheapening commodities, decreasing necessary and increasing surplus labor-time; (2) by enabling employment of women and children, thus generating surpluses from entire families; (3) by prolonging the working day, thus keeping labor at work longer; (4) by intensifying labor through speeding up work. [16: I, 405, 431–57]

$s/C + v$ varies directly with s/v and inversely with C/v. Any device which raises s/v while leaving C/v the same raises $s/C + v$. However, the process of capitalist industrialization, according to Marx, is characterized by an increase in C/v. If we assume (as did Marx in Volume I of *Capital*) that s/v remains constant, then $s/C + v$ must fall as C/v rises. This simple tautology is known in Marxian phraseology as the *"law of the falling tendency of the rate of profit."* It is an important component of the Marxian theory of income distribution and a linchpin of the Marxian analysis of unstable economic growth. It demonstrates the possibility of barriers to (1) stable equilibrium growth in the short run and (2) indefinite continued economic growth in the long run arising *endogenously*, that is, from the internal workings of the capitalist system.

As a tautology, this "law" follows from the definitions of the ratios. Marx itemized a number of "counteracting influences at work, which thwart and annul the effects of this general law, leaving to it merely the character of a tendency." [16: III, 272][7]

---

[7]These include: (1) "raising the intensity of exploitation"; (2) "depression of wages below their value"; (3) the creation of a "relative surplus-population" of unemployed workers which enables the opening of "new lines of production," with lower organic compositions of capital, and which creates competitive pressure on labor markets to decrease wages; (4) "cheapening of the elements of constant capital ... as a result of the increased productivity of labor"; (5) foreign trade, which enables the importation of cheap consumer goods and/or raw

The most likely case in a growing economy, within the framework of Marxian analysis, would be a simultaneous increase in *both* C/v and s/v. As noted, the employment of machinery can raise s/v in a number of ways. Even the American neo-Marxist Paul Sweezy, in his study of Marxian economics, argues that in this situation $s/C + v$ becomes "indeterminate. All we can say is that the rate of profit will fall if the percentage increase in the rate of surplus value is less than the percentage decrease in the proportion of variable to total capital." Unless there is some *special* reason to suspect so, "there is no general presumption that changes in the organic composition of capital will be relatively so much greater than changes in the rate of surplus value that the former will dominate movements in the rate of profit. On the contrary, it would seem that we must regard the two variables as of roughly coordinate importance." Sweezy adds, "This does not mean that there is no tendency for the rate of profit to fall." But it does show "it is not possible to demonstrate a falling tendency of the rate of profit by beginning the analysis with the rising organic composition of capital." [25 : 102, 104, 105]

Economic Growth: Investment of the Economic Surplus

Capitalism's historic function, contended Marx, is to grow, to industrialize, and thus, to provide the economic prerequisites for socialism. Few statements about the role of capitalism and capitalists in stimulating economic growth and development are as laudatory as the following from *The Communist Manifesto:*

---

materials. Items (1)-(3) operate by raising s/v; item (4) by decreasing C/v; and item (5) by doing either or both. Item (2), excluded from the model of competitive market capitalism, would require special monopsonistic power beyond that of the capitalists as a class. Item (4) is discussed in greater detail by Marx in Volume III of *Capital* in conjunction with "economies in the employment of constant capital"—in modern phraseology, economies of large-scale production.

The bourgeoisie has played a most revolutionary role in history. . . . It has been the first to show what man's activity can bring about. It has accomplished wonders far surpassing Egyptian pyramids, Roman aqueducts, and Gothic cathedrals; it has conducted expeditions that put in the shade all former migrations of nations and crusades. . . .

The bourgeoisie, during its rule of scarce 100 years, has created more massive and more colossal productive forces than have all preceding generations together. Subjection of nature's forces to man, machinery, application of chemistry to industry and agriculture, steam-navigation, railways, electric telegraphs, clearing of whole continents for cultivation, canalization of rivers, whole populations conjured out of the ground—what earlier century had even a presentiment that such productive forces slumbered in the lap of social labor?

On the supply side, the Marxian vision of the dynamics of the capitalist growth process essentially is a profit-investment-technology model, with Marx supplementing the magnitude of profit by a rate of profit concept. Under capitalist institutions and motivations, the rate of growth in potential output depends upon resources (including capital and labor) and technology. Technology, in turn, depends on and is embodied in investment. If technical improvements are to be made, economic surpluses over and above consumption must be made and accumulated in the form of capital investment. In a capitalist economy, investment depends on the rate of profit. Profits, in turn, depend on technology. Technological improvements, by raising labor productivity and decreasing costs, raises both potential output and profits for further investment.

There are two noteworthy points in this profit-investment-technology model. First, it is essentially a classical vision of the growth process. Second, it focuses upon the "aggregate supply function," and upon the generation of economic surpluses in the process of production. To this basic supply-oriented model, Marx added special emphases on employment, wages, and consumption, which focus upon the "aggregate demand function" and the "realization" of economic surpluses in the processes of market exchange and consumption.

Economic surpluses (profits) depend upon both their creation *and* their realization. Surpluses are created in the process of production through the utilization of variable capital (labor) and through increases in labor productivity via technological advances. The realization of surpluses depends primarily on the absorption of rising output by worker-consumers at prices corresponding to labor-time values. Other things being equal, $s/C + v$ varies directly with s. Therefore, the profitability of investment depends upon consumption as well as technology. Consumption, in turn, depends primarily on wage income. Capitalists, of course, also consume—at times, luxuriously. But the major markets for consumer goods must arise from the expenditures of workers.

Wage income depends on employment and wage levels. In contrast to the classical model of competitive market capitalism, which envisaged long-run changes in the size of the labor force via alterations in population, Marx directly incorporated the employment of labor, and fluctuations therein, into his analysis. Employment depends on the relation between the flow of investment and the stock of labor-saving capital innovations. The substitution of capital for labor increases the "reserve army of unemployed," while a general increase in the flow of investment during periods of prosperity raises employment. Thus, employment rises when investment increases in relation to the stock of labor-saving capital and decreases when capital is substituted for labor.

Given their upper and lower limits (net national product and subsistence wages, respectively), wage levels depend upon the interaction of market supply and demand

forces. Rising investment, by increasing the demand for labor, raises employment and wage levels. If the demand for labor exceeds the supply during periods of expanding investment and output, wages will rise. If the supply of labor exceeds the demand during depressed periods of falling output and investment, or if capital is substituted for labor in the production process, wages will fall.

In sum, the key to economic growth in Marx's analysis of capitalism is investment. Investment raises both production and, by employing the new technology, productivity. Rising production and investment are conducive to expanding employment and (if and when the demand surpasses the supply of labor) wages, which in turn leads to higher consumption. Technological advancement provides new opportunities for profitable investment, while higher consumption provides the basis for "realizing" on the marketplace through consumer sales the economic surpluses generated in the processes of production. Marxian capitalists generally can be relied on to reinvest their surpluses, despite their desire (which increases in mature, developed capitalism) to engage in luxurious consumption, sustaining and extending the growth process.[8] Were it not for certain

---

[8] In the Marxian view, capitalists generally can be relied on to reinvest their surpluses for at least four major reasons: (1) Competition compels investment in the latest techniques and methods of production. Capitalists who lag behind in adopting new technology lose out to their competitors. (2) Increased investment embodies the new technology, raises productivity, and provides the basis for increased s and s/v and, other things being equal, $s/C + v$. This is especially true for the capitalist who first introduces the technological improvement and obtains a temporary advantage over his competitors. (3) When wages rise, capitalists are induced to raise C/v and substitute capital for labor. (4) The capitalist has a psychological urge to accumulate. His power and position in a capitalist economy are direct functions of the size of his capital stock. "Accumulate, accumulate! That is Moses and the Prophets!" says Marx. [16 : I, 652]

"contradictions" which disrupt it, the process of capitalist growth would be continuous.

Economic Instability

Two basic facts stand out in the vast, complex panorama of economic change in the Western world during the past 150 years: first, the remarkably sustained increase in overall economic performance—economic growth; second, the recurrent, wave-like fluctuations around the long-run growth trend—economic cycles. One of the most enduring, though underdeveloped, elements of the Marxian analysis is that these two facts are interconnected, analytically and historically. Cyclical economic fluctuations, according to Marx, are inherent in the process of economic growth in an industrializing, developing capitalist economy. "The course characteristic of modern industry" is "a decennial cycle (interrupted by smaller oscillations)," divided into phases or "periods of average activity, production at high pressure, crisis and stagnation." [16: I, 694] These cyclically recurring "crises" constitute one of the most prominent "contradictions" of the capitalist system, and, at the same time, one of the most compelling reasons for the system's impending, inexorable downfall.

With Marx, the "cycle is the characteristic reference of the categories of his entire analysis, as distinguished from the long-run equilibrium" concept of the classic theory of competitive capitalism.[9] Economic fluctuations are not mere temporary deviations from a normal long-run trend, associated with monetary disturbances, financial panics, and isolated external events such as wars, plagues, famines, and crop failures. They are "real," fundamental, and pervasive elements of capitalist development, rooted deeply in production and exchange.

THE POSSIBILITY OF DOWNTURNS FROM STEADY GROWTH

The *possibility* of an interruption or disruption in stable, steady growth arises from two sources, in the Marxian analysis: "(1) the separation of purchase and sale, inevitable in any money economy, and (2) the fact that money, the universal store of value, is used as a means of payment to bridge this separation."[10] Supply, in short, does not necessarily create its own demand, as in the classic theory of capitalism. "Nothing can be more childish than the dogma, that because every sale is a purchase, and every purchase a sale, therefore the circulation of commodities necessarily implies an equilibrium of sales and purchase." The fact that $D_1 = S_1$ does not demonstrate that $D_2 = f(S_1)$ or that $S_1 \rightarrow D_2$. The first is an identity, a tautology, not a behavioral or functional equation. "No one can sell unless someone else purchases. But no one is forthwith bound to purchase, because he has just sold." Indeed, if "the interval of time between . . . the sale and the purchase becomes too pronounced, the intimate connexion between them, their oneness, asserts itself by producing—a crisis." [16: I, 127–28]

This first form of disruption to steady growth may be accompanied by a "monetary crisis." If seller *A* does not sell his commodity in a given period of time, seller *B* will be unable to pay his debts or make his purchases and so on through a network of mutually interdependent purchase-sale, debt-credit relationships. Because money functions as a store of value as well as a medium of exchange, it may fail to provide the continuity of payments necessary to prevent a downturn from becoming an actuality. [18: 376–88]

Furthermore, if a downturn from prosperity or departure from steady expansion occurs, there is no guarantee the allocational

[9]Leo Rogin, *The Meaning and Validity of Economic Theory* (New York: Harper & Row, Publishers, 1956), p. 376.

[10]Bernice Shoul, "Karl Marx and Say's Law," *Quarterly Journal of Economics*, November 1957, pp. 620–21.

processes of the competitive price system will automatically counteract the downswing (through, for example, falling prices, wages, and interest rates), and move the economy toward or to stable prosperity again, thus preventing partial over-production from becoming general. More likely is a mutually-reinforcing, cumulative downward movement, spreading throughout the economy, creating a *general* "glut," where the supply of *all* commodities exceeds demand. This can happen, argued Marx, "because the demand for the general commodity, money . . . is greater than the demand for all particular commodities." [18 : 391] This cumulative contraction in the economy is facilitated by the fact that the continuity of production at high levels ". . . is based on definite assumptions as to prices, so that a general fall in prices checks and disturbs the process of reproduction. This interference and stagnation paralyses the function of money as a medium of payment, which is conditioned on the development of capital and the resulting price relations. The chain of payments due at certain times is broken in a hundred places, and the disaster is intensified by the collapse of the credit system. Thus violent and acute crises are brought about, sudden and forcible depreciations, and actual stagnation and collapse of the process of reproduction, and finally a real falling off in reproduction." [16 : III, 298]

The characteristic form of the cyclical downturn, then, is a separation of purchases and sales, intensified by an excessive demand for money or liquidity crisis which, once started, spirals throughout the entire economy. But the underlying *cause* of cyclical fluctuations lies deeper in the real processes of capitalist production: "That which appears as a crisis on the money market is in reality an expression of abnormal conditions in the process of production and reproduction." [16 : II, 365]

Just what these underlying "abnormal conditions" are and how they interact to generate cyclical movements in economic

activity were never clarified in a consistent, systematic way in Marx's works. Contemporary American neo-Marxist economist Paul Sweezy distinguishes two major sources of cyclical fluctuations in Marx's writings, namely, fluctuations caused by oscillations in the *rate* of profit, $s/C + v$ (1) assuming that commodities sell at their "values" (that is, embodied socially necessary labor-time); (2) assuming that commodities do *not* sell at their values. Clearly, these are *alternative* bases for a theory of economic fluctuations. Commodities cannot sell both at *and* below their (Marxian) values. However, it is possible for either case (1) or (2) to occur.

CASE (1) CRISES: THE CREATION OF
SURPLUSES

Case (1) often is associated with Marx's theory of the long-run tendency toward a falling rate of profit. In its rigid form ($\uparrow C/v$, given s/v, or $\uparrow C/v \gg \uparrow s/v, \dashrightarrow \downarrow s/C + v$), this is a tautology and, even if true as a long-run historical tendency, provides no adequate basis for an analysis of cyclical fluctuations (which requires oscillations in, not just a downward trend in, the rate of profit), Fluctuations in the rate of profit, however, (bringing fluctuations in investment, and thus, in spending, output, and employment), can occur in the Marxian analysis because of fluctuations in real wages and employment, in turn dependent upon capital accumulation and investment in a growing economy. In short, cyclical fluctuations depend " . . . on the constant formation, the greater or less absorption, and the reformation of the industrial reserve army of surplus population. In their turn, the varying phases of the industrial cycle recruit the surplus population, and become one of the most energetic agents of its reproduction." [16 : I, 694]

If we divide economic cycles into the traditional four phases of expansion, downturn, contraction, and upturn, *one* Marxian model of the process might proceed as follows: (A) *Expansion.* An accelerated burst of investment (caused by one or a variety of reasons) leads to an increased demand for labor and (as demand for catches up with and eventually surpasses supply of labor), increased wages. (B) *Downturn*. Increased wages, in turn, lead to decreased surplus and/or s/v. Lower surpluses (and thus, lower profits) lead to lower investment.[11] (C) *Contraction*. Decreased investment, in turn, leads to decreased demand for labor, increased unemployment, and decreased wages. (Indeed, wages may, in a deep depression, temporarily fall below subsistence.) Surpluses and profits thus rise. Surpluses also increase because depression depreciates the value of constant capital, and rates of profit, calculated on the basis of these lower capital values, rise. In addition, smaller, bankrupt capitalists will sell their capital equipment to larger capitalists at sub-value prices, thus generating surpluses, even in the depths of depression, for those capitalists who survive. These bankrupt capitalists will join the labor force, swelling the "industrial reserve army," forcing wages down further, and generating larger surpluses for remaining larger capitalists. (D) *Upturn*. Increased surpluses eventually lead to higher investment and economic expansion. "And in this way the cycle would be run once more ... the same vicious circle ... under expanded conditions of production, in an expanded market, and with increased productive forces. [16 : III, 299] In sum: "An accelerated rate of accumulation brings on a reaction in the form of a crisis, the crisis turns into depression; the depression, through filling up the reserve army and depreciating capital values, restores the profitability of production and thereby sets the stage for a resumption of accumulation." [25 : 153]

Case (1) precludes the possibility of underconsumption or inadequate demand as a cause of the downturn (though, of course, falling investment will bring falling wages and

consumption during the contraction). Thus, it " ... is purely a tautology to say that crises are caused by the scarcity of solvent consumers, or of a paying consumption. ... if one were to attempt to clothe this tautology with a semblance of a profounder justification by saying that the working class receive too small a portion of their own product, and the evil would be remedied by giving them a larger share of it, or raising their wages, we should reply that crises are precisely always preceded by a period in which wages rise generally and the working class actually get a larger share of the annual product intended for consumption." [16 : II, 475, 476]

CASE (2) CRISES: THE REALIZATION OF SURPLUSES

In cyclical fluctuations associated with Case (2), however, commodities may not be sold at prices corresponding to their values because of inadequate consumption. In the long run, consumption is "chronically stagnant" or insufficient to maintain the actual output and employment at its potential level. In the short run, consumption fluctuates cyclically, partly as a *response* to fluctuating investment, employment, and real wages, and, under certain conditions, partly as an *initiator* of fluctuations in surpluses, and thus, investment. "The last cause of all real crises," argued Marx, "always remains the poverty and restricted consumption of the masses as compared to the tendency of capitalist production to develop the productive forces in such a way that only the absolute power of consumption of the entire society would be their limit." [16 : III, 568]

The essential point for Case (2) fluctuations is Marx's distinction between the production and the realization of surplus value:

> The creation of surplus value ... is but the first act of the capitalist process of production ... and this process has no other limits but ... the laboring population. ... Now comes the second act of the process. The entire mass of commodities ... must be sold. If this is not done, or only partly

---

[11]This model is based, in part, on Marx and on Sweezy. [25 : 105–6, 149–52] Whether the theory of the downturn specified in this model would be wholly acceptable to Marx is a matter of dispute.

accomplished, or only at prices which are below the prices of production, the laborer has been nonetheless exploited, but his exploitation does not realize as much for the capitalist. . . . The conditions of direct exploitation and those of the realisation of surplus-value are not identical. They are separated logically as well as by time and space. The first are only limited by the productive power of society, the last by the proportional relations of the various lines of production and by the consuming power of society . . . based on antagonistic conditions of distribution, which reduces the consumption of the great mass of the population to a variable minimum within more or less narrow limits . . . to the extent that the productive power develops, it finds itself at variance with the narrow basis on which the conditions of consumption rest. [16 : III, 285, 286, 287]

Inadequate consumption may be one basis for chronic stagnation; if correct, it may help explain how and why "depressions can last." Insufficient consumption may also appear during the expansion phase of the economic cycle and thereby help explain why "prosperity cannot last." If it appeared early in the expansion, it might choke off the boom, thus precipitating a premature downturn, a "weak cycle," or a "depression within a depression." But suppose, as in Case (1), that a spurt of investment carries the economy up toward or to a genuinely full employment, high-wage boom (a "strong cycle"). Consumption might still be inadequate, in the Marxian analysis, for the following reason: Capitalists may respond to rising wages by raising C/v, that is, by substituting capital for labor as labor becomes more expensive. This is self-defeating, however, since (a) unless s/v rises enough to match the increased C/v, $s/C + v$ will fall; (b) apart from the mechanics of the law of profit, a substitution of capital for labor decreases the demand for labor, raises unemployment, lowers wages, decreases consumption, and prevents the sale of commodities at their values, thus lowering surplus, profit, and investment, and helping to bring on a downturn.

Perhaps the most accurate conclusion to be drawn from all this is that Marx provided a number of provocative and suggestive hints on the generation and process of cyclical fluctuations. These were never integrated and synthesized into a consistent and adequate theoretical analysis. Particularly, he never fully recognized the necessity of interrelating the consumption and investment functions. Low consumption by itself is insufficient to cause a downturn so long as businesses continue to invest sums equal to the gap between consumption and national income (output). To "clinch the argument," notes Joan Robinson, "it is necessary to show that investment depends upon the rate of profit, and that the rate of profit depends, in the last resort, upon consuming power. It is necessary, in short, to supply a theory of the rate of profit based on the principle of effective demand." [20 : 50] These linkages were not fully and consistently demonstrated in Marx's analysis.

SUMMARY OF CHAPTER 5

1. Marxian economics is essentially a critique of the theory and practice of capitalist industrialization. The Marxian concept of capitalism focused upon ownership of the instruments of production and the division of society into property-owning and non-property-owning classes.

2. Marxian analysis was developed in terms of special definitions and ratios. Capital is divided into constant and variable (labor) components. Output is divided into consumption goods and investment goods. Gross income is composed of depreciation, raw materials, wages, and surplus. Net income is divided into wage income and surplus. The three ratios are the rate of exploitation or surplus value (s/v), the organic composition of capital (C/v), and the rate of profit ($s/C + v$). The last is composed of the other two ($s/C + v = s/v/(C/v + 1)$) for it varies directly with s/v and inversely with C/v.

3. According to Marx, the value of a commodity is determined by the amount of socially necessary labor time embodied in its production. This concept, rather than the competitive price system as an allocational process, was the central theme of Volume I of *Capital*. The labor theory of value requires a number of special assumptions which limit its applicability. The role and importance of the theory in Marxian analysis is also an open question.

4. Wages have a lower subsistence limit and an upper limit equal to the entire net national product. For capitalism to generate economic surpluses, wages must be pushed down toward subsistence or national income must be pushed above wages. In Marx's analysis of capitalism, the substitution of capital for labor accomplishes the former, while increased productivity, lengthening of the working day, and other devices achieve the latter.

5. Economic growth, in the Marxian view, is encouraged and generated by the capitalist process: on the supply side, through the interaction of profits, investment and technology; on the demand side, by increases in employment, wages, and consumption, which enable the "realization" of surpluses created in the process of production.

6. Economic growth is not stable and steady. Departures from an equilibrium or steady-state of economic growth are possible since the identity of aggregate sales and purchases provides no guarantee that supply will create its own demand or that demand for money will not be larger than the supply of money. Price flexibility will not restore full employment equilibrium once it is disturbed; instead, downturns tend to generate dynamic and cumulative processes of contraction into depression which eventually terminate and are succeeded by expansions and new crises.

7. Crises may occur from either the creation or realization of surplus value. In the former, capitalists respond to rising wages during prosperity by substituting capital for labor. But an increase in the organic composition of capital, unless offset by sufficient increases in rates of surplus value, will cause falling levels and/or rates of profits. In the latter, consumption is insufficient to enable capitalists to realize through market exchange the surpluses created in production.

8. In sum, in the Marxian interpretation, capitalism is a creative and dynamic economic system for generating, mobilizing, and investing surpluses of income over and above consumption. Its institutional structure, especially ownership of the instruments of production, initiates and encourages the accumulation of capital and the development and application of labor power in the process of industrialization. At the same time, the system rests upon the use of economic power by one class (capitalists) to exploit economic surpluses from another class (workers). This results in internal "contradictions" within the system, evidenced by its tendency toward recurrent departures from steady growth, cyclical fluctuations, and depression. Capitalism's dynamism rests upon exploitation of class by class and is characterized by instability and periodic economic crises.

5

Appendix:
The Marxian Theory of
Capitalist Development
and Transformation

In addition to his analyses of economic growth, cyclical instability, value, and distribution, Marx also had what might be called a theory of economic *development*, that is, an analysis of qualitative alteration in the structure of the economic system, as well as quantitative change in the magnitude of economic variables within a given institutional, motivational, and technological structure. This theory was based in part on his more technical economic analysis, but it also rested on his intuitive grasp of the dynamics of historical trends and his broad, visionary ideology and philosophy of history. Insofar as this is true, his theory of economic development is distinguishable from, though interrelated with, his technical economic theory. The fact that some of his visionary predictions have come true does not "prove Marx's economic theories right," any more than the fact that some of his forecasts have not come true does not "prove Marx's economic theories wrong."

Discussion in this chapter is divided into two main parts: an exposition of Marx's theory of history and social classes, which provided a broad framework for his theory of economic development; and an examination of the central and most prominent dimensions of the Marxian theory of capitalist development and transformation.

THE MARXIAN THEORY OF HISTORY AND SOCIAL CLASSES

The Marxian theory of history and social classes in part supports and is supported by Marx's economic analysis. The economic theory is sufficiently independent from the rest of Marx's thought to justify the separate and specialized treatment in Chapter 5. At the same time, it is necessary to recognize, with Schumpeter, "a unity of social vision which succeeds in giving some measure of analytic unity, and still more a semblance of unity, to the Marxian work," and "the fact that every part of it, however independent intrinsically, has been correlated by (Marx) with every other." [8:9] This correlation of economic and non-economic aspects of Marx's thought is especially prominent in the theory of economic development and prospects for capitalism.

The Marxian Vision of Historical Development

The Marxian vision of the process of historical development contained four major elements: (1) an economic structure or "mode of production"; (2) a non-economic "superstructure"; (3) a concept of historical causation concerning the relations between structure and superstructure; and (4) a theory of the "logic" of historical change in both structure and superstructure. In the following, Marx attempted to summarize these four ingredients and their interrelationships:

"In the social production which men carry on they enter into definite relations that are indispensable and independent of their will; these relations of production correspond to a definite stage of development of their material powers of production. The sum total of these relations of production constitutes the economic structure of society—the real foundation on which rise legal and political superstructures and to which correspond definite forms of social consciousness. The mode of production in material life determines the general character of the social, political and spiritual processes of life. It is not the consciousness of men that determines their existence, but, on the contrary, their social existence determines their consciousness. At a certain stage of their development the material forces of production in society come in conflict with the existing relations of production, or—what is but a legal expression for the same thing —with the property relations within which they had been at work before. From forms of development of the forces of production these relations turn into their fetters. Then comes the period of social revolution. With the change of the economic foundation the entire immense superstructure is more or less rapidly transformed."[1]

_____

[1] Karl Marx, *A Contribution to the Critique of Political Economy* (Chicago: Keri, 1904), Preface.

The first element, then, of Marx's historical framework is the concept of "mode of production" or "economic structure of society." This structure includes the techniques of production and technical knowledge concerned with the development and utilization of capital resources. But it also involves the quantity and quality of human and natural resources, and the social relations and institutions surrounding the technical processes of production, such as private property, specialization, and exchange. Apparently, Marx wanted to include under this heading both the "forces" of production (resources and technology) and the "social relations" of production (property, exchange, and so forth). A society's resources and technology and the processes of production related thereto, intertwined with the social relations or institutions and processes of production, exchange, distribution, and consumption consistent with those underlying resource/technology conditions, constitute the mode of production or economic structure, which is the primary cause of changes in society's non-economic superstructure.

This supersturcture apparently includes all social institutions and relations other than those embodied in the underlying mode of production—for example, art, morals, religion, the family, law, and politics—and *all* ideas, theories, and philosophies, economic as well as non-economic.

The basic line of causation in history, argued Marx, runs from structure to superstructure: $S \dashrightarrow SS$. This does not mean the economic structure is the only factor of importance in history or that the superstructure has no influence of its own. But it does mean the structure is the major cause of changes in the superstructure; that political, legal, and other non-economic institutions and ideas reflect the underlying economic conditions of society; and that, as a rule, if these non-economic relations and institutions are to exert an influence on historical development, they must do so indirectly, via their reverberations on the economic structure

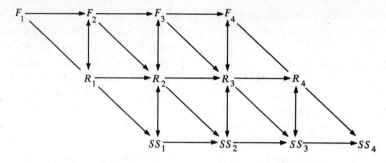

Fig. 5.1. Marx' theory of historical development

after having been initially brought into being (perhaps, with a time-lag) by changes in that structure.[2]

The relations between structure and super-structure and, within the economic structure, between the "forces" and "relations" of production, develop and change via an internal logic: First, changes occur in the forces of production, the underlying techniques or methods of production. Second, these changes cause further changes in the relations of production and exchange. Third, changes in the economic structure as a whole bring still further changes in the legal and political superstructure.

At each stage of historical development, forces of production, social relations of production, and the legal-political-ideological superstructure are in conflict. From conflict

comes change, in a "dialectical" process. This is illustrated in Fig. 5.1. F, R, and SS symbolize forces of production, social relations of production and exchange, and superstructure, respectively. The numbers 1, 2, 3, and 4 stand for different stages or "epochs" in historical development, for example, feudalism, capitalism, socialism, and communism. Suppose a society exists with a particular resource/technology base (F_1). an associated set of economic institutions (R_1), and a surrounding political, legal, and ideological superstructure (SS_1) consistent with the underlying economic structure. In the absence of change, such a society would be in "equilibrium." Its technology, economic institutions, and system of politics and supporting ideas would be mutually consistent and supportive.

Suppose a change occurred in the forces of production, for example, resource discoveries or technological improvements, illustrated by a horizontal movement from F_1 to F_2. The new resource/technology base would come into conflict with the old set of economic instituions, illustrated by the vertical, double-pointed arrows between R_1 and F_2. The resolution of the conflict would come with the emergence of a new set of economic institutions, R_2, consistent with the new technology. In a similar manner, the combined change from F_1/R_1 to F_2/R_2 would create a new economic structure, which would conflict with the old, surrounding superstruc-

[2]Marx's theme may be qualified in such a way as to lose a bit (some critics say much) of its power, but also some of its rigidity. Engels said: "According to the materialist conception of history the determining element in history is *ultimately* the production and reproduction in real life. If therefore somebody twists this into the statement that the economic element is the *only* determining one, he transforms it into a meaningless, abstract, and absurd phrase. The economic situation is the basis, but the various elements of the superstructure . . . also exercise their influence upon the course of the historical struggles and in many elements, in which . . . the economic movement finally asserts itself as necessary." [Karl Marx and Fredrick Engels, *Selected Correspondence* (New York City: International Publishers, 1935), p. 475.]

ture, SS_1 which would have lagged behind the dynamic changes in technology and economic institutions. Finally, the superstructure would change (from SS_1 to SS_2), and a new technological-economic-political system $(F_2/R_2/SS_2)$ would come into being. The new synthesis, which would emerge via a long period of evolutionary historical development, would constitute a revolutionary transformation from one system of technology, economy, and politics to another.

The new system cannot be in equilibrium, however, because of the continuity of dialectical change. Further changes in technology create further conflicts between forces of production and social relations of production $(F_3$ conflicts with $R_2)$, and further changes in economic institutions (from R_2 to R_3) create further conflicts between the economic structure and its surrounding superstructure $(F_3/R_3$ conflicts with $SS_2)$, with an eventual resulting transformation to a new superstructure (from SS_2 to SS_3), and thus, a new system $(F_3/R_3/SS_3)$. The process continues until an ideally functioning set of social relations of production and surrounding superstructure are established in a highly technologically developed and affluent communist economic society $(F_4/R_4/SS_4)$. At this point, the dialectic ends, a leap is made from "the realm of necessity" to "the realm of freedom," and man becomes the master of technology (through feedbacks from R_3/SS_4 to F_5, F_6, and so on, not shown in Fig. 5.1) instead of being controlled by it.

The transition from feudalism to capitalism illustrates the steps in this process. In the Marxian view, market exchange relations are not consistent with and do not develop in a self-sufficient agricultural economy. The technological innovations of modern times, combined with the development of an urban labor force, the factory system, and mobile money capital, provide the underlying conditions for the development of markets, specialization, exchange, competition, private property, individual free contract, and the

like. But the shift to predominance of these familiar capitalist institutions did not occur simultaneously with the changes in the productive forces. There was a time lag, Marx asserted, during which older, feudalistic institutions and relations (for example, internal restrictions on mobility of resources and products, and guild controls) remained as "fetters" on the development of the new forces of production. Finally, the developing productive forces became too powerful and creative for these older instituions. The result was a social revolution wherein the older institutions were supplemented or superseded by the new ones, and a new economic structure was born. This change in the economic system, in turn, encouraged change in the political and legal superstructure, that is, the transition from feudal to capitalist economy was accompanied by the emergence of a modern, centralizing nation-state. Once again, however, there was a time lag. The earlier feudalistic superstructure of law and government, centering around the political power of localized, landed aristocrats, remained to hamper the logical development of the economic system. Here, too, the final result is evident: By a process of social revolution, the superstructure was finally transformed to correspond with the underlying economic structure. Political power was transferred from local to national authorities, and laws were passed more conducive to the development of capitalist enterprise and less favorable to the feudal aristocracy.

This vision of historical change was used by Marx as a basis for predicting capitalism's coming demise, as well as its origins and development. In the Marxian vision, the productive powers of a complex, industrialized economy eventually become too great for its distributional system, too large to be effectively organized around the principles and institutions of private property and individual economic freedom. These institutions, and the legal and political superstructure associated with them, will increasingly become "fetters" on further economic development. The result: a series of increasingly severe "contradictions" in the form of crises and depressions which will eventually lead to capitalism's downfall. [19: 14–21]

Social Classes and Class Struggles

The central element in any economic system, the key to understanding its economic structure, and a fundamental source of conflict and change in history, in the Marxian view, is the socio-economic *class*. The class, not the individual, government, state, nor society is the central unit of economic decision. Individuals exert some influence, of course, but it is more of a personal, than of a fundamental historic nature. "Society" is too nebulous a concept to be of any use in identifying the source of economic change. "Government" is simply an administrative machinery or apparatus, while the "state" is an agency or instrument of oppression controlled by the dominant class in society.

In the Marxian analysis, social classes are not identified in terms of economic functions (such as landlords, workers, or employers). The definitional criterion is *property relations* and the power and freedom that accompany the ownership of property. In this view, society is divided into two classes: those who do and those who do not own property, particularly industrial capital, that is, the means or instruments of production. Capitalism, for example, is composed of two major social classes: the capitalists or bourgeoisie, whose distinguishing characteristic is the ownership of property, and the workers or proletariat, whose identifying feature is the lack of such ownership.

Socio-economic classes, thus defined, are antagonistic by virtue of the logic of their respective relations to each other. This conflict (sometimes supplemented and complicated by internecine warfare within a class; for example, big versus small capitalists) is continuous and uninterrupted.

Freeman and slave, patrician and plebian, lord and serf, guildmaster and journeyman, in a word, oppressor and oppressed, stood in constant opposition to one another, carried on an uninterrupted, now hidden, now open fight, a fight that each time ended, either in a revolutionary reconstitution of society at large, or in the common ruin of the contending classes . . . .
The modern bourgeois society that has sprouted from the ruins of feudal society, has not done away with class antagonisms. It has but established new classes, new conditions of oppression, new forms of struggle in place of the old ones. [19: 9–21]

Conflicts between socio-economic classes are the basic ingredients in the conflicts and changes in economic structure and superstructure, and Marx identified the birth and death of economic systems with the creation, movement to supremacy, senescence, and finally death knell of social classes. "The history of all hitherto existing society," asserted Marx and Engels in *The Communist Manifesto*, "is the history of class struggles."

The transformation from feudalism to capitalism, for example, required the "primitive" (pre-capitalist) accumulation of capital, and thereby, the creation of a new, dominant capitalist class to replace the feudal aristocracy, and the creation of a non-owning, but "freely contracting" industrial proletariat. In England, this socio-economic revolution employed a variety of techniques which, itemized by Marx, included the influx of gold and silver from the New World, the dispossession of monasteries and other church properties, and the enclosure movement, whereby large tracts of land (by purchase, force, theft, or by absorbing lands formerly used in common) were enclosed for sheep-raising, thus "freeing" large numbers of peasants, squatters, and others from the soil.

As an economic system matures, the antagonism intensifies because classes become more organized and "class conscious." The bourgeoisie under capitalism brought its proletarian antagonist into being and, in so doing, is not only digging its own grave, but providing its own "gravediggers." With the expansion and development of industry, "the proletariat not only increases in number; it becomes concentrated in greater masses, its strength grows, and it feels that strength more." Workers organize into labor unions and communicate with others so organized. This leads to a greater centralization of class conflicts, transforming them into struggles of greater national and political significance.

In addition, capitalism has "simplified the class antagonisms. Society as a whole is more and more splitting up into two great hostile camps, into two great classes directly facing each other—bourgeoisie and proletariat." Landlords become agricultural capitalists. Peasants, small businessmen, shopkeepers, and artisans "sink gradually into the proletariat" as big capitalists swallow up small capitalists in internecine conflict and as old skills are "rendered worthless by new methods of production." Others (for example, the military, the intellectuals, criminals) tend to support one or the other of the two conflicting classes.

As in the transformation from feudalism to capitalism, the change from capitalism to socialism involves (or will involve) not only a new form of economic organization, but also a move to dominance of the formerly oppressed class, the industrial proletariat. "What the bourgeoisie therefore produces, above all, are its own grave-diggers. Its fall and the victory of the proletariat are equally inevitable."

Thus Marx provided a unified vision of development and change blending history, sociology, and economics. His definition of social classes, like his interpretation of the historical process, was economic. At the same time, his definition of capitalism was essentially sociological; that is, Marxian capitalism is an economic system in which private capitalists own and control the means of production, while socialism is characterized by worker ownership and control. This definition, in Schumpeter's words, is "ingenuous tautology" and "a bold stroke of analytic strategy." By linking the fate of capitalism

as an economic system with that of capitalists as a socio-economic class, Marx was able, by contrast, to identify socialism with the dominance of the proletariat as a socio-economic class, and thus as the only form of classless society in a modern industrialized economy. At the same time, though Marx defined capitalism sociologically, he explained its workings in terms of economic analysis. The economic theory represented Marx's attempt to show how social relations among classes "work out through the medium of economic values, profits, wages, investment. . . . and how they generate precisely the economic process that will eventually break its own institutional framework and at the same time create the conditions for the emergence of another social world." Marx's theory of socio-economic clases, on the other hand, "is the analytic tool which, by linking the economic interpretation of history with the concepts of the profit economy, marshals all social facts, makes all phenomena confocal." It had the "organic function" of synthesizing the Marxian theory of capitalist development into a unified whole. [8: 20]

CAPITALIST DEVELOPMENT AND TRANSFORMATION

The key to the Marxian theory of capitalist development and transformation is a distinction between "early" and "mature" capitalism. Early capitalism (in Marx's conception, up to the mid-nineteenth century) was a phase of tremendous growth and youthful vitality when class antagonisms were not yet as sharp as they later became, when the system's contradictions, though growing, had not yet reached their heights, and when competition was the rule and expansion the theme. Later capitalism (in the Marxian view, *since* the mid-nineteenth century) is a phase of obsolescence and decay, leading eventually to collapse, death, and the emergence of a new, totally different post-capitalist economic system. During mature capitalism, class antagonisms sharpen and heighten; concentration and monopolization in industry, supplemented by concentration in finance and banking, replace competition; the gap between actual and potential economic performance grows chronic and increasing, as do the system's contradictions.

Marx's theory of mature capitalism identified historical trends that he believed were taking place as well as predictions of the future. In several instances, the details were filled in by various post-Marxian Marxists. The more prominent elements of this theory can be summarized within five central themes: (1) increasing severity of crises and cyclical fluctuations; (2) increasing concentration and centralization of capital; (3) increasing misery and antagonism of workers; (4) increasing imperialism and colonial exploitation; and (5) increasing state oppression.

Increasing Severity of the Economic Cycle

As capitalism matures, succeeding crises and depressions become increasingly severe. Their "periodical return put the existence of the entire bourgeois society on trial, each time more threateningly." Recoveries from depressions (through "enforced destruction of a mass of productive forces" and "by the conquest of new markets" and "the more thorough exploitation of the old ones") pave "the way for more extensive and more destructive crises" and diminish "the means whereby crises are prevented." [19: 14, 15]

This does not imply a non-cyclical stagnation or "stationary state." It could, but need not, require a downward long-run trend in overall economic performance. Perhaps the closest approximation to this element in the Marxian vision is an "asymmetrically explosive" cycle around an actual growth trend, which deviates increasingly from the potential output or income, as illustrated in Fig. 5.2. Measuring national income and time on the vertical and horizontal axes, respectively, the figure depicts a long-run growth in both

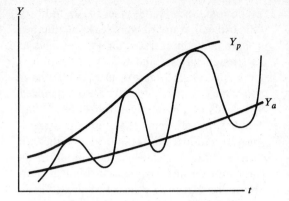

Fig. 5.2. Increasingly severe cycles

potential output (Yp) and actual output (Ya), yet an increasing gap between them resulting from the increased severity of cyclical fluctuations. Because "national income in real terms cannot rise above the full employment level, increasing amplitude of fluctuations in real terms means increasingly severe downswings, which bring the trend of actual income farther and farther below the trend of potential national income."[3]

The reasons for this prospect were never integrated by Marx into one consistent statement. However, three factors in the Marxian analysis would seem to be significant: first, the greater the economic growth and the larger the potential and/or actual output, the larger, in *absolute* terms, the depressions, and the greater the prospective departure, in *relative* terms, of the actual from the potential output—*if* there *are* underlying factors causing greater cyclical amplitude. Second, two long-run aspects of Marx's growth-cycle theories imply greater cyclical severity: the tendency toward lower rates of profit (which Marx held would be greater than the "countervailing influences") and the trend toward inadequate consumption. Third, two additional elements of Marx's theory of economic development, to be discussed, allegedly reinforce these factors:

[3]Benjamin Higgins, *Economic Development* (New York City: W. W. Norton & Company, Inc., Publishers, 1968), p. 130.

(1) the prospective trend toward monopolization; and (2) a secular increase in both the size of the labor force and the "industrial reserve army of unemployed."

As for the empirical validity of this hypothesis of increasing cyclical severity, it contains important insights. As the industrializing, capitalist economies of western Europe and the United States grew larger during the nineteenth century, the *absolute* size of both booms and depressions grew larger. As to the period 1776–1896, it is probably accurate to say that, as the process of cyclical change became increasingly rooted in the industrial structure, the extent of amplitude did become larger than the seasonal and random fluctuations of a pre-industrial era. Furthermore, there have been periods in the last century and a half in these countries (such as, the early 1870s to the late 1890s, and the depressed decade of the 1930s) when expansions *were* short and mild and depressions long and severe.

However, as a long-run forecase of nineteenth-twentieth century economic development, the hypothesis does not hold up well. The experience of western European countries and the United States from approximately the Civil War to World War II does not demonstrate a *secular trend* of increasing severity of cyclical fluctuations. More recently, one of the most striking features of the World War II and postwar economic scene has been the absence of a *major* depression, as contrasted to "minor recessions."

Marxists have often attributed the absence of increasingly severe economic crises and depressions to such "countervailing influences" as government spending, especially military spending. It is uncertain what would happen were peace to break out or Western governments to abandon the counter-cyclical monetary and fiscal measures they have developed over the last 30 to 50 years. Because most contemporary Western governments are not anxious to put Marx's prognostication to test by abandoning their military defense expenditures and/or counter-

cyclical policies, the forecast remains an untested hypothesis.

At the same time, the economic and political structures of formerly capitalist economies have changed so radically during the last 100 years as to make the assumptions of the forecast obsolete. However "socialized" and centralized the process of production, the process of exchange and the institutional superstructure purportedly remains *purely capitalist* in the Marxian model up to the system's ultimate collapse. Marx did not envisage (indeed, denied the likelihood of) the dramatic development in Western economies of collective and governmental institutions designed to reduce the severity of cyclical fluctuations.

Increasing Concentration and Centralization of Capital

A second element in the Marxian theory of mature capitalism is the transition from competition to monopoly. The general process of accumulation increases the stock of capital goods in the aggregate and of individual capitalists as well. Economies of large-scale production (which Marx assumed would increase with expanded technology over the passage of time) increase the minimum size of business necessary for efficient production and thus encourage "concentration" of capital, that is, an increased absolute size or scale of enterprise. These same economies of scale, supplemented by that "new and formidable weapon in the competitive struggle—the credit system" encourage, by merger and by the forceful exit of small firms from the market, a "centralization" of capital or concentration of capital and production in the hands of a smaller number of capitalists, that is, an increased relative size of enterprise or monopolization. (Marx apparently included in the concept of centralization an increased concentration of both ownership and control of enterprises, wherein both ownership of capital and control over production and investment decisions is vested in a smaller number of people.) "The battle of competition is fought by cheapening of commodities. The cheapness of commodities depends *ceteris paribus*, on the productiveness of labour, and this again on the scale of production. Therefore, the larger capitals beat the smaller." Centralization is also encouraged during depressions, when smaller capitalists close and/or sell their bankrupt businesses to larger capitalists. At any phase of the economic cycle, smaller capitalists, forced out of, or discouraged from entering into, more industrially and technologically advanced sectors of the economy, "crowd into spheres of production which Modern Industry has only sporadically or incompletely got hold of. Here competition rages in direct proportion to the number" of producers and "always ends in the ruin of many small capitalists, whose capitals partly pass into the hands of their conquerors, partly vanish." [16: I, 687, 686]

MONOPOLY

The first result, then, of concentration and centralization, is the monopolization of industry, which reaches its potential limit: (1) in any one industry when "all the individual capitals invested in it. . . have been amalgamated into one single capital" and (2) in the entire economy in any one society when "the entire social capital would be united, either in the hands of one single capitalist, or in those of one single corporation." [16: I, 688][4]

Allocation. Monopoly prices are determined solely by demand, since monopolists, through their control over supply, may select prices (above values) which, in terms of mar-

---

[4]Marx wrote very little about the corporation as an economic institution and its relation to capitalism. The major growth of the corporation came after his death. However, one of the effects of "stock companies," he wrote, [16: III, 516–17] is the transformation "of the actually functioning capitalist into a mere manager, an administrator of other people's capital, and of the owners of capital into mere owners, mere money-capitalists."

ket demand, give the highest profit. As a result, monopoly prices generally will be above, and monopoly output below, competitive levels. Resources, restricted from entry in monopolized industries, will move into competitive areas, lowering prices and profits. The competitive tendency toward an equalization of profit rates will be superseded by the development of a hierarchy of profit rates, varying directly with the extent of monopoly power.

Distribution. Under an earlier, more competitive economy, capitalists as a class, through their monopoly of capital, were in a position to exploit workers as a class. The development of additional monopoly power by a smaller number of larger capitalists enables additional exploitation either (1) by transferring profit from small to large capitalists, leaving total surplus value the same, or (2) by reducing real wages below competitive levels, or raising prices above competitive levels (adding to total surplus value), or both. "Thus the share of labor in total output is ground between the upper and the nether millstones of monopoly and monopsony." [20: 76]

Growth. Despite their output-restrictive tendencies, centralization and monopoly need not, in the Marxian view, decrease the rate of economic growth. Indeed, they may increase the rate of capital accumulation and, thereby, economic growth in at least two ways: First, as noted, monopoly may generate surpluses beyond those possible in comtetitive capitalism. Second, monopoly tends to increase the investment from any given surplus in two ways: (1) "Centralization supplements the work of accumulation by enabling the industrial capitalists to expand the scale of their operations" and, thereby, to engage in dramatic large-scale investment projects (such as railroadization), which would be impossible through the mere gradual summation of individual, non-centralized capitals and which, by rapidly generating new chunks of surplus, "become new and powerful levers of social accumulation."

(2) Monopoly encourages technological change, especially the application of labor-saving inventions: "Centralization, by thus accelerating and intensifying the effects of accumulation extends and hastens at the same time the revolutions in the technical composition of capital." [16: I, 688, 689]

Instability. If monopoly contributes to greater investment and economic growth by these devices, it also contributes to greater economic instability: first, anything that raises the rate of increase in capital accumulation strengthens the long-run tendencies toward decreased profit rates and underconsumption; second, labor-saving inventions decrease the demand for labor and raise the size of the reserve army of unemployed; third, movement of resources from restricted, monopolized industries to more competitive industries depresses the rates of profit in the latter; fourth, anything (such as monopoly or monposony) that redistributes income from workers to capitalists tends to raise investment, lower the rate of profit, and discourage consumption. Thus, monopoly capitalism and the economic cycle mutually reinforce one another in a vicious circle: Increased monopolization tends to increase the severity of cyclical fluctuations, but increasingly severe crises and depressions lead to greater monopolization.

SOCIALIZATION OF LABOR AND
PRODUCTION

The second broad result of concentration and centralization is the "socialization" of labor and production. As capitalism matures, the work process becomes more cooperative, collective, and "socialized," and thus, in the Marxian view, more in conflict with the anarchic characteristics of capitalist exchange and the market system. Just as the corporation transforms the "private profit of individual producers" into "the common property of associates," into "social property," so monopoly transforms and socializes work, labor, and production: "Hand in hand with this centralization, or this expropriation of many capitalists by few, develop, on an ever-extending scale, the cooperative form of the labour-process . . . the transformation of the instruments of labour into instruments of labour only usable in common, the economising of all means of production by their use as the means of production of combined, socialised labour. . . ." [16: I, 836]

One key implication of this tendency is that large-scale monopoly capitalism, with its centralization and organization of production and labor, is one short step from a socialized economy. In some ways, "there is less difference between large-scale capitalist enterprise and large-scale socialized enterprise on the one hand than between small-scale capitalist enterprise and large-scale capitalist enterprise on the other."[5] From the standpoint of continuity of the production and technological processes, the transition from a mature and monopolized capitalism to a socialist economy would be immeasurably simpler than from an earlier, more atomistically competitive economy.

As an analysis of either the process of becoming or being a monopolist, the foregoing is crude and sketchy—at least, in relation to the highly sophisticated models of the twentieth century. As a long-run prediction, it is also inadequate. Intensive statistical investigation has not revealed a secular trend toward increased monopoly in the United States in the twentieth century. Indeed, one could make a good case for the argument that competition has increased in the twentieth century through, for example, the unleashing of new products through research and technological change, urbanization, improved transportation and communication, and the increase in "discretionary income" (that is, income above that necessary for meeting basic consumption needs, such as food, clothing, and shelter). These elements of competition among products and industries

[5] William Ebenstein, *Today's Isms* (Englewood Cliffs, New Jersey: Prentice-Hall, Inc., 1967), p. 185.

have accompanied increased "concentration" and, at times, "centralization" within industries.

Despite these imperfections and inadequacies, an element of truth exists in the Marxian theory of the "propensity to monopolize": "For one thing, to predict the advent of big business was, considering the conditions of Marx's day, an achievement in itself. But he did more than that. He neatly hitched concentration to the process of accumulation or rather he visualized the former as part of the latter, and not only as part of its factual pattern but also of its logic." [8 : 34] The error lies not in recognizing these insights, but in rigidifying the sketchy Marxian prognostications into dogma and precise predictions.

Increasing Size, Concentration, Organization, Misery, and Antagonism of Workers

The third element in the Marxian theory of mature capitalism is a many-sided but not wholly clear prediction of the future position of workers and their relation to capitalists. Several aspects of this prediction, discussed earlier, in relation to Marx's theory of the class struggle, are summarized briefly: As capitalism matures, the *size* of the labor force grows, both absolutely and relative to the size of the population. Population growth could account for the former. Marx explained the latter partly as a by-product of the transformation from competitive to monopoly capitalism and the resultant move into the labor force of former craftsmen, small businessmen, farmers, and others, and partly in terms of the technology of the machine process, which enables, on an increasing scale, the employment of women and children. The concentration and centralization of labor accompanies that of capital. Large numbers of workers are massed together in centralized, hierarchically-structured factories as part of the process of the development of large-scale monopolistic enterprise.

Once brought together in this manner workers organize into labor unions and present collective and centralized positions, which become national and political in scope in their struggles with capitalists. Antagonism between workers and capitalists thus increases and is recognized and understood increasingly by workers. Antagonism also is fed by the increased misery of the workers.

BASES OF "IMMISERIZATION" OF LABOR: EXPOSITION

From the vantage point of the mid-nineteenth century, Marx regarded the economic lot and social position of workers under capitalism as miserable. Further, the "immiserization" (to use Schumpeter's apt term) of workers was not expected to diminish as capitalism matured. If anything, it would increase in several ways, for several reasons.

Whatever the nature and degree of misery as capitalism matures and population and the size of the labor force grow (the latter, in relative and absolute terms), larger numbers of people will experience it. Thus, even if "misery per worker" were to remain constant, aggregate misery is likely to increase as capitalism matures.

Both the social relations between workers and capitalists and the conditions of the work process under capitalism are socially and morally degrading to the worker. The worker, in contrast to the slave and serf of ancient and feudal economies, is a "free" economic agent. But if, to live, he must work, and if, to work, he must sell his labor-power to the capitalist, who is in a position to "exploit" him, then he is, in effect, a "wage-slave." The "wage worker has permission to work for his own life, that is, *to live only in so far* as he works for a certain time gratis for the capitalist. . . . consequently the system of wage labour is a system of slavery. . . ." [17 : II, 574]

Once hired, the worker's enslavement continues as he becomes a means to the end of creating surplus value. "Modern industry has converted the little workshop of the patriarchal master into the great factory of the industrial capitalist. Masses of labourers, crowded into the factory, are organized like soldiers. As privates of the industrial army they are placed under the command of a perfect hierarchy of officers and sergeants. Not only are they slaves of the bourgeois class, and of the bourgeois state; they are daily and hourly enslaved by the machine, by the over-looker, and, above all, by the individual bourgeois manufacturer himself." [19: 16]

The methods for doing this, including heavy reliance upon machinery and division of labor, convert

the labourer into a crippled monstrosity, by forcing his detail dexterity at the expense of a world of productive capabilities and instincts; . . . they mutilate the labourer into a fragment of a man, degrade him to the level of an appendage of a machine, destroy every remnant of charm in his work and turn it into a hated toil; they estrange from him the intellectual potentialities of the labour-process in the same proportion as science is incorporated in it as an independent power; they distort the conditions under which he works, subject him during the labour-process to a despotism the more hateful for its meanness; they transform his life-time into working-time, and drag his wife and child beneath the wheels of the Juggernaut of capital. [16: I, 396, 708]

Capitalism thus increasingly "alienates" the worker from his labor. Instead of being a source of self-realization and fulfillment, work is a social process beyond the worker's control, in which he becomes increasingly the slave rather than the master.

This slavery and degradation is independent of the worker's income position and, because methods of increasing surplus value involve increased investment, as capital accumulates, "the lot of the labourer, be his payment high or low, must grow worse." [16: I, 709] The "slavery" of wage-labor "becomes more severe in proportion as the socially productive forces of labor develop, whether the worker receives better or worse payment." [17: II, 574] The law of the industrial reserve army of the unemployed "rivets the labourer to capital" and "establishes an accumulation of misery, corresponding with accumulation of capital. Accumulation of wealth at one pole is, therefore, at the same time accumulation of misery, agony of toil, slavery, ignorance, brutality, mental degradation, at the opposite pole. . . ." [16: I, 709]

The same techniques which create greater surpluses also increase the burden of the worker's toil: "In proportion as the use of machinery and division of labor increases, in the same proportion the burden of toil also increases, whether by prolongation of the working hours, by increase of the work exacted in a given time, or by increased speed of the machinery." [19: 16] The mechanization of industry under conditions of advancing technology also "renders worthless" old skills, thus decreasing the demand for skilled labor and transforming the labor force into a more or less homogeneous mass of unskilled, uneducated machine-tenders. For many former craftsmen, tradesmen, and skilled workers, this represents a relative or absolute deterioration in real income.

Further, as economic fluctuations become increasingly severe, the variability of wage income also increases, as do uncertainty and insecurity. At any phase of the economic cycle, capital may be substituted for labor. During increasingly severe depressions, real wages fall increasingly below their potential for those employed and to zero for those who become unemployed.

With increased capital accumulation, substitution of capital for labor, and monopolization (which serves to redistribute income from small to large capitalists), the gap in incomes between rich capitalists and poor workers is likely to increase. This prognostication is consistent (a) with an increase in the percent of national income going to all workers as a class, as the size of the labor force increases and the number of capitalists diminishes; (b) with a decrease in the rate of profit, for it is quite possible for the rate of profit to fall as the absolute "mass" of profit rises; and (c) with the possibility of an increase in the absolute level of real wages and/or real wages per workers.[6] The important point is "the abyss between the labourer's position and that of the capitalist would keep widening." [16: I, 573][7]

As capitalism matures, wage rates are likely to fall in two ways: (1) Increased labor productivity leads primarily to a "cheapening of commodities," that is, price decreases (rather than, for example, increases in quality, new products, or leisure), thus lowering the "value of labor power." Insofar as wages are pushed toward subsistence levels, money wages can fall even though real wages in the sense of the "mass of the labourer's means of subsistence" rise; (2) Wages measured in *value* terms, that is, in the socially necessary labor-time embodied in the worker's means of subsistence, decrease.

In addition, if wages tend toward subsistence and "subsistence" shifts downward as capitalism matures because of the decreased demand for skilled labor and the "proletarianization" of small businessmen, then real wages will also exhibit a downward secular trend (though with cyclical fluctuations). In his early writings, Marx termed this a

likely possibility: "Instead of rising with the progress of industry," the "modern labourer ... sinks deeper and deeper below the conditions of existence of his own class. He becomes a pauper, and pauperism develops more rapidly than population and wealth." [19: 21] The position most consistent with his writings, however, is that real wages (1) are "indeterminate," varying with the respective bargaining power of workers and capitalists, or the demand for and supply of labor, and oscillating between "a lower limit vaguely defined in terms of the subsistence level and an upper limit which is not defined at all. . . ." [20: 34]; (2) need not decrease with capitalist development, but are likely to increase little, if at all.

LABOR IMMISERIZATION:
EVALUATION

These predictions about the future position of labor correspond reasonably well to historical developments in the late nineteenth century and the twentieth: the size of the industrial labor force has increased, has become more industrially and geographically concentrated and centralized, and more organized. At times and in varying degrees, social relations between labor and employers may be characterized as antagonistic, even violent. Further, Marx's views on the "alienation" of labor via division of labor and mechanization are challenging, though exaggerated and inaccurately identified with capitalism, rather than with industrialization in general.[8]

In at least two striking ways, however, the forecasts are faulty: First, antagonism neither requires nor necessarily leads to political revolution, and opposition to employers under capitalism neither requires nor supports "socialism" as an alternative to capitalism. It is possible for workers to oppose

---

[6]Marx recognized, but did not emphasize, the possibility "that, owing to an increase of productiveness, both the labourer, and the capitalist may simultaneously be able to appropriate a greater degree of . . . necessaries." [16: I, 573]

[7]Also representative are the following statements: "The position of the classes in relation to each other depends to a greater extent on the proportion which the wage forms than on the absolute amount of the wage." And ". . . assume the most favorable case: if productive capital grows, the demand for labour grows. Consequently, the price of labour, wages, goes up." But the "rapid growth of productive capital brings about an equally rapid growth of wealth, luxury, social needs, social enjoyments. Thus, although the enjoyments of the worker have risen, the social satisfaction that they give has fallen in comparison with the increased enjoyments of the capitalists . . . ." [See 18:230; 17:268, 269.]

[8]For a contemporary critique of these non-economic features of capitalism, see Erich Fromm, *The Sane Society* (New York City: Holt, Rinehart & Winston, Inc., 1955), p. 103ff.

primitive, *laissez-faire* capitalism, support reforms and modifications of capitalism, and, at the same time, be lukewarm toward revolutionary (or non-revolutionary) change to a socialist economy. Though the pattern varies from country to country, dependent in part upon different historical, political, and cultural conditions and experiences, organized labor in industrially developing capitalist economies during the twentieth century has been more concerned with improving its economic position within a (reformed and modified) capitalist framework than with a radical transformation to a new, different post-capitalist ("socialist") economy. This generalization, though more applicable to the labor movement in the Unites States than in Europe, applies with modifications to the European case, as well.

Second, the theory of increased worker immiserization is probably the least satisfactory of the Marxian forecasts. There is a logical problem: The Marxian prediction of a tendency toward a falling rate of profit is based on the assumption that the rate of exploitation, s/v, remains constant as investment in "constant capital" increases. But as Joan Robinson notes, this "proposition stands out in startling contradiction to the rest of Marx's argument. For if the rate of exploitation tends to be constant, real wages tend to rise as productivity increases. Labor receives a constant proportion of an increasing total. Marx can only demonstrate a falling tendency in profit by abandoning his argument that real wages tend to be constant. This drastic inconsistency he seems to have overlooked, for when he is discussing the falling tendency of profits he makes no reference to the rising tendency of real wages which it entails." [20: 36]

More embarrassing, however, is the evidence, notably the dramatic, undeniable increase in real wages over the last century in industrially developing capitalist economies. Of equal significance has been the accompanying increase in leisure and decrease in the length of the average industrial work-week (from about 60–70 hours in the mid-nineteenth century United States to about 40 hours in the mid-twentieth century). Even in relative terms, the Marxian prediction fails, for wages as a percent of national income have increased (though slightly) in economies which Marx considered capitalist. Further, these economies have not exhibited a secular trend toward increasingly severe cyclical or technological unemployment. In addition, labor has become increasingly heterogeneous rather than homogeneous. Unskilled labor as a percent of the labor force has decreased, not increased, with technological advancement, while skilled, managerial, and professional labor has increased. This, coupled with increasing real wage-income, has significantly reduced poverty. Workers generally are no longer poor, and the poor are no longer poor because they are workers. Income inequality—the gap between rich and poor—has decreased in the twentieth-century Western world. The "abyss" has narrowed, not widened.

One could seek to explain these inconsistencies by alleged "extenuating circumstances," that is, that immiserization *would* have increased had it not been for this or that development. This brings us directly to the Marxist-Leninist theory of capitalist-imperialism and colonialism and to the very non-Marxian development of social reforms by Western democratic governments.

Increasing Capitalist Imperialism and Colonial Exploitation

The emergence, development, and maturing of capitalism has important international repercussions. At the beginning, the transition from feudalism to capitalism was encouraged through the stimulus that the exploitation of the New by the Old World gave to "primitive accumulation" and by the expansion of trade and markets during the early-modern period of European exploration and colonization. As capitalism developed, foreign trade played an increasingly important role as a source of cheap food and raw materials, and colonies gained increased economic significance as markets for manufactured goods, places for foreign investment ("capital export"), and sources of cheap labor. All of these activities: (1) tend to raise the rate of profit, indeed, to promote "surplus-profit"; (2) tend to increase capital accumulation and the organic composition of capital, and thus, to lower the rate of profit. Foreign trade, though temporarily alleviating the tendency toward a falling rate of profit, does not eliminate capitalism's contradictions. It "only transfers" them "to a wider sphere and gives them a greater latitude." [16: II, 546]

As capitalism matures, according to post-Marxian Marxists Rudolf Hilferding and V. I. Lenin, special features of its maturity impel it toward even greater economic and political-military penetration and control of underdeveloped, pre-capitalist countries. Of course, argued Lenin, there "was a colonial policy and an imperialism before the modern phase of capitalism, and even before capitalism. Rome, founded on slavery, carried out a colonial policy and gave effect to imperialism. . . . But capitalism only became capitalist imperialism at a definite and very high stage of its development." Imperialism "undeniably represents a particular phase of capitalist development." It "emerged as the development and direct continuation of the essential qualities of capitalism in general." [15: 65, 71, 72]

The major components of the Neo-Marxist theory of imperialism may be summarized in the following manner: (1) As capitalism matures, its internal economic contradictions and problems induce increased economic penetration of underdeveloped economies, particularly in the area of foreign investment, both "portfolio" (especially government bonds) and "direct" (especially mining and the exploitation of raw materials). First, increased monopolization encourages the seeking of foreign investment outlets. Second, the intensification of long-run trends toward decreased rates of profit

and under-consumption encourage a movement of investment to underdeveloped areas, where labor and raw materials are cheap and profit rates high. Third, competitive rivalry among mature capitalist economies intensifies the economic imperialism of all. [15: 299–307] (As a parenthetical corollary to this first point, the same three factors lead to the abandonment of international free trade and the expansion of tariffs and other devices to protect the home market for domestic monopoly-capitalists.)

(2) The desire of monopoly-capitalists to secure their investments and to guarantee them against both the encroachments of rival capitalists of other countries and the hostility of native populations leads to capitalists' pressure upon their governments to protect their economic interests by territorial conquest and annexation. Thus, economic imperialism leads to political-military imperialism.

(3) Temporarily, imperialism moderates the internal economic contradictions of mature capitalist economies and postpones their inevitable collapses. The "extortion of super-profits from their world-dependencies enables the monopolists to. . . . bribe the proletarized masses, or at least their influential higher layers, into acquiescence."[9] These super-profits from imperial exploitation enable *both* wages and profits to rise. Thus, increasing misery, in the sense of lower real wages, is avoided, and the proletariat of the industrialized countries, corrupted by these gains and by the international rivalries among capitalist powers, in effect joins with domestic monopoly-capitalists in the exploitation of underdeveloped economies.

(4) Imperialism postpones but cannot eliminate mature capitalism's contradictions and impending demise. There are *limits* to imperialism: First, when capital export to underdeveloped economies has increased sufficiently to create a global capitalism, with

---

[9] Alfred G. Meyer, *Leninism*, (Cambridge, Massachusetts: Harvard University Press, 1957), p. 245.

equalized profit rates, further capital accumulation re-opens in expanded and extended form the old economic problems and contradictions. Second, the misery and exploitation of underdeveloped economies increase their hostility against the colonial powers and provide the seedbed for their eventual revolt. Third, the competitive rivalry of advanced capitalist countries for the control of the underdeveloped areas leads to hostility and, at times, open and increasingly severe warfare. International economic crisis. Revolt. War. These are the catalysts of capitalism's final hours.

Pertinent here is not the international dynamism and economic expansionism of industrialized economies of the Western world in the late nineteenth and early twentieth centuries, nor the political-military expansion and empire-building which accompanied them. Nor are we concerned with the appealing but inaccurate hypothesis that the former was the prime *cause* of the latter. Students of economics are admonished to avoid confusing *correlation* with *causation*. Our concern, rather, is with the limitations of a theory which explains the economic penetration of underdeveloped economies by industrialized economies on the basis of nonexistent or exaggerated trends (such as increasing monopolization, increasingly severe cyclical fluctuations, increasing underconsumption, or increasing worker misery) in the industrialized economies, and then explains the absence or postponement of these trends by reference to this economic penetration. A simpler, more direct route would be to argue the dynamism and economic growth of the Western world enabled Western capitalists to take advantage of what appeared to them to be profitable investment opportunities in the underdeveloped economies. Of course, no one knows what would have happened to the internal economic viability of Western countries *if* they had not been internationally dynamic and expansionist. But to explain the complex phenomenon of imperialism exclusively or primarily by the

alleged increasing contradictions of capitalism *and* the dynamics of capitalist expansion exclusively or primarily by the Leninist theory of imperialism is not convincing.

Increasing State Oppression and
Improbability of Genuine Social
Reform

An important feature in the historical development of Western economies since the time of Karl Marx has been the spread of political democracy and the utilization of democratic governments as institutional vehicles for the social and economic reform of capitalism. A non-Marxian critic of classic nineteenth-century capitalism might be tempted to term this development, in part, as another "extenuating circumstance" to the limitations of the Marxian forecasts of capitalist development. Increased monopolization; increased cyclical severity; increased immiserization: All of these *might* have occurred as Marx predicted had it not been for the economic reforms of democratic governments.

This is an untestable hypothesis. No one knows what might have happened in the absence of democratic economic reform because democratic economic reform has *not* been absent from the contemporary political and economic history of the Western world. The important point here is this hypothesis is not available to Marxists, for, in their view, *genuine* social reform would require the *elimination* of the *source* of capitalist exploitation—private property in industrial capital—and neither capitalists nor the capitalist-dominated "democratic" state are willing to do so.

Democracy cannot reform capitalism, in the orthodox Marxian view, because the democratic state, like all states, is controlled not by the citizens, but by the economically dominant social class—in capitalism, the bourgeoisie. The "public power of coercion," which is the identifying characteristic of the state, is used to maintain and protect the property relations that are the basis of class exploitation. In short, the state is an instrument whereby the dominant, property-owning class in society guarantees its monopoly position in the ownership of property and, thereby, the continuity of its dominance.

"The modern representative state," wrote Engels, is no exception to this rule: It "is the instrument of the exploitation of wage-labour by capital" and its power as an agency of oppression "grows stronger. . . . in proportion as the class antagonisms within the state grows sharper."[10] Its "executive," he argued, in collaboration with Marx, "is but a committee for managing the common affairs of the whole bourgeoisie." [19: 11] The trappings of modern democracies, such as bills of rights, legislative debates, and elections are but shrewd devices designed to conceal the absence of real (economic) freedom and democracy. As long as competing political parties accept the dominant economic and political position of the capitalist class, their divergences are inconsequential, and universal suffrage merely gives people the right to decide "once in every three or six years which member of the ruling class is to misrepresent them in Parliament."[11]

One important consequence of this view of the state and modern representative democracy is to deny the economy can be effectively controlled, modified, or reformed by governmental action. This does not mean the state does nothing in the field of economic reform: First, capitalists may discover the long-run continuity of the system of wage-labor requires short-run reforms, as, for example, factory legislation and maximum working hours. Second, faced with the threat of revolution, capitalists will throw concessions to workers as temporary palliatives to their revolutionary fervor. Third, in their struggle with the landed feudal aristocracy, capitalists may appeal for worker support by promising (and sometimes fulfilling) minor economic reforms. All three of these examples satisfy the double criteria that their enactment (1) is necessary to establish or maintain the stability and continuity of the capitalist system (that is, that their non-enactment might seriously threaten the system's stability and continuity) and (2) involves minor modifications at the fringes of capitalist organization, but does not seriously threaten the basis of its existence.

If this is true, it follows that genuine social reform is not attainable under capitalism and requires the establishment of a new, totally different post-capitalist economy. Capitalists voluntarily will never permit the "democratic" state to be utilized as a device for eliminating capitalism. Yet capitalism is historically transient: It cannot survive. How, then, does capitalism finally expire?

THE END OF CAPITALISM: MARX'S APOCALYPTIC VISION

Increasing state oppression and imperialist exploitation to the contrary, capitalism cannot avoid its inexorable demise. The historical end of capitalism as an economic system can be best understood and foreseen in terms of the qualitative changes which occur as capitalism matures. Increasing monopolization, cyclical severity, immiserization: All of these indicate a system which is either in the process of decay or inviting its revolutionary demise. In either event, capitalism eventually loses its dynamism and becomes, in effect, a "fetter" upon the continued expansion of the productive forces of society. At this point, capitalism ceases to function effectively as an economic system. Marx's description of this process reads like an apocalyptic vision:

Along with the constantly diminishing number of the magnates of capital, who usurp and monopolise all advantages of

---

[10]Fredrick Engels, *The Origin of the Family, Private Property, and the State*, in Emile Burns, *Handbook of Marxism* (New York City: International Publishers, 1935), pp. 329, 330.

[11]Karl Marx, *The Civil War in France:* cited in R. N. Carew Hunt, *The Theory and Practice of Communism* (New York City: The Macmillan Company, Publishers, 1951), p. 72.

this process of transformation, grows the mass of misery, oppression, slavery, degradation, exploitation; but with this too grows the revolt of the working-class, a class always increasing in numbers, and disciplined, united, organised by the very mechanism of the process of capitalist production itself. The monopoly of capital becomes a fetter upon the mode of production, which has sprung up and flourished along with, and under it. Centralisation of the means of production and socialisation of labour at last reach a point where they become incompatible with their capitalist integument. This integument is burst asunder. The knell of capitalist private property sounds. The expropriators are expropriated. [16: I, 836–37]

Marx has been criticized for lack of clarity and specificity about the details of capitalism's demise. The real issue is the validity of the Marxian theory of capitalist development. *If* the Marxian predictions are true, and if genuine social reform is improbable, then it would be reasonable to assert that mature capitalism is in a process of disintegration and/or approaching revolution. *If* the opposite were true, then such an assertion would not appear reasonable.

Throughout this and the preceding chapter, reservations, qualifications, and criticisms of the Marxian analysis and vision of capitalism have been made. Perhaps the best vehicle for systematically evaluating the Marxian critique is an examination of the two major post-Marxian, twentieth-century theories of capitalism, both in their own ways answering various dimensions of the Marxian critique. These two theories are provided by Joseph A. Schumpeter and John Maynard Keynes.

6

The Schumpeterian Theory
of Capitalist Development

WHAT IS SCHUMPETERIAN CAPITALISM?

Competitive market capitalism, as noted, may be studied as a theoretical economic system, an actual economic system, and/or a movement for economic reform. Marxism was both a theoretical analysis of capitalism and, incidentally, socialism, and a socio-economic reform (revolutionary) movement. Schumpeterian capitalism is more distinctly and purely intellectual and analytical. Austro-American economist Joseph Schumpeter (1883–1950) spent the greater part of his life in the *analysis* of capitalism as an economic system.[1] He drew a sharp distinction between scientific analysis (with which he was primarily concerned) and critical appraisal and proposals for public policy and economic reform. Since rigorous concern with logic, fact, and cause-and-effect, coupled with abstention from moral evaluation and recommendations for solving pressing short-run problems, do not generally arouse public interest, Schumpeter's powerful and penetrating analysis of capitalism is little known outside the ranks of professional economists.[2]

The Schumpeterian concept of capitalism is essentially that identified in Chapter 2. It includes private property in the means of production and regulation of the productive process by private contract; bank credit creation; the application of the "rational attitude" via quantitative monetary measurement to human behavior, including business decision; freedom of individual economic choice; the price system as a social process for coordinating economic decisions; limited government; and inequality in the distribution of income. It should be emphasized that, in contrast to early nineteenth-century classical economists who were studying a relatively underdeveloped economy, stressing atomistic, small-scale competitive industry, Schumpeter was concerned with an industrially and technologically developing capitalism, including the possibility of significant sectors of

---

[1] His major works include *The Theory of Economic Development* (Cambridge, Mass.: Harvard University Press, 1934), *Business Cycles* (New York City: McGraw-Hill Book Company, 1939), *Capitalism, Socialism and Democracy* (New York City: Harper & Row, Publishers, 1950), and *History of Economic Analysis* (Fair Lawn, New Jersey: Oxford University Press, Inc., 1954). See also: Clemence, editor, *Essays of J. A. Schumpeter* (Cambridge, Mass.: Addison-Wesley, 1951); Clemence and Doody, editors, *The Schumpeterian System* (Cambridge, Mass.: Addison-Wesley, 1950); and Harris, editor, *Schumpeter: Social Scientist* (Cambridge, Mass.: Harvard University Press, 1955).

[2] Indeed, state Clemence and Doody [12: 2], even among professional economists, in "recent years the Schumpeterian System has been the object of an interest amounting nearly to apathy."

industrial oligopoly and monopoly. Also, in contrast to the Keynesian analysis, Schumpeter dealt primarily with a relatively "unfettered, unreformed," late nineteenth- and early twentieth-century capitalism. The modified or (in Schumpeter's words) "laborist capitalism" of the New Deal and beyond is, he argued, a "moveable halfway house" which differs significantly from the principles of old-style, relatively unregulated "*laissez-faire* capitalism" and which "differs but little from genuinely socialist planning."

"Capitalism does not merely mean that the housewife may influence production by her choice between peas and beans; or that the youngster may choose whether he wants to work in a factory or on a farm; or that plant managers have some voice in deciding what and how to produce; it means a scheme of values, an attitude toward life, a civilization—the civilization of inequality and the family fortune." [8: 418–19]

As a body of economic analysis and an economic theory of capitalism, the "Shumpeterian System" draws upon both the central tradition in economic thought and Marxism. In the preface to the Japanese edition of his book, *The Theory of Economic Development*, Schumpeter emphasized (1) the influence upon his analysis of the concepts and writings of Leon Walras, a prominent member of the central tradition—especially Walras' "concept of the economic system" and his "theoretical apparatus which . . . effectively embraced the pure logic of the interdependence between economic quantities"—and (2) the similarity between his analysis and a basic idea in Marx's economics: "a vision of economic evolution as a distinct process generated by the economic system itself." [11: 159, 160]

Schumpeter divided these central ideas about economic processes "into three different classes: . . . the (allocational and distributional) processes of the circular flow, those of development (and accompanying growth), and . . . those (cyclical fluctuations) which impede the latter's undisturbed

course." [23: 218] In *Capitalism, Socialism, and Democracy*, this economic model was supplemented by political, sociological, and psychological insights which, with his economic analysis, provided a basis for provocative forecasts of future prospects for capitalism, as well as some interesting observations on the economics and politics of socialism.

ALLOCATIONAL AND DISTRIBUTIONAL PROCESSES OF THE STATIC AND STATIONARY CIRCULAR FLOW

"The essential point to grasp," argued Schumpeter, "is that in dealing with capitalism we are dealing with an evolutionary process. . . . Capitalism . . . is by nature a form or method of economic change and not only never is but never can be stationary." [8: 82] However, Schumpeter starts his analysis of the dynamism of capitalism with a summary of the stationary process of the circular flow under conditions of static, general equilibrium.[3] This excursion into the static and stationary preparatory to a study of the dynamic and evolutionary is justified by Schumpeter on four counts: first, as a simplified model of the "bare bones of economic logic" of the economic system as a whole to serve as a point of departure—a sort of general map of what the capitalist economy would be like in the absence of its

_____
[3]Schumpeter identified and distinguished between "static" and "stationary" in the preface to the Japanese edition of *The Theory of Economic Development*. "A static theory is simply a statement of the conditions of equilibrium and of the way in which equilibrium tends to re-establish itself after every small disturbance. Such a theory can be useful in the investigation of any kind of reality, however disequilibrated it may be. A stationary process, however, is a process which *actually* does not change of its own initiative, but merely reproduces constant rates of real income as it flows along in time. If it changes at all, it does so under the influence of events which are external to itself, such as natural catastrophes, wars and so on." [11: 159]

dynamism; second, the equilibrium concept is a useful analytical device for assessing the response of an economic system to change; third, since deviations from equilibrium may be compared with equilibrium positions, the concept serves as a "point of reference"; fourth, and most important analytically and historically, it is possible "to distinguish definite periods in which the system embarks upon an excursion away from equilibrium and equally definite periods in which it draws toward equilibrium." In short, within the process of dynamic economic change, there are periods where, within broad ranges or "neighborhoods," equilibrium conditions are fulfilled approximately. [22: I, 68–71]

In the absence of the dynamic changes Schumpeter called "economic development," the competitive economy would tend to settle into the routine of the circular flow in static and stationary "general equilibrium." On product markets, a flow of money would exchange for (consumption and investment) goods. On resource markets, a flow of (natural and human) resources would exchange for money. Demand for would be equal to supply of goods and resources on each product and resource market; given market prices, consumers, businesses, and resource owners would adjust their quantities demanded and supplied until they had reached positions of individual equilibrium, that is, where they had exhausted all opportunities for further augmentation of economic gain or diminution of economic loss.

Because an excess of revenue over cost would attract the entry of new firms (raising supply and lowering price), and because an excess of cost over revenue would cause the exit of old firms (decreasing supply and raising price), equilibrium would be consistent with only the "normal profits" included within the concept of ("opportunity") cost. All economic or pure profits, all "surplus values," would disappear; with their disappearance, the capacity to pay interest on the creation of demand deposits by commercial banks also would disappear. Individual "risks," of course, would exist, both of technical and commercial failure. But these could be met by insurance, by including risk premiums as costs, or by shifting resources from higher to lower risk sectors of the economy, and would provide no basis for pure profit or interest.

Resources would be allocated in this hypothetical competitive capitalism according to the market-revealed preferences of sovereign consumers. Income would be distributed according to the market value of the marginal product of the two basic resources, land and labor, in the form of rents and wages (capital being resolved into land and labor). Pure profits (and thus, interest) in the sense of an excess of revenue over cost of land and labor would disappear, as noted.

Gross investment would be equal to depreciation and production to consumption; because all resource markets are in equilibrium, stability and full employment utilization of resources would be jointly attained. In a stable, full employment economy, with no disruptions from economic development, money would have value "only as a medium of exchange," that is, building up money balances because of pessimism about an uncertain future would have no relevance. Money could be transferred in exchange for financial assets and property, of course, and individuals could engage in consumption loans. But there would be no basis for the creation of new money in the form of demand deposits by commercial banks, and its investment in new investment projects (and thus, also no basis for economic instability resulting from the credit creation and net investment process).

In such a general equilibrium system, there would be no leaders, directors, nor initiators, except insofar as consumers could be termed "leaders." Businessmen would react more or less passively to market demand and cost conditions, combining land and labor in a routinized, mechanical fashion, making no special contributions other than that of superintendence, and receiving no special income beyond wages and rents for their own labor and land.

The tendency of a competitive capitalist economy, in the absence of economic development, to move toward such a position of stationary general equilibrium does not imply the absence of *all* change: First, equilibrium, given underlying data (technology, consumer tastes, and supplies of resources), is a position toward which the economy is moving, not necessarily a position which has been firmly attained. Second, marginal changes may occur in underlying data, to which the economic system then adjusts—that is, the economy strives toward equilibrium, but the equilibrium position shifts with changes in tastes, technology, and so on. Third, stable equilibrium is consistent with economic growth in the sense of a long-run trend of slow, small-scale, continuous changes in population, savings, and capital accumulation. "Stable economic growth," depicted by curve GG in Fig. 6.1, involves expansion—but only in the sense of marginal, quantitative changes, calling forth "no qualitatively new phenomena, but only processes of adaption . . . " [23: 63] similar to those of adjusting to changes in consumer tastes and other "external data."

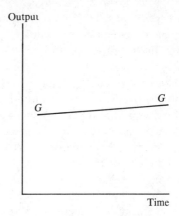

Fig. 6.1. Economic growth

work of the economy, which fundamentally displace the old equilibrium positions, creating new, different conditions. Economic development in this sense is accompanied by growth, that is, by a sustained upward movement in national income, saving, and population. But economic growth does not constitute development: "Add successively as many mail coaches as you please," said Schumpeter, "you will never get a railway thereby." [23: 64n]

Innovation

The central, essential ingredient in economic development in the Schumpeterian analysis is *innovation*, defined as the commercial or industrial application of something new—a new product, process or method of production, a new market or source of supply, a new form of commercial, business, or financial organization—a shift to new combinations of existing productive resources, to new, different production functions, or to new (and lower) cost curves. Innovation thus is to be distinguished from "invention" (even where inventor and innovator are the same person), especially when invention is restricted to new ideas of a mechanical or technical nature. Innovation involves the (1) commercial application of (2) any new idea. And it has been innovation, not invention, argued Schumpeter, which has

SOURCES OF CAPITALIST ECONOMIC DEVELOPMENT

The Concept of Economic Development

Economic development, argued Schumpeter, is the key to understanding capitalist economy. And economic development, in contrast to economic growth, has three salient characteristics: It comes from *within* the economic system and is not merely an adaptation to changes in external data. It occurs *discontinuously*, in spurts, rather than smoothly and continuously. It brings *qualitative* changes or "revolutions" in the frame-

been the central cause of economic expansion and change in capitalist economies in the nineteenth and twentieth centuries.

The big changes and innovations of the last 200 years, noted Schumpeter, for example, those associated with railroadization in the nineteenth and the development of the automobile in the twentieth centuries, have generally emerged from the commercial and industrial sectors of the economy, not from the "sovereign consumer" of classical and neoclassical economic theory. Especially during the era of "competitive capitalism" in the nineteenth century, these industrial and commercial innovations were embodied in new business firms by new business leaders via a revolutionary process summed up as "creative destruction," that is, where the creativity of the new commodity, market, or source of supply supplanted or destroyed the old. These new combinations, he added, take place as a rule by redirection of the employment of existing resources, not by the employment of formerly unemployed or underutilized resources.

Financing of Innovations

The commercial application of a new idea, involving the acquisition and redirection of the employment of existing means of production, must be financed—and it cannot be financed from the revenues received in the static, stationary circular flow, because these are just sufficient to cover existing costs and depreciation. They are not sufficient and not generally available for the daring experiments involved in shifting to new ways of doing things, especially when these new ideas involve (as they customarily do) new net investment beyond replacement requirements. Innovations, both logically and historically, must be financed by turning to a source of credit above and beyond the circular flow, namely, the commercial bank, the only private financial institution in the capitalist economy with the unique function and power of creating and lending new money, new

purchasing power over and above current saving out of current income.

Innovation thus is distinguishable from the financing of the innovation, and the innovator or "entrepreneur" distinguishable from the *capitalist* (defined "as the owner of money, claims to money, or material goods"), [23:75] even when, coincidentally, they happen to be one and the same person. The innovator-entrepreneur must convince the capitalist that the higher revenues and/or lower costs stemming from his innovation will enable him to pay both principal and interest on the loan. The innovator must convince himself that the profits expected from the innovation will be sufficient to do this *and* leave a net or pure profit for him. Thus, credit creation is a necessary but not, by itself, sufficient condition for economic development in a capitalist economy.

The Entrepreneur

The provision of credit by capitalists to entrepreneurs to finance innovations is a vital function in a capitalist economy, indeed, "important enough to serve as its *differentia specifica*." [23:69] But the linchpin of economic development, according to Schumpeter, is the "carrying out of new combinations," the putting into practice of the new ideas by entrepreneurs. These entrepreneurs are distinguishable not only from inventors and capitalists, but from businessmen-managers as well. Entrepreneurship is broader than business management because not all entrepreneurs operate established businesses. It is narrower than business management because not all managers, immersed as they are in the routine calculations of the circular flow, engage in entrepreneurial activities, that is, innovations.

Putting new ideas into practice is a special sociological and economic function, argued Schumpeter, and those individuals who have the unique qualities to do new things constitute a special sociological type. Innovation faces immense difficulties. First, the knowledge necessary for entrepreneurial decisions lies outside the known and accurate data of the circular flow and thus is shrouded in a haze of uncertainty and guesswork. Second, objective uncertainty is compounded by subjective reluctance of individuals to strike out into the unknown. Third is the antagonism and hostility of conformistic, non-innovators to the pioneer—in the form of legal and political obstacles, social mores, customs, and the like.

It takes a special kind of person to overcome these difficulties. In contrast to the "economic man," who carefully calculates marginal costs and revenues of alternative courses of action on the basis of known or reasonably accurate data, the entrepreneur must be a man of "vision," of daring, willing to take chances, to strike out, largely on the basis of intuition, on courses of action in direct opposition to the established, settled patterns of the circular flow. The entrepreneur is more of an "heroic" than an "economic" figure: He must have "the drive and the will to found a private kingdom" as a "captain of industry"; the "will to conquer," to fight for the sake of the fight rather than simply the financial gains of the combat; the desire to create new things—even at the expense of destroying old patterns of thought and action. In any society, including capitalism, said Schumpeter, such people are in the minority. [23: 74–94]

ECONOMIC FLUCTUATIONS

In the Marxian analysis, economic growth brings instability and instability is inherent in the process of growth in a capitalist economy. In the Schumpeterian analysis, economic development is embodied in the process of cyclical fluctuations, which, in turn, brings economic growth.

Schumpeter's analysis of cyclical economic fluctuations involved three stages or "approximations." The second and third models represent attempts to more closely approxi-

mate the complexities of reality by incorporating various elements to supplement the basic model in the first approximation. But the first approximation is useful because it isolates, in skeletal form, the most essential elements in cycles in the absence of the "innumerable layers of secondary, incidental, accidental and 'external' fact and reactions" that "cover the skeleton of economic life, sometimes so as to hide it entirely." [22: I, 137]

The First Approximation: A Two-Phase Cycle

If the innovations that constitute the key to economic development, and the capital investment in which innovations are embodied, appeared smoothly and continuously, that is, were evenly distributed through time, their absorption by the economic system could also proceed smoothly, continuously, and non-cyclically. But capitalist economic development proceeds via a cyclical, unstabilizing process, one which, in the first approximation, is *not* an aberration or economic sickness, but a normal, necessary element in development.

The basic reason economic development proceeds cyclically is that "capital investment is not distributed evenly in time but appears *en masse* at intervals." Investment occurs in large chunks at separate intervals because the innovations embodied in the new investments appear "discontinuously in groups or swarms." Innovations tend to cluster "because the appearance of one or a few entrepreneurs facilitates the appearance of others, and these, the appearance of more, in ever-increasing numbers" [23: 215, 223, 228] though not without limits. Once an innovation is successfully carried out by a pioneering entrepreneur, a herd of others will follow suit, not only in the entrepreneur's industry, but in others as well. Railroadization, for example, encouraged innovation and investment in the steel industry. The development of the automobile industry brought revolutionary developments in glass, rubber, petroleum, highway construction, filling stations, and so forth.

In sum, the placidity of the circular flow under general equilibrium conditions is disturbed by a clustering of innovations embodied in new investment, financed by bank credit, that is, by an excess of *ex ante* investment over *ex ante* saving. The expansion of monetary expenditures by entrepreneurs and the necessity of enticing the reallocation of resources to the innovating firms and industries causes increases in resource prices and thus costs. Increased expenditures by entrepreneurs plus increased purchases by resource owners who have received increased income cause rising prices. In a full employment economy, the expansion or prosperity phase of the economic cycle is characterized by inflation and a shift of resources from the production of consumption to investment goods. The monetary value of the output increases, but the aggregate level of real output remains the same.

But this investment-innovational boom, the monetary expansion financing it, and the price inflation accompanying it cannot continue unchecked: First, profits are squeezed by rising resource prices; second, after a period of "gestation," new products come into competition with old ones, bringing lower prices; third, the profit squeeze is aggravated by the payment by entrepreneurs of bank debt. This "liquidation" and resulting "credit deflation," are not likely to be offset by increased borrowing and investment by other entrepreneurs: Profitable investment opportunities are "definitely limited" to specific industrial sectors, not distributed indiscriminately throughout the entire economy. Continued new net investment is further discouraged by the profit squeeze and the uncertainties accompanying the expansionary movement away from equilibrium, which makes "accurate calculation impossible. . . especially for the planning of new enterprises." [23: 235–36]. The result is a downturn in investment, entrepreneurial activity, and industrial production, leading to decreased demand for resources, decreased employment, decreased money income, decreased demand for consumption goods, and so on through a mutually-reinforcing, cumulative contractionary movement gripping the entire economic system.

Though the contractionary phase of the economic cycle brings "discomfort," economic losses, and gloom to key investment-innovational sectors of the economy, it has two "cheerful sides to it": First, the recession is a process of absorption of the spurts of innovation, a period of incorporation of the new ideas, and a movement toward a new equilibrium position from which a new burst of developmental innovations may take place. (See Fig. 6.2.) Second, recession "fulfills what the boom promised" by enriching and enlarging the "stream of goods", by forcing reorganization of production and weeding out inefficient producers, and by lowering real costs of production. [8: 242–45] In sum: (1) The cause of recession, in the Schumpeterian analysis, is prosperity. If we want prosperity, we must accept the recession which necessarily and normally succeeds it. (2) Recession, in the first approximation, is not a malignancy. Despite its temporary discomforts, it performs a vital economic function and makes an important contribution to economic welfare.

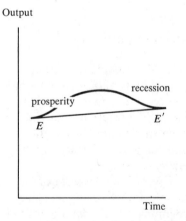

Fig. 6.2. The business cycle: first approximation

Cyclical economic fluctuations are much more complicated than the two-phase "primary wave" of this simplified innovational model. Schumpeter recognized some of these supplementary complicating features in his second approximation. The expansionary force of the prosperity may be hightened and enlarged by a variety of factors, including: increased investment and production by old firms stimulated by, and thus, dependent on, the continuance of increased consumer demand; increased borrowing to finance "speculative" ventures whose profitability depends not on the initial innovation, but on the expectation of rising prices; increased consumer borrowing and spending; "errors" and "excesses of optimism," "reckless enterprise," and the like. Result: A super-boom or secondary wave of expansion, built on top of, but often surpassing in amplitude, the underlying innovational expansion (see Fig. 6.3), a speculative, spurious prosperity, driven largely by subjective feelings which diverge increasingly from underlying objective realities.

The downturn from this speculative super-boom is caused by the same forces bringing readjustment in the first approxima-

tion. Once the force of the primary wave of innovational investment has been spent, the unproductive, unprofitable, and over-extended ventures crumble. The ensuring contraction will then involve more than a normal, necessary recessionary adjustment to and absorption of the innovations of the prosperity and will overshoot the "neighborhood of equilibrium," dropping into a major, severe, and "abnormal" depression. Liquidation and adjustment to a super-boom clearly will be greater than in the first approximation. In addition, the contraction may descend into a "vicious spiral" of decreased credit, decreased prices, and increased liquidation, heightened by speculative contractions in spending and errors of pessimism, perhaps even financial "panic" or "crisis." These developments during deep, protracted depressions "are pathological in the sense that they play no indispensable role in the capitalist process, which would be logically complete without them." [12: 13]

Because they are abnormal deviations from the logic of the capitalist process and depend on reactions to specific maladjustments, "no *theoretical* expectation can be formed about the occurrence and severity of depressions." [22: I, 150] Indeed, the vicious spiral in deep depressions conceivably may be so powerful that the system may never recover by itself and may require assistance from some external agent like government action or a random favorable event.

Restorative forces at work during the depression, however, often are strong enough to bring about a decrease in the rate of contraction, and thus, movement towards a depressionary trough or bottom point. One is the "diffusion or dilution of effects" as liquidations and bankruptcies spread, but at a slower rate throughout the system. Another is "depression business"—opportunities opened up for some producers with the bankruptcy of others. A third is the existence of incomes "insensitive to depression" (fixed income receivers) creating the result that income contracts by less than real output,

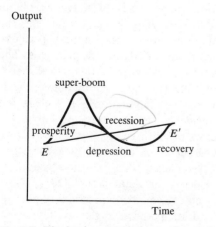

Fig. 6.3. The business cycle: secondary waves

and consumption expenditures by less than wages and salaries.

Recovery or revival, following an upturn from depression, is the last phase of the cycle and consists of a movement back toward equilibrium. (Schumpeter was insistent that cycles, each an "historic individual," should be counted from one equilibrium position to another, and not from peak to peak or trough to trough.) Presumably, the same restorative forces at work during depression assist the process of recovery. In addition, plant and equipment wear out and presumably must be replaced even to maintain existing output. Schumpeter observed that it "is easy... to show that recovery will necessarily set in if the depressive process stops (in practice it is sufficient that it slackens perceptibly)." [22: I, 152] The key point is that the forces of recovery are not powerful enough or qualitatively disruptive enough to generate another prosperity. Recovery is, rather, a period when the system limps and feels its way back to an equilibrium position, where the conditions exist from which a new burst of innovational investment can create another prosperity and another movement away from equilibrium. (Cf. Fig. 6.3.)

Third Approximation: Different and Simultaneous Cycles

Schumpeter's first and second approximations are constructed "as if" there were such a phenomenon as "the" economic cycle. Arguing that neither statistical-historical evidence nor the logic of economic theory supports such a contention, Schumpeter moved in his third approximation to a much lower level of abstraction by recognizing that economic cycles come in a wide variety of forms, with significant differences in length and amplitude. Indeed, the innovational model suggests a multicycle hypothesis: First, innovations come in different sizes, and thus, presumably would require different gestation and absorption periods. Second, innovations may be carried out in a series

of interdependent steps, each of which constitutes a cycle, but all of which together have a "family likeness." Third, cycles may come in sequences as a result of interdependent innovations in different industries which, added together, involve more fundamental structural change than that involved in any one cycle—for example, the clustering of superimposed cycles of various lengths "known as the Industrial Revolution."

Partly for expositional purposes and conceived more as a rough guideline for research than a developed general theory, Schumpeter distinguished among short, medium, and long cycles, or, in honor of their "discoverers," the 3–4 year "Kitchen," the 9–10 year "Juglar," and the 54–60 year "Kondratieff." Schumpeter dated the first long-wave Kondratieff from the 1780s to 1842, the second from 1842 to 1897, and the third from 1898 to the end of the 1930s. The first of these long-waves he associated with the "industrial revolution," the second, with railroadization, the third, with a broader set of innovations in the chemical, electric power, and automobile industries. The key to the Kondratieff is not a cyclical movement in the absolute level of aggregate real output, but, rather, a large-scale clustering or sequence of innovations, the appearance and absorption of which require a half-century or more.

Within the long-wave Kondratieffs appear innovational cycles of a less revolutionary order of magnitude, requiring shorter gestation and absorption periods—the Juglars and, perhaps, the Kitchens. Though there is no general, theoretical basis for expecting any rigid relation among the different kinds of fluctuations, "it is clear that the coincidence at any time of corresponding phases of all three cycles will always produce phenomena of unusual intensity, especially if the phases that coincide are those of prosperity or depression." [22: I, 173] The coincidence of the depressionary phases of a Kondratieff and a Juglar cycle, as, for example, in the 1870s and the 1930s, can produce exceptionally long, severe depressions, whereas Juglar depressions during a long-wave Kondratieff upswing, as, for example, between 1898 and the 1920s, are apt to be relatively short and mild.

ECONOMIC GROWTH

Out of the process of capitalist cyclical development comes economic growth, that is, a sustained upward movement in the aggregate level of economic activity, as measured by real output or real output per capita. This is illustrated in Figs. 6.2 and 6.3, where each new equilibrium position is (normally) higher than the preceding one, despite (or, because of) the intervening period(s) of recession (and depression). In sum, given a favorable social climate, the expectation of pure economic profits plus the tendency of initial success to bring imitation entices periodical upsurges in investment, financed by bank credit. The increased investment embodies the innovational activity, that is, the resource discoveries, technological improvements, market reorganizations, and so forth, which (though supplemented by secondary effects and disrupted temporarily by cyclical processes of adaptation) cause a sustained upward movement in real output, income, and its components, including real wages. Accompanying the upward increase in real output will be long-run upward trends in population, labor force, savings, and capital accumulation. But these are the results, not the basic causes, of economic development.

CAPITALISM'S PAST
PERFORMANCE AND FUTURE
PROSPECTS

The Record of the Past

Schumpeter painted a glowing picture of capitalism's past performance in his *Capitalism, Socialism and Democracy*. First was the economic growth which has resulted from capitalist development: the secular increase in total real output and real output per capita, supplemented by increases in the less tangible factors of increased leisure and quality of output.

Second, though the structure of income distribution, both personal and functional, "has not greatly changed ... expressed in terms of money" during the sixty-year period from 1870 to 1930, it has "substantially changed in favor of the lower income groups" measured "in real terms. ... This follows from the fact that the capitalist engine is first and last an engine of mass production which unavoidably means also production for the masses, whereas, climbing upward in the scale of individual incomes, we find that an increasing proportion is being spent on personal services and on handmade commodities, the prices of which are largely a function of wage rates." The "typical achievements of capitalist production" do not consist, to paraphrase Schumpeter, in more candles for Madame de Pompadour's ball or more silk stockings for Queen Elizabeth, but in the electrification of cities and continents and in low-cost nylons for working girls. If "we look at those avalanches of consumers' goods" from capitalism's past innovational revolutions, we "find that each of them consists in articles of mass consumption and increases the purchasing power of the wage dollar more than that of any other dollar— in other words, that the capitalist process, not by coincidence but by virtue of its mechanism, progressively raises the standard of life of the masses." [8: 67–68]

Third, and often neglected in a balance sheet of capitalism's past achievements, is the social legislation and reform not only made possible by the wealth accumulated from capitalist development, but often financed and proposed by capitalists. Last, insisted Schumpeter, capitalist development has been accompanied by and has assisted in the creation of a variety of non-economic benefits and characteristics of Western civilization, including the emphasis on logic and rationality, experimental science, personal freedom and democracy, even peace. In sum: "Not only the modern mechanized plant and the volume of the output that pours forth from it, not only modern technology and economic organization, but all the features and achievements of modern civilization are, directly or indirectly, the products of the capitalist process. They must be included in any balance sheet of it and in any verdict about its deeds or misdeeds." [8: 125]

The Promise of the Future

Suppose, said Schumpeter, capitalism were to continue to perform (in the United States) for another fifty years, starting in 1928, as it has in the past. Then, among other things, real output per capita could reasonably be expected to at least double, thus doing "away with anything that according to present standards could be called poverty, even in the lowest strata of the population...." In addition, all the programs of the social reformers, including care for the aged and the sick, education, "ample provision for the unemployed," and numerous other governmental functions "either would be fulfilled automatically or could be fulfilled *without significant interference with the capitalist process.*" [8: 66, 69] Indeed, for the United States, "the promise is not only spectacular but immediate.... *In the United States alone there need not lurk, behind modern programs of social betterment, that fundamental dilemma that everywhere else paralyzes the will of every responsible man, the dilemma between economic progress and immediate increase of the real income of the masses.*" [8: 384]

The experience of the depressed decade of the 1930s, insisted Schumpeter, provides no basis for objecting to these statements. Depressions of roughly equal length and severity have occurred on several occasions in the past, are explicable in terms of the simultaneous occurrence of a Kondratieff and a Juglar downswing, and already have

been included in the calculations. The expansionary phase of the Juglar cycle from 1932 to 1937 exhibited roughly the kind and amount of innovations and technological change to be expected in such industries as automobiles, rubber, steel, and chemicals (in the Schumpeterian schema) during a Kondratieff downswing. The subnormal performance of the 1930s also can be attributed in part "to the difficulties incident to the adaptation to a new fiscal policy, new labor legislation and a general change in the attitude of government to private enterprise...." The experience of the thirties thus "does not prove that a secular break has occurred in the propelling mechanism of capitalist production...." [8: 64] Further, in contrast to Marx's prognostication, unemployment as a percent of the labor force has shown no upward secular trend. If capitalism's future economic promise were to be fulfilled, the burden of providing ample compensation for the unemployed would decrease, as suggested, thereby providing the basis for eliminating the major "terror" of unemployment in terms of "the private life of the unemployed...." [8: 70]

The Plausibility of the Extrapolation

The extrapolation of past performance gives a useful and inviting picture of what capitalism *might* achieve. The plausibility of formulating a forecast of what capitalism *probably will* accomplish on the basis of this extrapolation depends, argued Schumpeter, on answers to three questions:

CAPITALISM AND PAST ECONOMIC GROWTH

Is there "an understandable relation between the capitalist order and the observed rate of increase in output?" [8: 72] Schumpeter's answer was "Yes." The capitalist economic system contains a "singularly effective" set of institutional and motivational arrangements, a simple, forceful system of rewards and punishments both for getting the job done and for injecting new blood into and ejecting old blood out of the entrepreneurial and business sectors of the economy. This is especially so because of the spectacular profits and failures which do occur occasionally and which thereby spur the large majority of businessmen who, in actuality, make much more modest gains (and losses).

A popular criticism of the preceding contention is that the maximum performance of the entrepreneurial-capitalist strata of society does not guarantee the maximization of overall economic performance. The maximization of profits does not promote, and indeed, may impede, the maximization of welfare. The traditional answer to this criticism is that (1) under competitive conditions, producers are compelled to produce and allocate resources efficiently in any one period of time and are enticed to contribute to economic growth over the passage of time; but (2) when producers hold monopoly power, profit maximization is likely to diverge from efficient and progressive performance.

In the Schumpeterian view, this traditional argument, though useful as an analytical exercise in its own restricted sphere, has historical and conceptual limitations. Historically, it infers either that (1) the impressive economic performance of "relatively unfettered 'big business'" capitalist economies like the United States between, say, 1870 and 1930, came despite, rather than because of, the actions of private capitalist entrepreneurs, or (2) the rate of economic growth decreased in the process of transition from "an entirely imaginary golden age" of nineteenth-century perfectly competitive capitalism to twentieth-century monopolistic and oligopolistic capitalism. This second inference, Schumpeter insisted, is doubly mistaken: The realities of twentieth-century capitalism are *more*, not less, competitive than during the nineteenth century, while the advent of large-scale, monopolistic and oligopolistic manufacturing enterprise

from, say, the 1890s, was not accompanied by a decrease in the rate of increase in real output, especially the real output made available to workers and people in lower income brackets.

The conceptual limitation of the traditional pro-competitive argument is its essentially static character. From a dynamic point of view, the real contributions to economic performance and welfare, said Schumpeter, are not lower prices and higher outputs from consumer-directed business firms in perfectly competitive markets, but daring and revolutionary innovations.[4] Because capitalism is a dynamic, evolutionary economic system, it, and the short-run market strategies of business firms, must be appraised in terms of "the perennial gale of creative destruction," that is, in terms of its long-run developmental dynamism. The really "relevant problem" is not "how capitalism administers existing structures," but "how it creates and destroys them." [8: 84]

Stated differently, it is quite possible that short-run semi-monopolistic positions, agreements, and strategies, with accompanying short-run inefficiencies in resource allocation and inequalities in income distribution, are necessary to provide a basis for the innovational investment that brings greater long-run performance and more vigorous long-run competition. Entrepreneurship may be, in large measure, a function of an institu-

---

[4]In "capitalist reality," argued Schumpeter, "it is not that kind of competition" (price competition under pure and perfect competition) "which counts but the competition from the new commodity, the new technology, the new source of supply, the new type of organization . . . —competition which commands a decisive cost or quality advantage and which strikes not at the margins of the profits and the outputs of the existing firms but at their foundations and their very lives. This kind of competition is as much more effective than the other as a bombardment is in comparison with forcing a door, and so much more important that it becomes a matter of comparative indifference whether competition in the ordinary sense functions more or less promptly; the powerful lever that in the long run expands output and brings down prices is in any case made of other stuff." [8: 84–85]

tional-social-political structure which permits *temporary* protection (through, for example, patents and secret processes) to the innovator and the generation of *temporary* pure economic profits above "normal profits" through the exploitation and manipulation of price, quantity, and quality variables via techniques which in the short run appear restrictive and monopolistic.

This idea is illustrated in Fig. 6.4. At any one point of time t_1, under given conditions of technology, resources, and tastes, a purely and perfectly competitive market, given the time to make the necessary long-run adjustments, could bring about a closer correspondence between production and existing consumer tastes, and thereby, a higher level of real output, t_1^x than that generated by a more monopolistic structure, t_1^y. If, however, temporary monopoly provides the basis for a higher rate of growth yy' than the competitive growth rate xx', the more monopolistic market structure may be preferable despite its short-run lapses from perfect allocational efficiency.

EXCEPTIONAL CIRCUMSTANCES?

Schumpeter's second question may be paraphrased by asking: Was the rate of growth in capitalist economies like the United States up to 1930 caused by exceptional circumstances, by "particularly favor-

able conditions which had nothing to do with capitalism"? [8: 73] Schumpeter's answer was "No." With the exception of World War I, governmental activity was relatively small, and wars were few and minor. Neither was a major factor in economic development. Population growth and an increase in the size of the labor force, other things remaining equal, would generally lead, under the usual assumptions of the law of variable proportions, to a smaller, not a larger, output per man and per person. The opening of new geographical territories and technological progress were vital sources of economic development. But these were not independent factors, separate from capitalist entrepreneurship; they were brought into commercial application by "business enterprise" and the "capitalist process." [8: 107–10]

CAPITALIST STAGNATION?

If there is an "understandable relation" between past development and capitalist economic organization, including "big business" oligopolistic and monopolistic markets, and if that past development cannot be attributed primarily to exceptionally favorable exogenous circumstances extraneous to capitalism, then the plausibility of the extrapolation of past growth trends is resolved into a third question: Is there "any reason why the capitalist engine should, during the next forty years, fail to go on working as it did in the past"? [8: 73] Schumpeter's answer to this question has both short- and long-run aspects.

First, the short-run aspect: If capitalist economic development proceeds via cyclical fluctuations, then short-run recessionary departures from the long-run growth trend do not constitute a secular break in that trend. Even major and severe depressions, like those of the 1930s, though not necessary to the logic of capitalist development, do not demonstrate the implausibility of an extrapolation of the past growth trends as noted earlier.

The long-run problem requires further

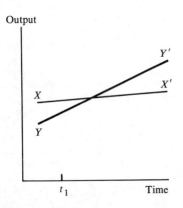

Fig. 6.4. Temporary monopoly and the growth rate

discussion. It is quite possible that capitalism has long-run ills apart from short-run cyclical depression which increase with time, thus invalidating any prediction of the future on the basis of past performance. Students of capitalism as diverse as Marx, Hobson, and Keynes have concured that capitalist economies face long-run difficulties which cause not only a divergence of actual below potential output in any given period of time, but also a divergence of the actual below the potential rate of growth over a period of time.

Very briefly, "chronic" or "secular stagnation" of the Keynes-Hansen varieties infers that decreases in the rate of increase in population growth, disappearance of the geographical frontier, and the improbability of new, heavily capital-intensive technological innovations may well create a situation where the opportunities for profitable private investment are more or less "chronically" insufficient to encourage the investment necessary for the maintenance of a full or near-full employment performance and/or growth rate.

The Schumpeterian theory of capitalism is, in part, an answer to Keynes, as it is to Marx. According to Schumpeter, there is nothing wrong with the economics of capitalism, the capitalist "engine," in the long run as well as in the short run, at least for the next 40 or 50 years. A decrease in the rate of increase in population provides no basis for long-run pessimism about capitalism's prospects. From the side of demand, a lagging population may be offset by an increase in the quantity, quality, and variety of wants; while, from the side of supply, increases in labor productivity can offset the implications of labor shortage.

Even if the disappearance of the geographical frontier is granted, technological improvements on old lands and geographical development of new ones are distinct possibilities. Further, the historical association of new geographical froniters with development does not demonstrate that natural-resource discoveries and exploitation were primarily responsible for that development or that the lack of it will result in long-run stagnation—"we must not confuse geographical frontiers with economic ones." [8:117]

Regarding technological change and the capital-intensity of output, Schumpeter said succinctly, "not proved." Statistical evidence up to 1929 has not adequately established a long-run tendency for new technological developments to become increasingly capital-saving, that is, to require less fixed capital per unit of output than in the past. [8:119] Further, even if it were accurate to classify the period since 1928, especially the depressed thirties, as characterized by the relative lack of technological innovations equivalent to those in the railroad, chemical, electric power, and automobile industries in the latter nineteenth and early twentieth centuries, this would provide no basis for expecting a "slackening of the rate of output through technological possibilities" because these "possibilities are an uncharted sea." [8:118] From a purely economic point of view, vast opportunities for technological development and innovative investment may await in such areas as chemicals, electricity, and housing.

It is necessary to emphasize the central Schumpeterian conclusion: If we reject Keynesian and other theories of secular stagnation and agree past economic development was connected in some direct, significant way with the capitalist organization of the economy and not primarily with extraneous factors, it follows that it is plausible to extrapolate past growth trends as reasonably accurate prognostications of future economic possibilities, at least in the absence of countervailing or offsetting factors. There is nothing in the pure economics of capitalism, said Schumpeter, to support the contention that capitalism has lost or is losing its potential or actual dynamism.

Can Capitalism Survive?

Paradoxically, when Schumpeter turned to prognosis, his conclusion was essentially similar to that of Marx. "Can capitalism survive?" "No, I do not think it can," he said. [8: 61] Though this conclusion is essentially Marxian, the basis for the conclusion is distinctly non-Marxian: Capitalism probably will prove to be historically transient, according to Schumpeter, not because of economic failure and not even despite economic success, but, paradoxically, *because* of that success. Capitalism, like most preceding economic systems, will probably disappear before it has "had time to fill to the full the measure of (its) promise." [8: 130] The fault lies not in the economics of the "capitalist engine," but in the psychology, sociology, ideology, and politics of "capitalist civilization." In short, capitalism's "very success undermines the social institutions which protect it, and 'inevitably' creates conditions in which it will not be able to live. . . ." [8: 61][5]

The bases for this fascinating and paradoxical hypothesis are four-fold: (1) "the obsolescence of the entrepreneurial function"; (2) "the destruction of the protecting strata"; (3) "the destruction of the institutional framework of capitalist society"; (4) "growing hostility" and "the legislative, administrative and judicial practice born of that hostility." [8: 131 ff.]

OBSOLESCENCE OF THE
ENTREPRENEURIAL FUNCTION

In the "trustified" capitalism of the twentieth century, innovations typically are made by large-scale corporations, whose research departments and specialists have routinized technological progress; whose bureaus and committees have replaced individual action; whose customers "have become accustomed to economic change" and, hence, less resistant to it; whose accumulated financial reserves have reduced the disruptive role of credit creation; and whose administrators and managers have substituted conscious, long-range investment planning for daring personal leadership. In short, economic progress is becoming "mechanized," "stabilized," "depersonalized," and "automatized."

But the social function of the capitalist-entrepreneur, as the innovative outsider who periodically revolutionizes the "economic organism," is bound to diminish in an environment in which economic progress becomes automatic, organized, and impersonal. With the obsolescence of the entrepreneurial function, the positions and incomes of both the active entrepreneurs and those portions of "the entire bourgeois stratum. . . their families and connections" dependent on them also are threatened, since, under these conditions, "the economic basis of the industrial bourgeoisie will be reduced eventually to wages such as are paid for current administrative work" plus lingering quasi-rents and monopoly returns. "Since capitalist enterprise, by its very achievements, tends to automatize progress, we conclude that it tends to make itself superfluous—to break to pieces under the pressure of its own success. The perfectly bureaucratized giant industrial unit. . . in the end . . . ousts the entrepreneur and expropriates the bourgeoisie as a class which in the process stands to lose not only its income but also what is infinitely more important: its function." [8: 134]

DESTRUCTION OF THE PROTECTING
STRATA

Capitalist entrepreneurs, according to Schumpeter, make poor soldiers, statesmen,

---

[5]This thesis was phrased somewhat differently in a 1928 article: "Capitalism is . . . in so obvious a process of transformation into something else, that is not the fact, but only the interpretation of this fact, about which it is possible to disagree . . . . Capitalism, whilst economically stable, and even gaining in stability, creates, by rationalizing the human mind, a mentality and a style of life incompatible with its own fundamental conditions, motives and social institutions, and will be changed, although not by economic necessity and probably even at some sacrifice of economic welfare, into an order of things which it will be merely a matter of taste and terminology to call socialism or not." [11: 71–72] "Capitalism produces by its mere working a social atmosphere . . . that is hostile to it, and this atmosphere, in turn, produces policies which do not allow it to function." [22: II, 1038]

diplomats, and clergymen. The industrialist is "rationalist and unheroic." He lacks the "mystic glamour" which "counts in the ruling of men." [8: 137] He requires an aristocratic, pre-capitalist class to protect him, manage the affairs of church and state, and leave him "unfettered" to carry out his revolutionary economic leadership—as illustrated by the classic case of nineteenth-century England. But when the process of transition from feudalism to capitalism is too thorough, or, as in the United States, when capitalism does not develop from a feudal base, the capitalist-entrepreneur is emancipated not only from those feudal institutions that "fetter" his development, but from those institutions and classes that support him, as well. In the Schumpeterian view, this is precisely what has happened. "In breaking down the pre-capitalist framework of society, capitalism . . . broke not only barriers that impeded its progress but also flying buttresses that prevented its collapse. That process, impressive in its relentless necessity, was not merely a matter of removing institutional deadwood, but of removing partners of the capitalist stratum, symbiosis with whom was an essential element of the capitalist schema." [8: 139] The very success of capitalist evolution in eliminating pre-capitalist institutions and classes leaves the bourgeoisie "politically helpless and unable not only to lead its nation but even to take care of its particular class interest." [8: 138]

DESTRUCTION OF THE INSTITUTIONAL FRAMEWORK

The very economic success of the capitalist process undermines its institutions: atomistic competition, freedom of contract, and private property. The traditional argument that the transition from the atomistic competition of the nineteenth to the large-scale, corporatized economy of the twentieth century has "reduced competition" and, thereby, economic performance "misses the salient point." Even *if* large-scale corporations were managed with angelic perfection, the elimination or

reduction in importance of small-scale producers and traders (the "perfectly bureaucratized giant industrial unit . . . ousts the small or medium-sized firm and 'expropriates' its owners . . .") reduces significantly political support for capitalism. Further, individual freedom of choice and freedom of contract have been replaced by dealings of "giant concerns" with each other, or with "impersonal masses of workmen or consumers." What is often referred to as the "separation of ownership and management in the large-scale corporation" has resulted in the disappearance of the "specifically proprietary interest" and the "evaporation" of "the material substance of property—its visible and touchable reality" and, thereby, the evaporation of "moral allegiance" for private property in the industrial sector of the economy, for capitalism as an economic system. Eventually, nobody is left either within or without the "precincts of the big concerns" who "really cares to stand for" capitaism as did the old-style, small-scale owner-managers of the nineteenth century. "Thus the modern corporation, although the product of the capitalist process, socializes the bourgeois mind; it relentlessly narrows the scope of capitalist motivation; not only that, it will eventually kill its roots." [8: 134, 139–42, 156]

GROWING HOSTILITY

The obsolescence of the entrepreneurial function, and the destruction of the protecting strata and the institutional framework of capitalist society reduces political support for the entrepreneur and for capitalism as an economic system. In addition, the very economic success of capitalism encourages and generates an "atmosphere of almost universal hostility to its own social order," both generally and among its intellectuals. The "critical frame of mind" and "rationalist attitude" which is a vital part of capitalist civilization is turned against capitalism: "the bourgeois fortress thus becomes politically defenseless." [8: 143]

General hostility toward capitalism stems

from four sources: First, the case for capitalism is a rational and utilitarian one ("*emotional* attachment to the social order" is "the very thing capitalism is constitutionally unable to produce"); but rational argument cannot meet political criticism based in part on emotional, sub- or extra-rational grievances. Second, the capitalist rationale rests on long-run considerations, whereas for most people, it is "the short-run view that counts." Third, capitalism, like any system, is characterized by short-run tensions and problems. Fourth, long-run improvements in living standards, including leisure, accompanied by "individual insecurity that is acutely resented is of course the best recipe for breeding social unrest." [8: 145]

General hostility toward capitalism is supplemented by that of intellectuals—"people who wield the power of the spoken and the written word," yet who generally lack "that first-hand knowledge . . . which only experience can give" [8: 147], who thrive on criticism, and who are given wide opportunities to "nibble at the foundations of capitalist society" through "freedom of public discussion" as well as increased living standards, increased leisure, and improved means of communication. [8: 151] Moreover, intellectuals affect politics and public policy, especially during periods of rapid social change, as during the New Deal, in the roles of political advisors, speechwriters, and public administrators.

General and intellectual hostility is related to the structure of capitalism's social classes. (1) "Capitalist evolution produces a labor movement" and "the rise of the labor interest to a position of political power and sometimes of responsibility." Labor unions, in conjunction with large-scale corporations, have collectivized the labor market, thus altering and socializing the institutional structure of capitalist economy. In addition, intellectuals have often invaded labor organizations and labor politics, providing "theories and slogans" and giving "bourgeois trade-union practices" a more radical, revolutionary bias

than would exist without their participation. (2) Capitalism, "also by its own working," evolves a phenomenon, the importance of which was not foreseen by Marx: "the 'clerical,' 'white collar' or 'New Middle Class,' " which, along with farmers and small businessmen, in some cases constitutes a majority of the population, and whose interests and attitudes, though quite different from those of the "working class" more narrowly conceived, are generally just "as hostile to the interests of the bigger and big bourgeoisie. . . ." [Cf. 8: 153–54 and 22: II, 697–99]

The transformation of, plus hostility toward, capitalism combine to give birth to public policies incompatible with it, "policies which do not allow it to function," [22: II, 1038] either through the imposition of injurious financial burdens upon the capitalist-entrepreneurial sector or the alteration of the institutional-attitudinal environment, and which contribute to the vanishing of profitable, private investment opportunities identified by the various theories of secular stagnation. As illustrations, Schumpeter cited developments during the New Deal, especially after 1935, including burdensome income, corporation, and estate taxes, labor legislation, public utility regulation, and anti-monopoly policies. The injurious effects of these programs upon private investment and innovation were heightened by the rapidity, hostility, and anti-business spirit with which they were enacted, and the overzealous, tactless manner in which they were administered. [22: II, 1038 ff.]

Faced by the transformation of capitalism and the hostility of intellectuals and non-capitalist classes, the inner psychology, the "motor forces" of capitalism begin to "decompose." The capitalist-entrepreneur "is rapidly losing faith in his own creed" and is absorbing many of the slogans, even the content, of contemporary radicalism. As evidence of this inner "decomposition," Schumpeter cited: the "meekness" and willingness to compromise in the face of the "crushing financial burdens" and the "incompatible" labor legislation of the New Deal; the postwar acceptance, "not only unquestioningly but also approvingly," of an entire battery of governmental economic policies and controls (for example, monetary and fiscal policies, redistributive taxation, social security, price controls); the 'disintegration of the bourgeois family,' the loosening of family ties; the decline of the family profit motive and the desire to save for and/or to build a family industrial dynasty; the "evaporation of consumers' property" as evidenced by the passing of the old, spacious bourgeois family home; and the shift to a "short-run view" among the industrialist-entrepreneurial segment of society and increasing acceptance of "anti-saving" theories and philosophies. [8: 157–62]

In sum, the process of capitalist economic development, by its very success, "undermines the position of the bourgeoisie by decreasing the importance of the functions of entrepreneurs and capitalists, by breaking up protective strata and institutions," and by "creating an atmosphere of hostility" and thereby "decomposes the motor forces of capitalism from within. . . . Faced by the increasing hostility of the environment and by the legislative, administrative and judicial practice born of that hostility, entrepreneurs and capitalists—in fact the whole stratum that accepts the bourgeois scheme of life—will eventually cease to function." [8: 161–62, 156] Capitalism, in short, "cannot survive."

CONCLUSIONS: AFTER CAPITALISM, WHAT?

If capitalism cannot survive, what is to follow? One alternative is agnosticism: "As regards the tendency toward socialism, we must first realize that this is a distinct problem. The capitalist or any other order of things may evidently break down—or economic and social evolution may outgrow it—and yet the socialist phoenix may fail to rise from the ashes. There may be chaos and, unless we define as socialism any non-chaotic alternative to capitalism, there are other possibilities. (Socialism) is certainly only one of many possible cases." [8: 56–57]

A second possibility, though Schumpeter discounted its probable postwar significance and did not examine it in any systematic way, is a "state-directed economy" of the Nazi German type. [22: II, 971 ff.]

A third alternative, and clearly the closest to the essence of the long-run Schumpeterian vision, is some variety of socialism. The factors discussed in the preceding section "make not only for the destruction of the capitalist but for the emergence of a socialist civilization. . . . The capitalist process not only destroys its own institutional framework but it also creates the conditions for another." [8: 162] In short, the capitalist "economic process tends to socialize *itself*—and also the human soul"; that is, as capitalism evolves, "the technological, organizational, commercial, administrative, and psychological prerequisites of socialism tend to be fulfilled more and more." [8: 219] The same factors which explain capitalism's coming demise also "strongly point to socialism as the heir apparent." [8: 61]

A final possibility, at least for the short run, is some form of "administered" or "laborist" capitalism. Several things to be said about such an alternative are: First, "administered" capitalism is *not* old-style, unfettered, and *laissez-faire*. Thus, even if this administered form of "capitalism" *were* to survive "indefinitely," Schumpeter insisted, his basic thesis on the historical impermanency of (unfettered) capitalism could not be denied. Second is a question of semantics. By 1950, said Schumpeter, the Western democratic nations had deviated so far from old-style capitalism that the economic order differed "but little from genuinely socialist planning." [8: 419] Indeed, it is largely a "matter of taste and terminology" as to whether this so-called administered capitalism is "socialism" or not. [11: 72] Third, the "extent to which capitalist interests can in fact be expropriated without bringing the economic engine to a standstill and the extent to which this engine may be made to run in the labor interest" is indeed remarkable. But can we reasonably expect the "spectacular development of society's productive powers" promised by capitalism to be fulfilled in an environment in which the capitalist-entrepreneurial sector of the economy is increasingly "burdened," "fettered," and "regulated"? May not the "frictions" and "deadlocks" inherent in such a mixed economic order generate a leap to "an outright socialist solution" and "complete planning as the smallest of possible evils," even for "the enemies of socialism. . . ."? [8: 419, 424]

The Schumpeterian vision is one of capitalism in general rather than of specific capitalist countries. This often has led his readers to overlook, as Daniel Bell suggests, that "he selected the economics of American industry and the sociology of European society and derived his justifications for capitalism from the first and his apocalyptic visions as to its fate from the second."[6] Identifying the driving force of capitalism with the great entrepreneurial families, he failed to appreciate how fully large-scale corporations could provide a new dynamism of their own. Identifying the State as an external force outside the economy, he failed to perceive the possibility of partnership between government and private enterprise, and of government as protector and sustainer of (a modified and socially reformed) capitalism. Having a continental and aristocratic disdain for democracy, intellectual social criticism, and the labor movement within the framework of European traditions and institutions, he did not really "see" the possibility of democratic compromise and negotiation among business, labor, agriculture, and government as anything beyond a

mere temporary arrangement or *modus vivendi*. Sophisticated in his analysis of the evolutionary development and transformation of old-style capitalism, he yet remained enmeshed in the tradition of the stark and grandiloquent alternatives of capitalism versus socialism.

Also, as in the Marxian prognostication, the Schumpeterian vision contains no timetable. Its constituent elements, "while everywhere discernible, have as yet nowhere fully revealed themselves." Superficial "temporary reverses" on the "surface" may easily mask "the tendency toward another civilization that slowly works deep down below." The Schumpeterian vision is a *long-run* forecast in an accounting system in which "a century is a 'short-run'. . . ." [8: 163] It is understandable if the American student of capitalism, concerned with practical, pressing short-run problems of economic organization and policy, concludes that, although this approach to the subject does not lessen the provocative, imaginative challenge of the Schumpeterian vision, it does make it difficult for present-day economists to put the thesis to a firm, clear empirical test.

SUMMARY OF CHAPTER 6

1. Schumpeterian economics was essentially an analysis of the development and transformation of industrializing capitalism. Schumpeter's theory of capitalism focused on the concept of creative destruction, that is, on how capitalism's creativity and success would eventually cause its demise.

2. Capitalism's creativity is best demonstrated, Schumpeter suggested, in its role in bringing industrialization and economic development. In contrast to the static, stationary allocational and distribtuional processes of the circular flow, economic development consists of revolutionary innovations in resources and technology, led by daring entrepreneurs and financed by

---

[6]Daniel Bell, *The End of Ideology*, rev, ed. (New York City: Free Press of Glencoe, Inc., 1962), p. 84.

bank credit. Innovative development brings economic growth in its wake, but growth does not constitute development.

3. According to Schumpeter, capitalism's past success is not vitiated by economic instability, monopoly/oligopoly, nor inequality. First, capitalist economic development is a cyclical process, characterized by the introduction (prosperity) and absorption (recession) of innovations. Large-scale depressions (secondary waves) are not a necessary part of the logic of capitalist development, and, overall, cyclical economic fluctuations do not appear to be growing larger.

Second, short-run monopolies and oligopolies are terminated in the perennial "gale of creative destruction" by new products, processes, sources of supply, and markets. Competition by innovation is more important and more indicative of the character of capitalism than price competition among existing firms with given resource/technology conditions.

Third, short-run inequalities in the distribution of income are tempered by the equalizing tendencies of economic growth in the long run; some degree of inequality may be the price that capitalist society pays for the creativity and progressiveness of its entrepreneurial leaders.

4. Capitalism cannot survive. Its economic creativity eventually will destroy the institutional, ideological, and political "superstructure" (in Marx's sense) which supports it—through, first, the obsolescence of the entrepreneurial function; second, the destruction of the protecting strata of pre-capitalist classes and institutions; third, the destruction of the institutional framework of atomistic competition and free markets; fourth, growing hostility of many classes to the interests of large-scale industrialists and increasing willingness to "reform" and "manage" the economic system.

5. Though the post-capitalist economic order could move in a variety of directions, its most likely successor is some variety of socialism. But even if a mixed economy or administered capitalism were to persist indefinitely, old-style unfettered industrializing capitalism would disappear, a victim of its own success.

7

The Keynesian Critique of
Laissez-Faire Capitalism
and Strategy
for Managed Capitalism

Keynesian capitalism is a movement—if not a political movement for social and economic reform, an intellectual-political movement for the propagation of a "Keynesian" theory of capitalism and its application to government economic policy in industrially-developed capitalist economies. John Maynard Keynes was the most influential economist in the first half of the twentieth century. Perhaps more than any other economist, he made respectable the critique of *laissez-faire* and support of government guidance of the macroeconomic affairs of industrialized Western societies. Insofar as his ideas and those of Keynesian economists on government guidance of and policy in capitalist economies have been put into practice, Keynesian-guided capitalism is an economic system, as well. Foremost in Keynes' mind was the theoretical economic analysis which provided, at least in part, the intellectual bases for both the movement and the actuality.

The Keynesian theory of capitalism may be studied from several vantage points. First is a critique of the traditional economic theory of capitalism. Second are the tools of economic theory, stripped of any empirical content and viewed from the standpoint of logical consistency and coherence. Third is the empirical content—the assumptions, observations, arguments, and inferences—plugged into the theories and equations, which give them practical applicability. Fourth are the recommendations for government economic policy which, in large measure, derive intellectual justification and support from the theoretical-empirical analysis. Last are the implications for capitalism as an economic system, for its institutions and prospects.

These elements of Keynesian theory, though interdependent, are distinguishable. For example, there is nothing in the logic of Keynesian tools of economic analysis to restrict their applicability to periods of depression and severe unemployment, though this problem, according to Keynes, was, during the 1930s, *the* central problem of industrially-developed capitalist economies. It is possible to turn the Keynesian analysis of depression "upside down" and derive a theory of (demand-pull) inflation. Further, policy proposals designed to cure capitalism's economic problems are on a distinctly "different plane from the diagnosis." Whereas, in Keynes' case, the analysis was "of a highly general character" and "meant to be definitive," the policy proposals "are not worked out completely" and "are not meant to be definitive" because they "are subject to all sorts of special assumptions and are necessarily related to the particular conditions of the time."[1] In other words, another time and another set of assumptions (for example, wartime inflation) might well be accompanied by different policy proposals.

Similarly, the basis for support or rejection of "Keynesian-type" policy proposals may be different in different cases. It is possible, as has been true for Keynesian economists since 1936 (the publication date of Keynes' major theoretical work, *The General Theory of Employment, Interest, and Money*), to support some or all of Keynes' policy prescriptions on the basis of formal economic theory. It is also possible, as in the case of Franklin D. Roosevelt during the later years of the New Deal, to support such "Keynesian" measures as government deficit spending, but largely upon political and humanitarian grounds. Conversely, it is possible to understand and to use Keynesian tools of economic analysis, to accept many of the Keynesian empirical assumptions and inferences, and yet to reject the Keynesian medicine on the grounds it is politically unfeasible or governments are not willing and able to promote the "public good" or "general welfare" as Keynes conceived it. Lastly, it is possible for different groups to support the same Keynesian policies for different reasons: Keynesian capitalists, for the purpose of guiding, stimulating, and

thus "saving" a modified form of capitalism; Fabian socialists, as one of a series of interlocking steps in the gradual movement toward and eventual establishment of socialism.

This chapter will proceed from Keynesian theory to empirical assumptions and applications, to policy proposals, and to implications for the organization and institutions of, and prospects for capitalism.

THE KEYNESIAN CRITIQUE OF TRADITIONAL ECONOMIC THEORY

John Maynard Keynes was a student of English neo-classical economist Alfred Marshall, educated in the neo-classical tradition of orthodox economic theory. Keynes accepted neo-classical analysis of how the competitive price system resolves the problems of allocation of resources and distribution of income under full employment conditions, but criticized the traditional view that competitive market capitalism contains an automatic, spontaneous social process which promotes stable equilibrium at full employment utilization of resources.

Allocation and Distribution Under Conditions of Full Employment Equilibrium

Like Schumpeter, Keynes essentially accepted the traditional analysis of resource allocation and income distribution *under conditions of full employment equilibrium.* Suppose the "volume of output to be given" at a level "corresponding to full employment as nearly as is practicable...." Then, the classic theory of competitive market capitalism "comes into its own" and provides an accurate analysis "... of the manner in which private self-interest will determine what in particular is produced, in what proportions the factors of production will be combined to produce it, and how the value of the final product will be distributed between them." Indeed, Keynes went further than Schumpeter in his acceptance of neoclassical theory by

---

[1] John Maynard Keynes, "The General Theory of Employment," *Quarterly Journal of Economics*, February 1937, p. 222.

suggesting that, assuming conditions of full employment equilibrium, "there is no objection to be raised against the modern classical theory as to the degree of concilience between private and public advantage in conditions of perfect and imperfect competition, respectively." Keynes continued, "I see no reason to suppose that the existing system seriously mis-employs the factors of production which are in use." "If," he emphasized, "nations can learn to provide themselves with full employment by their domestic policy", [14: 378–79, 382] then a system will have been created "which allows the classical medicine to do its work" and in which "the wisdom of Adam Smith" has been implemented rather than defeated.[2]

Thus, from the standpoint of resource allocation and income distribution, Keynes neither challenged nor added to the earlier classical and neo-classical analysis; and, insofar as Keynesian analysis can be distinguished from the microeconomics of the price system under full employment conditions, the two are complementary rather than competitive and may be combined, as evidenced by the writings of such followers of Keynes as Alvin H. Hansen and Paul A. Samuelson, in a sort of "grand (post-) neo-classical synthesis."

The Macroeconomics of Full Employment-Stability

While accepting the classic defense of the competitive price system as an allocational and distributional process, Keynes argued it does not automatically function to promote stable equilibrium at full employment utilization of resources. The empirical and practical dimensions are clear enough. In actuality, economies in which price systems have served as prominent social processes for economic

coordination have not been characterized by sustained full employment but instead, have experienced periodic and, at times, long, severe departures from it. Also, institutional barriers to wage and price flexibility—monopoly and oligopoly, tariffs, minimum wage laws, labor unions, and resale price maintenance laws—may prevent the classical medicine of price and wage deflation from raising aggregate demand in the event of recession or depression.

But Keynes, like Marx, wanted to critically evaluate market capitalism at its competitive best rather than at its non-competitive worst —and for essentially the same reason. A tendency toward depression and unemployment in a capitalist economy characterized by monopoly power and wage and price rigidity may as easily demonstrate the restrictive impact of monopoly as it does the inefficiencies of the price system in sustaining overall macroeconomic balance.

The Keynesian critique of the efficacy of the competitive price system as a social process for automatically and spontaneously generating a tendency toward stable equilibrium at full employment is threefold: the labor market; the money market; the saving-investment market.

THE LABOR MARKET

The traditional pre-Keynesian theory of the macroeconomics of the labor market has three central dimensions: the demand for labor as an inverse function of the real wage level; the supply of labor as a direct function of the real wage level; and an equilibrating process which promotes full employment through the interaction of the demand for and supply of labor.

Keynes' critique of traditional economic theory challenged each of these three hypotheses. First, Keynes criticized the traditional demand for labor function as being too narrow in concept. Employment, he argued, like output, depends upon the aggregate demand for goods and services. If demand is

---

[2]John Maynard Keynes, "The Balance of Payments of the United States," *Economic Journal*, June 1946, p. 186.

high, output and employment also will be high and, by virtue of diminishing returns (illustrated by a negatively sloped marginal product of labor curve), the marginal product, and thus real wage level of labor, will be low. Thus, in microeconomic equilibrium, the real wage level equals the marginal physical product (and the money wage level equals the value of the marginal product) for each firm. It does not follow, however, that decreases in real wage levels throughout the economy will necessarily sustain an increase in employment to full employment levels. This would be so only if supply created its own demand, that is, if the increase in output accompanying an expansion of employment were automatically accompanied by an equivalent increase in demand for goods and services.

Further, Keynes challenged the traditional conception of the supply of labor function. Labor supply, he contended, is more a function of the money wage level than the real wage level. Lower *money* wages plausibly will lead to a decrease in labor offered (for example, through strikes). On the other hand, lower *real* wages caused by increases in prices plausibly will not be accompanied by a withdrawal of labor. But if the supply of labor depends on money wages instead of real wages, the traditional "argument breaks down entirely and leaves the question of what the actual employment will be quite indeterminate." [14:8]

Lastly, Keynes argued the equilibrating mechanism on the labor market is no automatic guarantor of full employment. As already noted, Keynes challenged the accuracy of the traditional supply of labor function and the adequacy of the traditional demand for labor function. But a market without a supply function is like a scissors with only one blade (and in this instance, a rather dull one).

Even if the traditional analysis of demand and supply functions in the labor market is accepted, however, problems remain. First,

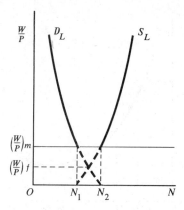

Fig. 7.1. The labor market

if wage rigidities (for example, minimum wage laws or labor unions) prevent sufficient deflation in wages and prices, unemployment may persist because of inconsistency between the demand for and supply of labor, as illustrated in Fig. 7.1. If real wages were permitted to fall to $(W/P)f$, an equality between demand for labor and supply of labor would conceivably ensue. But if the real wage level stops at $(W/P)m$, demand for labor falls short of the supply of labor and unemployment (N_1N_2) persists.

Second, the traditional concept of the equilibrating mechanism of the labor market presumes that money wage bargains between employees and employers determine real wages and that the general level of real wages determines employment. But full employment (and thus, a full employment level of real wages) is sustainable, Keynes argued, only if aggregate demand is sufficient to match aggregate supply at full employment. Because there is nothing in lower money wage rates which guarantees a full employment level of aggregate demand, workers may be unable to eliminate unemployment merely by accepting lower wages. In short, employment depends upon conditions in the money market and saving/investment market; and conditions in these markets may or may not be conducive to creating or sustaining levels of aggregate demand sufficient to establish full employment.

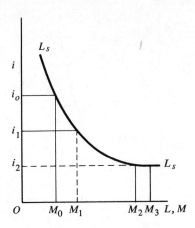

Fig. 7.2. The money market

THE MONEY MARKET

The Keynesian critique of traditional monetary theory focused on the concept of a speculative demand for money, as illustrated in Fig. 7.2. As we have seen, the existence of a speculative demand for money does not invalidate the traditional analysis of how a flexibily adjusting competitive price system promotes full employment equilibrium, but it certainly complicates it. For one thing, speculative demands are affected by uncertain expectations, which are subject to dynamic shifts or changes. A financial panic or "liquidity crisis," for example, characterized by an upward shift in the demand for money, has the effect of pushing interest rates up, thereby discouraging investment. Insofar as investment depends on interest rates which are uncertain, because of uncertainties surrounding a speculative demand for money, the level of investment—and the likelihood that investment will be sufficient to offset saving out of full employment output or income—also is uncertain.

As noted, the existence of a speculative demand for money places greater pressure on the wage/price mechanism for the maintenance of full employment. As long as money is demanded solely for transactionary purposes, shifts in investment can be absorbed by changes in interest rates. But with a speculative demand for money, changes in interest rates cause changes in the speculative demand for money. If investment shifts below the full employment level for any reason and interest rates fall (say, from i_0 to i_1, in Fig. 7.2), then the speculative demand for money will increase, leaving a smaller portion of any given supply of money available for transactionary purposes. To maintain high levels of aggregate demand under such circumstances, prices must fall. But lower prices must be accompanied by lower money wages, to keep real wages at their former (full employment) level. If prices and/or wages are inflexible, or if they fall insufficiently or slowly, unemployment may result. And if investment is unstable, as it is in industrializing capitalist economies, unemployment may be the rule rather than the exception.

Finally, full employment equilibrium may be difficult to sustain because of properties of the speculative demand for money function. At very low rates of interest, (say, i_2 in Fig. 7.2), nearly everyone may expect the interest rate to rise; as a consequence, the demand to hold money may be virtually perfectly elastic relative to the interest rate (illustrated by a horizontal segment of curve $L_S L_S$ beyond point M_2). Under these conditions, increases in the supply of money (beyond OM_2) will be virtually powerless to push interest rates below some minimum level. If the level of investment associated with such a minimum interest rate is insufficient to match full employment saving, output and employment will not be sustained at full employment levels. The problem may be one of degree rather than of kind. Thus, a decrease in interest rates from i_0 to i_1 in Fig. 7.2. requires an increase in the supply of money OM_0 to OM_1 either directly by action of the monetary authorities or indirectly via wage/price deflation, which, by decreasing the transactionary demand for money, frees money for meeting speculative demands. By contrast, a further similar decrease in interest rates to i_2 requires a larger increase in the supply of money (from OM_1 to OM_2). Again, if wage/price deflation is too little or too slow, interest rate deflation will be insufficient or too slow to sustain investment at full employment levels.

THE SAVING/INVESTMENT MARKET

The Keynesian critique of the traditional theory of saving and investment included reservations about the investment function, the saving function, and the saving/investment equilibrating mechanism. On the one hand, while recognizing investment is affected by the rate of interest, Keynes contended that changes in expected rates of profit may exert profound effects upon investment decisions. This may create problems. Because investment depends on uncertain profit expectations, investment, and thus, output and employment are also uncertain. On the other hand, Keynes challenged the traditional concept of the saving function. He argued that, while saving may be affected by the rate of interest, its primary determinant is the level of income. Essentially, saving and investment are done by different people for different reasons. Most investment is done by businessmen on the basis of comparisons of the relation between an (uncertain) interest rate and a (volatile and uncertain) expected rate of profit. Much saving, in a developed capitalist economy, is done by households and is determined by the levels of their incomes.

These dimensions of saving and investment behavior create problems for the use of the saving/investment market as a smooth, automatic equilibrating process at full employment. For one thing, the uncertainty and instability of investment makes full employment equilibrium uncertain. For another, if saving depends upon income as well as the rate of interest, then the interest rate by itself is insufficient to yield a determinate equilibrium solution. As illustrated in Fig. 7.3, the position of the saving function depends on the level of national income, given the rate of interest. Saving may equal investment at a low, unemployment level of income and employment (point E) or at a high, full employment level (point F). The interest rate by itself does not guarantee the

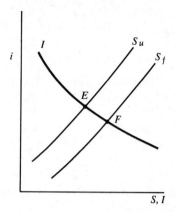

Fig. 7.3. The saving-investment market

saving function will be at one position rather than another.

Finally, if the investment function is very low relative to full employment saving, then even a zero rate of interest may be insufficient to establish full employment. This is illustrated in Fig. 7.4, where investment (at OI_u) falls short of that level necessary to match saving out of full employment income (OS_f) even at a zero interest rate. In this event, if the rate of interest were to stabilize at some low but positive figure (for example, i_m) because of the existence of an elastic or near-elastic speculative demand for money, the gap between full employment saving and the level of investment—and the resulting departure from full employment—would be even greater.

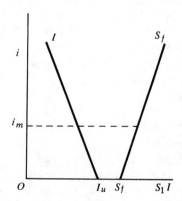

Fig. 7.4. Inconsistency between investment and full employment saving at a zero interest rate

TOOLS AND CONCEPTS OF KEYNESIAN ECONOMIC THEORY

The Scope of Keynesian Analysis

Like Schumpeter, Keynes was primarily concerned with issues other than the allocation of resources and the distribution of income under full employment equilibrium conditions. The scope of the Keynesian analysis may be summarized in four themes: aggregate analysis, employment and unemployment, equilibrium, short-run and long-run.

Keynesian analysis is concerned with the study of macro, or aggregate, economic principles determining "the scale of output and employment as a whole," rather than the mutual interdependencies of individual firms, households and resource owners. The key variables are the large economic aggregates of supply and demand on each of three major markets—final consumption and investment goods, labor, and money (and near-monies: "bonds")—that is, the supply of goods; the demand for goods, manifested by consumption and investment expenditures on currently produced output; the demand for and supply of labor; the demand for and supply of money.

In such an approach, "the pure theory of what determines the *actual employment* of the available resources" in the economy becomes a central problem. In the Keynesian view, an analysis restricted to the study of the operations of a *fully employed* economy is limited and partialistic. A truly "general" theory must encompass *all* levels of employment, including the "special case" of full employment, but including also positions of unemployment as well.

Much of the Keynesian analysis is devoted to the concept of equilibrium and to the identification of equilibrium conditions—in investment, output, employment, and "the" interest rate. This is not the same as saying that it is "static"—first, because those forces which govern an equilibrium position among aggregate economic variables may also be responsible for *changes* in those variables; second, because Keynes' analysis included a variety of dynamic elements and references, such as uncertainty and expectations; third, because post-Keynesian economists have "dynamized" Keynes' tools of analysis by applying them to such problems as cyclical fluctuations and economic growth. Still, the central concern of the basic Keynesian model is with positions of equilibrium, conceived in terms of a balance (or balances) between supply and demand, on product, labor, and/or money markets. Of special concern for Keynesian analysis is the distinct possibility (circa 1936), in the absence of countervailing forces in the form of government policies to offset or prevent it, the probability of the coexistence of equilibrium on the product and money markets with disequilibrium (in the form of an excess of supply over demand) in the labor markets, that is, "under-full employment equilibrium."

The Keynesian analysis of equilibrium in the aggregate levels of output and employment has both short-run and long-run inferences and applications, though the more rigorous, mathematical formulations of the basic Keynesian "model" typically are short-run affairs. From the standpoint of the study of capitalism as an economic system, however, long-run references and implications are as important as more rigorous and precise short-run models.

Keynesian Models of Aggregate Demand

Keynesian analysis focuses primarily on the aggregate level of ("effective") demand. Over a long-run period, the forces governing the potential supply of output are subject to change and are in large measure determining factors in national prosperity. But given the potential supply, the central factor determining whether that potential is realized or not would appear to be the aggregate level of demand, manifested by expenditures upon consumption and investment goods. Thus, for purposes of discussion, and (typically) within the framework of short-run problems, the forces governing the *potential* supply of output are generally taken as "given", beyond the scope of the analysis, and determined by forces other than those analyzed under the heading of aggregate demand. "We take as given," wrote Keynes in 1936, "the existing skill and quantity of available labour, the existing quality and quantity of available equipment, the existing technique, the degree of competition, the tastes and habits of the consumer, the dis-utility of different intensities of labour and of the activities of supervision and organization, as well as the social structure including the forces, other than" variables to be noted presently "which determine the distribution of the national income. This does not mean, of course, that these things are in fact constant, or that it is assumed that they are constant; but merely that, in this place and context, we are not considering or taking into account the effects and consequences of changes in them." [14: 245]

KEYNES I: THE BASIC INCOME AND EXPENDITURES MODEL

The simplest, most popular Keynesian model of aggregate demand focuses on the goods market and the relation between income and expenditures. This model abstracts from the money market, the labor market, and the capital market, and from diminishing returns in the production process. Ignoring government and foreign trade, aggregate expenditures are divided into consumption plus investment, while national income may be disposed of in the forms of either consumption or saving. This simple Keynesian model makes saving a function of the level of national income. Abstracting from the money market and the rate of interest, investment is regarded as an autonomous variable, independent of the level of income. It depends on the relation between the rate of interest and the expected rate of profit (the "marginal efficiency of capital," in Keynes' terminology). The equilibrium level of

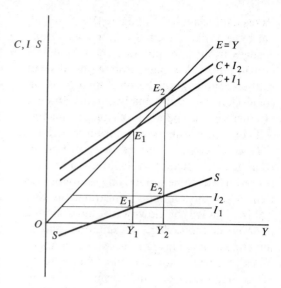

Fig. 7.5. C, I, S and equilibrium income

national income thus requires an equality between desired or planned saving and desired or planned investment: $S = I$. Equilibrium income occurs when $C + I = Y$. This is illustrated in Fig. 7.5 at point E_1 and income level Y_1, given investment at I_1 (and aggregate demand at $C + I_1$).

The equilibrium position depicted in Fig. 7.5 is a stable one; that is, income would tend to move toward an equilibrium position *if* it were temporarily away from it. At income levels below OY_1, demand ($C + I_1$) exceeds supply (income), investment exceeds saving, and income rises. At income levels above OY_1, demand falls short of supply, saving exceeds investment, and income falls.

The theoretical basis of this proposition is that the marginal propensity to save (the change in saving in response to a change in national income) exceeds the marginal propensity to invest. (The saving function is steeper than the investment line in Fig. 7.5.) The marginal propensity to spend (in this instance, the marginal propensity to consume) is less than the marginal propensity to create income. (The $C + I$ line is flatter than the 45° income = expenditures reference line in Fig. 7.5.) Insofar as this is true, increases (decreases) in income will be accompanied by increases (decreases) in aggregate demand, but by less than the change in income. Thus, changes in income, initiated by a modification in any underlying autonomous element in the economy, will become smaller as income changes, until, finally (in the absence of further autonomous changes), income will come to rest in an equilibrium position.

Once income achieves a position of equilibrium, a change in its level requires an alteration in some underlying autonomous element in the economy, illustrated in Fig. 7.5 by upward or downward shifts in the *positions* of the saving, consumption, and/or investment functions. An increase in autonomous investment, for example, from I_1 to I_2, raises aggregate demand from $C + I_1$ to $C + I_2$, and thereby raises the equilibrium position to E_2 and the level of income to OY_2.

Note the increase in income is *larger* than the initiating increase in investment. Keynes called this the *multiplier* effect. It results from the fact that the marginal propensity to spend (in this instance, the marginal propensity to consume) exceeds zero. An increase in investment of, say, $10,000,000,000 initially raises income by a corresponding amount. But this initial increase in income of $10,000,000,000, in turn, causes a secondary increase in demand (consumption) of, say, $5,000,000,000 (assuming, say, a marginal propensity to consume of 0.5), which yields a corresponding secondary increase in income. *This* increase in income of $5,000,000,000, in turn, causes another secondary increase in demand of, say, $2,5000,000,000, and so on, in a geometric series. Given autonomous investment at I_2, the process has a limit, since the marginal propensity to save exceeds zero. As income rises, saving also rises. Eventually, income rises high enough so that saving rises sufficiently to match (the higher level of) investment. $C + I$ once again will equal income, but at a higher level of income. The total increase in income may be divided into two parts: one, the initial or primary increase in income, $10,000,000,000, caused directly by the initial increase in autonomous invest-

ment; two, the secondary increases in income ($5 + $2.5 + ... = $10), caused indirectly by the secondary increases in demand (consumption) stemming from the existence of a propensity for people to adjust spending in response to changes in income

KEYNES II: THE NEO-KEYNESIAN
INTEGRATION OF MONEY AND GOODS
MARKETS

A narrow interpretation of Keynes' *General Theory* would isolate income and expenditures from money markets and interest rates. A broader interpretation, popularized by neo-Keynesian economists Alvin H. Hansen, in the United States, and John R. Hicks, in England, would integrate them.[3] In the Hicks-Hansen version of the Keynesian model, investment depends (inversely) upon the rate of interest as well as upon underlying profit expectations. (A variant is to make investment dependent also upon the level of national income.) Saving (and, thereby, consumption) depends upon the rate of interest as well as the level of income. The supply of money is determined exogenously by monetary authorities. The demand for money is divided into two parts: one, a transactionary component, depending directly upon the level of national income; two, a speculative component, depending inversely upon the rate of interest. A simultaneous and mutual equilibrium in the goods *and* money markets thus would require an equality between saving and investment, *and* between the total demand for money and the supply of money.

This is illustrated in Fig. 7.6a by the intersection of the *IS* and *LM* curves. The *IS* curve depicts a series of different equilibrium positions on the goods market, each characterized by the condition that $S = I (C + I = Y)$. It is negatively sloped on the basis of

[3]See John R. Hicks, "Mr. Keynes and the 'Classics'; A Suggested Interpretation," *Econometrica*, April 1937, pp. 147–59; and Alvin A. Hansen, *A Guide to Keynes* (New York City: McGraw-Hill Book Company, 1953), pp. 140–53.

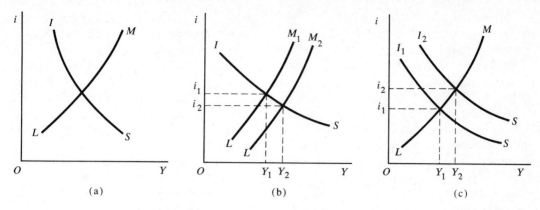

Fig. 7.6. (a) LM/IS curves, (b) an increase in the money supply, (c) an upward shift in the investment function

the proposition that low interest rates are associated with high investment and thus, high income and vice versa. The LM curve shows a series of different equilibria on the money market, each characterized by the condition that the demand for money equals the supply of money ($L = M$). It is positively sloped on the basis of the proposition that high (low) levels of income are associated with high (low) transactionary demands for money, and thus, given the supply of money, high (low) interest rates. The point of intersection of the IS and the LM curves is the only position consistent with the double condition of equilibrium on both the goods market ($S = I$) and the money market ($L = M$).

The neo-Keynesian LM/IS model is a useful device for illustrating the impact of monetary and fiscal policies. For example, an increase in the supply of money can be illustrated by an outward and upward shift in the LM curve from, say, LM_1 to LM_2 in Fig. 7.6b. Given all other propensities and functional relations in the economy, a larger supply of money can accommodate a lower rate of interest (i_2) and (through the stimulating impact of lower interest rates upon higher investment) a higher level of income (Y_2). A decrease in the supply of money would have the opposite effect.

In the area of fiscal policy, a decrease in taxes (by raising consumption and/or invest-

ment) or an increase in government purchases (by supplementing $C + I$) can be illustrated by an upward shift in the IS curve from, say, I_1S to I_2S in Fig. 7.6c. Given all other propensities and functional relations in the economy, a higher level of government purchases, for example, by raising the level of aggregate demand, causes a higher level of income (Y_2). Given the supply of money, a higher income level causes an increase in the transactionary demand for money (illustrated by a movement up the positively sloped LM curve). The higher demand for money, given its supply, causes a higher rate of interest (i_2). Used in unison, monetary and fiscal policy may bolster each other's effects upon national income.

KEYNES III: WAGES, PRICES, EMPLOYMENT, AND THE LABOR MARKET

The incorporation of the labor market into the Keynesian model is essentially a two-stage process: first, abstracting from the supply side of the labor market and assuming a given money wage level; second, incorporating, as in classical and neo-classical economic theory, the ideas that the supply of labor is a direct function of the level of real wages (W/P), and that money wages are perfectly flexible in downward as well as upward directions to clear the labor market.

Given Money Wages. Because of diminishing returns to the employment of labor in the production of output, given the stock of capital and natural resources under given technological conditions, the marginal product of labor decreases (increases) as employment increases (decreases). Under competitive conditions, as seen in Chapter 4, profit maximizing equilibrium for individual firms entails an equality between the money wage level and the market value of the marginal product; that is, between the real wage level and the marginal physical product: $W = P.MPL$ or $W/P = MPL$. Given the money wage level, diminishing returns and lower marginal physical product of labor results in lower real wage levels via higher prices. In the simple Keynesian income-expenditures model, which abstracts from diminishing returns, rising aggregate demand causes increases in real output and employment up to full employment and increases in the price level at full employment. Under conditions of diminishing returns, rising aggregate demand causes increases both in output and employment, and the price level, even before full employment is reached. In this event, the "trade-off" between inflation and unemployment depends essentially on the shape of the functional relation between output and employment. If the response of output to rising employment is large (small), the inflation accompanying the movement toward full employment will be mild (strong). If the money wage level is given, full employment of the labor force requires sufficiently high levels of aggregate demand. Unemployment cannot be eliminated through decreases in money wages, if the latter are given.

Flexible Money Wages. A variant on this model would be where the supply of labor depends directly on the real wage level and money wages are perfectly flexible. In this event, any unemployment because of an excess of the supply of labor above the demand for it would cause money wage levels to fall. Abstracting from the money market and the goods market, lower money wage levels, given the price level, would cause the real wage level to fall. Lower real wage levels would make it profitable to expand employment, just as in traditional theory. Whether higher employment would be sustainable, however, would depend upon whether lower money wages (and prices) are likely to cause aggregate demand to rise sufficiently to match increases in supply caused by increases in employment. As noted, Keynes had serious doubts about the efficacy of promoting full employment through the labor market route of deflation in money wage levels.

KEYNES IV: CAPITAL ACCUMULATION

In the short run, the stock of capital is fixed, but in the long run, positive net investment (investment in excess of depreciation) increases the stock of capital. Though Keynes hinted at the long-run impact of capital accumulation in the *General Theory*, the major strands of a Keynesian-type capital accumulation model have been provided by Keynes' successors, Evsey Domar, in the United States, and Sir Roy Harrod, in England.[4] The simplest means of incorporating capital accumulation into a Keynesian framework is to blend it with the basic income expenditures model.

In brief, net investment, by increasing the stock of capital, raises productive capacity and, thereby, potential output, the extent depending upon the productivity of capital. But as long as the marginal propensity to consume is less than one, spending will increase by less than the increase in income. Thus, the realization of the potential increase in output and the attainment and/or maintenance of full employment utilization of resources requires an increase in investment, the extent depending upon the value of the marginal propensity to save; that is, an increase in income generates an increase in

---

[4]See Evsey Domar, "Expansion and Employment," *American Economic Review*, March 1947, pp. 34–55; and Sir Roy Harrod, "An Essay in Dynamic Theory," *Economic Journal*, March 1939, pp. 14–33.

saving, which requires a further increase in investment.

Thus, the seemingly paradoxical conclusion that investment, by increasing income, creates a requirement for a further increase in investment. The higher the level of investment, the greater investment must be in the future to match the increased saving from the increased income caused by the past level of investment (past increased capital stock). The more rapidly investment grows, the more it must grow, if the growth in desired saving is not to be dissipated in the form of under-full employment of resources. It is not sufficient for investment merely to match full employment saving in any given short-run period. It must grow at a rate sufficient to match the growth in saving from the growth in income generated by the past growth in capital stock.

It is possible that investment could do this. But, as in the short-run case, with investors and savers being different people, saving and investing for largely different reasons, there is no guarantee the desired investment growth rate will match the desired saving growth rate for any sustained period of time. Thus, a developing capitalist economy is constantly on a razor's edge of its own making. If desired investment grows at a rate in excess of the rate of growth in desired saving, the result may be over-expansion and inflation. If desired investment grows at a rate lower than the rate of growth in desired saving, the result may be sluggish growth rates, unemployment, and recession.

KEYNESIAN ANALYSIS OF THE MAJOR ECONOMIC PROBLEMS OF CAPITALISM

Unemployment

The Schumpeterian analysis focused on cyclical economic fluctuations, including cyclical decreases in employment below, as well as increases in price levels above, full employment. But the "equilibrium level," the "normal" position or "neighborhood" around which these fluctuations take place, was conceived as one of full employment. The Keynesian argument diverges from the Schumpeterian and other pre-Keynesian studies of business cycles by emphasizing the possibility that industrially developed capitalist economies may tend toward positions of equilibrium, of economic balance, at levels less than full employment. The Keynesian point is not that capitalist economies are subject to periodic waves of unemployment as part of the process of cyclical growth, but, rather, that the economy tends to stabilize at equilibrium positions characterized by unemployment, and thus, by levels of income or output which lie below their potentials. Capitalist economies have no built-in mechanisms which automatically maintain full employment of society's resources, no automatic adjustment processes which prevent unemployment from occurring or which move rapidly to push the economy back to full employment levels of output if and when unemployment arises.

GOODS MARKET

The bases for this conclusion are drawn from the Keynesian analysis of the goods, money, and labor markets. On the goods market (illustrated in Fig. 7.5), an equilibrium level of income and expenditures may or may not entail full employment utilization of resources, notably labor. Equilibrium income requires an equality between aggregate demand and supply (in a no-government economy abstracting from foreign trade, an equality between consumption plus investment and national income, or between desired saving and investment). If equilibrium income (say, OY_1 in Fig. 7.5, where $I_1 = S$ and $C + I_1 = Y$) involves a high enough level of aggregate demand and supply to entail full employment, well and good. But suppose full employment requires a higher level of aggregate demand and supply (say, OY_2 in Fig. 7.5). Then, unless every increase in supply is automatically and spontaneously matched by a corresponding increase in demand, a "depressionary gap" will exist. Demand will be insufficient to match full employment supply; expected revenues flowing into business firms from consumption and investment expenditures will be insufficient to cover costs of production or payments to income recipients; and investment will be insufficient to offset saving out of full employment income. (S exceeds I_1, and $C + I_1$ is insufficient to match Y at income level OY_2 in Fig. 7.5). In the absence of an autonomous upward shift in consumption or investment, or some countervailing force outside the private sector of the domestic economy (such as a tax cut, or an increase in government spending or exports), full employment income could not be maintained, and income (along with output and employment) would tend to fall to some lower level below full employment (such as OY_1 in Fig. 7.5), which was sustainable. In a depressed state, Keynes argued, the economy may experience widespread unemployment and yet be in perfect balance or equilibrium, with an equality between demand and supply on the one hand and desired saving and investment on he other. (In Fig. 7.5, $S = I_1$ and $C + I_1 = Y$ at point E_1.)

Thus, one major obstacle to full employment equilibrium may be insufficient consumption and/or investment demand. Consumption may be insufficient for one or a combination of reasons: First, the overall level of the consumption function may be low. Economically developed capitalist economies are characterized by considerable inequality in the distribution of income. Because people in higher incomes brackets tend to save a larger percent of their income than those in lower brackets, it is possible that the height of the aggregate consumption function is low,[5] lower than if income were

distributed more equally. Second, the marginal propensity to consume is generally less than one. This means that as income rises during prosperity, some of the increase will go into saving; not all will be spent on consumption. Third, even if the *marginal* propensity to consume were to remain constant, the *average* propensity to consume (consumption divided by income) may decrease as income increases, thus generating a rising average as well as an absolute "gap" of saving between income and consumption, increasing with higher level of income. Fourth, it is possible (through not necessary for the Keynesian conclusions on unemployment equilibrium) that the marginal propensity to consume is not constant, but decreases as income rises. Fifth, in any short-run period, the consumption function is likely to be relatively stable, at least more so than the investment function. Thus, capitalist economies cannot depend upon *continuous upward* shifts in the height of the consumption function during periods of propensity to offset short-run decreases in the average and/or marginal propensities to consume as income rises.[6]

---

[5]It should be noted this does not necessarily support proposals for large-scale redistribution of income: First, the gap in the *marginal* propensities to consume of rich and poor may be much less than in *average* propensities to consume, so that any given

redistribution of income would have much smaller upward effects upon the aggregate level of consumption than one would suppose on the basis of average data. Second, there may be "social and psychological justification for significant inequalities of incomes and wealth . . ." independent of the aggregate level of output and employment. [14: 374] Third, measures exist which are superior to income redistribution for promoting full employment. Fourth, arguments about the *reform* of the *distribution* of income can and perhaps should be distinguished from those concerned with *recovery* in the aggregate *level* of *demand* and *income*. Given judgments about the distribution of income, as determined by social, ethical, and political criteria beyond the scope of Keynesian analysis, attention *then* can be focused on policies designed to raise the overall level of income.

[6]Three of these possibilities are illustrated in Fig. 7.7. In Fig. 7.7a, the line depicting the functional relation between consumption and income is a straight line, commencing at the origin. Along the line, the marginal propensity to consume (*MPC*) equals the average propensity to consume (*APC*), but the *absolute* saving gap between consumption and income (illu-

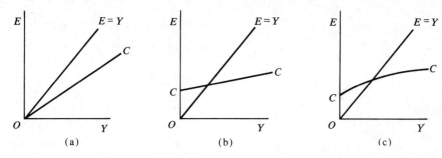

Fig. 7.7. (a) A long-run consumption function, (b) a short-run consumption function, and (c) a variable MPC

Given the propensity to consume, the level of output is determined in the Keynesian analysis by the volume of investment. But investment may be insufficient to match full-employment saving for several reasons. First, a point emphasized more by post-Keynesian economists than by Keynes: Investment and thus prosperity may be choked off by rising interest rates caused, in the absence of increases in the money supply, by increased demand for money balances generated by higher prosperity incomes. Second, in any given short-run period, with a given array of investment opportunities, the expected rate of profit will tend to fall as investment is extended from more to less profitable areas, as building and/or machinery costs rise because of diminishing returns in

capital goods producing industries. Third, this may be offset temporarily by optimistic subjective profit expectations extending beyond those probable in the light of more objective, long-run determinants of profitable investment such as population growth, resource discoveries, and technological improvements. However, investment made under such conditions is inherently "unstable and cannot endure, because it is prompted by expectations which are destined to disappointment." [14: 321] Fourth, investment depends on expectations of future profits. Probably the most important thing to be said about the future is it is uncertain. If it is, and if investment in large measure is independent of current income and depends upon profit expectations of such a future, then it is by no means certain investment will prove sufficient to match full employment saving.

In short, supply does not automatically or necessarily generate equivalent demand. The receipt of income, though equal to output and expenditures for any past period of time, does not guarantee a continuous reinjection of expenditures into the circular flow equal to that income: First, because as income increases, consumption is likely to increase, but by less, thus generating a larger gap, in absolute (and, perhaps, relative and marginal) terms, between income and consumption, that must be matched by investment if higher levels of income are to be maintained and/or achieved; second, investment is uncertain, unstable, and largely independent of the level of income. There is no guarantee it will

strated by the vertical distance between the C line and the $45°$ $E = Y$ reference line) increases as income increases. This is plausible in the long run, but less so in the short run, where time lags in response to changes in income and accommodation to accustomed living standards are stronger. In Fig. 7.7b, which represents a short run consumption function, the C line commences above the origin and intersects the $E = Y$ line at some positive income level. Below this point, C exceeds Y (through desired dis-saving and credit creation), and the APC exceeds 1; above this point, Y exceeds C, and the APC is less than 1; at this point, $C = Y$ and the $APC = 1$. Thus, increases in income bring a higher *relative*, as well as absolute, saving gap because the APC varies inversely with the level of income. Because the consumption function is a straight line, however, its rate of change, or MPC, remains constant at different income levels. Fig. 7.7c illustrates the MPC varying inversely with the level of income. In this event, the *marginal* saving gap also increases at higher levels of income.

be sufficient to match increased saving gaps as income rises. "This analysis," argued Keynes,

> supplies us with an explanation of the paradox of poverty in the midst of plenty. For the mere existence of an insufficiency of effective demand may, and often will, bring the increase of employment to a standstill *before* a level of full employment has been reached.... Moreover, the richer the community, the wider will tend to be the gap between its actual and its potential production; and therefore the more obvious and outrageous the defects of the economic system. For a poor community will be prone to consume by far the greater part of its output, so that a very modest measure of investment will be sufficient to provide full employment; whereas a wealthy community will have to discover much ampler opportunities for investment if the saving propensities of its wealthier members are to be compatible with the employment of its poorer members. If in a potentially wealthy community the inducement to invest is weak, then, in spite of its potential wealth, the working of the principle of effective demand will compel it to reduce its actual output, until, in spite of its potential wealth, it has become so poor that its surplus over its consumption is sufficiently diminished to correspond to the weakness of the inducement to invest. [14: 30–31]

MONEY, INTEREST, AND INVESTMENT

A classical argument is that, if full employment saving exceeds investment, interest rates will fall until saving and investment are again equal. The interest rate, in this view, serves as an equilibrating mechanism on the investment market. The Keynesian and neo-Keynesian answer to this is that the determination and role of interest rates and their relation to investment and income are much more complex. For one thing, income cannot be assumed to remain constant if, at full employment, saving were greater than investment.

Decreases in income, as well as (or instead of) falling interest rates, would be more likely. It is consistent, however, with more recent formulations of Keynesian theory, that interest rates and income are interconnected: A decrease in income will likely bring lower demand for money balances for transactionary purposes, which, given the supply of money, will lead to lower interest rates, and thereby, to a level of investment higher than that which would have taken place had interest rates been inflexible in a downward direction. The same results could be generated if monetary authorities were to pursue an easy money policy, increasing the supply of money to promote the lower interest rates necessary to bring higher investment. Conceivably, interest rates could be decreased far enough via either of these routes to raise investment to a level matching full-employment saving.

It has often been observed empirical studies do not support the contention that investment is highly responsive to small changes in the rate of interest. If investment were highly responsive to small changes in interest rates, then small decreases in interest rates would bring relatively large increases in investment. If, however, as many contemporary Keynesian economists suggest, investment is relatively unresponsive, relatively large decreases in interest rates would be necessary, particularly at rates in the vicinity of, say, three or four percent, to generate small increases in investment.

Further, in the Keynesian view, there may be limitations to the downward flexibility of interest rates. Two related, yet distinguishable, cases may be noted. First, interest rates can be lowered (either directly, through an increase in the money supply, or indirectly, via a decrease in the demand for money brought about by a decrease in national income and/or the price level), but not below some minimum positive figure, say one to two percent. This might be caused either from the side of the supply of money, by an "institutional minimum," wherein commercial bankers refuse to lend money below some minimum interest rate. Or, it might stem from the side of the demand for money, as in the case of the "liquidity trap," illustrated in Fig.

7.2. If at some low, yet positive, rate of interest, the demand for money becomes infinite (illustrated by the horizontal section of the LL curve) and if people prefer to hold on to their inactive money rather than part with it at such a low rate of interest, then increases in the supply of money (beyond, say, OM_2), are powerless to force the rate of interest lower. If the volume of investment forthcoming at this rate of interest lies below full employment saving, then interest rate flexibility cannot be said to provide a mechanism, automatic or contrived, to guarantee full employment equilibrium.

Second, even if there is no liquidity trap, and interest rates are flexible down to zero, expected rates of profit may be so low that the volume of investment, even at zero interest rates, falls short of desired saving at full employment. This is unlikely in the case of minor recessions; but in a deep depression, it is a possibility. Profit expectations in this case may be so pessimistic that no *positive* rate of interest, no matter how low, is sufficient to entice businessmen to borrow and invest enough to promote a movement to full employment prosperity. (Even in this case, a bizarre solution presents itself: a *negative* rate of interest. It is, however, theoretical: In a capitalist economy, what commercial banker is going to *pay* a businessman to borrow and invest?

WAGES, PRICES, AND THE LABOR
MARKET

It should be noted that under-full employment equilibrium on the goods market is characterized by an excess of supply of labor over demand for labor. Yet this condition on the labor market can be maintained if the national income is in equilibrium, and if the flow of investment plus consumption expenditures is the basic determinant of income and employment, that is, if aggregate demand on goods markets calls the tune, and employment falls into step with the output requirements thus determined.

But the question arises: Couldn't the process operate the other way around? If the supply of labor were in excess of the demand for it, wouldn't this force wages down, lowering costs of production; stimulating employment of unemployed workers, thus raising income and, thereby, demand for goods?

As suggested earlier, the Keynesian and neo-Keynesian answer to this contains both theoretical and practical elements. The key theoretical point is that, under the conditions illustrated in Fig. 7.5, decreased real wages cannot successfully push the economy back to full employment (equal, say, to OY_2) on the basis of their direct effects. The reason for this is that (unless the $MPC = 1$, or the volume of investment varies with income in such a way that it is always equal to the gap between income and consumption—which would guarantee full employment) any increase in the supply of output beyond, say, OY_1, as a result of an increase in employment, could not be sold at prices covering costs of production because, *given* the aggregate demand function (illustrated by the height and slope of the $C + I_1$ curve), the increase in supply would not be matched by an equivalent increase in demand.

Decreased real wages may operate as a full-employment equilibrating mechanism, in the Keynesian view, through their *indirect* effects on the basic independent variables in the economic system; decreased real wages must have the effect of shifting up the supply of money and/or shifting down the demand for money (thereby decreasing interest rates and, given the expected rate of profit, increasing investment), or shifting up the expected rate of profit and, thereby, investment, or shifting up the propensity to consume (shifting down the propensity to save) and, thereby, consumption.

Any of these indirect effects is theoretically possible. For example, decreased wages and prices would tend to lower the transactionary demand for money. This, given the aggregate supply of money and the general state of liquidity preference, would release funds for speculative purposes, (assuming interest rates are elastic or responsive to changes in the supply of money and its allocation between the transaction and financial asset sectors) which would lower interest rates and, thereby, (assuming investment is elastic or responsive to changes in the rate of interest) increase investment. (This would have the effect, per Fig. 7.6b, of shifting the *LM* curve to the right, thereby increasing national income.)

A second set of possibilities has to do with the expected rate of profit. If "business confidence" is encouraged by wage cuts (as is likely to be true if businessmen do not associate lower wages with lower monetary demand; if wage cuts are general and "once-and-for-all," and higher wages are expected in the future; if businessmen expect workers and labor unions to cooperate about wage cuts), wage cuts may be accompanied by an upward shift in the expected rate of profit, and thus, higher domestic investment. Similarly, wage cuts at home relative to wage cuts abroad may increase exports and, thereby, the level of net foreign investment (the excess of all export items over all import items).

Third, if lower money wages are accompanied by lower prices, the real value of liquid assets, such as U.S. government securities, will rise, which could lower the propensity to save, raise the propensity to consume, and, thereby, increase consumption. This is the "real balance effect" or "Pigou effect" identified by English economist A. C. Pigou. (Theses last two cases may be illustrated in Fig. 7.6c by an upward shift to the right of the *IS* curve, with a resulting increase in national income.)

On the other hand, there are alternative theoretical possibilities to these three cases. The expansionary effects in the money market of a decrease in the transactionary demand for money may come to grief on the shores of the liquidity trap and/or an exceptionally low investment-demand function. Business expectations and confidence can be shattered as well as encouraged by wage and price cuts during depressions, particularly in the "unfavorable contingency" where "money-wages are slowly sagging downward and each reduction in wages serves to diminish confidence in the prospective maintenance of wages". [14: 265] The same deflation in the price level which raises the real value of financial assets also redistributes income and wealth from variable to fixed-income receivers and from debtors to creditors, with possibly depressive effects upon the propensity to consume.

In addition to theoretical debate, there are practical problems. First, labor unions, minimum wage laws, business monopoly, and other institutional factors may prevent wage and price flexibility. Second, the quantitative size of several of the theoretically expansionary effects might be so small, even negligible, that large decreases in money wages and prices might be necessary to generate full employment. This is likely the case in the "Pigou effect" and also would be true in the event of a highly elastic liquidity preference function and a highly inelastic investment demand function. Third, insofar as the money market effects of wage cuts are to lower interest rates and thereby raise investment, wage flexibility is a cumbersome, uncertain, and roundabout substitute for monetary policy. A simpler, more direct route would be for monetary authorities to increase the supply of money. Fourth, insofar as the indirect goods market effects of wage cuts are to raise aggregate consumption and/or investment demand, wage flexibility again is a cumbersome, roundabout subjstitute for fiscal policy. In the Keynesian view, a simpler alternative is the direct manipulation of government taxing and spending. The net conclusion is that, whatever the theoretical pros and cons, wage and price deflation is likely to be limited and ineffectual as a process in economically developed capitalist countries for avoiding the trap of "under-full employment equilibrium," and as a technique for promoting and/or maintaining full employment prosperity.

Keynesian economists are often and perhaps understandably irked by the popular association of Keynes' major ideas with "depression economics." Keynes' *major* concern (outside of wartime finance and inflation), as an empiricist and policy adviser, was with the problem of depression and the possibility of an equilibrium at less than full employment. Even in the realm of pure economic analysis, Keynes' essentially static methodology and his emphasis on broad, macroeconomic relations and aggregate demand are probably more relevant to the big problems of depression and unemployment than to the more subtle, complex, and dynamic interrelationships between demand and supply which constitute the essence of "inflationary processes." On the other hand, the Keynesian tools are independent of the empirical values ascribed to the various variables, and may be applied to the study of inflation, as well as depression.

DEMAND-PULL INFLATION AT FULL EMPLOYMENT

The first and simplest case is that of pure (or, in Keynes' view, "true") inflation, where, at full employment, in the short run, and given the aggregate supply function, demand exceeds supply. This is illustrated in Fig. 7.5. Picture an equilibrium, full-employment level of income at OY_1. If aggregate demand were to shift up to $C + I_2$, then, given full employment income at OY_1, the excess of demand over supply would constitute an "inflationary gap." generating expansion in the level of income which, given full employment output, would be entirely inflationary. Because the elasticity of supply at this point would be theoretically zero, the increase in the price level would be proportionate to the upward shift in aggregate demand.

This simple "demand-pull" theory of inflation is similar to, yet distinguishable from, the more traditional pre-Keynesian theory of money-pull inflation. In various monetary theories of inflation, an increase in the supply of money at full employment will cause rising prices—either directly, by increasing monetary expenditures, or indirectly, by decreasing interest rates and, thereby, increasing investment (without decreasing desired consumption expenditures). In the Keynesian view, an increase in the supply of money is neither a necessary nor sufficient cause of inflation. It is not necessary because the height of the aggregate demand function $(C + I)$ may shift up at full employment, *given* the supply of money. It is not sufficient, at least in cases where interest rates are unresponsive to changes in the supply of money and/or investment is unresponsive to changes in the rate of interest. Of course, an increase in the money supply *may* cause inflation, but if it does, it is, in the Keynesian view, through its impact on aggregate demand when the economy is operating under full employment conditions.

What about an increase in demand from $C + I_1$ to or toward $C + I_2$? Might not this generate inflation *before* full employment is reached? In this first and simplest case, the Keynesian answer is "no." If we assume that all unemployed resources are "homogeneous and interchangeable," that is, equal in quality and efficiency, and if we abstract from problems of "variable proportions" and "diminishing returns," "bottlenecks" in strategic sectors of the economy, and monopoly positions (labor unions) which could push up costs and/or prices, an increase in aggregate demand below full employment will generate an increase in employment, and thus, output. *Below* full employment, rising demand causes rising employment and output—that is, prosperity; *at* full employment, rising demand causes rising prices—that is, inflation.

Subject to certain important qualifications, this simple, crude model holds important practical implications, namely: "It tells us when to fear and when not to fear inflation. It tells us that, subject to the qualifying assumptions, inflation is not to be feared when there is large-scale unemployment; and it tells us that once full employment has been attained, inflation does become a threat. Thus it relieves us of the dread of inflation when we are plagued with mass unemployment, and it warns us that once we have conquered unemployment we must be on guard against inflation."[7]

A classic case that points up this bit of wisdom is that of Germany in the early 1930s. Depression, unemployment, and Hitler's promises to do something about them were strategic factors in catapulting the Nazis to power, while fear of prospective inflationary consequences was a major factor in preventing application by the Weimar Government of the large-scale increases in government expenditures which might have cured depression.

IMPURE INFLATION

A second, more complicated case is that of impure inflation, where prices, as well as output and employment, can rise prior to the attainment of full employment. Demand exceeds supply at less than full employment and, because supply does not increase in proportion to increases in demand (the elasticity of supply of output to a change in demand is less than 1), *both* prices and output-employment rise as demand increases. Keynes presented three prime examples of factors working for impure inflation: First, as full employment is approached, the bargaining position of organized labor is increased, leading to pressures for higher wage rates, with resulting upward shifts in production costs and, thereby, prices. Second, not all resources are equally variable. A change in the proportions of resource-inputs (for example, an increase in the ratio of labor to fixed plant and equipment), may, in the short run, lead to diminishing productivity and

thus increasing costs and prices, even if wage rates remain constant. Third, full employment is not reached simultaneously in all sectors of the economy. Conditions of perfectly inelastic supply, and thus, inflation may be reached in certain "bottleneck" sectors prior to full employment in the economy as a whole. If steel prices are rising and other prices are not falling, or not sufficiently to offset rising steel prices, then the average price level will rise.

These various alternative relations between demand, output, and the price level are illustrated by the shape of the aggregate supply curve ZZ in Fig. 7.8. In Stage I, with considerable unemployment, rising demand leads to rising employment and, thereby, output, but with perfectly elastic supply of output, no change in the price level. In Stage III—"pure inflation"— rising demand leads to a higher price level, but, with zero elasticity of supply of output, no change in employment or output. In the intermediate zone of State II—"impure inflation"—rising demand is accompanied by rising output and rising prices. Under these conditions, the cost of reducing unemployment in Stage II may be inflation, while the cost of reducing inflation may be unemployment. This is illustrated more directly in Fig. 7.9 by the *IU*, or "inflation-unemployment," curve. In the case of pure inflation, the *IU* curve would cross the

[7]Dudley Dillard, *The Economics of John Maynard Keynes*, (Englewood Cliffs, N. J.: Prentice-Hall, Inc., 1948), p. 227.

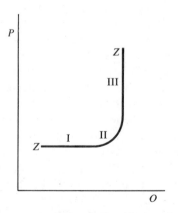

Fig. 7.8. An aggregate supply function

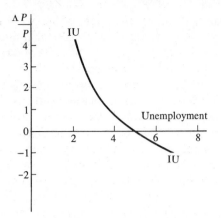

Fig. 7.9. Trade-off between inflation and unemployment

horizontal axis at, say, three or four percent unemployment (substantially full employment). Rising demand would bring increases in the price level (measured on the vertical axis) only above this position. In the case of impure inflation, however, the price level commences rising at less than full employment—say at five percent unemployment, instead of three or four percent. In this case, a reduction in unemployment below five percent, illustrated by a movement to the left on the horizontal axis, is accompanied by rising prices, while a reduction of inflation is accompanied by a departure from full employment.

These comments merely skim the surface of the complicated problems of inflation in economically developed capitalist or modified-capitalist economies. But they emphasize that: (1) Keynes' and Keynesian analysis is not merely "depression economics" and may be applied to problems of inflation; (2) (a modified version of) the basic Keynesian model includes the possibility of a conflict between the goals of full employment and price stability; and (3) the basic Keynesian model of aggregate demand is perhaps more applicable to the big, macroeconomic problems of under-full employment equilibrium than to the more subtle, intricate problems of inflationary processes, especially of the non-demand-pull variety.

Contemporary economists J. R. Hicks and Roy Harrod in England and Lloyd Metzler and Alvin H. Hansen in the United States have used one or more of Keynes' fundamental concepts as building blocks in constructing dynamic models of cyclical fluctuations. While major depressions of the 1930s variety have receded into recollection, cyclical movements in economic activity definitely have persisted into the post-World War II period.

In his *Business Cycles and National Income*, Alvin H. Hansen, who perhaps has done more than any other author to communicate the Keynesian theory and philosophy of capitalism, suggested a synthesis of various cycle theories around three central concepts: (1) the relationship between the expected rate of profit and the interest rate; (2) the consumption function and multiplier; (3) the accelerator.

THE EXPECTED RATE OF PROFIT AND THE INTEREST RATE

Suppose we view the economy in a position of equilibrium at less than full employment. Now, suppose an upward shift in investment occurs. This increase, unless offset by a decreased propensity to consume, will lead to increased employment, output, and, as the system moves to or toward full employment, rising prices. But this investment-generated expansionary movement cannot last, because, built into the internal workings of the system are self-correcting factors leading to termination of expansion and precipitating a downturn into contraction. In any given short-run period of time and with any given set of investment opportunities, the expected rate of profit will vary inversely with the volume of investment. As investment rises, expected profit rates eventually will fall as the stock of capital increases and the supply price or replacement cost of capital assets increases. Meanwhile, rising incomes generated by rising investment are accompanied by increased demands for money balances, and, given the supply of money, by higher interest rates. Thus, an investment boom, initiated by an excess of expected profit rates over the interest rate, reaches its terminus, partly through increased interest rates and partly through falling profit rates.

Keynes emphasized, somewhat in the manner of Schumpeter's "second approximation," the possibility of a sharp downturn, accompanied by a liquidity "crisis." The immediate cause of such a downturn, which Keynes apparently felt was typical of the cyclical experience of the nineteenth century, is a sharp drop in the expected rate of profit following a period of speculative and exuberant expansion. During later stages of the boom, "optimistic expectations" may be "sufficiently strong to offset" the increased stock of capital, rising production costs, and rising interest rates. The bases of these expectations, however, are extremely "precarious." When more tempered, objective evaluations of profit expectations replace the boom-induced subjective estimates, as eventually they will, the result may be a "sudden collapse in the marginal efficiency of capital." When "disillusion falls upon an over-optimistic and over-bought market, it should fall with sudden and even catastrophic force. Moreover, the dismay and uncertainty as to the future which accompanies a collapse in the marginal efficiency of capital naturally precipitates a sharp increase in liquidity-preference—and hence a rise in the rate of interest (which) may seriously aggravate the decline in investment." [14: 315–16]

The reader can easily construct the basic phases of the contraction and upturn: A decrease in investment leads gradually to an increase in the marginal efficiency of capital through a decrease in capital stocks and production costs. Meanwhile, falling incomes are accompanied by decreased demands for money and, assisted perhaps by an increase in the supply of money by monetary authorities, by decreased interest rates. For a significant period of time—the length depending mainly upon (a) "the length of life of durable assets in relation to" (b) "the normal rate of growth" and, (c) "the carrying costs of surplus stocks" [14: 317] of inventories—these counteracting forces may be more than offset by downward shifts in the marginal efficiency of capital. The upturn must await the "return of confidence," that is, an upward shift in the marginal efficiency of capital, which comes after sufficient time has passed for machinery and tools accumulated during the boom to wear out, for surplus inventories to be liquidated, and for the normal rate of growth, accompanied by falling production costs and lower interest rates, to entice an upturn in investment. In an especially severe depression, like that of the 1930s, this may be a long time in coming.

THE CONSUMPTION FUNCTION AND THE MULTIPLIER

Hansen has argued that "the great contribution of Keynes' *General Theory* was the clear and specific formulation of the consumption function. This is an epoch-making contribution to the tools of economic analysis. . . . The consumption function is by far the most powerful instrument which has been added to the economist's kit of tools in our generation."[8] Endeavors of empirical researchers to put statistical content into this concept and growing realization that the consumption function may be less stable than Keynes presumed, have diminished somewhat the exuberance of this evaluation. Still, it is true the consumption function, and its companion, the multiplier, play important roles in the analysis of cyclical fluctuations—though, they were not explicitly discussed by Keynes in conjunction with his "Notes on the Trade Cycle."

The consumption function is relevant both for the analysis of expansions and contrac-

---

[8] Alvin H. Hansen, "The General Theory (2)," in Seymour E. Harris, editor, *The New Economics* (New York City: Alfred A. Knopf, Inc., 1952), p. 135. Cf. Alvin H. Hansen, *A Guide to Keynes*, p. 27.

tions and for downturns and upturns. In regard to the former, the multiplier, which Keynes derived from the consumption function, gives more explicit, systematic, and precise content to the concept of cumulative, self-reinforcing waves of expansion and contraction, which were part of every pre-Keynesian cycle theory. The basic idea is a shift in any autonomous variable, (for example, autonomous investment) will tend to be accompanied by larger, multiple shifts in income and employment, explicable in terms of secondary repercussions upon consumption of the initiating disturbance, the extent of such secondary effects depending on the size of the marginal propensity to consume. In regard to the latter, as long as the marginal propensity to consume is less than one and the consumption function relatively stable, or more stable than autonomous investment, fluctuations in income will tend to be self-limiting in both directions. Decreases and increases in income tend to be accompanied by smaller decreases and increases in consumption, thus placing a damper on contractions and expansions.

THE ACCELERATOR

Keynes did not develop or utilize the concept of the accelerator. He contented himself with the "fact that an increase in consumption is apt in itself to stimulate . . . further investment merely fortifies the argument" (of the multiplier).[9] But the accelerator is an integral part of the contemporary neo-Keynesian analysis of cyclical fluctuations. Its essential features are summarized herein.

Students of cyclical economic fluctuations have noted two prominent characteristics of investment: (1) it tends to be relatively more unstable than consumption; (2) it is often a "leader" in cyclical movements, turning down (up) when income and consumption are still rising (falling). The accelerator helps explain these two phenomena.

---

[9]John Maynard Keynes, "The General Theory of Employment," *Quarterly Journal of Economics*, 1937, p. 222.

The basic idea of the accelerator is that investment (more accurately, the non-autonomous component of it) depends upon the *change* in the level of output (or some component thereof, for example, consumption) given some desired ratio between the flow of output and the stock of capital. Suppose, for example, the desired ratio of capital stock to the annual flow of output (the capital-output ratio), under given technological conditions, is 2 : 1; that output = 100 and desired and actual capital stock is 200 in year 1; and that the rate of depreciation of capital is 10 percent (or 20 when capital stock is 200) per year. Now, suppose that demand for final output increases in years 2 and 3, as shown in Table 7-1 (where *Ig* = gross investment, and *In* = net investment).

As demand for final output increases from 100 to 110, desired capital stock rises from 200 to 220. With depreciation (10 percent of 200) at 20, an increase in capital stock to 220 requires an increase in *Ig* to 40 (20 to offset depreciation, 20 to enable an expansion in output to meet rising demand). *Ig* doubles (from 20 to 40), and *In* rises from 0 to 20. An increase in demand for output (of 10 percent) has induced a larger increase in *Ig* (of 100 percent). Now, notice what happens in year 3 as demand for final output continues to increase, but at a *decreasing rate*, from 110 to 115. Desired *K* is now 230. But actual *K* is 200 (200 − 20). (If depreciation stayed at 10 percent of *K*, it would be slightly more (22), and actual *K* would be slightly less (198).) Thus, *Ig drops* to 30, and *In drops* to 10. *A decrease in the rate of increase* of final demand has caused a *downturn* in *I*, even though the *level* of demand is higher in year 3 than 2.

Table 7-1.

Year	Output	Capital Stock	Ig	In
1	100	200	20	0
2	110	220	40	20
3	115	230	30	10

Table 7-2.

Year	Output	Capital Stock	Ig	In
1	100	200	20	0
2	90	180	0	−20
3	85	170	10	−10

Alternatively, suppose demand for final output decreases, as shown in Table 7-2. As output falls from 100 in year 1 to 90 in year 2, the desired K falls from 200 to 180. With depreciation at 20, desired K = actual K, giving Ig at 0 and In at −20. A *decrease* in demand for final output has been accompanied by a larger decrease in I. Now, notice what happens as demand for final output falls from 90 to 85 in year 3. Desired K decreases to 170. But with depreciation at 20 (18, to be technically accurate), actual K is now 160, making Ig = 10 and In = −10. A *decrease in the rate of decrease* of final output has induced an *upturn* in I, even though the *level* of output is lower.

Integration of these three tools (profit rates in relation to interest rates, the multiplier, the accelerator) provides a useful framework for understanding the *general* process of cyclical economic fluctuations in developed capitalist economies, illustrated in Table 7-3.

Long-Run Problems and Prospects

It is true, as Schumpeter argued, the "exact skeleton of Keynes' system belongs . . . to macrostatics, not to macrodynamics . . ." and that Keynes "confined his *model* . . . to the range of short-run phenomena." Indeed,

we can sympathize with Schumpeter when he concluded, "*All the phenomena incident to the creation and change in* (the industrial) *apparatus, that is to say, the phenomena that dominate the capitalist processes, are thus excluded from consideration.*"[10] At the same time, Keynes' "vision" and the Keynesian argument of the 1930s was set within the framework of long-run historical change and prospects. The Keynesian philosophy of capitalism, like that of Marx and Schumpeter, has its own theory of "breakdown." Like Marx, and unlike Schumpeter, Keynes felt the capitalist economy, its "engine," was sick. But unlike both, Keynes felt that, with minor surgery and proper medication applied in the right dosages by a wise and knowledgeable physician, a modified form of capitalism could be made to work and endure.

The long-run malaise of capitalism, in the Keynesian view, is the possibility of a more or less secular "stagnation." This term, suggested by and associated with Keynes' leading American expositor, Alvin H. Hansen, does *not* mean perpetual contraction, the terminus of economic growth, absence of cyclical fluctuations or inflation, or perpetual absence of full employment. It may, but need not, be characterized by a decrease in the rate of increase in *potential* output, and/or by a growing gap between actual and potential output. It is a description only of capitalism under certain given conditions, at a particular stage of historical development, and in the absence of countervailing forces. It is not a

---

[10]Quotations from Schumpeter, "Keynes, the Economist (2)," in Harris, editor, *op. cit.*, pp. 92–93. Italics in original.

Table 7-3.

Expansion	Downturn	Contraction	Upturn
r > i ⟶ ↑I	↑I ⟶ ↓r; ↑Y ⟶ ↑i	i > r ⟶ ↓I	↓I ⟶ ↑r; Y ⟶ ↓i
↑I ⟶ mult. ↑Y	↑Y ⟶ ↑gap bet. Y & C (MPC < 1)	I↓ ⟶ mult. ↓Y	↓Y ⟶ ↓gap bet. Y & C
↑Y ⟶ ↑I	↓rate ↑Y ⟶ ↓I	↓Y ⟶ ↓I	↓rate ↓Y ⟶ ↑I

forecast, but more on the order of a *prediction* ("on the basis of our analysis of the past, and insofar as the future is like the past, then, given certain underlying conditions or data, and other things remaining equal, capitalism could, and in the absence of certain prospectively effective countervailing forces to be identified presently, probably would more or less stagnate in the future.")[11]

Secular stagnation in the Keynesian sense means and requires more or less persistent failure to sustain full employment, and therefore a more or less chronic tendency for the long-run trend in actual output to fall below its potential level over time as well as within a particular period of time. Secular stagnation, in short, is the situation in which, over the long run, unemployment is the general rule and full employment the exception. The gap between actual and potential output may remain the same or increase. Keynes described the problem: ". . . it is an outstanding characteristic of the economic system in which we live that, whilst it is subject to severe fluctuations in respect of output and employment, it is not violently unstable. Indeed, it seems capable of remaining in a chronic condition of sub-normal activity for a considerable period without any marked tendency either towards recovery or towards complete collapse. Moreover, the evidence indicates that full, or even approximately full, employment is of rare and short-lived occurrence. Fluctuations may start briskly but seem to wear themselves out before they have proceeded to great extremes, and an intermediate situation which is neither desperate nor satisfactory is our normal lot." [14: 249–50]

The immediate cause of secular stagnation is a more or less chronic tendency for full employment saving to exceed autonomous investment; that is, the Keynesian version of capitalist "breakdown" may be interpreted as meaning "over-saving," "under-investment," or both. In regard to over-saving, even if consumption were to increase proportionately to the increase in national income (leaving the *average* propensity to consume constant), it still would be true (as long as the *marginal* propensity to consume was less than one) that the absolute size of the "saving gap" would grow as income grew. The other side of the coin is that the price system does not automatically guarantee investment will be forthcoming to meet the growth in the absolute size of saving under full employment conditions. In short, the proposition that supply will tend to create its own demand at full employment "is not valid because consumption in real terms rises absolutely less than output, or real income . . . and this widening gap may or may not be filled by investment depending upon the prevailing strength of the factors (technology and population growth) which determine the investment outlays."[12]

Short-run inconsistency between full employment saving and investment may be explained in terms of uncertain expectations, "sudden collapses" in the marginal efficiency of capital, cyclical saturation of markets, cyclical or prosperity-induced rising investment costs, and the like. But the Keynesian theory of long-run or secular stagnation was based on the expectation of continuing, long-run causal forces, a persistent arteriosclerosis of investment opportunities. This dearth of profitable investment opportunities and resulting secular stagnation in a mature, capitalist economy was interpreted somewhat differently by Keynes and Hansen, as will be apparent.

---

[11]On "secular stagnation," see Benjamin Higgins, *Economic Development* (New York City: W. W. Norton & Company, Inc., 1968), pp. 120–42. Also, Higgins' earlier expositions: "Concepts and Criteria of Secular Stagnation," in *Essays in Honor of Alvin H. Hansen* (New York City: W.W. Norton & Company, Inc.,1948); and "The Concept of Secular Stagnation," *American Economic Review*, March 1950.

---

[12]Alvin H. Hansen, *A Guide to Keynes, op. cit.*, pp. 75, 34.

KEYNES

In Keynes' sketchy statements of the problem, the marginal efficiency of capital was held to vary inversely with the stock of capital. First, as capital accumulates, given a full employment labor force and under given technological conditions, it yields a positive, but diminishing marginal physical product. "Owing to its accumulation of capital being already larger, the opportunities for further investment . . . in a wealthy community . . . are less attractive." [14: 219] Indeed, Keynes argued, it is quite conceivable that, in a highly industrialized economy, the capital stock could be increased to the extent "to be able to bring down the marginal efficiency of capital in equilibrium approximately to zero. . . ." [14: 220][13]

Second, each increase in the stock of capital increases output. But, as long as the long-run $MPC > 1$, each increase in output is accompanied by an increase in consumption which is less than the increase in output, and thus, by an increased need for ever higher investment if higher potential outputs are to be continually realized. "Each time we secure today's equilibrium by increased investment, we are aggravating the difficulty of securing equilibrium tomorrow." [14: 105]

_____

[13] Actually, it is the marginal *productivity* of capital which would be brought down to zero as capital stock increased. The marginal efficiency of capital is an expected rate of monetary return on investment, embodying a relationship between expected net revenues and current supply price or replacement cost of capital assets. A decrease in the marginal productivity of capital is more accurately illustrated by a downward shift in the marginal efficiency of capital curve than by a movement down along it. It also should be noted that the possibility of a zero marginal productivity of capital would require not only that the marginal productivity decreased as the stock of capital increased, but that it decreased at a constant or increasing rate. If the marginal productivity decreased at a decreasing rate, it would approach, but never be equal to, zero. Capital always would have a net marginal yield, and the demand for capital would have no boundary or limit.

Given the propensity to consume, a decrease in the marginal efficiency of capital, in the Keynesian view, can be offset only by a decrease in the rate of interest. But decreased interest rates are not automatically forthcoming. (Indeed, decreased profit rates may possibly be accompanied by increased preferences for liquidity, and thus, by pressure for upward movements in interest rates.) They require a positive monetary policy, an increase in the supply of money. But monetary policy faces a number of obstacles, as noted earlier; two of the most important are: (1) "Institutional and psychological factors" may "set a limit much above zero to the practicable decline in the rate of interest." [14: 218] (2) Even if the interest rate could be reduced to zero, the volume of investment might be insufficient to match full employment saving in a wealthy society. In sum: "If—for whatever reason—the rate of interest cannot fall as fast as the marginal efficiency of capital would fall with a rate of accumulation corresponding to what the community would choose to save at a rate of interest equal to the marginal efficiency of capital in conditions of full employment," then investment will tend to fail to meet full employment saving. Indeed, in the extreme case where the stock of capital is so abundant as to bring its marginal efficiency down to zero, employment and income "will have to shrink until the community becomes so impoverished that the aggregate of saving has become zero. . . ." [14: 219–20, 217]

A major limitation of Keynes' version of the secular stagnation hypothesis is the absence of an induced investment function. It is reasonable to assert that increased income brought forth by an increase in the stock of capital will induce an increase in investment as well as consumption. Autonomous investment must rise in a growing economy to meet the gap, not between consumption and income, but between consumption plus induced investment and income. Ackley summarizes this "basic error of the Keynesian position" well:

It is a failure to realize that a growth of income—a growth which the very act of investment permits—can prevent capital saturation. There is twice as much capital in use in the United States today as two decades ago. But we are not for that reason necessarily closer to capital saturation than we were then. For the whole economy has grown, too. An economy twice as big in annual income can use twice as much capital. To be sure, if we were trying to use twice as much capital to produce the *same output* as that of two decades ago, we would have to be using capital in ways such that the marginal yield would be very low, perhaps negative. But this is not our problem, and Keynesian stagnation is not the *inevitable result* of capital accumulation. This is not to say that there can never be a problem of too much capital; merely that today's investment (to solve today's full employment problem) does not *necessarily* make it harder to find profitable investment outlets tomorrow, as Keynes frequently argued.[14]

A second consideration in assessing the empirical plausibility of Keynes' vision of chronic stagnation is the height of the marginal efficiency of capital schedule and shifts therein. The depressive effects of an increase in the stock of capital could be offset by long-run upward shifts in the entire schedule of profit rates. Dynamic growth factors in the economy may outweigh diminishing returns to capital under given institutional, psychological, technological, and resource conditions. Keynes' view, stated briefly in the *General Theory*, is that these underlying determinants of the marginal efficiency of capital, and thus, of autonomous investment may be less powerful in the twentieth than in the nineteenth century:

During the nineteenth century, the growth of population and of invention, the opening-up of new lands, the state of confidence and the frequency of war over the average of (say) each decade seem to have been sufficient, taken in conjuction with the propensity to consume, to establish a schedule

of the marginal efficiency of capital which allowed a reasonably satisfactory average level of employment to be compatible with a rate of interest high enough to be psychologically acceptable to wealth-owners. . . .

Today and presumably for the future, the schedule of the marginal efficiency of capital is, for a variety of reasons, much lower than it was in the nineteenth century. The acuteness and the peculiarity of our contemporary problem arises, therefore, out of the possibility that the average rate of interest which will allow a reasonable average level of employment is one so unacceptable to wealth-owners that it cannot be readily established merely by manipulating the quantity of money. [14: 307, 308–9]

HANSEN

Emphasis on the underlying long-run determinants of the marginal efficiency of capital and, thereby, autonomous investment, is the common bond between Keynes' and Hansen's theories of secular stagnation. For Hansen, the problem (in the context of the late 1930s) was *not* the stock of capital but, rather, the possibility of insufficient autonomous investment because of insufficient growth in such underlying long-run determinants of the rate of profit as population growth, resource discoveries, and technological development. Hansen directed his attention specifically to the United States.

In contrast to such early nineteenth-century economists as Malthus and Ricardo, who were concerned about *excessive* population growth, Hansen (in the late thirties) was concerned about the possibility of an *insufficient* population growth rate. In the nineteenth century, rapid population growth, accompanied by repeated waves of urbanization, was a powerful factor in encouraging investment, especially in residential construction, transportation, and public utilities. With a decrease in the population growth rate (dropping from about 30 percent per decade in the early 1800s to about 7 percent in the decade ending in 1940), one growth stimulus for investment may be less powerful in the future than in the past.

---

[14]Gardner Ackley, *Macroeconomic Theory* (New York: The Macmillan Company, 1961), p. 511.

Resource discoveries and the development of new geographic territories also were powerful stimuli to autonomous investment in the nineteenth century, especially in the railroad industry. Development of a geographic frontier is important because it stimulates investment even under *given* conditions of consumer tastes and technology. With the disappearance of the geographic frontier in the United States, and with political obstacles both at home and abroad to large-scale American participation in the development of new territories in underdeveloped economies, we must rely more heavily on "economic frontiers" in the future, that is, on cost-reducing technological improvements, inventions, and innovations. If population growth and geographic frontiers play smaller roles in the future than the past, technology must play a larger role—the rate of growth in technological improvements must be higher.

Can technological improvements be sufficient to yield long-run profit rates high enough to generate levels of autonomous investment, which, in turn, are sufficient to attain and maintain long-run full employment utilization of resources? Hansen's answer is "Not necessarily." First, technological improvements and the heavy investment associated with them are closely related to the emergence and development of great "new industries," such as railroads in the nineteenth century and automobiles in the twentieth. As these revolutionary new industries reach maturity and cease growing, "as all industries finally must, the whole economy must experience a profound stagnation, unless new developments take (their) place."[15] This may occur, but neither logic nor history guarantees it will.

Second, whereas Keynes (at least, in the

General Theory) had no criticism of monopoly and oligopoly in business and labor, Hansen felt such important developments as the growth of labor unions, increasing substitution of sales promotion for "vigorous price competition," and the monopolistic tendency of avoiding new investment when it makes old investments obsolete were restricting the rapid introduction of cost-reducing techniques.

It is difficult to put the Hansen hypotheses to a clear and firm empirical test. Other than the technical problem of isolating the role of specific causal forces in the economic growth process, underlying structural conditions of political economy have altered radically since the 1930s. What would happen to autonomous investment, income, and employment if the federal government abandoned its responsibilities under the Employment Act of 1946, state and local governments sharply restricted their large-scale programs of highway-freeway-educational facilities construction, or peace were to "break out," etc.? This is essentially an academic question, for their opposites are more likely within the framework of contemporary "managed-socially reformed capitalism" and contemporary international relations. Thus, the absence of large-scale economic stagnation in the postwar economy does not invalidate the theory of secular stagnation, though, in conjunction with the structural changes of the last 30 years, it makes it more difficult either to verify *or* disprove it.

GOVERNMENT ECONOMIC POLICY

For Keynes, policy recommendations to deal with capitalism's central economic problems are on a distinctly "different plane from the diagnosis." Of the 24 chapters in the *General Theory*, only one (the last) was devoted to broader issues of government policy and social philosophy; and it was extremely sketchy as a guide to action. Post-Keynesian discussions and debates over government economic policy have become

---

[15]Alvin H. Hansen, "Economic Progress and Declining Population Growth," *American Economic Review*, March 1938. Reprinted in Gottfried Haberler, editor, *Readings in Business Cycle Theory* (Philadelphia: Blakiston, 1944), p. 379.

an integral part of the economic theory and social philosophy of contemporary managed capitalism (see Chapters 13 and 14, below); however, the major elements in the Keynesian theory of government economic policy are an integral part of the Keynesian view of capitalism and are stated briefly here.

Institutional Complementarity: The Agenda of Government

Perhaps the most important underlying idea in the Keynesian theory of government economic policy is what might be called *institutional complementarity* in the relations between public and private sectors of the economy, government and private enterprise, public policy and the price system. In the Keynesian view, the ideal relationship is one in which each complements the other by performing those functions it is best equipped to do. This viewpoint was clearly expressed by Keynes in *The End of Laissez-Faire* in 1926:[16] "Perhaps the chief task of Economists at this hour is to distinguish afresh the *Agenda* of Government from the *Non-Agenda;* and the companion task of politics is to devise forms of Government within a *Democracy* which shall be capable of accomplishing the agenda."

"We must aim at separating those services which are *technically social* from those which are *technically individual*. The most important Agenda of the State relate . . . to those functions which fall outside the sphere of the individual. . . ."

The major contribution and distinguishing feature of the Keynesian theory of government economic policy has been the identification of the "agenda of government" in the light of its theoretical and empirical analysis of the economic process in developed capitalist societies.

---

[16] John Maynard Keynes, *The End of Laissez-Faire*, (London: Woolf, 1926), pp. 40, 46.

Goals of Economic Policy

FULL EMPLOYMENT AND PRICE STABILITY

In the Keynesian view, the most important objective of government economic policy is full employment without inflation. On logical grounds, price stability deserves co-billing with full employment. Price inflation, generated by excessive aggregate monetary demand, and depression and unemployment, generated by inadequate monetary demand, are avoidable evils. On empirical grounds, however, full employment deserves top listing. If, as assumed throughout Keynesian literature, unemployment is the rule and full employment the exception, and if inflation is essentially a problem of excessive aggregate demand at or near full employment, then the promotion of a full-employment utilization of resources is the primary goal, with price stability following as an important, but less pressing, objective.

DECREASED INCOME INEQUALITY

To full employment, Keynes added the reduction of inequality in income distribution —though he left the extent of such desired reduction unspecified. Though underdeveloped, Keynes' basic contention was (1) in an economic society generally characterized by an excess of full employment saving above desired or intended investment, the traditional defense of income inequality (namely, to encourage saving) loses much of its force; (2) the reduction of inequality, by raising the propensity to consume and decreasing the propensity to save, may raise aggregate demand and, thereby, contribute to the promotion of full employment.

This inclusion of income equality on the same agenda as full employment has been pleasing to contemporary democratic socialists and social reformers, who are happy to have their traditional arguments against inequality bolstered by the analysis of a dominant and important school of economic thought. It has been a source of embarrassment to those post-Keynesian economists who wish to retain their scientific "neutrality" by distinguishing between *recovery* in the aggregate performance of the economy and *reform* in the distribution of income *at* full employment levels. Insofar as it is possible to make this distinction, it follows that (1) equality should be evaluated for itself, independent of its relations to full employment; (2) full employment may, but need not, be accompanied by the reduction of income inequality as a policy goal. A Keynesian outlook toward full employment may be accompanied by a status quo or even reactionary approach to inequality in income distribution. In any event, what Keynes gave with his left hand, he took away with his right, suggesting that "there is social and psychological justification for significant inequalities of incomes and wealth," (although, it is true, "not for such large disparities as exist today"). [14: 374]

INDIVIDUAL FREEDOMS AND DEMOCRACY

Along with full employment, price stability, and reduction of large-scale inequality, Keynes added individual economic and political freedoms and political democracy. Freedom and democracy figure both negatively and positively in the Keynesian system of policy goals. Negatively, government economic policy should avoid conflict with individual freedoms and political democracy. Positively, full employment without inflation is a prerequisite for the maintenance of freedom and democracy, because failure to attain this basic goal within the framework of free and democratic institutions may lead to non-democratic solutions. If this is true, and if private enterprise is not automatically self-regulating at full employment levels, then the incorporation of the promotion of full employment in the "agenda of government" may be defended "both as the only practicable means of avoiding the destruction of existing economic forms in their entirety

and as the condition of the successful functioning of individual initiative." [14: 380] The Keynesian view is that, as a policy goal, full employment, far from being inconsistent with a "free enterprise" economic system, is logically and empirically necessary for its maintenance.

ECONOMIC GROWTH

Contemporary neo-Keynesian economists, in the radically different context of postwar prosperity, cold war rivalries, and emergence of new nations desirous of rapid economic development in underdeveloped economies, have added economic growth as an important goal of government economic policy. In part, of course, this is the traditional Keynesian objective in modified terms: The *promotion of economic growth to or toward full employment is, essentially, the promotion of the goal of full employment.* Beyond this, however, is the goal of sustaining and perhaps increasing the rate of economic growth at full employment.

In Keynes' view, as noted, the second of these two dimensions of economic growth is intimately linked to the question of the likelihood of increases in the stock of capital leading eventually to a "state of full investment," at which the rate of return from capital goods would have decreased to levels just sufficient to cover labor costs "plus an allowance for risk and the costs of skill and supervision." [14: 377, 375] Net saving, net investment, and the interest rate would have decreased to zero, and further economic growth would be based on changes in population, labor force, technology, and tastes. Keynes felt such a "state of full investment" could be reached within a generation or two via government policies to promote full employment by encouraging (private and public) investment. *If* it were established, then raising the rate of economic growth, were it desired, would cease to be capable of being a general goal of macroeconomic policy and would partake of more intricate judgments and decisions in regard to technology, tastes, and work versus leisure—judgments and decisions beyond the scope of the Keynesian analysis.

If, on the other hand, it proved to be possible (for example, because of increases in the propensity to consume) to attain full employment with relatively small increases in the stock of capital (annual levels of net investment), below those yielding a "state of full investment," then the question of the extent to, and the means by, which the present generation should restrict its consumption so as to increase the allocation of resources to investment *at* full employment would be a "separate decision. . . ." [14: 377]

REALLOCATION OF RESOURCES

Keynes did not identify changes in the *allocation* of resources as a goal of economic policy. "I see no reason," he said, "to suppose that the existing system seriously misemploys the factors of production which are in use. . . . It is in determining the volume, not the direction, of actual employment that the existing system has broken down." [14: 379] As observed, *if* full employment utilization of resources were attained through government policy, then the Keynesian social philosophy would have "no objection" to the classical analysis of how private self-interest and the competitive price system determine both *what* is produced and *how* it is produced (that is, how the proportions of resources in the production of quantities of particular outputs are determined).

Of course, the promotion of full employment as a policy goal requires the allocation of resources to the production of something. That "something" might be consumption goods, investment goods, or both; it might be marketable goods produced and sold by private businesses or "collective goods" (such as education or highways) provided by government, or both. Thus, any decision to promote full employment also implies judgments and decisions regarding the allocation of resources—between consumption and investment, and between the public and private sectors of the economy.

But these judgments and decisions, in the Keynesian view, are distinguishable from the *central problem* of promoting full employment. It is possible to accept the Keynesian view as to the primacy of full employment as a policy goal, to support programs to expand *either* consumption or investment or both, and to expand *either* marketable commodities and services of collective goods or both. It is, for example, possible to identify full employment as the central goal of government economic policy and favor tax cuts as a policy instrument to promote private consumption and/or investment. It is equally possible, as in the case of Alvin H. Hansen, to propose increases in "public investment" as a major route to full employment.[17] Conversely, it is possible to support or propose shifts in the allocation of resources, from consumption to investment (or vice-versa), or from the production of marketable to collective goods, and yet, to criticize the primacy Keynes placed on full employment and its associated high-level production as policy goals.

Indeed, so important is full employment in the Keynesian view that almost *any* employment of unemployed resources may be socially beneficial via the increased spending of the newly employed workers and the impact of this spending on output, further employment, and further spending, *even if* the newly-employed resources are producing *nothing* (for example, "digging holes in the ground") or something which in itself appears foolish. In the *General Theory*, Keynes suggested, tongue-in-cheek:

---

[17] "As we look at the deplorable physical condition of our great cities, the substandard housing both urban and rural, the congested urban transportation facilities, and the wastage of natural resources, it becomes abundantly evident that our greatest deficiencies are precisely in those areas that require large public investment outlays." Alvin H. Hansen, *Economic Policy and Full Employment*, (New York City: McGraw-Hill Book Company, 1947), p. 23.

If the Treasury were to fill old bottles with bank notes, bury them at suitable depths in disused coal mines which are then filled up to the surface with town rubbish, and leave it to private enterprise on well-tried principles of *laissez-faire* to dig the notes up again (the right to do so being obtained, of course, by tendering for leases of the note-bearing territory), there need be no more unemployment and, with the help of the repercussions, the real income of the community, and its capital wealth also, would probably become a good deal greater than it actually is. It would, indeed, be more sensible to build houses and the like; but if there are political and practical difficulties in the way of doing this, the above would be better than nothing. [14: 129]

ALTERATIONS IN THE FUNCTIONAL
DISTRIBUTION OF INCOME?

The Keynesian view on the social desirability of alterations in the functional distribution of income (the distribution of income among wage, profit, rent, and interest receivers) is essentially similar to that of the question of the reallocation of resources. If the *primary* goal is an increase in employment and national income, then the question of *whose* income should increase is a logically distinguishable and *subsidiary* issue. *If* full employment is attained through government policy, then the Keynesian social philosophy has "no objection" to how the competitive market system distributes national income among different resource owners. A Keynesian route to full employment is equally consistent with measures to aid, support, and raise incomes of business, labor, agriculture, and/or any other groups in the economic system.

However, Keynes was sympathetic to the more active enterpreneurial and laboring groups in the economy and alluded to the possible "euthanasia of the rentier, and, consequently, the euthanasia of the cumulative oppressive power of the capitalist to exploit the scarcity-value of capital" [14: 376] with the arrival, fostered by pro-investment full employment government policies, of a "state of full investment." Keynes felt: (1) as long as the economy operates at less than full employment, it is not necessary to restrict consumption (via saving more) to increase investment, and thus, that interest "today rewards no genuine sacrifice," [14: 376] but is merely the price paid to entice liquidity preference seekers to part with money; (2) as the stock of capital increases, its "scarcity-value" decreases as its rate of return falls toward zero.

This gradual "euthanasia" which "will need no revolution" [14: 376] was more a *prognostication* than a *recommendation*. Aside from his proposal to expand private and government investment as part of a full employment program, Keynes had no policy recommendations regarding the redistribution of income. If, because of increases in population and the labor force, changes in consumer tastes and institutions, technological improvements, and, as noted earlier, the growth in national income and employment, the marginal efficiency of capital and the capacity to pay interest do not fall to zero within a generation or two, then the "euthanasia of the rentier" remains more a harmless eccentricity than a developed diagnosis and prescription. In any event, it has not been taken up by neo-Keynesian economists as a central element in the Keynesian social philosophy in regard to goals of government policy.

WHY THE PRIMACY OF FULL
EMPLOYMENT AS A POLICY GOAL?

In the Keynesian theory of government economic policy, full employment heads the list of desirable policy objectives for several reasons: First, full employment is desirable in its own right, as a basis for providing incomes for those willing and able to employ their resources and as a vehicle for avoiding the human costs and miseries of unemployment, which even generous systems of unemployment compensation cannot circumvent.

Second, full employment, in the Keynesian view, either contributes to or is consistent with other important policy goals. A major social cost of unemployment is the loss of potential output or income for an entire society; a major social benefit of full employment is the attainment of that level of output and income consistent with productive capacity. Full employment is prerequisite to the maintenance of freedom and democracy. It may serve to promote greater equality in the distribution of income. Up to full employment, it *is* economic growth. Sustained full employment provides the context within which increases in the growth rate are most likely to occur. It can be consistent with and neutral toward a variety of different value judgments regarding the allocation of resources and distribution of national income.

Third, in the context of the 1930s, unemployment and depression were the central economic problems. It seems reasonable to suggest that, even in the absence of rigorous statistical investigation, with about one-fourth of the civilian labor force unemployed in the United States, the potential economic gains from the promotion of full employment far exceeded any marginal gains to consumer satisfaction derivative from a reallocation of resources or a redistribution of income. But even if the extent of unemployment were lower—say, five to ten percent—the potential gains in a highly developed economy like the United States might be as high as $50 billion per year or more.

Fourth, the promotion of full employment is widely beneficial to large numbers of people in an economic society, perhaps, everyone. In moving from unemployment to or toward full employment, some people, perhaps everyone, become better off and no one need lose. It is not necessary to decrease

one group's income in order to increase another's, to increase investment at the expense of consumption, and/or to increase public expenditures at the expense of private expenditures. "The business cycle," suggests Frank Knight, "is not a problem of conflict of interest, since practically no one profits from depressions."[18]

Fifth, unemployment is not only an evil, but an avoidable one. Full employment not only is desirable, but attainable within the framework of existing economic and political institutions in developed capitalist economies. We now have the knowledge, in the form of the Keynesian analytical apparatus and in the statistical data on national income and related measures of aggregate economic performance which has accompanied and been stimulated by the development of Keynesian analysis, to terminate and/or avoid depressions, to attain and maintain full employment, if only we would put that knowledge to work. We can do so, in part, precisely because the relevant knowledge is not the specific and specialized knowledge of the concretized circumstances of time and place emphasized by critics of government economic policy like Friedrich Kayek. If and when we fail to apply our knowledge to promote full employment, our failure is a political one—a failure of will, imagination, and organization, not of economic knowledge.[19] The essence of this view is that depres-

[18] Frank Knight, "Economic and Social Policy in a Democratic Society," *Journal of Political Economy*, December 1950, p. 520. For a criticism of this modified "harmony doctrine," see Paul Streeten, "Keynes and the Classical Tradition," Kenneth Kurihara, editor, *Post-Keynesian Economics*, (New Brunswick: Rutgers University Press, 1954), pp. 345–64.

[19] Keynes was not optimistic about the political feasibility of the implementation of a public expenditure program (his major proposal) adequate to promote full employment in the great depression of the 30s. "The conclusion is that at recent times investment expenditures have been on a scale which was hopelessly inadequate to the problem . . . . It appears to be politically impossible for a capitalist democracy

sion and unemployment are not "necessary" or "natural." They are "... nothing but a frightful muddle, a transitory and unnecessary muddle. For the Western World already has the resources and the technique, if we could only create the organization to use them, capable of reducing the Economic Problem, which now absorbs our moral and material energies, to a position of secondary importance."[20]

The Instruments of Government Economic Policy

Modern governments have at their disposal varied instruments of public policy and measures for social control of the economic system. In the Keynesian view, the most important, as well as effective, instruments are those of general macroeconomic strategy, which have a primary effect on the aggregate level of monetary demand, rather than on sectors, industries, or groups within the economy and/or the determination of the quantities and prices of particular commodities and resources in particular markets.

This emphasis on the general lines of macroeconomic strategy via the manipulation of a relatively small number of key policy instruments, formulated and executed to exert overall control on the level of aggregate demand, derives from the identification of unemployment and depression as the central economic problems, of full employment as the major policy goal, and of the aggregate level of demand as the strategic determinant of the overall level of income and employment in the economic system.

The major instruments of macroeconomic

policy essentially are four:[21]

1. Increasing or decreasing the level of government purchases of products and/or labor services.

2. Increasing or decreasing the level of government transfer payments or, alternatively, decreasing or increasing the level of government taxes.

3. Increasing or decreasing the supply of money.

4. Increasing or decreasing the level of government lending, or alternatively, decreasing or increasing the level of government borrowing (from the general public).[22]

The first two sets of instruments are called *fiscal* policy, from the Latin *fiscus*, meaning *the money basket of the monarch*, now denoting the inflow and outflow of revenues and expenditures of the government. The control of fiscal instruments, such as government purchases, taxes, and transfer payments, generally is vested in legislative and executive

---

[21]This is a variation on a theme presented in a now-classic article by Abba P. Lerner, "An Integrated Full Employment Policy," *International Postwar Problems*, pp. 69–73. Reprinted in Arthur L. Grey, Jr. and John E. Elliott, *Economic Issues and Policies* (Boston: Houghton Mifflin Company, 1965), pp. 140–43.

[22]If government borrows from the central bank (instead of the general public), the supply of money will rise in the form of increased demand deposits of the Treasury at the central bank. If government borrows from commercial banks which have reserves exceeding those required by the central bank, so that loans to government do not require decreasing loans to private citizens, the supply of money also will rise. Government borrowing from the general public leaves the supply of money in the entire system constant, but transfers funds from households and/or businesses to government. Conversely, changes in the supply of money by the banking system (commercial banks and/or central banks) involve alterations in lending by the banking system to private citizens or governments. The banking system may increase the supply of money by lending to businesses or households (purchasing their notes) or by lending to governments (purchasing government securities).

---

to organize expenditure on a scale necessary to make the grand experiment which would prove my case except in war conditions." John Maynard Keynes, "The United States and the Keynes Plan," *The New Republic*, July 29, 1940, p. 159.

[20]John Maynard Keynes, *Essays in Persuasion* (New York: Harcourt, Brace & World, Inc., 1932), p. vii.

branches of the government. The third set of instruments, called *monetary* policy, is concerned with changes in the stock of money, essentially that portion of the money supply created by the commercial banking system in the form of demand deposits or checking accounts, rather than with the money income and expenditures of governments, and generally is controlled (within given limits) by a central bank. The fourth set of instruments partakes of and is relevant to both monetary and fiscal policy.

Each of these sets of policy instruments may have microeconomic as well as macroeconomic dimensions and implications. For example, governments may alter the *composition* of government purchases (increasing, say, defense expenditures and decreasing public works expenditures), of transfer payments (increasing, say, unemployment compensation benefits and decreasing old-age benefits), and/or of taxes (increasing, say, sales taxes and decreasing income taxes). Governments may make non-proportional changes in tax rates (for example, decreasing income tax rates more on lower than on upper income brackets). Central banks may endeavor, through selective monetary controls (such as controls over down payments and length of payoff time on housing and consumer loans) to affect specific lines or types of credit creation. Treasuries may try to increase their sales of long-term government securities in relation to short-term. But the central concern in the Keynesian theory of government economic policy is the macroeconomics, or *overall levels*, of government purchases, taxes, transfer payments, money supply, and government borrowing-lending, rather than microeconomic questions of composition.

The Basic Strategy of Macroeconomic Policy

The general strategy of macroeconomic policy, in the Keynesian analysis, is to manipulate these four central sets of instru-

ments to *raise* aggregate demand during periods of depression and unemployment and to *lower* aggregate demand during periods of inflation. If aggregate demand is insufficient to match full employment supply, Keynesian advice would be: (1) increase the level of government purchases; (2) increase the level of government transfer payments and/or decrease the level of taxation upon the private sector of the economy;[23] (3) increase the supply of money by increasing banking system lending to the general public and/or governments;[24] (4) increase the level of government lending to, and/or decrease the level of government borrowing from, the general public. If aggregate demand exceeds full employment supply, Keynesian advice would be the reverse: (1) decrease the level of government purchases; (2) decrease the level of government transfer payments to, and/or increase the level of taxes upon, the private sector

---

[23]Keynes did not specify tax cuts as an anti-depressionary device in the *General Theory*. He mentioned increased progressivity of the tax structure as a possible device to decrease income inequality, thereby possibly lowering the propensity to save and raising the propensity to consume. However, there is nothing in the manipulation of the level of taxation which is inconsistent with Keynes' approach. The utilization of alterations in tax levels as a part of macroeconomic strategy for full employment without inflation now is regarded as an integral part of the "Keynesian" social philosophy of government economic policy.

[24]Because Keynes felt that (1) the interest rate is not very responsive to increase in the supply of money; (2) investment may not be highly responsive to decreases in the rate of interest; and (3) deep depressions may be accompanied by sharp upward shifts in the demand for money, which may offset the impact of increases in the money supply and/or sharp downward shifts in profit rates, which may offset the impact of decreases in the rate of interest, he concluded that monetary policy, *by itself*, might not be fully effective as a device for moving from deep depression to full employment. This view, however, is consistent with the position that monetary policy (1) may help to prevent minor recessions from becoming deep depressions and (2) may, *together with* expansionary fiscal policy, contribute to a movement toward full employment, even from an initial position of deep depression.

of the economy; (3) decrease the supply of money by decreasing lending by the banking system to the general public and/or governments; (4) decrease the level of government lending to, and/or increase the level of government borrowing from, the general public.

IMPACT OF THE INSTRUMENTS

Alterations in the level of these instruments of macroeconomic policy affect aggregate demand in different ways:

1. Government purchases are components of aggregate demand. They enter the income stream directly and, thus, are the most powerful and direct of the instruments of macroeconomic policy. An increase in government purchases, other factors remaining equal, raises aggregate demand; a decrease in government purchases decreases aggregate demand.

2. Government transfer payments and taxes are not components of aggregate demand. But they may affect aggregate demand indirectly via their effects on personal and/or business income. For example, an increase in unemployment compensation benefit payments and/or a decrease in personal income taxes raises personal income. An increase in personal income will be disposed of in the form of increased consumption and/or increased saving. Of course, if the marginal propensity to save, or $MPS = 1$ ($MPC = 0$), all the increase in personal income will go into saving, and aggregate demand will not change. If the marginal propensity to consume, or $MPC = 1$ ($MPS = 0$), all the increase in personal income will go into consumption, and the initial rise in aggregate demand will be as large as in the case of increased government purchases. But if, as Keynes assumed and as seems most plausible, the MPC exceeds zero, but is less than one (that is, the MPS exceeds zero), some of the increase in personal income will go into increased aggregate demand in the form of increased consumption, and some will

be disposed of in the form of increased saving, the composition of disposition depending on the MPC (MPS). A decrease in unemployment compensation benefit payments and/or an increase in taxes would have the reverse effect.

3. The impact on aggregate demand of a change in the supply of money, government lending, and/or government borrowing is indirect, perhaps more so than in the case of alterations in the levels of government taxes and/or transfer payments. An increase in the supply of money, with its accompanying increases in lending to the general public and/or to governments, or an increase in government lending to the general public, provides funds which may be used to increase I, C, and/or G. G is both an instrument of government policy and a variable component of aggregate demand. An increase (or decrease) in G is automatically an increase (or decrease) in aggregate demand. Alterations in government taxes and transfer payments, by changing personal income, have their primary effects on aggregate demand by affecting C. An increase (or decrease) in transfer payments and/or a decrease (increase) in taxes, by raising (lowering) personal income, raise (lower) consumption and, thereby, demand. Alterations of government subsidies to, loans to, or taxes upon businesses may also affect private investment. But the major macroeconomic instrument for controlling private investment is monetary policy. An increase in the money supply, both by increasing available funds and by decreasing interest rates, may entice an increase in investment. A decrease in the money supply may have the opposite effect. In sum:

$$\uparrow(\downarrow)G \longrightarrow$$
$$\uparrow(\downarrow)TP \text{ or } \downarrow(\uparrow)T \rightarrow \uparrow(\downarrow)PY \rightarrow \uparrow(\downarrow)C \rightarrow \uparrow(\downarrow)D$$
$$\uparrow(\downarrow)M \rightarrow \downarrow(\uparrow)i \longrightarrow \uparrow(\downarrow)I \rightarrow$$

INITIAL, SECONDARY, AND COUNTERVAILING EFFECTS

Initial Effects. The initial or immediate effect of an increase in G during a period of depression and unemployment is an increase in output, income, and employment, either in the private industries from which government purchases are made or in the public projects in which government engages. The initial or immediate effect of an increase in *C* induced by an increase in personal income from tax cuts or transfer payments increases, or an increase in *I* initiated by the decrease in interest rates from an increase in the money supply, is an increase in output, income, and employment in the industries producing those consumption and investment goods. Keynes argued that the social costs of putting unemployed resources to work is zero because their employment does not decrease employment elsewhere in the economic system. Thus, *even if* there were *no* secondary or additional effects of expansionary monetary and fiscal policy beyond the immediate and initial increases in output, income, and employment, these policy measures would be justified.

Secondary Effects. In the Keynesian view, however, as long as consumers spend some portion of every increase in income, these initial effects may be supplemented by other and additional increases in output, income, and employment. As observed earlier, this means that any initiating increase in *C*, *I*, and/or *G* brought about by expansionary monetary and fiscal policy may generate increased output, income, and employment, which is some *multiple* (larger than one) of the initial and immediate increase in output, income, and employment.

In Keynes' original formulation, the strategic initiating variable was (private or public) investment; the strategic multiplying variable was consumption via the marginal propensity to consume; and the stratagic "dragging" or "dampening" variable, the action of which prevented an infinite increase in income, was saving via the marginal propensity to save.

In contemporary formulations of the multiplier theory, *any* component of aggregate demand may serve as the initiating variable; any component of aggregate demand (including *I* and *G*) may rise in response to an initiating increase in income and thus reinforce the effect of the *MPC* and raise the value of the multiplier; and a variety of ways of disposing of increases in income other than saving (such as increases in imports and/or taxes) may dissipate the effect of the *MPC* and lower the value of the multiplier.

The multiplier analysis should be distinguished from that of "pump priming," an idea prominent in popular discussions of the 1930s and often confused with the multiplier concept. The central theme of pump priming was that during a period in which private investment was abnormally low, government could "prime the pump" by increasing government spending. As income, output, and employment rose in response to government spending, business confidence would be restored, and private investment would expand. As private investment expanded and full employment was achieved, further increases in investment could be accompanied by decreases in government spending, now that the "pump" was primed. Though not the same as the multiplier concept, this idea is not inconsistent with it. *If* investment rises because of the increase in income generated by initiating increases in aggregate demand or because of a restoration of business confidence, it *is* conceivable government purchases could decrease and still leave aggregate demand high enough to match full employment supply. But this need not be the case, and, in a deep depression characterized by the collapse of private investment, it probably would not be. Whether it would be or not would depend upon the values of the initiating increases in *C*, *I*, or *G*, and upon the various multiplying and retarding propensities.

Countervailing Effects? What about countervailing effects? Is it not possible that increases in aggregate demand generated by expansionary monetary and fiscal policy, especially increases in government purchases, may damage "business confidence," causing decreases in private investment or preventing investment from rising and thereby offsetting, in whole or part, the expansionary effects of the initial change in demand? In the Keynesian view, this is conceivable. Whether and/or to what extent it is likely depends on a variety of factors, such as (1) whether the initiating change is an increase in government purchases, which may be associated more strongly in the business community with "socialization" than decreases in taxes and/or increases in the money supply; and (2) if the initiating change is an increase in government purchases, whether or not it (a) is rapid and large-scale; (b) is accompanied by an increase in the public debt in a society and at a time when such increases are widely regarded as "unsound finance"; (c) is made in areas traditionally reserved for private enterprise or leads businessmen to think this will happen in the future; (d) is accompanied by various microeconomic measures of social reform, such as increased progressivity of the income tax structure or increased taxes on or regulation of business, generally regarded by the business community as "anti-business" or at least not pro-business; (3) occurs at a time and in such a way as to appear to decrease the power and status of business, business values, and the role of businessmen in the provision of national political leadership.

A major limitation of Keynes' analysis is that it largely excluded consideration of these various "political" and "human" factors. The experience of the United States economy in the 1930s is a classic illustration of this. One could make a strong case for the hypothesis that the main difficulty with government spending and federal governmental deficits in the 1930s was that they were too *small*. Had the federal government created the deficits during the mid-thirties that it did later, during World War II, the depression could have been terminated much sooner. On the other hand, a problem of the application of Keynesian-type policies to promote full employment in the United States during the mid-thirties was that several of the items previously cited were present. Robert Heilbroner contended that in the New Deal during the 1930s, government spending and government deficits "never truly cured the economy—not because it was economically unsound, but because it was ideologically upsetting."[25]

Contemporary Keynesian economists are more sanguine. They argue that the thirties was a very special case. In the radically different context of the postwar period, in the light of ideological adjustments businessmen have made to the altered role of government in economic life and in view of the more temperate, moderate, and essentially conservative stance of contemporary macroeconomic policies and contemporary American economists trained in the Keynesian tradition, these potentially deadlocking countervailing effects need not occur and are not occurring.

INTERDEPENDENCE OF MONETARY AND FISCAL POLICY

The impact of monetary and fiscal instruments generally is greatest if they are used in *unison*. As already noted, Keynes felt monetary policy by itself might not be fully effective in promoting a movement to full employment from a position of depressionary equilibrium. But the reverse also is true: An expansionary fiscal policy may face obstacles in the endeavor to promote full employment if it is not accompanied by an increase in the supply of money. Suppose fiscal authorities increased government spending as an anti-depressionary device. First, how is the increase in government spending to be financed? Where are the funds to come from? If they come from an equal increase in tax revenues, most, though not necessarily all, of the expansionary impact of the increase in spending will be offset. If they come from an equal increase in government borrowing from the general public, the net expansionary effect is likely to be somewhat larger because funds

[25]Robert Heilbroner, *The Worldly Philosophers* (New York: Simon and Schuster, Inc., 1967), p. 253.

spent upon the purchase of government securities are less likely to have been spent upon consumption and/or investment goods than funds obtained as tax revenues. Still, government borrowing from the general public leaves the money supply constant, but transfers it from private consumers or businesses to government. Unless purchasers of government securities would have held their funds entirely in idle money balances in lieu of purchasing government securities; that is, unless the marginal propensity to consume and invest (and/or the marginal propensity to consume and invest of people to whom they might have loaned their funds) is zero, the expansionary effect of the increase in government spending must be offset, at least in part.

On the other hand, if the increase in government spending is financed by borrowing from commercial banks with excess reserves, or, better, from the central bank, then it is accompanied by an increase in the supply of money. Neither the income of nor the money in circulation in the private sector of the economy decreases. But money to finance government spending increases, and the increase in government spending is not offset, in whole or part, by decreases in spending elsewhere in the economic system.

Second, as aggregate demand rises toward full employment levels, the transactionary demand for money rises and, in the absence of increases in the supply of money, interest rates rise (as seen in upward movements along the LM curve in Fig. 7.6c). But increases in interest rates choke off rising investment and thereby may prevent the attainment of full employment. In sum, monetary and fiscal policies supplement and complement each other in the promotion of the policy goals of full employment without inflation.

KEYNESIAN SOCIAL PHILOSOPHY, CAPITALISM, AND SOCIALISM

Does the Keynesian social philosophy, taken as a whole and including both diagnosis and prescription, constitute a basis for "saving capitalism"? Or is it really an entering wedge in the transition to or toward socialism or some other post-capitalist system? Any endeavor to answer this question must distinguish between two quite different issues: first, the personal convictions and proposals of Keynes and his followers; second, the uses to which "Keynesian policies" are put by national governments and the conditions under which they are applied.

The Keynesian Position

In regard to the former, it seems clear that to Keynes and to many, probably most, contemporary neo-Keynesian economists, especially in the United States, the Keynesian social philosophy as a whole and the Keynesian macroeconomic strategy are essentially *conservative* (or mildly liberal) in motivation and content. Keynes was critical of Marx, Communism, socialism, and even the British Labour Party. (He was a member of the Liberal Party and called himself a representative of the "educated bourgeoisie.") Aside from his general macroeconomic strategy, his mild support for reduction of income inequality, and miscellaneous underdeveloped eccentricities and biases (as, in the prognostication of the "euthanasia of the rentier"), Keynes advocated no large-scale departures from or modifications of capitalism.

Specifically, Keynes insisted a successful resolution of capitalism's central economic problem of depression and unemployment does *not* require: [14: 374–80]

1. an extension of government ownership of industry—"It is not the ownership of the instruments of production which it is important for the State to assume";

2. large-scale redistribution of income— ". . . there is social and psychological justification for significant inequalities of income and wealth. . . .";

3. a substitution of systems or processes of

government economic planning and control over microeconomic decisions of what, how, and for whom for the competitive price system—"But if our central controls succeed in establishing an aggregate volume of output corresponding to full employment as nearly as is practicable, the classical theory comes into its own again from this point onwards. If we suppose the volume of output to be given, that is, to be determined by forces outside the classical scheme of thought, then there is no objection to be raised against the classical analysis of the manner in which private self-interest will determine what in particular is produced, in what proportions the factors of production will be combined to produce it, and how the value of the final product will be distributed between them";

4. large-scale and rapid change—"In some . . . respects the foregoing theory is moderately conservative in its implications. . . . Moreover, the necessary measures of socialisation can be introduced gradually and without a break in the general traditions of society";

5. the elimination of economic individualism —"For whilst it indicates the vital importance of establishing certain central controls in matters which are now left in the main to individual initiative, there are wide fields of activity which are unaffected";

6. a radical departure from the classical philosophy toward the role of government—"The central controls necessary to ensure full employment, will, of course, involve a large extension of the traditional functions of government. [But] the modern classical theory has itself called attention to various conditions in which the free play of economic forces need to be curbed or guided."[26]

---

[26]According to Streeten, Keynes "is unmistakably in the classical liberal-utilitarian tradition" (1) in the

Keynes and contemporary neo-Keynesian economists argue that *one more important, but limited,* departure from *laissez-faire* must be made, one strategic new function must be added to the "agenda of government," namely, a system of "central controls," a macroeconomic strategy for promoting and maintaining full employment. But this departure and addition: (1) is the only one necessary; (2) leaves intact the essential institutions and processes of private enterprise and the competitive price system; (3) is imperative for resolving capitalism's most important single problem—severe depressions with accompanying large-scale unemployment—and therefore will *"strengthen and preserve* the 'free enterprise system' by curing what has always been its worst defect . . . and removing the main cause of subversive, radical attacks upon it."[27]

Uses to Which Keynesian Policies Might Be Applied

The uses to which "Keynesian policies" and instruments are or might be put (and the conditions for their application) is, however, a *distinctly different* issue. Macroeconomic strategies to promote full employment *may* be used to preserve and strengthen capitalism. But they may be used as vehicles in a transition to or toward socialism or some other

---

specific *utilitarian* sense, "which Keynes shared with Bentham and Mill, that the economic welfare of a nation is something that the government can and should discover and promote;" (2) in the specific *liberal* sense that "the promotion of economic welfare requires only a little tampering here and there," leaving the rest to "the automatic play of self-interest"; and (3) in the specific *harmony* sense that "he looked upon the economic activities of a nation . . . as if they had a common purpose which, properly understood, is also the purpose of each individual." Cf., Streeten, "Keynes and the Classical Tradition," in Kurihara, editor, *op. cit.,* pp. 356, 363.

[27]Overton Taylor, *A History of Economic Thought* (New York: McGraw-Hill Book Company, 1960), pp. 505–6.

post-capitalist economic system. They may be liberally or conservatively applied. They may be employed within a framework of managed capitalism. But they may also be applied by "socialist government." In short, Keynesian economics and its accompanying theory of government economic policy and social philosophy, may be used to sustain capitalism *or* to move toward the establishment of a radically more socialist economic system (through, for example, repeated large-scale extensions of government spending and investment as a percent of total spending and investment during periods of actual or threatening depression) depending, among other things, on the aims of political leaders, political and economic conditions, and the cultural traditions, heritage, and history of the system.

Keynes recognized and emphasized this in a letter to Friedrich Hayek shortly after the publication of Hayek's *The Road to Serfdom* (in which Hayek had argued (1) the social reform of capitalism may or will lead to socialism and (2) socialism will lead to totalitarianism, that is, modern "serfdom"):

> I should say that what we want is not no planning, or even less planning, indeed I should say that we almost certainly want more. But the planning should take place in a community in which as many people as possible, both leaders and followers, wholly share your own moral position. Moderate planning will be safe if those carrying it out are rightly oriented in their own minds to the moral issue.... I accuse you of perhaps confusing a little bit the moral and the material issues. Dangerous acts can be done safely in a community which thinks and feels rightly, which would be the way to hell if they were executed by those who think and feel wrongly.[28]

---

[28]John Maynard Keynes, Letter to F. A. von Hayek, January 28, 1944. Cited in Roy Harrod, *The Life of John Maynard Keynes* (New York: Harcourt, Brace & World, Inc., 1951), pp. 436–37.

SUMMARY OF CHAPTER 7

1. Keynesian analysis is the last of the major theories of old-style capitalism and the first of the prominent contemporary theories of managed capitalism.

2. As a theory of competitive market capitalism, the Keynesian analysis has three central dimensions: first, a critique of traditional (classical and neo-classical) economic theories of capitalism, especially traditional theories of the spontaneous and automatic tendencies toward full employment equilibrium under a regime of private enterprise and competitive markets; second, a set of tools and concepts which provide a series of models of the overall or macroeconomic behavior of the economic system; third, the application of these tools and concepts to an interpretation of contemporary economic problems, most notably the tendency toward depression and unemployment.

3. In regard to the goods market, Keynes argued the interaction of aggregate supply and demand or saving and investment determine the equilibrium level of national income (and thereby, employment) and that an equilibrium level of national income may or may not entail full employment, depending essentially upon the level of aggregate demand. Because saving and investment are engaged in largely by different people for different reasons, and because investment depends significantly upon profit expectations (in relation to interest rates) in a world characterized by uncertainty, investment may well be insufficient to match full employment saving, with the result that income will tend to settle at a level below full employment, where saving is low enough to match what businessmen are willing to invest.

4. In regard to the money market, Keynes argued the speculative demand for money places an added burden on the wage/price mechanism as a vehicle for promoting full employment through automatic and spontaneous market forces and that, at very low

rates of interest, the tendency for the preference for liquidity to approach perfect elasticity (the "liquidity trap") may make it virtually impossible to depress interest rates and, thereby, to raise investment.

5. In regard to the labor market, Keynes challenged the classical supply of labor function (where supply of labor was depicted as a direct function of real wages) as inaccurate, the classical demand for labor function (where demand for labor was depicted as an inverse function of real wages) as inadequate, and the classical analysis of the equilibrating mechanism (where flexible money wages brought equality between supply of labor and demand for labor at full employment) as cumbersome and unpersuasive, at best.

6. The Keynesian theory of and strategy for a reformed or managed capitalism has two major ingredients. The first: prescriptions and recommendations for the creation and application of modern macroeconomic planning and strategy. The primary goal in the Keynesian strategy is full employment utilization of resources. The major means proposed to attain and sustain this are monetary and fiscal policies, that is, manipulation by central governmental authorities of such strategic policy variables as the supply of money and the levels of government spending and taxing.

7. The second ingredient of the Keynesian theory of managed capitalism is a rationale of contemporary macroeconomic policies in the light of the social philosophy of classical liberal individualism and in relation to capitalism as an economic system. Keynesian economists have contended the purpose of proposed extensions of central controls over money, government spending, and taxing is to "save" capitalism, though in a modified and managed form. The major defect of old-style capitalism, they argue, is its tendency toward depression and unemployment. But once full employment is established through

the judicious application of *macro*economic controls, then the classical theory "comes into its own" as a means of explaining the *micro*economic relations of resource allocation and income distribution. Keynes felt it was unnecessary for capitalist economies to go beyond these macroeconomic measures. Yet, failure to apply them almost certainly would result in more radical socialization or other transformations of the existing economic and political order.

SELECTED READINGS FOR
PART II

In addition to several works previously cited, notably Dahl and Lindblom (1), Galbraith (3), Hayek (4), Hoover (5), Myrdal (6), Rostow (7), and Schumpeter (8), the following sources are especially useful:

11. CLEMENCE, RICHARD V., *Essays of J. A. Schumpeter* (Cambridge, Mass.: Addison-Wesley, 1951).

12. CLEMENCE, RICHARD V. and DOODY, F. S., *The Schumpeterian System* (Cambridge, Mass.: Addison-Wesley, 1950).

13. GIRVETZ, HARRY G., *The Evolution of Liberalism* (New York: Crowell-Collier & Macmillan, Inc., 1953).

14. KEYNES, JOHN M., *The General Theory of Employment, Interest and Money* (New York: Harcourt, Brace & World, Inc., 1936).

15. LENIN, V. I., *Imperialism: The Highest Stage of Capitalism* (New York: International Publishers, 1932).

16. MARX, KARL, *Capital*, Volume I (New York: Modern Library, Inc., N.d.; originally published by Charles H. Kerr & Company, 1906). Volumes II and III (Chicago: Kerr, 1909).

17. MARX, KARL, *Selected Works*, Volumes I and II (New York: International Publishers, 1932).

18. MARX, KARL, *Theories of Surplus Value* (New York: International Publishers, 1952).

19. MARX, KARL and ENGELS, FRIEDRICH, *The Communist Manifesto* (New York: International Publishers, 1948).

20. ROBINSON, JOAN, *An Essay on Marxian Economics* (London: The Macmillan Company, Publishers, 1957).

21. ROSSITER, CLINTON, *Conservatism in America* (New York: Vintage, 1962).

22. SCHUMPETER, JOSEPH A., *Business Cycles*, Volumes I and II (New York: McGraw-Hill Book Company, 1939).

23. SCHUMPETER, JOSEPH A., *The Theory of Economic Development* (Cambridge, Mass.: Harvard University Press, 1934).

24. SMITH, ADAM, *An Inquiry Into the Nature and Causes of the Wealth of Nations* (New York: Modern Library, Inc., 1937).

25. SWEEZY, PAUL, *The Theory of Capitalist Development* (New York: Monthly Review, 1956).

III

SOCIALISM

Part III provides a comparative review and analysis of the major Western theories of socialism since Marx. (Socialist theory in the context of contemporary socio-capitalism and Communism is discussed in Parts IV and V.) Four theories have been selected to parallel the organization and approach of the preceding discussion of capitalism.

The first is the classical Marxian vision of the ideally functioning socialist (and communist) economic system(s). Despite its relatively vague and speculative character, it provides a classic exposition of and rationale for socialism as an economic system. Many post-Marxian socialist theories and strategies have been reactions to or extensions or modifications of this classic vision.

The second—the neo-Austrian critique of socialism—provides, by contrast, the most prominent critical theory of socialism to emerge in the early twentieth century. The neo-Austrian indictment of socialism is essentially twofold. It contends that socialism, first, is (or would be, if established) economically inefficient in the allocation of scarce resources; second, is characterized by or would lead to the absence or loss of individual economic and political freedoms and democracy.

The most prominent contemporary economic theories of socialism are decentralized, market, or liberal socialism and centralized, hierarchical, or authoritarian socialism, respectively. The former versions of socialist theory have been most notably associated with the classic contributions of late Polish economist Oskar Lange. In his theory of decentralized socialism of the 1930s, Lange assumed freedom of individual choice in consumption and occupation, wide discretion to managers of government-owned enterprises, consumer sovereignty, and a significant role for market or price systems in coordination of economic decisions. Until post-World War II, most variants of decentralized socialism were conceived as successors to capitalism in economically developed societies, and socialist theories focused upon the possibility and practicality of efficient allocation of resources in accordance with consumer demands.

By contrast, theories of centralized socialism developed by such Western neo-Marxists as Paul Sweezy, Paul Baran, and Maurice Dobb, inspired in significant measure by the experiences of Soviet Russia and other Communist countries, have regarded socialism as an instrument for the industrialization of economically underdeveloped societies, that is, as a substitute for capitalism. Theories of and strategies for centralized socialism in this context have been characterized by the substitution of the plans and directives of central governing authorities for the freedom and discretion of individual consumers, workers, and managers, and by a critique of consumer sovereignty and the price or market system as a social process for economic coordination.

8

The Classical Marxian Vision

of

Ideally Functioning Socialist

and Communist Economic Societies

Marxian economic theory deals primarily with the analysis of capitalism and capitalist industrialization. But this analysis is accompanied by a "vision" of post-capitalist economic society. This chapter examines some of these broader visionary elements in Marxian economics.

A BASIC DUALITY IN THE MARXIAN VISION OF INDUSTRIALIZATION AND ECONOMIC DEVELOPMENT

The Marxian vision and analysis of economic development is based on a fundamental duality.[1] On the one hand, Marx accepts,

indeed glorifies, the process of industrialization. He accepts capitalism as the necessary vehicle of historical progress and nearly worships its capacity to generate economic growth through technological development and capital accumulation. On the other hand, Marx provides (1) an economic critique of capitalism's inequalities and injustices in income distribution, monopolistic tendencies, and crises and depression, and (2) a social critique of the dehumanizing impact upon man of the development of modern industry and technology. Having already examined the economic critique in detail, we will concentrate on Marx's views on "alienation" or the dehumanizing effects of the industrial process.

The basic underlying premise in Marx's concept of alienation is that man achieves the essence of his humanity or self-realization in the creative process of self-activity, of work. Man's satisfaction is derived from creative work rather than from consumption. But capitalist industrialization, based on private property, competition, market exchange, and division of labor, causes and intensifies "alienation" or estrangement.

[1] Adam Ulam [46: 64] neatly summed up this duality in Marx: "Anti-industrialism and the most absolute faith in industrialization are the two interwoven themes of Marxism. They are so closely knit together that it is difficult to discern either in its full complexity or intensity. The anti-industrialism of the doctrine matches or surpasses in intensity the most violent anarchist sentiments. Its underlying faith in progress through science and industry sometimes leaves behind as pale and unsubstantial the most uninhibited liberal optimism about the benevolent effects of industry and free market."

According to Marx, alienation takes several forms. He identified them in the *Economic and Philosophical Manuscripts* of 1844. [43: 90–196] First, the process of work under capitalism separates the worker from the *product* of his labors. The output created by workers becomes the property of the capitalist. Thus, the output of labor becomes an *"alien* object," outside of and opposed to workers, and the worker, through his receipt of the means of subsistence (labor-power) and through his utilization by capitalists in the creation of output, becomes an object for the production of more "alienated" output. Second, workers under capitalism are alienated from *themselves*, from their own creative powers and self-realization. Work under capitalism is "external" to the worker; instead of being an end in itself, it becomes merely a means for satisfying other ends in the process of consumption. Third, by alienating man from himself and from the product of his labor, capitalist industrialization also dehumanizes man, alienates him from the "essence" of humanity. Fourth, capitalism also generates estrangement *between men*—between worker and capitalist, between workers in their competitive struggle for jobs, and between capitalists in their competitive struggle for markets.

To Marx, then, the conditions of the work process under capitalism are socially and morally degrading, regardless of the absolute level of wages or of wages as a percent of national income. The property relations of capitalism make a "wage slave" of the worker, necessitating the sale of his labor-power. Competition among workers, especially during periods of unemployment, alienates the worker from his fellows. Increased use of machinery and division of labor rob the worker of creativity and self-realization in the work process. They convert him into a "crippled monstrosity," reduce him to a "fragment of a man," lower him "to the level of an appendage of a machine," transform "his lifetime into working-time," and drag "his wife and child beneath the wheels

of the Juggernaut of Capital." [16: I, 396, 708] The accumulation of capital and wealth in the process of capitalist industrialization is characterized by "accumulation of misery, agony of toil, slavery, ignorance, brutality, mental degradation. . . ." [16: I, 709]

Utopian Socialism and Crude Communism

By a "bold stroke of analytic strategy," Marx identified the alienation and estrangement of modern Western culture with capitalism rather than the process of rapid, large-scale industrialization. He also identified capitalism with the socio-economic conditions of early nineteenth-century England. Thus, his vision of a post-capitalist economic system was also one of a non-alienated man in an (ideally functioning) industrialized society.

UTOPIAN SOCIALISM

Ideal socialism, as he envisioned, was sharply distinguished from two other varieties: "utopian socialism" and "crude communism." Marx sought to distinguish between his own "scientific socialism" and the ideas of those socialists whom he contemptuously labeled "utopians." According to Marx, the ideas and experiments of men such as Robert Owen in England, and Saint Simon and Fourier in France were "utopias." They were unrealistic because (1) they gave no really systematic, scientific analysis of how or why their ideals could be established, and (2) although their visions and proposals often specified details of proposed socialist economic organization, they had no contact with or support from a socio-economic class as a base of economic power. They could have no such power base, Marx argued, because the time had not yet become ripe for transformation to socialism. When utopian theories were formulated in the early nineteenth century, capitalism was imma-ture. The struggles and antagonisms between workers and capitalists were too underdeveloped to permit mass, revolutionary support for their ideas and programs. Consequently, these utopian socialists were compelled to appeal to "the ruling class . . . to the feeling and purses of the bourgeois . . ." and to attempt to demonstrate the validity of their ideas through voluntary experiments and cooperative associations. These attempts, Marx argued, "are of a purely utopian character" and are therefore "necessarily doomed to failure." [19: 40–41] Conversely, Marx considered his brand of socialism "scientific" rather than "utopian" because of its (1) systematic analysis of the historical process of transformation, which could demonstrate in terms of historical laws how and why capitalism would inevitably be transformed into socialism; (2) contact with and support from an important source of economic power: namely, the industrial workers. In the process of capitalist development, the working class would become increasingly antagonistic to the system, and thus increasingly receptive to the establishment of socialism.

It is in part a tribute to the impact of Marx's ideas that many anti-Marxists have accepted so uncritically his dismissal of people like Owen, Fourier, and Saint Simon as "utopian." But as Schumpeter, among others, emphasized so effectively [8: 308–11], there is a good deal to be said in defense of the realism of the so-called "utopian socialists." First, their romantic dreams and visions were not completely in the clouds, but were based upon existing social problems and human yearnings. Second, if institutional and ideological change is not a one-way street—if ideas can influence institutions, as well as the other way around, then it is conceivable that the criticism of existing economic systems in terms of their deviations from a "utopia" may later, if not sooner, have a very practical impact by influencing the development of economic institutions. The English labor union, cooperative and factory reform movements, for example, owe much to the work and writings of Robert Owen, while contemporary ideas and practices of collectivized and centralized economic planning owe an intellectual debt to Saint Simon. Third, some pre-Marxian socialists grappled (admittedly in unsystematic, not always clear ways) with analyses of some of the problems of operating a post-capitalist economy. Because Marx felt socialism would emerge from the dying embers of capitalism, he considered a detailed analysis of socialism to be premature. Fourth, the Marxist approach to the socialist movement is not the only one. Industrial workers are not necessarily pro-socialist simple because they oppose primitive, laissez-faire capitalism. By identifying the transformation from capitalism to socialism with the growth to dominance of the industrial proletariat, Marx excluded from his model the very practical possibility of non-socialist, yet laborist, reform of capitalism, a possibility which, in terms of contemporary developments in economic organization in such countries as England, Sweden, and the United States, can hardly be called a "utopian dream."

CRUDE VERSUS TRUE COMMUNISM

Marx also distinguished between "crude" and "true" communism. Crude communism [43: 127–27, 131, 149] is the form which communism takes when established in a historical era when society is not yet economically prepared. It is characterized by communal ownership of industrial capital, an enforced community of work, and enforced equality of wage income; it is not "true" communism. It is merely a crude extension of capitalism. It transfers ownership of industrial capital from private capitalists to the community as a "universal capitalist." The community then enforces work, with payment in money wages. "The role of worker is not abolished, but is extended to all men." By enforcing rigid equality in wage income, crude communism "wishes to eliminate talent, and so forth, by force." It focuses on satisfactions derived from consumption rather than creative work. By leveling everyone "on the basis of a *preconceived* minimum," it represents the culmination and universalization of envy. (Under capitalism, poorer workers envy richer workers and capitalists. The culmination of envy is the desire to eliminate income differences under crude communism and reduce everyone to a common level in the enjoyment of consumer goods.)

By contrast, Marx's vision of post-capitalist society was characterized by two central features. First, socialism is an industrialized society; it is industrialized capitalism without private capitalists and certain other associated institutional trappings of capitalist economy. Thus, industrialization via capitalism is a necessary historical prerequisite to the establishment of socialism. Second, "true" socialism and "positive" communism are industrialized societies without the alienation of labor. "Marxism is the type of socialism that believes in industrialization, but can live as a revolutionary movement of importance only in symbiosis with a widespread anti-industrial feeling. As such, it is unique among socialist systems of the nineteenth century." [46: 130–31] The Marxian vision thus is one of post-capitalist economic societies which contain the economic benefits of industrialization without the attendant social and moral costs of alienation. It is, in its own way, a utopian vision of an ideally functioning economic society.

THE TRANSITION FROM CAPITALISM TO SOCIALISM

If capitalism cannot survive, the question of the transition to the new post-capitalist order becomes highly relevant. We will divide this question into three sub-questions: When? Where? How?

When?

Marx, at least in his earlier writings, apparently thought the transition from capitalism to socialism was imminent. Certainly, this is the tone of *The Communist Manifesto*, written in 1848. As events successively dampened his optimistic expectations, and more systematic and detailed analysis supplemented his more youthful visions, he increasingly withdrew from specifying a precise timetable. The crucial point about the transition, especially in Marx's later writings, is that it will come when the time is "ripe." As emphasized, Marx regarded as "utopian" attempts to create a socialist economic system prior to the full development and maturation of capitalism. "No social order," he argued in 1859, "ever disappears before all the productive forces, for which there is room in it, have been developed; and new higher relations of production never appear before the material conditions of their existence have matured in the womb of the old society."[2]

Where?

According to Marx, transition to the post-capitalist order will occur in the industrialized economically developed capitalist nations of the Western world. England and Germany, for example, are countries which seemed to nineteenth- and early twentieth-century socialists to be in the process of ripening. Capitalism, in the classic Marxian view, has a vital historic function to perform; namely, the development of society's "productive forces": the accumulation of capital, the development of technology, the expansion of the factory system, the socialization of the work process, and so forth. The route to industrialization and economic growth, important prerequisites to socialism, is that of capitalism. Socialism will appropriate a fully developed capitalist technology and productive machine and has distinctly different historic functions to perform. This implies, incidentally, that it is in the interest of workers in underdeveloped economies to encourage the

---

[2]Karl Marx, *A Contribution to the Critique of Political Economy* (Chicago: Kerr, 1904), p. 12.

establishment of capitalism as a prerequisite to socialism, despite the misery and degradation capitalism brings them.

Clearly, this classical Marxist interpretation does not correspond to the facts of twentieth-century Communist revolution. As noted, Communists generally have come to power in essentially agricultural, underdeveloped economies, where neither capitalism nor industrialization were firmly entrenched nor highly developed. The Russian revolutions of 1917 are a classic case in point. Communist writers, notably Lenin and Trotsky, revised the classic Marxist-socialist theory of transition, largely in the attempt to make it correspond more closely to the strategy and tactics of Communist revolutionary experience.

The contemporary Leninist theory of transition may be summarized as (a) the "law of uneven development" of capitalism; (b) the "law of combined development." [44: 257–73] The former refers to the idea inherent in Lenin's theory of imperialism that the extent of capitalism and industrialization differs in different countries and that less developed economies, chafing under the imperialist exploitation of the industrially advanced capitalist powers, may ripen for *political revolution* despite their lower level of *economic* development. By analogy, capitalist world economy resembles a chain which can be broken at its *weakest link*, perhaps during a severe depression or war (like Russia, for example), rather than a tree, from which the ripest fruit falls off first.

The latter principle asserts that in the underdeveloped economies penetrated by capitalist imperialism, elements of feudalism and capitalism coexist. A transition to socialism thus requires *two* revolutions: first, a bourgeois or capitalist revolution against feudalism; second, a "proletarian" (this term broadened to include peasants, as well as industrial workers) revolution against capitalism. Just as elements of capitalism and feudalism are "telescoped" together, to use Leon Trotsky's famous phrase, in the under-

developed countries, so, too, can both revolutions be "telescoped" into one. In short, the transition to socialism will occur first in relatively less developed economies, like Russia, not necessarily in the industrially developed nations of the Western world. Clearly, the aims envisaged in this transition, and the economic and political problems of the "socialist" society in the event of successful revolution, are radically different from those of the classic Marxian and non-Marxian-socialist outlook.

How?

For Marx, the primary issue was that capitalism cannot survive. The details of *how* the prospective transition from the capitalist to the post-capitalist economy is to occur are of secondary importance, and any one of a variety of hypotheses is consistent with his general philosophy. Two things, however, are clear: First, the more or less rapid, dramatic transformation from one economic system to another (from feudalism to capitalism, from capitalism to socialism, from socialism to communism) is a social phenomenon of *revolutionary* significance. Second, "social revolutions" in this sense occur only in the "fullness" and "ripeness" of time; that is, only on the basis of *evolutionary* preparation. It is consistent with Marx's analysis of the process of the historical emergence, development, maturation, and final death of economic systems to say it involves, indeed requires, both revolution *and* evolution.

As to the question: Will "social revolution" in this technical sense *also* require revolution in the *popular* sense; that is, physical violence, popular uprisings, street riots, workers at the barricades, and so on? The answer most consistent with Marx's writings: *It all depends* —first, on the specific conditions, circumstances, history, and background of the country involved; second, on the particular segment of Marx's voluminous writings you prefer to quote. Generally, Marx emphasized that an economic and politically dominant capitalist class will not voluntarily and peacefully abdicate its position of wealth and power, and that its dislodgement probably would require a violent overthrow by its workers.[3]

On several occasions, however, especially in his later, perhaps mellower, years, Marx and especially Engels recognized the possibility of a *peaceful* transition. In 1872 before the Hague Congress of the International, Marx said: "We know that the institutions, the manners and the customs of the various countries must be considered, and we do not deny that there are countries like England and America, and if I understood your arrangements better, I might even add Holland, where the worker may attain his object (that is, effectuate the transition from capitalism to socialism) by peaceful means. But not in all countries is this the case."[4] It would appear to be consistent both with Marx's writings and with historical experience to say that economic and social transformations of societies of revolutionary consequence involve varying degrees of violence and peacefulness between the extremes of "perfect peace" and "perfect violence," the point on

the continuum varying with time and place. At any rate, whatever Marx's position on violence (to him, apparently, a secondary issue), post-Marxian socialists divided into two major schools: (1) evolutionary socialists such as the Fabians in England, and the "revisionist Marxists," notably Edward Bernstein; (2) revolutionary socialists. The first group insisted socialism could be established by peaceful, evolutionary means in industrially developed, democratic nations. The second group argued, like Lenin, that, "as a general rule," the "replacement of the bourgeois by the proletarian state is impossible without a violent revolution." [42: 20] (The emphasis on violence in the writings of Lenin and his successors, incidentally, is consistent with the view that "socialism" first will emerge in a relatively underdeveloped and, most likely, pre-democratic country, like Russia or China, rather than in the industrially developed nations, with their longer histories and traditions of democratic institutions.)

THE MARXIAN CONCEPTION OF SOCIALISM

The Marxian conception of socialism essentially is that identified earlier herein as "pure or classical socialism." The major elements of this conception are summarized in Table 8-1.

We have already commented on the Marxian view of socialism as an industrialized, post-capitalist economy. Motivations and social processes will be discussed in the following section. The other dimensions warrant consideration here.

As in the Marxian definition of capitalism, ownership-control of the means of production is a strategic element in the Marxian vision of socialism. A transition from capitalist to socialist economy includes a shift to worker-state ownership of industrial capital; that is, under Marxian socialism, the workers (or the state, responsible to and

---

[3] "Would it . . . be a matter for astonishment", argued Marx in *The Poverty of Philosophy* (Chicago: Kerr, 1910), pp. 190–191, "if a society based on the *antagonism* of classes should lead ultimately to a brutal *conflict*, to a hand-to-hand struggle as its final *denouement*? . . . It is only in an order of things in which there will be no longer classes or class antagonism that *social evolutions* will cease to be *political revolutions*. Until then, on the eve of each general reconstruction of society, the last word of social science will ever be: 'Combat or death; bloody struggle or extinction. It is thus that the question is irresistibly put'." "Force," stated Marx [16: I, 824], "is the midwife of every old society pregnant with a new one." Bober (*Karl Marx's Interpretation of History* (Cambridge, Mass.: Harvard University Press, 1948), pp. 262–63) suggests two additional reasons for an emphasis upon violent revolution in Marx's writings: (1) "the building of communism demands a change of heart on a mass scale, and only in the shock of revolution can this change be wrought . . ."; (2) "revolution shortens the pains of transition."

[4] *Ibid.*, pp. 264–65.

Table 8-1.

MARXIAN SOCIALISM

1. Level of economic development	Developed economy with a high per-capita income and an advanced technology
2. Resource base	Heavy reliance upon capital and capitalistic methods of production
3. Ownership-control of the means of production	Worker-state ownership and control
4. Locus of economic power	Workers and the worker-state
5. Motivational system	Remnants of "bourgeois" psychology (economic gain maximization) modified by beginnings of satisfactions from the creative work process
6. Organization of economic power	Combination of decentralization (worker control) and centralization (central planning)
7. Social processes for economic coordination	Primary reliance upon an overall system of public economic planning for the entire economy, coupled with "democratization" or worker control of industry
8. Distribution of income and wealth	Elimination of income from private ownership of land and capital, coupled with some income inequality based on differences in quantity and quality of work.

controlled by the workers) own the instruments of production. This raises the whole question of the relation between the state and the workers. On the one hand, Marxian socialism includes a *state*, which, via its ownership-control of the instruments of production, guides, organizes, and coordinates economic decisions in an industrialized society. On the other, Marxian socialism presumably is characterized by the absence of the social and moral costs of "alienation" of labor. But this would seem to require that *workers* own and control the instruments of production with which they work.

Marx and his successors attempted to resolve this dilemma by *identifying* worker and state ownership.[5] In his discussion of the

Paris Commune (the governing body of a short-lived popular-worker uprising in Paris in 1871), Marx distinguished between the political apparatus of the state and the workers (and, by implication, between state and worker ownership); he emphasized that the members of the Commune were mostly "working men, or acknowledged representatives of the working class," chosen through "universal suffrage" by workers, to whom they were "responsible and revokable at short terms." [17: II, 498] In other words, state ownership and worker ownership coalesce because either (1) the state *is* the collectivity of workers, or (2) the state is *responsible to* and controlled by the workers.

---

[5]This is illustrated by the following: "The proletariat will . . . centralize all instruments of production in the hands of the state, that is, of the proletariat as the ruling class . . . ." [19: 30] "The proletariat

seizes the state power and transforms the means of production in the first instance into state property." [17: I, 181] Under socialism, the "means of production are no longer the private property of individuals." They "belong to the whole of society." [42: 76]

The nature of the institutional processes for making and coordinating economic decisions under socialism is not specified in detail in the writings of Marx and Engels. Their central point in relation to these issues was the elimination of the price or market system, which was held to be ineffective as a social process for economic calculation, coordination, and control because it generates "anarchy of production in society as a whole." [17: I, 173] "The point of bourgeois society," argued Marx, "consists precisely in this, that *a priori* there is not conscious regulation of production."[6]

The most essential institutional features of Marxian socialism, would appear to be (1) freely associated groups of workers in control of the allocation of labor and the determination of production decisions, and (2) a conscious central plan formulated by society for the organization and control of the entire economy.[7] Apparently, Marx saw no conflict between these two different principles of economic organization and, partly because of this, did not examine such problems as the role and power of central planners, the relations between central plans and decentralized bodies of "freely associated" workers, or the scope and limits of managerial responsibility.

---

[6]Cited in Bober, *op. cit.*, p. 281.

[7]Cf. the following typical references: "production by freely associated men . . . consciously regulated by them in accordance with a settled plan." [16-I, 93] ". . . socialized man, the associated producers, regulating their interchange with nature rationally, bring it under their common control" [16: III, 954] ". . . united cooperative societies are to regulate national production upon a common plan, thus taking it under their own control . . . ." [17: II, 504] Cf. also the juxtaposition of the following two elements—first: "Until the 'higher' phase of Communism arrives, the Socialists demand the *strictest* control, *by society and by the state*, of the quantity of labour and the quantity of consumption . . ."; second; "only this control must . . . be carried out, not by a state of bureaucrats, but by a state of armed workers." [42: 80]

THE ECONOMICS OF SOCIALISM IN THE MARXIAN VISION

Marx essentially had no economic theory of socialism—certainly nothing corresponding to his analysis of the economics of capitalism. Particularly noticeable is the absence of any systematic analysis of economic planning—indeed, even of recognition of the types of problems with which post-capitalist planners might have to deal. Yet, it may be useful to summarize the few scattered statements that exist in Marxian literature on the economics of socialism.

Allocation of Resources

Marx recognized the universality of the problem of resource allocation; that is, its applicability to all economies, including capitalist and post-capitalist systems. In regard to the latter, he emphasized the necessity of maintaining "the proper proportion between the different kinds of work to be done and the various wants of the community," stating that this problem "cannot be done away with by the *particular form* of social production, but can only change the *form it assumes* . . . "; the desirability of establishing "the natural law" of "equilibrium" in the exchange of commodities, which requires a "direct relation between the quantity of social labor time employed in the production of definite articles and the quantity of the demand of society for them"; the importance of accomplishing tasks "with the least expenditure of energy"; and the necessity of bookkeeping for the purpose of "control and ideal survey." [16: I, 90; II, 153; III, 221, 954; "Letters to Dr. Kugelmann," pp. 73–74, cited in 39: 132] True to Marxian form, the emphasis in all these references is on the allocation of *labor* resources. That capital, natural, and entrepreneurial resources are also scarce and require economic calculation and control is either downplayed or denied.

Marx expected a socialist economy would be immensely more productive and efficient than capitalism had been at an earlier stage of industrialization and economic development. But the major gain expected from the shift to socialist institutions and allocational processes was in the enlarged freedom of man as a producer or worker. The key point for Marx is *not* that socialism will be more efficient than capitalism in production and in satisfying consumer wants (though he obviously felt that it would be), but rather that, if resources were allocated and production decisions made on the basis of a "conscious plan" in which workers participated and which they controlled, man no longer would be a slave to the "blind power" and "blind laws" of the social processes of production and exchange. Instead, in free association and cooperation, man would most fully realize his potential and achieve his *human* power to control and direct his destiny.

The naive "innocence" of the visions of both Marx and Lenin on the post-capitalist economy is shown by their expectations that economic calculation and control would be essentially *simple*, so that "everyone" should "*be able* really to take part in the administration of the state." Part of this simplicity is accounted for by the development under capitalism of "universal literacy" and "the 'training and disciplining' of millions" of industrial workers. The "accounting and control necessary for" the efficient organization of the socialist economy, wrote Lenin, "have been *simplified* by capitalism to the utmost, till they have become the extraordinarily simple operations of watching, recording and issuing receipts, within the reach of anybody who can read and write and knows the first four rules of arithmetic. When the *majority* of the people begin everywhere to keep such accounts and maintain such control over the capitalists ... this control will really become universal, general, national. ... The whole of society will have

become one office and one factory. ..." Ultimately, "when all have learned to manage, and independently are actually managing by themselves social production, ... then the escape from this national accounting and control will inevitably become so increasingly difficult ... that very soon the *necessity* of observing the simple fundamental rules of everyday social life in common will have become a habit." [42: 83–85]

Distribution of Income

The starting point for understanding the Marxian conception of income distribution under socialism is the shift from private, individual capitalist to worker-state ownership of industrial capital. Since the workers (or the state, responsible to and controlled by the workers) own industrial capital under socialism, exploitation of workers as a class by any non-working class becomes impossible. The "*exploitation* of man by man will have become impossible," argued Lenin, "because it will be impossible to seize as private property the *means of production* ...." [42: 77] This implies it would not be possible (1) for workers to be exploited by the state; (2) for some workers to be exploited in relation to other workers.

INCOME DISTRIBUTION AND ECONOMIC SURPLUS

In regard to the first possibility, one might suppose workers under socialism would be exploited by the state if the state kept from them any surplus of national income above wages. In an important and interesting critique of the 1875 platform of the German Workers' Party, Marx emphasized this was *not* the case. In the post-capitalist economy, the "total social product" would be divided into seven categories: (1) a depreciation allowance for "the means of production used up" in production; (2) an "additional portion for expansion of production" or increase in capital stock; (3) a "reserve or insurance fund to provide against misadventures, disturbances through natural events," and the like; (4) the "general costs" of government administration (which Marx anticipated would decrease as socialism developed); (5) a portion "for the communal satisfaction of needs, such as schools, health services, and so on" (which Marx expected would increase under socialism); (6) "funds for those unable to work"; and, finally, (7) the remaining "diminished proceeds" from the national product, "namely that part of the means of consumption which is divided among the producers of the cooperative society." The first three categories, he emphasized, "are an economic necessity," that is, necessary for any economic system, and "are in no way calculable by equity," that is, social justice. [17: II, 562]

The existence of the first six categories means that a difference occurs between total output and consumption goods available to workers in a socialist economy. Under capitalism, such a difference would be called a "surplus," the generation of which by private capitalists, through a production and exchange process that degrades and enslaves workers, would constitute "exploitation." Under socialism, however, the difference between total output and worker-consumption does *not* constitute exploitation because "what the producer is deprived of in his capacity as a private individual benefits him directly or indirectly in his capacity as a member of society." [17: II, 562] Indeed, its existence does not even constitute a "surplus" —at least, not a surplus comparable to that generated under capitalism. In the ideally organized socialist economy, "the producers do not exchange their products," and labor does not appear in the form of the "*value* of these products, as a material quality possessed by them," the receipts from the sale of which accrue to capitalists. Workers, rather, contribute *directly* to the creation of *their* total output. After deducting for the "common fund," that is, the first six items (presumably by some political decision in which workers participate and control), the "social stock of means of consumption" which remains is available for distribution to workers. [17: II, 563] Rent, interest, and profits (capitalism's surplus) will not exist in an ideally organized socialist economy, where income can accrue to individuals (except those unable to work) only on the basis of labor, not ownership of instruments of production.

In sum, the elimination of capitalism and the emergence of socialism does not create an economic system where consumption equals national income. An excess of national income over consumption is both necessary and desirable, if the economy is to grow, government is to function, communal needs are to be satisfied, and those unable to work are to be provided for. But when workers, in free association and in control of the apparatus of the state, consciously, on the basis of an overall "plan," choose to allocate a portion of total resources to the provision of these non-consumption purposes, the process does not involve exploitation. It is perhaps unnecessary to add that the major limitation of this view lies not in its economics (which, in contrast to the crude notion that under socialism all output should and will go to worker-consumption, is much more sophisticated), nor in the beauty of its moral vision, but in its failure to understand and specify how workers in such a system are to prevent their state from becoming as exploitative in practice as private capitalists ever were in Marxian theory.

EQUITY AND EQUALITY

In regard to the second possibility, workers will share in the "diminished proceeds" from total output on the basis of their work or contribution to production. ("He who does not work shall not eat," said Lenin. [42: 78]) The individual worker "receives back from society . . . exactly what he gives to it . . . ," that is, "his individual amount of labour . . . . He receives a certificate[8] from society" that he has provided a certain amount of labor, and "with this certificate he draws from the social stocks of means of consumption as much as costs the same amount of labour." [17: II, 563]

Because workers are mentally and physically different, they make different contributions to production, and, on the basis of this distributional criterion, receive different incomes. Socialism, therefore, will not create income equality. This, argued Marx, is unjust, because: "everyone is only a worker like everyone else"; it accepts "unequal individual endowment and thus productive capacity as natural privileges"; since it makes no allowance for wife and size of family, it would involve family inequality even if workers were to share equally; and it ignores human need. Such injustice is unavoidable because socialism "emerges from capitalist society" and is thus "still stamped with the birthmarks of the old society from whose womb it emerges." Because of bourgeois psychology and bourgeois conceptions of "rights," income differentials are still necessary as an incentive system for production and the allocation of labor in the early stages of a socialist economy. Justice "can never be higher than the economic structure of society and the cultural development thereby determined." [17: II, 563–65][9]

---

[8]In a socialist economy, "money-capital is eliminated. Society distributes labor-power and means of production to the different lines of occupation. The producers may eventually receive paper checks, by means of which they withdraw from the social supply of means of consumption a share corresponding to their labor-time. These checks are not money. They do not circulate." [16: II, 412]

[9]Lenin similarly emphasized [42: 77] that socialism "cannot produce justice and equality; differences, and unjust differences, in wealth will still exist . . . ." Socialism eliminates *only* the 'injustice' that consists in the means of production having been seized by private individuals . . . ." It "is not capable of destroying at once the further injustice consisting in the distribution of the articles of consumption 'according to work performed' (and not according to need)."

Economic Growth and Full Employment Stability

The treatment of economic growth and and stability in the Marxian vision is even more sketchy than that of allocation and distribution: Marx emphasized that, if socialism is to grow, like capitalism, it must engage in positive net investment, that is, must allocate a portion of total resources to the augmentation of the capital stock. Socialism will not eliminate the capitalist function, but rather will *transfer* it from private capitalists to the worker-state, and, by implication, will include it in an overall "investment plan." The principles governing the plan for determination of the portion of society's resources to be allocated for this purpose are not specified beyond the general directive that "their magnitude is to be determined by available means and forces, and partly by calculation of probabilities . . . ." [17: II, 562]

The Marxian vision suggests socialism is more conducive to economic growth than capitalism. First, socialist growth is characterized by the absence of cyclical deviations from the potential full-employment growth curve. Capitalism, said Marx, had a vital historic function to play in the process of industrialization and the development of society's "productive forces" (resources and technology). But as capitalism develops and matures, its "relations of production" (institutions) increasingly conflict with those productive forces. It stifles the potential full development of economic performance and prevents, in recurrent depressions, the actual performance from equaling the potential. With the substitution, under socialism, of a "socially planned regulation of production" for the "anarchy" and "blind laws" of capitalism, society's productive forces "can be transformed from demoniacal masters into willing servants." The "release" of these forces of production from the "bonds" of capitalist institutions is the sole condition necessary for an unbroken, progressive development of productive forces. In simple form we might say capitalism causes increasingly severe cyclical depressions. Eliminate capitalism, and cyclical depressions vanish. It is relevant to note the Marxian vision ignores this embarrassing question: Might not the institutions of a socialist economy (such as the relations between decentralized groups of workers and central planners) also be a potential source of cyclical instability?

Second, socialism eliminates the domination of man by his natural and social environment and makes him the conscious planner, the understanding controller, the freely associating "master of his own social organization." In short, men emerge from enslavement and become, for the first time in history, "really human," truly free to "fashion their own history." This "leap from the realm of necessity into the realm of freedom," by implication, unleashes a vast reservoir of human energy, creativity, and productivity, which could raise the potential level and growth in production.

Third, socialism "sets free for society as a whole a mass of means of production and products by putting an end to the senseless luxury and extravagance of the present ruling class and its political representatives." [All preceding quotations are from Engels' writings. Cf. 17: I, 184–86]

PURE OR IDEAL COMMUNISM: THE MARXIAN VISION OF THE PERFECT SOCIETY

The classic Marxian conception of communism is of a perfect society which may, at some unspecified future time, become accessible to man *if* two preconditions are met: (1) a tremendous expansion of production and productivity, based upon economies of large-scale production, the elimination of depressions, the unleashing of human creativity, and the continued growth of science and technology; (2) an accompanying dramatic alteration in individual and social psychology, notably the substitution of cooperation for competition and the creativity of the work process for satisfactions from consumption.[10]

Division of Labor and Distribution of Income in Affluent Communism

The Marxian vision of communism is one of a society of extreme affluence. Economic motivation, private property in the form of consumption goods, and the pursuit of economic gain have disappeared; social classes and exploitation are a thing of the past; social cooperation has replaced competition; the state as a coercive agent of oppression has "withered away"; and the maximization of individual freedom coalesces with a communally planned regulation and coordination of the entire society. Economic instability is nonexistent; economic growth has become automatic and self-sustaining; and resource allocation and income distribution are determined largely, if not entirely, on the basis of non-economic criteria. The traditional problem of scarcity, if not eliminated, at least has been reduced so dramatically that significant modifications may be made in the processes of resource allocation and production, on one hand, and the distribution of income, on the other.

[10]According to Lenin, the "expropriation of the capitalist will inevitably result in a gigantic development of the productive forces of human society." This provides—though "how rapidly" and "how soon . . . we do not and *cannot* know"—the "economic basis for that high state of development of Communism" where it is possible to break "away from the division of labor," to remove "the antagonism between mental and physical labor" (a major source of "social inequality"), and to transform "work into the 'first necessity of life'." With this tremendous increase in labor productivity, people gradually will discard the "narrow horizon of bourgeois rights" and will "voluntarily work *according to their ability*" and "take freely 'according to . . . needs' " without need for "exact calculation by society of the quantity of products to be distributed to each of its members . . . ." In short, Communism presupposes "both a productivity of labour unlike the present and a person not like the present man on the street . . . ." [42: 79–80]

The Marxian vision of modifications in resource allocation and production incorporate several elements, including an increase in leisure and accompanying reduction in the quantity of work required to provide the output to satisfy consumer wants to very low levels. The most striking element in the Marxian vision of communist production and resource allocation, however, has to do with the division of labor. In rhapsodic terms, Marx described his utopia: In "communist society, . . . nobody has one exclusive sphere of activity. . . ." Everyone "can become accomplished in any branch he wishes. . . ." Society "regulates the general production and thus makes it possible for me to do one thing today and another tomorrow, to hunt in the morning, fish in the afternoon, rear cattle in the evening, criticize after dinner, just as I have a mind, without ever becoming hunter, fisherman, shepherd or critic."[11] This quotation and others like it often are misunderstood. A modern industrialized society requires a division of labor. Further, socialist-communist economic societies, lacking price systems as social processes for coordinating economic decisions, would require a social plan to regulate production and apportion labor to various tasks. Thus, communism would not be accompanied by elimination of the division of labor, and workers would not be free to work when and where they pleased. What *would* be abolished would be the "tyrannical subordination" to the division of labor. [17: II, 566] Within the framework of a general economic plan for society, it would be possible, Marx thought, for an individual worker (especially with the enlargement and universalization of education) to change to and experiment with *various* occupations which he found attractive.[12]

The second dimension of communist affluence is the transformation to a system of income distribution based on need, rather than on correspondence to productive contribution. In an often-cited quotation from the *Critique of the Gotha Programme*, Marx eloquently described this vision: "In a higher phase of communist society, after the enslaving subordination of individuals under division of labour, and therewith also the antithesis between mental and physical labour, has vanished, after labour has become not merely a means to live but has become itself the primary necessity of life, after the productive forces have also increased with the all-around development of the individual, and all the springs of cooperative wealth flow more abundantly—only then can the narrow horizon of bourgeois right be fully left behind and society inscribe on its banners: from each according to his ability, to each according to his needs. [17: II, 566]

The poetic beauty and seeming unreality of this vision should not overlook that economic growth and technological change in an affluent society may well bring about profound changes in individual motivations and social organization. It should also be noted that how we evaluate the practicability of such a vision depends, in part, on how we define that much maligned term, "needs" and whether we attempt to apply it to the entirety of society of to parts thereof. It is wholly possible and not unlikely that as a society becomes richer, it will rely less upon

---

[11]Cf. *The German Ideology*, reprinted in Robert Freeman, *Marx On Economics* (New York: Harcourt, Brace & World, 1961), p. 270.

[12]In a review of the Marxian vision of communism, Iring Fetscher expresses this theme succinctly: "As a member of society every one is indeed bound to work; but he is able—within the framework of necessity which arises from the needs of the community—to choose freely." Within the framework of a socially planned division of labor, "everyone will, nevertheless, be in a position to choose various functions that he can fulfill, and not have to spend his whole life bound to a single task which would hinder the development of his potential capacities . . . . A situation in which socially necessary work attracts no or too few volunteers is, for practical purposes, not envisaged in the Marxian anthropology of a communist society." Cf. "Marx, Engels, and the Future Society," in Walter Laqueur and Leopold Labedz, *The Future of Communist Society* (New York: Frederick A. Praeger, Inc., 1962), pp. 106, 104.

division of labor and will attempt to satisfy an increasing number and variety of "basic needs" outside of the marketplace and on the basis of criteria other than productive contribution.

The Transformation of Man

The transformation of man and his relations to output, labor, and other men are both preconditions for and central characteristics of "true" communism as conceived by Marx. The creation of a non-alienated man in an ideally functioning communist economic society has several facets. First, workers, through the ownership and control of the natural and man-made means of production, are no longer alienated from their output. Second is the transformation of the work process and attitudes toward work; in cooperative association with others, the worker controls the creation of his output and thus can obtain real creative satisfaction from work. (This factor also is aided by modifications in the division of labor, reductions in working hours, more equitable apportionment of manual versus mental tasks, and the continued substitution of capital for unskilled labor.) Work ceases to be drudgery and becomes an enjoyable, creative experience in which men may freely engage. Third, the subjection of the forces of nature to conscious social control terminates the alienation of man from the essence of humanity and provides for workers the human need to control their environment. Fourth, "In place of the old bourgeois society, with its classes and class antagonisms, we shall have an association in which the free development of each is the condition for the free development of all." [19: 31] Ideal communism is an economic society characterized by the substitution of cooperative association for the class antagonisms of the past.

In the *Economic and Philosophical Manuscripts*, the youthful Marx gave his vision of pure communism:

Communism is the *positive* abolition of *private property*, of *human self-alienation*, and thus the real *appropriation* of *human nature* through and for man. It is, therefore, the return of man himself as a social, that is, really human, being, a complete and conscious return which assimilates all the wealth of previous development. Communism as a fully-developed naturalism is humanism and as a fully-developed humanism is naturalism. It is the *definitive* resolution of the antagonism between man and nature, and between man and man. It is the true solution of the conflict between existence and essence, between objectification and self-affirmation, between freedom and necessity, between individual and species. It is the solution of the riddle of history and knows itself to be this solution. [43: 127]

CONCLUDING NOTE

To ignore the Marxian vision of the ideally functioning socialist and communist economic societies in a comparative review of economic systems would be inadequate. On the other hand, to suggest this broad, speculative vision constituted a rigorous and clear model of a socialist economy, that it has corresponded to any real world economic system, or that it has been the only view of the appropriate route to or organizational form of post-capitalist economics would be misleading and inaccurate. Still, post-Marxian socialism is in many instances an extension of, modification of, or reaction to this rather vague, speculative vision. This will be seen in succeeding chapters on socialism and Communism.

SUMMARY OF CHAPTER 8

1. The classical Marxian analysis of economic development was characterized by a basic duality involving a glorification, yet critique, of industrialization. Thus, capitalism was perceived as the historic route to industrialization, yet was held to cause "alienation"

and to be characterized by contradictions which eventually would cause its demise. Socialism was perceived as an industrialized, not merely post-capitalist, economic system.

2. The Marxian prediction of the transition from capitalism to socialism may be divided into three issues: when, where, how. As to *when*, the key point of classical Marxism was that socialism will emerge when the time is "ripe," that is, when the technological, institutional, and ideological requisites have been fulfilled. As to *where*, the Marxian vision of socialism predicted its emergence in industrialized capitalist societies. As to *how*, the transformation from capitalism to socialism was perceived as being characterized by decades of evolutionary economic development, as well as by a final political revolution, which might or might not be violent, depending upon circumstances.

3. The classical Marxian definition of socialism contained two major, but never fully or clearly integrated, dimensions: first, worker control over production and allocation of resources (the decentralized, democratic, anarcho-syndicalist element); second, a consciously formulated central plan for the coordination of the entire economy (the centralized, dictatorial, authoritarian element).

4. The classical Marxian analysis of economizing processes for allocation, distribution, growth, and stabilization under socialism was sketchy, at best. The substitution of central planning for market processes was expected to promote stability while coordinating investment programs for economic growth. The elimination of private ownership of the instruments of production was expected to terminate surplus value, but not economic surpluses (to provide for investment, collective goods, and so forth). Income differences were expected to reflect differences in the quantity and quality of labor. Workers, both directly by control of production and indirectly by control over the state and thereby society-wide planning agencies, were expected to allocate resources so as to equalize consumer demands (expressed in labor units) and supplies of commodities (valued in terms of socially necessary labor time) and to produce with the least expenditure of energy, that is, to minimize cost.

5. The classical Marxian vision of communism is that of a post-socialist, super-affluent, super-industrialized society. Its emergence was perceived to require (1) an exceptionally advanced technology, and (2) a dramatic alteration in human motivations, characterized by a shift from competition for income to cooperation and derivation of prime human values from work. Given these requisite conditions, pure communism could abolish the "tyrannical subordination" to division of labor and distribute income according to need without untoward effects upon production or productivity.

9

The Neo-Austrian
Critique of Socialism

INTRODUCTION

As seen in the preceding chapter, Marxian economic analysis lacked a rigorous, developed model for socialist economic organization and planning. This deficiency in the socialist literature has been rectified in the twentiety century by the emergence of a variety of neo- and non-Marxist theories, united in their criticism of capitalism and support of "socialism," but divergent in their conceptions of the structure and behavior of socialist economy.

These theories have been affected in varying ways and degrees by the general development of post-Marxist, but non-Marxist, economic thought, some sympathetic to, but much critical of, the prospective economic efficiency of socialism. Probably the most prominent and "fundamental" of the post-Marxist critiques of the economic theory of socialism was that by neo-Austrian economists Ludwig von Mises and Friedrich A. von Hayek.[1]

The neo-Austrian indictment of socialism essentially is twofold. First, its primary criticism, developed in the 1920s and 1930s by Mises, Hayek, and others, is that socialism is (or would be, if established) economically inefficient in the allocation of scarce resources. A second line of criticism has been expressed, especially since the 1940s, by Hayek and others, for example, American neo-liberal economist Milton Friedman. It is that socialism is characterized by or would lead to the absence or loss of individual economic and political freedoms and democracy, and

---

[1] Mises and Hayek are the intellectual descendents of the Austrian school of economic theory which flourished in the late nineteenth century, centered around the University of Vienna. Its founding father was Carl Menger, one of the triad (Menger-Jevons-Walras) significant for first clearly formulating and incorporating the concept of marginal utility into economics in the 1870s. The Austrian school was noted for its focus on *individual* economic calculation

and choice, the role of *subjective* factors (notably utility) in the explanation of value, its highly *theoretical* emphases, and its strong attachment to *liberal individualism* in social philosophy. Mises and Hayek, following in the Austrian tradition, taught in Europe in the 1930s and 1940s and emigrated to the United States. Along with Milton Friedman and other contemporary economists at the University of Chicago and elsewhere, they have made important contributions to the contemporary social and economic philosophy of neo-liberalism. Aside from works cited in this chapter and in the selected readings at the end of Part III, Mises is most noted for his major work *Human Action* (New Haven: Yale University Press, 1949). Hayek has published numerous books and articles in economic theory and social philosophy. Most representative of his recent writings is *The Constitution of Liberty* (Chicago: University of Chicago Press, 1960), in which his earlier critique of socialism is modified and extended to include a critical analysis of democratic social reforms in the context of contemporary managed capitalism.

that the "road to socialism" really is a "road to serfdom" and totalitarian dictatorship.

This chapter is primarily an exposition of the neo-Austrian analysis, with major emphasis on the Mises-Hayek critique of the prospective possibility-practicability of "rational economic calculation," coordination, and control. Also examined briefly are responses to the neo-Austrian critique, though alternative theories and views on socialism, in the main, are deferred for separate treatment in later chapters. The broader question of the prospective impact of socialism upon freedom and democracy is examined in the Appendix to this chapter.

The Basic Character of the Neo-Austrian Critique

The phrase "critique of the economic theory of" socialism implies three things. First, unlike other theories reviewed in Part III, the neo-Austrian contribution is unsympathetic to and critical of the aims and aspirations of the socialist movement(s). An exposition of the critical ideas of the neo-Austrian economists thus provides a function similar to that of the inclusion of the Marxian critique of capitalist industrialization among the theories of capitalism in Part II. Two other similarities might be noted. Just as Marx insisted his was a scientific analysis rather than a moral condemnation of capitalism, so, too, Mises and Hayek affirm the essentially scientific character of their critique of socialism. Further, just as Marx had great influence on post-Marxian theories of capitalism, notably those of Schumpeter, so, too, the neo-Austrian critique has affected later theories of socialism, especially those of Lange and other contributors to the analysis of decentralized market socialism.

Second, the neo-Austrian critique focuses on economic issues, indeed, as will be discussed, on a very special conception of and set of emphases in regard to economic issues. According to Hayek, reviewing "The Nature and History of the Problem" in 1935, discussions of socialism for many years ". . . turned almost exclusively on ethical and psychological issues. On the one hand, there was the general question whether justice required a reorganization of society on socialist lines and what principles of the distribution of income were to be regarded as just. On the other hand, there was the question whether men in general could be trusted to have the moral and psychological qualities which were dimly seen to be essential if a socialist system was to work." [4: 119–20]

But neither social goals nor the "practical possibility of the execution of the plans . . . really touch the heart of the problem." [4: 120] "On the validity of the ultimate ends science has nothing to say. They may be accepted or rejected, but they cannot be proved or disproved." [4: 130] Whether people can be induced to execute plans, on the other hand, is a matter for study by the moralist and/or psychologist, but not the economist. But the real "heart of the problem," though under- and/or unrecognized, is economic, namely whether a socialist economy, "even in the ideal case" where these practical moral and psychological problems are absent, "would achieve the desired end." [4: 120] The key problem here, according to Hayek, is the use of knowledge in society to make "rational economic calculations" in a social context which includes a process for the coordination of knowledgeable decisions and actions.

Third, the neo-Austrian critique is essentially, if not exclusively, one of the economic theory of socialism, rather than socialist practice, as a theoretical economic system, rather than an actual economic system or a movement for economic reform. This reflects in part the heavy emphasis in Austrian economic thought on pure theory, as opposed to historical-empirical research, and on logic, rather than specific cases. It also constitutes a powerful element of rhetoric. Were the problems of socialism merely "practical" difficulties, socialists could respond by emphasizing the imperfections of *any* economic system, capitalist or socialist, and the problems of transition to a new form of economic organization, which presumably would decrease as the system developed. But if the economic problems of socialism are of a "fundamental theoretical character," then even in "ideal" circumstances, socialism cannot be expected to work, or, at least, to work efficiently. If the problems were merely practical ones, the solution would be to learn from experience and formulate by trial and error practical solutions to those problems. But if the problems are of a fundamental theoretical character, there is nothing, Mises and Hayek imply, but to abandon socialism as an illogical and inconsistent utopia.

The theoretical emphasis of the neo-Austrian critique was heightened by the fact that Mises and Hayek essentially continued the traditional Marxian conception of socialism as a possible successor to capitalism in the economically developed democratic nations of the West. Though referring from time to time to Soviet Russia (the only example of a functioning socialist economy prior to World War II), the primary neo-Austrian focus has been on examining the inconsistencies, inefficiencies, and tensions which would *prospectively* accompany the emergence of socialism in a developed and (formerly) capitalist country.

The Political Framework of the Neo-Austrian Critique of Socialism

This prospective and future-oriented cast of the neo-Austrian critique was related also to the political framework of socialism in Europe prior to the close of World War II. As already observed, Marx was vague and inconclusive regarding the transition to socialism, as well as its prospective economic (and political) organization once established. On this question, the post-Marxian socialist movement divided, broadly speaking, into "revolutionary" and "evolutionary" schools of thought. Many moderate democratic socialists (or "social democrats," as they came to be called in Europe) were influenced as much by the ideals of egalitarian democracy and an ethical or religious critique of old-style capitalism as by Marxian economics. These Western-socialists (for example, the Fabian socialists and guild socialists in England) as well as the Marxist "revisionists" (notably, Edward Bernstein) contended that genuine social reform, indeed, eventual transformation from capitalism to socialism, is possible through the peaceful utilization of the franchise.[2]

Though some democratic socialists initially were enamored with the possible emergence of Soviet Russia as a new socialist civilization, most regarded Stalinist Communism, at best, as an aberration of socialism rather thn its realizationa.

The political dimensions of the neo-Austrian critique have been directed primarily to the Western democratic socialists and social reformers. In effect, the neo-Austrians (notably Hayek) have said: "If you democratic socialists and social reformers continue with your programs and proposals for the modification of capitalism, socialism (or some other variety of collectivism) will probably emerge. But socialism is unlikely to provide for a rational and efficient allocation of resources. In any event, socialist planning is incompatible with individual political, as well as economic, freedoms and, if established, may well lead to the substitution of totalitarian dictatorship for pluralistic democracy and, thereby, the abridgement if not destruction of the democratic and egalitarian values which you seek."

---

[2]These same factors—the strong emphasis on a humanistic and partly non-economic critique of capitalism, combined with faith in the democratic process as a vehicle for the reform of capitalism and its eventual transformation to socialism—help explain why democratic socialists also did not construct rigorous economic theories or blueprints of socialism. Because of the intimate relation between democratic socialism and the democratic economic reform of capitalism, more detailed study of democratic socialist proposals and programs is deferred to Chapter 14.

A critique of socialism, insists Hayek, must distinguish sharply between ends and means, between aims and methods. It must do so partly because the determination of the validity of "ultimate ends" transcends scientific discussion, but largely because the same means may be used to attain a variety of ends. Government ownership and centralized government planning, for example, *may* be used to promote the traditional socialist aim of redistribution of income from property owners to workers. But these same methods *may* as easily be used for non- or anti-equalitarian purposes. [4: 129; 35: 33] "The (economist's) dispute about socialism has thus become largely a dispute about means and not about ends. . . ." [35: 33]

Yet, human action is purposeful; economic activity is directed toward the attainment of ends or purposes. How, then, can we test or evaluate socialism as a *method* for achieving ends in distinction to the moral assumptions and judgments by particular socialists about alleged socialist aims? Hayek's answer is that the central "problem of socialism as a method" stems from the "formal" fact that *any* principle of social justice in the distribution of income "must be stated in the form of a scale of importance of a number of competing individual ends." Therefore, the "central authority" somehow must resolve the fundamental "economic problem of distributing a limited amount of resources between a practically infinite number of competing purposes. . . ." The "fundamental question" is whether a central planning board can organize production so as to correspond to such a given scale of values "with a reasonable degree of accuracy, with a degree of success equaling or approaching the results of competitive capitalism. . . ." In short, there are "only two legitimate tests of success": "the goods which the system actually delivers to the consumer and the rationality or irrationality of the decisions of the central authority." [4: 130–31, 150]

Thus, though insisting he is concerned with means rather than ends, Hayek is proposing the goal of *allocational efficiency* (rather than, say, equality, growth, or full-employment stability) as the central purpose of socialist planning and the basic criterion for his critical evaluation of the prospective success of socialism as an economic system, and, further, his conception of allocational efficiency rests upon the assumption of consumer sovereignty. Hayek implies allocational efficiency, rather than other social goals, is or should be acceptable to socialists as the central criterion for judging socialism's prospective success, first, when he identifies it as a "formal" problem of methods, applicable to all economic systems and, second, when he suggests the key question in the critique of socialism is "the possibility of successful planning, of achieving the ends for which planning was undertaken." [4: 149] It is not clear that socialists, especially of the Marxist, neo-Marxist, or democratic varieties, (cf. Chapters 8, 11, 14) would agree. It is perhaps more accurate to say, borrowing Maurice Dobb's words, that Hayek has *deduced* allocational efficiency as socialism's central planning goal "Mises-like, from the 'nature of the economic problem'" as an implicit normative imperative (31: 243) rather than from an empirical perusal of socialist literature or practice. In other words, Hayek proposes to evaluate the prospective success of socialism and socialist planning primarily in terms of neo-Austrian, rather than distinctly socialist, normative criteria.

The Structure of Socialist Economic Organization

The Neo-Austrian conception of the structure of socialist economic organization is summarized briefly in Table 9-1 in terms of the definitional criteria used in earlier chapters.

(1) and (2). Between World Wars I and II, Mises and Hayek held the traditional

Table 9-1.

THE NEO-AUSTRIAN CONCEPTION OF SOCIALISM

1. Level of economic development	Developed economy
2. Resource base	Capitalistic
3. Ownership-control of instruments of production	Government-collective ownership-control
4. Locus of economic power	Dispersed or concentrated
5. Motivational system	Maximization of individual economic gain given moral-political determination of income distribution
6. Organization of economic power	Decentralized or centralized
7. Social processes for economic coordination	Government price system and/or government hierarchy
8. Distribution of income and wealth	Equalitarian or non-equalitarian as determined by government policy

view of socialism as a possible, perhaps probable, successor to capitalism in the economically developed nations of the West. (3) A central feature of socialist economy is government-collective ownership and control of "productive resources, no matter in whose interest this control is used." [4: 131] The neo-Austrians regard "worker ownership" and "worker control of industry" as mere Marxist window-dressing, at best, a confusion between ends and means. (5) and (8). The neo-Austrians thus remain agnostic about the criteria and patterns of income distribution and other social goals. Hayek especially emphasizes that *any* given moral-political judgment regarding income distribution must be accompanied by an inferred judgment regarding a scale of individual ends, which presumably would guide and motivate individual actions. (4), (6), and (7). The neo-Austrians recognize various possible types of socialist economy in regard to the locus-organization of economic power and processes for economic coordination, ranging from highly centralized to decentralized ("competitive") forms, the former associated especially with the writings of English neo-Marxist Maurice Dobb (cf. Chapter 11), the latter, with the writings of English economist H. D. Dickinson and especially Polish economist Oskar Lange (cf. Chapter 10). In the former case, the fundamental

question, according to Hayek, is whether "all problems of production and distribution can be rationally decided by one central authority. . . ." In the latter case, the key issue is "whether decisions and responsibility can be successfully left to competing individuals who are not owners or are not otherwise directly interested in the means of production under their charge." [4: 162]

RATIONAL ECONOMIC CALCULATION, THE PRICE SYSTEM, AND SOCIALISM

The neo-Austrian critique of the economic theory of socialism contains three central propositions: (1) the imperative necessity of economic calculation; (2) the necessity of a competitive, money price system for rational and efficient economic calculation and coordination; (3) the impossibility-impracticability of a competitive, money price system within the framework of a socialist economy.

The Necessity of Economic Calculation

From the standpoint of neo-Austrian economic theory, the fundamental problem for socialism is that of establishing devices for rational calculation, that is, for analysis of the gains and costs of alternative courses of action. The imperative necessity of calculation is derived from two basic sources: First, it is logically derivative from the definition of *human* action. In Mises' methodology, the essential element in human action is the application of reason in the attempt to attain purposes. All human action, all economic activity is based *by definition* upon a dissatisfaction with some existing state of affairs, and a program initiated by the actor or economic agent, guided by reason, and designed to establish a more desirable state of affairs, a fuller, closer attainment of purposes. This would be true even in an economic paradise characterized by a superabundant stock of goods in relation to wants, because of priorities in wants, diversity in the capacity of goods to satisfy wants, and given mortality, scarcity of time. Thus, in all cases, including those in which all commodities were "free goods," rational human action would be characterized by the endeavor to economize, to "forego the satisfaction of lesser needs so as to satisfy the more urgent needs" and thereby achieve the "highest degree of satisfaction." [45: 114, 113]

Second, the necessity for calculation is heightened by the existence of scarcity—in the first instance, of consumer goods themselves; in the second instance, of *all* goods and/or resources (not just labor) used to produce goods that satisfy human wants. Indeed, Hayek defines "economic actions" as all "acts of choice which are made necessary by the scarcity of means available for our ends" [4: 68] much as Lionel Robbins, contemporary English neo-liberal economist, defines economics as "a relation between ends and scarce means which have alternative uses."[3] The scarcity of resources places a premium on the process of economizing, on allocating resources so as to maximize the satisfaction of human wants. Economical allocation, in turn, requires the calculation of the gains and costs of alternative alloca-

tional patterns, where "gains" embrace "all those things which men hold to be desirable, all that they want and strive for" [45: 112], and "cost" refers to opportunities or alternatives foregone, that is, "the advantages to be derived from the use of given resources in other directions." [4: 123]

Because human action in general and allocational choices in particular must be made in all economic systems, it follows that economic calculation is universally necessary for all economic systems. The "economic calculus" or "pure logic of choice," to use Hayek's phrase, is not peculiar to one form of human society (capitalism), but necessary for all, including socialist societies. It is particularly important to distinguish between the various non-wage components of national income (rent, interest, profits, depreciation) as payments to property-owning individuals and as elements for cost calculations. The *payment* of interest, for example, "is not a necessity in a socialist society where by definition the state is the only entrepreneur and the sole owner of the means of production, but that does not mean that it is unnecessary to include interest as a cost item in the *calculations* of the central authority." [37: 91] As long as investment funds are scarce and must be allocated among competing uses (reflecting the scarcity of resources for future in relation to present production), the rate of interest is an essential element in rational cost calculations. To generalize: Land, capital, and entrepreneurial talents, as well as labor, are scarce in relation to human wants. Choices must be made in regard to their economical utilization and allocation. These choices require processes for calculation in socialist as well as capitalist economic societies.

The Necessity of a Competitive Price System

Assuming the necessity and universality of economic calculation, the neo-Austrians argue that *rational* economic calculation and

---

[3]Lionel Robbins, *The Nature and Significance of Economic Science* (New York: The Macmillan Company, Publishers, 1935), p. 16.

social coordination of actions and decisions based upon economic calculations requires a competitive money price system.

This neo-Austrian assertion stems from a seminal article by Mises in 1920 [36: 87–130, esp. 95–115], elaborated in a later book on socialism. [45] According to Hayek, Mises owns the "distinction of having first formulated the central problem of socialist economics in such a form as to make it impossible that it should ever again disappear from the discussion. . . ." [4: 143] And according to Lange, it was Mises' powerful challenge that forced the socialists to recognize the importance of an adequate system of economic accounting to guide the allocation of resources in a socialist economy. "Even more, it was chiefly due to Professor Mises' challenge that many socialists became aware of the very existence of such a problem." The merit of having caused the socialists to approach this problem systematically belongs entirely to Professor Mises." Indeed, Lange avers somewhat facetiously, "Both as an expression of recognition for the great service rendered by him and as a memento of the prime importance of sound economic accounting, a statue of Professor Mises ought to occupy an honorable place in the great hall of the Ministry of Socialization or of the Central Planning Board of the Socialist state." [39: 57–58]

CALCULATION

Mises' position is simple and direct: Rational calculation requires units. Despite its limitations, the monetary unit is the best, indeed, the only, practicable unit for rational economic calculation. Money can be used as a realistic unit for calculation only insofar as the goods and resources whose relative values are to be calculated are part of a social exchange process, that is, a system of prices established on markets through the interactions of supplies and demands. Alternatives to monetary calculation are inadequate and/or innaccurate. Marginal utility, for example, "provides no unit of value" since utility judgments merely "arrange" but "do not measure" values. [45: 114] Calculations in kind are an "illusion" because of the heterogeneity of the goods and resources to be evaluated. Even supposing the problem of *what* goods to produce to satisfy consumer wants were somehow resolved without a money price system, the problem of *how* to produce these goods still would remain. And because that "method of production which is technically inferior may be economically superior," the determination of the "least-cost combination of inputs" requires information about the relative scarcity of resources as well as their physical productivity, that is, requires "the guidance afforded by the pricing process." [36:145]

COORDINATION AND CONTROL

Augmenting the calculational arguments are those based on social *coordination* and control. Social coordination of economic decisions, argues Hayek, is essentially a problem of knowledge. The knowledge relevant for rational economic planning is *dispersed* among millions of decision-makers. This is so for three basic reasons: First, in those socialist models where consumer and worker preferences are to be counted, consumers and workers are the repositories of the relevant data. Second, no man or small group of men could possibly have in mind or at hand all the relevant information regarding the countless decisions of production which, because of mental division of labor, is dispersed in the minds of thousands of managers and workers. Third, the knowledge especially relevant for economic decisions is not scientific knowledge or "general rules," but "knowledge of the particular circumstances of time and place." Nearly every individual, argues Hayek, "has some advantage over all others because he possesses unique information of which beneficial use might be made, but of which use can be made only if the decisions depending on it are left to him or are made with his active cooperation." [4: 80]

"The economic problem of society is thus not merely a problem of how to allocate 'given' resources—if 'given' is taken to mean given to a single mind which deliberately solves the problem set by these 'data'. It is rather a problem of how to secure the best use of resources known to any of the members of society, for ends whose relative importance only these individuals know. Or, to put it briefly, it is a problem of the utilization of knowledge which is not given to anyone in its totality." [4: 77–78]

If we grant with Hayek that "the economic problem of society is mainly one of rapid adaptation to changes in the particular circumstances of time and place" and that therefore maximum efficiency is most likely to result if "the ultimate decisions (are) left to the people who are familiar with these circumstances, who know directly of the relevant changes and of the resources immediately available to meet them" [4: 83–84], then a social process must exist to coordinate the plans and decisions of those individuals, that is, to adjust individual plans to changes in data, which now include the choices and actions of others. The process which achieves this herculean feat is a price system in a competitive market. The essential function of prices in Hayek's model is to communicate to individuals the information they need to adapt to changes in data and to adjust their plans to the economic plans and decisions of other individuals in the economic system. The function of competition is to provide a social control process, to compel individuals to adjust their economic plans and decisions to changes in market forces beyond their control.

The Incompatibility of Socialism
and the Competitive Price System

IMPOSSIBILITY

The argument that rational economic calculation is *impossible* in a socialist economy based on government ownership is generally attributed to Mises. Even assuming that the question of *what* to produce has been resolved, argues Mises,

... there still remains the problem of ascertaining how the existing means of production can be used most effectively to produce these goods in question. In order to solve this problem it is necessary that there should be economic calculation. And economic calculation can only take place by means of money prices established in the market for production goods in a society resting on private property in the means of production.... If the Coal Syndicate delivers coal to the Iron Syndicate a price can be fixed only if both syndicates own the means of production in the industry. But that would not be Socialism but Syndicalism.... (In short:) Without calculations, economic activity is impossible. Since under Socialism economic calculation is impossible, under Socialism there can be no economic activity in our sense of the word. [45: 142, 132, 119] Rational economic activity is impossible in a socialist commonwealth.... [36: 130]

To support these assertions, Mises draws upon two lines of reasoning, one general, the other more specific. Generally speaking, market prices arise from and are based upon the assumption of the "ceaseless search" by capitalist entrepreneurs to maximize profits. Without the constant searching and striving for profits (and for rents, interest, and wages) by resource owners, the market mechanism "loses its mainspring, for it is only this prospect which sets it in motion and maintains it in operation." [45: 138] According to Mises, a socialist economy has no substitute for the powerful motive-force of personal economic gain maximization by private resource owners. More specifically, a socialist economy can find no substitute for the private enterprise capitalist who, in a world characterized by dynamic change, removes *his* capital from one sector of the economy and *re*allocates it to another, and who, seeking not merely profit, but a balance between the desire for profit and the risk of loss, directs the use of capital goods in those ways which most closely correspond to consumer market demands. No single, universal rule (for example, to "direct capital to those undertakings which promise the highest return")[4] could be substituted for the artistic discretion of the private enterprise capitalist, and "if it is to remain socialistic," the central authorities of a socialist economy could not delegate the responsibility for reallocation of capital for enlargements and contractions of the scale of enterprises and for the establishment of new plants and industries, to decentralized managers. But retaining the power to determine the amount of capital accumulation and the allocation of investment funds in the hands of the central authorities "signifies the elimination of the market" [45: 141] and, therefore, of rational economic calculation.

IMPRACTICABILITY

The argument that rational economic calculation and efficient social coordination is *impracticable* in a socialist economy based upon government ownership[5] (or, more accurately, that, because of the practical

---

[4]Such a "state of affairs," argues Mises, "would simply mean that those managers who were less cautious and more optimistic would receive capital to enlarge their undertakings while more cautious and more skeptical managers would go away empty-handed." [45: 140]

[5]Minor disagreement exists over "the nature of the original criticism" [4: 182] presented by Mises in 1920. Lange, supported by Schumpeter [8: 172–73], holds that the essence of Mises' position is that "economic calculation is impossible in a socialist society" [39: 58] and that Hayek, Robbins, and others "have given up the essential point of Professor Mises' position and retreated to a second line of defense" [39: 63] by emphasizing problems of practicability rather than impossibility. In his review and critique of Lange's model, Hayek insisted the real issue, from the outset, was the practicability, not the logical conceivability, of socialist pricing and that it was Lange and other "younger socialists" who (presumably under the fire of Mises' powerful criticism of the early 1920s) were forced to "retreat" from the pure logic of "mathematical solutions" by turning to the trial-and-error methodology of decentralized socialist price systems. [4: 143–47, 183]

problems involved, the level of rationality in economic calculation and efficiency in social coordination is likely to be lower in a socialist economy than in competitive market capitalism) generally is attributed to Hayek and Robbins. Suppose, for example, a "mathematical solution" is conceived for the problems of economic calculation. Suppose a mastermind exists with all the relevant data (consumer tastes, technology, resource scarcities). Then, a mathematical solution of equilibrium output levels and input combinations, with an equation for every unknown, "is not an impossibility in the sense that it is logically contradictory." But the tasks of compilation of data and solution of "hundreds of thousands" (Hayek) or "millions" (Robbins) of equations, especially under conditions characterized by dynamic changes in tastes, technology, and resource scarcities, would be "humanly impracticable and impossible." [4: 153]

Alternatively, suppose an economic dictator determines what commodities are to be produced and thus avoids the complex problems of discovering consumer preferences and ordering and combining them into a "common scale" to serve as a guide to production. Still, the problem of evaluating the means of production, and their social coordination, in an economic world in which relevant knowledge is dispersed rather than concentrated and subject to dynamic change, still would remain. Compared with the intimacy and artistry of decentralized decision-making and the "automatic coordination" of the competitive price system, "the more obvious method of central direction is incredibly clumsy, primitive, and limited in scope." [35: 50]

Now, conceive a decentralized or "competitive" solution, in which the central planning authorities leave input and output decisions to decentralized managers but periodically change prices via a "trial-and-error" process to promote market equilibrium. Even abstracting from the fact that the transition from capitalism to socialism would completely alter the price system, making it "inadmissable" to use preexisting price relations as a starting point, the number and frequency of required price adjustments under such a trial-and-error system, if it were to approach simulation of the competitive market, would be voluminous. "To imagine that all this adjustment could be brought about by successive orders by the central authority when the necessity is noticed, and that then every price is fixed and changed until some degree of equilibrium is obtained, is certainly an absurd idea." [4: 157–58] At the very least, whether "the solution offered will appear particularly practicable, even to socialists, may perhaps be doubted." [4: 208] (Hayek's critique of the Lange model of decentralized socialism is developed more fully in Chapter 10.)

RESPONSES TO THE NEO-AUSTRIAN CRITIQUE

Broadly speaking, there have been two major responses to the neo-Austrian critique of socialist calculation and coordination in the literature of socialism (in addition to simply ignoring it). One response has been to accept the neo-Austrian conception of the nature and scope of socialism's prospective economic problems, the underlying neo-Austrian normative assumptions (consumer sovereignty, the priority of allocational efficiency), and the necessity of a price system for rational, efficient resource allocation and social coordination of economic decisions, but to insist that a workable substitute for a competitive, money price system could be established in the framework of a socialist economy. This is the approach of decentralized, liberal, or market socialism (Cf. Chapter 10). A second response has been to accept the decentralized models as useful exercises in meeting the challenge of the neo-Austrians, but to reject (or sharply

dissent from) the neo-Austrian conceptions of socialism's economic problems and emphases on consumer sovereignty-allocational efficiency, and the alleged necessity of a competitive, money price system as the exclusive or dominant social process for making and coordinating planful economic decisions in a socialist economy. This is the approach of centralized, authoritarian, or hierarchical socialism. (Cf. Chapter 11.)

An exposition of these two alternative models of socialist economy is contained in the succeeding two chapters. At this point, brief references should be made to three economists who participated in the twentieth-century debate over "rational economic calculation in a socialist economy": Barone, Taylor, and Lange. These comments, with the preceding exposition of the neo-Austrian critique, provide an introduction to the decentralized socialist model of the chapter to follow.

Barone

Enrico Barone, a student of Italian economist Vilfredo Pareto, published an article in 1908 on "The Ministry of Production in the Collectivist Society" [36] which has been claimed by both neo-Austrians and decentralized socialists as vindicating their respective positions. On the one hand, Barone insisted it "fantastic" to assume problems of the organization of production in a socialist economy would be significantly different from those in competitive capitalism. "All the economic categories of the old regime" (such as prices, wages, interest rates, rents, profits, and saving) "must reappear," and, if the political leadership wants to achieve a "maximum advantage" in the allocation of the scarce resources, then "the same two fundamental conditions which characterize free competition reappear" (for Barone: minimum cost of production and equality between price and average cost). [36: 289] Further, he insisted, following

Pareto[6] and preceding Hayek, "it is frankly *inconceivable* that the *economic* determination of the technical coefficients can be made *a priori*." [36: 207] In other words, understanding the mathematical form of a system of simultaneous equations expressing minimum cost resource combinations does not provide the information needed to discover the empirical content of those relationships.

On the other hand, Barone provided the germs of an economic theory of decentralized socialism by suggesting some "experimental" or "trial-and-error" pricing techniques the Ministry of Production (MOP) might use in its attempt to organize production and allocate resources to correspond to consumer preferences. In regard to saving and investment, for example, Barone proposed the MOP select "at random" a rate of interest and let people freely determine how much they want to save and lend to the government. This saving would be used to finance the production of investment goods, which then would be used to provide an increased output of consumption goods in the future. The MOP would be charged with discovering whether this future stream of output was large enough to enable the payment of the selected interest rate. By trial and error, the interest rate could be raised and lowered and eventually would settle at a sustainable equilibrium level. [36: 268–69] In other words, by a trial-and-error process of readjustment, the MOP could move toward establishing an equilibrium rate of interest equating the marginal efficiency of capital with the marginal time preference of consumers.

---

[6]Considering the "fabulous number of equations" involved in an economy with millions of people and thousands of commodities, a solution to the problem of rational economic calculation and social coordination is beyond the "power of algebraic analysis." (This was before the era of the electronic computer.) "In other words, if one really could know all these equations, the only means to solve them which is available to human powers is to observe the practical solution given by the market." [Cited in 4: 182]

Taylor

The discussion of the trial-and-error pricing process was further developed by American economist Fred M. Taylor in the late 1920s. In Taylor's model of socialist economy, "(1) the state should determine the money income of the citizen; and (2) the citizen should dictate to the state what should be produced in return for that income." [39: 48] Consumers, given money incomes and facing given prices for consumption goods, freely purchase the combinations of commodities they desire. Prices of consumption goods are set at levels equal to costs of production and presumably readjusted to reflect cost changes. (Taylor did not distinguish between marginal cost and average cost pricing.) In other words, prices of consumption goods are to be determined by the interaction of market demand and government supply.

The socialist government could then establish resource prices by a trial-and-error process embodying five major steps: (1) Prices could be assigned to resources and (2) socialist managers could be instructed to behave in their input-output decisions as though the initial valuations were correct. (3) The central authorities could then watch for indications that the initial values were incorrect. If a resource price were too low, for example, managers would make lavish use of it, creating a shortage at the end of the "current productive period." If a resource price were too high, managers would economize in its use, creating a surplus. "Surplus or deficit—one or the other would result from every wrong evaluation of a factor." [39: 53] (4) If such deficits or surpluses appeared, resource prices could be changed—up, in the case of a deficit, down, in the case of a surplus. (5) This process could be repeated until deficits and/or surpluses had been eliminated, that is, until demands for resources were equal to supplies.

Writing in the 1930s, Polish economist Oskar Lange formulated a rigorous, sophisticated, and certainly now "classic" model of economic calculation and social coordination of the allocation of resources in a socialist economy. It should be emphasized that, for the purpose of this model, he accepted the neo-Austrian contention of the necessity of a price system for economic calculation and coordination. But he denied the necessity of a money price system based upon the market actions of private resource owners for the efficient determination of resource prices. Lange's answer to Mises is that the latter confused two quite different kinds of prices, that is, the specific concept of "exchange ratios of commodities on a market" and the generic concept of the "terms on which alternatives are offered," which are "determined ultimately by the technical possibilities of transformation of one commodity into another, that is, by the production functions." [39: 61] Because, in a socialist economy, capital goods are owned by the government, a market for them does not exist in the specifically capitalist sense. But for purposes of economic calculation, this does not prevent a socialist government from establishing "accounting prices" which can serve the same calculational and coordinative functions as actual market prices serve in a competitive capitalist economy. Lange's answer to Hayek is that an "accounting price system" *can* be established in a socialist economy via a trial-and-error process similar to, but more elaborate than, that described by Professor Taylor. An exposition and critical evaluation of such a system is presented in the following chapter.

SUMMARY OF CHAPTER 9

1. One of the most prominent and fundamental critiques of the economics of socialism after Marx was provided by neo-

Austrian economists, notably Ludwig von Mises and Friedrich von Hayek. Like Marx, they viewed socialism as a possible successor to capitalism in economically developed capitalist economies. Their critique, developed and popularized in the 1920s and 1930s, was essentially theoretical. It focused on basic theoretical issues connected with the relations between means and ends in a socialist economy, rather than on evaluation of socialist ends or descriptive analysis of socialist means in practice.

2. The classic neo-Austrian critique of socialism contends that it has (or would have) inherent inefficiencies and irrationalities in making and coordinating economic decisions, and in adapting socialist means (public ownership, central planning) to socialist ends (whatever these may be).

3. This "fundamental theoretical critique" has three main dimensions: (1) The basic economic problem for socialism, as for any economic system, is the imperative need for economic calculation of benefits and costs. An accompanying problem is to coordinate or integrate for society as a whole decisions based on economic calculations. (2) "Rational economic calculation" and efficient social coordination and control in the allocation of scarce resources requires a competitive price or market system. (3) A competitive price/market system requires private ownership and operation of industry.

4. The neo-Austrian view of the relations of socialism to these three requirements may best be summarized in reverse order: (3) Because socialism is characterized by public rather than private ownership, it lacks the vital social process of the competitive price/market system. (2) Because socialism lacks (or would lack) a competitive price/market system, "rational economic calculation" and efficient social coordination and control of resource allocation will be impossible (Mises) or at least impracticable (Hayek). (1) Therefore, however noble or appealing its aims,

and apart from imperfections of administration—that is, psychological and political problems—socialism would, even in principle, be incapable of efficiently resolving fundamental economic problems facing a society.

5. Response to the neo-Austrian critique of the economics of socialism has been essentially twofold. One has been to accept the neo-Austrian assumptions, but deny their conclusions. Another has been to challenge the assumptions of the neo-Austrian analysis. The first response has been accompanied by theories of decentralized, market socialism, which have sought to demonstrate the practicality of a blend of public ownership and price/market processes. The second response has been associated with theories of centralized, hierarchical socialism, developed, in several instances, by Western neo-Marxist economists from a radically different theoretical framework. These two alternative models of socialist economic organization are examined in the next two chapters.

Appendix:
Economic Systems,
Individual Freedoms, and Democracy

The net conclusion of the neo-Austrian critique of the economic theory of socialism is that competitive market capitalism is an indispensable requisite for rational economic calculation and efficient allocation of resources in accordance with consumer preferences. Its corollary is that socialism, characterized by public ownership and lacking the competitive price system, is or would be characterized by irrationalities in economic calculation and inefficiencies in resource allocation.

Especially since the 1940s, this economic critique has been supplemented and complemented by a political one. The neo-Austrian version of the social philosophy of liberal individualism contends that:

1. Competitive market capitalism also is an indispensable requisite for the attainment and maintenance of individual economic and political freedoms and the sustenance of democracy;

2. A blend of capitalist and socialist ingredients is structurally untenable, and attempts to modify or reform capitalism, carried too far, will snowball or escalate into (presumably a highly centralized form of) socialism;

3. Socialism would be characterized by or lead to the absence or diminution of individual freedoms and political democracy, and the creation of totalitarian dictatorship.

COMPETITIVE MARKET CAPITALISM, INDIVIDUAL FREEDOMS, AND DEMOCRACY

The historical correlation between the emergence and development of competitive market capitalism and the political freedoms of modern representative democracy (noted by Karl Marx, among others) is clear: "personal and political freedom has never existed in the past" without "freedom in economic affairs." [35: 13] This relation is no historic accident, Hayek argues; nor can it be explained on the basis of other, extraneous factors. Essentially, the competitive market system provides a framework for spontaneous, voluntary exchange relations among individuals free from coercion. Law, under competitive market capitalism, consists essentially of a general framework of rules within which individuals are free to plan and choose. (In contrast are systems of administrative regulation, characterized by *ad hoc* and potentially arbitrary and discriminatory decisions consciously formulated and enforced in terms of concrete circumstances.) In addition, private economic power provides a means for safeguarding other freedoms and asserting the rights of citizenry against the power of potential tyrants. "What maintains liberty in France, Scandinavia, and in the English-speaking countries," wrote Walter Lippman in the mid-1930s, "is more than any other thing the great mass of people who are independent because they have, as Aristotle said, 'a moderate and sufficient property.'"[1] "Democracy won its place," suggests Robert MacIver, "because those who believed in it and fought for it had acquired also some power of resistance against tyranny, some private economic power."[2]

THE STRUCTURAL UNTENABILITY OF MIXED ECONOMIES

In the neo-Austrian view, mixed economies, blending elements from capitalism and the price system on the one hand and socialism and central planning on the other, are unlikely to persist. They constitute, at best, a *modus vivendi* or temporary arrangement in the historical development of economic systems. The bases for this contention are essentially the following:

From Monopoly to Socialism

The struggle against competition has led in many countries (often with government instigation or support) to the expansion of private monopoly power. Private monopoly is unlikely to satisfy either old-style liberals or new-style socialist planners. But once private monopoly power has become entrenched, "the only alternative to a return to competition is the control of the monopolies by the state—a control which, if it is to be made effective, must become progressively more complete and more detailed." [35:41]

From Government Control to Market Failure to Socialism

Whereas the central organizing principle of competitive market capitalism is the price system, the major organizing principle of socialism is central planning. Though these two can be combined to some extent, there are limits. Once government regulation and central planning exceeds these limits, competition ceases "to operate as an effective guide to production," thereby increasing the pressure for escalating the extension of government controls and the further departure from reliance on the market system. [35:42]

The Part and the Whole

Once the communal sector, in which the state controls all the means, exceeds a certain proportion of the whole, the effects of its actions dominate the whole system. Although the state controls directly the use of only a large part of the available resources, the effects of its decisions on the remaining part of the economic system become so great that indirectly it controls almost everything. [35:61]

From Interdependence to Comprehensivity

The different sectors and industries of the economic system are interdependent, not isolated. Because of this, it is difficult to stop central planning at any particular point. To make central controls work in one area of economic activity (for example, prices), controls must be extended to other areas (for example, wages). Thus, "once the free working of the market is impeded beyond a certain degree, the planner will be forced to extend his controls until they become all-comprehensive." [35:105]

---

[1]Walter Lippman, *The Method of Freedom* (New York: The Macmillan Company, Publishers, 1935), pp. 101–2.

[2]Robert MacIver, *Democracy and the Economic Challenge* (New York: Alfred A. Knopf, Inc., 1952), p. 59.

As the scope of government planning and control is extended, people will increasingly recognize their incomes and positions in society depend on conscious decisions of government authorities, rather than the impersonal forces of the market. This plausibly has a double effect. First, governments "cannot refuse responsibility for anybody's fate or position" and, thus, are open targets for pressure groups. Second, people will increasingly bend their efforts to influencing government action in their favor. The combined result is to expand the network of government protective mechanisms. [35: 107]

THE IMPACT OF SOCIALISM UPON FREEDOM AND DEMOCRACY

The neo-Austrian contention of incompatibility between socialism and centralized socialist planning on one hand and individual freedoms and democracy on the other has three major dimensions: first, the prospective impact of socialism on individual economic freedoms; second, confusion in the socialist literature and movement about relations between means and ends; third, relations between economics and politics and the prospective impact of socialism on political freedoms and democracy.

Socialist Planning, Economic Dictatorship and Individual Economic Freedoms

Given the aspirations of socialists and the propensities of government policy-makers, it is extremely unlikely socialist planning would be limited to providing a general framework of law within which individuals would be free to plan and choose. It is much more plausible to expect it would be: (1) extended to formulating plans designed to accomplish concrete objectives in specific ways; and (2) accompanied by delegation of legislative and executive powers to various authorities and agencies to realize plans and apply directives in concrete circumstances.

But these features of socialist planning, by their very nature, constitute restriction of individual freedoms. First, if government is to predict successfully the impact of its actions in particular ways, "it can leave those affected no choice" because, insofar as people are free to choose their own ends, the effects of government action on particular ends "cannot be foreseen." Second, the delegation of legislative and executive powers to administrative agencies without "fixed rules" gives them "almost unlimited discretion" to use coercive power in arbitrary and discriminatory ways. [35: 76, 77]

In terms of areas of economic decision, Hayek argues, socialist planning must, or is highly likely to, entail conscious control of property and the determination of production decisions (prices, outputs, inputs, location of enterprises, volume and allocation of investment, and so on) by government authority, rather than individual economic choice. But other economic freedoms are likely to be abridged, as well.

This likelihood is partly concealed by the tendency of economic theorists in western democracies to assume that practitioners and policy-makers share their value judgments. For example, in the 1930s, a number of economists constructed models of ideally functioning decentralized socialist market economies, complete with freedom in the choice of consumption and occupation, consumer sovereignty, and delegation and decentralization of input/output decisions to managers of governmentally owned plants and industries.

But many socialist practitioners since Marx have been wary of such "capitalist" concepts as consumer sovereignty and market coordination and have deemed a "planned economy" strategic to socialism. "What our planners demand is a central direction of all economic activity according to a single plan, laying down how the resources of society should be 'consciously directed' to serve particular ends in a definite way." [35: 35] The construction of economic models combining central planning with individual choice and market exchange is a useful exercise. But these models, Hayek suggests, may correspond closer with the personal predilections of economic theorists than with the plausible institutional patterns of socialist economies in practice.

Even decentralized socialism would concentrate a high degree of power in central governmental authority and, thereby, reduce the scope, or be devoid, of freedom of individual choice in such areas as saving and investment, foreign trade, and prices of capital goods, land, intermediate goods, and interest rates, as well as freedom of private enterprise. But socialism in practice and proposals by centralized socialists restrict individual freedom still further. In centralized models of socialism, "planner sovereignty" replaces consumer sovereignty.

Since under centralized models of socialism, prices no longer represent the relative valuations attached by individuals to their desires for various goods, and since it is the government which determines what goods are to be produced, it is obvious it will be the government which will determine not only the qualities and quantities of goods and services to become available, but also which regions, groups, and individuals are to receive designated amounts of these goods and services. Further, if planning is to be effective, it "must control the entry into the different trades and occupations or the terms of remuneration, or both." Under such conditions, the "free choice of occupation," which also determines where one lives and with whom one associates, becomes meaningless. Centralized socialist planning simply means "we are to be relieved of the necessity of solving our own economic problems and that the bitter choices which this often involves are to be made for us." [35: 92, 95]

Confusion About and Between Means and Ends

The likelihood that socialism would diminish or destroy freedom and democracy is obfuscated, Hayek contends, by confusion within the democratic socialist movement about and between "means" and "ends," both under socialism and in the process of movement toward it.

First, the confusion stems from socialism's involving movements and programs for the economic reform of capitalism, as well as theories of how socialism, once established, would function. Because democracy has been used by socialists to reform capitalism in an effort to move toward socialism, it is presumed that socialism could or would be democratic too. Complicating this is that many democratic socialists are sincere in their professions of democracy. But both of these dimensions conceal rather than reveal the most likely relation between socialism and democracy, for the dangers which socialism creates for a free and democratic way of life (1) are likely to become clearest only after socialism has been established and (2) are derived from objective properties of the socialist system rather than from the (often sincere) intentions of socialists.

In addition, considerable confusion surrounds the concept of socialism itself, for it has been used to describe both the aims or ends of the democratic socialist movement (that is, justice, equality, security) *and* the means to attain those ends (public ownership and control, central government planning). But the same means (for example, public ownership and control) may be used to promote different ends. For example, public ownership and central planning may be used to promote large-scale *inequality* rather than greater equality. It is the collectivist means of socialism, Hayek argues, not the (often commendable) ends of socialists which are inconsistent with democracy and individual freedom. In essence, socialism "is a species of collectivism and . . . therefore everything which is true of collectivism as such must apply also to socialism." [35: 33–34] The various forms of collectivism (socialism, communism, fascism, and so on) differ in the ends "toward which they want to direct the efforts of society." But they are similar in means, that is, in "wanting to organize the whole of society and all its resources" for the attainment of their respective ends and, thereby, "in refusing to recognize autonomous spheres in which the ends of the individuals are supreme. In short, they are totalitarian . . . ." [35: 56]

Though "means" should be distinguished from "ends," the two are intimately and necessarily connected. This connection often is misunderstood, as in the popular but incorrect view that it should be possible for the citizenry or society to determine the ends and delegate to experts the task of determining the most efficient means to attain them. This distinction is invalid because the "ends of an economic plan . . . cannot be defined apart from the particular plan." The formulation of such a plan "involves the choice between competing or conflicting ends—different needs of different people." But the determination of which ends shall be sacrificed and which alternatives shall be chosen can be made only by "those who know all the facts," that is, the experts to whom the task of planning has been assigned. Thus, it is "inevitable" that planners "should impose their scale of preferences on the community for which they plan." [35: 65]

Further, the major ends of the socialist movement—equality and security—undergo radical changes in their basic characters as the degree of socialization is extended, changes which increase the inconsistency of socialism with individual freedoms and place the individual increasingly at the mercy of coercive government authority. As long as socialism is a minority movement of social protest and reform within a dominantly capitalist economy, the pressure for greater equality is manifested in measures to redistribute income from the relatively rich to the relatively poor, leaving the initial distribution of income essentially to the market. But once the state becomes responsible for the direction of production, it simultaneously acquires responsibility for determining the relative importance of different goods, and hence, responsibility for determining the distribution of income for the entirety or majority of the citizenry. Under these conditions, the earlier goal of "greater equality" becomes more or less meaningless. Government must decide the merits of particular individuals and groups and, thereby, their incomes.

With the advent of socialism, changes also occur in the nature of security. In the early stages of the movement toward socialism, political pressure for greater security conceivably may be restricted to prevention of severe privation and promotion of minimum living standards. This kind of security is perfectly consistent with individual freedom, and there is no reason a rich society should not be able to provide it. But security also may be desired in another, quite different sense: the maintenance of given living standards or positions of individuals or groups.

This kind of security (1) can be provided for one segment of society only by denying it to others, and "others," with the advent of socialism, become the majority of society; (2) is inconsistent with freedom of occupational choice. If occupational choice is to remain free, relative remunerations in different jobs must correspond to their social importance. If movement of labor between different jobs is not to be accomplished by shifts (down, as well as up) in relative income position, it must be done by other methods, most notably, direct commands.

Socialist Planning, Democracy, and Political Freedoms

Suppose we were to grant, with Hayek, that socialism is more likely to emerge in centralized than decentralized forms, and would be accompanied by the absence of or decrease in individual economic freedoms as understood from the vantage point of old-style capitalism and liberalism. Would it not be possible to separate politics from economics and to maintain political freedoms (such as speech, voting, assembly, petition, and dissent) despite the absence of or decrease in economic freedoms? What difference does economic dictatorship make if we can maintain political democracy, that is, control—through suffrage and the ballot box, competing political parties and interest groups, an educated and informed electorate, a responsive political leadership inculcated in democratic ideals—by the citizenry over political leaders and government policy?

Hayek's answer to these questions is negative: First, the prime value is freedom, not democracy. Second, it is impossible to separate economic and political ends. Third, democracies cannot engage in comprehensive planning efficiently and successfully As a corollary, pressures for economic dictatorship in a centrally planned socialist economy will plausibly lead to political dictatorship and a decrease in effective democratic political control by the citizenry over their leaders. Fourth, pressures upon planners under conditions of economic and political dictatorship are likely to lead to a decrease in political freedom and the extension of the totalitarian character of government planning.

FREEDOM AND DEMOCRACY

In the neo-Austrian hierarchy of values, political democracy ranks substantially below individual freedom, including economic freedoms. Political democracy essentially is a means for safeguarding individual freedoms, but no fetish should be made of it. On the one hand, individual freedoms (cultural, religious, and economic) have on occasion been quite high under autocratic political systems. On the other hand, democracy is capable of being totalitarian, oppressive, and despotic. Democracy *may* function to prevent the excesses of autocratic political power and to safeguard individual freedoms, but it need

not do so. *Even if* socialism were democratic, it could (and plausibly would) become arbitrary and coercive in the exercise of central planning.

ECONOMIC AND POLITICAL ENDS

It is logically impossible to maintain political freedoms (that is, freedom to pursue "political ends") while sacrificing economic freedoms (that is, freedom to pursue "economic ends") for the simple reason that there are no "purely economic ends separate from the other ends of life." [35: 89] *Economics* really means the allocation of our scarce means to pursue *any* ends.

What are sometimes erroneously regarded as "economic interests" or "economic ends" and identified with money and exchange seem "muggy and grubby" and unimportant only because, in a free market economy, we have the power to determine which ends are least important, at the margin of our interests. By contrast, socialist planning would delegate a generalized control over the allocation of resources to governmental authorities. Such control would (indeed could) not be restricted to "marginal" or "economic" ends, but instead would give government the power to determine the utilization of resources for the pursuit of all ends. "Economic control is not merely control of a sector of human life which can be separated from the rest; it is the control of the means for all our ends. And whoever has sole control of the means must also determine which ends are to be served, which values are to be rated higher and which lower—in short, what men should believe and strive for." [35: 92]

CAN DEMOCRACIES PLAN?

The neo-Austrian position on the theme of obstacles to democratic planning is two-fold. First, a comprehensive plan requires a "comprehensive scale of values in which every need of every individual is given its place." [35: 57] But because of the "indisputable fact" that the imagination and knowledge of needs by any central government authority is limited and that value scales exist in the minds of individuals, the formulation of such a "comprehensive scale of values" is impossible.

Second, it would be virtually impossible to formulate and integrate plans to attain ends efficiently, *even if* these ends could be arranged in terms of a comprehensive value scale because, as observed earlier, the requisite knowledge to do this is dispersed among millions of individuals throughout the economic system. In sum, socialist planning of a comprehensive sort is likely to be characterized by contradictions and complexities.

This creates, says Hayek, a fundamental problem for democratic planning: The citizenry may want (or think it wants) a comprehensive plan; yet neither it nor a democratic legislature plausibly will be able to agree on one. Legislatures thus will increasingly come to be regarded as inefficient and incapable of formulating consistent overall plans. But "agreement that planning is necessary, together with the inability of democratic assemblies to produce a plan, will evoke stronger and stronger demands that the government or some single individual should be given powers to act on their own responsibility." [35: 67]

In short, the complexities of comprehensive planning plausibly would increase pressures to delegate the power to formulate plans to experts (central planning boards) and to increase the role of the executive branch of government and administrative agencies relative to the legislature, thereby removing the planning process from effective control by the legislature, competing political parties, and the citizenry. In effect, the legislature would "at best be reduced to choosing the persons who are to have practically absolute power" while the role of the citizenry would be restricted to selecting those relatively ineffectual legislators and

confirming the position of a chief executive who would have "all the powers at his command to make certain that the vote will go in the direction he desires." [35: 69]

FROM PLURALISTIC DEMOCRACY TO DICTATORSHIP VIA SOCIALIST PLANNING

A complex, comprehensive, unified plan, Hayek argues, cannot easily be adjusted to compromise. Because of mutual interdependences among different parts of the plan, adjustments in one part will require further modifications in others. But as the scope of the plan is extended, pressures on the planners from groups who realize their income positions and economic security depend solely on political decision heighten the inherent problems in the formulation of a rational plan. The process of economic planning can be threatened by political power clashes between various groups and between rival socialist factions and political leaders who arise to support different groups.

Therefore, contends Hayek, socialist planning must be free from the sabotage of critical groups if it is to survive; that is, the plan must become unitary as well as all-comprehensive. But a unified plan is inconsistent with the conflicting interests and values of different groups. Thus, if planning is to survive, it must be formulated by a small group or an individual and imposed upon conflicting groups. In short, "the democratic statesman who sets out to plan economic life will soon be confronted with the alternative of either assuming dictatorial powers or abandoning his plans . . . ." [35: 135] Socialist planning "leads to dictatorship because dictatorship is the most effective instrument of coercion and the enforcement of ideals, and, as such, essential if central planning on a large scale is to be possible. The clash between planning and democracy arises simply from the fact that the latter is an obstacle to the suppression of freedom which the direction of economic activity requires." [35: 70]

Lastly, says Hayek, to be successful, dictatorial planning must become totalitarian and be accompanied by the abridgement of political as well as economic freedoms. On the one hand, as a species of collectivism, socialist planning *is* totalitarian in nature; that is, it extends or would extend a totality of control over the entire economic system, and, thereby, over the allocation of resources to attain any or all ends. This would be true *even if* socialist planning were successfully adopted by a democratic political system.

On the other hand, the totalitarian propensities of a comprehensively planned economic system plausibly would take on additional properties in the light of political dictatorship, itself stimulated by the very process of total planning. Just as successful planning requires the imposition of a unitary plan on conflicting groups and, therefore, dictatorship, so dictatorial planning would be more successful were government plans free from criticism and dissent.

The stifling of dissent, in turn, can be most effectively accomplished, says Hayek, if three conditions are met: (1) the creation by political leaders of a supporting group willing to submit to a "totalitarian discipline" which they then would impose on the rest of society through controls by the totalitarian party, the armed forces, and the secret police; (2) the creation of a creed or "myth," popularized through propaganda facilitated by government control over mass communication media, whereby people would come to regard the ends of the political leadership as their own; and (3) the extension of government control over *all* aspects of life (such as churches, education, family life, leisure, and travel) so as to reinforce the impact of propaganda and minimize areas of autonomy which could lead to dissent or criticism. [35: 137, 153, 92, 100] The frightening conclusion of Hayek's critique is that the logic of comprehensive socialist planning is cultural and political, as well as economic, totalitarianism.

CRITICAL EVALUATION OF THE NEO-AUSTRIAN ARGUMENT

Critical evaluation of the neo-Austrian argument as to relations among socialism, freedom, and democracy will be divided into two main parts. First, we shall attempt to clarify the discussion by distinguishing among several of its leading dimensions, which were somewhat indiscriminately mixed in the original Hayekian presentation. Second, at greater length, we will examine views of other scholars on these subjects.

Dimensions of the Neo-Austrian Critique

Hayek's indictment of socialism and central planning relative to freedom and democracy contains trenchant, provocative criticism. Unfortunately, it was marred by a polemical style and, as exists in most polemics, an indiscriminate mixture of elements which, in the interest of clarity, should be distinguished.

The most prominent example of this is his failure to distinguish clearly among *can, has,* and *must.* It is undoubtedly true that democratic planning and social reform *can* lead to "socialism," that socialism *can* be or become highly centralized, and that a highly centralized socialism *can* be or become dictatorial and perhaps totalitarian in its political and cultural life, as well as economic organization. Hayek's critique is at its strongest in identifying some of the pressures and conflicts which make these contingencies possible and some of the circumstances under which their likelihood acquires plausibility.

But "can" or "could" is neither "has" nor "must." First, *has* it happened? "Although not impossible," suggests Peter Wiles, the contention that democratic social reform and government control of capitalism "slips inevitably" into a centrally planned economy "is a piece of inverted Marxism which history does not exemplify by a single instance."[3] The need for large-scale, rapid change, compounded by the problems of interdependencies among the different parts and sectors of the economy, has indeed generated pressures for something of this sort in "innumerable capitalist war economies, but when wars cease, the process is regularly reversed."[4]

Suppose "socialism" and "socialist planning" were necessarily inconsistent with freedom and democracy; no country with strong democratic traditions ever has established "socialist planning" as Hayek conceives it. It is true that Communist, and, to a lesser extent, Nazi and Fascist, societies have combined political dictatorship and government regulation of the economy. But although this supports the hypothesis that political dictators establish government control over the economy, by itself, it neither confirms nor refutes the argument that democratic planning and social reform constitute or cause dictatorship or totalitarianism.

Second, *must* it happen? Hayek's argument is weakest at this point because a "can" or even a "has" is not a "must." In effect, Hayek argues *if* planning is to be efficient and successful, it must be or become dictatorial and totalitarian. Suppose this were true; the question arises: Why *must* planning (or comprehensive planning) be or become efficient and successful? Why couldn't it be unsuccessful or, like most human enterprises, function inefficiently, with various imperfections? Underlying Hayek's prognosis of almost deterministic inevitability is the undemonstrated (perhaps undemonstrable) implicit assumption that potential conflicts between "efficiency" in planning and freedom, democracy, mixed economy, and so

forth, invariably *must* be resolved in favor of planning efficiency. It is this dimension of Marxian-like determination of the political and social superstructure by the underlying economic structure and the ends or goals of society by (some of) its means that has most grievously affronted Hayek's critics, whose views we will now examine.[5]

Alternative Views on Socialism, Freedom and Democracy

The following views reflect alternative positions on several issues raised by the neo-Austrian critique, namely, relations between: (1) socialism and democracy; (2) democracy and economic reform; (3) economic planning and individual freedoms; (4) democracy and economic planning.

SCHUMPETER: RELATIONS BETWEEN SOCIALISM AND DEMOCRACY

Socialists have traditionally distinguished between (1) the transition to socialism and (2) the organization and operation of the socialist order, once established. Joseph Schumpeter, whose analysis of capitalism was previously examined, followed this tradition and, in effect, identified conditions affecting the viability of democracy in each instance.

Transition to Socialism. The likelihood that socialism and democracy could viably coexist would be heightened, Schumpeter suggested, if the transition to socialism occurred in a state of "maturity" in eco-

---

[3] Peter Wiles, "Economic Activators, Planning, and the Social Order," Bertram M. Gross, Editor, *Action Under Planning: The Guidance of Economic Development*, (New York: McGraw-Hill Book Company, 1967), p. 181.

[4] *Ibid.*

[5] It also affronts some of his defenders. Henry Wallich, a member of the Council of Economic Advisers in the United States during the Eisenhower administration, maintains (in *The Cost of Freedom*, New York: Harper, 1960, pp. 54–55) that although the "old-fashioned liberal's case against the centralized economy is a persuasive one," it is marred "by the frequent use of the word 'must' where 'may' would be appropriate." A "case that may be almost watertight in countries where democracy and freedom are weak does not necessarily apply to countries where both are strong."

nomically developed capitalist nations in which important preconditions had been met, namely:

1. The incorporation of socialists into the democratic process. This has three effects. First, that socialists in countries with strong democratic traditions (such as Scandinavia, England, the United States), "have consistently upheld the democratic faith" [8: 238] and worked within the democratic process increases the likelihood they would continue to use familiar and successful democratic methods once they came to power. Second, it provides a basis for a considerable program of socialization and nationalization *prior* to the transition, thereby reducing significantly the magnitude and perceived radicality of change when the transition finally occurs. Third, it increases the likelihood socialists will accept an evolutionary process of socialization, including both these preparatory measures, prior to the transition and postponement of socialization of some areas (such as agriculture, small business) to an indefinite time *after* the transition, thereby simplifying transitionary problems and bringing additional support.

2. The decomposition of capitalism and increasing socialization of capitalism from within, thereby fulfilling more and more "the technological, organizational, commercial, administrative and psychological prerequisites of socialism...." [8: 219] Most significantly, maturity gradually weakens resistance and promotes cooperation from all classes of society, thereby reducing "violent excitement" and maximizing the likelihood of transition to socialism in a democratic way, perhaps "by a constitutional amendment, that is, in a peaceful way without a break in legal continuity." [8: 221]

3. An advanced technology and a high level of economic development, thereby minimizing conflicts over income distribution, reducing the fervor for radical and large-scale redistribution of income, avoiding the need for draconian sacrifices for the purpose of industrialization under the aegis of socialism, and providing an economic base, if desired, to compensate private owners for land and capital, thus avoiding confiscation of their property.

4. The existence of "experienced and responsible" political leaders to lead and organize the transition in a rational and disciplined way and a bureaucracy "of adequate standing and experience" willing and able to accept and administer orders from "the legal authority, whatever it is...." [8: 301, 221]

Organization and Operation of Socialism. Suppose the transition to socialism occurs in a state of maturity, and, thereby, these preconditions for socialism and socialist democracy have been met. Schumpeter turned to the question of the prospective relations between the operation and functioning of a socialist economy and the democratic method. The basic logic of his position may be stated succinctly:

1. Socialism is "an institutional pattern in which the control over means of production and over production itself is vested with a central authority." [8: 167] (This does not exclude: appointment, supervision, and approval of the CPB by democratic legislatures; or delegation of considerable freedom of action to plant and industry managers.)

2. Democracy is an institutional method "for arriving at political decisions in which individuals acquire the power to decide by means of a competitive struggle for the people's vote." [8: 269]

3. "Between socialism as we defined it and democracy as we defined it there is no necessary relation: the one can exist without the other. At the same time, there is no incompatibility; in appropriate states of the social environment the

socialist engine can be run on democratic principles." [8: 284]

In short, socialism may or may not be democratic (as Schumpeter defined these terms) depending on whether requisite conditions for democracy are or are not met. In countries (for example, Russia) in which these conditions have not been met, socialism is unlikely to be democratic. In other countries (such as the United States or England) in which they have been met, socialism, if and when established, is likely (or much more likely) to be democratic. These conditions are:

(1) a high quality, in terms of ability and character, of political leadership;

(2) a highly developed, trained, and dutiful bureaucracy, with expertise, tradition, and spirit;

(3) a reasonable restraint on the "effective range of political decision";

(4) widespread agreement on the basic institutional structures of society and, thereby, willingness to "abide by the rules of the democratic game," to practice "democratic self-control" and, at the same time, to tolerate a "large measure" of dissent and "difference of opinion." [8: 290–95]

In regard to the first condition, socialism would have no special contribution (relative to capitalism) because it "has no obvious solution to offer for the problem solved in other forms of society by the presence of a political class of stable traditions." [8: 302] At the same time, it would have no necessarily deleterious impact upon several of these conditions, for, in general, they are (as, for example, the creation of a sophisticated and highly developed government bureaucracy) precisely those developments which tend to take place via the process of democratic reform in economically developed capitalist nations under the aegis of preparation for and transition to socialism.

Of course, as Hayek contends, democracy —because of the competitive struggle to win

and keep political office, the waste of energy through "incessant battle" inside and outside parliaments, and the administrative diseconomies of democratic control over economic decisions by central authority—may be an administratively inefficient way of running a socialist economy. But dictatorship also has its distorting, wasteful internal political warfare; democracy can be reformed to reduce somewhat the pressures on political leaders; and, in any event, even socialists may well prefer democratic "inefficiency" to "dictatorial efficiency." Further, "public management" (a necessary condition for socialism) should be distinguished from "political management" (a condition unnecessary for socialism). "Democracy does not require that every function of the state be subject to its political method." [8: 292] For example, the banking system, federal regulatory agencies, and state universities have delegated powers and relative autonomy to function at present within a general framework of political supervision, thus keeping a reasonable restraint on the "effective range of political decision." Presumably, this practice could be extended in a socialist economy.

As to the final set of conditions (democratic self-control, widespread agreement, and tolerance of diverse opinion), socialism actually may score better than capitalism. If, as assumed earlier, socialism emerges in the "fullness and ripeness of time," the popular support for it is likely to be high. With the establishment of socialism, "clashing capitalist interests" (large versus small industry, agriculture versus industry, protectionists versus exporters) will largely disappear since bases for political pressure groups and the degree of controversy over economic policy might well be lower than under capitalism.

FINER: DEMOCRACY AND ECONOMIC REFORM

In the Hayekian vision, it is socialism which emasculates or terminates freedom and democracy, but it is democracy, through economic reform, which is a major contributing factor to the establishment of socialism. Many economists and political scientists have challenged this position, especially students and advocates of various forms of "managed capitalism" or "mixed economy." One prominent critic has been Herman Finer, whose *Road to Reaction* is a direct rebuttal to the neo-Austrian critique. Unfortunately, Finer's presentation is somewhat marred by excessive rhetorical zeal in responding to Hayek's strictures. Still, Finer's rebuttal contains two prominent and thoughtful reservations concerning the validity of the neo-Austrian critique.

First, Finer argues, the central issue in the relations between economic and political systems in the Western democracies is democratic economic reform and the degree and character of government's role in economic life. On the one hand, *laissez-faire* now is a thing of the past, abandoned ingloriously in country after country. On the other hand, comprehensive socialist planning as defined by Hayek is a figment of the imagination, not established in any country, not even Soviet Russia. The real issue in nations such as the United States and Great Britain, noted throughout their histories for their empirical, experimental, and pragmatic approaches to combining different solutions to pressing problems, is the "middle way" determined in practice "by actual human beings."[6]

Indeed, the establishment of the requisite conditions and framework for the viably functioning competitive economic system desired or assumed by Hayek would require a significant role for government action in the economy, in some ways greater than exists at present. At the same time, to restrict government policy to "fixed rules," determined in advance, would require a reactionary, anti-democratic enforcement of an essentially *laissez-faire* system in the face of widespread public support for the continuance and extension of the modern, positive state. In the name of "freedom," this would arbitrarily restrict democracy.

Second, Finer criticizes Hayek's analysis of the relations among economic and political systems. Socialism and democratic economic reform were *not* contributing factors to the emergence of totalitarian dictatorship in Italy, Germany, or Russia. In Italy, "the Fascist regime was set up by the violent and personal ambitions of Mussolini. Had there been no Mussolini, there would have been no Fascism."[7] In Germany, the Nazis came to power in a society with a strong nationalist and militarist, but weak democratic, tradition and proceeded to create and extend a totalitarian dictatorship (of which a centrally planned economy was a part, but not a causal inspiration) in accordance with the racist and nationalist ambitions of Hitler—hardly an illustration, much less confirmation, of the hypothesis that economic reform and democratic planning lead to dictatorship. In sum, democratic planning and economic reform played an insignificant role in these countries prior to the establishment of dictatorship.

In Russia, the Bolsheviks came to political power by violent revolution after years of exile and revolutionary activity in a society characterized by economic underdevelopment, political autocracy, civil war, and surrounding hostile foreign powers. Once in power, they made rapid industrialization with the imposition of draconian sacrifices upon the population the major objective of a highly centralized and comprehensive apparatus of nationalization, collectivization, and economic planning. Since neither the conditions and circumstances nor the goals and techniques of Communist economic planning remotely resemble the conditions, goals, and methods which characterize

---

[6]Herman Finer, *Road to Reaction* (Chicago: Quadrangle Books, 1945) p. 123.

[7]*Ibid.*, p. 89.

planning, economic reform, and proposals for further change in Western, economically developed, democratic nations, any inference from the Communist to the American or British experience is fallacious.

As far as the democratic countries are concerned, Hayek's gloomy prognosis emanates, Finer argues, from three false premises: first, that the sole determinant of the character of an economic system and its relation to the surrounding social and political order is the economic structure, that is, that goals, traditions, and political leadership (the "superstructure" in Marxian terminology) have no significance in determining the democratic character of the society; second, that economic planning must be total, comprehensive, and unitary; third, that if and when democracy and the requirements of efficient planning come into conflict, efficiency always must win and democracy always must lose.

By contrast, Finer suggests, the democratic character of a society is profoundly affected by goals, traditions, and leadership; economic planning and reform in practice in democratic nations are characterized by experiment, compromise, and mutual adjustment in the light of competing interests and values; and, consequently, in societies with strong democratic traditions, conflicts between planning "efficiency" and democracy typically are resolved in favor of democracy. In short, economic reform and government control over economic life can be and is democratic, as the experiences of England, the United States, and other countries attest. Given the pragmatic and experimental approach to public policy in these countries, it is extremely unlikely democratic economic reform will lead to "socialism" in some comprehensive sense. Even if "socialism" were to emerge, there is no *empirical* evidence that a socialism established under democratic auspices in economically developed countries with strong democratic traditions would become dictatorial and totalitarian.

WOOTON: ECONOMIC PLANNING AND INDIVIDUAL FREEDOMS

In the neo-Austrian analysis, government ownership and control of industry and central planning, considered as a unit, are contrasted with private ownership and the competitive market system. In her classic study, *Freedom under Planning*, Barbara Wooton distinguishes between private versus government ownership and operation of industry on the one hand and government planning versus the market system on the other. Her purpose is to focus more closely upon the prospective impact of government planning—"the conscious and deliberate choice of economic priorities by some public authority" [47: 6]—upon individual freedoms. The distinction is pertinent to our discussion for two major reasons. First, much of Hayek's criticism of socialism focuses upon government economic planning rather than government ownership. Second, government economic planning, as defined by Wooton, can be and has been extended—as during wartime—quite apart from the enlargement of the nationalized sector.

Mrs. Wooton begins by distinguishing sharply between (1) the "fact of planning," assuming that planners are "public-spirited people who seek only to discover the common good, and to do their best for it" and (2) the question of "who is to plan the planners?" to ensure that this underlying assumption is valid. [47: 19, 158] Much of the "anti-planning" argument, Wooton suggests, in a manner similar to Keynes' critique of Hayek, indiscriminately mixes these two issues. In the interest of clarity, they should be distinguished.

A summary of Mrs. Wooton's conclusions on the first issue is given in Table 9a-1. The bases for these conclusions are:

Freedom of Collective Bargaining: The area of greatest prospective conflict between freedom and economic planning occurs with respect to wages and collective bargaining.

RELATIONS BETWEEN GOVERNMENT ECONOMIC
PLANNING AND INDIVIDUAL FREEDOMS

Type of Freedom	Prospective Relation to Government Economic Planning
Freedom of collective bargaining	Direct conflict. Arbitration is a possible alternative.
Consumer sovereignty	Direct conflict. But a mixture is possible.
Freedom of private enterprise	No inherent incompatibility, but some conflict is likely.
Political freedoms	Some conflict possible, but its extent has been exaggerated and can be reduced by appropriate institutional innovation.
Choice of employment and jobs.	Possible conflict, but unlikely. Essentially neutral.
Choice of consumption and saving	Possible conflict, but unlikely. Essentially neutral.
Determination of aggregate conumption, saving, investment, employment	Direct conflict between government determination and market determination; but government action is essentially neutral regarding individual freedom to save, consume, invest, or employ.
Cultural freedoms	Essentially neutral.
Civil freedoms	Essentially neutral. Conflict least likely.

The conflict is twofold. First, conflict inescapably arises from the fact that a "conscious determination of production priorities implies also conscious regulation of wage rates." [47: 104] If wages are determined by free collective bargaining, they will be consistent with governmentally determined production priorities only by coincidence. Second, if wages are determined by collective bargaining, then government planners are denied the use of planned wages as a means of providing economic inducements to entice labor mobility. The attainment of government production priorities thus will require other, non-monetary means of allocating labor (such as labor conscription and direct controls) possibly or probably inconsistent with freedom in the choice of occupation and employment.[8] The extent of conflict could possibly be reduced, however, through compulsory arbitration or a metamorphosis of collective bargaining into a condominium or cooperative joint determination of wages by labor unions, management, and government.

Consumer Sovereignty: "Full consumers' sovereignty" is "definitely not compatible with economic planning as we have defined it. It is not possible for the *same* questions to be settled *both* by the conscious *and* deliberate decisions of planners, *and* as the unconscious, unforeseen results of the behavior of millions of consumers acting independently of one another. . . . Planned decisions and unplanned market reactions are in fact alternative ways of determining economic priorities . . . in the determination of any particular issue they are mutually exclusive." [47: 43] The reduction of freedom involved

---

[8]For a similar view, see Sidney E. Rolfe, "The Trade Unions, Freedom, and Economic Planning," reprinted in Wayne A. Leeman, *Readings in Compara-* *tive Economic Systems* (Boston: Houghton Mifflin Company, 1963), pp. 224–37.

in the extension of government economic planning, however, because of its conflict with consumer sovereignty, is likely to be small. First, because of monopoly, sales promotion, income inequality, externalities, and so forth, the extent of consumer sovereignty in capitalist economies in practice is much less than its advocates contend. Second, it is perfectly possible to blend consumer sovereignty and planner sovereignty, for example, determining the *aggregate levels* of investment and consumption by government choice and the composition of consumption goods output in accordance with marketability.

Freedom of Private Enterprise: Though "any attempt to make the output of non-socialized industries conform to a comprehensive plan will always be a somewhat precarious affair, . . . there is no *inherent* incompatibility between public determination of economic priorities and freedom of private ownership of industry." [47: 123] In a society which places a high value on freedom of private enterprise, potential conflicts can be reduced by primary reliance upon economic inducement, such as government purchases from private businesses, as a means of realizing public priorities. In addition, no freedom is absolute—especially one which, like freedom of private enterprise, is exercised by a small minority of the population. Because of the widespread social effects of business decisions, they will be regulated by government policy to a greater or lesser extent in any event.

Political Freedoms: These include the freedom to dissent and criticize government, to form opposition parties, and to replace one government and legislature with another. This raises a *potential* dilemma because (long-run) "economic planning demands continuity, and political freedom appears to imply instability." [47: 131] This potential conflict between economic planning and political freedom will become an actual one, however, only in the absence of (a) general agreement on the purposes of government

economic planning and (b) methods to promote greater continuity in long-run planning within the democratic framework.

As to (a), considerable agreement on social values (for example, full employment, minimum standards of public health) exists already, as illustrated by the broad similarity between programs of different political parties in such developed democracies as Great Britain. Further agreement doubtless can be discovered and extended, as political parties increasingly criss-cross lines of traditional economic interest groups. As to (b), "where there is a will there is a way." It should be possible to create appropriate machinery to give greater long-run stability to legislative determination of economic priorities.

Freedom in the Choice of Occupations and Jobs: If freedom is defined as the "ability to do what you want" [47: 4], then government economic planning, insofar as it succeeds in promoting full employment, increases individual freedom. Under conditions of widespread unemployment, "freedom in occupational choice" becomes a sham.

During full employment, government economic planning conceivably could restrict freedom of choice of occupations and jobs in two ways: by laws or by economic pressure. The former is not only unnecessary, but unlikely. It is unnecessary because workers may be enticed to enter or leave occupations or jobs to a significant degree by wage incentives. It is unlikely because labor conscription and compulsory direction of labor is much more complicated than simply setting wages at planned levels, letting workers move at will, and adjusting wages by a trial-and-error process to equate demand and supply. The dovetailing of labor with jobs may be further simplified by careful attention to the location of industry, where possible, by bringing jobs to workers rather than relocating workers to jobs.

As to economic sanctions, the fact is that public welfare and unemployment compensation have radically reduced the likelihood of restrictions upon freedom of choice of employment. With continued economic growth, it should be possible to provide sufficiently for the unemployable or voluntarily unemployed and more abundantly for those who are willing to work, whether working or (temporarily) unemployed.

Freedom in the Choice of Consumption and Saving: The prospective impact of government economic planning upon individual freedom to consume and save is similar to that of freedom of choice in employment. Insofar as government economic planning is successful in promoting full employment, the freedom of consumers is increased, for the loss of income during periods of depression and unemployment makes a mockery of freedom in the choice of consumption. Supposing full employment to be achieved, government rationing and restrictions upon freedom of choice in consumption are conceivable, but aside from wartime and other special cases (for example, dangerous drugs) are unnecessary and unlikely: unnecessary, because there is nothing in the conscious determination of priorities in production which requires the abandonment of markets as a social process for distributing goods already produced; unlikely, because government rationing systems are cumbersome and more complicated than markets for this purpose. In sum, "the conscious planning of economic priorities involves no necessary threat to freedom of consumption . . . ." [47: 50]

Freedom in the Determination of Aggregate Consumption, Saving, Investment, and Employment: Because of the vagaries of expenditures, especially investment, an equality between the desires to save and invest may or may not occur at full employment utilization of resources. If production "is left to follow the dictates of market purchase," full employment may well be inconsistent with consumer sovereignty, even in the restricted form in which it exists in practice. "The liberty of the consumer to distribute his spending as he likes through time is thus a potential threat to the liberty of the worker to do more than look for work." This conflict can be resolved, but not without "a considerable amount of economic planning," that is, adjusting the aggregate level of demand to the capacity to produce and the conditions of employment on the labor market. [47: 73–75] This may, but need not, restrict the freedom of individuals to consume, save, or invest as they wish. What it means is that the determination of the *aggregate levels* of investment, saving, consumption, and employment cannot be left to the vagaries of the marketplace, but must become a public responsibility. The exercise of this responsibility, however, by control over government spending, taxing, the money supply and the supplementation of private by public employment need not conflict with individual economic freedoms in particular instances.

Cultural Freedoms: Because it is easier to plan for uniformity than for diversity, government economic planning can be used to reduce cultural freedoms (such as freedom of speech or religion). For example, governments could withhold newspaper ink from dissident editors. Whether governments would restrict cultural freedoms, however, is a different matter, depending essentially upon the quality and character of the planners and the citizenry rather than planning itself.

Civil Freedoms: Civil liberties (for example, right to a trial by jury) are least likely to be affected by government economic planning. "There is no logical connection between," say, government control of output in the steel industry and the elimination of trial by jury. Again, since people in positions of power reasonably can be presumed to enjoy exercising it, it is conceivable that government power to plan could be abused. But whether it would be abused depends less upon planning than on "how far political power is in practice absolute, and what kind of people exercise that power for what kind of ends." [47: 37]

Who is to Plan the Planners? In sum, "there is nothing in the conscious planning of economic priorities which is inherently incompatible with the freedoms which mean most to the contemporary Englishman or American." [47: 158] This leads to the question "Who is to plan the planners?," that is, how can we be sure planners will not become tyrants? This, suggests Wooton, is at least an open question and depends essentially upon social and political psychology rather than the logic or content of economic planning.

The problem is one of "adjusting democratic theory and practice to the realities of the modern world. . . ." [47: 167] and has three central dimensions:

(1) the emergence of better procedures for wise selection of political leaders (such as greater emphasis upon the quality, character, and integrity of governmental leaders than on the "details of what potential governments propose;" increased specification of qualifications for public office; increased focus upon comparison of past performance with stated goals; sharper distinction between goals and means to attain them);

(2) widespread involvement and participation of the citizenry in the administration and execution of plans;

(3) an increase in "democratic competence and courage" among the citizenry through the extension of an "environment of social equality," especially through education. [47: 178]

None of these tasks, Wooton concludes, are impossible, and several are the likely results of government economic planning. In short, the relations between freedom and economic planning partake of a circle "that can be either vicious or virtuous: it is the citizens of a wisely planned society who are least likely themselves to fall victims to the dangers of planning; and vice-versa." [47: 180] In any event, there is nothing in government economic planning which warrants its designation as a road to serfdom, dictatorship, or totalitarianism.

DAHL AND LINDBLOM: DEMOCRACY AND ECONOMIC PLANNING

While Finer and Wooton provide a direct rebuttal to Hayek's overall argument, Dahl and Lindblom have examined in a pointed way the strategic issue of relations between democracy and economic planning. The general question of the compatibility of economic planning with democracy, they suggest, is "virtually without meaning." [1: 277] Like Schumpeter, they focus instead upon the prospective impact of economic planning upon the conditions and preconditions necessary for democracy.[9]

Contemporary democracy in practice is essentially a social process to blunt or temper inequalities in political power through establishing or maintaining a "high degree" of control by the citizenry over political leaders. This requires two fundamental *conditions*: first, competition among political leaders for support by the citizenry as the basis for control by leaders; second, opportunity for citizens to transfer support from incumbent political leaders to their rivals. The vitality of the process of political competition depends, in turn, on underlying *preconditions*. Three of these are directly pertinent to typical arguments about relations between democracy and economic planning: (1) indoctrination in democratic ideals and procedures by political leaders, subordinates, and associates, and the citizenry as a prime means of preventing rulers from becoming tyrants; (2)

---

[9]Strictly speaking, *democracy* (rule by the people) would require the condition of political equality and the method of majority rule, that is, an equal distribution of control over governmental decisions through rule by a "majority of political equals." [1: 43] *Polyarchy* (rule by many), defined as a social process in which the citizenry exerts a "high degree" of control over political leaders, is an approximation to democracy. It "is distinguished from democracy by the fact that leaders by no means share equal control over policy with non-leaders," [1: 284] though leaders are selected by citizens through voting.

agreement by the politically active on basic methods and procedures for political competition (such as freedom to vote, freedom to dissent and criticize government, freedom to organize political parties); (3) a high degree of "social pluralism," that is, more or less autonomous social groups or organizations, to encourage strength by union, the likelihood of competing leaders, and alternative sources of information.

It is commonly argued by critics, of whom Hayek is a prime example, that "economic planning" and democracy are incompatible. Dahl and Lindblom have translated these arguments into assertions regarding the probable effects of economic planning upon the preconditions for viable political competition. In each instance, they contend, the assertions are based upon logical or factual errors and/or misunderstanding of the character of democracy, economic planning, or both.

Indoctrination in Democratic Ideals and Procedures. It is popularly contended by Hayek and other neo-liberal economists that an extension of central planning must or will undermine faith in the institutions and habits of democracy—through the corruptive influences of power, the tendency for the "worst to get on top," the conflicts between efficient planning and democratic procedure, and the weakening in the will and spirit of the citizenry to resist progressive enlargement in the scope of central authority. Something of the sort is logically conceivable and appears to have relevance to countries with weak democratic traditions. But in societies with strong democratic traditions, the opposite seems true: it is not the extension of central planning and government control that limits democracy, but the democratic political process that limits the scope and power of central planning. In short, whenever central planning begins "to seem oppressive to enough people" in societies with strong democratic traditions, "citizens employ the political process to call a halt, and even to

throw out the politicians in office," as attested by numerous post-World War II experiences in the United States, Great Britain, the Scandinavian countries, Australia, and New Zealand. [1: 293]

Basic Agreement. It is often argued that planning requires a single, monistic goal. If this were so, then democracies could plan in war (characterized by consensus on a single overriding objective) but not in peace (characterized by a multiplicity of competing goals). Therefore, planning in peace would require dictatorship to impose agreement on a (wartime-like) imperative objective. But wartime planning aside, goals are typically multiple, in dictatorships as well as democracies. The notion of the requirement of a single, overriding objective, or "comprehensive value system," is misleading. Economic planning, especially in a democracy, "usually requires a carefully thought-out adjustment of potentially or actually conflicting actions aimed at a variety of purposes." [1: 300] Naturally, planning would be easier with one goal than with several and more complicated with the need to blend or compromise among several than with one. But this is a commentary on the difficulties of planning in any political system, not upon the impact of planning on the political system.

A closely allied argument is that economic planning requires agreement on basic policies or "plans" extending over long-run periods; but democracies, characterized by political competition and alternation in political parties, create an instability in agreement on policies, thus making (long-run) economic planning difficult, if not impossible. This argument, while containing an element of apparent plausibility, rests on two misconceptions. First, much economic planning is short-run in character: indeed, given short-run instability and shifts in underlying functional relations and conditions, much economic planning must focus upon short-run problems. Second, political competition in modern democracies does not create massive shifts in policy disruptive to long-run economic planning. On the one hand, frequent alternations in political parties (say, every two to four years) are not a necessary condition of democracy, as illustrated by long stretches of Republican or Democratic party dominance in national politics in the United States. On the other hand, shifts in political parties are not necessarily or even generally accompanied by large-scale shifts in basic policies. A Republican victory at the polls in the United States, for example, or a Conservative one in Great Britain, is highly unlikely to yield massive policy changes, as demonstrated by experiences of the 1950s and 1960s.

Social Pluralism. A final fear of government economic planning is that its extension must or will destroy the pluralism necessary for effective functioning of political competition and, thereby, democracy. The argument is threefold. First, the extension of government control over the economy increasingly leaves the citizen defenseless against arbitrary administrative decisions. Second, the egalitarian redistributive measures of the contemporary welfare state reduce the autonomy and independence of groups from whom income and wealth is taken and make society increasingly dependent upon government decision. Third, because of its complexities and the interdependencies of the different parts of the economy and of economic plans, the effective power to plan is increasingly removed from legislatures and transferred to executive and administrative branches of government, thus reducing the political pluralism and separation of powers necessary for the maintenance of democracy.

The first two arguments, Dahl and Lindblom contend, are belied by actual experiences with democratic planning. In fact, social pluralism is higher in such countries as Sweden and the United States today than it was prior to the 1930s. It is probably true that income redistributive measures and the functioning by government as a means for the promotion of countervailing power has weakened the relative position of some groups in the economy by strengthening the position of others. But this on balance has served to substitute greater social pluralism (that is, democratic negotiation among labor unions, corporations, and farm organizations) for the essentially monistic dominance of business interests and values of earlier decades.[10]

The third argument, though very popular in the United States, is open to serious reservation. If a viable *social* pluralism does not exist, the mere political or constitutional separation of executive and legislative powers is not a *sufficient* condition for the sustenance of democracy. But if a viable social pluralism does exist, then the separation of powers (as in the United States) may not be a *necessary* condition for a viable democracy, as illustrated by parliamentary systems such as Great Britain, which sustain democracy despite the absence of a political separation of powers.

In sum, government economic planning does not necessarily constitute a limit on or obstacle to the effective functioning of democracy. Indeed, as we shall explore briefly later, the opposite, in certain circumstances, may well be true: that is, particular forms and institutions of contemporary democracy may place strategic limits upon or obstacles to the effective functioning of government economic planning.

---

[10]Cf. Thomas Petit, *Freedom in the American Economy* (Homewood, Illinois: Richard D. Irwin, Inc., 1964).

10

The Economic Theory
of Decentralized Socialism

One of the most prominent, provocative, and classic models of the organization and operation of an ideally functioning socialist economic system formulated by economists sympathetic to the aims and aspirations of the socialist movement(s) is that of decentralized, market, or liberal socialism. Contributions to the analysis of this kind of system have been made by numerous authors. Probably the most rigorous and sophisticated treatment has been that presented by Polish economist Oskar Lange. Accordingly, this chapter will provide an exposition and a brief critique of the Lange model.[1] Also examined will be some issues involved in gradations between centralized and decentralized socialism and some of the prominent bases and pressures involved in the transition from centralized to more decentralized forms of socialist economic organization.

---

[1] Though the most prominent, the Lange model is not the only theory of decentralized socialism. Varieties of decentralized socialism are as possible as gradations between decentralized and centralized socialism. Unless otherwise indicated, however, the phrase "decentralized socialism" in this chapter refers to the Lange version of the late 1930s. Recent contributions to decentralization versus centralization in the contest of contemporary Communism, including the Yugoslav experience, managed-socially reformed capitalism, and democratic socialism, are developed in later chapters.

CENTRALIZATION AND DECENTRALIZATION IN SOCIALIST ECONOMIC ORGANIZATION

Centralization and Decentralization in Criteria for Identifying and Comparing Varieties of Socialism

Socialism, as a body of economic theory, a movement of social protest and economic reform, or an economic system, exists or may exist in various forms. Even if discussion were restricted to post-Marxian developments, the variety and diversity of socialistic programs, processes, and institutions are great.

A means of distinguishing among varieties of post-Marxian economic theories of socialism is that of centralization versus decentralization. In preceding chapters, we have used centralization versus decentralization as a strategic dimension in the identification and comparison of economic systems. Actually, each of the identifying criteria we have used may exhibit or have implications for centralization and decentralization, as illustrated in Table 10-1. Theories of decentralized socialism tend to emphasize the dimensions of the identifying criteria shown in the second column, while theories of centralized socialism will generally focus on the features listed in the third column.

Table 10-1.

CENTRALIZATION AND DECENTRALIZATION IN
SOCIALIST ECONOMIC ORGANIZATION

Criteria	Decentralized Features	Centralized Features
1. Level of economic development	1–2. Economy sufficiently developed to afford "inefficiencies" or complex enough to require the agility of decentralized economic institutions and processes.	1–2. Developing, industrializing economy, characterized by large-scale changes which are simple enough to benefit from centralized, collective decision-making processes.
2. Resource base		
3. Ownership and control of the means of production	3. Mixture of private and public ownership; important role for 'social' but nongovernmental ownership (labor unions, cooperatives, and so on); important role for local/municipal ownership.	3. Dominant national governmental ownership and control.
4. Locus of economic power	4. Freedom of individual choice in consumption, occupation, and saving; wide discretion for plant and industry managers; consumer sovereignty.	4. Concentration of economic power in government; detailed plans, with little managerial discretion; restrictions upon freedom of individual choice; planner sovereignty.
5. Motivational system	5. Significant reliance upon cooperation and/or spontaneous pursuit of individual economic gain.	5. Significant reliance upon manipulation by governmental authorities and/or governmental directives and commands.
6. Organization of economic power	6. Pluralism; localization and separation of powers; functional parliament.	6. Centralization and concentration of powers; important role for delegation to experts.
7. Social processes	7. Price systems; bargaining; democratic worker control over industry.	7. Government bureaucracy.
8. Distribution of income and wealth	8. Equality; decentralized processes.	8. Inequality; centralized processes.

Gradations of Centralization and
Decentralization in a Socialist
Economy

Centralization versus decentralization is more a difference in degree than one in kind, and a whole series of gradations and combinations of the two are conceivable within the general framework of socialist economic organization.

Professor W. A. Johr has provided a useful topology of some of these gradations. [38: 130–31] He distinguishes among four major models of socialism:

1. *The entirely centrally-directed economy.* In this model, the *CPB* determines the aggregate volume of consumption, saving and investment, and the level of production of each commodity; it allocates the labor force and distributes the output of consumer goods.

2. *The centrally-directed economy with free consumer's choice.* Here, individual consumers receive money incomes and are free to allocate them among existing commodities. In all other respects, this model is the same as the first.

3. *The centrally-directed economy with free consumer's choice and free occupational choice.* This model differs from the preceding in the addition of freedom of occupational choice and the resulting allocation of labor by wage differentials rather than by state direction.

4. *The centrally-directed economy with free consumer's choice, free occupational choice and freedom to save.* In this model, the state relinquishes its direct control over the volume of saving and investment, encourages individuals to save, and indirectly affects the volume of voluntary saving by manipulating the rate of interest.

In each of these four models, Johr designates two subdivisions: (a) sovereignty of the *CPB* over individual economic agents; (b) sovereignty of individual economic agents over the *CPB*. In (a), the *CPB* determines the desired production targets, labor allocations, and volume of saving and investment, but achieves these goals by bringing them into harmony with individual preferences through regulating prices, wage rates, and interest rates. In (b), the CPB functions as a representative agent of individuals, concerned only with realizing the individual preferences (deduced from market-determined consumer goods prices, wage rates, and interest rates) "by providing the desired variety of consumer goods, by creating jobs, and by determining investment." [38: 131] A movement from model (1) to (4) and, within each model, from (a) to (b), invlves increasing decentralization and decreasing centralization in the power to make and enforce economic decisions.

Polish economist Jan Drewnowski has provided a somewhat similar exposition of gradations between centralization and decentralization in a socialist economy. According to Drewnowski, "the central institutional problem of a socialist state" is to "determine the sphere of influence of state decisions as against that of individual decisons." [32: 124] Accordingly, he divides the economy into three zones: "the zone in which state preferences are supreme (the zone of state influence), the zone in which individual preferences are supreme (the zone of individual influence), and the zone in which state and individual preferences meet (the zone of dual influence.)" [32: 129]

Drewnowski then defines capitalism and socialism, and gradations within each, in terms of their respective placement in these three zones. What earlier was called "old-style capitalism," for example, often was viewed as a system in which all or nearly all of the national economy was in the individual zone. By contrast, contemporary, modified capitalist economies contain a state zone and a significantly enlarged dual-influence or dual-preference zone, as well as an individual zone. A ("full") socialist economy, on the other hand, contains no individual zone, no zone where individual preferences are supreme. It may be best conceived as a system combining a state- and a dual-preference zone. But such a system may have a series of gradations, ranging from "the limiting case in which the economy is in the state zone and that in which the state zone is not much more extensive than in capitalism." [32: 130]

Drewnowski's limiting case, where all of the national economy is in the state zone, is the same as Professor Johr's completely centrally-directed economy. In this case, the quantities of all goods produced, the allocation of all resources, and the distribution of all commodities through a rationing system are determined by government. Consumer preferences play no role, and no markets exist. This is an empirically unrealistic, but theoretically limiting, case. The typical case is divided into two major zones: the state zone, which usually is found in the investment goods industries, and the dual-preference zone. The latter, in turn, is divided into three sub-varieties: in a "first-degree market economy," which corresponds roughly to Johr's model (2)(a), the distribution of consumer goods is transferred from the state- to the dual-preference zone. Consumers are free to spend their incomes as they wish, and markets replace government rationing as a process for distributing goods. Quantities of consumer goods output are determined by the state, but prices, which are set and periodically readjusted to equate supply and demand, are "determined" by consumer demand, and thus, individual preferences.

In a "second-degree market economy," which corresponds roughly to the "decentralized reforms" proposed in recent years by the "liberal Communists" in some of the east European countries, "the next adjoining range of variables (that is, quantities of consumer goods, quantities of resources other than new investment used in their production, and the allocation of resources among plants) is transferred from the state- to the dual-influence zone." [32: 131–32] In this model,

the aggregate volume of consumption goods, the aggregate volume of natural resources used in the production of consumption goods, and the quantities of investment goods remain in the state zone. Given these factors, variables transferred to the dual-influence zone would be determined by adjusting production to consumer demand via the principle of profit maximization.

The "third-degree market economy," corresponds roughly to Lange's decentralized model. It leaves the aggregate volume of consumption and investment goods in the state zone and transfers the determination of the allocation of investment goods to the dual-influence zone. Decisions on the forms of investments and their allocations among different plants would be made on the basis of consumer demand for finished products.

THE ORGANIZATIONAL STRUCTURE OF DECENTRALIZED SOCIALISM

Economic Theory of Decentralized Socialism

The phrase "economic theory of decentralized socialism" implies four things: First, it deals with *economic* problems and characteristics, and abstracts, largely though not entirely, from historical, political, ethical, psychological, and administrative issues. Though this restricts severely the scope and empirical applicability of the model, it accords with the principle of scholarly division of labor and is a refreshing change from the pre-Langean literature of the socialist movement, which was often such a jumble of non-economic and economic themes and problems that no clear picture of a socialist economic system emerged.

Second, the Lange contribution lies primarily in the area of *theoretical* rather than actual economic systems or movements for economic reform. Further, as a theoretical system, it has both explanatory and normative characteristics and implications. It purports to explain how an ideally functioning socialist economic system could or might be organized and operated. It is not a theoretical description of a real economy. (However, present interest in the Lange-type model stems largely from recent debates over and apparent trends toward greater decentralization in economic organization in Communist East Europe, and, in part, from the possible applicability of Lange's rules of economic calculation and coordination under a system of partial nationalization as, for example, in the United Kingdom.)

Third, it is a theory of a *socialist* economy and thus shares certain common traits and characteristics with other visions, models, and proposals within the socialist family, including that of centralized socialism. These similarities will be clarified in the following sections.

Fourth, it is a model of a distinctly *decentralized*, market, or liberal socialism, and thus is distinguishable from other forms of socialism, such as Marxian and centralized varieties. Market socialism shares much in common with competitive, market capitalism. One of the major aims of the Lange model was to demonstrate (in response to the criticisms of Mises and others), that a "socialist" economy, characterized by public ownership of the means of production and some degree of central, governmental economic planning, still could reproduce via a decentralized system of institutions and techniques the logic and results of competitive, market capitalism.

Goals of Economic Planning and
the Structure of Economic
Organization Under Decentralized
Socialism

The social goals of economic organization are not specified by Lange. But clearly, though implicitly, he carries over into his analysis of socialism the major goals discussed by most twentieth century economists; that is, a simul-

taneous and balanced attainment of efficiency in the allocation of resources, equity in the distribution of income, full employment stability, economic growth, and the maintenance of (certain) individual economic freedoms within the context of political democracy.

The structure of decentralized socialism, as a system for attaining these goals, may be summarized briefly as follows:

LEVEL OF ECONOMIC DEVELOPMENT

The decentralized socialist model, like the Marxian vision, was considered a prospective successor to capitalism in the economically developed nations, not primarily as a substitute for capitalism in underdeveloped economies. This view is in sharp contrast to that of centralized socialists.

OWNERSHIP

Lange assumed government or "public ownership of the means of production." [39: 72] As noted earlier, this is a possible, but not necessary, form of social ownership in a socialist economy. Other possibilities, such as worker or cooperative ownership, are not considered in the Lange model. Lange did not specify the level of government ownership, though presumably it is national or central rather than, say, municipal authority that he had in mind. The simplifying assumption is made that all capital and natural resources are governmentally owned. Any actual socialist economy would in all probability be a "mixed" system containing a "large number of means of production owned, for example, by farmers, artisans, and small-scale entrepreneurs. But this," he argued, "does not introduce any new theoretical problem." [39: 73_n]

ECONOMIC POWER

In the Lange model of decentralized socialism, the freedom and power to formulate economic decisions is dispersed widely among a variety of economic decision-making units: individual workers and consumers; plant and industry managers of government enterprises; a Central Planning Board (CPB), and governmental units other than the CPB. Individual workers, for example, are free to choose their occupations, and consumers are free to allocate their incomes among different commodities and services, and savings. (The total amount of investment and saving is to be determined "corporately" and centrally by the CPB.) Presumably, both workers and consumers will exercise this freedom and power in the pursuit of the maximization of individual economic gain through market exchange. Further, "consumer sovereignty" supplements freedom of consumers' choice. Not only are consumers free to spend as they wish among existing goods; in addition, "the preferences of consumers as expressed by their demand prices, are the guiding critieria in production and in the allocation of resources." [39: 72–73] An "efficient" allocation of resources is one which, among other things, corresponds closely to consumer preferences.

With the possible exception of owner-managers of small-scale private businesses, plant and industry managers are government employees and are instructed by the CPB to follow certain "rules" (the content of which will be explained). Given these rules, however, and given prices of inputs and outputs, which are beyond their control, government managers are free to determine the quantities and combinations of inputs and outputs. The Lange model does *not* include a physical "plan" specifying quantities of inputs and outputs to be produced and consumed by government plants and industries. This is a distinctive feature of *decentralized* socialism.

Thus, the CPB does not determine quantities of inputs and outputs in a national economic plan. Further, it does not set either prices of consumer goods or wage rates. It is, however, a locus of significant central power and responsibility in an essentially decentralized system and has at least six main functions: First, it sets and periodically readjusts prices of intermediate goods (for example, coal, steel, electric power) and capital goods (machinery and buildings) as well as the rate(s) of interest. Second, it determines "corporately" the total volume of investment. Third, it or a financial subsidiary, such as the Central Bank, evaluates the respective claims of different plants and industries for loanable funds for capital expansion. Fourth, it is responsible for distributing a "social dividend" (to be described) to worker-citizens as their share in the income from capital and natural resources. Fifth, it supervises the actions of plant and industry managers to ensure they are complying with the rules. Sixth, it provides for various "collective wants" in the public sector of the economy, such as national defense and education.

The Central Planning Board need not be dictatorial. It is presumably part of and controlled by a government apparatus, including a chief executive and national legislative body, supplemented by a system of public administration, and in turn, presumably controlled by citizenry through the ballot box. Decentralized socialism could even include, suggested Lange, "a Supreme Economic Court whose function would be to safeguard the use of the nation's productive resources in accordance with the public interest. It would have the power to repeal decisions of the Central Planning Board that were in contradiction to the general rules of consistency and efficiency . . . just as the United States Supreme Court has the power to repeal laws held unconstitutional." [39: 98]

In sum, decentralized socialism presumably would contain three sectors: a decentralized private sector, consisting of consumers, workers, and private owner-managers of small-scale businesses, all interested in the pursuit of their individual economic gains through market exchange; a centralized public sector, consisting of government in general and the CPB, concerned with the provision of collective wants; and a decentralized-centralized socialist sector, divided into decentralized plant and industry managers, given wide latitude and flexibility to determine input-output quantities and relationships, and a central planning board, guiding and supervising government-owned enterprises. Clearly, the socialist sector is the distinctive feature of Lange's model and merits our major attention. The behavioral principles of the private and public collective sectors presumably would be the same as under capitalism.

SOCIAL PROCESSES

The social processes for making and coordinating economic decisions essentially are three: One is political democracy (which Lange cites only briefly), a vehicle for the expression of citizen preferences and general government supervison of the economy. A second is government hierarchy, within the government in general, the CPB, and government-owned plants and industries. The third is the price system, which, in Lange's model, assumes two forms. The first is "a 'genuine market (in the institutional sense of the word) for consumers' goods and for the services of labor." [39: 73] In these markets, prices are set by the interaction of the market or industry supply (or demand) of producers and the market or industry demand of consumers (or supply of labor). This spontaneous nongovernmental price system provides a basis, as under competitive market capitalism, for the calculation by consumers, workers, and government managers of marginal costs and marginal benefits of alternative purchases and/or sales. It also provides, through the threat of substitution by workers and consumers, a system of control over the managers of business units.

Beyond this, the market price system acquires added significance through the acceptance of the principle of consumer sovereignty. The rationality and efficiency of resource allocation within the socialist sector is evaluated in terms of its correspondence to consumer preferences, as revealed through demand prices of consumer goods.

Prices of means of production, though set by the CPB, must be consistent with the prices of consumer goods. Second, then, are the prices of capital and national resources and the rates of interest. They are set by the CPB and consitute a government-hierarchical price system supplementing, but, in an ideally functioning socialist economy, consistent with and controlled by a market price system.

INCOME DISTRIBUTION

In a capitalist economy, "the incomes of consumers are equal to their respective receipts from selling the services of the productive resources they own, plus entrepreneur's profits (which are zero in equilibrium)." [39: 66] Under socialism, where natural and capital resources are government-owned, personal incomes "are divorced from the ownership of those resources," and a socialist society thus is given "a considerable freedom in matters of distribution of income." Specifically, Lange divided consumers' income into two parts: one, wage income, determined by the market price system in the labor market; two, a "social dividend," constituting the individual's share in the income derived from the capital and natural resources owned by society," [39: 74] determined by principles to be described later.

Decentralized Socialism and Capitalism: Similarities and Differences

We noted in Chapter 2 that socialism is *not* the opposite of capitalism, and that, especially in the decentralized version, features of socialism bear a striking family resemblance to certain of those of competitive market capitalism. There are, however, a number of important differences between them as well. Some of the major similarities and differences between decentralized market socialism and competitive market capitalism are listed in Table 10-2.

If the contrast is made between decentralized socialism and the modified or reformed

Table 10-2.

MAJOR SIMILARITIES AND DIFFERENCES BETWEEN DECENTRALIZED SOCIALISM AND COMPETITIVE MARKET CAPITALISM

Criteria	Similarities	Differences
1–2. Level of economic development and resource base	Developed economy, with dominantly capitalistic resource base	
3. Ownership and control of the means of production	The likelihood of some private ownership	But primary reliance on social or government ownership
4. Locus of economic power	Dispersion of economic power among individual economic units, freedom in the choices of consumption and occupation, the assumption of consumer sovereignty, and a wide latitude of discretion for industrial managers	But existence of a CPB, with varied economic functions not found in the model of competitive market capitalism, coupled with the sharp reduction or absence of freedom of private enterprise
5. Motivational system	Pursuit of maximization of individual economic gain by consumers, workers, and managers	But CPB responsible for social goals transcending individual economic calculations; managers motivated by desire to maximize their incomes rather than profits
6. Organization of economic power	Essentially decentralized organization of power to make economic decisions	But greater centralization in organization and existence of a CPB with important centralized functions
7. Social processes	Heavy reliance on price systems	But substitution of a government-hierarchical price system for the spontaneous market-price system in the money, capital, and the intermediate goods markets
8. Distribution of income and wealth	Some inequality of income through the operation of a system of market-determined wage differentials	But the promotion of greater equality through the elimination or sharp reduction of property incomes, coupled with the distribution of a "social dividend"

capitalism of today's various "mixed economies," a somewhat different picture emerges. On the one hand, it might be argued decentralized socialism is even *more* radically decentralized and closer to the Adam Smith version and vision of competitive market capitalism than are today's modern mixed economies, with their concentrated, centralized (private and public) economic power and departures from reliance on the competitive price system as a coordinative social process.[2] Further, if we turn from the essentially static and "bloodless concept of perfect competition" [8: 183] to the "dynamism" and "creative destruction" of the Schumpeterian version of the capitalist process, we can identify still other differences.

On the other hand, decentralized socialism is much more of a "mixed economy" and is much closer to the theory and practice of contemporary managed capitalism than are either the classic Marxian or the neo-Marxian centralized versions of socialism. Like the economic systems of Western Europe, the United Kingdom, and, to a lesser but still significant degree, the United States, the decentralized socialist model is characterized by: a mixture of private and government ownership and control of industry; a combination of private and government economic power; the pursuit of social goals and provision of collective wants by government bodies, a greater centralization of government economic decision-making than in market capitalism; the supplementation of the price system by political democracy and government hierarchy as social coordinative processes; the promotion of greater income equality through government action.

Decentralized Socialism and Orthodox Economic Theory

Similarities and differences between market capitalism and decentralized socialism

[2]Dahl and Lindblom phrase it even more vigorously: "The doctrine of decentralized socialism, of decentralizing the great number of governmental controls now exercised over economic life in the United States and Western Europe, is more radical than the socialism and reform now advocated by the major democratic parties of the Left. That the price system has very radical potentialities for undermining a hierarchy-ridden society has always been hinted at in its family resemblance to anarchy." [1: 217] Again: ". . . the use of mandatory price mechanisms is an alternative—perhaps the only feasible one—to an excess of centralization that threatens to grow out of recent attempts to extend government hierarchical controls over business enterprise." [1: 215]

are found in economic theory as well as institutional assumptions. It should be emphasized that Lange, though presenting a case for socialism, was trained in and familiar with non-socialist economic theory, including Austrian and neo-classical contributions, and that his rhetoric was directed not at already-convinced socialists but at professional economists. As a socialist, Lange emphasized the desirability and prospective efficiency of an ideally organized socialist economic system. As a socialist economist, Lange emphasized the contribution of Marxian economics, both from the standpoint of Marx's recognition, though inadequate solution, of problems of resource allocation under socialism, and in terms of the Marxian analysis of the dynamics of capitalist development. As a socialist economist familiar with Keynesian analysis, Lange argued capitalism has no built-in mechanism for guaranteeing full-employment stability.

An economist trained and versed in orthodox economic theory, Lange argued that any economic system faces recurrent economic problems stemming from *the* fundamental problem of scarcity of resources in relation to human wants, and that economics, as the "science of administration of scarce resources in human society," is widely applicable to *both* capitalism and socialism despite different institutional conditions. Indeed, Lange argued the orthodox economic analysis of choice, allocation, equilibrium, price and value provides a *better* basis for understanding the day-to-day workings of a socialist economy than does Marxian economic theory.

Further, Lange evidently felt the *primary* economic case for socialism must rest on a demonstration that it can solve the neo-classical problems (analyzed in terms of neo-classical theory) rationally and efficiently. Lastly, as an economic scientist, Lange wanted to provide a "scientific" case for socialism; that is, to demonstrate that a socialist economy could be structured to more closely attain certain given objectives than capitalism, rather than to politically or ethically evaluate these objectives.

PRINCIPLES OF ECONOMIC BEHAVIOR UNDER DECENTRALIZED SOCIALISM

Brief Review of the Competitive Capitalist Model

Because a central purpose of his theory was to show a socialist economy could establish a substitute for the competitive price system as a social calculational and coordinative process, Lange preceded his analysis of socialism by a brief review of the role of the competitive price system under market capitalism. The treatment is traditional and admirable for its clarity and brevity. The essence of economics is described as "administration of scarce resources in human society." In a capitalist economy, the power to administer scarce resources lies essentially among consumers, concerned primarily with consumption and want satisfaction; business firms, concerned primarily with production and money profits; and resource owners, concerned primarily with acquisition of money income through the utilization by and/or the sale of their resources to business firms. The actions of these individual units are, of course, interdependent. The economy or economic system is, in essence, the "totality of interdependent units of economic decision." [41: 25] The central form of interdependence is the market exchange process, in which a market is defined as "a pattern of regular, recurrent transactions of exchange relations between units of economic decision." [41: 26] In a competitive market: (1) the number of sellers and buyers (of presumably homogeneous products and services) is so large that each individual regards the market exchange ratios or prices as *given* parameters, beyond his control; (2) entry into and exit from each market is free. [39: 65]

Given this institutional assumption, and given information as to the preference scales of consumers (the "psychological data"), the amount of resources available, and the technical possibilities of transforming resources into commodities in the productive process (the "technological data"), the essential ingredients of "competitive equilibrium" theoretically are resolvable and have two central parts: (1) the "subjective" equilibrium of individual units of economic decision, defined in terms of maximization of utility (satisfaction), profit, or income, *given* equilibrium prices; and (2) the "objective" equilibrium of the competitive market, that is, the determination of equilibrium market prices via the equation of market demand and market supply.

INDIVIDUAL (SUBJECTIVE) EQUILIBRIUM

Households and firms function both as buyers and sellers. As buyers, households maximize their total utility when marginal utility per dollar is the same in all directions $(MU_1/P_1 = MU_2/P_2 = MU_n/P_n.)$ Given prices and incomes, consumer demand is thus determined. As sellers, households maximize their incomes by selling their resources to the highest bidder(s). Given resource prices, allocation of resources among different firms and industries is thus determined. As buyers, firms seek the "least-cost combination of inputs" at any level of output by combining resources to equate marginal physical product per dollar in every direction. $(MPP_1/P_1 = MPP_2/P_2 = MPP_m/P_m)$. As sellers, firms produce that level of output (and as buyers, employ that total level of input of resources) which maximizes profit, where marginal cost equals marginal revenue which, under competitive conditions, equals price $(MC = MR = P)$, as shown in Figs. 4.2a and 4.3a. Given commodity and resource prices, the supply of commodities and the demand for resources thus is determined. Assuming freedom of entry and exit, resources will be shifted from industry to industry until, in the long-run equilibrium, total output has reached the level where price is pushed down (or up) to equal minimum long-run average cost. Thus, under competitive conditions, the pursuit of profit by business firms tends to be accompanied, in long-run equilibrium, by two socially beneficial results: (1) the minimization of the sacrifice of alternatives (minimum cost for any level of output and minimum-cost scale of plant and output); and (2) the organization of production to correspond most closely to consumer preferences ($MC = P$). (See Fig. 4.4.)

MARKET (OBJECTIVE) EQUILIBRIUM

The "objective" condition of equilibrium, in Lange's terminology, is attained when the decisions of individual economic units are coordinated or consistent with one another. Equilibrium prices are determined by the condition that the demand for each commodity or resource equals its supply. Only under this condition are the "subjective" maximization conditions of all individual units compatible. Such a general equilibrium system, however, though it may be illustrated in mathematical equations, actually is "solved," that is, determined, by a "trial-and-error" process, based on what Lange called "the parametric function of prices." In other words, prices are regarded as given parameters by separate individual units, but equilibrium prices actually are determined by the collective market actions of all individual units, via a series of successive trials. Beginning with randon or historically given prices, individual units attain their subjective maximization positions. If demands and supplies (determined from these maxima) are equal, the process ends. If they are not, price adjustments take place: Prices will rise where demands exceed supplies and will fall where supplies exceed demands. This process will continue until demand and supply are equal in each product and resource market and a general equilibrium of the competitive economy has been attained, as illustrated in Figs. 4.2 and 4.3. The crucial problem is to "see whether a

similar method of trial-and-error can be applied in a socialist economy." [39: 72]

How Would Decentralized
Socialism Work ? Choice,
Allocation, and Equilibrium

The basic idea of the Lange-type model of decentralized market socialism is that an efficient allocation of resources could be practicably promoted within the framework of a socialist economy through the incorporation of rules of managerial behavior and a trial-and-error market exchange process incorporating the same two central ingredients found in the classic model of competitive market capitalism just reviewed. These are: (1) the subjective equilibrium of individual units of economic decision, on the basis of given "indices of alternatives" (market prices for labor and consumer goods and "accounting prices" for all other resources and commodities); that is, the maximization of utility and incomes, as under competitive market capitalism, for households as buyers and as sellers of labor services, and the determination of resource combinations and resource and output levels according to certain rules by the managers of governmentally-owned plants and industries; (2) objective equilibrium; that is, the determination of prices via the establishment of equality between demand and supply in the various markets throughout the economic system.

INDIVIDUAL (SUBJECTIVE) EQUILIBRIUM

Subjective equilibrium is achieved when individual units of economic decision have attained equilibrium positions in terms of desired objectives.

Assuming free choice of consumption, households as buyers maximize their utility in relation to the consumer goods market in exactly the same way as in competitive market capitalism. Given prices, incomes, and tastes, consumers freely allocate their scarce money income and choose that combination of commodities and services which yields the highest satisfaction. This determines consumer demand for products and services.

Any private owner-managers in a dominantly socialist economy presumably would attain an equilibrium position, given prices of inputs and outputs, at input and output levels and combinations which maximized profits, as in the theory of competitive market capitalism.

For managers of government-owned plants and industries, Lange substituted two rules, imposed and enforced by the CPB, for the profit maximization assumption. Because the purpose of the rules, however, is to enable efficient and consumer-directed allocation of resources, the social results are similar to those of the model of competitive market capitalism, and managers behave, in effect, "as if" they were attempting to maximize profits on the basis of given prices.

Rule 1. Optimum Resource Combinations. The first rule instructs plant managers (in the operation of existing plants) and industry managers (in the construction of new plants) to select that combination of resources for *each* level of output which minimizes costs of production, thus attaining an optimum combination of resource inputs. As in the competitive capitalist model, this occurs, given resource prices, for those resource combinations in which marginal physical product per dollar is equal in all directions.

The purpose of Rule 1 is the "minimization of the sacrifice of alternatives." Assuming resource prices are accurate "indices of terms on which alternatives are offered," a minimization of the cost of producing any given output also must minimize the alternatives sacrificed and maximize the resources available for the production of alternative commodities. Cost minimization in the sense of Rule 1, however, does not necessarily mean production at that level of output or scale

of plant at which the traditional U-shaped average cost curve(s) is at *its* lowest point (level OQ_1 in Fig. 10.1). It does mean a choice of resource combinations leading to the lowest average cost curve(s) (LAC_2 in Fig. 10.1), given resource prices and under given technological conditions. ($C_2Q_2 < C_2'Q_2$ at OQ_2, $C_3Q_3 < C_3'Q_3$ at OQ_3, and so on.)

In applying this rule, it is necessary to distinguish between the short and long run. In the short run, the plant (equipment, buildings) is fixed, and output is varied by employing larger or smaller quantities of variable resources (labor, raw materials). In this case, the rule can be applied to the optimum combination of any two or more variable resources, but not to fixed resources, because the latter cannot be changed. The full application of Rule 1 can occur only in the long run, when all resources, including the size or scale of plant, become variable. If the long-run average-cost curve is U-shaped, as in Fig. 10.2, reflecting economies, then diseconomies, of large-scale production, it will be less costly to increase output by expanding the plant size than by increasing the utilization of existing plants to their minimum cost points during the declining phase of the LAC curve. (Note, for example, that cost is lower for output Oq_2 in Plant 2 than in Plant 1, despite the fact that c_1 lies at the minimum point of SAC_1 while c_2 lies above the minimum point of SAC_2.) The same occurs in reverse during the rising phase of the LAC curve. (Compare, for example, c_4 and c_5 for output Oq_4.) Thus, the least-cost combination of inputs occurs at *every* point along the LAC curve, but only at *one* point for each SAC curve (namely, at the points of tangency, as c_2, c_3, c_4, and so on.) Since that one point may or may not correspond to the optimum output level in the short run (see Rule 2), the *plant* manager cannot be held strictly to Rule 1. By contrast, the *industry* manager is responsible for adjusting the combination of resources in

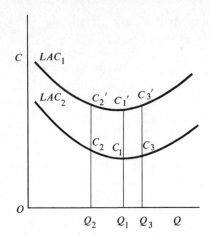

Fig. 10.1. (*Left*) Costs and optimum resource combinations

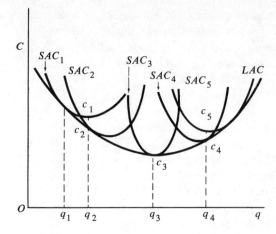

Fig. 10.2. (*Right*) Short-run vs. long-run costs

the long run by changes in the scale of plant and/or in the construction of new plants to achieve least-cost combination of inputs at *every* level of output.

Rule 2. Optimum Output and Input Levels. The second rule instructs plants managers (in the operation of existing plants) and industry managers (in the construction of new plants or the enlargement of old plants) to produce that level of output of each commodity (and thus, purchase that level of input of each resource) at which the marginal cost of production equals the given price (and thus, at which the value of the marginal product of each resource equals its price), hence securing an "optimum scale of output" and input.

The application of this rule to plant managers serves "the same function that in a competitive system is carried out by the private producer's aiming to maximize his profit, when the prices of factors and of the product are independent of the amount of each factor used by him and of his scale of output." [39: 76] Thus, in each product market in which he sells (Fig. 4.2a), the plant manager sells that level of output at which $MC = MR = P$; while in each resource market in which he buys (Fig. 4.3a), the plant manager purchases that level of each variable resource at which its $VMP = MRP =$ its price. This determines short-run plant and industry

output and short-run plant and industry demand for resources. The application of this second rule to managers of entire industries, that is, the instruction to expand or contract the size of plants (or to build new plants or refrain from replacing old ones) until long-run marginal cost of the entire industry equals price, determines the output (and input) level of each industry as a whole. It thus "performs the function which under free competition is carried out by the free entry of firms into an industry or their exodus from it." [39: 77]

The purpose of Rule 2 is to organize production and allocate resources to conform to consumer preferences. Assuming marginal costs accurately measure the marginal importance of alternative production opportunities, and prices of consumer goods accurately reflect the marginal significance of consumer preferences, an equation of marginal cost and price also yields a maximization of consumer satisfaction from scarce resources since "the marginal significance of each preference which is satisfied" is equal to "the marginal significance of the alternative preferences the satisfaction of which is sacrificed." [39: 79] Were price to exceed marginal cost, the marginal addition to consumer satisfaction would be greater than the marginal sacrifice of expanding output,

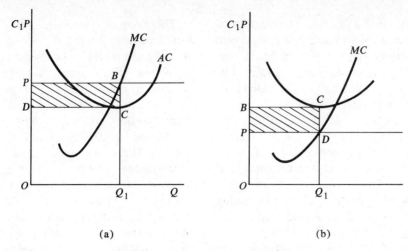

Fig. 10.3. (a) Profits, and (b) losses

and total satisfaction would increase through an increase in output. Were prices below marginal cost, the reverse would be true.

Consumer preference maximization in the sense of Rule 2, however, does *not* necessarily mean production at that level of output, scale of plant, or number of plants at which the *LAC* curve is at *its* lowest point (as illustrated in Fig. 4.4 at output OQ_e), which presumably would be the result, under perfectly competitive capitalism, of the entry and/or exit of firms into and out of industries in the long run. To maximize consumer satisfaction, marginal cost pricing must be followed regardless of the relationship between price and average cost. If price is above (or below) minimum average cost, the application of the $MC = P$ rule will yield economic profits (or losses), as illustrated in Fig. 10.3a (and 10.3b) of *PBCD*.

Turning to the economic behavior of resource owners, we may distinguish two cases: First, assuming free choice of occupation and given wage rates, individual workers maximize their incomes on the labor market by offering to sell their labor services to the highest bidder, as under competitive market capitalism, thus determining the supply of labor. Second, in regard to land and capital, government managers and officials are instructed to offer to direct these resources to

those industries able to pay or "account for" them at the prices given and set by the CPB, thus determining their supply. The purpose of this ruling is to allocate natural and capital resources in accordance with consumer preferences, as revealed by consumer demand prices on consumer goods markets. If, for example, consumer demand for automobiles is high, while that for bread, rice, or corn is low, it will be the producers of automobiles rather than those of harvesting equipment who will be best able to pay for large quantities of steel at given prices.

MARKET (OBJECTIVE) EQUILIBRIUM

Individual consumers, workers, and government managers are able to attain positions of equilibrium and, thereby, utility and income maximization, cost minimization, optimum output levels, and most efficient resource allocations only on the assumption of *given* prices. The equilibrium prices themselves are determined by the condition that demand for each commodity or resource equals its supply, since only under this condition are the subjective equilibrium-maximization positions of all individual units of economic decision consistent. Under competitive market capitalism, the equations in such a general equilibrium system actually are "solved" by a "trial-and-error" process based on the "parametric function of prices," that is, on the fact that all individual units regard prices as given parameters, even though equilibrium prices actually are determined by the collective market actions of all individuals via a series of successive trials.

In competitive market capitalism, the "parametric function of prices" arises "automatically and spontaneously" from the institutional structure of the economy and its markets. The model of decentralized socialism substitutes the "parametric function of prices" as an "accounting rule." All government managers and officials must regard all prices "as if" they were given and beyond their control, and make their decisions accordingly, even in cases where they know it is not true. One of the functions of the CPB is to impose the "parametric function of prices" as an accounting rule; to see to it managers truly base their calculations and decisions on given prices, and "not (to) tolerate any use of other accounting." [39: 81] If individuals, including government managers, regard prices as given and independent of their actions, then market equilibrium can be established for each commodity and resource by the same kind of successive "trial-and-error" process operative in the competitive capitalist model.

The social process of movement toward equilibrium in the consumer goods and labor markets presumably would occur "spontaneously and automatically," as under competitive market capitalism, given the assumptions of the model. In markets for other commodities and resources, the CPB itself functions as the "market." It first establishes accounting prices in these markets, either at random or on the basis of historical data. If the prices initially selected are "correct," supply will equal demand, and no adjustments will be needed. Any divergence of actual prices from equilibrium prices will be indicated "in a very objective way—by a physical shortage or surplus of the quantity of the commodity or resource in question— and would have to be corrected." [39: 82]

The mode of correction is simple: "Prices would have to be raised if demand exceeds supply and lowered if the reverse is the case." Each new set of prices "serves as a basis for new decisions which result in a new set of quantities demanded and supplied. Through this process of trial and error, equilibrium prices are finally determined." [39: 86] The conclusion: A substitution of decentralized socialist "planning for the functions of the market is quite possible and workable. . . . There is not the slightest reason why a trial and error procedure, similar to that in a competitive market, could not work in a socialist economy to determine the accounting prices of capital goods and of the productive resources in public ownership. . . . The argument that in a socialist economy (these prices) cannot be determined objectively, either because this is theoretically impossible, or because there is no adequate trial and error procedure available, cannot be maintained." [39: 83, 89–90]

AN ILLUSTRATION

These basic concepts of choice, allocation, and equilibrium in the Lange model are illustrated in Figs. 10.4a and 10.4b. The initial equilibrium positions are depicted for a market (say, steel) in 10.4b and for a plant within the industry in 10.4a.[3] For the market, the CPB, by a trial-and-error process, has settled upon an equilibrium price of OP_1, where $S = D_1$. Given price at OP_1, the industry manager has adjusted the number

[3] For ease in exposition and illustration, the following simplifying assumptions are made: (1) the industry initially contains one plant; (2) constant cost conditions exist for the industry—that is, diseconomies or economies of scale for the *industry* (factors which cause costs for *all* plants to rise or fall as industry output rises and which would be illustrated by upward or downward shifts in the *position* of cost curves for individual plants) are absent; (3) any succeeding plants have cost curves identical to those of the existing plant; (4) the example begins with a price tangent to the minimum point of the LAC curve, so that pure economic profits for the plant and industry are zero and each plant operates at its "optimum scale."

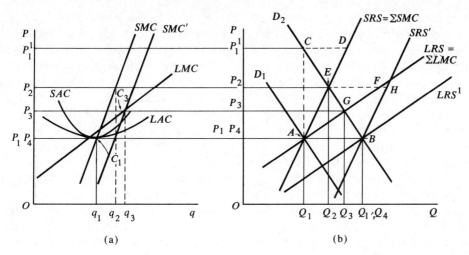

Fig. 10.4. (a) Enterprise adjustments, and (b) industry adjustments

and scale of plants so the marginal cost of the industry (or horizontal summation of the marginal costs of all individual plants, of which that in Fig. 10.4a is representative) is equal to OP_1. (This constitutes an equilibrium solution because the total industry output of OQ_1, as thus determined, just equals market demand at this price.) Given the scale of plant, represented by curves SAC and SMC, each *plant manager* has selected that level of output at which $SMC = price$, or Oq_1. At this level of output, resources are combined in the least costly way. (This is illustrated by the low position of the LAC curve, just as in Fig. 10.1, and by the equality between SMC and LMC.)

Now suppose a change in demand occurs; for example, an increase in the demand for automobiles and, thereby, an increase in the demand for steel of, say, 100 percent, illustrated by a shift in the market demand curve in Fig. 10.4b from D_1 to D_2. (Or, conversely, suppose a decrease in the demand for new homes and, thereby, a decrease in the demand for lumber, not illustrated in the diagrams.) What plausibly would happen in response to these changes?

In the *very short run*, where the proportions of variable to fixed resources, the scale of existing plants, and the number of plants all remain given, the increase in demand has created a deficit or shortage of $Q_1Q_1'(=AB)$ at the former going price of OP_1 (and a surplus of supply above demand in the lumber industry at the former market price). Accordingly, the CPB would raise the price of steel (and lower the price of lumber.) In the absence of any change in output, shortages of the commodity would continue to be reported until, by trial and error, the CPB had increased the price to OP_1'.

In the *short run*, where output may expand or contract through increases or decreases in variable resources, but where the scale of existing plants and the number of plants remain given, the new price lies above SMC. Accordingly, the *plant manager*, taking the new price as given and beyond his control and following the rule, expands output, by employing more variable resources in a given plant, to the point at which $SMC = price$. This expansion, illustrated by a movement up along SMC in Fig. 10.4a and SRS in Fig. 10.4b, would eventually create a surplus (CD in 10.4b.) The CPB then would reduce the price. By trial and error, the price would settle at OP_2, where $D_2 = SRS$ (point E in Fig. 10.4b). Given price at OP_2, the *plant manager* would adjust output to Oq_2 (equal to OQ_2), where $SMC = price$. (How would plant managers respond in the lumber industry?)

In the *long run*, one or both of two additional adjustments would be made, presumably, as one combined decision, but for the sake of illustration, let us separate them. First, given the number of plants (one, in this example), the *industry manager*, observing the excess of price above LMC at output Oq_2, would authorize an expansion in scale of the plant(s). (Similarly, the industry manager in the lumber industry would decrease the scale of plant by, say, failing to replace machinery when it wore out.) The *plant manager* also would have requested an increase in plant scale to meet Lange's Rule 1, that is, to minimize cost for any level of output by more efficient combination of resources. (At output Oq_2, $LMC < SMC$, indicating lower costs are possible by increasing the scale of plant and, thereby, increasing the ratio of fixed to variable resource.)

Presumably, the final selection of the new plant size would be determined by a trial-and-error process and by consultation between plant and industry managers (who in this instance are the same). If price were to remain at OP_2, the *industry manager*, following the rules, would select that scale of plant which would enable expanded output, with an optimum or least-cost combination of resources, to the point of equality between LMC and price OP_2. This scale of plant would be associated with a new SMC curve (not shown in the diagram) intersecting the LMC at that price. Given the new plant, the *plant manager* would select that output at which the new $SMC = price$. At this output/price/cost combination, the plant manager also would be minimizing cost according to the principle of least-cost combination of resources, since SMC would equal LMC. The expansion of output, however, illustrated by a movement up along the flatter LRS in Fig. 10.4b, eventually would create a surplus (of EF). The CPB then would reduce the price. By trial and error, the price finally would settle at OP_3, where $D_2 = LRS$ (at point G). The new market equilibrium would be attained partly through an increase

in quantity demanded (from E to G) and partly through a decrease in the output supplied by the industry (from F to G), caused by some reduction (though not to the original scale) in the scale of plant. The appropriate scale of plant authorized by the industry manager (illustrated by SMC' in Fig. 10.4a) would be that which would enable a level of output characterized by an equality between LMC and price OP_3 under conditions of least-cost combination of resources. Given the new plant scale, the *plant manager* would select output Oq_3 (equal, in this instance, to OQ_3,) where $SMC = price$ and $SMC = LMC$. (What adjustment would have occurred in the lumber industry?)

Second, the result of these adjustments, though in accordance with the rules ($S = D$, $LMC = SMC = P$) for *existing* plants, would not yet constitute a final equilibrium solution, for the *industry manager* must determine the optimum *number* of plants, and thus, the allocation of output between them as well. If all prospective plants have cost curves identical with those of existing plant(s), then it would be less costly, following the rules, to produce additional output beyond Oq_1 (equal to OQ_1) by building a new plant than by enlarging an existing one. In this event, the *industry manager* would keep the existing plant at the initial scale (illustrated by SAC and LAC in Fig. 10.4a) and authorize construction of a new plant. (In the lumber industry, an old plant would halt production.)

Were the increase in market demand large enough to justify it, the *industry manager* would build the new plant at the scale of the existing one. The price at OP_2 being given and beyond his control, the *manager of the new plant*, operating independently from the other plant manager and following the rule to equate SMC and *price*, also would wish to expand output to Oq_2. But, were this to occur, total industry output, measured along the new, higher SRS' curve in Fig. 10.4b, would exceed demand at price OP_2 (by EH). In that event, the CPB, following its own rule of price adjustment, would reduce the price. As price decreased, two equilibrating adjustments presumably would take place. On the one hand, the quantity demanded would increase (from E to B). On the other hand, the industry supply would decrease (from H to B). The price would finally settle at OP_4 (equal, in this instance, to the original price OP_1), where $D = S$ at industry output OQ_4 (equal to OQ_1'). Given this price, *each* of the *two plant managers* would adjust output to Oq_1, where $SMC = LMC = P$. Each plant would produce one-half of the total industry output, ($Oq_1 = 1/2\, OQ_4$), thus minimizing the cost by allocating total output between the two plants to equalize their marginal costs ($MC_1 = MC_2$). (Can you describe the analogous adjustments by the *CPB*, industry manager, and plant manager(s) in the lumber industry?)

AN EFFICIENT ALLOCATION OF RESOURCES

To summarize the implications of the Lange model of decentralized socialism for efficiency in the allocation of resources, using the marginal conditions described in Chapter 4:

1. Assuming freedom of consumer choice, an *optimum allocation of goods among households* would occur automatically by consumers buying those combinations of goods which they regard as most satisfactory in the light of given market-price ratios.

2. An *optimum specialization in production of goods* would be met when each plant increased production of each commodity to the point of equality between marginal cost and the given price.

3. Given a common ratio of commodity prices to resource prices for all plants and industries, the application of the $MC = P$ and, thereby, $VMP = resource\ price$ rule would simultaneously yield an *optimum allocation of resources among plants in the production of goods*.

4. If each plant and industry manager combined resources in the least costly way (where marginal productivity ratios equal resource price ratios), and resource price ratios were common to all managers, an equalization of marginal productivity ratios, the marginal condition for an *optimum combination of resources in the production of goods*, would also occur.

5. If households equalized marginal utility ratios with given price ratios (condition 1), and plant and industry managers followed the rule to equate marginal costs and (given) prices in all directions (condition 2), an *optimum composition in the production of goods* would ensue automatically because both households and managers face common price ratios which are given and beyond their control.

6. If households equalized the ratios of marginal disutility from the employment of their labor resources with given price ratios (the condition for their own maximization of satisfaction), and if resources were optimally allocated in the production of goods (condition 3), the fact that households and managers face common price ratios on labor markets automatically would generate *optimum employment of (labor) resources*. If managers of plants and industries providing other (non-labor) resources followed the rule to sell to anyone who wishes to buy at going prices up to the point of equality between marginal cost and price, the fact that resource suppliers and resource demanders face common prices would automatically promote an efficient or *optimum employment of (non-labor) resources*.

EFFICIENCY AND PROFITABILITY

In effect, the rules of the decentralized socialist model are those which would follow from the attempt to maximize profits under competitive market capitalism were prices beyond the control of suppliers and demanders. If plant and industry managers take prices as given and follow the rules to combine resources in the least costly way and to determine output and input levels as instructed, profits will be maximized, as in the competitive market capitalist model, and profitability and efficiency will coincide. (Granting this, one wonders why Lange didn't simply recommend the more general rule of profit maximization for plant and industry managers under a regime of given prices.)

Profit maximization, however, is equally consistent with positive, negative, or zero profit levels, depending on the relation between price and *average* cost. Profit maximization (or loss minimization) requires that *marginal* cost equals price. But this may coincide with positive profits ($P > AC$), negative profits ($P < AC$), or zero profits ($P = AC$).

In previous illustrations (Figs. 10.4a and 10.4b), price was tangent to the minimum point of the LAC curve, as well as equal to LMC. Thus, each plant operated at the optimum scale, and pure economic profits were zero. This resulted from our simplifying assumptions. (Fn. 3) It also would tend to result were the number of plants large and existing and impending plants had identical cost curves. Were the number of plants large, the addition or subtraction of any one of them would have an insignificant effect on total industry output. In this event, it would be possible to expand or contract the output of the industry in response to upward or downward shifts in market demand by magnitudes small enough to keep each plant at optimum scale with, for all practical purposes, perfect adjustment to changing demand in accordance with the $LMC = P$ rule. If all plants had identical cost-curves, none would have pure economic profits or losses while others were just breaking even. Even increasing cost or decreasing cost conditions in the industry wuld not affect this conclusion, because increases or decreases in cost-curves would be proportional for all plants, leaving their relative positions unchanged.

By contrast, modification of these assump-

tions or conditions can be accompanied by pure economic profits or losses at output levels where $LMC = P$. Suppose, for example, market demand is insufficient to match supply (equal to LMC) at minimum LAC. In this event, no output level permits the elimination of losses (though they are minimized where $LMC = P$), and the retention of the plant would require its subsidization. Alternatively, as a second example, suppose an increase in market demand causes the CPB to raise the price of a commodity above the minimum point of the LAC curve for existing plants, but that new plants have higher costs than existing plants. At least temporarily (until eliminated by increases in prices of those resources permitting the lower costs or by taxation), existing plants would receive pure economic profits. Thus, in Figs. 10.5a and 10.5b, an increase in price above OP_1 would entice industry managers to construct new plants rather than expand the scale of existing plants only when price had increased to OP_2, where the marginal cost of the new plants was no longer higher than those of the existing ones. The scale of existing plants (Fig. 10.5a), following the rule to equate LMC and price, would be expanded to increase output beyond the minimum LAC point, thereby attaining pure economic profits. To eliminate these profits, however, would require a change in scale of plant and output so that $LAC_1 = P_2$, thus

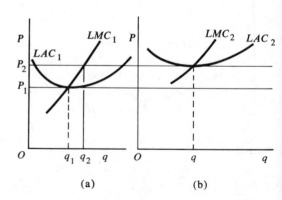

Fig. 10.5. (a) Low-cost plant, and (b) high-cost plant

breaking the rule to equate P and LMC. The rule also would be broken if the plant manager maintained output at Oq_1 and operated at the minimum point of LAC. The excess of price above LMC at this output and scale of plant indicates that an optimum allocation of resources, in accordance with consumer preferences, would require an increase in output to OQ_2, facilitated in the least costly way by expanding the scale of plant, even though the new scale would exceed the "optimum" level.

WHY BOTHER? THE CASE FOR SOCIALISM

At this point, one may ask: Why bother? Why shift from the present system to a socialist economy if the intended result merely is a reproduction of a decentralized system of economy structured to attain the characteristics, behavior patterns, and economic effects of competitive market capitalism? Lange himself recognized and raised this question when he asked: "But if competition enforces the same rules of allocating resources as would have to be accepted in a rationally conducted socialist economy, what is the use of bothering about socialism? Why change the whole economic system if the same result can be attained within the present system, if only it could be forced to maintain the competitive standard?" [39: 98–99]

Unsurprisingly, Lange had a ready answer for his own question. A change of the "whole economic system," he stated, is necessary and desirable for three reasons. First, socialism can do more than merely reproduce the efficient and consumer-directed allocational patterns of the competitive capitalist model; it can do these things "much better" and faster. Second, a socialist economy would or could be in a better position than capitalism (even at its best) to attain a variety of other social goals, namely greater equality and equity in the distribution of income,

economic growth, and full-employment stability. Third, the alternatives are not, in fact, socialism and competitive market capitalism, but socialism and the existing economic system, the "actual capitalist system." But the actual capitalist system is *not* purely nor perfectly competitive, nor is it probable (perhaps not even possible) for government action to make it so. Nor is government action of a non-socialist, but non-competitive, type likely to be effective in planfully resolving capitalism's pressing economic problems.

It should be noted that arguments one and two, in conjunction with Lange's general model of decentralized socialism, provide the essential ingredients of the decentralized socialists' answer to Hayek, Mises, and others, while the third argument, supplemented by the second, answers the Keynesians, social reform liberals, and others who believe capitalism can be "patched up" and, in a modified and guided form, "socially controlled." It should also be noted these arguments extend the discussion from the relatively restricted terrain and rigorous analysis of how (decentralized) "socialism can work" to a broader "case for socialism," a case which involves a greater number of political and ethical arguments and value judgments, and which, at points, relies upon arguments about socialism in general and/or centralized elements in economic organization not unique to a decentralized model. The reasoning which supports this "case" now will be summarized.

Allocation of Resources

THE EFFICIENCY OF A CPB PRICE SYSTEM

Lange presented two arguments to support his contention that a "trial-and-error" process could work "much better" under decentralized socialism than in competitive market capitalism. First, because the CPB has a "much wider knowledge of what is going on in the whole economic system than any private entrepreneur can ever have," equilibrium prices could be reached by a "much shorter" series of successive trials than a competitive market actually does thus avoiding "unnecessary waste" by "deliberately" using "anticipations . . . of demand and supply schedules. . . ." [39: 89, 89–90n] According to its rule of price adjustment, the CPB will raise price if demand exceeds supply and lower price if supply exceeds demand. But having a wider knowledge of market conditions than plant managers, it can move directly and quickly to what it expects would be the new equilibrium price in the event of shifts in supply or demand. This would reduce the *number* of iterations prior to establishment of equilibria. Further, having wider knowledge of general economic conditions than industry managers, it presumably would be in a better position (1) to assess whether shifts in market supply or demand were temporary or more permanent; (2) to determine interdependencies of demand and supply. (For example, an increase in demand for automobiles is likely to be accompanied by an increase in demand for steel, gasoline, and so on.) Thus, the CPB need not necessarily wait until demand and supply diverge to make *ex post* price changes, but could alter prices *ex ante* in anticipation of demand and supply shifts or divergencies, thus reducing the *time lags* in adapting to change.

Second, a decentralized socialist price system could be more comprehensive than that of a competitive capitalist economy, because it could or would be based upon calculations of social, not merely private, costs and benefits. Though the divergence of private and social costs in a capitalist economy may be largely "removed by proper legislation, taxation, and bounties . . . a socialist economy can do it with greater thoroughness." [39: 104] Presumably, the political pressures against charging enterprises for their external damages or social costs would be less under a system of government ownership, where plant and industry managers are agencies of and responsible to government authorities, than under capitalism. In addition to the costs directly incurred by plants and industries, the CPB could add a charge representing social costs. Automobile producers, for example, could be assessed for traffic congestion, carnage on the highways, smog, and, perhaps, unwed motherhood, as well as for steel, glass, rubber, machinery, and so on. Cigarette plants could be charged for cases of lung cancer. Lumber companies could be assessed for funds needed to conserve natural resources. Given these charges, plant and industry managers would function as before, in accordance with the rules. Consumer sovereignty would continue to prevail. But with upward shifts in cost-curves because of social costs (and downward shifts because of social benefits beyond those of the product itself), $LMC = P$ output levels would be lower (higher) than if social costs (and benefits) were ignored.

It should be noted these advantages in resource allocation are not "built-into" the workings of the model of *decentralized* socialism, nor are they unique to it. They are, rather, based on a presumed superiority of centralized over decentralized knowledge, and presumably would apply to other forms of socialism, for example, centralized, as well.

EFFICIENCY IN RESOURCE ALLOCATION
BETWEEN MARKETABLE AND COLLECTIVE
GOODS

In addition to setting and adjusting prices, the CPB also determines (or advises the government on the determination of) the magnitudes of collective goods (national defense, law and order, education, public health, and so on.). Socialists join a number of prominent non-socialists in contending that people are likely to want to extend irrationally the consumption of marketable goods relative to collective goods. (Cf. Part IV.) In a capitalist economy, pressures for keeping production and consumption of collective goods below optimum levels are supplemented, socialists argue, by the association of marketable goods with the private sector and collective goods with the public sector. By contrast, under socialism, both marketable and collective goods are produced, in a manner of speaking, by the "public sector." While marketable goods are sold to other enterprises or consumers, collective goods are ordered by and sold to the government. But both are produced under conditions of government ownership and control. Thus, deliberations about and determination of the allocation of resources between collective and marketable goods can be made free from the extraneous issue of "public" versus "private" enterprise. As a result, political and ideological opposition to the provision of collective goods would be less and a better balance would exist between collective and marketable goods than under capitalism.

Other Social Goals: Equality,
Full-Employment Stability, and
Economic Growth

The second major basis for the alleged superiority of the socialist model over the capitalist is that central authorities in a socialist economy would be in a better position to attain other important social goals in addition to efficient and consumer-directed allocation of resources.

EQUITY AND EQUALITY

Of these other goals, Lange, like most Western socialists, emphasized equity and equality in the distribution of income, but on bases drawn as much, if not more, from the welfare economics of English neo-classical economists Alfred Marshall and Arthur C. Pigou than from the literature of socialism. "Only a socialist economy," he argued, "can distribute incomes so as to maximize social welfare." [39: 99] Under capitalism, inequality in the distribution of ownership of land and capital helps to create inequality in the distribution of income. Assuming comparability and equality in the marginal

utility of income for all consumers, demand prices under capitalism do not "reflect the relative urgency of the needs of different persons. . . ." Thus, *even at its best*, a capitalist allocation of resources, determined by consumers' demand prices, "is far from attaining the maximum of social welfare. While some are starving, others are allowed to indulge in luxury." [39: 100]

Wage Differentials. Assuming freedom in the choice of occupation and consumption, the income distributional pattern required for "maximizing the total welfare of society" is twofold: (1) the same demand prices offered by different consumers must represent "an equal urgency of need"; (2) labor services must be allocated among different occupations so "as to make the differences of the value of the marginal product of labor in the various occupations equal to the differences in the marginal disutility involved in their pursuit." [39: 101–2]

Assuming comparability and equality in the marginal utility of income for all consumers, the first requirement would be met under conditions of income equality. Total utility is maximized when the marginal utility of income is equalized among different consumers; that is, when it is impossible to increase utility of anyone without decreasing the utility of someone else. If the marginal utility of income were the same for all households, this condition would occur when incomes were the same.

Though this conclusion follows logically from the underlying assumptions, contemporary economists are skeptical of the assumptions themselves. Lange defended them on practical grounds. Interpersonal comparisons of utility are necessary, he argued, as a basis for interpreting the effects of equilibrium conditions upon human welfare and for judging and choosing among different economic policies. Such comparison is made implicitly in the competitive capitalist model: "To deny the comparability of the urgency of the need of different persons and at the same time to regard the allocation of resources based on demand prices as the only one consistent with economic principles would be contradictory." [39: 101n]

Similarly, Lange recognized the assumption of equality of marginal utility of income "does not correspond to reality . . ." but argued that an income distributional pattern based on it "would strike the right average in estimating the relative urgency of the needs of "different persons, leaving only random errors, while the distribution of income in capitalist society introduces a constant error —a class bias in favor of the rich." [39: 102,103][4]

Because different occupations have different marginal disutilities, the second condition requires income inequality. Assuming freedom of choice in occupation, wage differentials are needed to attract workers to industries and occupations which they consider less desirable.

At first glance, these two conditions for income distribution appear contradictory, for the first requires equality, the second, inequality. But the contradiction is "only apparent," for, in a competitive labor market, the wage differentials under the second condition might be said to "compensate" for the differences in "leisure, safety, agreeableness of work," and so on, so that differences in money wage rates not only are

---

[4]Lange speculated on the possibility of recognizing interpersonal differences in the marginal utility of income by combining an equality in marginal utility of incomes with higher incomes for more "sensitive" individuals. (Boulding has termed this criterion the "to him that enjoyeth most what he has, to him should be given more" principle.) He discarded this possibility, however, partly because of its impracticability (how can one measure differences in "sensitivity"?) and partly because "differences in 'sensitiveness' existing in present society are chiefly due to the social barriers between classes, for example, a Hungarian count being more 'sensitive' than a Hungarian peasant. Such differences would disappear in the relatively homogeneous social stratafication of a socialist society, and all differences as to 'sensitiveness' would be of purely individual character." [39: 103]

compatible with, but *necessary* for, the attainment of equality in real (or "psychic") wage rates. [39: 101–2]

The compensatory principle would not explain wage differentials (under conditions in which wages equal the value of the marginal product of labor) in the cases of the "natural monopoly" of "exceptional talents" (for instance, prominent artists or surgeons), or of differences in education and training and their associated costs. However, because large portions of wage income in the first instance would probably constitute an "economic rent," that is, an excess of actual income above the minimum necessary to draw forth and maintain the supply of the resources in production, "a socialist society . . . might pay them incomes which are far below the value of the marginal product of their services without affecting the supply of those services." [39: 102n] In regard to the second instance, a properly organized socialist economy presumably would make educational opportunities and facilities free and equally available to all.

Non-Wage Income: The Social Dividend. Beyond the greater equality in wage income and the resulting "maximization of social welfare" associated therewith, a socialist economy presumably would be in a position to promote greater income equality through the elimination or large-scale reduction in incomes from privately-owned land and capital. A socialist economy characterized essentially by government ownership of the means of production would largely dispense with the distribution of rents, interest, and profits to private landlords and capitalists. Still, land and capital are productive, as well as scarce, resources, and generate income. Because they are scarce, they require economic calculation and coordination in any economic system. And because they are productive, a socialist economy requires a process to distribute the income generated by them.

Consider, for a moment, the government of a socialist economy as one giant enterprise. Revenues flow into it from the profits of plants and industries, from rent and interest payments for government-owned land and capital, from new money creation, and from taxes on households. Expenditures flow out of it in the form of orders to socialist enterprises for collective goods, transfer payments to households, and subsidies to enterprises where the $P = LMC$ point lies below LAC. If government demand for collective goods is higher than income from (net) profits, rents, and interest, the difference may be financed by new money creation or additional taxation (or borrowing from the public). If, by contrast, government demand for collective goods is smaller than profit-rent-interest income, the surplus may be distributed to households as a "social dividend" on the government-owned land and capital. Such a dividend, to be consistent with a system of consumer-directed allocation of resources and the "optimum distribution of labor services between the different industries and occupations," [39: 83] would have to be distributed so as to not affect the wage-directed choice of occupation and allocation of labor. For example, it could be divided equally, or "according to age or size of family or any other principle which does not affect the choice of occupation." [39: 84]

FULL-EMPLOYMENT STABILITY

Lange and other socialists also contend that a socialist economy would be in a better position than competitive market capitalism, even at its best, to maintain full-employment stability.

The bases for this argument are essentially threefold. First, potentially disruptive changes in the economy could be more easily localized, thus preventing partial overproduction from turning into general overproduction and obviating the need or tendency for general cumulative contraction in income, output, employment, and spending to spread "over the whole economic system" as in competitive market capitalism, where a private enterpreneur "*has* to close his plant when he incurs grave losses." Thus, "cumulative shrinkage of demand and output caused by a cumulative reduction of purchasing power could be stopped in a socialist economy." [39: 105–6]

Second, the CPB in a socialist economy surely would have all the macroeconomic controls available to central governing authorities in managed capitalist economies, that is, control over taxes, government spending, and the supply of money. If aggregate demand were insufficient to match aggregate supply at full employment utilization of resources, the CPB could reduce tax rates on households, increase government demand or government subsidies to households, expand the "social dividend," and/or increase the funds available for investment by socialist enterprises. If, by contrast, aggregate demand were temporarily in excess of aggregate supply at full employment, the CPB conversely could raise tax rates, reduce government demand for collective goods, retain government surpluses instead of paying out a social dividend and/or reduce the funds available for investment by socialist enterprises.

Thus, control over these instruments of macroeconomic policy should enable a socialist economy to be as efficient in the pursuit of full-employment stability as managed capitalism at its best. In addition, some of the major obstacles to the efficient application of these policy instruments in practice in capitalist economies presumably would be lower under socialism. For example, frictions between private business interests and government policy-makers presumably would ease. Increased government demand to ward off recession would not raise business fears of reductions in private demand or influence by the private sector, since plant and industry managers would be government employees. An expansion in the supply of money could be readily accomplished by "sales" of non-interest-bearing government bonds to the central bank, and need not inspire debates or fears over an increase in the "public debt" and interest payments on that debt. Further, a society willing to support widespread socialization of industry presumably would have no qualms about vesting the various instruments of macro-economic policy in one central planning body, thus promoting coordination and consistency in their application and reducing the time lags in government response to divergences between aggregate demand and supply.

Third, socialists contend divergencies between aggregate demand and supply at full employment would be extremely unlikely in a socialist economy. In capitalism, savers and investors are different people and save and invest for different reasons. Aggregate investment is the sum of a multitude of individual investments, and may or may not equal the aggregate volume of saving forthcoming in a fully employed economy. By contrast, even in decentralized socialist models, aggregate investment is determined by the CPB. At less than full employment, investment would be financed by the creation of money. At full employment, the decision to invest would be simultaneously accompanied by a decision to tax households to provide an amount of collective "saving" to just match the planned level of investment. Because aggregate investment and saving would be made centrally and simultaneously by the CPB, on the basis of the social goal of "the best use of all the productive resources available in the whole economic system" rather than the competitive capitalist aim of maximizing profit "on each separate investment", total investment "would be always" kept at levels "sufficient to provide full employment for all factors of production. . . ." [39: 106n] In sum: "There will be no question of 'saving' outrunning 'investment'; for investment will not be made out of individual saving, but out of planned appropriations of productive resources. . . . Nor

will 'investment' be able to outrun 'saving'; for the investment will be the saving."[5]

ECONOMIC GROWTH

An economy grows in two basic ways. One is by expanding actual output, given potential, full-employment output under given technological conditions. This occurs, for example, when an economy moves from a depressed state, characterized by unemployment, to or toward a full employment position. The second way is to increase potential (and actual) output at full employment by increasing the quantities of resources, improving efficiency in their allocation, and improving technology.

CPB control over the aggregate level of saving and investment, Lange and other socialists contend, maximizes the likelihood of the first kind of economic growth just explained. But, in addition to maintaining full employment, and thus, attaining whatever output level and rate of growth is potentially attainable at full employment of given resources and under given technological conditions, a socialist economy may also be able to promote as rapid, if not more rapid, a rate of growth in potential economic performance than capitalism. First, if, as seems plausible, the collectivization of aggregate investment enabled the CPB to increase capital accumulation as a percent of GNP, the rate of growth would be higher than under capitalism, even if capitalism functioned at full employment. Second, capital accumulation could be extended in a socialist economy without worrying about its effects upon the profitability of private (or past public) investment opportunities. At the plant and industry level, Lange argued, economic growth is encouraged by "any" cost-reducing innovation, regardless of its

---

[5]G.D.H. Cole, "The Place of Money in a Planned Economy," *New Statesman and Nation*, June 30, 1934, pp. 987–89. Reproduced in Wayne A. Leeman, *Capitalism, Market Socialism, and Central Planning* (Boston: Houghton Mifflin Company, 1963), p. 270.

effects on the value of past investments. Following Rule 1, to produce at minimum cost, plant and industry managers would be able to make productive innovations without worrying about their effects on the devaluation and obsolescence of old plant and equipment.

INVESTMENT AND CONSUMER SOVEREIGNTY

By substituting CPB determination of the aggregate level of investment and rate of capital accumulation for the saving-consuming preferences of households, the socialist economy departs from consumer sovereignty and, thereby, might be said to involve a "diminution of consumers' welfare." [39: 85] Many socialists have argued this disadvantage is more apparent than real because, under capitalism, saving-consuming preferences are profoundly affected by inequalities in the distribution of income inconsistent with the socialist egalitarian ethic and because of the failure of full-employment saving to be matched by investment in any event.

Though the CPB would determine the aggregate level of investment in the Lange model of decentralized socialism, its composition or allocation among industries and plants would be accomplished by the market. Each industry manager would decide the scale and number of plant(s) in his sector of the economy, given the interest rate for borrowed funds. If the sum of these demands for the entire economy exceeded the aggregate quantity of funds authorized by the CPB, the interest rate would be raised. If the economy-wide demand for loanable funds was lower than the CPB-determined saving, the interest rate would be lowered. Thus, the equilibrium rate would be determined by the same type of trial-and-error process described earlier. Given equilibrium interest rates, industry managers would then authorize the expansion of old plants or the construction of new ones, up to the point at which $LMC = P$, where costs would now include

interest (and, presumably, depreciation), thus allocating investment funds among the various producing units of the economy in accordance with consumer preferences.

The Alternatives: Decentralized Socialism versus Actual Capitalism

The last and "much more powerful argument" in Lange's "case for socialism" is that "the actual capitalist system is not one of perfect competition; it is one where oligopoly and monopolistic competition prevail." [39: 107] By inference rather than detailed analysis, Lange asserted that oligopolistic and monopolistically competitive markets (1) misallocate resources and generate economic inefficiency; (2) extend and intensify capitalist inequalities in income distribution; (3) remove the price flexibility that, in the more atomistically competitive economies of the nineteenth century, contributed to full-employment stability; and (4) through endeavors to maintain the values of past investments, slow down the rate of innovation and technological progress and, thereby, decrease the rate of economic growth.

A capitalist economy has two major ways to deal with the problem of monopoly—and neither is satisfactory. One would be "to return to free competition." This alternative, however, "does not seem to be possible because of the large size of modern business units." On economic grounds, a "return to free competition" could be accomplished only by atomizing present large-scale units of production. But this could be done only at the expense of losing economies of large-scale production and the contributions which mass production make to technological progress. On political grounds, the leaders of large-scale monopolistic and oligopolistic businesses are unlikely to support such vigorous monopoly-busting and are much more likely to utilize their considerable economic power to secure profitable government intervention and assistance. In the real world of pressure-group politics, governments are likely to "yield to the pressure of those powers." [39: 116, 118]

A second alternative would be government control and planning of production and investment within the framework of private ownership. But detailed government regulation and planning of business decisions under capitalism "can scarcely be successful." Because of their "great economic power," large-scale manufacturing and financial corporations would actually control managerial decisions, not public planning authorities. Even if government planners could and did control managerial decisions, such control would be unsuccessful because it would force private managers to do things (for example, to introduce innovations destroying old capital values) which conflicted with the goal of profit maximization and which would even impose financial losses. The resulting "constant friction" between government planners and private managers would "upset the financial structure of modern capitalist industry" and "paralyze business." In any event, large corporations and private financial institutions "could use their economic powers to defy the government authorities" and engage in various acts of "economic sabotage." This would compel the government to choose between yielding to business pressures and relinquishing government control or transferring recalcitrant and uncooperative businesses into government ownership and management, thus leading to socialism. [39: 119–20]

If it is impossible to return to free competition or to have effective public control and planning of private production and investment decisions, "then socialism will remain as the only solution available." [39: 121] In addition, when the model of a properly functioning decentralized socialist economy is compared with the "monopoly, restrictionism, and interventionism" [39: 120] of actual capitalism, rather than with the "formal principles" of the competitive capitalist model presented by economic theor-

ists, some of the traditional arguments against socialism lose much of their force. For example, argued Lange, "*the real danger of socialism is that of a bureaucratization of economic life. . . .* Unfortunately, we do not see how the same, or even greater, danger can be averted under monopolistic capitalism. Officials subject to democratic control seem preferable to private corporation executives who practically are responsible to nobody." [39: 109–10] Similarly, the efficiency of public officials in a socialist economy should be compared with that of executives of large-scale corporations, rather than with those in small-scale private enterprise. [Quotations from 39: 121, 120, 109–10][6]

CRITIQUE OF THE ECONOMIC THEORY OF DECENTRALIZED SOCIALISM

The Lange model of decentralized socialism has been subjected to critical evaluations from a variety of sources and on a number of bases. An interesting facet of this criticism is that some of the sharpest attacks have come from neo-liberals like Hayek and centralized socialists like Maurice Dobb and Paul Sweezy. The subject of comparative economic systems makes for strange bedfellows! Equally interesting is the intellectual support given the Lange model by the champion of industrializing, old-style capitalism, Joseph

---

[6]This implies the often-noted assertion that "socialism has simply to take over where big business leaves off. Economic units under socialism will be rationalized versions of the large corporation, with salaried executives and qualified specialists occupying the decisive managerial positions and with the functions of the board of directors in the hands of duly constituted public authorities." [9: 211–12] It is interesting to note that Schumpeter, in his critique of socialist theory, conceded even more than this. It is conceivable, he argued, "that socialist management may . . . prove as superior to big-business capitalism as big-business capitalism has proved to be to the kind of competitive capitalism of which the English industry of a hundred years ago was the prototype." [8: 196]

Schumpeter. Critical evaluation herein will be organized around a number of central questions and issues: Is the Lange model really socialism?—the question of terminology. Could it work?—its logical possibility. Would it work?—its empirical applicability. How well would it work?—a normative appraisal.

Is Decentralized Socialism Really Socialism?

Decentralized socialism (and the type of government economic planning associated with it) differs, in a number of striking and important ways, from both the classic Marxian version and contemporary centralized models of socialism, and draws heavily from the analysis, value systems, and experience of market capitalism and "bourgeois" economic theory. Neo-liberals have drawn upon this as evidence of the abandonment of traditional socialist hopes and illusions. Thus, according to Hayek, the "younger socialists ... have abandoned the belief in a centrally planned economic system and pinned their faith on the hope that competition may be maintained even if private property is abolished.... The hope of a vastly superior productivity of a planned system over that of 'chaotic' competition has had to give place to the hope that the socialist system may nearly equal the capitalist system in productivity. The hope that the distribution of income may be made entirely independent of the price of the services rendered and based exclusively on considerations of justice, preferably in the sense of an egalitarian distribution, has to be replaced by the hope that it will be possible to use part of the income from the material factors of production to supplement income from labor. The expectation that the 'wage system' would be abolished, that the managers of a socialized industry or firm would act on entirely different principles from the profit-seeking capitalist, has proved to be equally wrong." [4: 177, 186]

"It is idle," Hayek feels, to ask whether decentralized socialism "still falls under what is usually considered as socialism." On the whole, it seems, it should be included under that heading. "More serious," however,

> ... is the question whether it still deserves the designation of planning. It appears not to involve much more planning than the construction of a rational legal framework for capitalism. If it could be realized in a pure form in which the direction of economic activity would be wholly left to competition, the planning would also be confined to the provision of a permanent framework within which concrete action would be left to individual initiative. And the kind of planning or central organization of production which is supposed to lead to an organization of human society more rational than 'chaotic' competition would be completely absent. [4: 161]

"[At the very least] much of the original claim for the superiority of planning over competition is abandoned if the planned society is now to rely for the direction of its industries to a large extent on competition." [4: 186]

Similar doubts about the *bona fide* status of decentralized market socialism are expressed by various representatives of the centralized school of thought, though for strikingly different reasons. Centralized socialists consider the Lange model useful as a logical exercise and as a refutation of the criticisms by Mises and Hayek. But they clearly regard it as a weak-livered, "bourgeois" deviation from how a real socialist economy is or should be run. Thus, Dobb contends, Lange has replaced the *a prioristic* arguments about the "impossibility of socialism" of Mises and others with a modified *a prioristic* argument of his own; namely, with the "categorical imperative" that a socialist economy must utilize the "particular mechanism" of the competitive price system. But "there is no valid reason" to support the necessary utilization of the competitive market—"to deduce it, Mises-like, from the 'nature of the economic problem' as the imperative solution." [31: 241, 243] "Such a system," urges Paul Sweezy in a similar vein, "is certainly conceivable, but most socialists will probably feel that it reproduces some of the worst features of capitalism and fails to take advantage of the constructive possibilities of economic planning." [9: 253] "Not much useful purpose," suggested Paul Baran, "is served by considering planning in a socialist society as directed towards the attainment of 'optima' the contents of which are borrowed from the individualistic value system of the capitalist world or from some personal predelictions of the writers." [26: 384]

The essence of socialist economic planning, according to Dobb, is *ex ante* coordination of the national economy, especially of investment priorities. In decentralized market socialism, "much of the uncertainty that is characteristic of a system of 'anarchy of production' (arising from atomistic diffusion of decisions and from competition) would still remain. . . ." [31: 241] Maladjustments resulting from this uncertainty could, of course, be corrected, but only *ex post*, thus depriving the socialist economy of the important advantage of planful foresight. In a similar vein, Sweezy insists that, "in any actual socialist society," the CPB would formulate and execute a more or less comprehensive "plan" embodying directives regarding output and input quantities, combinations, and allocations, not merely or primarily adjustments of accounting prices. "The truth is that Lange's Board is not a *planning* agency at all but, rather, a price-fixing agency; in his model production decisions are left to a myriad of essentially independent units, just as they are under capitalism." In practice, "a socialist economy will be centrally planned in a sense very different from that in which Lange's model may be said to be centrally planned." [9: 238, 233]

Whatever one's preferences as to terminology, it is clear that, though a member of the socialist family and sharing with the socialist movement and literature certain common features and aspirations, decentraliz-

ed or market socialism is definitely a "mixed" system, sharing certain features traditionally and historically associated with the theory and practice of market capitalism. The Lange model provides the useful *tour de force* of distinguishing clearly between ownership of the means of production and social processes for coordinating economic decisions as criteria for identifying, classifying, and comparing economic systems. Just as recent students of capitalism have argued that it should be possible to combine private ownership with social and government control and coordination, the model of decentralized socialism posits the possibility of a mixture of public ownership and coordination and control by the institutions and/or rules of the competitive price system. This is illustrated in Fig. 10.6. If Mises and Hayek are right, the price system may be combined with private ownership (Case 1, Competitive Market Capitalism), and government ownership may be combined with government bureaucracy (Case 2, Centralized Socialism). But if the Lange model makes sense, then Case 3, combining government ownership and the price system, is also possible. (Case 4, combining private ownership and government bureauc-

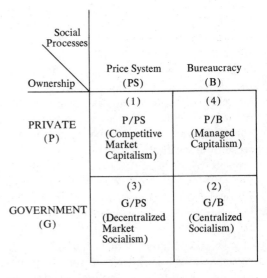

Fig. 10.6. Combinations of social processes and ownership criteria

racy, is another mixture, to be examined in the discussion of managed capitalism in Chapter 13.)

Could and/or Would Decentralized Socialism Work?

No real debate now exists among Western economists as to whether the Lange model of decentralized socialism could work. "No doubt is possible" [8: 167] that it could, argued Schumpeter, assuming the successful resolution of transition problems and the attainment of a requisite high level of economic development. Private ownership is not now regarded as a *logically necessary* requisite for the existence of a pricing system as a social process for economic calculation. This conclusion is hardly startling if we remember the logic of decentralized socialism is essentially that of the model of the competitive price system, formulated and developed to fine-tuned precision by *non-socialist* economists. As Schumpeter stated, both capitalism and socialism borrow from "the perfectly general logic of choice," and thus, exhibit an "essential sameness . . . of economic logic. . . ." [8: 182] The crucial point is accounting prices. If we abstract from the acceptability, workability, and prospective efficiency of decentralized socialism, there would seem to be no reason to doubt the *possibility* of the establishment and utilization for purposes of economic calculation of such a government price system. The economic theory of decentralized socialism appears to meet the test of logical consistency. Even contemporary neo-liberal critics of socialism focus the brunt of their critique on the practicability of the socialist model. Friedrich Hayek, for example, commends the Lange model for its "intellectual quality" and its "thoroughness—its thoroughly unorthodox" and "courageous" attempt "to face some of the real difficulties and completely to remodel socialist doctrine in order to meet them . . ." but concludes: "whether the solution offered will appear particularly practicable,

even to socialists, may perhaps be doubted." [4: 207, 208]

Granting, then, that decentralized socialism's logical credentials are in order, does or would it work in practice? There are at least three difficulties in the path of reaching a valid answer to this. First, the Lange model was a theory of a *prospective, not an actual*, economic system. Thus, its practicability cannot be verified (nor disverified) by testing the extent of its correspondence to some actual, existing national economy. The fact that, say, the Polish or British economic systems of the 1970s do not closely correspond to the Lange model of the 1930s does not prove that either or both at some future time might not or will not so correspond. On the other hand, one may challenge, on methodological grounds, an exclusive study of prospective, as opposed to actual, economic systems. Many contemporary socialists, especially of the centralized variety, consider this prospective-normative cast of the decentralized socialist model to be a major defect. Thus, Baran labeled "most of the literature on socialist economics" as "utopian" and escapist. [26: 382] Polish economist Jan Drewnowski argues that a "theory of socialism should start from an analysis of the existing socialist systems." Existing socialist literature, of which the Lange model is the prime example, "takes an approach that is far from realistic and might even be termed utopian. Incredible as it may seem, the convictions of the authors, rather than the realities of socialist economies, are taken as the basis for theories. . . . Lange's theory was a considerable intellectual achievement, but it did not explain any reality because its premises were never based in existing conditions." [32: 341–42]

Second, how workable is "workable"? It might mean simply that decentralized socialism would or might survive, that it would not degenerate into economic anarchy and chaos, and that the problems of economic calculation and coordination would be manageable at some unspecified level of efficiency and success. If we accepted this relatively unambitious test, then, again, our answer probably would be in the affirmative: decentralized socialism would be workable. Thus, according to Schumpeter, the Lange-type model of socialism is "eminently operational; that is to say, it not only establishes a logical possibility but in doing so also shows the steps by which this possibility can be realized in practice." [8: 185] And, according to Hayek: It is "not the possibility of planning as such which has been questioned . . . but the possibility of successful planning. . . . There is no reason to expect that production would stop, or that authorities would find difficulty in using all the available resources somehow, or even that output would be permanently lower than it had been before planning started." [4: 149–50] If we go beyond the simple, unambitious test of economic survival, however, the question of workability enlarges into the greater test of *how well* a socialist economy could and/or would work.

Third, what is meant by "workable"? It might mean simply that the rules of the CPB, *if followed* by decentralized managers, would be a workable basis for a rational calculation of costs and benefits and an efficient, consumer-directed allocation of resources. If so, decentralized socialism would be workable, just as competitive market capitalism would be workable *if* the institutional bases for the enforcement of the rules, that is, pure-perfect competition, existed in reality. But a very important question is that of the *administrative feasibility* of enforcing Lange's rules. If a socialist price system is to work, decentralized managers must be induced to follow the rules of the CPB. They must regard accounting prices as given and beyond their control even when they know that prices are subject to change by government action and subject to control by managerial discretion. "Clearly," argues Hayek, "this will not do." [4: 197] At the very least, how plant and industry managers "are to be induced to respond to their prescriptions in a mandatory price system is a large and relatively un-

examined issue." The economic theory of decentralized socialism "has not attacked the question of whether adequate incentives can be constructed to make the signals effective for control. It is this limitation in the theoretical prescriptions that makes it possible, though somewhat misleading, to say, as has been said, that economic theory has shown a socialist price system to be economically, but not politically, workable." [1: 188]

How Well Would Decentralized Socialism Work?

GENERAL OBSERVATIONS

Presuming that decentralized socialism would and could work, the question remains: How well? To begin with, it is essential in critical evaluations of comparative economic systems to distinguish between models of ideally working systems (purely competitive capitalism, decentralized socialism, and so on) and actual, competing national economies (such as the economic systems of the United States or Soviet Russia). Often, defenders of capitalism compare the practical problems of economic organization in, say, Soviet Russia, with highly idealized pictures of non-existent, atomistically competitive price systems. Socialist economists—and here, Lange is a prominent example—equally often compare models of ideally functioning socialist economies free from frictions, uncertainties, and imperfections with the practical problems of economic instability, inequality, and monopoly in, say, the United States or Great Britain. Such comparisons are inadequate and misleading. A comparison of ideal models with ideal models and practical problems with practical problems as well as ideals with practice would provide a fuller and better basis for critical evaluation.

Second, a critical evaluation of the economic theory of decentralized socialism should be clear about the goals postulated and the assumptions or basic premises of the model. In regard to goals, the Lange model has been subjected to two quite different kinds of criticism. Neo-liberals, such as Hayek, accept the central goal of consumer-directed production and the result of individual freedom of choice in general, but have serious reservations about the prospective efficiency of decentralized socialism in attaining its goals. The Western centralized socialists, on the other hand, dissent from consumer sovereignty, at least as the primary, overriding objective of economic organization, and substitute the goal of rapid industrialization and economic development as the most important single test of the performance of an economic system.

In any event, the objectives of a society presumably will have a profound effect on the organization and behavior of the economic system—on the institutions and instruments chosen to attain goals and on priorities in the fundamental organizational structure of the economy, for example, the blend of centralization and decentralization. Part of the "utopian" quality of the Lange model lies in the unexplored premise that socialist governments place or would place a high priority on resource allocational efficiency (relative, say, to rapid growth, full employment, or income redistribution), and consumer-directed production.

In regard to assumptions and basic premises, the Lange model has been criticized from both Right and Left. Hayek, for example, criticizes its "excessive preoccupation" with problems of "the pure theory of stationary equilibrium" and "perfect competition." With "given and constant data" and standardized commodities, he argues, the equilibrium which Lange described "could indeed be approached by the method of trial-and-error." But the real, "practical problem" is not this "hypothetical equilibrium," but the question of which system of economic organization "will secure the more rapid and complete adjustment to the daily changing conditions in different places and different industries." As a matter of "practical judgment," Hayek finds it difficult to believe anybody would

doubt the "inferiority" of decentralized socialism as compared to imperfect, but workably competitive, capitalism. [4: 188]

Similar criticisms have been made by the centralized socialists. Maurice Dobb, for example, argues that the entire debate about "economic calculation in a socialist economy" was conducted at such a formal, abstract level that important qualifications were "ignored and a false impression of precision and certainty conveyed." [31: 60] Paul Baran concurred, arguing that, under "static assumptions, with 'consumers sovereignty' determining the allocation of resources . . . rational calculation is just as possible under socialism as under competition. . . . Under dynamic assumptions, in particular under conditions of rapid change in all 'data', no mechanical device can assure such rationality, either under capitalism or under socialism." [26: 386n]

Third, how well decentralized socialism would work in practice depends upon political, sociological, and psychological factors, as well as economic ones. We have already observed one important gap in the Lange model, namely, that in any actual economy, rules for economical calculation must be supplemented by psychologically acceptable and administratively workable incentive systems, by techniques of reward and punishment. It seems reasonably clear, as Schumpeter argued, that the "human element" in the workability of decentralized socialism would *not* require "demigods and archangels." Still, the "problems of bureaucratic management" (or, in Schumpeter's words, the "rational exploitation of the bourgeois stock") [8: 205] would certainly be a difficult problem— and one which the Lange model largely ignores, on the unsatisfying grounds that it "belongs to the field of sociology rather than of economic theory and must therefore be dispensed with here." [39: 109] Another prominent example: In insisting the power of capitalists and large-scale corporate enterprise would prevent effective programs of government anti-monopoly policy or non-socialized government planning in capitalist economies, Lange went "beyond the boundaries of economic theory" into politics and sociology. "All the more conspicuous is his failure to do so in other parts of his system."[7] The failure to recognize the possibility of political and administrative obstacles or imperfections in a socialist economy is "naive," suggests Kenneth Boulding. "Any realistic theory of the socialist . . . economy must operate in terms of an equilibrium of political and administrative processes," and there is "no reason to suppose that these pressures will be any more perfect in a socialist than in a market economy."[8]

DECENTRALIZED SOCIALISM AND
EFFICIENCY IN RESOURCE ALLOCATION

Criticism of the decentralized socialist model of resource allocation has been essentially twofold. On the one hand, problems of economic calculation and management, especially in relations between plant and industry managers and the CPB, raise important questions about the prospective vitality and effectiveness of the simulated competitive price system within the setting of government ownership. On the other hand, though this model was based on the simulation of competitive markets as a dominant social process for resource allocation, Lange was very unperceptive as to the possibility of monopoly elements or propensities existing or emerging in a socialist economic system.

The CPB: An Effective Substitute for the Competitive Market? Critics of decentralized socialism contend that price determination by a CPB would be a cumbersome and inefficient substitute for the spontaneous processes of

the competitive market. Hayek has been especially noted for his identification of some prospective limitations of the Lange-type model of socialist competition. His major arguments include:

1. If prices are determined by the CPB rather than the market, delays and time lags plausibly will occur. Plant and industry managers will have to report shortages or surpluses of commodities or resources to the CPB. This data then will have to be verified and sorted out to remove contradictions (unless that task is performed by industry managers). Finally, new prices will have to be set for some specified future date (unless an "elaborate system" is to be established, whereby managers are "constantly notified" of new prices, upon which they then determine output and input requirements.) [4: 192–93]

2. Time lags and sluggish adjustments by the CPB will be heightened by two crucial factors: complexity in the number and variety of commodities, and the variety and rapidity of changes in tastes, resource discoveries, technological improvements, and so on. Because of these factors, the CPB will be inclined to make price changes at infrequent intervals, rather than in terms of "rapid and complete adjustment to the daily changing conditions in different places and different industries." [4: 188]

3. In competitive market capitalism, much competition occurs in terms of "special circumstances of time, place, and quality." Because the number of such circumstances is "practically infinite," the CPB plausibly would simplify its task by setting prices for broad classes of goods. As a result, price differences based on such differences in quality, time, and place would be reduced, and managers would have little or no inducement or even "real possibility to make use of special opportunities, special bargains, and all the little advantages

---

[7]Carl Landauer, *European Socialism*, Volume II (Berkeley: University of California Press, 1960), p. 1656.

[8]Kenneth E. Boulding, *Principles of Economic Policy* (Englewood Cliffs, N.J.: Prentice-Hall, Inc., 1958), p. 26.

offered by their special local conditions, since all these things could not enter into their calculations." [4: 193]

4. At the same time that competition in quality, time, and place is reduced and prices become less sensitive to these differences, and thus, less accurate as indices of alternative opportunities, managers who follow the rules and take prices as given become mere "quantity adjustors." They thereby forego the often socially beneficial practice of price competition, that is, inducing their customers to buy more by price cuts or their suppliers to offer more by price increases. By following Lange's second rule (equating marginal cost to a *given* price), managers may well violate the spirit of the first rule (cost minimization) because "one of the most important forces which in a truly competitive economy brings about the reduction of costs to the minimum discoverable will be absent, namely, price competition." In competitive market capitalism, a powerful force for cost minimization "is the opportunity for anyone who knows a cheaper method to come in at his own risk and to attract customers by underbidding the other producers. But, if prices are fixed by the authority, this method is excluded." [4: 196]

Monopoly: Consumer Goods and Labor Markets. In the decentralized socialist model, free markets exist for consumer goods and labor. The CPB does *not* determine prices in these sectors of the economy. These markets *may* be characterized by competitive conditions, but they may as easily be characterized by elements of monopoly or oligopoly. This places a socialist government in a dilemma somewhat similar to that of monopoly/oligopoly capitalism. If the government or CPB establishes tight control over price and production policies of individual plants and industries, the result (presuming

it is workable)[9] is government regularation and ownership, rather than free markets. If, on the other hand, managers of government-owned enterprises are given a free hand in price and production policies, then, except in industries characterized by large numbers of sellers and homogeneous products, the enterprises will wield varying degrees of market power. In this event, the "parametric function of prices," dependent upon (actual or simulated) pure competition, will not exist.

This is not an argument against the efficiency of resource allocation under socialism *as compared to* capitalism. Further, the substitution of government ownership for private ownership may facilitate somewhat the public control and regulation of monopoly and oligopoly. But the elimination of private ownership does not in itself establish competitive markets in consumer goods or labor, and it is plausible to expect a socialist economy to have attendant monopoly/oligopoly problems. (Also, it presumably would have to resolve issues associated with labor unions, collective bargaining, worker control over industry and participation in management decisions, and so on. These issues, neglected in the Lange-type model of decentralized socialism, are of considerable significance in contemporary theories of managed capitalism, democratic socialism, and Yugoslav and revisionist Communism.)

Monopoly: Markets for Producer Goods and Non-Labor Resources. In Lange's model of decentralized socialism, prices in markets

---

[9]Just as the complexities of modern industrial organization have led to a separation of ownership and management in large-scale private corporations in capitalist economies and place distinct limitations upon control over corporate decisions by stockholding capitalists, so, too, might the exigencies of public corporations under socialism lead to a separation of public owners and mangers and place strategic limits on control over socialist enterprises by society or its representative, government. See J. K. Galbraith, *The New Industrial State* (Boston: Houghton Mifflin Company, 1971), pp. 98–108.

for producer goods, land, and capital are determined by the CPB, rather than by spontaneous market forces. But once set, the "parametric function of prices" is to be imposed as an "accounting rule": that is, for plant and industry managers, prices are given and beyond their control.

In industries satisfying the structural conditions of pure competition (a large number of sellers and homogeneous products), this accounting rule would be quite plausible for *plant or enterprise managers*. In these rare but conceivable instances, the size of the individual producing unit would be so small that its impact on the total output (and hence, indirectly, the price) of the industry would be negligible. Consequently plant managers would have no option but to adjust output and input levels and combinations as best they could, given prices, whether these prices were determined by spontaneous market supply and demand forces or by the market-simulated decisions of the CPB.

But, in all other industries, ranging from monopolistic competition through oligopoly to pure monopoly, plant managers, by virtue of the large relative size of the enterprise and/or product differentiation, would be able to exert significant control over industry supply and, thereby, indirectly, the price that the CPB would set. In all industries, including purely competitive ones, *industry managers* would function as monopolists in determining the scale or size of plants and, thereby, the output of the industry as a whole.

Three examples are shown in Figs. 10.7a, 10.7b, and 10.7c. Fig. 10.7a illustrates an industry with a single plant, that is, monopoly. If the CPB adjusts price in the event of divergence between supply and demand so as to clear the market, the price would eventually move toward and settle at OPc, where industry supply (equal to the marginal cost of the monopolistic enterprise) equals market demand. If the plant and industry manager (they are the same in this instance) follow the rules, take the CPB-determined price as beyond their control, and adjust the output level and scale of plant to equate marginal cost with price, output would move toward OQc, that is, the competitive level. But suppose the plant/industry manager produces a smaller output. Because market demand is negatively sloped, marginal revenue lies below and diverges from it (as in Fig. 4.7). Profits would be higher at output OQm, where $MC = MR$, that is, the monopoly level. Were output restricted to this level, demand would exceed it at price OPc. Consequently, the CPB, following its own rule of price adjustment, would raise the price. Eventually, the price would be raised to OPm, that is, the monop-

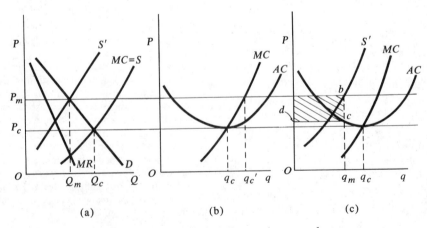

Fig. 10.7. Decentralized socialism and monopoly power

oly level. In the absence of a careful audit of the records and behavior of the enterprise-industry, the CPB would have no way of knowing that the equality of market demand and output level OQm at price OPm constituted a divergence from the rules.

Now let Fig. 10.7b illustrate a single small-scale plant in a purely competitive industry. For its manager, price is truly given, not because it is set by the CPB and imposed as an accounting rule, but because the plant is too small to have an appreciable effect upon industry supply. Given price at, say, OPc, it will dutifully follow the rule to equate its marginal cost with price by setting its output at Oq_c. But the manager of the competitive *industry* as a whole faces the same negatively sloped demand curve as the monopolistic plant-industry manager in Fig. 10.7a. If the industry manager behaves monopolistically but simulates a competitive solution, he will permit each *plant* manager to produce up to the point of equality between MC and *price*, but will withdraw some plants from production (by failing, for example, to construct new plants when old ones deteriorate) and restrict industry output to, say, OQm. At this lower output, demand would exceed supply, and the price would be raised to, say, OPm. The plants that remained in production would each expand output to, say, Oqc', but total *industry* output would be at the lower monopoly level because of the smaller number of plants.

Now suppose (with an appropriate change in the scale on the horizontal axis) Figs. 10.7b and 10.7c represent two plants in an oligopolistic industry, and Fig. 10.7a, the industry as a whole. Suppose the industry manager and the plant manager in Fig. 10.7b wish to follow the rules and the plant manager in 10.7c wishes to simulate them. By restricting output to, say, Oq_m, the deviant plant manager causes a significant decrease in industry output. In effect, his desired supply (and the resulting industry supply), as distinguished from his actual marginal cost curve, shifts down to $s'(S')$. As a result, market demand exceeds industry supply, and

the CPB, following its own rule, would raise price. As price rises, demand would decrease and the non-deviant plant manager in Fig. 10.7b, following the rules, would expand his output. Eventually, price would rise to the point where the combination of the decrease in demand and the increase in output by the other plant would just equal the illicit cut in output by the plant manager in Fig. 10.7c. Suppose price initially were equal to average cost; both plants now would receive pure economic profits, output in each would diverge from minimum long-run average cost, and the successfully deviant oligopolist would produce inefficiently at an output where price exceeded marginal cost. Still, the CPB, the industry manager, and the non-deviant plant manager all would be following the rules. The market would be cleared, the non-deviant plant manager would equate marginal cost with (the higher) price, and the industry manager would equate what he thought was industry marginal cost with the CPB-determined price.

Costs, Profits, and Managerial Incentives. Clearly, if the dispersion and delegation of economic power to plant and industry managers is to be consistent with the social goal of an efficient allocation of resources, managers must follow the rules. To accomplish this, an incentives and control system is required. Managers must find it advantageous and rewarding to follow the rules and disadvantageous to diverge from them. At the same time, the CPB needs some simplifying device to detect and measure the success of managers.

One such device would be to instruct managers to maximize profits. Salaries and promotions then could be tied directly to profit levels: Higher profits would be associated with higher managerial salaries and faster promotions, and vice-versa. This would directly link managerial performance and reward and, at the same time, simplify the process by shifting emphasis from the structure of the rules to results (profits). It would certainly be conducive to managerial pursuit of Lange's first rule (cost minimization) because anything which lowers cost, given output, raises profit. *Given prices*, whether determined by market forces or by the CPB, it would also automatically encourage the pursuit of Lange's second rule because, in this instance, price equals marginal revenue, and the condition for profit maximization ($MC = MR$) and the efficiency rule ($MC = P$) coalesce.

The difficulty with all this is that it presumes what should be proven, that is, that managers *will* regard prices as given and beyond their control, when, in many instances, as described earlier, their actions can serve to indirectly manipulate prices. If managers are encouraged to maximize profits through an incentives system which links profits to salaries and promotions, they may be also encouraged to cheat. All industry managers and plant managers (except those in purely competitive industries) have a built-in incentive to behave monopolistically, that is, to gain higher profits by restricting output and letting the CPB raise prices, thereby sacrificing efficiency and consumer satisfaction (the prime goal) for profitability (the intermediate success indicator).

Pressures for Centralized Control. Decentralized socialist models contain significant opportunities for centralized control. These include, as already noted, the determination of the total level of investment, the level of collective consumption, the level of foreign trade, and the prices of capital, land, intermediate goods, and interest rates. In addition, problems of promoting compliance with the rules will plausibly inject further pressure for centralization. Profit *maximization* does not necessarily result in large *profits*, and *large* profits do not necessarily demonstrate profit *maximization*. For purposes of economic efficiency, the crucial comparison would be between actual and potential profits, not simply between profit levels of different plants and industries. Further, to ensure efficiency

and low-cost production and to offset monopoly power and cheating by plant and industry managers, the CPB will be tempted to extend an apparatus of investigation, auditing, and supervision. On the one hand, critics argue, it is questionable that an auditing system necessary for this task is practicable in a modern, complex, industrialized economy. On the other hand, if actually achieved, the CPB, for all practical purposes, would be doing or placing itself in a position to do the tasks decentralized managers should be doing. The resulting duplication of data gathering and evaluation, red tape, and conflicts between central planners and plant/industry managers would result in inefficiency and waste of resources and, at worst, in the elimination of the delegation and dispersion of economic power that is the hallmark of the decentralized socialist model.

DECENTRALIZED SOCIALISM AND OTHER SOCIAL GOALS

As we have seen, the theory of decentralized socialism, at least the Lange version, provides a more rigorous analysis of efficiency in resource allocation than of such other policy goals as economic growth, full-employment stability, and equity-equality in income distribution. Partly for this reason, these dimensions of the Lange model have not been subjected to the probing critique that has emerged in regard to the central issue of resource allocation. Still, critics of decentralized socialism have raised a number of key questions in these areas as well, especially regarding the appropriate blend of centralization and decentralization.

Economic Growth and Stability: Centralization and Decentralization in Investment. The issue of the appropriate blend of centralization and decentralization is most controversial in regard to the goals of economic growth and stability.

The Neo-Austrian Critique. Neo-Austrian economists, notably Friedrich Hayek, criticize the separation of the issues of the level and allocation of investment, and ask how the incentives and control process can be expected to work effectively in investment decisions. If industry managers are rewarded (by higher salaries and promotions) on the basis of profits and punished (by salary cuts and demotions) in the event of losses, they may well behave like monopolists, play it safe, avoid risky investments, and refrain from technical progress.

On the other hand, if profits are not a success indicator and managers do not bear financial responsibility for losses, two unfortunate results may ensue. First, freed from financial responsibility, managers, perhaps conscientiously and in accordance with a desire to follow the rules, "will be tempted to embark upon all sorts of risky experiments on the bare chance that one of them will turn out successful."[10] Second, since large profits are not necessarily an indication that managers have followed the rules, the CPB may be tempted to extend supervision and auditing over the vital area of allocation of investment funds. How, then, would investment allocations be decided in the (likely) result of divergence of opinion and expectations between industry managers and the CPB? If the CPB simply rubber-stamps applications for funds by industry managers, it abdicates control over investment decisions. But if applications must be "examined and approved" by the CPB, it will, in effect, have taken over the function of investment and, thereby, have substituted centralized bureaucratic for decentralized market control of the investment process. [4: 198]

The Centralized Socialist Critique. The Western neo-Marxist centralized socialists also criticize the separation of the level and allocation of investment, though from a radically different vantage point. Whereas

control over the former is necessary to determine the overall rate of economic growth, control over the latter is necessary to determine its direction. The Western neo-Marxists present three major criticisms of the decentralized/centralized process of investment in the Lange model.

First, they contend, the central issue of socialist economies in practice has been and is likely to continue to be rapid industrialization and economic growth, rather than allocational efficiency in accordance with consumer sovereignty. Thus, the Lange model and other theories of allocational efficiency in decentralized socialism, though useful in answering the exaggerated claims of the neo-Austrians, are characterized by misplaced emphasis.

Second, rapid industrialization and economic growth may benefit from, indeed, may require, a considerably larger dose of centralization in decision-making than envisaged in the Lange model. For example, the rate of growth may well depend upon such strategic factors as the geographic location of industry and the allocation of investment funds among different sectors and industries (determined in the Lange model by competitive bidding rather than by the CPB), as well as the determination of the aggregate level of saving and investment. In addition, the essence of economic planning, they contend, lies in *ex ante* coordination. Under (the Lange version of) decentralized socialism, the CPB would make readjustments in prices and allocation of investment funds according to altered supply and demand conditions. But, argue the advocates of more centralized forms of socialist economy, these would take place essentially *ex post* and after time lags.

Third, the market-simulating character of decentralized socialist models, if or when adopted, might well contribute to economic instability as well as fail to provide the centralized thrust necessary for rapid economic growth. Maurice Dobb summarized the centralized socialist position on this issue:

---

[10]H. D. Dickenson, *Economics of Socialism* (Fair Lawn, N.J.: Oxford University Press, Inc., 1939), p. 214.

It would seem as though much of the uncertainty that is characteristic of a system of 'anarchy of production' (arising from atomistic diffusion of decisions and from competition) would still remain, and with it the possibility of similar maladjustments as occur [under capitalism] (for example, between demand for capital goods, depending on the aggregate volume of investment, and the demand for consumption goods, dependent on the size of the total wages-bill) . . . . One can, therefore, imagine fluctuations in accounting prices, reminiscent of the fluctuations under capitalism. [3] : 241, 244]

The Managed Capitalist Critique. The critique of the decentralized socialist model of investment provided by many students and advocates of contemporary "managed" or socially reformed capitalist economies lies somewhere between these two relatively more extreme positions. Many contemporary economists of widely differing political and ideological persuasions would concur that the attainment of full employment without inflation and the promotion of rapid growth rates under full-employment conditions would, in most instances, require considerable application of centralized methods of control over aggregate demand in general and the level and direction of investment in particular. Many also would have reservations, together with Hayek, about the efficiency of socialist incentives systems for promoting risky investment and technological progress.

At the same time, managed capitalists would blunt and temper both the neo-Austrian and neo-Marxian criticisms and, yet, provide their own special critique of the appropriate blend of centralization and decentralization in investment decisions. As to the neo-Austrian critique, contemporary managed capitalists would compare and contrast managers of large-scale private corporations under managed capitalism with industry managers under decentralized socialism and contend that problems of monopoly and avoidance of risky investment might well be an attribute of either or both systems.

The main criticism voiced by students of managed capitalism of any form of socialism is that, whatever the appropriate blend of decentralization or centralization in investment, *public ownership* is more or less beside the point. Monetary and fiscal policy may provide, and, in many instances, has provided, centralized methods for controlling the relation of aggregate demand to aggregate supply without widespread public ownership. Lange's comparison between a theoretical model of decentralized socialism and the problems of monopoly and depression in capitalist economies in practice circa the mid-1930s is doubly misleading. It compared (socialist) theory with (capitalist) practice. A fairer and fuller comparison would be between (1) the theory of investment, economic growth, and stability under decentralized socialism at its best and contemporary managed capitalism at its best; and (2) the successes and failures of implementation of decentralized/centralized schemes for investment decision-making in practice in economies corresponding to or incorporating major elements of decentralized socialism or managed capitalism (for example, a comparison between investment, growth, and stabilization in, say, Yugoslavia and Sweden).

Equity and Equality in the Distribution of Income. As observed earlier, part of the "case for socialism" is the contention that it would combine efficiency in resource allocation with equity in income distribution. The elimination or sharp reduction in private ownership of land and capital (and consequent elimination or reduction in private rents, interest, and profits) would radically decrease the extent of inequality and, thereby, inequities in property ownership. Under a system of freedom in the choice of occupation, necessary wage differentials under competitive conditions would correspond largely to differences in marginal disutility of different jobs and, consequently, would not entail true inequalities or inequities. And government taxation—or declaration of "social dividends"—could be based on any equitable criterion (for example, the sizes of families) independent of the choice of occupation.

Criticism of these propositions is essentially similar to those directed toward decentralized socialist views regarding economic growth and stability. Western neo-Marxists, at one extreme, are perfectly willing to accept large-scale wage differentials, indeed, insist they are indispensable as a means of promoting incentives, especially under conditions of freedom in the choice of occupation. Under centralized socialism, however, wage differentials would correspond to CPB evaluations of plan attainment, rather than to differences in marginal productivity as determined in the process of market exchange under conditions of consumer sovereignty.

Neo-Austrians, notably Hayek, concur with this assessment, though from the vantage point of a radically different set of value judgments, and contend that socialism in practice is more likely to correspond to the centralized than the decentralized model. Socialist means, argues Hayek, may be used to attain a variety of ends. An economic system characterized by public ownership and a concentration of decison-making power vested in the CPB may use its power to promote greater equality in income distribution than under capitalism. But nothing in the institutions or behavioral processes of socialism requires or necessitates this be done. A socialist government may as easily use its tremendous concentration of powers to promote exactly the opposite end, for example, to redistribute income in favor of a party elite or some other favored group.

The main critical commentary made by many students of contemporary managed capitalism is that the extent of inequality in income distribution under decentralized socialism plausibly would be considerably more than its advocates envisage, even under the institutions and processes assumed. This, combined with the theory and practice of egalitarian democratic social reforms under managed capitalism, heightens the plausibility

of a negative response to Lange's question, "Why bother?"

It is true that socialism, by eliminating private ownership of productive assets, thereby would reduce inequality in income. At the same time, only the consumed part of property income is available for distribution. Insofar as property income is taxed away or saved and invested under capitalism, it serves functions which would have to be provided in a socialist economy as well; and if the CPB sets the rate of capital accumulation above that which would emerge from individual choices in a capitalist economy, even the formerly consumed portion of property income might be unavailable for distribution. Consequently, the "social dividend" might well be at or close to zero. Indeed, if, as seems plausible, taxes were imposed on households to supplement government income from rent, interest, and profits of public enterprises, the social dividend, as a kind of transfer payment, would become negative.

In regard to wages and salaries, considerable diversity in income is perfectly consistent with, indeed, necessary for, the efficient functioning of the decentralized socialist model, characterized by (real or simulated) competition, freedom in the choice of occupation, and consumer sovereignty. Of course, some wage differentials under competitive conditions represent differentials in marginal disutility. But marginal disutility differences are not unique to socialism; presumably, they exist under capitalism as well. In any event, many wage differences do not and would not correspond to differences in marginal disutility. Under socialism as under capitalism, some high-paying jobs, such as those of industry managers, will also be quite pleasant. To some extent, these differences might be reduced, for example, through education; by increasing the supply of skilled, managerial, and professional labor relative to unskilled labor, this would tend to increase wages of the latter relative to those of the former, thereby reducing inequality in wage income. But again, education is not unique to socialism. Managed capitalism, at its best, can do and has done much to reduce income inequality through changing relative labor supplies via education. And, again, in any event, wage differentials presumably would persist under decentralized socialism, even with lump-sum taxes designed to confiscate economic rents of managers, because of differences in persons, that is, different talents, abilities, and energies. This would be especially likely for plant and industry managers, who serve as linchpins in the decentralized socialist model. Enticements to managers to follow the rules with vigor might well result in large-scale differences in income, the elimination of which could seriously dampen managerial incentives and, thereby, reduce efficiency.

In short, any economic system which places a high value upon freedom in occupational choice and efficiency in responses by producers to consumer preferences plausibly will be characterized by a considerable degree of income inequality quite apart from property income. At the same time, some of the major devices or proposals used by decentralized socialists to provide a rationale for existing inequalities (such as differences in marginal disutilities) or to reduce them (such as education) would be applicable to managed capitalism as well as to decentralized socialism.

Conclusion

In conclusion, perhaps the simplest and briefest, though least satisfying, answer to the question of how well decentralized socialism of the Lange variety would work is that we do not know. This frustrating conclusion stems from the facts that decentralized socialism is a prospective rather than an actual system, that several of the relevant variables determining its prospective success are non-economic in nature, and that it is a mixed system, "a compromise whose performance cannot be theoretically predicted. Claims meet coun-ter claims when its prospective advantages and disadvantages are compared with the achievements and shortcomings of capitalism." [34: 247]

Still, experience is accumulating in Eastern European countries, most notably in Yugoslavia, that decentralized forms of socialist economy, combining social ownership with a significant role for price or market processes, do function—and in some ways, at a high level of performance. For two decades after its publication, the Lange model of decentralized socialism appeared at best a rigorous statement of a possible form of socialist economy, at worst, an utopian curioso. Recent trends toward decentralization in Revisionist Communism have helped revive interest in this classic model of socialist planning and pricing and place in it better perspective. Market socialism, which began as an analysis of post-capitalist economic organization, is now providing inspiration in various forms for strategies and proposals for reform in contemporary Communist economies. We shall explore this in Part V. At this juncture, it will be instructive to examine Lange's postwar contributions to the theory of socialism, most notably the bases for and problems of transition from centralized to decentralized socialism.

FROM CENTRALIZED TO DECENTRALIZED SOCIALISM?

The next chapter will examine some of the major pressures for centralization which exist or might exist in a socialist economy: the political requirements of revolutionary transformation to a new socioeconomic system; the imperatives of rapid, large-scale industrialization; the central, strategic role of large investment in heavy industry; the lack of a disciplined working force and a skilled, sympathetic managerial class, and so forth. Centralized socialists have often emphasized the simplicities, possibilities, and prospective advantages of central plan formulation and execution in the context of an all-out drive for industrialization and economic development in underdeveloped economies. But many of these pressures for and possible advantages of centralized decision-making, planning, and control undoubtedly diminish as the institutional framework of the new political and economic system stabilizes and as the economy develops.

Suppose a centralized socialist economy, established by political revolution in an underdeveloped economy, is successful in coexisting with its external rivals and in establishing and maintaining government ownership of industry, collectivization of agriculture, and a system of near-comprehensive centralized planning and direction of the processes of industrialization and economic development. Suppose such a system is successful in the industrialization process, and, via its centralized strategies, has achieved a high rate of industrial growth and transformation to a fairly high level of economic development, with a large total output, an expanded capitalistic resource base, an advanced technology, a disciplined working force, and a skilled, educated managerial elite. Under these conditions and circumstances, the transition to a more decentralized form of economic organization is a distinct possibility.

The pressures for and prospective advantages of greater decentralization in a centrally planned economy have been stated by a number of socialist economists, notably Oskar Lange, in his postwar writings. First, the very success of the revolutionary transformation to a socialist economy terminates or diminishes the pressures for centralization which accompanied its transitional birth pangs. The extent of central control needed to *maintain* a system of government ownership of industry, collectivization of agriculture, and national economic planning may well be less than that needed in the process of *establishing* the institutional bases of the new system.

Next, argued Lange, are the "dialectics of

the processes of construction of socialism." The very success of centralized methods of industrialization generate an expanded, skilled, and disciplined work force which grows in "consciousness and political maturity" and a "new socialist intelligentsia," a new professional, managerial, and administrative class skilled in the arts of management and sympathetic to the goals of the political leadership. [40: 19]

Further, neither the aims of centralized socialists nor their underlying assumptions and value judgments about the proper institutional structure of the economic system requires a plan which is near-comprehensive in scope. The "active guidance and direction of the main lines of economic development" necessitates certain minimum requirements or pre-conditions (division of national income into investment and consumption; allocation of main investments among different branches of the economy; physical and financial coordination of the main branches of the economy), just as the conduct of a major war by a capitalist nation requires a certain minimum degree of centralized control over the allocation of resources. But, beyond these minimum, fundamental requirements, there is no objective need for further centralized planning and control. The aims and institutions of centralized socialism are consistent with leaving all other details to regional, local, decentralized units. Even the determination of output targets for various commodities, says Lange, is a "technical," not a "fundamental," problem. [40: 21] Indeed, a near-comprehensive plan may be inefficient and wasteful as well as unnecessary. Attempting to plan for the microeconomic details of specific products and resources is complex, cumbesome, and confusing. Centralized target-setting lacks flexibility of response to concrete and changing needs and circumstances, and requires a "wasteful bureaucratic apparatus" to supervise and enforce.

In its early revolutionary and transitional stage, a centralized socialist economy will often involve heavy use of "administrative orders and administrative allocations" as bases for plan fulfillment. As the economy develops in size and complexity, and as the institutional bases of the new socialist economy become established and stabilized, centralized administrative orders and commands become increasingly cumbersome and ineffectual. Indeed, the "greatest obstacle to further progress results from the lack of proper economic incentives in this bureaucratic centralistic type of management. This hampers proper economic utilization of resources, encourages waste, and also hinders technical progress." [40: 19]

A main indicator that a socialist economy is "maturing" is when it "starts to overcome these centralistic, bureaucratic methods of administrative planning and management . . ." [40: 19] and turns to greater reliance upon decentralized systems of economic incentives. On the one hand, tapping economic incentives is a less frustrating and more efficient system for plan execution, except in the isolated situation of big, rapid changes under upsetting conditions—which become less prevalent as the economy develops and the political system stabilizes. Thus, a preference "should be given to the use of economic means" (incentives systems) over administrative commands. On the other hand, the greater complexity of a developed economy makes it increasingly difficult, even impossible, for central planners to directly supervise and administer the details of plan execution. Therefore, the imperatives of plan consistency and efficiency require that "the situation has to change in the sense that the economic means are the rule and administrative means become subsidiary to the economic means." [40: 22, 23] Central planners must consider how people in decentralized situations will respond to plans and how they can be enticed to execute them.

It also has been contended that the formulation of plans can and "must" be increasingly decentralized as socialism develops. Plan formulation *can* be decentralized insofar "as it is possible to set up economic incentives such that the decisions of the decentralized units are the same as the decisions which would be made centrally." Plan formulation "*must* be decentralized in all cases where the central decision responds to a situation too late." Unless there is decentralization in cases of lags in centralized response and plan reformulation, "central planning becomes fictitious. . . ." Before changes in the different sectors of the economy are communicated to, or discovered by, the CPB, "irreversible things" have already occurred, robbing the central planners of any real guiding and directing function in plan reformulation. Under these conditions, discretionary power must be given to decentralized planners and administrators to reformulate specific aspects of the general plan as it applies to their sectors, and to formulate their own subsidiary plans within the framework of the aggregative national plan. [40: 24–25]

In addition, as a socialist economy develops, its capacity for expanding the output of consumption goods without contracting investment goods production increases. As this occurs, political pressures for increased quantity, quality, and variety of consumption goods increase. As the early heroic revolutionary fervor subsides, continued imposition of the burdens and sacrifices of rapid, large-scale industrialization on consumers must become less politically expedient. At the same time, a Schumpeterian-like process of creative destruction is at work. The very economic success of the old-style centralized macroeconomic strategies for industrialization and development creates an economy whose magnitude and complexity render those earlier strategies increasingly obsolete. New, more sophisticated and decentralized devices and processes for calculating consumer and worker preferences and marginal costs of scarce capital and land must be devised. And since centralized economic organization has no indigenous processes for making such marginal calculations, it is quite possible that even centralized socialists would turn increasingly in the process of economic development to greater reliance on the more flexible and decentralizing device of price systems. It is "essential," argued Lange, that "the plan be based on correct economic accounting. Correct accounting of economic costs and economic benefits, and consequently, a correct price system, are indispensable." [40: 26]

Indeed, it is wholly possible that processes for and advantages of greater decentralization in an economically developed centralized socialist system will be felt in the area of the underlying institutional features of the system itself. Even in a totalitarian society, there are "islands of separateness"[11]— sectors that maintain some degree of independence from the political leadership. In centrally planned industrialization in general, the peasantry and the agricultural sector is very likely to strongly resist its absorption into the planning system via the device of collectivization of agriculture. A government engaging in a rapid, large-scale process of industrial transformation, and enveloped in revolutionary fervor, may well regard the inefficiencies and hostilities engendered by large-scale collectivization of agriculture as a necessary price to pay for the establishment of political control over the mobilization of its economic surpluses. But a government facing the immensely complex problems of coordinating a developed economy, and more pragmatically concerned with the performance of the system than with rigid adherence to a specific institutional structure, might well feel it could afford to relinquish or decrease the rigor and scope of its control over agriculture by turning to greater reliance upon cooperative and/or private farming. Another example might be that of wholesale and retail trade, where rigid ideological insistence on government ownership undoubtedly contributes to economic inefficiency in centrally planned systems, but

where private ownership would not necessarily interfere with central governmental control over the main lines of economic development. A third example is that of households, wihich might be increasingly freed from central direction and control, as both consumers and sellers of labor services.

The extent to which this vision of transformation or transition in the process of economic development from centralized socialism to or toward some more decentralized form of economic organization applies to any actual case obviously depends on non-economic factors, including the nature of the political system, the power relations among the political leadership, and the evaluation by the political leaders of international politics. The preceding paragraphs present more of an exposition of an interesting possibility than a rigorous prediction of actual cases. Though not conclusive, the overall experience of Communist economic development would seem to indicate the political leaders of centrally planned systems are loath to relinquish their control over the national economy; they are deeply suspicious of proposals for decentralized economic reforms; and the psychology of the "big push" in economic development, with its attendant centralized strategies, sacrifices, and disturbances, is modified rather than abandoned in the process of economic development.

The "administrative methods" of central planning are "seriously challenged," argues Nicolas Spulber, "only when national crises of great proportions threaten the economy and the entire political and social structure. . . ." But even in these instances, a shift from central direction based on specification of input and output quantities to decentralized organization characterized by greater managerial discretion is "reluctant, unstable, and half-hearted." The "bureaucracy created in the early phases of a forced industrialization drive seems to visualize itself as eternally indispensable for exacting a continuously high rate of saving, for carrying out some transcendent goal, like an every-growing

---

[11]Carl J. Friedrich and Zbigniew K. Brzezinski, *Totalitarian Dictatorship and Autocracy* (Cambridge, Mass: Harvard University Press, 1956), Part VI.

heavy industry, an unsurpassed military establishment or a spectacular feat in outer space."[12] Further, the problems of growing complexity and microeconomic imbalances *may* lead to greater decentralization; but they *may also* lead to frenzied efforts at *re-centralization*. On the other hand, postwar developments in Communist East Europe demonstrate that a socialist economic system is not rigidly "set" for all time in an immutably unchanging institutional structure. An identification of the possibility of movements toward decentralization and "marketization" in centrally planned systems is at least equal in importance to an understanding of the major pressures for centralization.

SUMMARY OF CHAPTER 10

1. Centralization versus decentralization is a fruitful means of distinguishing among varieties of twentieth-century economic theories of socialism.

2. One of the most prominent classic blueprints of socialism is that of decentralized, market, or liberal socialism. This theory focuses on the following features of socialist economic organization: a developed economy with a capitalistic resource base; primary reliance on government ownership of the means of production; a dispersion of economic freedom and power among decision-making units, with freedom of individual economic choice in consumption and occupation, wide discretion for plant and industry managers in the determination of input-output decisions, and a CPB which sets the aggregate level of investment and determines prices of intermediate goods and the interest rate; a motivational system characterized by the pursuit of individual economic gain by households as consumers and workers and the imposition by the CPB of "rules" designed to promote economic

efficiency upon plant and industry managers; a basically decentralized organization of economic power; a mixture of price systems, government hierarchy, and democracy as social processes for making and coordinating economic decisions; greater equality of income through reduction of property income, coupled with a system of market-determined wage differentials.

3. The behavioral principles of decentralized socialism are essentially those of competitive market capitalism, modified by the incorporation of government ownership, a CPB, and income redistribution in the light of the reduction of private ownership of land and capital. Given freedom of consumer and occupational choice, and instructions by the CPB to plant and industry managers to produce any particular output level at least-cost combination of resources and to produce that level of output where marginal cost equals price, economic results will ensue similar to those of free markets in competitive market capitalism.

For land, raw materials, capital goods, and investment funds, "accounting prices," estabished by the CPB and adjusted to promote equality between industry demands and supplies, would simulate the behavior of competitive markets, provided such prices were taken as "given" by plant and industry managers and assuming the same rules for determination of plant and industry input combinations and input/output levels as previously noted.

4. The decentralized socialist "case" for socialism is essentially threefold. First, it is contended that socialism can allocate resources efficiently and in accordance with consumer preferences as well as, indeed, better than, competitive market capitalism. Second, a socialist economy would or could be in a better position to promote greater income equality, full-employment stability, and economic growth than capitalism. Third, capitalism in practice is not and is not likely to become competitive.

---

[12]Nicolas Spulber, *The Soviet Economy: Structure, Principles, Problems* (New York: W. W. Norton & Company, Inc., Publishers, 1969), p. 237.

5. The major questions in a critical evaluation of the economic theory of decentralized socialism are: Could and/or would it work? And, if so, how well would it work? As to the first question, there is little doubt the logical credentials of decentralized socialism are in order and the system is economically operational. The major problems are motivational and administrative: How are plant and industry managers to be enticed or compelled to follow the rules? How is the CPB to be enticed or compelled to restrict its role as described by the theory? As to the second question, theories of decentralized socialism have been criticized from both Left and Right. Centralized socialists criticize the theory for failing to take advantage of the contributions of centralized economic planning and suggest that the tendencies toward economic instability in capitalist economies might well be found in decentralized socialism. Many economists in capitalist countries doubt the efficacy of socialist transformation of the economic system for the purpose of obtaining benefits which might he more simply attained within the framework of private enterprise capitalism by vigorous antitrust policy, monetary and fiscal policies, and measures to reduce the degree of inequality in income.

6. Still, the theory of decentralized socialism has important implications and insights for the study of socialist economic organization. Originating as a blueprint for post-capitalist economic organization in the 1930s, the theory (and its successors) is providing inspiration for the economic reform of contemporary Communist economies, where the bases and pressures for transition to a more decentralized form of economic organization are increasing with the process of economic development.

11

Western Neo-Marxist
Economic Theories
of Centralized Socialism

The second prominent twentieth-century model of the organization and workings of a socialist economic system developed by socialist economists is that of centralized, hierarchical, or authoritarian socialism. Contributions to the analysis of this kind of system have been made by a variety of authors. One of the most prominent treatments of the subject in the West is that developed by a group of neo-Marxist economists, notably Maurice Dobb, Paul Sweezy, and Paul Baran.[1] An exposition and critique of the theory of centralized socialism developed by this group is utilized in this chapter as an organizational framework for the discussion. The ideas of other contributors, however (including Oskar Lange, whose postwar

writings have provided an interesting comparison and contrast with his more well-known decentralized socialist model described in the preceding chapter) are incorporated or cited herein where appropriate.

Economic Theory of Centralized Socialism

The phrase "economic theory of centralized socialism" has four key aspects: First, it deals essentially with *economic* rather than, say, political, psychological, or ethical issues. Second, it is concerned primarily with the *theory* of centralized socialism, with centralized socialism as a theoretical economic system rather than as an actual economic system or movement for economic reform or revolution. Third, it is a member of the *socialist* family of economic philosophies and systems, sharing certain common features with other members of this group, including decentralized socialism. Fourth, it is a theory of a distinctly and distinctively *centralized*, hierarchical, and authoritarian system, and is thus distinguishable from other forms of socialism, for example, the *decentralized* model of the preceding chapter, and the various theories and proposals of the Western,

---

[1] Dobb is a Lecturer and Fellow of Trinity College, Cambridge University. Baran, now deceased, was a Professor of Economics at Stanford University. Sweezy, formerly a member of the Economics Department at Harvard University, is now a free-lance contributor to left-wing and socialist publications. For a brief discussion of the first two of these men and their contemporary significance, see "Viewing the U.S. Economy with a Marxist Glass," Business Week, April 13, 1963, pp. 67–68, 71.

democratic socialists, identified and compared in Chapter 14.

As in the case of decentralized socialism, the abstraction of the distinctly economic aspects of centralized socialism from its non-economic context and environment restricts the scope and empirical applicability of the model. At the same time, it performs the useful service of focusing attention on central and important, yet often neglected, economic problems.

Though a theoretical economic system, centralized socialism is more explanatory and empirical and less normative in tone than the decentralized socialist model of Chapter 10. It draws directly on and is held by its expositors to be applicable to actual experience in the Soviet-type economies. As developed and formulated by Dobb and others, however, it is not merely descriptive of particular practices in the Communist systems; nor is it simply an apologia for Communist economic organization. It is, rather, a generalized theoretical exposition and defense of centralized government planning and decision-making in an economy characterized by government ownership and control of the instruments of production.

Goals of Centralized Economic Planning

The major goals of economic policy and planning as presented by centralized socialists are not radically different from those of writers on economic systems in general. Presumably, centralized socialists prefer efficiency to inefficiency, equity to inequity, full employment and economic stability to unemployment and instability, growth to stagnation, and freedom to tyranny. However, the centralized socialist priority system in regard to these goals, as well as their content and interpretation, is quite different from that of other systems.

THE INDUSTRIALIZATION IMPERATIVE

At the apex of the pyramid of goals for centralized socialists is *rapid industrialization*

and economic growth. In part, this reflects the Leninist and contemporary neo-Marxist view that (the centralized version of) socialism is more likely to emerge first in the under-developed economies than in the rich, capitalist economies of the West. In part, it represents the empirical and realistic view that rapid economic development is, in fact, the central goal of economic planning in the highly centralized and hierarchically structured Soviet-type economies. In part, it rests upon the centralized socialist idea that, even in economically developed nations, the central economic problem is and will continue to be that of production. Thus, in his review of Soviet economic experience, Baran identified rapid, large-scale economic growth and development as the imperative goals of Soviet planning. [26: 289–92]

Dobb is especially critical of the concentration, both by neo-liberals and decentralized socialists, upon the traditional problems of "securing an *optimum* allocation of resources between alternative uses, with both resources and uses treated as given" and contends that "successful development from one economic situation, with its given combination of resources and configuration of demand, to another might be a more crucial test of the contribution by an economic system to human welfare than the attainment of perfect equilibrium in any given situation." [30: 244–45]

OTHER GOALS OF CENTRAL PLANNING

The remaining major economic goals receive special interpretations and emphases by centralized socialists. By *efficiency* in the allocation of resources, they do not necessarily or generally mean consumer-guided production; indeed, they are more likely to mean the correspondence of production decisions to the preferences of the CPB or the political leadership. Regarding low-cost production and the "minimization of the sacrifice of alternatives," they are clearly more concerned with the dynamic and historical decrease in costs through increased productivity than with the static achievement of lowest-cost production under given technological conditions.

Like socialists in general, the Western neo-Marxist group identifies an *equitable* distribution of national income as one involving a substantial *equality* of income (in comparison with the theory and practice of capitalism). Like Marxists in general, they associate equality in income distribution with the emergence to political power and dominance of labor as a socio-economic class and with the elimination or sharp reduction of private-property income. The equalitarian component of the socialist vision is definitely muted, however, in the analysis of centralized socialism by two factors: one, a recognition that the distribution of income must be consistent with the patterns of resource allocation adopted in the national economic plans formulated by the CPB, if those plans are to be achieved; two, the view that rapid industrialization requires differential monetary and non-monetary rewards to encourage incentives.

Full-employment stability is more often discussed in centralized socialist literature in terms of the failure of capitalist economies to attain it than in its role as a positive goal for centralized planning. However, it is clear that the neo-Marxists regard centralized socialism as the type of economic system in which full employment stability is most likely to be achieved. Capitalism, managed capitalism, and decentralized socialism all are criticized for their actual and/or prospective failure to attain this goal. In addition, it should be noted that, in capitalist and decentralized socialist formulations of the goal of full employment, freedom of occupational choice is presumed. Under centralized socialism, full employment could mean (though it need not necessarily mean) the employment of unemployed workers at government projects by government decree.

Individual economic freedoms clearly rank very low in the centralized socialist priority list. "It must be stressed," noted Baran, "that a radical reorientation of all aspects of social existence could not unfold under the rein of unfettered individual freedom." [26: 385] Freedom of consumer choice (that is, freedom of consumers to allocate their given incomes among different combinations of existing commodities and services) generally is presumed by centralized socialist economists, as is freedom of occupational choice. Though human as well as capital and natural resources could be directed by central authority, most models of centralized socialism presume the allocation of labor can be better achieved by monetary and non-monetary incentives than by command. Insofar as this is true, freedom of occupational choice is theoretically compatible with a governmentally planned allocation of resources. But freedom of private enterprise to own, produce, hire, and exchange, freedom of consumers, businesses and private financial institutions to determine the aggregate volume of savings and investment, and freedom of consumer sovereignty (that is, guidance of production decisions according to market-revealed consumer choices) is either denied or sharply criticized and restricted.

Structure of Centralized Socialist Economic Organization

The structure of centralized socialism as a system for planfully attaining its goals may be identified in terms of the eight definitional criteria used in previous chapters, as illustrated in Table 11-1.

In regard to criteria one and two, the Western neo-Marxists have not abandoned their hopeful expectation of the eventual establishment of a centralized form of socialist economy in the Western, capitalist nations. However, on the basis of Communist economic experience, they clearly envisage the emergence of their brand of socialism in underdeveloped, often pre-capitalistic economies as much more typical and probable. They view socialism primarily as a substitute

Table 11-1

CENTRALIZED SOCIALISM

1. Level of development	Underdeveloped, but developing
2. Resource base	Landistic, in the process of transformation into capitalistic
3. Ownership-control of instruments of production	Dominantly government ownership-control
4. Locus of economic power	Government, CPB
5. Motivational system	Government promotion of social goals, coupled with incentive systems to achieve compliance
6. Organization of economic power	Dominantly centralized
7. Social processes for making and coordinating economic decisions	Dominantly government hierarchy
8. Distribution of income and wealth	Greater equality of income through sharp reduction of property income, coupled with a system of CPB-determined wage differentials

for capitalism in underdeveloped economies rather than as a successor to capitalism in developed economies. They specifically deny the necessity of capitalism as the only historic route to industrialization and economic growth, and conceive the major problems of socialist planning to be those of fostering rapid, large-scale economic growth and the development of capitalistic methods of production.

Three points should be especially noted in regard to criterion three: First, government ownership is particularly emphasized by neo-Marxists in their definitions of socialism, almost to the point of constituting its *differentia specifica*. Thus, Polish economist Jan Drewnowski defines *socialism* simply as a "system in which all the means of production are owned by the State." Unlike most contemporary non-Marxists who distinguish between ownership and control of industry, and who note the decreasing role and significance of ownership *per se* in the identification and definition of comparative economic systems, the centralized socialists continue to adhere to the traditional Marxist view that ownership of industrial property is the basis of economic power, and thus, a major criterion for identifying and comparing different economic systems. Second, centralized socialists place greater emphasis upon

central government ownership and control of industry than do other members of the socialist family and a correspondingly smaller emphasis upon municipal, worker, cooperative, and other forms of ownership. Third, like many defenders of capitalism who treat private ownership as sacrosanct and an end in itself, centralized socialists often write as though government ownership were more than an institution or means, as though it were itself a goal of economic policy.

In regard to criteria four through six, the locus of economic power in centralized socialism is the central government and its associated decision-making and administrative bodies, especially the CPB. Individuals and private organizations of individuals play a distinctly minor and dependent role. This does not mean individuals have *no* freedom or discretion in economic decision-making and no personal or private economic goals or desires, or that central planners can or do ignore entirely the preferences of workers, consumers, or plant and industry managers. But it does mean that the power to make the major economic decisions is concentrated in a highly centralized government planning body, and that the promotion of national economic development through the formulation and execution of a national economic "plan" takes precedence over personal and private goals and such other goals as consumer sovereignty and worker control of industry.

In regard to criterion seven: Under centralized socialism, government hierarchy largely replaces the price system as the dominant social process for making, coordinating, and enforcing economic decisions. Whereas, under decentralized socialism, "market prices guide the planners," under centralized socialism, "the planners guide the prices." Under centralized socialism, the CPB does have the responsibility for formulating a consistent "national economic plan" and for specifying quantities of inputs and outputs, and physical "targets" to be attained during a forthcoming time period. This is a distinctive characteristic of *centralized* socialism.

Though political democracy as a social process is not necessarily inconsistent with government hierarchy, it should be noted that citizen-worker control of political leaders and the political process is not stressed in the centralized socialist literature. Similarly, bargaining—especially "collective bargaining" in the now traditional, modified capitalist sense of the give-and-take between organized labor unions and representatives of the management of private businesses—plays a small role in centralized socialism. Labor unions would continue to exist, but their role would change from that of bargaining agents to that of policy formulation and/or execution agents in a system of national government economic planning. It is at this point, incidentally, that the neo-Marxists find it difficult to combine Marx with central planning. The original Marxian vision included both central government planning *and* worker control of industry. By their major emphasis on government hierarchy and central planning, the neo-Marxists tacitly relegate worker control to a lower rank in their priority system.

Criterion eight, distribution of income and wealth, was cited in the preceding section on economic goals of centralized socialism. On the one hand, centralized socialists, like socialists in general, claim the elimination or sharp reduction of private property in land and capital will promote greater equality in income. On the other hand, the execution of national economic plans and the achievement of governmentally planned goals requires a system of rewards and punishments. Recognizing that planning by government command and decree can be, at best, only a marginal system for social control, centralized socialists emphasize the use of wage differentials as a basis for tapping human incentives and executing government plans. In contrast with market capitalism and the decentralized socialist model, however, wage differentials are determined by the CPB, not by a competitive labor market. The resulting inequalities under centralized socialism are governmentally determined, not market determined.

Centralized Socialism and Decentralized Socialism: Similarities and Differences

As thus defined, centralized socialism shares with decentralized socialism: government ownership and control of capital and natural resources, a central government planning body and government hierarchy as a social process for making and coordinating economic decisions, and greater income equality through the reduction of private property, coupled with wage differentials as a source of incentives. Centralized socialism diverges from decentralized socialism: in its assumption that socialism will typically emerge in underdeveloped economies with a pre-capitalistic or only rudimentary capitalistic resource base, in its critique of consumer sovereignty and its concentration of economic power in government and a highly centralized governmental planning body, with responsibility for the formulation of plans for the promotion of governmentally-determined goals, in its rejection or sharp restriction of the price system and its correspondingly heavier reliance on a hierarchically structured government bureaucracy as the dominant social process for making and coordinating economic decisions, and in its determination of wage differentials by government planning rather than by the process of market bidding.

Centralized Socialism, Orthodox Economic Theory, and the Marxian Vision

Beyond these institutional differences in the definition and conception of socialism are methodological and doctrinal contrasts between centralized and decentralized socialists. Economists who have formulated economic theories of decentralized socialism generally have been steeped in the assumptions, methodology, and tools of traditional, neo-classical economic analysis. Individual freedom of economic choice, consumer sovereignty, competition, equilibrium, marginal analysis, the price system, market exchange: All these are drawn from the heritage of orthodox economics. Centralized socialists draw much more heavily upon (a modernized neo-Marxist version of) Marxist literature and are much more critical of the methodology and content of orthodox economics than are decentralized socialists. Economists like Dobb, Sweezy, and Baran place their greatest emphasis on the big, dynamic macroeconomic problems of economic growth and development and are quite critical of the decentralized socialists' reliance on the traditional, microeconomic tools and concepts of marginal analysis, static equilibrium, competition, and efficient resource allocation in terms of market-revealed consumer preferences.

Though drawing heavily on Marxian economic theory, however, the Western, neo-Marxist group has made several modifications, including important changes in the classic Marxian vision of the ideally functioning socialist economy. Perhaps the most prominent difference lies in the replacement of the vision of historical process from feudalism through capitalism into socialism with the neo-Marxian view of socialism as an alternative route to industrialization and development of a capitalistic resource base in underdeveloped economies. Another major difference is the absence of the anarchistic, anti-statist bias of the classic Marxian vision in the writings of the neo-Marxists. *Worker* ownership, *worker* control of production decisions and *worker* cooperation in the development of moral community has definitely faded and been overshadowed by a much more explicit, vigorous emphasis on *government* ownership, *government* control, and *government* planning. Centralized socialists are children of their age in recognizing and emphasizing the role of the state in the coordination of the national economy. Further, whereas Marx was an analyst and forecaster, and a bit of a prophet, he was not much of a planner. Beyond his very vague and visionary statements about socialism and communism, Marx refrained from developing blueprints for post-capitalist economic organization. But for centralized socialists, government economic planning is a key distinguishing feature of a socialist economy; and in contrast to Marx, they have provided an important and systematic contribution to the analysis of a centrally and comprehensively governmentally planned economic system.

Is Centralized Socialism Really Socialism?

One of the semantic tangles in the study of comparative economic systems is the question of the *bona fide* status of centralized socialism as a member of the socialist family. As noted earlier, this issue has arisen because both neo-Marxists and Communists on one hand and Western democratic socialists on the other have appropriated the word "socialism" to describe their visions or systems.

Whether centralized socialism is "really

socialism" or not obviously depends upon how we define the word *socialism*. Centralized socialists are free to define their terms as they choose. These writers are on strong ground when they note the normative and "utopian" elements in the economic theory of decentralized socialism, and when they emphasize that the economic and institutional conditions of revolutionary social change, rapid, large-scale industrialization, and economic development in underdeveloped economies and in the Communist bloc diverge from the visions of Marx, the decentralized socialists, and democratic socialists alike.

They are on weaker ground when they identify centralized socialism with socialism in general and when they adjudge the economies of the Communist countries good (indeed, the "only") illustrations of socialism in practice. It should be reemphasized there are important differences among the varieties of socialism; centralized socialism is one conceivable form of socialist economy, but not the only one. This tendency to identify centralized socialism with socialism in general would be accurate only if all other forms of socialism were unattainable or were institutionally unstable if and when attained. But these are conjectures which the centralized socialists have not proved. The other side of this coin is that, even if the economic system of Soviet Russia or some other Communist country did correspond to the model of centralized socialism, it would still lack several features associated with the word "socialism" in the Western democratic socialist movement. As to the neo-Marxist presumption that centralized socialism is the only "true," *bona fide* form of socialism, democratic and decentralized socialists have their personal predilections and value judgments, too. The real, substantive questions for the study of economic systems are how (and how well) economic systems with the properties described by the neo-Marxist centralized socialists would or do work.

PRESSURES FOR CENTRALIZATION IN A SOCIALIST ECONOMY

Though any of the various gradations of centralization/decentralization described at the beginning of Chapter 10 is conceivable, the Western neo-Marxists (supported by some non-Marxist and non-socialist economists) contend that, in an actual socialist economy, the pressures toward centralization in making and implementing economic decisions are or would be considerable. Though most noted for his model of decentralized socialism, Oskar Lange asserted in 1958 that, at least in early stages of development, the planning and management of a socialist economy is likely to be "highly centralized" for two major reasons. First, reasoning from Communist experience, the revolutionary liquidation of the presocialist system and the revolutionary establishment of socialism "requires centralized disposal of resources by the new revolutionary state, and consequently, centralized management and planning" as a basis for maintaining and defending the revolution. Second, centralization in the planning and use of resources is required by the goal of rapid, large-scale industrialization, partly because of the imperative need to concentrate resources on development projects and "avoid dissipation of resources" away from them, and partly because of the lack of a skilled, disciplined working class and a managerial class sympathetic to the revolutionary government. [40: 17]

Even if a decentralized form of socialism were established by peaceful and democratic methods in an economically developed country, certain pressures for centralization would remain. [Cf., for example, 31: 241–42; 4: 203–5; 9: 233–36] The "crux of the whole problem," argues Sweezy, is "the management of investment." [9: 234] The major economic advantage of a socialist system, adds Dobb, is the planful, *ex ante* coordination of investment decisions. These advantages, plus the problems of maladjustments of over- and under-investment in decentralized socialism, stimulate the centralization of investment decisions. Further, government ownership and control of the means of production place the responsibility for investment decisions in the hands of the state. Because of the crucial importance of investment in the process of economic growth, it is highly unlikely that a socialist economy would reproduce the decentralization and atomization of investment decisions found under capitalism.

But "the centralization of investment decisions," concludes Sweezy, "makes comprehensive planning all but inevitable." The reasoning supporting this assertion is developed neatly:

> Assume, for example, that the government of a socialist society makes a basic policy decision to invest a certain percentage of the national income over a period of, say, five or ten years and lays down certain general goals such as the building up of heavy industry, the rehousing of a specified proportion of the population, and the development of hitherto backward regions. The next step would naturally be to charge the Central Planning Board with the task of drawing up an investment plan for carrying out these decisions. This investment plan will begin by translating the general goals laid down by the government into quantitative terms: so many new factories, railroads, power plants, mines, apartment houses, schools, hospitals, theaters, and so forth. The dates at which these various construction projects are to be started and finished will then be specified. From these data, it will be possible to draw up schedules of the different kinds of materials and labor which will be required. At this point the investment plan may be said to be complete. But would it be sensible for the Central Planning Board to stop here and to rely on price and income controls to ensure that what is needed will be ready at the right time, at the right place, and in the right quantities?

> The answer is surely that it would not be. When the needs of the investment plan have been determined, the Central Planning Board will, almost as a matter of course, take steps to see that they are met; and this can be done only by extending the scope of the plan to include the various sectors of the economy which are directly concerned. Such an extension is not possible, however, if only the requirements of investment are taken into account, since materials and manpower are needed for both consumption and investment purposes. Hence the Central Planning Board will find it necessary to estimate consumer demand for all products which compete for resources with the investment plan and to draw up a second set of schedules showing the different kinds of materials and labor which will be required. It should now be possible, by consolidating the investment and consumption schedules and by comparing them with current and prospective supplies, to work out a general plan for the development of the economy over the period in question.

> ... When a consistent and practical plan has finally been adopted, it cannot be left to the discretion of individual industry and plant managers whether or not they will conform to it; rather it must be their first duty imposed by law, to carry out their part of the plan to the best of their ability . . . . [9: 236]

The above reasoning, supported by trends and pressures toward centralization in economic life in the twentieth century, is highly persuasive. It should be recognized, however, that any hypotheses about pressures toward centralization in a decentralized socialist system are highly conjectural. Because no economically developed Western democracy has established a decentralized system of socialist economy, no one can say with certainty what would happen were one to evolve. Economies in practice often involve pragmatic mixtures which defy the logic of laws of evolution toward extreme, limiting cases. The preceding chapter described an interesting alternative hypothesis; namely, that there are limits to the effectiveness and continuity of centralization in economic organization, and that, under certain circumstances, there may well be pressures toward increasing *de*centralization in socialist economy.

THE BEHAVIORAL PRINCIPLES
OF CENTRALIZED SOCIALISM:
THE METHODOLOGY OF
CENTRAL PLANNING

Western neo-Marxists generally contend the most important single economic advantage of centralized socialism is its system of economic planning. For this reason, as well as for ease and convenience of exposition, this discussion of the behavioral principles of centralized socialism is organized around the major steps of the planning process. To avoid repetition, critical appraisal of the economic analysis of centralized socialism is incorporated in this discussion rather than separately.

Formulation of Planning Goals:
Critique of Consumer Sovereignty
and Defense of Centralized
Goal-Setting

Because large-scale industrialization and economic development head the centralized socialist's list of planning goals, and take priority over other, more orthodox criteria of economic welfare, such as static allocational efficiency, the centralized socialist denies the ultimate test of the success of an economic system is the degree of correspondence between production decisions and consumer wants. This denial rests, in part, upon a critique of consumer sovereignty and, in part, upon an accompanying assumption or judgment that the CPB is generally in a more effective position than consumers to formulate planning goals and targets consistent with the general goal of economic growth.

CRITIQUE OF CONSUMER SOVEREIGNTY

Centralized socialists raise several doubts about the validity or "sacredness" of consumer sovereignty. First, even in a capitalist economy, consumers are not as sovereign as orthodox competitive theory portrays them. Consumer preferences are, to a considerable extent, molded by the sales promo-tional activities of producers. Insofar as this is true, producers, in responding to market-revealed "choices" of consumers, produce what *they* have persuaded consumers to want, rather than what consumers "independently" desire. Further, preferences of low-income consumers are affected by the consumption patterns of the rich, who "set the pace" and are emulated by others. Then, too, market choices of consumers are most communicative of individual preferences in regard to *existing* commodities. They provide little guidance for meeting new preferences through the creation of new products or new varieties of old products. Also, the "dollar ballots" of the marketplace provide for a sort of "plural voting." The rich, who have more to spend, exert greater impact and bias upon the market than consumers in low-income brackets. The implication of these criticisms (none of which are the private monopoly of neo-Marxists) is that the degree of consumer sovereignty in capitalist economies is distinctly and significantly less than that suggested by the textbook treatment of pure competition. Thus, its elimination or reduction in a centralized socialist system will involve a distinctly and significantly lower loss of human welfare than critics of such a system allege.

Second, because of their lack of knowledge, limited experience, unreflectiveness, or simple gullibility, consumers are often markedly "irrational" in their market behavior, both in "not knowing what is good for them" and in adopting means which are inappropriate to the attainment of ends. Consumer irrationality is especially prominent in regard to choices extending over time (notably, investment versus consumption), where consumers exhibit a chronic tendency to "myopic underestimation of the future . . . ."Further, consumer sovereignty is an inadequate guide to "collective wants," which "cannot be satisfied by individuals as separate units and which accordingly are not represented (at any rate not adequately) in the demands of individual consumers as expressed on a market." Consumer choice may also be defective in instances of "external economies or diseconomies" of consumption, where consumer satisfactions (or disutilities) depend on the consumption patterns of others. [31: 71–73]

Third, and of special importance for an underdeveloped economy embarking upon programs of industrialization, the dynamic context of economic growth and development alters the nature of the problems with which economics deals and does so in a way which significantly decreases the role and relevance of consumer sovereignty. For one thing, consumer wants which, in static allocation theory, are treated as given *data*, become *variables* subject to change and development in the process of economic growth. A government which has embarked upon a planned course of development inevitably affects consumer preferences in the process—hopefully, for the better, since the "setting of new and higher standards (of consumption) will undoubtedly be one of the central preoccupations of a socialist society, and one that is inseparable from the promotion of a higher standard of life." [31: 79] In any event, market choice yields no clearly valid standard for production decisions in this context. Market choices *prior* to the unfolding of a course of economic development would reveal preferences ignorant of the new world to come, while consumer choices made *after* a phase of developmental change has occurred would embody the new social habits and conventions which have accompanied the past changes in production.

Another prominent example of how growth and development alter the context in which economists analyze problems and also reduce the validity of consumer sovereignty is that the big, strategic decisions of economic change and development—decisions in regard to the aggregate level of investment, the distribution of investment between capital goods and consumption goods industries, and the location of industry, as well as such traditionally collective decisions as national defense, education, urban development, and transportation facilities—are very remote from the market choices of consumers. Based on imperfect knowledge of an uncertain future, they are, in any system, but especially in an underdeveloped economy establishing industrialization programs, largely *autonomous* and independent of consumers' market choices. But key "decisions of this type will constitute the framework of economic development, defining its general shape and direction; and only within this general framework can decisions affecting the adaptation of production to consumers' wants have play." [31: 78]

DEFENSE OF CENTRALIZED CHOICE

If a critique of consumer sovereignty is one side of the centralized socialist coin in regard to planning goals, defense of the rationality and social desirability of collective, centralized decision-making is the other. The neo-Marxist case for centralized goal-setting has several major interdependent strands, all of which acquire special significance in relation to the issues of industrialization and economic development. [Cf. 31: 75–80] First is the minimum magnitude argument: The sheer size of the developmental effort required to jolt an underdeveloped economy into sustained growth may easily be larger than that which is possible or manageable by private enterprise, producing in response to market demand. (This is complicated by indivisibilities in the processes of production and consumption, to be examined herein.)

Second is the rapidity argument: A decentralized pricing system appears to be a mechanism most effectively suited to making small marginal adjustments over an extended period of time. Centralized processes of decision-making, on the other hand, may be more suitable for making the large changes necessary for industrialization and economic growth *rapidly*.

Third is the complementarity and interdependence or "external economies" argument. The central idea here is that production decisions are interdependent and that there may be substantial advantages or economies in developing a whole series of investment projects together. (A classic illustration is the development of an entire river valley, with its attendant dam construction, power plants, irrigation and soil conservation projects, highway construction, transportation facilities, and so on.) This argument is clearly related to the first one. The sheer magnitude of large-scale, interdependent projects often is such that they require centralized decision-making in underdeveloped economies in order to be made efficiently—indeed, in order to be made at all.

Because there are interdependencies and external economies in time as well as space, "the occurrence of some change at any point will depend (to the extent of any such relation of interdependence) on the expectation of changes occurring elsewhere." If the probability of such changes occurring is less than certainty, "no one of an interrelated set of changes may ever take place." [31: 75] Centralization of economic decisions can raise the probability of interrelated changes taking place closer to certainty.

Related to this theme is the concept of continuity. Investment in one sector of the economy often is predicated on the maintenance or continuity of investment in the economy as a whole. But because, in a world of imperfect knowledge and uncertainty as to future development of the rest of the economy precisely this kind of continuity is denied to individual producers in a decentralized pricing system, the centralized socialist reaches the conclusion that "certain kinds of development may only come upon the agenda if development is centrally planned as a whole . . . . In other words, the type of mechanism whereby economic decisions are taken may be the crucial factor in determining the form and direction of development" [31: 89]—indeed, its very possibility.

Fourth is the argument of long-run versus short-run interests. Individual consumers are much more concerned with their own economic interests than with those of future generations and more aware of their immediate, short-run desires than of their long-run interests. This is especially true in regard to saving versus consumption decisions, where individual consumer choices are "notoriously unreliable." [31: 39] In many underdeveloped economies, the saving that may be necessary in the short-run to achieve the growth which, in the long-run, would substantially raise income levels and living standards is not likely to be voluntarily forthcoming through individual consumer market choices. Insofar as this is true, the centralized decision to generate and allocate, through collective, governmental devices, an "economic surplus" into investment projects may be the only method possible (abstracting from foreign economic assistance) to move the economy into continued growth and may, indeed, contribute more to long-run consumer welfare than a decentralized system, more faithfully attuned to short-run consumer preferences.

A final argument, closely related to the others, is that of *ex ante* coordination. According to Dobb, "the crux of the matter" may be expressed

> . . . by saying that the quintessential function of planning as an economic mechanism is that it is a means of substituting *ex ante* coordination of the constituent elements in a scheme of development—that is, *before* decisions have been embodied in action and in actual commitments—for the tardy *post facto* coordinating tendencies that are operated by the mechanism of price movements on a market in a capitalist world—tendencies, moreover, which in the presence of substantial time-lags may merely achieve extensive fluctuations. In this the essential difference between a planned economy and an unplanned evidently consists. The successful employment of such *ex ante* coordination may not only enable a given objective to be attained more smoothly and more speedily, but because the degree of uncertainty confronting economic decisions is of a much smaller order of magnitude—uncertainty regarding the character of parallel decisions in other sectors of the economy and regarding future decisions that will be made—it will open the

door to certain types of development which would not be possible at all (or at least be extremely unlikely) for an unplanned capitalist economy. [31: 76. See also 30: 9]

CRITICAL EVALUATION

Centralized socialists begin with the underlying value judgments that: rapid, large-scale industrialization and economic development is more important for human welfare than the immediate satisfaction of consumer desires; major decisions about the scope, rapidity, and form of economic development should be made by political leaders; and the success of developmental programs and processes should be measured by the degree of their correspondence to the preferences of political leaders, not to those of consumers and/or citizens (except as decided by political leaders). *If* these value judgments are accepted, then consumer sovereignty is irrational, and a free market pricing system cannot be permitted to guide and control production decisions. The counter-answer of the critic of centralized socialism, at this most fundamental level of analysis, is simply a different value judgment, namely, that the good life, economically speaking, is properly a mutual blending or balance of a number of social goals, including efficiency, justice, stability, freedom, and growth; that no one man or small body of men knows what is "best" for society as a whole; and that the control of production decisions by consumers and/or citizens is socially desirable.

Critics of goal formulation under centralized socialism often try to go beyond this general counter-value judgment by asserting that, in the absence of a competitive price system to communicate consumer preferences, production targets and aims are "arbitrary" (to use Lange's term). [39: 85] "Concerning the basic policy decisions which are to shape the structure of the plan," argues George Halm, "we have no way of showing that one combination of aims is better than another." [34: 284] This is true. But, unfor-

tunately, the same is true of consumer choice. The preferences of consumers are just as "arbitrary" as those of a CPB. Centralized decision-making "does not substitute something arbitrary or even subjective for something demonstrably right or wrong and, in any case, objective. Instead, it begins, as does the price system, with arbitrary and subjective choices, which may be wise or foolish." [1: 396] Scientific economic analysis has no built-in mechanism for validating one or the other of these systems of value judgments —though it is true logic and empirical evidence can be brought to bear on the question of the comparative rationality of centralized versus market choice. Generally speaking, centralized socialists take CPB preferences as "given," just as orthodox economists take consumer preferences as "given."

Substitution of CPB sovereignty for consumer sovereignty does not preclude the possible use of a price system as a means of quantifying CPB preferences, communicating them to plant and industry managers, and securing rational economic calculation and accounting. In this event, all prices would become "accounting prices," and managers would be instructed to behave "as if" they were given, as in the model of decentralized socialism described in the preceding chapter.

Centralized socialists are probably right, however, in emphasizing that, in the context of underdeveloped economies, the basic elements in a centralized development strategy are, in many instances, crude and simple enough to be communicable to subordinates without the use of a price system. "In regard to the basic necessities of life, such as housing, primary foodstuffs and a modicum of clothing, the care of children and the requirements of public health . . . [it] should be possible to find fairly widespread agreement in a given community as to what is most conducive to welfare." [31: 87] In this view, centralized socialists receive support from some non-socialist economists. Dahl and Lindblom, for example [in 1: 396], argue that, once the CPB has made its choices, it is not necessary to translate them "into a set of prices indicating what responses are demanded . . . . [In] the absence of competing leaders, all striving through price offers to win their preferred responses from the productive enterprises, there is no need for leadership to communicate its own preferences to enterprises through prices. On the basis of cost information available to it, leadership can much more simply and directly place its orders in physical terms."

Similarly, substitution of CPB sovereignty for consumer sovereignty in the big decisions of production, investment, and collective consumption does not preclude the possible use of freedom of consumer choice, consumer sovereignty, and the price system in the microeconomic decisions of consumption. The popular view that the only alternatives are 100 percent consumer sovereignty and complete economic dictatorship imposed by a CPB is a "false antithesis," suggests Dobb. Within the framework of basic developmental and other collective decisions already made by the CPB, there is no special reason why market retail prices, taken as an expression of consumer preferences, could not be used as a basis for guiding the allocation of resources within this remaining consumer goods sector. What is in question is whether individual consumer preferences, as revealed by market choices, "are the exclusive or even preponderant factor to be taken into account by central planners." [31: 70–71]

Qualified in this manner, the centralized socialist critique of consumer sovereignty and defense of centralized choice is less divergent from Western theoies of centralized versus decentralized choice in managed capitalism than popularly thought. Most students of economic systems would grant the partial validity and perceptiveness of the centralized socialist position and recognize that:

1. There are possible combinations of centralized and decentralized choice which lie between pure consumer sovereignty and pure CPB sovereignty;

2. there are limitations both to the existence and the validity of consumer sovereignty in contemporary, modified capitalist economies;

3. the price system is a social process which is highly specialized for making certain kinds of choices and ill-suited for making certain other kinds of choices (collective goods); in these latter cases, some mechanism for collective choice may be more rational than consumer sovereignty;

4. rapid, large-scale industrialization and economic development in many underdeveloped economies today may be facilitated, indeed, may require, a fairly high degree of centralized choice in regard to the "mobilization and allocation of the economic surplus"; and

5. the appropriate position between the extremes of pure market choice and pure CPB determination of production goals is an empirical and pragmatic issue which cannot be determined by the application of an *a priori* generalization.

Still, important differences remain. For the neo-Marxist, centralized choice is the general rule and market choice the exception. For most non-socialists (and many contemporary Western democratic socialists), the opposite is true. Critics of centralized socialism would generally contend that:

1. Recognition of limitations upon the applicability of consumer sovereignty provides a case for the reform of capitalism and the improvement of consumer rationality (through, for example, the control of advertising, the provision of product information by governmental bodies, or the promotion of greater equality in income distribution) rather than the establishment of centralized socialism;

2. no conceivable listing of collective wants would provide a basis for supporting a

policy of near-comprehensive centralized choice; and

3. an acceptance of the rationality for contemporary underdeveloped economies of even a high degree of governmental determination of the division of national income into investment and consumption and government formulation of investment criteria and priorities does not provide a case for near-comprehensive governmental determination of production targets or near-comprehensive government ownership.

In short, recognition of the prospective rationality of centralized choice in various instances does not provide a conclusive case for centralized socialism as an economic system.

Analysis of Conditions and Formulation of Plans

SUBSTITUTION OF GROWTH STRATEGIES FOR THE STATIC ALLOCATIONAL CALCULUS: INDIVISIBILITIES AND COMPLEXITY

Even by its advocates, the price system is typically considered a social process best equipped to enable *continuous*, *marginal* adjustments and adaptations to changing conditions based upon calculations of marginal gain and marginal cost. The cruder processes of centralized decision-making generally are acknowledged by centralized socialists to be more suitable for making big, *discontinuous* changes than for continuous marginal adjustments. Thus, the effectiveness of a centralized socialist system in analyzing economic conditions and formulating economic plans depends in part on "the actual complexity of the situation with which any group of central planners is likely to be confronted." [31: 81] This, of course, is an empirical matter, and cannot be resolved by theoretical generalization. We can conceive, however, of two classic alternatives as limiting

cases. At one extreme are the smooth, perfectly continuous variations in coefficients and variables found in most economics textbooks. At another extreme is the case of fixed coefficients of production, constant marginal cost, and "perfect complementarity" in consumer preferences. The closer the actual situation lies to the former extreme, the larger the number of possible alternatives in production and consumption, and thus, the greater the complexity of the calculational problems and the more amenable those calculations are to the sophisticated marginal calculus of orthodox price theory and of the price system as a calculational mechanism. The closer reality lies to the other extreme, the smaller the number of alternatives, the simpler the calculational problems, and the more amenable those calculations are to the cruder devices of centralized processes. In the case of perfectly fixed coefficients of production, for example, as illustrated in Fig. 11.1, the "least-cost combination of resources" for producing a particular level of output is determined solely on the basis of technological data. In the case of constant marginal cost, illustrated in Fig. 11.2, there is no "optimum scale of output" because every level of output is "optimum" (in the sense of lowest average cost). In the case of "perfect complementarity" of consumer demand, illustrated in Fig. 11.3, there is no substitutability between commodities, regardless of price and price changes.

Economists (including socialist economists) are not in agreement on the extent of continuity versus discontinuity in economic coefficients and variables, and empirical studies on this issue are not conclusive. Writing in the late 1930s, Lange accepted the traditional view that constant coefficients of production (and constant marginal cost conditions) is a "special case" rather than the general rule. [31: 94n–95n] At the other extreme, Paul Baran, in his review of national economic planning for the American Economic Association, expressed the view

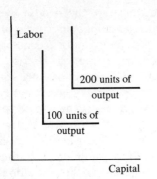

Fig. 11.1. (*Left*) Fixed coefficients of production

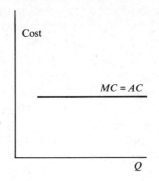

Fig. 11.2. (*Center*) Constant marginal cost

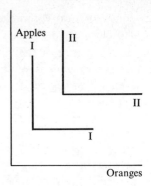

Fig. 11.3. (*Right*) Zero substitutability in consumption

that, in both developed and underdeveloped economies, the problem of the CPB "would not be slow adjustments to small changes . . . but choice among few technological alternatives involving large indivisibilities and 'fixed coefficients'." [26: 385] Dobb holds an intermediate position on this issue, probably acceptable to many non-Marxist and non-socialist economists, concluding that "actual situations may be a good deal nearer to the extreme of rigid proportions that economists have generally assumed" and that the discontinuities of reality make it a good deal "cruder" and simpler than the smooth curves seen in textbook graphs infer. [31: 85]

Dobb gives several examples of prominent types of discontinuities to support his conclusion. One is the familiar case of indivisibilities in capital equipment: For example, shall we build one or two blast furnaces? Shall a railroad be constructed from New York to Chicago or not? This kind of indivisibility is especially prominent in underdeveloped economies and is related to the "magnitude argument" for centralized decision-making already noted. It may easily continue, however, in the process of industrialization, where new plants may be used to produce new products or varieties of old ones rather than simply expanding the production of some existing commodity.

Another example is fixity, or, at least, discontinuities, in the technological coefficients of production. Again, this is particularly

prominent in the case of capital and especially in the short-run time period, in which capital is "fixed" in supply. Third is the case of complementarity in supply and/or demand, where a combination of products are supplied and/or demanded (for example: steel, automobiles, rubber, glass, highway construction, filling stations, and restaurants) and where gradations and combinations are significantly less than infinite.

A fourth, and "peculiar" but probably "characteristic," case of discontinuity in consumer demand may arise in a socialist economy under conditions of relative equality in incomes. Above a certain price level, market demand for consumers' durables (for example: automobiles, refrigerators, TV sets) is likely to be highly inelastic; while, near and below that price, many or most consumers may want to buy it, and demand will become highly elastic. From the standpoint of economic analysis, the market demand curve will have a sharp discontinuity or "kink" at or near that price, as illustrated in Fig. 11.4. "The practical conclusion will be that no intermediate position may be practicable for planning between not putting the commodity into mass production at all and producing it on a very large scale indeed." [31: 85]

A final example is the limitations placed upon present choices by decisions made in the past. In any given short-run period of time, alternatives are distinctly limited

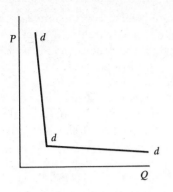

Fig. 11.4. Discontinuity in consumer demand

because of past decisions (investment is limited by existing steel capacity, consumption by the size of consumer goods industries, and so on.) In theoretical analysis, the "range of practicable decision—the degree of freedom"—increases over time until, in the long-run, all factors become variable.

> In practice, however, no planning, however ambitious, can have more than a fairly limited time horizon, since the number of incalculables in the situation will increase progressively as the perspective of any plan is extended into the future. It may well be that this practicable time horizon is considerably shorter than the economists' abstract long-period in which productive resources become indefinitely mobile and adaptable. To the extent that it is shorter, the constraints upon planning agenda will be more numerous: the element of determinism in policy-decisions will be more prominent and the patterns to be woven of the future will be fewer. [31: 85–86]

The result of this line of reasoning is that, to the extent economic reality corresponds to the preceding description of these varied discontinuities and indivisibilities, the "problems of economic planning seem to acquire a resemblence to the problems of military strategy, where, in practice, the choice lies between a relatively small number of plans, which have in the main to be treated and chosen between as organic wholes, and which, for a variety of reasons, do not easily permit of intermediate com-

binations. The situation will demand a concentration of forces around a few main objectives, and not a dispersion of resources over a very wide range." [30: 6] Further, this shift in the nature of economic problems and problems of economic planning affects the degree of precision that can be reasonably expected in the attainment of planning goals and targets. And this, in turn, can affect the effectiveness and choice of the instruments used. Thus, a Western neo-Marxist may admit to the Hayekian charge that centralized calculation and decision-making is "incredibly clumsy, primitive, and limited in scope" [35: 50] in relation to making continuous marginal adjustments in a developed economy under given technological and institutional conditions, and yet, still defend its imprecise and dynamic-developmental rationality and effectiveness.

CENTRALIZED STRATEGIES FOR
INDUSTRIALIZATION AND ECONOMIC
DEVELOPMENT

Rapid, large-scale industrialization and economic development in an underdeveloped economy, with its attendant technological, social, and institutional changes, requires the formation of a surplus of income or output over and above consumption and its effective utilization in a series of investment projects in industry, agriculture, education, and so on. Accordingly, neo-Marxists like Baran have identified the "mobilization" and allocation of the "planned economic surplus" as the key issues in a strategy for centralized economic development in underdeveloped countries.

Mobilization. Baran distinguished three varieties of "economic surplus." The *actual economic surplus* is defined simply as the difference between actual consumption and actual output in any given economy, and thus is identical with real saving or capital accumulation. *Potential economic surplus* is "the difference between the output that *could* be produced in a given natural and technological environment with the help of employable productive resources, and what might be regarded as essential consumption." [27: 23] In any existing capitalist economic society, he contended, the potential economic surplus is significantly larger than that actually realized for four major reasons: one, the "excess" and "non-essential" consumption of upper- and middle-income brackets; two, the output foregone to society because of the existence of "unproductive workers"[2]; third, "the output lost to society because of their irrational and wasteful organization of the existing productive apparatus" (for example, excess capacity or monopoly); and fourth, "the output foregone owing to the existence of unemployment caused primarily by the anarchy of capitalist production and the deficiency of effective demand." [27: 24] *Planned economic surplus*, the concept most relevant for centralized government strategy in a rationally organized socialist economy, is defined as "the difference between society's 'optimum' output attainable in a historically given natural and technological environment under conditions of planned 'optimal' utilization of all available productive resources, and some chosen 'optimal' volume of consumption." [27: 41–42] The words *optimum* and *optimal* in the preceding sentence infer a radical reorganization of production and income distribution, with attendant revolutionary social and institutional changes, and the collective "judgment of a socialist community" embodied in "a rational plan expressing what society would wish to produce, to consume, to save, and to invest at any given time." [27: 42]

Though the *actual* economic surplus invested in productive plants and equipment in underdeveloped economies is small, the *potential* economic surplus is often surprisingly large. Though not generally large in absolute terms, it is often a high proportion of the national incomes of these countries and is "sufficiently large" to enable high "rates of growth" if not always "large absolute increments to their output . . . ." [27: 227] The central problem is *not* "shortage of capital," but, rather, a failure to realize the potential economic surplus in the form of productive investment, a failure brought about by the factors listed earlier, especially "by various forms of excess consumption of the upper class, by increments to hoards at home and abroad, by the maintenance of vast unproductive bureaucracies and of even more expensive and no less redundant military establishments. A very large share of it . . . is withdrawn by foreign capital." [27: 228] The "first" and "decisive" step in a strategy of centralized development is therefore the actual "mobilization" of the potential economic surplus.

Baran cited two typical obstacles to the realization of the potential economic surplus, one transitory, the other more fundamental. The transitory obstacle is the "upheaval and disorganization" which accompany the revolutionary transformation to the new economic system. The revolutionary crisis may be so severe—especially when accompanied by war and civil war as in Soviet Russia—as to preclude any increase in either investment or consumption; indeed, both may fall, and even essential consumption may be disrupted. Once the immediate revolutionary crisis is over and pre-revolutionary levels of output are restored, a second and more fundamental obstacle appears. Though the "social revolution" generally will transfer control over large industry to the revolutionary government, the "agrarian revolution," which typically and probably unavoidably

---

[2]Baran defined unproductive work as consisting "of all labor resulting in the output of goods and services the demand for which is attributable to the specific conditions and relationships of the capitalist system, and which would be absent in a rationally ordered society." As illustrations, he cited workers "engaged in manufacturing armaments, luxury articles of all kinds, objects of conspicuous display and marks of social distinction. Others are government officials, members of the military establishment, clergymen, lawyers, tax evasion specialists, public relations experts, and so forth. Still further groups of unproductive workers are advertising agents, brokers, merchants, speculators, and the like." [27: 32–33]

accompanies it, destroys the "social foundations" of the economic surplus (through the elimination of rent and interest payments, the division of large landed estates, and so on) and thus has the primary effect of increasing peasant incomes and mass consumption. Especially in countries where most of the output, and thus, economic surplus was generated in agriculture, the potential economic surplus "absorbed" by the peasant population must be "recaptured." Until it is, the actual economic surplus will fall far short of its potential, and the transition to a centrally planned economic surplus, which is the key to centrally planned development, is delayed. [27: 263–67]

In an industrialized urban economy with a highly developed monetary and fiscal system, the simplest and probably most efficient device for transferring income from private to public control is the income tax. In an underdeveloped, dominantly agricultural economy, showing the institutional and economic effects of an "agrarian revolution," the assessment and collection of an income tax is an unmanageable and "all but useless" task. In addition to political opposition from the peasantry, the low monetary receipts of the subsistence farms makes its collection in money impracticable, while the collection of taxes in kind from a large, geographically scattered rural population is "an administratively hopeless undertaking." [27: 266] Wage-price-profit policy also faces distinct difficulties. A policy of high agricultural prices, low industrial prices, low wages, and high government profits would place the burden of the industrialization program upon the urban workers (a minor segment of the population), would probably not generate sufficient revenue, and would typically be politically unacceptable to the revolutionary leadership. But reversing the relationship by shifting relative prices in favor of industry through a policy of low agricultural prices, high industrial prices, and high government profits can be counteracted by the richer peasants (the "kulaks" in the context of the Soviet Russian case) who hold marketable surpluses and who can refuse to exchange them at government prices, thwarting government plans by reducing agricultural output and/or increasing their own consumption.

In essence, then, as long as the peasantry remains economically independent, it will remain "inaccessible to planning by the socialist government." An economically independent peasantry, ideologically and industrially undisciplined, holding recollections of pre-revolutionary exploitation, and being the recipients, through an agrarian revolution, of the benefits of expanding income and consumption, are hardly likely to cooperate in "mobilizing and recapturing an economic surplus" when it places the burdens and sacrifices of the industrialization process squarely on their shoulders. The only way to incorporate agriculture in a strategy and system of centralized economic development, concluded Baran, the "only way to include it in the general nexus of the national economy is by liquidating subsistence farming as the principal form of agricultural activity and transforming agriculture into a specializing, labor-dividing, and market-oriented industry in which the structure of output as well as its distribution between the consumption of those who work in it and the surplus accruing to society as a whole can be determined by the planning authority, as in the case of other industries. Under conditions of socialism this transformation cannot be accomplished except by means of productive cooperation of the peasants, through collectivization of peasant farming . . . ." [27: 267–68] "By transferring the disposal of agricultural output from individual peasants to government-supervised collective farm managements, collectivization destroy(s) the basis for the peasants' resistance to the accumulation policy." [26: 395] With collectivization of agriculture, the portion of agricultural output consumed by the peasant population can be fixed by government allotment to collective farmers, while peasant consumption of non-agricultural products can be controlled by government regulation of agricultural and industrial prices.

Suppose, for example, the population wants to spend $95,000,000,000 out of a $100,000,000,000 national income on consumption goods and save $5,000,000,000, while the CPB, following the directives of the political leadership, plans production of $70,000,000,000 of consumption goods and $30,000,000,000 of investment goods. A wage policy which pays out $100,000,000,000 to workers in investment and consumption goods industries, including the agricultural sector, and a price policy which adds a tax of $25,000,000,000 billion to the cost of consumption goods, so that they sell at prices yielding revenues of $95,000,000,000, will provide a planned profit of $25,000,000,000 billion to supplement voluntary saving. Thus, wage-price-profit policy can become the major device for simultaneously mobilizing the potential economic surplus and making the transition to a system of governmentally planned economic surpluses. Total real wages can be set at levels corresponding to planned consumption, and the profits of government enterprises can be used to finance the investment projects of the industrialization program. The peasantry, shorn of their economic independence, can be integrated into a system of national economic planning and development, a central element of which is their absorption of the major burdens of the industrialization process.

Allocation. Once "mobilized," the economic surplus must be utilized efficiently if the developmental goals of centralized planning are to be achieved. Baran distinguished three strategic questions in the centralized allocation of the economic surplus: (1) "whether economic development should be striven for via industrialization, or whether progress should be sought by raising the productivity of agriculture . . . ." (2) "whether economic development should be sought through the expansion of producers' goods (heavy)

industries, or through an increase of consumers' goods (light) industries . . ." (3) "whether capital-intensive or labor-intensive methods of production should be chosen for the development programs of the underdeveloped countries." [27: 271, 283, 285]

In regard to the first question, centralized socialists contend that an exclusive or primary reliance on raising agricultural productivity (as advised by some non-socialist economists) is self-defeating. The rate of increase in output obtained through such productivity-raising devices as better seed and livestock, cheaper credit, and so on is so small as to be typically offset by growth in population. A really large increase in agricultural productivity presumes the use of modern agricultural technology and capital equipment, that is, the mechanization, capitalization, chemicalization—in short, the *industrialization*—of agriculture. But if industralization is an important prerequisite for the improvement and modernization of agriculture, it is no less true that economic surpluses to finance investment projects in industry must come essentially from the agricultural sector of the economy. Thus, increased agricultural productivity and surpluses are prerequisites for industrialization, and exclusive emphasis on investment in industry is as one-sided as exclusive reliance on agriculture. The way out of this "vicious circle" is to recognize the interdependence and complementarity of agriculture and industry and to embark on a program of large-scale investment and industrialization in industry *and* large-scale modernization, collectivization, and industrialization in agriculture *simultaneously*. The question—industrialization *or* increased agricultural productivity—is "meaningless." Both are needed. "It is the growth of industry that supplies agriculture with the technical wherewithal for its development and with manufactured consumer goods for the rural population, and it is the expansion of agriculture that provides food for the increasing industrial labor force, and many raw materials for the rising industrial production." [27: 275]

The second question involves the allocation of the economic surplus between investment and consumer goods industries, for example, between the production of machines to produce steel, electric power, or more machines versus the production of machines to produce automobiles, TVs, and hair dryers. But this question is essentially the same as the more general one of the optimum rate of economic growth. Investment in industries making consumer goods increases the productive capacity of those industries, and thus, the aggregate potential annual level of consumer goods output. But investment in the capital goods industries "raises not merely the potential level but the potential *increase* in the consumption level each year in the future (since that increase is dependent on the output of new productive equipment for the industries making consumers' goods)." [31: 130–31] Its effect is thus *continuing* rather than once-and-for-all. Whether the rate of growth in total output is to rise, fall, or remain constant depends upon the proportions in which net investment is allocated between the capital goods and consumer goods industries. Thus, the same rationale which supports rapid growth in total output simultaneously supports an allocational policy which gives the investment goods sector and heavy industry top priority.

Within the investment goods sector, centralized allocation consists essentially of making a relatively small number of strategic decisions, concentrating on a number of "crucial links." For example, in one planning period, steel and machine tools may receive high priority; transportation and electric power may be relatively neglected. In a succeeding plan, these "transitory 'disproportionalities'" will become apparent, and emphasis will shift to pulling up the temporarily backward "links" in the "chain" of economic development. [26: 397–98]

Beyond the issue of the allocation of the economic surplus among different branches and industries is the question of what *form* the investment should take, what methods of production should be used. Western economists have often answered this third question by recommending labor-intensive, rather than capital-intensive, methods. The reasoning behind this is basically two-fold: First, capital is generally scarce in relation to labor in most underdeveloped economies. Low-cost production in these cases involves economizing in the use of the scarce factor, that is, adopting techniques of production which are labor-using and capital-saving. Second, underdeveloped economies often have large surpluses of unemployed labor— both "disguised unemployment" among the rural peasantry and "undisguised unemployment" among people who have left the farms but are unable to find work in the cities. Both as a means of contributing to the reduction of unemployment, and as a device for expanding output with little or no investment, labor-intensive methods are indicated.

Centralized socialists take sharp exception to what they term this "dogma" [31: 139] of the "conventional literature." [27: 285] Opportunities for expanding output by transferring the "disguised unemployed" to urban industries are distinctly limited, they contend. Indeed, argued Baran, if we consider the expenditures for housing, hospitals, and schools which must accompany their transfer, and the food and clothing which must be assured once they arrive, "the labor-intensive techniques may well involve a larger outlay of capital per unit of output than the capital-intensive alternatives." [27: 286]

Beyond this, there are several positive arguments supporting the case for capital-intensive methods. The central problem, suggests Dobb, is the goal of rapid, large-scale economic growth. Once this is accepted, it follows that the choice between capital-intensive and labor-intensive forms of investment depends essentially not on the ratio of the stock of capital to the stock of labor, but rather "on precisely the same considerations as those which determine the choice between a high and a low rate of investment . . . namely, the importance to be attached to raising consumption in the immediate future compared with the potential increase of consumption in the more distant future which a particular rate of investment and form of investment will make possible. In other words, the same ground which would justify a high rate of investment . . . would justify also a high degree of capital intensity in the choice of investment-forms; and *vice versa*." There is no *a priori* reason, Dobb adds, to support the contention that underdeveloped economies should have a lower rate of investment than developed economies. Indeed, because the productivity effects of "a given increase in the (relatively small) stock of capital is likely . . . to be abnormally large" [31: 149] the converse, if anything, would be true.

Further, the factor proportions argument rests upon a static criterion, namely the ratio of the stock of capital to that of labor at a given moment in time. But in the dynamic process of economic development, factor scarcities may change. The "abundance and 'cheapness' of currently available labor may well be only a temporarily prevailing condition *preceding* the realization of any given stretch of the developmental program. Aware of the aggregate demand for labor entailed by its own plans, the authority has to consider therefore that relatively soon, during the life span of the equipment that is to be installed, labor may turn from a relatively ample to a relatively scarce factor, particularly when this involves skilled labor." [27: 287]

Lastly, once a commitment has been made to rapid, large-scale economic growth as the imperative objective of centralized planning, and once top priority has been given to heavy industry, the choice of techniques is distinctly limited. Workers do not just "sit down" and turn out machine tools, electrical equipment, or tractors with their bare hands. Often the choice is between producing a particular product, taking advantage of the possibility of drawing upon the technology and scientific knowledge of the developed countries, or not producing that particular commodity at all.

CRITERIA, TECHNIQUES, AND PROBLEMS IN CENTRALIZED PLAN FORMULATION

Scope and Character of Centralized Socialist Planning. Government economic planning under centralized socialism—in contrast, say, to the type of economic planning currently popular in many of the economically developed nations of the West—does not consist only of the coordination of different public economic policies and of the various sectors of the economy. It is much broader in scope and involves "an active determination of the main lines of development of the national economy. Otherwise, if planning were mere coordination, the development of socialist economy would be elemental; it would not really be directed by the will of organized society." [40: 20] In short, the CPB has the responsibility of formulating a "plan" or plans for the development of the whole economic system.

The scope of central plans may vary over a fairly wide range and still meet this general requirement of serving as an "active" and "directive" agent in the strategy of centralized development. The *minimum* plan, suggested Lange in his postwar analysis, "must include at least two things: first, the division of national income between accumulation and consumption; second, the distribution of investments among the different branches of the economy. The first determines the general rate of economic growth; the second determines the direction of development." In addition, the plan "may or may not include the targets for the production of certain basic commodities, like basic raw materials, basic means of production, and so on. These," he concluded, are "technical problems, not fundamental problems." [40: 21] Beyond targets and plans of physical output, of course, are those of finance and of labor—plans, for example, for cash, credit, the government's budget, foreign exchange, and the balance of payments position; plans for the supply of and demand for labor; and targets for the education and training of labor, the transfer of labor from agriculture to industry, from over-populated to unsettled regions, and so on.

The heart of centralized planning and control lies in the physical plan, the overall blueprint which translates the generalized directives of the political leadership into more concrete objectives, expressed in terms of physical quantities of outputs and inputs of consumer goods and services, of labor, and, especially, of investment in plant and equipment. Of course, the sale of consumer goods output, the purchase and sale of labor services, the receipt and expenditure of government funds, the provision of currency and credit, and the sale of intermediate products and investment goods among enterprises all involve or may involve the use of markets and money. Thus, the "physical plan" must be accompanied by a "financial plan," expressing the same targets and objectives in monetary terms and indicating the planned utilization of money and credit, and the planned flows of monetary expenditures and receipts throughout the economic system. Clearly, however, the physical plan takes priority over the financial plan. A centrally and comprehensively planned economic system controls the use of its resources and actively guides and determines the process of economic development through its system of physical plans and allocations. In short, noted Dobb, the "Financial Plan will need to be appropriately geared to the Production Plan and the gearing altered to conform with any fundamental alteration in the latter." [30: 351]

Consistency and Efficiency in Plan For-mulation. The formulation of centralized economic plans involves two central and fundamental criteria: consistency and efficiency. What do these criteria entail? Why are they important, and how do they raise problems and difficulties in plan formulation? What techniques do central planners have for attempting to meet these criteria and reduce or resolve the problems associated with them?

By *consistency*, we mean the internal coordination or balance among the different parts of the plan. The demand for labor must be equal to the supply of labor. The output of coal must be sufficient to produce the planned targets for steel production. Steel must be available in the proper quantities and varieties to achieve plans for tractor output. Tractors, seeds, fertilizers, and irrigation systems must all be available mutually and simultaneously to produce the planned targets of wheat production. The demands for specific consumer goods must be commensurate with their supplies. Financial equilibrium must accompany and accommodate physical coordination: the supply of cash and credit must equal the monetary value of consumer goods output; the monetary value of inputs must be consistent with the monetary value of output; money wages must be equal to planned consumption; and so on.

Consistency emerges as a distinct problem for centrally planned economies because of the immense complexity and mutual interdependence of economic variables. In economic affairs, all variables literally are interwoven in a system of mutual interdependence. Further, a centrally and comprehensively planned economy has no built-in social process (such as the competitive price system) which automatically works to promote coordination and equilibrium. Central planners must consciously identify and measure these mutual interdependencies and formulate plans accordingly. They must recognize and understand the ramifications of economic interdependence because an increase in the aggregate performance of the national economy depends upon balance among its constituent parts and sectors. "Bottlenecks" (for example, the under-supply of skilled labor, the lack of spare parts for trucks) can disrupt and slow down the process of economic development.

According to Gregory Grossman, maintaining physical balance or consistency is the "chief daily task and core" of a "command economy" (where decisions are made on the basis of "directives from above.") Before any economy can turn to the more sophisticated and exacting requirements of static allocational or dynamic developmental efficiency, it must first attain at least a minimal level of microeconomic balance between supplies and demands of particular goods. "It is *this* task that in fact constitutes by far the largest part of the so-called planning in the command economy, *not* what we in the West usually understand by this term, namely, the delineation of economic goals and the selection of strategies and instruments for their realization." Much of the planning activity in a command economy "is devoted to an arduous activity that substitutes for the most elementary accomplishment of the market mechanism." This imperative fundamental role for consistency in centralized planning explains why *physical* planning is so important in the context of the command economy. "To attain and preserve balance, a command economy must collate the physical availabilities and requirements of very many commodities, and this in turn necessitates physical targets for production and input utilization . . . ." [33: 142, 143, 144]

Efficiency goes beyond consistency. An efficient utilization of resources presumes at least some minimum degree of coordination of the parts and branches of the economy and the absence of at least the most strategic and glaring bottlenecks. But the reverse is not true. An economic system may meet the criterion of internal consistency quite well in that supplies may equal demands and its various parts may mesh together smoothly, and it still may operate at a very low level of efficiency. Efficiency generally involves a maximization-minimization problem—for example, minimizing the input of resources in the production of particular commodities, maximizing output from a given body of inputs—and arises in a variety of contexts, for example, in calculating the most efficient combination of inputs, level of outputs, scale of plant, location of plant, degree of geographic specialization, allocation of investment funds among different branches and industries, and so on.

Efficiency is a special problem for centrally planned economies. In the absence of a pricing mechanism, central planners have no readily available system for translating physical quantities (pounds, tons, bushels, and so on) into comparable quantitative magnitudes, and thus, no one simple measure of success or efficiency, no indigenous institutional mechanism for calculating alternative costs. Hierarchical price systems may be established, of course; but these, for a variety of reasons to be noted shortly, may not adequately nor accurately reflect real costs, based on underlying relative scarcities of different resources. In a centrally planned system, plans do not follow prices; prices follow plans. There are obvious limitations in attempting to calculate the efficiency of a system of physical plans on the basis of monetary cost data, the content of which is regarded as secondary and accommodative to the physical plans themselves. Yet, efficiency in plan formulation is an important criterion for centralized socialists. The promotion of high rates of growth over the passage of time requires reasonably close concern with the "minimization of the sacrifice of alternatives" in any given period of time. It is true that the strategy of centralized development in an under-developed economy places static allocational efficiency at a distinctly lower level of priority than the more dynamic criterion of economic growth and development. Still, an underdeveloped economy with fewer resources, a lower standard of living, and lower reserves of plant equipment and stocks of goods can ill afford waste and a cavalier attitude toward the criterion of efficiency in the use of the meager resources it does have.

Central planners propose a variety of techniques for reducing the magnitude and severity of the problems of consistency and efficiency in a centralized socialist economy. First is the use of governmental, hierarchical pricing systems as bases for economic accounting. One of the most thorough-going proposals in regard to the utilization of price systems in centralized socialism was made by Lange in the late 1930s. Suppose the preference scale of the CPB is given and has been communicated to plant and industry managers in the form of a system of prices. In this case, *all* prices become "accounting prices," and the same rules of consistency and efficiency apply as under decentralized socialism. Internal consistency is achieved by instructing plant and industry managers to produce at that level of output at which marginal cost is equal to the given accounting price and to direct "ultimate productive resources . . . only to industries which can 'account for' the prices fixed" by the CPB. [39: 92] Efficiency is promoted by instructing plant managers to choose that combination of resources which minimizes the cost of producing each level of output. Accounting prices can have an "objective meaning" if the CPB imposes the "parametric function of prices" upon itself. In other words, the CPB fixes prices on the basis of its own preference scale; but, once set, they are regarded as given and are changed only via a trial-and-error process of movement toward market equilibrium. At the end of the accounting period, the prices of commodities in short supply are raised, while those for which there are surpluses are lowered. "The consistency of those decisions with the plan can be, instead, measured by fixing quotas of output and comparing them with the actual achievement (as is done in the Soviet Union). But there is no way of measuring the *efficiency* in carrying out the

plan without a system of accounting prices which satisfies the objective equilibrium condition, for the rule to produce at the minimum average cost has no significance with regard to the aims of the plan unless prices represent the relative scarcity of the factors of production." [39: 94]

Actually, most centralized socialists do not go this far, for to do so would assign the determination of prices to the CPB, but would delegate the determination of quantities of inputs and outputs to plant and industry managers. The usual conception of a centralized socialist "plan" includes centrally determined quantitative output and input targets. Still, even in this case, a hierarchical price system may aid calculation, if only in the modest role of accommodating and facilitating the physical plan.

Second, the "ability to build on the past and to change things around if plans are out of line enormously simplifies the task of planning."[3] Even centralized and comprehensive plans do not begin completely from scratch; they typically represent, instead, modifications of and deviations from established patterns of the past. With the passage of time, plans may be modified and changed in the process of execution. Flexibility in plan reformulation is related to priorities in planning goals. Given the primary objective of rapid, large-scale industrialization, and the lower emphasis upon consumer sovereignty and consumer welfare, it is possible to shift resources from consumer goods industries to the production of investment goods if, toward the end of the planning period, it becomes apparent initial planning targets were excessively optimistic and joint attainment of investment and consumer goods goals is unlikely. This way, consistency can be maintained in the crucial investment goods sector by sacrificing, if necessary, the production of consumer goods.

[3] Alfred R. Oxenfeldt and Vesevolod Holubnychy, *Economic Systems in Action* (New York: Holt, Rinehart & Winston, Inc., 1965), p. 97.

Third, the scope of centralized planning can be restricted to a relatively small number of "key links" and basic commodities. Detailed plans of the "nuts and bolts" and "red-versus-blue lollypops" variety can be left to local planners more familiar with the "concretized circumstances of time and place," with local conditions and needs.

Fourth is decentralization of data gathering. Even in centralized socialism, the CPB need be responsible, especially at the outset, for only the broadest and most aggregative of plans. The plan can acquire more specialized microeconomic content in the process of disaggregation downward into regional, industry, plant, and collective farm plans. Equilibrium outputs and inputs may be approached via a process of "trial and error" and "successive approximations" somewhat analogous to the decentralized socialist analysis of price determination.

Fifth, centralized socialists propose that internal consistency may be checked through the device of "national balance sheets" or, at a more sophisticated level, by input-output analysis. In the simplest and most aggregative form, the national balance sheets constitute a sort of national economic ledger, with a list of sources of supply of a particular commodity (such as planned output, stocks of reserves, planned imports) on one side of the page and a list showing planned allocation of that commodity among different users on the other. In a more complex form, the "method of balances" has been described by Dobb as "the use of a complex system of equations between the various magnitudes in a plan as the tests of internal consistency or coherence between its various elements." [30: 331]

Because incomes are paid in the form of money and are freely spent on consumer goods markets, production balance sheets must be accompanied by financial balances. From a macroeconomic view, the problems of consistency and balance arise most prominently in regard to the division of resources between investment and consumption. The most typical centralized socialist proposal,

as noted earlier, is to set the total wage-bill (the average wage level multiplied by the total number of workers) at a level sufficient to enable total consumer expenditures to equal the monetary value of consumer goods output (the sum total of consumer goods output multiplied by their prices) and to set a margin between the retail prices of consumer goods and their costs equal to the planned cost of investment goods. Microeconomically speaking, once the financial balances are coordinated with physical balance sheets of the quantities of various resources required to attain output targets, "planned costs" can be determined by adding the products of input quantities and input prices. A "planned profit," calculated as a percent of "planned cost," may be added to determine the selling price of each commodity. Under such a system of calculations, noted Dobb, actual profit will vary inversely with the relation of actual cost to planned cost. If enterprises meet output targets with smaller quantities of inputs than those designated in the plan, actual costs will be lower than planned costs, and actual profits will be higher than planned profits. If plant managers are permitted to retain a portion of this "unplanned profit" and use it for managerial bonuses, welfare facilities, and the like, it can serve as a "collective incentive" to increase efficiency and "'beat the plan'." With both output and price set by the production and financial plans, "the enterprise can do nothing to improve its financial position by restricting output: on the contrary, to restrict output will reduce its receipts and hence any profit to be left in its hands. Here the enterprise is harnassed firmly within the shafts of the Plan. The sole way in which it can improve its financial position, and hence the sole direction in which profit can operate as an incentive, is by an economy in its consumption of productive resources." [30 : 355]

Problems in Plan Formulation. Probably the most important factor to keep in mind in appraising the prospective success of plan formulation under centralized socialism is the criteria for appraisal. In terms of *their own* criteria, centralized socialists present a provocative and persuasive argument. In the context of an underdeveloped economy and a traditional pre-capitalist society, where private investment-and production-oriented entrepreneurship is scarce, a centralized, collectivist analysis of economic conditions and formulation of plans can be a powerful stimulus to economic growth. Given the goal of large-scale, rapid industrialization and granting the relative unimportance of meeting consumer wants, both the simplicity and the content of the centralized socialist strategy for "mobilizing and allocating the planned economic surplus" acquires a logic and rationality which it would not have in a more complex, economically developed, consumer-oriented society. Granting the existence of even some of the indivisibilities and discontinuities in production and consumption stressed by the centralized socialists, the task of achieving consistency and efficiency in economic calculation and plan formulation would indeed be simpler than that envisaged in the orthodox marginal analysis, with its marginal calculations, continuous variations, and innumerable alternatives. Assuming a dynamic sequence of development over the passage of time is a more important measure of success than static allocational efficiency at any given moment or period of time, the "key links" strategy of centralized planning loses some of its crudeness and acquires a rationality which otherwise it would not have. Lastly, given institutional mechanisms for decentralized data-gathering and flexibility in plan revision and recalculation; restricting the scope of the central plan to, say, 1,000 to 2,000 "basic" commodities; making some crude but not inaccurate assumptions about underlying technological coefficients; and granting the existence of reserves of strategic resources to soften the blow of unexpected contingencies, it is reasonable to conclude that the problems of maintaining a necessary minimum of internal consistency would be of a significantly lower order of magnitude than that popularly supposed.

But all of this grants the assumptions as well as the criteria of the centralized socialists. The shoe is definitely on the other foot when these assumptions and criteria are replaced by those of a more traditional kind. Of course, as already noted, an underdeveloped economy is placed even less favorably than a developed one to absorb waste and inefficiency in the allocation of its resources. The greater scarcity of its resources—especially skilled labor, managerial talent, and capital—makes their economical utilization as important if not more important than in a developed economy. But beyond this, and of greater importance, the very success of centrally planned strategies for industrialization and economic development must progressively create and magnify their own obsolescence. As a centrally planned economy develops, it becomes more complex, the number of alternatives in production and consumption increases, the grand, macroeconomic strategies of the earlier stages of industrialization become increasingly less sufficient to encompass a meaningful overview of the microeconomics of the whole system, the pressures of expanding consumer goods production become greater, the varieties of products increase, and the difficulties of meshing production decisions with consumer wants, as well as output targets with input requirements, enlarge. A concrete empirical example: The Dobb-Baran-Sweezy model is admirably suited to provide a simplified rationale for the Soviet industrialization process of the 1920s and 1930s; it is less effectively equipped for providing guidelines to understanding and appraising the considerably more complex, more industrialized, and more sophisticated Soviet Russian economy of the 1970s.

In addition to increasing difficulties of maintaining an integrated overview of the whole economic system as it increases in size and complexity, the principal limitation of centralized socialism in plan formulation would appear to be the absence of an indigenous system or social process for calculating with any real degree of sophistication the preferences of consumers on the one hand and the alternative or opportunity costs of production on the other.

As already noted, the "basic needs" of minimum living standards can perhaps be assessed directly by political leadership and or the CPB without any great loss in consumer welfare. ("Are we going to put shoes on the peasants this year or not?") But, as the magnitude and variety of consumer goods increases (as the centralized socialists expect and promise it will in the process of centrally planned development), CPB-determination of consumer goals undoubtedly becomes increasingly crude and inaccurate. Voting and questionnaires have their uses in specialized instances, but as general indices of consumer preferences over a wide variety of products and services, are crude and cumbersome devices. The only alternative is consumer market choice via a price system. This is, of course, precisely the conclusion Dobb reaches when he accepts the rationality of a retail market as a process for communicating consumer preferences. But in doing so, he implicitly accepts what his more orthodox critics have contended all along, namely, that beyond the (admittedly important) crudities of "minimum living standards" and certain broad areas of "collective wants," centralized decision-making has no indigenous mechanism for quantifying, comparing, and communicating consumer preferences, and thus, for making marginal calculations of the desirability, from the consumers' view, of alternative choices in the allocation of resources.

As emphasized earlier, success in plan formulation requires more than maintaining internal consistency in a physical sense, more than avoiding "bottlenecks" in the combinations of inputs and in the relations between inputs and outputs—which, in itself, presumably would become increasingly complex and, *ceteris paribus*, more difficult in the process of economic development. It requires

also a calculation of the relative costs of alternative allocational patterns. But this kind of calculation cannot (except in the extreme limiting cases noted earlier) be made in physical terms. A particular level of output of a particular commodity may typically be produced by a variety of resource combinations, all of which are thus equally physically productive. Which of the alternatives is most efficient requires a knowledge of the relative scarcity of the resources. But a comparison of the relative scarcity of diverse resources—for example, steel, electric power, labor, machinery—requires quantification in comparable values and an institutional mechanism for making such quantitative and comparable measurements.

A major limitation of centralized allocational systems is that they lack indigenous institutional mechanisms for calculating costs. Centralized socialists recognize this problem when they include, in varying degrees, price systems as social processes for economic calculation in their models. But this reinforces our general conclusion. A socialist economy relying on centralized government bureaucracy has no system for cost calculations built into its institutional framework. To make meaningful comparisons of alternative costs, it must incorporate elements traditionally associated with capitalism and orthodox economic theory.

But the successful incorporation of price systems in centrally planned economies faces two major difficulties. First, the doctrinal and ideological biases of centralized socialists are obstacles to the use of price systems. Traditionally, centralized socialists were reluctant to extend recognition of the role of prices in economic calculation to capital and land, and attempted to formulate criteria for the allocation of investment funds, for example, in terms of the labor theory of value.[4]

---

[4] At one point (the late 1940s), for example, Dobb suggested that if the CPB has data on the productivities and construction costs of different investment projects, an efficient allocation of investment funds

Recently, however, this traditional view has been modified. Drawing on Soviet Russian experience, Dobb suggests that a centralized socialist economy would typically use "a retail market in which finished consumer goods are priced, and . . . a wage structure, related both to the nature of different types of work and to the relative scarcities of different sorts of labour-power, which forms the basis for the calculation of prime (variable) costs." [30: 13] He also recognizes the need for calculation of "prices of capital goods entering into construction costs as well as prices generally . . . ," allowance for natural resource scarcities, and the use of some sort of "cost of capital" to enterprises as a means of encouraging "the best use of plant and equipment . . . ." [30: 14n]

The use of prices for land and capital as well as for labor does not appear to be necessarily inconsistent with the institutions of centralized socialism. As long as capital is a a scarce productive resource, economy in its use requires some device to allocate it to its most productive uses. An interest rate, uniformly applied to different industries, provides a consistent basis for rationing scarce capital and "would set a rational limit to the amount of capital which the planner would find attractive to use in the projected plant."[5] Traditional opposition of neo-Marxists to rent and interest calculations appears to stem as much from doctrinal bias as from factors inherent in the logic of a centrally planned economy. In practice, though, doctrinal and

ideological biases may be of compelling significance. Inaccuracies and inadequacies of cost calculation in Soviet Russia, for example, probably have been caused as much by ideological opposition of the political leadership to "bourgeois" economic concepts as by factors indigenous to the institutional structure of the Soviet economy. On the other hand, a pragmatic concern for economic development is a powerful stimulus for muting the more strictly ideological obstacles to use of price systems.[6]

Second, the institutional structure and behavioral principles of centralized socialism, as described by Dobb and others, make the successful and efficient incorporation of price systems difficult. A few selected examples: Unless the CPB accepts the type of proposal made by Lange in the late 1930s or some reasonable facsimile thereof, prices will retain a large element of subjective bureaucratic guesswork. Once set, hierarchical accounting prices are not likely to be changed except at periodic intervals, and thus, are unlikely to accurately record changes in underlying demand and supply conditions over the passage of time. For simplification, prices are apt to be set for general categories of goods and are therefore unlikely to accurately reflect special considerations of quality and

---

might proceed as follows: First, calculate the "net productivity" of each project, defined as the value of plant output at current prices minus the "prime costs of building and building materials and equipment" of "producing that output, expressed as a ratio to the construction of the plant, again calculated in terms of current cost in wages and materials involved in construction." Second, formulate on this basis a priority list of projects in terms of their comparative yields. Third, simply work "down this list until the resources for investment in that given period are exhausted." [30: 14, 14n]

[5]Robert W. Campbell, *Soviet Economic Power* (Boston: Houghton Mifflin Company, 1965), p. 102.

[6]In recent years, Russian and East European economists have moved closer to the traditional Western view on the role of the interest rate in economic calculation, through the technique of the "payoff period." The essence of this device is a comparison of the cost savings of different investment projects with construction costs. Suppose two investments: With project A, construction costs are $20 million, and operating costs are $2 million less per year; the "payoff period" is thus ten years—it would take ten years for the saving in costs to pay off the investment. With project B, construction costs are $25 million, and operating cost savings are $5 million per year; the payoff period is thus five years. Clearly, the payoff period is the interest rate "standing on its head." A payoff period of ten years indicates a productivity of and thus a capacity to pay an interest rate of 10 percent, while one of five years constitutes an interest rate of 20 percent. A rule by the CPB that payoff periods must be no longer than, say, ten years means in effect the use of an interest rate of 10 percent.

product differentiation. Unlike a capitalist economy, where producers, seeking profit maximization, need not actually measure marginal cost, but need only act "as if" they were equating marginal cost and marginal revenue, managers in centrally planned economic systems would have to measure marginal cost—which is no easy task. Lastly, even in an age of high-speed electronic computers, there will be time lags between the communication of information regarding the "concrete circumstances of time and place" from decentralized data-gatherers to centralized decision-makers.

Execution of Plans and Techniques of Social Control

Analysis of problems of plan execution and social control by centralized socialists are relatively underdeveloped in relation to their treatment of plan formulation. This is, in part, explicable by the fact that plan execution is as much a matter of public administration and social psychology as of economic theory. It may also be that the subject of plan execution is a source of some embarrassment to centralized socialists. Worker control of industry and equality in the distribution of income are traditional goals of the Western democratic socialist movement. But these goals, formulated in the context of nineteenth- and early twentieth-century industrialization in Western capitalist economies, were expected to be realized in highly industrialized and post-capitalist economies. They do not fit well with the aim of large-scale, rapid industrialization in underdeveloped economies and with the technique of comprehensive and centralized direction and control of national economic development.

PLAN REVISION

A common misconception about centralized planning is that plans, once formulated, are rigid targets which must be fulfilled—and woe unto those workers, managers, and collective farmers who fail to attain them. Most centralized socialists would probably agree with this previously cited statement by Sweezy: "When a consistent and practical plan has finally been adopted, it cannot be left to the discretion of individual industry and plant managers whether or not they will conform to it; rather, it must be their first duty, imposed by law, to carry out their part of the plan to the best of their ability . . . ." [9: 236] Still, insists Dobb, plan execution does not mean merely an *ex post* "audit or inspection to allot praise or blame for achieving or falling short of the target." Nor is it concerned simply "with keeping industry on the rails of the plan." It is more accurate to say that "the process of putting a plan into operation is itself part of the process of fitting it to actual data and of testing-out its correspondence with reality. Such a process cannot be confined to the stage when the Plan is being put on paper for the first time." [30: 336, 337] Clearly, as noted earlier, this technique can add flexibility to centralized planning and can contribute to the consistency and efficiency of plans in practice, as well as to plans on the drawing boards. However, it also raises a problem for plan execution. If rigid adherence to initial plans is demanded, plans will depart increasingly from reality with the passage of time; bottlenecks and dislocations will arise, which, if not met by flexible reformulation of plans and directives, will be extended and magnified in widening circles of interdependence through the economy. If, on the other hand, the CPB is too flexible in the reformulation of plans, managers will begin to look on planning targets as exhortations and advice rather than as directives, and evasions of the plans "are likely to be multiplied for no sufficient reason; and these evasions will themselves introduce new unforeseen elements, with their consequential hitches and maladjustments affecting other parts of the Plan." [30: 337–38]

Dobb's compromise solution is that the

CPB must be in a position to judge quickly whether divergences between plans and reality are "justified" or "unjustified." If failures to meet the plan are justified in the light of actual events and unforeseen developments, then plans must be revised, with an eye to minimizing disruptive repercussions and adjustments in other sectors of the economy. If planning failures are unjustified, it is the failures which must be quckly corrected, again, with a minimum of interdependent disturbance. Naturally, a system of effective plan revision requires "a developed machinery and techniques of observation and of analysis of the current situation at every point, as well as a machinery and technique of control. It will also, of course, be greatly facilitated by the possession of certain reserves (such as key raw materials and mobile equipment) to give elbow-room to maneuver." [30: 338] It also requires a balance or fusion between "political" and "realistic" elements. Every plan is a statement of purpose, a policy designed to guide, exhort, persuade, and shape human action. It is also, however, a realistic analysis of economic conditions and prognostication of future developments and potentials based on logic and facts. Thus, a strategic feature of centralized planning "can be said to consist of moving towards a successful blend of policy with reality, of subjective design with the objective situation, of directives with prognosis, by a *succession of approximations;* but a succession of approximations written, not simply on paper, but in action." [30: 339]

CENTRALIZATION AND DECENTRALIZATION

Plan execution, no less than plan formulation, requires a balance between centralization and decentralization. [Cf. 33: 144–48] On the one hand, control over revision of plans and correction of planning failures requires the unifying, comprehensive insights of a central planning body. In the absence of sufficient and effective centralized control, managers and planners in various industries and regions are likely to proceed in plan execution and revision without sufficient consideration of mutual interdependence and balanced development of the entire system. Steel producers, for example, may concentrate production in a small geographic area, and achieve low production costs at the expense of high transportation costs for the rest of the economic system. Planners in particular geographic regions may ignore the advantages of territorial division of labor and build little autarkic empires of their own. On the other hand, no CPB, even in an age of electronic computers, has at its disposal *all* the knowledge of the concrete circumstances of time and place of particular regions, industries, plants, and farms. In acquiring information about plan failures, in making judgments about the justification of those failures, and in making decisions as to plan revisions, some decentralization is imperative. The "lower units of the planning mechanism," states Dobb, "act as the eyes and ears" of the CPB. "These tentacles of the planning octopus," as he aptly describes them, extending out and down both industrially and geographically, "feel out the ground over which it moves . . . . They will be the 'progress officers' of the Plan." Indeed, in "many cases, where no more than local adjustments are required, they will play the operative role in initiating or sanctioning any revisions that have to be made." [30: 339]

TECHNIQUES OF SOCIAL CONTROL

Centrally and comprehensively planned economic systems are sometimes called "command economies." [Cf., e.g., 33: 137] In a general and popular sense, this phrase is descriptively useful. The dynamics of centralized socialism reside in the power, decisions, and "commands" of its centralized leadership. In the more technical nomenclature introduced earlier, however, this label is apt to be misleading. Actually, the economic theory of centralized socialism (as well as the behavior of centrally planned economies in practice) includes a mixture of a variety of types of social control, with "command" in a technical sense playing a significant, but limited, role.

Even in centralized socialism, social control is not exclusively unilateral. Some degree of reciprocity, though small, would or could exist. Government control of the economy is, in part, countered by the possibility of *some* consumer control over production decisions, both in the general aggregative sense of the necessity for maintaining *minimum* consumption standards as a condition for plan fulfillment and of generalized pressures for greater emphasis on consumer goods production as the industrial base is built and higher levels of production and education achieved, and in the microeconomic sense of the utilization of a retail market for revealing consumer preferences, the satisfaction of which, once fundamental investment and industrialization requirements have been met, is not inconsistent with the aims of centralized socialism. Further, centralized socialists recognize that the CPB is not omniscient, and that some decentralization in data gathering and plan formulation, revision, and execution is necessary. The specific contents of centralized socialist plans are perhaps more accurately described as the result of a bargaining process between planners and managers at different levels of the planning hierarchy than as a predetermined downward communication of unilateral decrees.

Even within the realm of conscious unilateral control, centralized socialism may well use a combination of compulsion and inducement to control individual economic agents and to achieve its plans rather than compulsion alone. Lange, for example, distinguished between two types of social control, calling one the method of "administrative orders and administrative allocation of resources" and the other the method of "economic means." In the former, various production units in the economy "are ordered to do certain things—for instance, to produce so much of something. The resources which are necessary for that purpose, both material

and financial, are allocated in an administrative way." The latter method sets "up a system of incentives which induces people to do exactly the things which are required by the plan." [40: 22]

The compulsion of a system of "administrative orders and allocations" cannot be dispensed with in a centralized socialist economy. The minimum "fundamental decision" of the strategy for centrally planned economic development (that is, the division of national income into investment and consumption, and the allocation of investment funds among different sectors of the economy) would seem to require some degree of compulsion—command or prohibition—to be implemented and executed. Further, "economic means are rather subtle instruments responding to 'normal' changes in the situation and frequently break down when very fundamental or revolutionary changes are needed. In such cases, the use of administrative means must be accepted." [40: 22] Thus, in the transition to centralized socialism and in the early years of its development when large-scale, rapid institutional changes are taking place and incentives systems are insufficient, unreliable, and slow, great reliance on "administrative means" and compulsion is likely.

In general, however, and increasingly in the process of economic development preference "should be given to the use of economic means." [40: 22] Lange supported this recommendation by two arguments: First, by using "economic means, planning makes use of the automatic character of people's responses to given incentives. Thus, certain automatic processes in the economy are established." [40: 23] Second, the system of "administrative orders" has distinct disadvantages and limitations which become increasingly apparent as a socialist economy develops:

Methods which are necessary and useful in the period of social revolution and of intensive industrialization become an obstacle to further economic progress when they are perpetuated beyond their historic justification. They become obstacles because they are characterized by lack of flexibility. They are rigid; they lead, therefore, to waste of resources resulting from this inflexibility; they require a wasteful bureaucratic apparatus and make it difficult to adjust production to the needs of the population. However, it seems that the greatest obstacle to further progress results from the lack of proper economic incentives in this bureaucratic centralistic type of management. This hampers proper economic utilization of resources, encourages waste, and also hinders technical progress. [40: 18–19]

Of course, value judgments and proposals do not in themselves explain how a centrally planned economic system would or does behave. The point, rather, is one of logic and fact: Insofar as the aims of centralized socialism can be better attained through the use of inducement than of compulsion, and insofar as the political leadership recognizes this and is rationally prepared to act on it, it is logical to conclude that inducement is or will be the dominant technique of social control in centralized socialist economies.[7]

It should be emphasized, however, that the conscious, manipulated incentives system of a centralized socialist economy—and the resulting pattern of income distribution accompanying it—is quite different from the more spontaneous controls of the competitive price system. The uncautious reader of socialist literature is apt to obtain the impression that centralized socialism and competitive capitalism are essentially similar in the area of social control—both presumably would rely primarily upon systems of economic incentives to coordinate and control economic decisions. This impression is highly misleading. Though central planners make use of "the automatic character of people's responses to given incentives" and thereby establish "certain automatic processes in the economy," these processes should be distinguished from the market-determined (Lange calls them "elemental") processes and incentives systems of competitive capitalism: "These two things should be distinguished. The difference is that in a socialist society, where the automatic processes are part of the method of realization of the plan, the conditions establishing incentives are set up by economic policy; whereas in capitalist society, these conditions develop in an elemental way. There is a basic difference: In one case (capitalism), the incentives develop in an elemental way and are not subject to conscious control of society; in the other case (socialism), they are consciously established by organized society in such a way as to produce the desired results." [40: 18–19]

PROBLEMS IN PLAN EXECUTION AND SOCIAL CONTROL

The popular view that a centrally planned economy cannot successfully administer a coordinated system of plan execution nor provide an incentives system to mesh the directives of the political leadership and the actions of managers, workers, and peasants seems grossly exaggerated. One thing seems clear from the developmental experience of Communist countries: Centrally planned economies can be and are powerful agents for harnessing, directing, and channeling human, capital, and natural resources into developmental programs. Through sophisticated combinations of command and induce-

---

[7]Cf. the convenient and concise list of limitations of the pure command system as a technique for social control in Dahl and Lindblom. [1: 107–8] These authors give six major reasons to support their contention that "command is an important but marginal system" [1: 106] of social control: (1) Commandees have no incentive to obey commands if they can escape the penalties. (2) Command is difficult to legitimize. (3) Command requires costly and specialized machinery of supervision, enforcement, and punishment. (4) Command gives "little incentive to industry, enthusiasm, loyalty . . .", and so on. (5) Command is frustrating because the controller has nothing to offer subordinates except punishments for failure to conform to commands. (6) For all these reasons, "Superiors themselves find it unprofitable and inefficient to rely exclusively on command . . ." and therefore attempt to modify pure commands by introducing incentives systems.

ment, the political leadership of centrally planned economies has been successful in harnessing the personal aspirations and incentives of individuals, especially managers and industrial workers, to the requirements of central plans.

On the other hand, on both logical and empirical grounds, there are important shortcomings in centralized systems of plan execution and control. First is the inevitable conflict between the "political" and "realistic" elements of planning targets mentioned earlier. The input-output figures in central plans are or may be a confusing mixture of political goals, exhortations, and statistical data. Planning data serve the important political purpose of guidance, persuasion, and exhortation, of urging subordinates to greater achievement than that which would be likely if data represented merely reasonable expectations of output possibilities and input requirements. Output targets and input allocations resting upon expectations of actual performance provides no basis for penalizing or prodding the inefficient producers and can conceivably lead to progressive deterioration of efficiency. If actual performance is taken as the criterion for potential, a failure to meet planning targets will be accompanied by a downward revision in expectations, which, in turn, can lead to greater laxity in plan execution, and another failure to meet planning targets, and so on *ad infinitum*, or at least to some minimum level of efficiency that even the least efficient plants would have no difficulty meeting. Yet, if planning targets are mere hopeful anticipations, not generally realized nor, in fact, realizable, production planners and managers will soon discover that, as realistic statistical data, plans are unreliable. Each manager then will have to make his own best-guess judgment as to how and to what extent he should attempt to adhere to planning targets. Multiply this several thousandfold, and rigorous *ex ante* coordination, so important to centralized socialists, evaporates. Coordination by a pricing system does not raise this conflict

because there are no physical targets to be met. Physical output quotas and input assignments are not necessary.

Second is the conflict between the requirements of centralization and decentralization. In centralized socialism, successful execution of economic plans requires both a centralized overview of the whole economic system and decentralized concern with the concrete circumstances of time and place. These two principles are in conflict, and even the most efficiently organized centralized socialist economy can be, at most, a crude, best-guess mixture between them. Again, the price system as a process for social coordination and control avoids this conflict by abstaining from the necessity of centralized decisions. All decisions in a competitive price system are decentralized, marginal adjustments by individual economic units. No conflict need arise between the decisions and judgments of individual units and the CPB because there is no CPB.

Third, the more successful the political leadership and the CPB are in establishing manipulative systems of economic incentives, and the more vigorously individuals are convinced that their own monetary and nonmonetary rewards will best be maximized by attaining planning targets and goals, the greater are the pressures upon them to *simulate* such attainment. Accompanying formal systems of economic administration in centrally planned economies are, typically, informal techniques of industrial management. The process of simulation begins with the formulation of the plan itself. Taking advantage of their specialized knowledge of particular conditions, managers may be tempted to understate output possibilities and overstate requirements to provide a margin of safety (what the Russians call *strakhovka*) for unforeseen contingencies and for general inefficiency and the "quiet life." Simulation of plan achievement proceeds through a variety of additional imaginative devices, including producing the wrong assortment of goods, sacrificing quality for quantity, misappropriating funds, using pull or influence to work up special deals not recognized in official plans, and even outright falsification of accounts.[8]

Fourth, a centrally planned economic system has no one simple criterion of success equivalent to, say, profit maximization in a capitalist economy or to Lange's triple-rule system in decentralized socialism. A central plan consists of a large variety of targets and expectations in regard to output levels, input combinations, labor force requirements, product varieties and assortments, and so on. No plan ever will be met perfectly. But when it is not, central planners "must establish some set of priorities for relating underfulfillment of one goal to overfulfillment of another." But "once the managers have learned what the set of priorities is, they will take these priorities into account in making their decisions . . . . Whenever controllers give high priority to one particular goal in their evaluation of plan fulfillment, and make that priority effective through bonuses, enterprise managers will violate other parts of the plan in order to fulfill the high priority indicator."[9] A classic illustration is the sacrifice of quality for quantity when high priority is placed upon meeting quantitative targets.

Fifth, centrally planned economic systems can establish and have established incentives systems which work with reasonable success in regard to two heavily favored social groups: managers and industrial workers. But both *a priori* reasoning and historical evidence confirm that control and manipulation of the peasantry is an exceptionally difficult task. For one thing, centrally planned development places the burden of the industrialization process squarely upon the shoulders of the peasantry, which is scarcely an act conducive to "socialist cooperation" and which leaves the political leadership little room for income differentials in the agricultural sector if minimum consumption needs are to be met. Further, the peasantry is a unique and special "sociological type," a tradition-oriented, pre-capitalist "misfit" surviving, but not assimilated, into post-capitalist societies, suspicious of the ideological blandishments and exhortations of "city-slickers," communist or capitalist. Collectivization provides a solution of a sort to the problem of social control of the peasantry, but a solution fraught with difficulties. For one thing, the traditional land hunger of the peasantry makes it generally antagonistic and uncooperative to collectivization programs. For another, the opportunities for economies of large-scale production are generally less in agriculture than in manufacturing and some other sectors of the economy, and there is no guarantee that the most efficient-sized production unit will coincide with the size that political leaders think is necessary for effective political control. Add to these factors the dislocations of making a transition to a system of collectivized agriculture, which, in the face of peasant antagonism, can reach massive proportions and have debilitating long-run consequences (as in the case of Soviet Russia), and there is a serious limitation upon plan execution and social control.

CENTRALIZED SOCIALISM AND OTHER MAJOR ECONOMIC GOALS

As a theoretical economic system, centralized socialism has a high rating in regard to economic growth and stability and a low rating in regard to allocational efficiency and individual economic freedoms. Its rating in regard to the goal of an equitable distribution of income depends essentially upon one's value judgments in regard to social justice. Already explored in detail have been the

---

[8]Cf. the classic statements by Joseph Berliner, "The Informal Organization of the Soviet Firm," *Quarterly Journal of Economics*, August 1952, pp. 342–65; and Alec Nove, "The Problem of 'Success Indicators' in Soviet Industry," *Economica*, February 1958, pp. 1–13.

[9]Campbell, *op. cit.*, pp. 123, 129, 130.

shortcomings of centralized socialism in regard to allocational efficiency and individual economic freedoms. Examined briefly herein are the issues of growth, stability, and equity.

Economic Growth

Both empirical evidence and the arguments of the centralized socialists would seem to support the following three conclusions: (1) Centralized socialism is *a* workable and powerful route to industrialization and economic development in underdeveloped economies. (2) Rapid and large-scale industrialization in underdeveloped countries requires some minimum degree of central governmental planning, especially in regard to large, integrated investment projects. (3) The traditional marginal calculus and the competitive price system as social processes for economic calculation and control have a much lower applicability to the problems of initiating and propelling economic growth in underdeveloped economies than they have to understanding and guiding the microeconomic details of resource allocation in economically developed countries. These conclusions are probably shared by a number of analysts of economically underdeveloped countries, including many non-socialists and non-Marxists.[10]

As we have seen, centralized socialists

---

[10]Benjamin Higgins, for example, argues, "The economics of development is distinguished by the overwhelming importance of the choices which must be made by large groups rather than by individuals; which must be made in terms of 'lumps', 'jumps', or structural changes rather than marginal adjustment; and which may involve fundamental changes in social organization and perhaps even in social philosophy .... The 'calculus' involved in economic development is one of comparing the effects of one gestalt of investment with another over a period beginning at least ten years hence and extending well into the future. The market provides very limited guidance in allocating resources so as to maximize the degree of development. For this reason, development planning is necessary." *Economic Development* (New York: W. W. Norton & Company, Inc., Publishers, 1959), pp. 635–36, 454.

insist on or infer two additional hypotheses: First, centralized socialism is the *only* prospectively successful route to industrialization and economic development in underdeveloped countries. (Cf. Baran [27: 261]: "The establishment of a socialist planned economy is an essential, indeed indispensable, condition for the attainment of economic and social progress in underdeveloped countries.") Second, central planning of the "mobilization and allocation of the economic surplus" requires a more or less comprehensive system of government ownership and governmentally planned determination of output targets; in other words, central planning of investment and development programs requires centralized socialism as an economic system.

Our concluding verdict on both of these is: not proved. The former is an *a priori* assertion rather than a verified hypothesis. The latter confuses central planning as a developmental technique with centralized socialism as an economic system. The evidence of postwar developmental programs (for example, in India), though limited and inconclusive, is still illustrative. Neither this evidence nor logical reasoning supports the contention that central planning requires a predominance of government ownership or a comprehensive replacement of market choice by government plans. The need for developmental planning, argues Benjamin Higgins, in a comprehensive survey of the entire field of economic underdevelopment, "has nothing to do with the relative importance of the private and public sectors; intervention to alter the decisions of private entrepreneurs is still a plan." Indeed, there is no reason why centrally planned government development programs cannot be formulated and executed in "countries where private enterprise predominates" and where market criteria and institutions continue to play large, significant roles in economic choice and allocation. The "basic decisions" of government developmental planning in underdeveloped economies (determining the level and allocation of government investment; providing a framework for private enterprises and private investment) cannot be left to private initiative and the price system any more than the promotion of full employment and stable prices in the economically developed nations can be left entirely within the realm of private market decisions. But in economic development, as in stabilization, a "mixed economy" is a distinct possibility, indeed, argues Professor Higgins, "is most likely to succeed. *Laissez faire* will not do the job, and totalitarian physical planning is unlikely to do the job well. It is the essence of good development planning that the government should take those decisions which it alone can make effectively, leaving to the market the decisions that can be made more effectively there."[11]

Full-Employment Stability

In regard to economic stability and full employment, the centralized socialists present a persuasive argument to support their case that processes of central planning are likely to be free from unemployment and cyclical fluctuations, or at least distinctly and significantly freer from these problems than economies placing a larger reliance upon decentralized processes of coordination and control. Certainly the sources and forms of *capitalist* cyclical fluctuations and employment—that is, the separation of saving and investment decisions; the decentralized and "uncoordinated" nature of *ex ante* investment plans, correctable only after time lags *ex post;* the instabilities generated by the private creation and destruction of bank credit; the capriciousness of the aggregate demand function, especially the investment component, and the special sensitivity of profit-oriented private business firms to changes in aggregate demand; the inadequacies, inflexibilities, and time lags in the dynamic workings of the price system, which help to generate mutually reinforcing, cumulative movements in economic activity; the fact that labor is largely a variable cost, and

is readily laid off during periods of insufficient or declining demand; and so on—are largely absent in centrally planned systems.

Under centralized socialism, saving and investment are subject to simultaneous centralized, and *ex ante* coordination. The financial elements of the plan (planned cost, profits, wages, consumption, investment, and so on) are dependent on and adjusted to the calculations and controls of the physical plan. For a centrally planned system as a whole, labor becomes a fixed, rather than a variable, cost. Workers laid off from employment in one sector of the system would not knowingly be left unemployed, but presumably would be absorbed in another sector. Contraction in one part of the system (say, consumption) would provide no reason for mutually reinforcing contraction in another (say, investment)—indeed, the reverse would be more true. Because they directly control the income-creation process, central planners have vehicles for manipulating aggregate demand so that it need not fall short of aggregate supply at full employment. In the turnover tax or some similar device, the CPB can adjust demand to supply, raising the general level of the tax when consumer demand exceeds the output of consumer goods and lowering it when the reverse is true. In a sense, *Say's Law* is more applicable to a centrally directed economy than to a capitalist one. Supply tends to create its own demand: first, because aggregate wages-consumption are programmed at those levels which will be just sufficient to match the difference between the monetary value of total output and the planned value of investment goods; and, second, because any unforeseen mismatching of consumer expenditures and the monetary value of consumer goods output may be corrected by readjusting the price level of consumer goods through, for example, a manipulation of the turnover tax.

On the other hand, it would be misleading to regard economic fluctuations as unique to decentralized economic systems. Though free from the instabilities associated with

[11] *Ibid*, pp. 454–56.

decentralized calculation and control, centralized socialism *may have its own sources and forms of cyclical fluctuations.* Centralized *ex ante* calculations of either aggregate demand or aggregate supply, or both, may be incorrect. On the side of supply, estimates of population growth, labor force, technology, stocks of natural resources, and changes in techniques of industrial organization and administration may be wrong. On the side of demand, actual consumption expenditures may exceed or fall short of planned consumption, the absolute magnitude of such divergences increasing with economic growth and rising consumer incomes. But between the *ex ante* formulation of the central plan and its *ex post* reformulation to take into acount these divergences, a more or less significant time lag may occur, the length of the lag depending on: (1) recognition of plan miscalculations by decentralized data-gatherers and plan supervisors; (2) communication of information to central planners; (3) reformulation of plans by the CPB; (4) execution of reformulated plans with their resultant effects upon the economy. The problem can be further complicated by the obstinancy and inflexibility of central planners in their continued adherence to initial plans and estimates and by the tendency of lower-level administrators and managers to simulate plan performance and to tell their superiors what they think the superiors want to hear. The result is, first, an aggregate imbalance between supply and demand, either in the form of an excess of goods over monetary expenditures or (more typically) an excess of monetary claims over the output and resources available; and, second, periodic *ex post* readjustments and plan reformulations with accompanying fluctuations, if not in the absolute level of output, at least in the rate of growth in output, as illustrated in Fig. 11.5.[12]

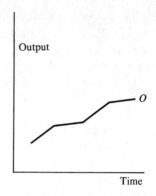

Fig. 11.5. Variations in the rate of growth

Equity and Equality in the Distribution of Income

It seems clear that centralized socialism *could* reduce significantly the inequalities in income and power emanating from private ownership of land and industrial capital and could, *ceteris paribus*, promote smaller income inequality than would exist in a capitalist economic system. Whether a centrally planned system *would* or *does* promote substantially smaller inequality than other modern industrialized or industrializing economic systems, and whether the resulting patterns of income and power distribution correspond to the goal of social justice, however, are quite different matters—of logic, factual evidence, and value judgment.

From a logical point of view, nothing in centralized socialism requires large-scale equality. It is true that government direction of economic activity entails power to regulate income distribution and thereby to realize some ideal of distributive justice. But the same means—centralized economic planning and control—may be used to achieve a variety of different objectives and income distributional patterns, including highly inequalitarian ones that would diverge from our conceptions of social justice, perhaps even from the

---

[12]There is now quite a literature on cyclical economic fluctuations in centrally planned economies. See, for example, G. Staller, "Fluctuations in Economic Activity: Planned and Free Market Economies, 1950–60," *American Economic Review*, May 1964, pp. 385–95; and Josef Toman, J. Goldman, and J. Fleck, "Conjunctional Research in a Socialist Economy," *Czechoslovak Economic Papers*, No. 10, 1968, pp. 19ff.

pre-revolutionary ideals of the centralized socialists themselves. Indeed, the literature of centralized socialism contains two elements of a sharply inequalitarian nature readily admitted even by neo-Marxists: first, the requirements of centralized mobilization and allocation into investment projects of a large surplus of income exceeding consumption and the accompanying imposition of this massive industrialization effort upon the shoulders of the general populace, especially the peasantry; second, the necessity of tapping individual incentives for the execution of plans through a system of income differentials. Further, centralized socialists agree that a centrally planned economic system is characterized by a concentration and centralization, and thus, inequality, in the power to make economic decisions far exceeding that of competitive capitalism or decentralized socialism. Lastly, it seems probable that combining the concentration of political and economic power with a centralized governmentally-determined system of income differentials would generate a definite system of socio-economic classes, with political leaders at the apex and a professional and managerial elite forming secondary supporting blocks, structured as tightly, if not more tightly, than those of industrial capitalism.

Of course, to centralized socialists, the elimination or sharp reduction of income from private ownership in land and industrial capital is a strategic element in social justice, and government ownership emerges as socially desirable in itself. This involves two related, but distinguishable, problems. The first represents a classic confusion of means and ends. Like private ownership, there is nothing desirable or undesirable about government ownership *per se*. Systems of public versus private ownership "should be judged," Kenneth E. Boulding contends, "by their fruits and their costs, not by any absolute principle of rightness or wrongness."[13]

[13]Kenneth E. Boulding, *Principles of Economic Policy*, (Englewood Cliffs, N.J.: Prentice-Hall, Inc., 1958), p. 400.

Beyond this means-end problem, the association of government ownership with social justice is based upon two premises: first, a Marxian labor theory of value which identifies all forms of "surplus value" as exploitative; second, the interesting but peculiar view that "economic surpluses" under centralized socialism do not constitute "surplus values," and thus, are not exploitative.

The first of these two premises may be criticized in terms of recognition of the inadequacies and inaccuracies of a purely labor theory of value. As long as land, capital, and entrepreneurial talent are scarce in relation to their uses in the productive process, they will command a price or return, under competitive conditions roughly correspondent to their productive contribution. As long as they are privately owned, some minimum payment or opportunity cost will be required to entice the owners to continue to supply them. A system of government ownership eliminates the necessity for interest, rent, and profit returns to private owners, but not the scarcity or productive contribution of capital, land, and entrepreneurship. Of course, granting this does not preclude the value judgment that capitalist economies generate excessive inequalities in the distribution of income, the factual judgment that private ownership of land and capital is an important source of income inequality, and the recognition that concentration and monopoly in this ownership accentuates these inequalities and makes the relationship between productive contribution and income received extremely tenuous. But the crude identification of all non-wage income as exploitative surplus value is no closer to the truth than the crude identification of all incomes with the marginal products of the respective factors of production.

The second premise goes back at least to Marx's *Critique of the Gotha Program* and rests upon the curious view that economic surpluses constitute exploitative surplus values under capitalism, but not under socialism. In Marx's original case, some basis for this contention existed in the emphasis upon cooperative worker control of industry and plan formulation—that is, economic surpluses do not constitute surplus values under socialism because workers do not sell their labor services for wages to owners of industrial capital; and the content of national plans, including the allocation of resources between investment and consumption and the distribution of income between saving and consumption, is made freely and cooperatively by workers themselves. But in the neo-Marxist version of centralized socialism, workers *do* sell their labor services for wages on labor markets to owners of industrial capital (the state), and it is the *CPB, not the workers*, which formulates and executes decisions regarding the aggregate distribution of income between economic surplus and planned wages-consumption. It is difficult for a non-socialist to avoid the conclusion that a CPB can be just as "exploitative" in the "mobilization and allocation of the economic surplus" as the collective impact of the investment decisions of any group of decentralized industrial capitalists. Soviet Russia is a case in point. The "Soviet Union has probably exploited its farmers and workers more ruthlessly than any capitalist country, in the sense that a large proportion of the product of the society has been channeled into the single control of the state, and farmers and workers have received only a fraction of what they have produced."[14]

SUMMARY AND CONCLUSIONS
TO CHAPTER 11

1. Centralized socialism is characterized by: government dominance in the ownership and control of the means of production and in the exercise of economic power; government promotion of social goals as a basic motivational dynamism; and a centralized government hierarchy as a social process for making and coordinating economic decisions.

2. Western neo-Marxists have made important contributions to the economic theory of centralized socialism in the twentieth century. Drawing inspiration from the experiences of Communist countries, they have regarded socialism as essentially a process for the industrialization and economic development of underdeveloped economies.

3. The focus of Western neo-Marxist theories of centralized socialism is upon the methodology of central and comprehensive government economic planning. This has had three major dimensions: first, a critique of consumer sovereignty and a defense of centralized determination of goals by government authorities; second, a substitution of centralized development strategies emphasizing the "mobilization and allocation of the economic surplus" for static allocational efficiency in the analysis of conditions and formulation of plans; third, an emphasis upon government hierarchy and manipulation as the major techniques for the execution of economic plans and the implementation of social controls.

4. Even abstracting from the experiences of Communist countries, it would seem clear that centralized socialism could and would "work." Whether in the form of a crude, military-type economic strategy, or via a more sophisticated system of mathematical equations, based on electronic computers and input-output analysis, or in terms of a more or less comprehensive governmental, hierarchical system of accounting prices, its logical credentials appear to be in order. It is "operational" in the Schumpeterian sense of showing not only a logical possibility, but also in identifying the steps and techniques whereby that possibility could be realized. It is also a distinct possibility in the Hayekian sense that there "is no reason to expect that production would stop, or that the authorities would find difficulty in using all the available resources somehow, or even

[14]*Ibid.*

that output would be permanently lower than it had been before (centralized) planning started." [4: 149–50] Lastly, if doubt were to remain, the empirical existence and success of the Soviet-type economies demonstrates conclusively that centrally/comprehensively planned economic systems do work.

5. As a theoretical economic system, centralized socialism has a high rating in regard to economic growth and stabilization and a low rating in regard to static allocational efficiency and individual freedoms. Its rating in regard to the goals of an equitable distribution of income depends essentially upon one's value judgments in regard to social justice.

6. In conclusion, it is easier to "come to grips" with a critical appraisal of the economic theory of centralized socialism than of decentralized socialism. The former is characterized by a healthy empiricism and pragmatic crudity largely missing from the more rigorous and theoretically pleasing, but also more ethereal, models of the latter. Centralized socialists are relatively clearer on the distinctions between theoretical and actual systems and between theoretical criteria of static allocational efficiency and dynamic development, on one hand, versus, say, American and Soviet Russian economic performance on the other. Centralized socialists are also clearer on the goals which they postulate, the underlying assumptions of their analysis, and the degree of refinement and precision in goal attainment which it is reasonable to expect in practice. We have no assurance, argues Sweezy, that the goals of centralized socialism "will always be attained in practice. There will be areas of indeterminacy, miscalculations, errors of execution. But this is true of all systems, including competitive capitalism, monopolistic capitalism, unplanned collectivism, and planned socialism; and in this respect it seems safe to say that planned socialism need not fear comparison with its hypothetical and actual rivals." [9: 239] The critic of centralized socialism can appreciate the cautious empiricism of this statement while retaining reservations about its conclusion.

SOURCES CITED IN PART III

Several works already cited in Parts I and II, notably Dahl and Lindblom (1), Hayek (4), Myrdal (6), Schumpeter (8), Sweezy (9), Tinbergen (11), and Marx (16, 17, 19) are pertinent to socialism and have been cited throughout Part III. In addition, the following sources are particularly useful.

26. BARAN, PAUL, "National Economic Planning," Bernard F. Haley, editor, *A Survey of Contemporary Economics*, Volume II (Homewood, Illinois: Richard D. Irwin, Inc., 1952).

27. BARAN, PAUL, *The Political Economy of Growth* (New York: Monthly Review Press, 1957).

28. BERGSON, ABRAM, "Socialist Economics," Howard S. Ellis, editor, *A Survey of Contemporary Economics*, Volume I (Philadelphia: Blakiston, 1949).

29. BERGSON, ABRAM, "Market Socialism Revisited," *Journal of Political Economy*, September 1967.

30. DOBB, MAURICE, *Soviet Economic Development Since 1917* (New York: International Publishers, 1966).

31. DOBB, MAURICE, *On Economic Theory and Socialism* (New York: International Publishers, 1955).

32. DREWNOWSKI, JAN, "The Economic Theory of Socialism: A Suggestion for Reconsideration," *Journal of Political Economy*, August 1961. Reprinted in Morris Bornstein, editor, *Comparative Economic Systems: Models and Cases* (Homewood, Illinois: Richard D. Irwin, Inc., 1965).

33. GROSSMAN, GREGORY, "Notes for a Theory of the Command Economy," *Soviet Studies*, October 1963. Reprinted in Bornstein, *Comparative Economic Systems*.

34. HALM, GEORGE N., *Economic Systems: A Comparative Analysis* (New York: Holt, Rinehart, & Winston, Inc., 1960, 1968).

35. HAYEK, FRIEDRICH A., *The Road to Serfdom* (Chicago: University of Chicago Press, 1944, 1961).

36. HAYEK, FRIEDRICH A., editor, *Collectivist Economic Planning* (London: Routledge & Kegan Paul, 1935).

37. HOFF, T. J. B., *Economic Calculation in the Socialist Society* (London: Hodge, 1949).

38. JOHR, W. A. and H. W. SINGER, *The Role of the Economist as Official Advisor* (London: Allen and Unwin, 1955).

39. LANGE, OSKAR and FRED M. TAYLOR, *On the Economic Theory of Socialism*, Benjamin Lippincott, editor (Minneapolis: University of Minnesota Press, 1938).

40. LANGE, OSKAR, *The Political Economy of Socialism* (The Hague: van Keulen, 1958).

41. LANGE, OSKAR, "The Scope and Method of Economics," *Review of Economic Studies*, 1945–1946.

42. LENIN, V. I., *State and Revolution* (New York: International Publishers, 1932).

43. MARX, KARL, Economic and Philosophical Manuscripts, in Erich Fromm, *Marx's Concept of Man* (New York: Ungar, 1961).

44. MEYER, ALFRED G., *Leninism* (Cambridge: Harvard University Press, 1957).

45. MISES, LUDWIG, *Socialism: An Economic and Sociological Analysis* (New Haven, Conn.: Yale University Press, 1951).

46. ULAM, ADAM, *The Unfinished Revolution: An Essay on the Sources of Influence of Marxism and Communism* (New York: Random House, Inc., 1960).

47. WOOTON, BARBARA, *Freedom under Planning* (Chapel Hill: University of North Carolina Press, 1945).

IV

MANAGED CAPITALISM AND DEMOCRATIC SOCIALISM

In Parts II and III, capitalism and socialism were treated essentially as alternatives. We shall now turn to a study of contemporary economic systems "between and beyond" capitalism and socialism, notably managed capitalism and democratic socialism, and their associated economic theories, social philosophies, and proposals for economic reform. Managed capitalism and democratic socialism are characterized by a mixture of "capitalist" and "socialist" elements and incorporate some dimensions of economic organization found in neither classic system.

Theories of managed capitalism focus upon the modifications and reforms which have characterized the shift from old-style capitalism to contemporary forms of economic organization in the Western, economically developed democracies, especially in the United States. The unifying theme in new-style capitalism is the blend of private and public management, guidance, and control of the national economy. We shall examine, first, the structure and organization of the system; and second, theoretical descriptions of its behavior and functioning.

Contemporary democratic socialists, especially in Scandinavia and Great Britain, have started their analysis and evaluation of the economic order from a different perspective. But in the process, they have reformulated the theory and philosophy of democratic socialism in the light of the transformation of old-style capitalism and have proposed further economic reforms from the vantage point of their (reformulated) vision of a democratic socialist society. In this way, a rapprochement between the economic theory and social philosophy of "capitalism" and "socialism" appears to take place.

12

Managed Capitalism:
Structure and Organization

WHAT IS MANAGED CAPITALISM?

Introduction

Capitalism is in the process of significant qualitative institutional change, if not revolutionary transition, toward a new and different economic system(s). The origins, magnitude, and rapidity of change, and the specific forms, agencies, and processes of change have varied in different cases. But many economies, including those of West Europe, Great Britain, Scandinavia, the United States, Canada, and Australasia, have experienced significant institutional changes in the twentieth century, especially since 1929, several of the most prominent dimensions of which have been:

1. a significant departure from earlier, more capitalist economic structures and organization;

2. an incorporation of certain elements traditionally associated with the economic theory and social philosophy of socialism;

3. a failure to establish, even approximately, the institutions and processes of pure or classic socialism;

4. a retention of certain elements traditionally associated with the economic theory and social philosophy of capitalism;

5. an incorporation of certain elements not prominent in the theory or practice of old-style capitalism *or* in any of the major classic visions of socialist economy;

6. a continuation, extension, and/or incorporation of elements found generally in all or most modern industrialized economic societies.

Clearly, a reality exists "in search of recognition" [63: 3–19] and analysis. The major theories of capitalism and socialism provide part of the background and tools for such a task. At least in part, contemporary "socio-capitalist" economies lie between capitalism and socialism, incorporating elements from both. But economic systems between and beyond capitalism and socialism need to be recognized and analyzed in their own light, in terms of the interblending (not merely juxtaposition) of capitalist and socialist elements and new elements traditionally associated with neither capitalism nor socialism, not merely as appendages to one of the two classically conceived systems or as temporary transitions between one and the other.

The first step toward recognition of this phenomenon has been an increasing proliferation of labels and titles, including "mixed economy," "mixed enterprise capitalism," "hybrid economy," "corporate capitalism," "collective capitalism," "organizational economy," "laboristic economy," "laboristic capitalism," "state capitalism," "new industrial state," "collective democracy," "statism," "dual economy," "managed economy," "managerial capitalism," "welfare state," "welfare capitalism," "socio-capitalist democracy," "oligopoly capitalism," "pluralistic economy," "guided capitalism," and so forth.

Theoretical analysis of the institutions, processes, issues, and strategies of economic systems between and beyond capitalism and socialism, however, in contrast to the origin of new descriptive labels, has proceeded from two main sources. First, a variety of writers and contributors, especially in the United States, has started from the capitalist end of the continuum: They have identified one or more ways in which contemporary Western economies have departed from the theory and practice of old-style competitive market and *laissez-faire* capitalism and have formulated theories and proposals in relation to these changes. Though recognizing the existence of certain "socialist" elements in the new postwar economic systems, their focus has been on the modifications and reforms of old-style capitalism which have led to and characterize the new, presently emerging systems, the various devices for private (especially corporate) and public management, guidance, planning, and control of the economy, and upon proposals for further reform. Their emphasis, in other words, has been on a new, modified, socially-reformed and collectively "managed" capitalism.

A second group, especially in West Europe, Scandinavia, and Great Britain, has started from the socialist end of the continuum: They have reformulated the theory and philosophy of democratic socialism in the light of contemporary modifications of capitalism and have proposed further social reforms of capitalism from the vantage point of their (reformulated) democratic socialist vision. Though recognizing the retention and existence of "capitalist" elements in the new postwar economic systems, their focus has been upon the accommodation and modification of traditional democratic socialist theory to the present and emerging economic systems in the West and upon proposals for further change and reform.

In this two-fold process, a rapprochement between the economic theory and social philosophy of "capitalism" and "socialism" appears to be taking place, as illustrated by a growing literature which specifically challenges the validity of the traditional capitalism-socialism dichotomy and/or presents models or visions of systems which, while incorporating elements of both, are not readily identifiable under either heading or any variation thereof.

In succeeding discussion, we will identify and describe (in the remainder of this chapter) the broad contours and major dimensions of the structure and organization of contemporary, modified, socially reformed, and managed capitalism, as developed by some of the prominent contributors to the first group. Next, we will compare different economic theories and social philosophies which describe the behavior and evaluate the performance of managed capitalism and offer strategies and proposals for further reform. We then will examine the contributions and proposals of contemporary (especially British) democratic socialists on the reformulation of democratic socialist thought in the light of the theory and practice of managed capitalism.

Managed Capitalism: Theory, Practice, Movement

The new and emerging managed capitalist economic systems simultaneously are actualities, theories, and movements. In each of these approaches, however, we should emphasize diversity and pluralism. The postwar United States economy, though similar to, is by no means identical with, that of the United Kingdom or West Germany, or, indeed, with the United States economy of the New Deal period. Spatially and temporarily, there is no economic system in practice which may be designated as *the* example of managed capitalism. The term is broad enough to cover a variety of subdivisions and specific cases, each different in numerous ways, yet all sharing certain broad mutual characteristics.

Similarly, there are varied theories of managed capitalism, each emphasizing one or more dimensions in which the structure and/or behavior of the economic system diverges from old-style capitalism. These theoretical contributions have not yet been integrated to formulate an overall model or vision, much less a rigorously and fully developed social philosophy of managed capitalism. But several prominent dimensions are present in the literature of the last few decades, and the broad contours of such a vision, economic theory, and social philosophy are emerging.

As a movement for further social change, managed capitalism also has a number of variants, emanating from both economic practice and theoretical analysis, providing a social-intellectual rationale for, and critique of, the current state of the system,

and yielding proposals as to where, how, and how fast further reform and change should take place. These sub-movements range from quite conservative support of the new status quo to more liberal-radical proposals for further rapid, large-scale institutional change.

Structure and Organization of
Managed Capitalism: Synopsis

The structure of managed capitalism as an economic system, as described by prominent contemporary contributors, is identified more specifically in Table 12-1.

LEVEL OF ECONOMIC
DEVELOPMENT AND RESOURCE
BASE: THE TECHNOLOGICAL AND
ECONOMIC REVOLUTIONS

Most students and proponents of managed capitalism are concerned essentially with the problems of a highly developed, highly capitalistic economy. This does not preclude

Table 12-1.
THE STRUCTURE OF MANAGED CAPITALISM

1. Level of economic development	Highly developed
2. Resource base	Highly capitalistic
3. Ownership-control of instruments of production	Predominantly private and corporate: separation of "ownership" and "control"
4. Locus of economic power	Dispersed, yet concentrated in large-scale private and public organizations
5. Motivational system	Individual economic gain (but with decreased role for profit maximization by owners-managers), modified by the pursuit of group and social goals
6. Organization of economic power	Mixture of centralization and decentralization
7. Social processes for making and coordinating economic decisions	Mixture of competitive/monopolistic price systems, democracy, bureaucracy, and bargaining
8. Distribution of income and wealth	Mixture of market-determined resource prices, group action, and a significant but limited role for government redistributive measures

the possible adaptation of managed capitalist ideas to underdeveloped economies. However, the context of the emerging economic theory and social philosophy of managed capitalism is usually, if not exclusively, that of developed, even "affluent" economic societies.

A system of economic organization may have powerful effects upon both the character and the rate of economic growth and development. As noted in Parts II and III, this is a central recurring theme in the writings of Marx, Keynes, Schumpeter, and the contemporary neo-Marxist centralized socialists, among others. But the reverse also is true: The character and pace of economic growth and development may profoundly affect the system of economic organization, its institutions and ideas. This proposition may be developed more systematically and with application to managed capitalism by reference to three central sub-themes:

1. The character and pace of economic growth and development in Western capitalist economic societies in the twentieth century has been remarkable, even "revolutionary." In terms of our first two critieria for identifying and comparing economic systems, this has meant, first, a transformation from developing but relatively underdeveloped to industrialized, highly developed, even affluent economic societies; second, a transformation from earlier, simpler, less capitalistic economies to highly capitalistic economies, with very large ratios of physical capital to labor and large-scale applications of science and technological innovations, often embodied in new forms of capital investment.

2. These processes of more or less continuous, rapid, large-scale scientific, technological, and economic growth and development have generated changes in the organization and structure of the economic system, and the emergence of new institutions, agencies, and techniques for mobilizing and allocating capital, making and coordinating economic decisions, and resolving recurrent, yet changing, economic problems. These changes, among others, have led to the transformation from an old-style, more individualist, more atomistically competitive, and essentially *laissez-faire* capitalism to a new-style, more collectivist, more concentrated and oligopolist, and essentially managed capitalism.

The more conservative among the managed capitalists generally contend these institutional changes, or at least some of them, may have been too great or too rapid. The more liberal managed capitalists suggest that, in some instances, institutional adjustment and accommodation to technological and economic change has been too slow, too small, and/or too haphazard. But most agree that large-scale and rapid institutional change has taken place and that the pressures and requirements of science, technology, and economic growth and development will and must be accompanied by further institutional change in the future.

3. The transformation to a highly developed, highly capitalistic, affluent, and socially reformed-managed capitalism has generated pressures for the emergence of new bodies or systems of thought, both to understand and explain the structure and functioning of the new system(s) and to evaluate its performance and make proposals for further change.

Recurring debate exists as to the extent of and need for intellectual and ideological change. The more intellectually conservative among the students of managed capitalism suggest that intellectual change may, at times, have been too rapid and that we have been too quick to abandon or criticize the wisdom of the past, the validity of traditional economic theories and/or their associated or accompanying social philosophies. But many managed capitalists argue that the reverse is true; that is, that our economic theories and social philosophies have not kept up with the dynamic changing pace of events. The result of this "intellectual lag" is a growing obsolescence of our ideas in describing and understanding the economic system.

"We live," asserts Adolph Berle, "under a system described in obsolete terms." [49: 27] Despite evidence of concentration, centralization, and collectivization, we still describe capitalist economies as atomistic, decentralized, and individualistic. Despite evidence of affluence and abundance, we continue to conceive the capitalist system(s) in terms of poverty and "scarcity economics." But adherence to the "conventional wisdom" (defined by John K. Galbraith as "ideas which are esteemed at any time for their acceptability" rather than their logical consistency or empirical applicability) [56: 9] may prevent institutional change necessary in the light of rapid economic growth and development and, indeed, may thereby place obstacles in the path of the continuity and successful realization of the potentials of that growth and development itself.

OWNERSHIP AND CONTROL OF INDUSTRY: THE CORPORATE AND MANAGERIAL REVOLUTIONS

Managed capitalists accept private (nongovernmental) ownership of the instruments or means of production as the predominant, if not exclusive, pattern in industry. Government ownership and enterprise (as contrasted to government provision of "collective services")[1] plays an almost non-existent role in models of managed capitalism, and

extensions of government ownership are characterized more by their absence than by their inclusion in even the more liberal or radical managed capitalist proposals and agenda for further economic reform. At the same time, models of managed capitalism do recognize and incorporate a variety of general and specific methods and techniques of government *regulation and control* of private enterprise, as well as more sophisticated mixtures of private-government ownership (as, for example, in Atomic Energy Commission contracts).[2]

Within the near-exclusive sphere of private enterprise, managed capitalist models emphasize two central points: first, the predominant role of the large-scale *corporation* in production, asset ownership, investment, and other dimensions of economic activity; second, the *"separation of ownership and control"* within large-scale corporations, with resulting implications for the locus and organization of economic power.

---

[1] In government ownership-enterprise (for example, the Tennessee Valley Authority), government agencies *produce* commodities in government-owned plants, typically financing productive activities largely, if not exclusively, through the *sale* of those commodities on markets. A government service (for example, defense or education) involves the *purchase* by governments of commodities and/or labor services (typically from private businesses or individuals), which are distributed collectively and financed largely, if not exclusively, through *taxation*.

[2] In West Europe, notably France, the United Kingdom, and Scandinavia, government enterprise accounts for 15 to 25 percent of the ownership of industrial assets and for about the same portion of national output. In the United States, where government enterprise and ownership is very small, government regulation (by regulatory commissions) exists in nearly every industry which, in Europe, is under government ownership. If we add to government enterprise, producing 1.2 percent of national income in 1954, these regulated industries (transportation, communications, electric power, water, and gas), producing 11 percent of national income, we have a total of 12.2 percent of national income originating in "economic sectors subject to positive regulation." [Jesse W. Markham, "Market Structure and Economic Institutions," in *The American Economy* (New York: George Braziller, Inc., 1963), p. 10.] If to this we add agriculture (a heavily subsidized and regulated industry, producing 5.5 percent of United States output in 1954), the total rises to 17.7 percent. In short, government ownership and/or regulation of industry accounts for about one-fifth of total economic activity in the economically developed, mixed economies of the West. This is a significant, but limited, proportion, yielding the rough-hewn conclusion that private ownership and control of industry are the dominant, though not exclusive, patterns in the practice, as well as the theory, of managed capitalism.

If the private (that is, non-governmental) corporation does not rate top billing, it at least deserves co-billing with government as the dominant social institution and form of economic organization in the theory and practice of managed capitalism. Corporate dominance has at least two major dimensions. First, corporations are the dominant form of business and industrial organization. They produce over 50 percent of the gross national product, account for over 50 percent of business sales, own over 50 percent of total industrial assets, make over 50 percent of total annual investment, and employ over 50 percent of the total labor force. Private corporations are the dominant producer, seller, owner, investor, and employer as well as the vehicle of technological change in contemporary managed capitalism.

This position of dominance, of course, is a relative one, that is, based not on numerical superiority, but on the control and direction of the preponderant share of total output, industrial assets, capital formation, and so on. Corporations co-exist with other forms of business organization, notably the individual proprietorship, about which we may say exactly the opposite to that said about corporations, namely, that individual proprietorships have preponderant numerical superiority (roughly 10 out of 11-million in 1970 in the United States), but control and direct a relatively small share (approximately one-fifth to one-fourth) of total output, industrial assets, capital formation, and so forth.

Of course, the relative role of corporations varies among different industrial sectors, ranging, in the United States, from 80 to nearly 100 percent in electricity, gas, communications, mining, manufacturing, and finance, to roughly 60 percent in wholesale and retail trade, to approximately 30 percent in services, and to around 10 percent in agriculture. Even if the relative role of corporations in industry (excluding agricul-

ture, finance, services, and trade) remained stable over time (there are, after all, obstacles to increasing one's relative position above 90 to 100 percent), the relative decrease in agriculture as a percent of national income-output in the process of continued economic growth and development might easily be accompanied by an increase in the role of corporations in the total economy. In any event, the relatively dominant position of corporations in the theory and practice of new-style, managed capitalism is clear and striking.[3]

Second, considerable concentration and centralization of economic power exists among a relatively small number of large-scale corporations. In the early thirties, Berle and Means estimated 200 large-scale non-financial corporations controlled about 50 percent of corporate, 38 percent of total business, and 22 percent of total national wealth. More recent studies yield similar conclusions: A dominant share of total output, sales, assets, capital formation, and so on, is accounted for by a relatively small number of very large, often "multi-billion dollar" corporaions. The role and power of large-scale corporations is even more striking in those industries in which a *very small number* of corporate enterprises (say, less than 20; in many cases, 1 to 4) produce more than 50 percent of total output. In the United States, this pattern occurs for a whole series of industries, including aluminum, automo-

---

[3] In their classic book, *The Modern Corporation and Private Property*, published in 1932, the lawyer-economist team of Berle and Means estimated that, as of 1929, "at least 78 percent and probably a larger proportion of American business wealth is corporate wealth." [50: 31] Subsequent studies have yielded similar conclusions. For example, A. D. H. Kaplan estimates corporations controlled about 80 percent of the total assets of industrial enterprises in 1950. [A. D. H. Kaplan, *Big Enterprise in a Competitive System*, rev. ed. (Washington, D.C.: The Brookings Institution, 1964), p. 117.] Drawing upon Internal Revenue data, Jesse Markham depicts corporations as receiving about 75 percent of total business receipts in 1959. [*Op. cit.*, p. 7] And so on through every major dimension of economic activity.

biles, steel, cigarettes, tin cans, even beer and ale.

The following is a summary of the managed capitalist position on the emergence and role of the large-scale corporation:

1. The process of industrialization has been both generated and accompanied by rapid, large-scale technological revolutions in inventions and innovations, typically embodied in new labor and managerial skills and knowledge and in new forms of capital investment.

2. These developments, coupled with the opportunities of large-scale national and international marketing, have encouraged the development of new institutions and forms of economic organization to supplement and/or supplant the individual proprietorship in the ownership and/or control of large-scale aggregations of capital, employment, production, and sales.

3. Because of its advantages—in raising capital, organizing and applying science and technology to industry, and organizing and coordinating large-scale, often far-flung enterprises—the corporation has emerged in Western developed economies as the dominant form of industrial organization.

4. Within many, if not all, industries, these same tendencies (aided by the opportunities for and propensity toward monopoly) have generated a concentration and centralization of economic power in a relatively small number of large-scale corporate giants.

5. The economic dominance of the large-scale corporation within particular industries and the economy as a whole does not preclude, indeed co-exists with, a strategic but limited role for government ownership and/or regulation of industry and a continued numerically superior but relatively limited role for proprietorships, partnerships, small-scale corporations, and other (for example, cooperative) forms of industrial organization.

Separation of Stock Ownership and Managerial Control in the Large-Scale Corporation: The Managerial Revolution

Classically, industrial "property" had two central dimensions: (1) possession of, access to, and control over the utilization of capital goods; (2) preferential treatment in the benefits—income, wealth, and power—flowing from the utilization of these goods. In a series of books written since the early thirties, Adolph Berle, Gardner Means, and others, have described the revolutionary impact on industrial property of the emergence and movement to dominance of the large-scale corporation.

According to these students of managed capitalism, the growth of the large-scale corporation has had two major effects on industrial property: First, the nature of control and power has been transformed. The process of the aggregation of capital under the "titular ownership" of the large-scale corporation has "created a body of things so large and so complex that no individual could have cognizance, let alone possession, of them." [49: 66] Industrial property has been transformed in the process from a relation between men and things to a control of things via the power relations between men and men, within the framework of the corporate organization.

Second, the active and creative function of economic control in the large-scale corporation, that is, the exercise of power in the formulation and execution of policy decisions in regard to production, employment, sales promotion, purchasing, sales, saving, investment, research and development, and so on has been separated from the essentially passive and receptive function of beneficial (stock) ownership.[4] Control over and power in large-scale corporate enterprise now resides essentially in the hands of managerial-executive groups, who are largely self-appointive and own little or no stock in the corporations which they control. The modified and relatively reduced benefits from stock ownership go primarily to a stockholding group who, collectively and individually, exercise little or no managerial power and control in the corporations they "own." Edward S. Mason sums this up by saying: "Almost everyone now agrees that in the large corporation, the owner is, in general, a passive recipient; that, typically, control is in the hands of management; and that management normally selects its own replacements."[5]

The process of transformation from individual owner-control to the separation of management from stockholder ownership has proceeded through several main stages, as identified by Berle. [49: 69–76] The first stage, typical in the early years of the twentieth century in the United States, is one in which corporate management and/or its board of directors is effectively controlled by and accountable to a stockholder group

---

[4]From a terminological point of view, it is perhaps unfortunate that this division of the two classic dimensions of industrial property and power initially was called the "separation of ownership and control." Actually, control *is a dimension*, indeed, probably the *primary* determining dimension of *property ownership*. Burnham exaggerates, but has a point when he says that ownership "*means* control; if there is no control, then there is no ownership . . . . Those who control *are* the (de facto) owners . . . . If ownership and control are in reality separated, then ownership has changed hands to the 'control', and the separated ownership is a meaningless fiction." [James Burnham, *The Managerial Revolution* (New York: The John Day Company, Inc., 1941), pp. 92–93, 94.] Berle's present identification of a fission of industrial property and power into active, creative *management* and essentially passive, receptive *stock ownership* would seem to be more descriptively accurate and terminologically consistent.

[5]Edward S. Mason, editor, *The Corporation in Modern Society* (Cambridge, Mass.: The Harvard University Press, 1959), p. 4.

holding more than 50 percent of the voting stock in the corporation. In a few exceptional cases (small-scale and family-held corporations), this form of control continues today. In the United States, Ford Motor Company, DuPont, Alcoa, and A & P are examples. But they are rare exceptions. In the Berle and Means estimate of the early thirties, such exceptions accounted for only 11 percent of the 200 largest non-financial corporations in the United States. The proportion, if anything, is lower today.

The second stage, prominent from 1914 to 1928, is control through ownership of a sufficient minority (say, 20 percent) of the voting stock, combined with an effective working relation with directors and managers. An effective working relation between large stockholders and corporate executives obviously is imperative in this case, for an independent-minded board of directors may send out proxies to large numbers of dispersed stockholders who either typically do not bother to vote or will return a signed proxy to existing management to obtain support for corporate officers and policies which diverge from those favored by large, but minority, stockholders. Minority control thus is a power which, first, is shared with corporate management, and, second, is extremely *precarious* and difficult to maintain. In any event, since the late 1920s it has not been a dominant form of corporate control. (In 1932, Berle and Means estimated 23 percent of the 200 largest non-financial corporations were under minority control.)

The third stage is "management control" (accounting for 44 percent of the 200 largest non-financial corporations in 1932). In this case, the ownership of stock is so widely dispersed[6] that "no large concentrated

---

[6]Dispersal of stock ownership could, but need not, constitute or create a "people's capitalism," that is, an economy in which stock ownership and its benefits are dispersed widely among the preponderant majority of the population. In the United States, for example, stock ownership though fairly widespread in absolute terms (15 to 20 million stockholders), is concentrated

stockholding exists which maintains a close working relationship with the management or is capable of challenging it, so that the board of directors may regularly expect a majority, composed of small and scattered holdings, to follow their lead. . . . This is the locus of power over and the norm of control of the bulk of American industry now. Nominal power still resides in the stockholders; actual power is in the board of directors." [50: 73, 74][7]

Government Ownership and Control

Private ownership is the dominant, but not exclusive, pattern in managed capitalism. Further, the separation of ownership and management within the private corporate sector carries with it a broader implication, namely, a relative decline in the importance of ownership. In the Marxian critique of capitalist industrialization, ownership is strategic because it is the basis of power and control. By contrast, managed capitalist theory contends—and practice tends to cor-

---

among a relatively small proportion of the total population (five to ten percent). In addition, the majority of stock is held by a relatively small proportion of total stockholders. In an intensive investigation, Lewis H. Kimmel [in *Share Ownership in the United States* (Washington, D.C.: The Brookings Institution, 1952), pp. 43, 46] estimated (for 1951) that the largest two percent of American stockholders own 58 percent of the common stock of publicly-owned corporations, the next largest 31 percent owned 32 percent, and the smallest 67 percent owned only 10 percent.

[7]Berle identifies a fourth possible stage in which formerly dispersed stockholdings become concentrated in the hands of pension trust funds and mutual funds, giving the professional managers of those funds the potential to control the corporations whose stock they hold in trust for individuals who neither control corporations nor (individually) purchase stock in them. [49: 52–56] Galbraith identifies yet another stage in which technology (rather than capital *per. se.*) becomes the strategic resource and power comes to reside in a "Technostructure"—those "who bring specialized knowledge, talent, or experience to group decision-making." [56: 71]

roborate—that government control of the economy may extend far beyond ownership and need not necessarily be associated with a high degree of government ownership of industry.

Table 12-2 summarizes the major areas or sectors of government control in the theory and practice of contemporary managed capitalism. All sectors and types of control refer to activities falling under government policy and decision-making. The most direct, obvious area of "government ownership and control" (sector A) includes production by government enterprises for the market, provision of output by government agencies and departments, and government purchases from the private sector of the economy, which, in turn, (though national income accounting does not make this distinction) may be more accurately described as production than consumption.

Government control of production and the economy extends far beyond these activities. Governments control private sectors of the economy in varied ways, including (B) regulation, support, or mediation in private enterprise production; (C) expenditures upon collective consumption (purchased as goods or labor services from the enterprise or household sectors of the economy) and transfers to households to support household consumption, and (D) transfers to and support of not-for-profit institutions, for example, hospitals and universities.

THE LOCUS AND ORGANIZATION OF ECONOMIC POWER: THE ORGANIZATIONAL REVOLUTION

Corporate Power

IMPACT OF CORPORATE AND MANAGERIAL REVOLUTIONS

The implications of the corporate and managerial revolutions for the locus and organization of economic power are reasonably clear. In contrast to the classic model of

Table 12-2.

SECTORS AND TYPES OF GOVERNMENT CONTROL IN MANAGED CAPITALISM*

Sector	Type of Control	Examples
Government	Government ownership and production for the market	TVA, atomic power reactors, water and power
	Contribution to national income by government departments and agencies	Department of Defense, space research
	Government purchases of collective goods for production	Social intrastructure (public housing, highways)
Private enterprise production	Government control of the decentralized market-directed sector	Agricultural price supports
	Government regulation, subsidy, or support of particular industries	Public utilities, transportation, subsidies to airlines
	Government provision of general rules for industry	Antitrust legislation and enforcement
	Government mediation and balance of power between private groups	Wage-price guidelines, mediation and arbitration, labor legislation
Consumption	Government consumption of collective goods and services	National defense, education, parks and recreation
	Government transfers to households	Social insurance, interest on public debt
Other institutions	Government transfers to and support of non-profit institutions	Hospital care for veterans, research contracts to universities, support of the arts

*Adapted from [67: 265–76]

competitive market capitalism, in which power to make economic decisions is diffused so widely among large numbers of competing firms that no one is in a position to control or rig the market, or exploit his customers, rivals, or suppliers, contemporary theories of managed capitalism clearly recognize and focus upon the phenomenon of economic power. And in contrast to the Marxian model, which traces power nearly exclusively to ownership of industrial capital, contemporary theories focus on the exercise of economic power and social control by and in large-scale corporations, characterized by a fission of the two classic dimensions of property. In short, it is suggested that old-style, atomistic, market-directed capitalism has been transformed into a new-style "corporate" capitalism.

As students of contemporary managed capitalism see it, the power of large-scale corporations is great, fundamental, and pervasive. It includes more or less hierarchial direction of economic activity *within* the corporation, and thereby, control over employment, wages, and working conditions. It also includes control of traditionally market-determined variables, such as prices of commodities and resources. More broadly, it determines: the location of corporate activity, and, thereby, the creation, industrialization, or economic denuding of entire towns or regions; sales promotion activities, and thereby, in part, consumer tastes and preferences; the extent and rate of capital investment and technological development, and thereby, in large part, the rate of economic growth. The corporate and managerial revolutions have generated and accompanied a transformation from an economic system, the overall results of which were attained without the "conscious intent or decision" of any individual or group to one in which a relatively small number of executives in a relatively small number of large-scale corporate organizations make planful decisions which profoundly affect the behavior and functioning of the entire economy.

Beyond business organizations and markets, indeed, beyond the economy as a whole, is the influence which large-scale corporations and their executives exert on politics and society at large. The concentration and centralization of economic power in large-scale corporations carries with it the possibility of extension of control into such "non-economic" areas as public opinion, communications, education, and government. There is insight in the view of C. Wright Mills that the combination of corporate dominance, the ascendance of war, cold war, and the military in public policy and economic activity, and the relative shift in political power from legislatures to executive branches of government has created a "power elite," consisting of a relatively small number of leading corporate executives, political leaders, and military men, who exert a substantial degree of influence and control over contemporary managed capitalist economic societies, but who, in turn, are not (yet) subject to meaningful and effective democratic control by those societies. [62: 269 ff.] In any event, the question of the locus and organization of economic power, particularly corporate power, is crucial to the theory of managed capitalism.

LIMITS UPON CORPORATE POWER?

OLIGOPOLY, CORPORATE CONSCIENCE,

AND COUNTERVAILING POWER

In an economic system dominated by a relatively small number of large-scale corporations, whose programs for capital expansion are financed primarily, if not exclusively, from internal funds, the tradi-tional limitations upon the economic power of business firms, that is, the capital market and atomistic competition, seem relatively pale. Yet, corporate power is blunted and contained in a variety of ways. First, the dominant pattern of market organization in those sectors of the economy in which large-scale corporations generally prevail is oligopoly, not pure monopoly, and the struggles for economic leadership by a small number of corporate behemoths, however imperfect and different from old-style atomistic price competition, provide a vehicle for containing the economic power of any one of them.

Second is the power of public opinion and the beginnings, however imperfect, of the emergence of a concept and common law of "corporate conscience," which corporate managers, freed from traditional market and stockholder controls, may be in the process of developing and, in terms of which, they function less as profit maximizers and more as "trustees" of an amalgam or plurality of interests, including those of customers, suppliers, competitors, governments, local communities, and so forth. [A defense of this thesis is found in 48: 61–115; for a critique, see 63: 121–56.]

Third is the theory of *countervailing power* proposed by John K. Galbraith. The classic restraint on the exercise of private market power has been competition, that is, the existence or emergence of a large number of competitors on the same side of the market. Another sometimes quite important restraint is countervailing or offsetting power, that is, the existence or emergence of opposing positions of power on opposite sides of markets. Galbraith's central theses are (1) private economic power on one side of the market (original power) encourages offsetting or countervailing positions of economic power on the other side (countervailing power); (2) countervailing power has supplemented, if not superseded, competition as a restraint on market power and, thereby, "performs a valuable—indeed, an indispensable—regulatory function in the modern economy." [3: 137]

Two prominent examples are labor unions, which, by developing organized positions of market power in the sale of labor, have in part countervailed the power of corporations as buyers; and large retail discount houses and chain stores, which, by developing organized positions of market power in the purchase of commodities from manufacturers and wholesalers, have, in part, countervailed the power of corporations as sellers. Countervailing power develops, suggests Galbraith, both by *inducement*, to share some of the gains from a position of original market power, and for *self-protection*, as a defense against exploitation. [Cf. 3: 111–12]

The benefit to society from the emergence of countervailing power is the neutralization of one position of power by another; that is, the creation of a *plurality* of power positions which prevents and contains the power of large-scale corporations. Countervailing power may, but need not, generate the economic results of atomistic competition (that is, low prices and high outputs for consumers). Its major justification is essentially social and political: By countervailing power with opposing power, it destroys positions of monistic power and, thereby, contributes to the amelioration of the grievances or alleviation of the "tensions of some social group." [57: 4]

These ideas are imaginative and provocative, even if overplayed. Galbraith recognizes some of the main limitations himself: Countervailing power emerges imperfectly and is not as self-generative as suggested in the initial central thesis. Galbraith's answer to this, in part, is to shift from empirical explanation to normative evaluation by suggesting that governments ought to encourage the emergence of countervailing power where the number of buyers or sellers is large and their market power weak, as, for example, in retailing, labor markets, and agriculture. This explains, he suggests, the exclusion of these sectors from antitrust prosecution and their encouragement by government action (retail price maintenance laws, labor legislation, agricultural price supports).

Countervailing power is least effective during periods of high or rising demand and inflationary pressure, when large buyers and sellers, such as corporations and labor unions, may join together at the expense of consumers. Galbraith's answer to this criticism includes recommendations for placement of price stability above full employment in our priority list of social goals, a more liberalized system of unemployment compensation, and, a limited program of price and wage controls.

The theory of countervailing power does not invalidate the normative case for competition or eliminate the need for antitrust laws or enforcement. Galbraith's answer is that "if economic power could be totally mitigated by law, . . . the case against accepting countervailing power as a fact of life might be strong." [57: 5–6] But if monopoly power is a pervasive characteristic of contemporary economic life and cannot or will not be eliminated by legislative and judicial action, then countervailing power provides or may provide a possibly valuable supplement to or substitute for traditional competititon.

The Organizational Revolution

THE ORGANIZATIONAL ECONOMY

The corporation is neither unique nor monistic in its position of concentrated and centralized economic power. Large-scale organization is pervasive throughout much of contemporary economic activity, and the economic power position of corporations is supplemented, shared, and to a certain extent, "countervailed" by other private and public organizations.

Contemporary studies of managed capitalism emphasize the interblending of individualism and collectivism, decentralization and centralization. On the one hand, managed capitalism is characterized by a dispersion of economic power among a variety of decision-making units, including consumers, workers, businesses, financial institutions, governments, and so on. This dispersion of power indicates a fundamental decentralization in making and carrying out economic decisions. On the other hand, managed capitalists emphasize the concentration of economic power in the hands of a relatively small number of large-scale private and public organizations. This concentration of power facilitates and illustrates the existence of centralization in economic decision-making. Recognition of this blending of dispersion-concentration and centralization-decentralization makes "balance" among a plurality of large-scale organizations a central issue for the theory and practice of managed capitalism.

A prominent and strategic dimension in the transformation from old-style, individualistic capitalism to contemporary, managed capitalism has been the emergence and growth in the size and importance of large-scale collectivistic organizations concerned with making and executing economic decisions and promoting or protecting the economic interests of their members. The *rapidity* with which collective organizations have supplemented, if not supplanted, individual economic choice and individual units of economic decision, the present absolute and relative *magnitude* of such organizations and the impact which they have had upon the structure and behavior of contemporary managed capitalist economies justifies describing this transformation as an "organizational revolution" [52: 3–5] and the result as an "organizational economy" or "organized capitalism."

The organizational revolution, as described in the literature of contemporary managed capitalism, has had two major effects on the locus and organization of economic power. The first has been the surge to prominence of organizations. Within the "public sector" of the economy, this has taken the double form of (1) an increase in the size and roles of governments and governmental-political organizations (governments, political parties, executive departments, administrative agencies and commissions, and, as a large-scale employer of labor and allocator of resources, armed forces), not only in absolute terms, but in relation to the economy as a whole; (2) an increase in the size and economic role of central or national governmental organizations, in relation to local ones. Within the "private sector" of the economy, the emergence and surge to dominance of the large-scale corporation spearheaded the organizational revolution. But the growth of the corporation was accompanied and followed by the emergence and development of a variety of other organizations within and without the precincts of business including trade and business associations, professional associations (for example, the American Medical Association), labor unions, farm organizations, and cooperatives.

The second effect has been an enlargement and qualitative alteration in the bases of economic power or capacity to engage in social control. Even in old-style capitalism, under more or less atomistically competitive conditions, there were differences in power and control, but they primarily reflected differences in personal resources, such as wealth, income, family, and ability. In an organizational economy, these differences in personal resources are supplemented and "vastly magnified" by the power and social control available to people in positions of decision-making responsibility in large-scale organizations. [1: 232]

THE INTERPENETRATION OF POLITICS AND ECONOMICS

The organizational revolution has facilitated and been accompanied by a growing "interpenetration of politics and economics." In part, this is discernible in the phrase "locus and organization of economic power," for "power" is as much, if not more, a political concept as an economic one,[8] as seen in the interdependence of private and public institutions and processes: Economic issues and organizations shape, manipulate, and give direction to government policies, while, simultaneously, government agencies and organizations control and regulate the economy, including such large-scale private organizations as corporations and labor unions. This kind of interpenetration is especially noticeable if and when the scope of a public (private) organization's activities are expanded to encompass functions traditionally associated with private (public) organizations, as, for example, when governments establish public enterprises to generate and sell electric power, or when private corporations establish large-scale programs and agencies for subsidizing higher education. Interpenetration of politics and economics is also discernible in the growing recognition of the governmental and political problems of private organizations and the economizing problems of public organizations.

In some instances, notably atomic energy programs and research and development in general, interpenetration of politics and economics borders on merger. When a business sells most or all of its output to government (as in the aircraft industry), uses government-owned plants and facilities (as in atomic energy), has as its "product" a "cost plus fee" contract determined independently of a marketplace (as in space research), or is charged with the attainment of public purposes (such as non-discrimination in

employment), is it "private" or "public"?

But perhaps most important, the interpenetration of politics and economics is discernible in that largely because of the growth of large-scale organizations, man endeavors to manage, administer, and control economic society. Further, social control processes extend: not only to means to obtain ends, but to the selection of ends; not only to the magnitudes of particular economic variables (such as prices, outputs, wages, employment, GNP, taxes, or government spending), but to the historic process of economic development; not only to adjusting to the existing economic order, but to constructing the major dimensions of an emerging one. [56: 21–33]

Of course, actual choices and decisions regarding the direction and redirection of economic society are "neither so simple nor so grand" [1: 3] as the lofty alternatives of capitalism versus socialism or the price system versus government planning, envisaged in the classic debate over economic systems previously described in Parts II and III. But in contrast to the atomistic economy, where individual atomic units adjust to impersonal social forces beyond their control, our modern organizational economies have created the means whereby, within limits, men themselves determine the course and direction of their own society. In short, the impersonal forces of the marketplace have been supplemented, if not superseded, by conscious social guidance and management, and the resulting system may be described in part as "guided" or "managed" capitalism. This is a problem of politics, or political economy, rather than of pure economics.

Government as Manager

The policy objectives and functions of government, and the means or instruments used to achieve those objectives and/or realize those functions in managed capitalism, are varied. Tables 12-3, 12-4, and 12-5 provide brief checklists of objectives, func-

---

[8] J. K. Galbraith has aptly noted [3: 24] that much of the appeal of the competitive model to non-economists was in "its solution to the problem of power." In an atomistically competitive market economy, power to make and enforce economic decisions is diffused. In our contemporary organizational economies, economic power, though concentrated and centralized (in comparison with the competitive model), is shared by a plurality of private and public organizations. This power has important economic and political implications and is not exclusively a question for investigation by students of public governmental organizations.

Table 12-3.

OBJECTIVES OF ECONOMIC POLICY

Source	Policy Objectives	Notes
Dahl and Lindblom [1: 28–54]	Freedom; rationality; democracy; subjective equality; security; progress; appropriate inclusion	"Seven basic ends for social action" or "instrumental goals" as contrasted with "prime goals," such as love, power
Dahl and Lindblom [1: Chap. 5]	Resource development; high resource output; choice; allocation; stabilization; distribution	Economizing processes "necessary to rational calculation and control in economic life"
Smithies ["Economic Welfare and Policy," *Economics and Public Policy* (Washington, D.C.: The Brookings Institution, 1954), p. 14]	Continued economic growth; high and stable employment; reasonable stability of the price level; equitable distribution of income and social security; allocation of resources through the market mechanism; conservation of cultural and material resources	"Leaving aside its international policy, the economic policy of an advanced industrial economy ... should achieve a compromise among these objectives"
Boulding [*Principles of Economic Policy* (Englewood Cliffs, N.J.: Prentice-Hall, Inc., 1958), p. 19]	Economic progress; economic stability; economic freedom; economic justice	"Major objectives of economic policy." "Useful system of classification which leaves surprisingly few loose ends."
Johr and Singer [38: 111]	Supply of goods (level; growth; distribution); method of producing goods (freedom; opportunity for employment stability of economic status; preservation of certain branches of industry)	
The Commission on Money and Credit [*Money and Credit, Their Influence on Jobs, Prices, and Growth* (Englewood Cliffs, N. J.: Prentice-Hall, Inc., 1961), pp. 9–12]	An adequate rate of economic growth; sustained high levels of production and employment; reasonable stability of prices; adequate national security; harmonious international economic relations and contributions to economic development abroad; desirable degree of economic freedom and reliance on the market mechanism and strengthening of competition; equitable distribution of opportunity and income	"An adequate rate of economic growth, sustained high levels of production and employment, and reasonable stability of prices are clearly the three objectives of central concern for monetary, credit, and fiscal policies, These three goals, however, must be sought in the context of other important national objectives which necessarily impose constraints on their pursuit."

Table 12-4.

FUNCTIONS OF GOVERNMENT IN MANAGED CAPITALISM

Source	Functions of Government	Notes
Thompson ["Government and the Market" in *Federal Expenditure Policy for Economic Growth and Stability*, Papers on Fiscal Policy (Washington, D.C.: U.S. Government, 1957), pp. 130–52]	'Framework' activities ('rules of game'; defining the group whose welfare is to be maximized; freedom of entry; regulation of natural monopoly; regulation of external economies and diseconomies, provision of information); 'Allocation' activities (provision of 'indivisible' services; promoting external economies; operating natural monopolies; promoting equality; humanitarian activities); miscellaneous activities (price fixing; government enterprises)	"Framework activities alter or help to establish the given conditions which govern the equilibrium of market forces." "Allocative activities involve substantial use of resources, or modify the distribution of income, or affect the level of economic activity."
McConnell [*Economics* (N.Y.: McGraw-Hill Book Co., 1966), p. 98]	Strengthening and facilitating the price system (legal and social framework; maintaining competition); supplementing and modifying the price system (providing minimum living standards, adjusting for social costs and revenues; providing social goods and services; controlling unemployment and inflation; promoting economic growth)	"The economy of the U.S. can be accurately described as mixed capitalism." But "government assists and modifies the functioning of the price system in a variety of significant ways."
Johr and Singer [38: 125–27]	Steering the market mechanism (for example, subsidy); supplementing the market mechanism (such as fixing prices and wages in minor or subsidiary cases); subsequent correction of the results of the market mechanism (such as income redistribution through tax and expenditure policy)—adjustment intervention (to accelerate and facilitate a market-initiated development); preservative intervention (to maintain situations or industries); transformative intervention (to change the economy in a direction determined by government)	Measures designed to guide or 'correct' the market economy

Table 12-4. *cont.*

Source	Functions of Government	Notes
Watson [*Economic Policy* (Boston: Houghton Mifflin Co., 1960)]	Regulation of competition and monopoly; regulation of economic organizations, transportation, and public utilities; policies for economic growth and stability (monetary and fiscal); income policies (redistribution; social security; farm policies); foreign economic policy	"Secondary ends of economic policy"—which "act as a means to one or more of the primary ends of economic policy."
Wilcox [*Public Policies Toward Business* (Homewood, Ill.: Richard D. Irwin, Inc., 1960)]	Maintaining competition (antitrust policy); moderating competition (subsidy; control of agriculture; control of collective bargaining); substitution of regulation for competition (public utilities, transportation, direct controls in wartime); substitution of public for private enterprise	Government controls over business

tions, and policy instruments used by representative contemporary authors. The unifying thread which weaves together the apparent complexity and diversity of objectives, functions, and instruments is that government, in managed capitalism, functions as a prominent, though not exclusive, manager or governor of the economic system. This places managed capitalism in direct contrast to classic models of capitalism and socialism.

In the classic model of competitive market capitalism, government plays an important but limited role in providing the framework (law and order, national defense, public works) within which the competitive market system essentially governs itself. Economy and government are more or less separable. In the various classic visions and theories of socialism, government emerges as a major, if not dominating, agency or instrumentality for making and coordinating economic decisions. Economy and government economic

policy are more or less indistinguishable. In managed capitalism, government is a major sector within the economic system, strategically guiding, regulating, and controlling the processes of allocation, distribution, growth, and stabilization. But it is a sector of the system, a partner in the processes of economic governance and social control. It is by no means the entire system; and it shares the responsibility of economic governance and social control with a variety of other organizations and institutions (such as corporations, labor unions) and social processes (price systems, collective bargaining, private bureaucracy). [56: 298–308]

The contribution of government to the management of the economic system in contemporary managed capitalism has two central dimensions: (1) macroeconomic policy or strategy, whereby governments endeavor, essentially through control over money, taxes, and government spending, to guide or manage the aggregate level of economic

Table 12-5.

INSTRUMENTS OF GOVERNMENT ECONOMIC POLICY

Source	Instruments of Public Policy	Notes
Wilcox [*op. cit.*, pp. 19–28]	The common law; statutes and ordinances; administrative regulation; franchises, certificates, and licenses; taxes and subsidies; contracts; industry codes; investigations and publicity; emergency controls; government ownership and operation	Methods for control of business by government
Watson [*op. cit.*, p. 102, 152ff.]	Regulation of business practices; taxes; subsidies; loans; guarantees of loans; insurance; charters of incorporation and franchises; licenses and related methods of control; procurement; government corporations; publicity and investigation	"The instruments of economic policy are those means that cannot be ends in themselves."
Tinbergen [*Economic Policy: Principles and Design* (Amsterdam: North Holland, 1956), p. 7]	Quantitative policy (changes in the values of the instruments of economic policy; for example, taxes, expenditures, prices, wages, tariffs); qualitative policy (changes in the structure of the economic system given the 'foundations,' such as new taxes, new expenditures; establishment of 'built-in' stabilizers); reforms (changes in the foundations of an economic system, such as establishment of social security systems; nationalization of major industries; provision of guaranteed minimum income; centralization of production decisions); Utopias (misconceptions of human nature, rejected by most economists and politicians as inappropriate, such as abolition of money; complete equalization of incomes; completely free services)	

activity; (2) microeconomic policy or strategy, whereby governments endeavor to control or influence particular groups or sectors of the economic system and their interrelations. (1) is concerned essentially with full-employment stability and economic growth, while (2) is concerned essentially with resource allocation and income distribution.

MACROECONOMIC STRATEGY

Government macroeconomic strategy should be distinguished from mere macroeconomic actions by governments. As long as governments exist, the conduct of their monetary and fiscal affairs will inevitably constitute actions which do or can have effects upon the economic system. But macroeconomic strategy is more than mere action. It is characterized by the conscious, deliberate manipulation of policy instruments for the purpose of affecting the aggregate performance of the economy and for achieving desired policy goals.

Bases of Macroeconomic Strategy. Macroeconomic strategy has several bases. One, undoubtedly, has been the Keynesian critique of the economic theory and practice of old-style market capitalism.

Another has been national and international crises, most notably the depression of the 1930s, World War II, and the cold war of the 1940s and beyond.

A third has been the expansion in the size of governments and, thereby, an expansion in the magnitude of impact of government actions upon the economic system. The increase in the size of governments is explicable in terms of a variety of factors, most notably war and urbanization, of which the desire to formulate and apply macroeconomic strategy is only one. But once government accounts for 20 to 35 percent (rather than, say, five to ten percent) of national income and expenditures, a macroeconomic strategy becomes almost imperative.

Fourth, the absence of pure competition and the accompanying absence of perfect flexibility in prices, wages, and interest rates have decreased faith in the self-adjusting character of the capitalist system. Keynesian and neo-classical economists may debate over the "academic" question of whether the economy *would* automatically move to or toward full employment equilibrium *if it were* characterized by pure competition and perfectly flexible prices, but in fact, contemporary managed capitalist economies do not have these properties. They are, instead, characterized by oligopoly, monopolistic competition, "administered pricing," labor unions, agricultural price supports, resale price maintenance, and the like. This does not mean such economies have no adaptability or that the market system has

been completely superseded by other social processes. (Actually, the new-style monopolistically-oligopolistically competitive capitalism may be more conducive to economic growth than old-style atomistically competitive capitalism and, in some ways, make for greater, rather than lesser, stability.) But it does mean the private sector of the economy no longer has (if, indeed, it ever had) the structural or behavioral properties of the classical theory of automatic self-adjustment and that, even in idealized theoretical formulation, more or less continuous full employment cannot be expected to emerge spontaneously through the operation of impersonal market forces.

Fifth, recognition of the need for the provision of at least some minimally effective macroeconomic strategy by the government sector of the economy seems now firmly embedded in the political consensus of contemporary managed capitalist economies. Different political parties, political leaders, and economic interest groups, as well as economists, may have divergent priorities among goals and different views on the magnitude, timing, and composition of macroeconomic policies. But the general premise that governments (and central banks) can and should use their monetary and fiscal powers to prevent stagnation, depression, and inflation, and promote economic growth, full employment, and price stability seems irrevocably established and often is stated in national legislation, as, for example, in the United States Employment Act of 1946:

> The Congress declares that it is the continuing policy and responsibility of the Federal Government to use all practicable means consistent with its needs and obligations and other essential considerations of national policy, with the assistance and cooperation of industry, agriculture, labor, and State and local governments, to coordinate and utilize all its plans, functions, and resources for the purpose of creating and maintaining, in a manner calculated to foster and promote free competitive enterprize and the general

welfare, conditions under which there will be afforded useful employment opportunities, including self-employment, for those able, willing, and seeking to work, and to promote maximum employment, production, and purchasing power.

Framework and Goals of Macroeconomic Strategy. The declaration of policy in the Employment Act of 1946 provides a neat synopsis of both the central framework and goals of macroeconomic policy. The framework of macroeconomic strategy, especially as practiced in the United States, involves two major dimensions: institutional complementarity and joint responsibility. The concept of institutional complementarity acknowledges the existence of the private and public sectors of the economy and emphasizes their mutual and prospectively productive interrelations. As noted in the preceding quotation from the Employment Act, macroeconomic strategy is conceived as a complement and contributor to, not a substitute for, competition and private enterprise. The concept of joint responsibility emphasizes that the attainment of the goals of macroeconomic policy requires a joint cooperative effort by both sectors.

Although the Employment Act neither refers to growth or price stability nor mentions "full employment" by name, the concluding phrase "maximum employment, production, and purchasing power" may be loosely interpreted as incorporating these three objectives. In any event, United States macroeconomic policy since 1946 has been dominated by these goals.

Full employment as a policy goal does not mean *zero* unemployment of the civilian labor force, but instead, makes some allowance for "frictional" unemployment, that is, the unemployment involved in moving from one job to another. Estimating frictional unemployment at about three percent of the civilian labor force, most students of managed capitalism would regard a situation in which 96 to 97 percent of the labor force was employed as one of substantially full employment.

Similarly, substantial stability of the overall or general price level as a policy goal does not necessarily mean perfect stability. Further, both demand-pull and supply-push pressures for inflation are greater in a full or near-full employment economy than in one characterized by substantial slack, unemployment, and under-utilization of plant capacity. Also, institutional and other barriers may prevent deflation in some sectors, while inflation occurs in others. In addition, a certain amount of inflation reflects increases in the quality of products and services, a factor difficult to account for in cost of living indices. For these reasons, many postwar economists would regard a mild inflation of one to two percent per year as constituting substantial price-level stability.

As in the cases of full employment and price stability, the central question for economic growth as a policy goal, as viewed by managed capitalists, is not so much the qualitative issue of whether it is an appropriate objective for government action, but rather, the quantitative one of "how much." Among postwar contributors to the theory and strategy of managed capitalism, the range for the desired growth rate in a full employment economy is about three to five percent. The lower figure represents the historical growth rate in the United States since the late nineteenth century and, presumably, is that rate of growth which would be "naturally" forthcoming in a full employment economy via increases in the labor force and improvements in technology in the absence of concerted and conscious government action beyond that required to promote full employment utilization of resources. The upper figure represents a higher target rate of growth to meet pressing international commitments (defense, foreign aid) and national goals (education, urban renewal), requiring a positive government program to increase the rate of growth *at* full employment rather than merely to attain and maintain stability along a more modest full employment growth-curve.

To an extent, these major goals of macroeconomic policy are interdependent and complementary. However, they may conflict. Full employment may generate inflationary pressures. Rapid growth may be accompanied by instability and unemployment. Policies to temper inflation may curb full employment and high growth rates. Insofar as this is true, goals must be coordinated and priorities identified and established. Priorities and emphases among goals depend in part upon empirical assessments of their relations and "trade-offs."

They depend also on the degree of desired "tautness" or level of aspiration in the pursuit of goals. The least ambitious, but in the light of historical experience, not inconsequential macroeconomic strategy would be to "even out" the peaks and troughs of cyclical economic fluctuations, thereby avoiding severe or large-scale inflations and depressions. This strategy dominated economic development and policy in the United States, for example, between the end of World War II and the early 1960s. Economic growth was interrupted during this period by four recessions in output and employment (in 1948–1949, 1953–1954, 1957–1958, and 1960–1961). But partly through fortuitous circumstances (pent-up demand after World War II, Korean War and Cold War expenditures) and partly by policy design, both "automatic" and "discretionary," there was no major large-scale depression/deflation equivalent in length or severity to the prewar ones. The absence (or possible obsolescence) of large-scale depression/deflation marked a seismic change in the behavior of the economic system. The business cycle continued, but in dramatically subdued and manageable form.

A more ambitious level of aspiration, creating a greater likelihood of conflicts among policy goals, would be to sustain economic growth at full employment levels, with relative price stability, and prevent downturns into minor recessions. Something like this occurred in the United States during the first half of the 1960s as the economy—

again stimulated in part by fortuitous circumstances and in part by deliberate measures of monetary and fiscal management—moved from a recessionary trough (in 1961) toward a full-employment position in a sustained period of expansion without downturn longer than that of any preceding period except for World War II. The strategic innovation of monetary and fiscal management during this period was the application of expansionary policies in anticipation of a possible downturn, that is, when the economy was still rising, as a means of warding off a downturn and accelerating the rate of expansion toward full employment. If the early postwar period in the United States demonstrated the likelihood of the obsolescence of large-scale depression, the "new economics" of the 1960s raised the hope, tentative though it may be, of the possible obsolescence of downturns into recessions as well.[9]

At the same time, successful pursuit and implementation of this relatively more ambitious strategy can create its own costs and problems. By the mid-sixties, the United States economy had substantially closed the gap between potential and actual production. Combining the objectives of sustained economic growth and full employment with only mild inflation and moderate deficits in the balance of payments involves a balancing act of precision and delicacy. Paradoxically, the more creatively successful the expansionary macroeconomic strategy, the greater the care and precision required to walk the economic tightrope. An economy floundering in large-scale depression can engage in a wholeheartedly expansionary monetary and fiscal policy (increases in the supply of money, tax cuts, increased government spending) without

---

[9]For a description of macroeconomic policy during this period, see Walter W. Heller, *New Dimensions of Political Economy* (New York: W. W. Norton & Co., Inc., 1967); E. Ray Canterbury, *Economics on a New Frontier* (Belmont, Calif.: Wadsworth Publishing Co., Inc., 1968); and Seymour E. Harris, *Economics of the Kennedy Years* (New York: Harper & Row, Publishers, 1964).

worrying excessively about inflationary pressures, allocational inefficiencies, or balance of payments deficits. A prosperous, full employment economy, because of its prosperity, has less "slack"; accordingly, government policymakers have a smaller degree of freedom in vigorously pursuing expansionary measures. The implementation of macroeconomic policy in the United States since the mid-1960s illustrates these strains and tensions.[10]

MICROECONOMIC STRATEGY

Like macroeconomic strategy, government microeconomic strategy should be distinguished from mere actions by government. As long as governments exist, the conduct of their affairs inevitably will constitute actions which do or can have effects upon groups or sectors of the economic system. But microeconomic strategy is more than mere action. It is characterized by the conscious, deliberate manipulation of policy instruments for the purpose of affecting microeconomic structure, behavior, or performance and for achieving desired policy goals.

Bases of Microeconomic Strategy. The bases of microeconomic strategy essentially parallel the major dimensions of structural transformation and reform from old-style to contemporary managed capitalism previously described. The technological, corporate, managerial, and organizational revolutions and the new blend of social processes (oligopolistic and monopolistically competitive price systems, collective bargaining, growth of private hierarchies) have radically altered the institutional structure of the economic system and have both been accompanied by and encouraged the expansion of government's role in the economy, as promoter of competition, regulator of monopoly, subsidizer or promoter of the interests of particular groups or sectors,

---

[10]See, for example, Irving Siegel, "Fuller Employment with Uptrending Prices," *Journal of Economic Issues,* March 1968, pp. 31–44.

and "equalizer" in the balance of power among them. Indeed, a strong case may be made for the hypothesis that such institutional and structural change in the private sector of the economy ". . . compels the state to large-scale measures of intervention. They become necessary simply to prevent the actual disorganization of society, which would result from the organization of the individual markets, if this development were not controlled and coordinated. And they are needed in order to prevent those who have acquired a stronger bargaining power from exploiting the others." [6:32–33]

In addition to institutional and technological changes, there have been motivational and ideological changes, that is, in attitudes and outlooks. With the increased democratization of the political process and the expanding political role of larger numbers and sectors of society, it became almost inevitable that democratic government would be used as a vehicle for social reform and income redistribution. At the same time, growth in the "urge for economic equilization" has been "one of the major driving forces behind the general trend towards increasing the volume of state intervention." [6: 38]

Similarly, the same technological and institutional changes, coupled with urbanization and the shift from an agrarian to an industrial way of life, which have encouraged an expanded role for government, also have encouraged changes in attitudes toward risk and insecurity. In a dominantly agricultural, underdeveloped economy, the major sources of insecurity or discontinuity in income are "natural"—floods, drought, and other natural disasters. In a developed, industrial, urban society, the major threats to the continuity of income and employment—depressions, industrial accidents and disease, even old age—become "social" in character and encourage accommodation to the attitude of need for social or collective solutions.

More fundamental, however, in its general significance for microeconomic strategy, has been the increase in "economic rationality" in the shift from old-style to managed capitalism. Oddly, the traditional view of the psychological foundations of economic behavior under old-style capitalism is that of the rational calculation of economic gains and costs. But maximization of economic gain through market exchange is only one dimension of the attitudinal properties of old-style capitalism. Another was the traditional, conventional, pre- or non-rational willingness to accept impersonal social forces, processes, or taboos beyond one's control. In the process of industrialization, older taboos (for example, regarding the gold standard, the categorical imperative of the annually balanced budget, the sanctity of private property) have broken down, and people have become more economically "sophisticated" and "economically rational," demanding vehicles and instruments of private and public control over their economic destinies.

In the United States, at least, the trend has been from action and intervention to planning and strategy. As governmental microeconomic actions and interventions have expanded, the need for strategic and planful coordination of public policies has also increased. "The regular sequence has been that intervention caused planning. . . . What happened was that, as measures of state intervention in a particular field grew in volume and in complexity, attempts to coordinate them more rationally had from time to time to be thrown into this development" when measures turned out to be more than temporary, when policies had important secondary, tertiary, or countervailing effects beyond those anticipated, when aims and policies or policies and policies turned out to be inconsistent, or when government policies raised administrative difficulties. [6: 22]

Framework and Goals of Microeconomic Strategy. The framework and goals of microeconomic strategy in practice are not as neatly or clearly summarized as those of macroeconomic strategy. No microeconomic

counterpart to the Employment Act of 1946 exists, though the rhetoric of the preamble to the Act has important microeconomic implications. (Thus: "with the assistance and cooperation of industry, agriculture, labor, and State and local governments . . . in a manner calculated to foster and promote free competitive enterprise. . . .")

By a process of induction, however, it is possible to identify the framework of microeconomic strategy as that of "balanced pluralism" and the major goals of microeconomic strategies as efficiency, equity-equality, balance of power, and freedom. Clearly, contemporary managed capitalist economies differ from the theory and practice of old-style capitalism and the traditional nineteenth-early twentieth century visions of socialism by the incorporation of a plurality of independent but interdependent groups or organizations, each seeking to control markets in which it buys and sells, to bargain with other organized groups, and to utilize the methods and processes of democratic government to promote its interests through government action.

In this context, the relevant institutional framework is neither individual choice coordinated by market processes nor government choice coordinated by centralized hierarchy nor a combination of the two, but a third system in which government functions as one of a number of organized clusterings of economic and political powers and, in turn, as a regulator of and responder to organized private interests. In this context, also, traditional microeconomic goals of efficiency and freedom take on broadened meanings and are supplemented by concerns for equality, equity, and balance of power.

In the theory and practice of old-style capitalism, competition and the marketplace were the social processes expected to coordinate microeconomic decisions in a socially efficacious way. In the theory and practice of managed capitalism, microeconomic strategy has been intimately related to issues of competition and monopoly.

Broadly speaking, at least in the United States, two main patterns have emerged. Where the number of sellers has been small and their absolute and relative sizes and market power large (as in manufacturing industry), the microeconomic strategy advocated and/or adopted has been to promote competition and control monopoly. This is illustrated, for example, by the Sherman, Clayton, and Federal Trade Commission Acts in the United States. The Sherman Act (1890) made illegal both monopolization and conspiracies or combinations to restrain trade. The Clayton Act (1914) specified certain practices (price discrimination, tying contracts, exclusive dealing arrangements, interlocking directorates, mergers) as unlawful when they would "substantially lessen competition or tend to create a monopoly." The Federal Trade Commission Act (1914) declared "unfair methods of competition in commerce" to be unlawful and established the Federal Trade Commission (with the Antitrust Division of the Department of Justice) to help enforce the antitrust laws.

By contrast, where the number of sellers has been large and their absolute and relative sizes and market power small (as in agriculture, wholesale and retail distributive trades, and labor), the microeconomic strategy advocated and/or adopted has been to restrain competition or otherwise protect or support competitors. This is illustrated by agricultural price supports, laws to exempt "resale price maintenance contracts" specifying minimum retail prices from antitrust prosecution, and legal and political encouragement of collective bargaining by labor unions as agents of countervailing power to corporate managements.

THE NEW BLEND OF SOCIAL PROCESSES

Analysis and proposals in the literature of managed capitalism emphasize a blending of a variety of social processes for making and

coordinating economic decisions. The blend incorporates two major features: first, an emphasis upon price systems other than purely competitive ones—especially price systems in markets characterized by the blending of competitive and monopolistic elements (monopolistic competition and oligopoly); second, a recognition of social processes for economic decision-making and coordination which may serve as potential complements to or substitutes for price systems, namely, democracy, bureaucracy, and bargaining. We shall examine in the following chapter the new blend of social processes in greater depth as part of a discussion of the behavior and functioning of managed capitalism.

FROM ECONOMIC MOTIVATIONS TO SOCIAL GOALS: INCOME DISTRIBUTION AND THE WELFARE STATE

Economic Motives and Social Goals

The motivational assumption underlying the theory of competitive market capitalism was the maximization of individual economic gain through market exchange—profit maximization for business firms, earnings maximization for resource owners, utility maximization for consumers. While recognizing the continued importance of the pursuit of individual economic gain, students of managed capitalism have enlarged the concept of the motivational underpinnings of the structure and organization of the economic system.

First, the "separation of ownership and management" in large-scale corporations plausibly reduces the relative importance of old-style profit maximization. The executive leadership of large-scale corporations undoubtedly is interested in profits. At the same time, however, since corporate managers typically are neither owner-proprietors or major stockholders, it has been suggested their interests and motives, while including profits, are different and broader than those encompassed in the traditional profit-maximization assumption. Their motivational framework also includes such aspirations as managerial salaries, maintaining managerial control over the corporation, sales maximization, growth and enlargement of market share, harmonious labor-management relations, and avoidance of antitrust prosecution.

Second, recognition of concentration and centralization of economic power and, thereby, the capacity to control and shape economic development through conscious, planful human choice and action, has encouraged a shift in emphasis from the assumption of individual economic gain maximization to the pursuit by large-scale groups and organizations, especially governments, of goals for large sectors of and/or the entire national economy.

It is this second dimension of contemporary managed capitalism which both supporters and critics evidently have in mind when they refer to those economic systems as "welfare states" or "welfare capitalism." The term "welfare state" has occasionally been applied rather narrowly to programs of "social welfare," and "social security"; that is, unemployment compensation, old-age insurance, workmen's compensation, and general public assistance. More typically and recently, it has acquired a broader, more inclusive connotation. "Welfare state" or "welfare capitalism" generally now may be held to mean a state of affairs in which government, subject to greater or lesser degrees of democratic control by the citizenry, pursues and promotes "social welfare," generally conceived as stability, income and employment security, income equalization, and some roughhewn balance in the power, position, and interests of private economic groups.

The pursuit of social welfare by governments in contemporary welfare states is profoundly affected by sustained prosperity and high rates of economic growth. By raising living standards, including those of lower income brackets, economic growth blunts pressures for reducing the extent of income inequality. At the same time, economic growth permits a mild equalization in income without reducing, or reducing substantially, the incomes of people in upper income brackets. More broadly, high levels of economic activity and high growth rates permit the more or less successful simultaneous pursuit of varied social goals. Contemporary managed capitalist economies may be, and in varying ways and degrees are, "welfare states," "warfare states," and "mass consumption economies" simultaneously. Such systems may indulge in such luxuries, within limits, of pursuing both guns and butter and declaring a "war on poverty" along the way.

Income Distribution

The literature of managed capitalism emphasizes a blend of market-determined resource prices, group action (by, for example, corporations, labor unions, and farm organizations) to affect income distribution and government measures to redistribute income.

The shift from old-style to contemporary managed capitalism has been accompanied by shifts in income distribution: first, in functional income distribution, a decrease in rent and interest and an increase in wages as a percent of national income; second, in personal income distribution, a decrease in the percent of personal income received by people in upper income brackets and large-scale increase in the percent of personal income received by people in middle income brackets; third, within the upper income brackets, a decrease in the percent received by proprietors-owners of businesses and an increase in the percent received by people in professional and managerial occupations and positions. These shifts in the distribution of income, coupled with economic growth and rising living standards, have substantially reduced, though by no means eliminated, poverty as an *economic* problem.

As noted, prosperity and sustained economic growth mutes emphasis upon income redistribution as a social goal and minimizes pressures for social reform in contemporary managed capitalism. If economic growth falters, however, or full employment is not sustained, the implicit political compact between the relative "haves" and "have-nots" breaks down, and pressures build for more radical approaches to the reduction of poverty and the redistribution of income and wealth.

In practice, managed capitalist economies such as the United States still retain substantial inequalities in the distribution of income and especially wealth; the post-World War II period (at least in the United States) has been remarkably free from further shifts in the relative positions of the lowest and highest income brackets; and poverty continues to afflict up to (depending upon how loosely "poverty" is defined) 20 to 25 percent of the population.

In regard to theories and strategies, managed capitalism is divisible into at least two main sub-groupings: one, the more liberal social reform capitalists, who, while supporting the new system of political economy, are sharp critics of poverty and inequalities in income and power; another, the more conservative managed capitalists, who, while accepting the major tenets of Keynesian macroeconomic strategy to sustain full employment prosperity, are also generally supporters of corporate privilege and dominance (or at least the postwar status quo in regard to the distribution of income, wealth, and economic power), and critics of schemes and measures to further decrease the extent of economic inequalities.

SUMMARY AND CONCLUSION: OLD AND NEW ELEMENTS

Let us apply the preceding discussion of the structure and organization of managed capitalism to the six propositions cited at the opening of this chapter:

1. What are the primary ways in which managed capitalism departs from the theory and practice of competitive market, *laissez-faire* capitalism?

a. in the relative decrease in individual owner-managed proprietorships and the separation of "ownership" from executive control and management.

b. in the relative decrease in economic individualism and in decentralization in economic decision-making.

c. in the relative decrease in the automaticity of competitive market exchange as a social process for making and coordinating economic decisions.

2. In what major ways has managed capitalism incorporated elements of socialism?

a. in the extension of public control over industry.

b. in the increase of social and group action in the pursuit of social goals.

c. in the increase in the organization, power, and status of workers and labor organizations in the economy and the reduction of inequality in the distribution of income and wealth.

d. in the increase in processes for conscious, planful direction, coordination, and control of the national economy.

3. In what major ways has managed capitalism failed to establish a thoroughgoing socialist economic system?

a. in its failure to establish even approximately more or less widespread and comprehensive systems of social government ownership of industry, worker control of industry, or centralized government planning and control of the entire national economy.

b. in its failure to establish even roughly conditions of equality in the distribution of income and wealth and/or a "worker's state" or classless society.

c. in its failure to establish even

approximately cooperation (or other social goals or aspirations) as the more or less widespread and comprehensive principle for human motivation and economic decision-making.

4. What are the major capitalist elements remaining in the theory and/or practice of contemporary managed capitalism?

a. a predominant role for private, non-governmental ownership and control of the instruments of production coupled with a substantial absolute (even though diminished relative) role for individual, owner-managed businesses.

b. the maintenance of substantial areas and opportunities for freedom of individual, decentralized choice and decision-making—for consumers, workers, savers, investors, property owners, and businessmen—and for the pursuit of economic gain through market exchange.

c. a heavy (even if relatively reduced) role for markets and price systems in making and coordinating economic decisions and for competition (even though monopolistic or oligopolistic) as a social control process.

d. the maintenance of a strong and influential business and entrepreneurial class, of property income, and of large-scale inequalities in the distribution of income and wealth.

5. In what major ways does managed capitalism incorporate dimensions or features not prominent in the theory or practice of competitive market, *laissez-faire* capitalism or the major classic visions or models of socialist economy?

a. in the coexistence of a pluralism of large-scale, collectivist, centralized, bureaucratic private and governmental organizations, with the power to make strategic, socially significant economic decisions, whose interrelationships are characterized by an interplay of competition, cooperation, and negotiation or bargaining.

b. in the coexistence of private, corporate planning and management (most typically of the major microeconomic decisions of "what," "how," and "for whom") and public, governmental planning and management (especially of overall, macroeconomic strategies).

6. What are the major features which managed capitalism shares with all or most modern industrialized economic societies?

a. a high level of economic development and high rate of economic growth.

b. a high ratio of capital to labor and embodiment of technical improvements in new capital investment.

c. a predominance of large-scale, hierarchically or bureaucratically structured centralized organizations, including governments, for making economic decisions.

d. a utilization of money, markets, and exchange.

e. an emphasis on conscious, planful social management, guidance, and control of economic life in the pursuit of social or collective aims.

f. an existence of inequalities in income, wealth, economic status, and/or power to make economic decisions.

13

Managed Capitalism:
Behavior and Functioning

This chapter describes leading theoretical ideas on the behavior and functioning of managed capitalism by focusing upon the altered blend of social processes for making and coordinating economic decisions and on the relations between managed capitalism and policy goals. First, we will examine market structures or price systems, notably monopolistic competition and oligopoly, which combine competitive and monopolistic elements and are characterized by the unifying theme of pluralistic market control. Next, we will explore countervailing and supplementary factors in market control. Then, we will briefly compare non-market processes, notably bureaucracy, bargaining, and democracy. Lastly, we will relate the structure and behavior of managed capitalism to social goals (efficiency, equity/equality, full employment/stability, and economic growth).

VARIETIES OF PRICE SYSTEMS

Classically, the price system was regarded as a social process for the control of business firms by consumers and resource owners. The social control process envisaged in the classic competitive model involved the possibility of substitution among (1) products and (2) firms. The former is more fundamental and "primary" [1: 178–81] than the latter. It exists or may exist even in the case where

an industry is dominated by one firm (that is, pure monopoly) because of the possibility of inter-industry competition. If the number of business firms is large, then (2) spontaneously accompanies (1) as an important form of "supplementary" [1: 182ff.] control. It functions via the actual or possible shift of purchases or sales by consumers or resource owners from one business firm to another within an industry or market.

The literature of managed capitalism continues to place heavy emphasis on these two forms of social control over business firms. Indeed, through innovation and technological development, rising living standards with accompanying increases in "discretionary income," urbanization, and improvements in transportation and communication, the primary control of inter-industry competition may well be greater in contemporary-managed capitalism than in old-style capitalism. However, the corporate and managerial revolutions have fostered and been accompanied by the emergence or expansion of social techniques whereby business firms actively manage or control prices or markets rather than passively adapt to given impersonal market forces beyond their control. At the same time, the organizational revolution has fostered and been accompanied by the emergence or expansion of social techniques for the control or containment of the market power of business firms.

Were competition pure and perfect, the degree of control over prices and markets by individual business firms would be zero, for all practicable purposes. Thus, the management of prices and markets by business firms may be described essentially in terms of price systems which incorporate impurities and/or imperfections.

Two prominent types of impurities are instances where (1) the number of firms is not large; and/or (2) the products (or places of employment) of firms are differentiated in the minds of consumers (or resource owners.) In (1), firms control prices and markets by virtue of their relatively large size (the limiting case is one firm), even if products or places of employment are identical. In (2), firms control prices and markets by virtue of their differentiation (the limiting case is "perfect differentiation")—for example, consumers may be willing to pay a higher price for a more highly advertised product or one which they regard as qualitatively superior—even if the number of sellers is relatively large. Of course, (1) and (2) may be combined, as when a relatively small number of firms sell a related but differentiated product (for example, cigarettes) and control over prices and markets is based upon both factors.

Every market other than pure competition (characterized by large numbers of firms with identical products and places of employment) has a degree of monopoly, however small, a degree of control over prices and quantities of products and/or resources bought or sold. Yet, every market, other than pure monopoly (characterized by one firm with a "completely differentiated" product or place of employment), involves a degree of intra-industry competition, however small, a degree of substitution among firms and/or products within an industry or market. Thus, the characteristic form of modern industry is an interblending of competition and monopoly, or monopolistic competition,

with oligopoly as the special and strategically important form of monopolistic competition where the number of firms is relatively small.

The major form of market imperfection consists of a variety of factors (lack of knowledge or mobility, legal or other institutional barriers to entry) which prevent or discourage entry of firms into an industry or market area to compete with existing firms. Large size and/or product differentiation may give business firms control over prices and markets in the short run. Absence of, or barriers to, freedom of entry may perpetuate such control in the long run.

Monopolistic Competition

The first market structure involving an interblending of elements associated with both competition and monopoly is *monopolistic competition*. The structural features of monopolistic competition are: (1) many sellers, selling (2) a related but differentiated product. (1) is a competitive element, while (2) incorporates a degree of monopoly power, the degree depending on the extent of differentiation.

The combination of these two ingredients makes monopolistic competition special. The special feature has to do with demand conditions as seen by individual firms.[1] Under pure competition, where price is determined by impersonal forces of demand and supply beyond the control of individual sellers, the demand curve as seen by each firm is a straight horizontal line at the going

---

[1] Cost conditions depend upon (1) resource prices, and (2) quantities of resources required to produce various levels of output. Unless monopoly power in the sale of output is accompanied by monopsony power in the purchase of resources, (1) will be the same for firms selling under monopoly, monopolistic competition, and pure competition. (2) depends upon the physical relations between inputs and outputs, which, we will assume, are the same for firms regardless of the degree of market power. Thus, cost conditions are not likely to be radically different, and the main differences relate to conditions of demand.

market price (recall Fig. 4.2a.) Under pure monopoly, where the individual firm has no rivals or substitutes for its product, its demand curve is the demand curve for the market as a whole. (DD in Fig. 4.7.)

But under monopolistic competition, the demand curve for a firm's related but differentiated product plausibly would lie somewhere in between. Because the individual firm has a differentiated product which claims some degree of "brand loyalty," its demand curve is tilted or downward sloping: It can increase its sales (but less than infinitely) by decreasing its price and will discover its sales decrease (but not to zero) when its price is increased. In this, it is akin to monopoly. But on the other hand, its product, though differentiated, is not unique. Instead, the firm has (a large number of) rivals and close substitutes for its products. Assuming that prices of other firms remain constant,[2] price increases by one firm will cause many of its customers (though not all, because of brand loyalty even at higher prices) to substitute the product of one or more of its competitors; price decreases will entice many (but not all) customers, old and new, to substitute its product for that of one or more of its competitors. In this, it is somewhat akin to competition.

As in pure monopoly and pure competition, the most profitable level of output for the individual firm under monopolistic competition is that at which marginal cost equals marginal revenue (OQ_1 in Fig. 13.1). As in monopoly, the individual firm has the freedom and power to control price, that is, to select that combination of price and output which maximizes its profits. Also as in the monopoly case, marginal revenue (MR) lies below and diverges from the demand = average

<hr>

[2]This assumption follows from the underlying structural condition of many sellers. If the number of sellers is large, the loss or gain in sales for any *one* firm as a result of a decrease or increase in price of another firm is not likely to be great, and the firm thus may ignore the prospective reactions of rivals to their actions.

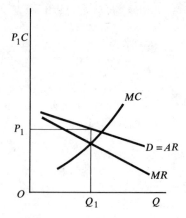

Fig. 13.1. Profit maximization under monopolistic competition

revenue (AR) curve. As a result, price ($= AR$) at P_1 lies above marginal cost (MC). Output is lower and price higher than if output were pushed up to a point at which $MC = P$. However, if the extent of differentiation and, thereby, the tilt of the demand curve, is relatively mild, the divergence between demand and marginal revenue curves and, thereby, between price and marginal cost will also be mild, and the price and output will not differ greatly from that reached under pure competition.

The tendency for prices and production under monopolistic competition to approximate the results of pure competition is heightened by the fact that, although each firm may plausibly regard prices and outputs of other firms as given, the *position* of its own demand curve is affected by the simultaneous independent actions of all firms. Suppose, for example, as illustrated in Fig. 13.2, that each representative monopolistic competitive firm, commencing at price-output combination P_1Q_1, believes that an increase in output to Q_2 and a decrease in price to P_2 will raise profits, by moving down the slightly tilted demand curve d_1. But as *all* firms simultaneously and independently expand their output, the *total* output of related but differentiated products increases in relation to total market demand. Thus, (1) the demand curve or market share of any individual firm

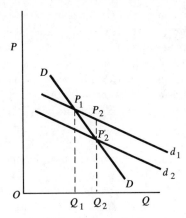

Fig. 13.2. Group adjustment

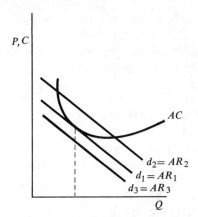

Fig. 13.3. Demand, cost, and profit

shifts down (say, to d_2), and (2) the price which consumers are willing to pay for output OQ_2 actually falls to, say, P_2'. [Alternatively, this may be depicted by demand curve DD, which shows the response of sales to changes in price when *all* firms (simultaneously and independently) raise or lower price.] Firms, taking their competitors' prices and outputs as given, produce larger quantities and end up by accepting lower prices than they would if they assumed their competitors generally would follow them in price-output changes.

This process of group adjustment presumably would continue until (1) consumers were willing to purchase the total output of related but differentiated products at prices expected by sellers who (2) were maximizing profits via price-output combinations characterized by an equality of marginal cost and marginal revenue. Whether profit maximizing output entails (above-normal) profits, however, depends upon the relation between average revenue (AR) and average cost (AC). Three major possibilities are shown in Fig. 13.3. If demand = d_1, losses are made at all output levels except that one at which AR just barely equals AC, and the firm breaks even with "normal profits." If demand = d_2, a range of output exists over which above-normal profits can be made. If demand = d_3, losses are made at all levels of output and the best the firm can hope to accomplish

in the short run is to minimize its losses. Of course, in the long run, when firms inside and outside the group of related but differentiated competitors have had time to adjust to the profit conditions represented by Fig. 13.3, exit and/or entry could or would shift the positions of demand curves in relation to cost curves and, thereby, change profit conditions. We will return to this after examining prices and output under oligopoly.

Oligopoly

The second form of market structure between pure competition and pure monopoly is that of oligopoly. In one consistent choice of terminology, *oligopoly* is a form of monopolistic competition because it is characterized by an interblending of competitive and monopoly elements. But the nature of the blend is so special as to require a special name to distinguish it, not only from the purely competitive and monopolistic extremes, but from monopolistic competition in general, or from the form of monopolistic competition described in the preceding section (many sellers, with differentiated products).

Just as oligarchy is rule by the few, oligopoly is competition among the few. The crucial identifying characteristic of oligopoly is a small number of relatively large sellers (and of oligopsony, a small number of relatively large buyers). How few and how relatively large must firms be to warrant this classification? The practical answer is: small enough in number and large enough in relative size so that the market actions of any one seller (for example, price increases or decreases) have an appreciable effect upon the sales and profits of other sellers. If this is true, the prudent oligopolist, recognizing his fundamental interdependence with his rivals, will consider their prospective reactions to his actions.

What is the effect of all this upon the oligopolist's demand curve? If we could abstract from "oligopolistic interdependence," the firm under oligopoly clearly would face a negatively-sloped demand curve for its product: First, if a seller is large relative to the market and supplies an appreciable proportion of total industry output (say, 20 percent), its control over output will make it a price maker rather than a price taker. Like the monopolist, its market size gives it control over price and the discretion to select profitable price-output combinations denied to the small-scale (relative to the market) monopolistic competitor were it not for product differentiation. This source of market power exists under oligopoly even if the product is homogeneous (pure oligopoly). Second, if a relatively large seller *also* sells a related but differentiated product (differentiated oligopoly), it has, in product differentiation, an additional source of market power and capacity to control price, akin to that of monopolistic competition. From these two points of view, oligopoly is a member of a family of market structures characterized by the absence of adjustment by firms to impersonal market forces beyond their control.

The unique and special feature of oligopoly, however, is the interdependence of the oligopolists. This interdependence does not exist for the firm under pure monopoly because, for all practical purposes, it has no rivals. It does not exist for the pure competitor or the relatively small-scale mono-

polistic competitor because, in these markets, the number of rivals is so large and the impact upon their sales of price-output decisions by any one of their competitors is so small that their prospective reactions may be ignored.

Because of interdependence, the oligopolist's demand curve cannot be determined independently of the prospective actions and reactions of rivals. Thus, it would be misleading to draw a unique and independent demand curve for an oligopoly seller as we have for firms under other market structures. And without such a demand curve, we cannot depict a unique profit maximizing solution for a "representative oligopolist." Alternatively stated, without plausible predictions of rivals' reactions, we cannot depict a determinate price-output solution for the case of oligopoly.

We can identify, however, a relatively small number of classic or representative types of oligopoly behavior, classified in terms of rivals' prospective action-reaction patterns, notably the degree and form of collusion. We shall distinguish three cases: (1) independent, uncoordinated, or non-collusive oligopoly; (2) perfectly or completely coordinated, collusive oligopoly; (3) imperfectly coordinated, collusive oligopoly. [61: 364–65]

(1) INDEPENDENT OLIGOPOLY

Under independent oligopoly, the firm's market behavior, though *inter*dependent with that of its rivals, is not coordinated with them through any form of explicit or tacit collusion. Each firm is independent to seek its own best price-output policy. Because of interdependence, however, the policy selected will depend upon expected reactions of rivals.

Two Demand Curves. Fig. 13.4 depicts two main types of prospective reactions to price changes by an independent oligopolist. JD_1 represents the demand curve faced by the individual firm on the assumption that its rivals are expected to *match* its price changes instantaneously. In this event,

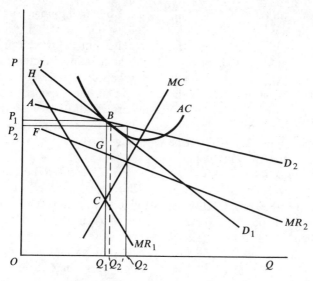

Fig. 13.4. The temptation to cut prices

the firm will not gain customers from its rivals by lowering its price and will not lose customers to its rivals by raising its price. JD_1 thus is a replica in miniature of the market demand curve. (Technically and precisely, this is true only under pure oligopoly. Under differentiated oligopoly, there is no demand curve for *the* industry output, but only for the related but differentiated products of individual firms. In many cases of high substitutability, however, the observation is roughly, if not precisely, accurate.) On the other hand, AD_2 represents the demand curve faced by the individual firm on the assumption (as in monopolistic competition) that its rivals do *not* match its price changes, at least not immediately. In this case, the firm would gain customers from its rivals by price cuts and would lose sales to them by price increases. Thus, D_2 is closer to the horizontal than D_1.

If the oligopolist anticipated that either one of these two demand curves were certain and given, then a profit maximizing price-output solution could be depicted at the point of intersection of the marginal cost and the appropriate marginal revenue curve. Suppose, for example, that marginal cost is represented by curve MC and the marginal

revenue curves appropriate to demand curves D_1 and D_2 are MR_1 and MR_2, respectively. Then the oligopolist who expects his rivals to *match* his price changes immediately will select price-output combination P_1Q_1, appropriate to the intersection of MC and MR_1. The oligopolist who expects his rivals will *not match* his price changes, at least not immediately, would maximize his profits at a lower price (P_2) and a larger output (Q_2), appropriate to the intersection of MC and MR_2. Because different oligopolists may have different expectations of rivals' reactions, one firm (say, a discount house) might select P_2Q_2, while another (say, a conservative, "high quality" furniture retailer) might select P_1Q_1.

The Temptation to Undercut One's Rivals. Now suppose that one oligopolist, who traditionally has operated on the assumption of immediate price-matching by his rivals and who has adjusted his price-output combination accordingly, becomes convinced his traditional assumption is no longer valid, and that he can be a price-cutter with no fear of retaliation. This provides a powerful temptation to decrease his price, for as long as his rivals do not retaliate by decreasing their prices, his profits must rise. That this is so is illustrated in Fig. 13.4. The initial profit maximizing equilibrium is at the intersection of MC with MR_1 with price at P_1 and output at Q_1. Assume, for purposes of simplification, that D_1 is tangent to the AC curve at this point so that the firm is just breaking even and making normal profits. If it now believes that a price cut will not be matched by its rivals, the relevant demand curve becomes D_2, and the relevant MR curve becomes MR_2. MR_2 exceeds MC at output Q_1, indicating the profitability of expanding output to a new profit maximizing price-outout combination of P_2Q_2. Because the additions to revenue exceed the additions to cost, profits must be higher at Q_2 than at Q_1; and since the firm just broke even at Q_1, it must be receiving above-normal profits at Q_2. (Note that D_2 lies above AC at output Q_2.)

Price War. What is sauce for the goose, however, is sauce for the gander. The endeavor by one oligopolist to steal his rivals' customers by price-cuts may well lead to retaliatory price-cutting, indeed, as price-cuts spread throughout an oligopolistic market characterized by independence of action, to a "price war," as each firm attempts to undercut the others. In this event, D_2 proves to be a lorelei. If all firms decrease their prices more or less simultaneously, in the mistaken belief their rivals will not follow suit (at least, not as much or as rapidly), then the relevant demand curve is D_1, not D_2. As price drops from P_1 to P_2, for example, in Fig. 13.4, the representative oligopolist discovers its sales are Q_2' instead of Q_2. What about profits? Clearly, profits must have decreased, for, at Q_2', MC exceeds MR_1, the marginal revenue curve appropriate for demand curve D_1. (Indeed, if we assume D_1 was tangent to AC at output Q_1, it must be below AC at Q_2'; the representative oligopolist must now be making losses.) At this point, one of the oligopolists may endeavor to recoup his losses by decreasing

price again, hoping, *this time*, no one will follow and he can move along a new D_2, parallel but below the first one, intersecting D_1 at a point directly opposite price P_2. If his expectation is correct, he increases his profit at the expense of his rivals. If it is incorrect, all firms will increase their outputs and decrease their prices (and profits) down along curve D_1.

Price Stability: The Kinked Demand Curve. The theory of price war under independent oligopoly rests upon the assumption of *symmetry* in expected reactions of rivals to price increases *and* decreases. But asymmetrical combinations also are possible; that is, oligopolists may expect different reactions from rivals to a price-cut than to a price increase.

Suppose, for example, a "mature" oligopolistic industry in which firms have learned through bitter experience to avoid price wars, have more or less "settled down" to a generally accepted and acceptable price or cluster of prices, and are concentrating their competitive energies upon technological change, new products, quality improvement or variation, and sales promotion. In this event (which is not *the* theory of oligopoly, but simply a distinct possibility), each seller will avoid price cuts because of the expectation that his rivals will *match* them, resulting in a movement down D_1, instead of D_2, with prospective decreases in profits for all and increases in the share of the market for none. At the same time, each seller will avoid price increases for fear that his rivals will *not match* them, resulting in a movement back along a D_2, instead of a D_1, curve, with large-scale losses in sales to his rivals. Result: price stability or rigidity instead of warfare.

The demand "curve," in this case, is composed of two parts. If the initial generally accepted price is at point B in Fig. 13.4, then the expected demand curve for prices above B is segment AB, while the expected demand curve for prices below B is segment BD_1.

(Segments JB and BD_2 become irrelevant.) These two segments together constitute one curve with a more or less sharp "kink" at the going price.

What now happens to marginal revenue? Clearly, the two MR segments associated with the two relevant demand segments now become the appropriate ones. In Fig. 13.4, suppose the going price is OP_1 (or Q_1B). The kinked demand curve is ABD_1. The appropriate MR segments are FG down to point B and CMR_1 below B. The MR "curve" thus becomes $FGCMR$. Note that the MR has a discontinuous vertical segment GC. This gap exists because the two segments of MR are associated with two different demand curves, and thus, have two different shapes *and* positions.

The kinked demand curve and its associated MR curve provide an analytical tool to help explain two types of price rigidity. First, as long as MC intersects MR somewhere in its discontinuous segment, the price and output will not change. (At lower outputs and higher prices, MR exceeds MC; at higher outputs and lower prices, MC exceeds MR.) Only if MC were to rise (fall) to where it intersected segment $FG(CMR)$ would it be profitable to increase price and decrease output (decrease price and increase output).

Second, shifts in demand may also be accompanied by price stability (but changes in output) if the shift keeps the demand curve kinked at the same price and the shift is sufficiently limited so that MC still intersects MR in its discontinuous segment.

It has often been observed that oligopolists respond to fluctuations in demand by changing output and employment but keeping prices relatively stable. The kinked demand curve theory provides an analytical tool which helps us to understand why this may take place.

(2) PERFECTLY COLLUSIVE OLIGOPOLY: CARTELS AND EXPLICIT AGREEMENTS

Under perfectly collusive oligopoly, the market behavior of firms is coordinated through tight-knit agreements, often (though not necessarily) formulated and enforced by an organization or cartel. Each firm is interdependent with the others but *not* independent to make its *own* best price-output policy. Instead, a collective endeavor is made to promote the interests of the group of oligopolists as a whole (for example, through price-output combinations which will maximize joint or industry profits). Collusion is a matter of degree. Most collusive agreements are neither completely coordinated nor organized. The model of perfect collusion is helpful more for setting a logical limit at the opposite end of the continuum from completely independent, non-collusive oligopoly than for describing typical cases. In this, it serves the same analytical function as the theory of pure monopoly for pure and monopolistic competition.

Pressures or incentives for collusive or coordinated, rather than independent, action are powerful under conditions of oligopoly. Uncertainty over prospective reactions of rivals may create a strong urge for the promotion of certainty through joint action. The promise of the maximization of joint profits adds prospectively valuable benefits, while the possibility of concerted action to prevent the entry of potential competitors holds out the lure of keeping whatever joint profits are made.

The Centralized Cartel. In an extreme case, the cartel would make centralized decisions regarding production and marketing of output, with a joint sharing of revenues. In effect, this would constitute a monopoly, and the sub-decisions and allocations between firms as members of the syndicate would be analogous to those of different plants or divisions of a monopolist.

In a less extreme but still quite organized and centralized case, each oligopoly would produce and market its own output, but within the framework of cartel-determined price and output policies. The basic rationale in this case would again be to maximize joint or industry profits by determining price and output for the group of oligopolists as a whole so as to equate estimated industry marginal cost with estimated industry marginal revenue. Quotas for dividing total output among cartel members would have to be devised, for example, upon some pre-arranged basis of negotiation and bargaining or according to the principle of cost minimization of the industry as a whole. In the latter event, output quotas would be assigned to equalize the marginal cost of each firm. The joint profit maximizing price-output combination is characterized by an equality of industry marginal revenue with industry marginal cost, where the latter is the summation of the marginal cost curves of the individual oligopolists. Total output is divided between the two firms so that, for each, marginal cost equals the given industry price. The low-cost (high-cost) firm thus will receive a larger (smaller) quota. The rationale for this is that, if, given a particular division of output between them, firm one has a lower marginal cost than firm two, total industry costs can fall (and joint profits rise) by a redistribution of output, which continues until firm one's marginal costs have risen and firm two's marginal costs have fallen to a point of equality.

The Market-Sharing Cartel. A somewhat less stringent form of cartel behavior is simply to divide or share markets among cartel members. Again, this may result in a price-output combination that corresponds to a joint or industry "monopoly in fact if not in name" profit-maximizing solution under special circumstances, namely, if oligopolists produce a homogeneous product (causing a common price), have identical cost functions, and agree on market shares at each possible price. In the simplest case, the market is divided equally. With identical cost curves, each firm is a model of the total market in miniature. Given total market demand and its associated marginal revenue,

each firm faces *its* individual demand curve with its associated marginal revenue, which is one-half of the market demand curve at every price for two firms, one-third for three firms, and so on. Each firm maximizes profit at that price-output combination associated with the intersection of *its* marginal cost and marginal revenue; the industry as a whole maximizes its profits at that price-output combination associated with the intersection of industry marginal cost (which is double each firm's marginal cost for two firms, triple each firm's marginal cost for three firms, and so on) and market or industry marginal revenue.

Divergences from Joint Profit Maximization. These cases, though useful for comparison and classification, undoubtedly exaggerate the extent of "perfection" and organization in collusive oligopoly in practice and of success in achieving the *de facto* monopolistic joint profit maximization solution. For one thing, more blatant forms of organized collusion are illegal in several countries. For another, different estimates of cost and demand conditions, different cost conditions in different plants and for different products produced by different firms, and product differentiation between firms may very easily yield large-scale differences among oligopolists on the question of the best joint profit maximizing solution. Further, the establishment of cartel policy, like any collective decision, depends heavily upon bargaining skill and power, negotiation and compromise, and other political factors having little to do with joint profit maximization. But perhaps most important is the temptation to depart from the cartel policy by extending one's quota and undercutting the stated cartel price, for, as explained earlier, *if* the other oligopolists do not follow suit (in this case, by observing the price and quota allocation policies of the cartel), any one oligopolist faces a demand curve with significantly greater elasticity than the market or industry demand curve. The result is for cartels to disintegrate through the evasions and circumventions of their members.

(3) IMPERFECTLY COLLUSIVE OLIGOPOLY: PRICE LEADERSHIP

In imperfectly collusive oligopoly, no *explicit* agreement or organization coordinates the actions of the interdependent oligopolists; but each firm, though nominally independent, *tacitly* behaves *as if* it were a party to coordinated action. One of the most common forms of tacit collusion is *price leadership*, in which changes in prices of one firm (the price leader) are deliberately followed by changes in prices of other firms (price followers).

Price Leadership by the Low-Cost Firm. One basis for functioning as a price leader is to have lower costs than your rivals. Suppose, for purposes of simplification, two oligopolists produce the same product and tacitly agree to "live and let live" and share the market together. *If* cost conditions were the same for the two firms, the profit maximizing solution would be the same as in our earlier discussion, with the exception that it would be reached by a tacit trial-and-error process rather than through explicit agreement.

But cost conditions might easily be different for the two firms. Assuming the desire by both to maximize profits, the high-cost firm would like to pursue a high price-low output combination, while the low-cost firm would prefer to charge a lower price and sell a larger output. If products are homogeneous, the high-cost firm has no choice but to follow the lead of the low-cost firm and charge the same price. Both sell the same output. The low-cost firm maximizes its profits, and the high-cost firm settles for below-maximum profits.

Price Leadership by the Dominant Firm. Often, however, as, for example, in the steel industry in the United States, the price leader is the *dominant* firm. The non-dominant firms decrease their prices when the large firm decreases its price for fear of losing sales to their Brobdingnagian rival, increase their prices when he increases his for fear that failure to do so may result in retaliatory action (such as a price war), and keep their prices stable when he does so. If the non-dominant firms are many and relatively small and their products are the same or nearly the same as those of the price leader, they then regard the price as given and beyond their control. Under differentiated oligopoly, a price cluster, with some prices lower and some higher than that charged by the dominant firm, would replace the single price of the pure oligopoly case, but non-dominant firms still might follow the lead of the price leader simply by endeavoring to maintain a given price differential as, for example, in the retail market for gasoline or cigarettes.

MONOPSONISTIC COMPETITION AND OLIGOPSONY

Business firms may and do exercise varying degrees of control over the markets in which they buy as well as those in which they sell. In the extreme case of pure monopsony, illustrated in Fig. 4.8, there is only *one* buyer in a particular market. Assuming the conditions of sale in the markets in which it buys and sells approximate those of pure competition, the monopsonistic firm may select a price-quantity combination for the materials or resources it buys free from the effects of the countervailing power exercised by raw material and/or resource sellers, as well as from prospective reactions of rivals. But pure monopsony, like pure monopoly, is extremely rare. More typical are the intermediate market structures of monopsonistic competition and oligopsony. Monopsonistic competition is characterized by many substitutable but differentiated buyers. Because firms are often differentiated in some way, however mildly, this market structure is probably more or less pervasive throughout contemporary managed capitalist economies. Oligopsony (pure or differentiated) is characterized by a small number of buyers, as, for example, in the purchase of tobacco by a relatively small number of cigarette producers or the purchase of the services of automobile workers by a relatively small number of automobile producers.

The basis for market control by monopsonistically competitive firms lies in the fact that buyers, though similar or substitutable, are in some ways (such as by location, conditions of employment, and so on) differentiated in the minds of sellers. Because the number of buyers is large, any individual firm (1) cannot control the market because of its relative size and (2) has an insignificant effect upon the purchases of its competitors and may thereby plausibly ignore the effects of its actions upon their prospective reactions. However, because it is differentiated in some ways in the minds of its suppliers or workers, it exercises some degree of control over the market, the extent varying directly with its degree of differentiation. But because the differentiation is incomplete (since each firm competes with a large number of other substitutable though differentiated buyers), its control is less than under pure monopsony.

As in pure monopsony, the monopsonistically competitive firm faces a positively sloped supply curve (the extent of slope depending upon the extent of differentiation) and a marginal outlay or marginal resource cost curve which lies above and diverges from the supply curve. Instead of accepting a market price as given and beyond its control, as under pure competition, the profit-maximizing monopsonistically competitive firm as a price-maker presumably would select that price-quantity combination at which its positively sloped marginal outlay (or marginal resource cost) equalled its marginal revenue (or marginal revenue product). As in pure monopsony, the prices and the purchases of raw materials or resource inputs presumably would both be lower than

under pure competition and, in the case of a resource, the price would lie below its marginal revenue product, and the firm would obtain "monopsony profits." However, as in monopolistic competition, the extent of divergence from the results of pure competition may be quite small if the degree of differentiation among firms, and thus, the tilt of the supply curve, is mild.

The major basis of market control by oligopsonists is their large size relative to the markets in which they buy. In differentiated oligopsony, this is supplemented by differentiation of the (small number of) buyers in the minds of the sellers. Thus, market control is typically more fundamental and pervasive than under monopsonistic competition. But the essential and unique dimension of oligopsony (like that of oligopoly) is that the market actions of any one firm have appreciable effects upon the purchases and profits of other firms. The prudent oligopsonist, recognizing the fundamental and mutual interdependence with his rivals, will consider their prospective reactions to his actions. Thus, the supply curve facing the oligopsonist is not uniquely determinate because it depends upon the diverse reactions of his rivals.

As in oligopoly, however, some major types or forms of oligopsony behavior are identifiable. At one extreme, in perfectly collusive oligopsony, firms would engage in tight-knit, explicit agreements on the prices and quantities of materials and resources so as to maximize joint or industry profits. This would create "in fact, if not in name" the results of pure monopsony. At the other extreme would be independent, non-collusive oligopsony. If the oligopsony were "immature," the temptation to steal suppliers and personnel from one's rivals might result, as in oligopoly, in price warfare. Alternatively, as the oligopsonistic market matures and settles down, something akin to the kinked demand curve case might develop on the side of supply, resulting in relatively stable or rigid raw material and resource prices. In between would be various forms of tacit, imperfectly collusive oligopsony, of which price or wage leadership would be illustrative. In each of these instances, with the possible exception of price warfare, purchases and materials-resources prices in an oligopsonistic market presumably would be lower than if it were organized under pure competition; but, except for perfectly collusive oligopsony, the restriction of purchases and prices presumably would be less than under pure monopsony.

COUNTERVAILING AND SUPPLEMENTARY FACTORS IN MARKET CONTROL

The preceding discussion of control over markets in the private sector of the economy has focused primarily upon (1) competition (or lack of it) among *existing* firms; (2) *prices* and output; (3) *static* models; and (4) *business firms* as wielders of market power. In this section, each of these will be modified or supplemented in turn.

Competition from the Entry of New Firms

Profit positions, prices, and outputs of existing firms producing either the same or differentiated products may be affected significantly by the exit of old competitors and/or the entry of new competitors. Indeed, entry or exit of firms into or out from a group of competitors may transform their relations from one type of market structure to another (such as from monopolistic competition to oligopoly, or vice versa.) We will first examine the general problem of exit and entry in monopolistic competition and then the impact of entry or its absence under conditions of oligopoly.

EXIT AND ENTRY UNDER MONOPOLISTIC COMPETITION

The impact of long-run adjustments in the number of firms under monopolistic competition is illustrated in Fig. 13.3. Assuming the demand and cost curves are representative of each firm and no efforts are made by firms to alter the position or shape of these curves, then $demand = d_1$ illustrates the long-run equilibrium condition for the group as well as for each individual firm. If $AR = AC$, then there are no pressures for existing firms to leave or enticements for new firms to enter production. If $demand = d_3$, however, losses at every level of output cause firms to move out of production entirely. As they do so, given the total or market demand for the related but differentiated set of products of the group as a whole, the share of market demand obtained by any one remaining firm increases, and its demand curve shifts up to the right. This process would tend to terminate when enough firms had left so that the demand curve faced by a representative individual firm had shifted up sufficiently to be tangent to the AC curve, at which point the elimination of losses would terminate the pressure for further departures of firms.

If $demand = d_2$, on the other hand, the excess of AR above AC would entice new firms to enter production, if and/or to the extent it were possible to do so. The existence of many firms does not guarantee the absence of barriers to new firms. Thus, it is conceivable that individual firms could continue to reap above-normal profits in the long run under monopolistic competition. The same factors that characterize monopolistic competition, however (many firms, high though imperfect substitution of products), also plausibly contribute to ease of entry of new firms. Presuming this is so, new firms would enter. Given the total or market demand, the share going to any individual firm would decrease, illustrated by a shift downward to the left of the demand curve for its product. This process would tend to terminate when enough firms had entered so that the demand curve faced by a representative individual firm had shifted down sufficiently to be tangent to the AC curve, at which point the elimination of above-normal profits would end the enticement for further entry of firms. Naturally, the process, in reality, might easily be less precise than this. Strong product differentiation by some firms, coupled with (imperfect) barriers to entry of new firms, might perpetuate above-normal profits for some firms while others were just breaking even.

The process and results of exit and/or entry under monopolistic competition resemble those under pure competition. There are differences, however: First, the process of adjustment cannot be described accurately in such terms as "the increase (decrease) in *the* output of industry results in a decrease (increase) in *the* price of the product" for there is no (homogeneous) industry output and no single price for that output, but instead, a constellation of substitutable but differentiated products with closely related but non-identical prices. Second, the point of tangency between a negatively sloped demand curve and the *AC* curve cannot occur at the *minimum* point of the latter, but must occur at some point *to the left* of "optimum scale" or the lowest point on the *AC* curve. Thus, output is lower and cost and price are higher than in comparable circumstances under purely competitive conditions, even though free entry tends to eliminate above-normal profits. Clearly, however, the extent of divergence from the long-run, purely-perfectly competitive solution depends upon the extent of differentiation of products, illustrated by the degree of tilt of the demand curve. If, for example, the demand curve were nearly horizontal, output would be only slightly lower and cost and price only slightly higher in long-run equilibrium under monopolistic competition than under pure competition.

OLIGOPOLY AND FREE ENTRY

As in monopolistic competition, new firms will be attracted into an oligopolistic industry by the existence of above-normal profits. Under given conditions of market or industry demand, the entry of new firms tends, as in monopolistic competition, to decrease the share of the market going to existing firms and, thereby, to decrease their profits (and perhaps, their prices). Indeed, if the process continues, oligopoly may be transformed into monopolistic competition. At the least, the likelihood of independent action increases and that of collusive action decreases.

For these reasons, oligopolists endeavor to prevent or forestall free entry; barriers to entry of new firms are strategic bases for establishing and/or maintaining oligopoly and, where they exist, oligopoly profits.

Barriers to the entry of new firms may be inherent in the oligopolistic industry ("natural" barriers) or established by oligopolistic firms ("artificial" barriers). A prominent inherent barrier to entry is the limited size of the market. The smaller the market size, the smaller the number of firms that can operate at or near optimum (minimum cost) scale of plant and, thereby, secure economies of large-scale production. This creates a dilemma for prospective new firms. If their size is small, their costs may be significantly higher (and their profits significantly lower) than existing firms. If their size is large, total output may be raised sufficiently by their entry to eliminate profits (or create losses) both for them and for existing firms. Allied to this is the problem that the initial investment in plant and equipment, and thus, financial resources required, to establish an entrant in effective competition with existing firms may be so great as to limit entry to only very large firms.

In an economy characterized by a high level of economic development and a high rate of economic growth, however, the strategic importance of the first inherent barrier decreases—unless technological improvements continually favor large firms to an extent greater than the rate of increase in the size of the market. Further, there may be limits to economies of large-scale production. Often, medium-sized firms may be as or more efficient than very large firms, as appears to be the case, for example, in the steel industry in the United States. In addition, a minimum required large size, though a barrier to *new small* firms, is not typically a limitation upon the entry of *existing large* firms from other fields of production (as, for example, the entry of Ford Motor Company into the production of radios and television sets).

Barriers established by oligopolistic firms may be of several varieties. Prominent examples are monopsonistic or oligopsonistic control over strategic raw materials or other resources, restrictive or exclusionary practices (such as patents) supported by government action, vigorous product differentiation, large-scale advertising and sales promotion, and aggressive reactions to entrants (such as price wars).

If above-normal profits exist in an oligopolistic industry and barriers to entry (natural or artificial) are successful, profits may be retained even in the long run. Even the potentiality of entry, however, may place *some* limit upon the *extent* of exploitation by oligopolists of existing opportunities for above-normal profits. Oligopolists may not always be able to depend upon effective product differentiation, sales promotion, or a reputation of toughness toward newcomers to forestall entry. If so, output may be extended (and price reduced) beyond the position of *short*-run profit maximization to discourage entry and thereby contribute to the maintenance of lower but still above-normal *long*-run profits.

Competition in Product Quality and Sales Promotion (Non-Price Competition)

The purely competitive firm sells a homogeneous product and, accordingly, incurs no selling expense. The purely monopolistic firm may vary either or both product quality or sales promotion activities, but only in an endeavor to increase its sales and/or profits in relation to other *industries* (or to *potential* competitors). Business firms in the interme-diate zones of monopolistic competition and oligopoly, however, may compete with other firms within their own industries in their endeavor to exert greater control over markets and to increase their sales and/or profits at the expense of their rivals. Thus, (1) non-price competition (competition in product quality and variety and/or sales promotion) is much more likely under monopolistic competition and oligopoly than under pure competition or pure monopoly; and (2) variation in product quality and sales promotion, though a form of competition, is also a device for the exercise of control by business firms over markets and the process of exchange.

The character and impact of non-price competition varies, depending, among other things, (1) upon whether sellers may (monopolistic competition) or may not (oligopoly) plausibly ignore the prospective reactions of their rivals to their changes in product quality and/or sales promotion; (2) in the case of oligopoly, upon the extent and form of organization-collusion in price and non-price variables.

The central feature of oligopolistic non-price competition is the *mutual interdependence* of product quality and sales promotion changes just as in the case of changes in prices. If oligopolists were to act in perfect joint profit-maximizing collusion in regard to non-price variables, then the quality of the product and the level and form of sales promotion outlays would be adjusted so as to yield a solution which would approximate "in fact, if not in name" that of pure monopoly. Improvements in product quality and increases in advertising outlays generally are accompanied by upward shifts in both demand and cost curves, that is, they enable firms to sell larger quantities at the same price or a given quantity at a higher price or some combination, but typically at the expense of higher production and/or selling costs. Thus, at a given price, alternative product qualities and sales promotion outlays are associated with different cost and demand curves. One of these cost-demand combinations will normally yield the maximum profit at that price. The same will be true at other possible prices. Of these various profit-maximizing price-product and/or price-sales promotion combinations, one—the *maximum maximorum*—will yield the highest profit of all. It is this combination that the perfectly joint profit-maximizing, non-price collusive oligopolistic cartel presumably would endeavor to attain.

If oligopolists do *not* act in perfect joint profit-maximizing, non-price collusion, however, outlays on both product quality and variety and sales promotion are likely to be higher. Sellers may endeavor, in ways varying from minor deviations from the policies of the non-price "leader" to aggressive non-price warfare, to increase their sales at the expense of their intra-industry rivals by improving product quality and/or increasing selling outlays *on the assumption that rivals will not respond*, at least not immediately, fully, or successfully. But, most typically, rivals will respond "competitively" by improving their products and/or increasing their advertising or other forms of sales promotion. As at least some rivals do this, the effects in part or whole cancel out. Sellers fail to acquire expected increases in sales. But product and selling costs are higher and profits consequently lower than in pure monopoly or perfect oligopoly.

Under monopolistic competition, the likelihood of independent action increases because the number of sellers is large enough and the impact on any one rival small enough so that any *one* firm plausibly may ignore the prospective reactions of rivals to its changes in product quality and sales promotion. But when all firms simultaneously improve product quality and/or increase sales promotion outlays, the increases in sales to any one are less than anticipated, and, again, product and selling costs are higher and profits lower than in pure monopoly or perfect oligopoly and, perhaps

(though not necessarily), than in imperfectly collusive and independent oligopoly.

Under either oligopoly or monopolistic competition, the increased costs and demand associated with improvement or greater variety in product quality and increases in sales promotion outlays are likely to be accompanied by increased prices. In the case of product quality, the higher price is at least partially offset by higher quality, or, if sales promotion-price changes are characterized by substantial diversity, consumers may have the bonus of diversity and variety in the product-price advertising combinations of sellers. Some sellers, for example, may offer the combination of low prices-low quality-low advertising to price-conscious buyers, and so forth.

In one special case, price actually may be lower with product quality improvement and/or sales promotion increases. This may occur if the higher level of demand is also more elastic and/or if the larger sales accompanying the upward shift in demand permit lower costs by enabling firms to produce at or closer to the minimum point of the (higher) average cost curve.

In any event, product quality and sales promotion changes, though forms of (non-price) competition, also are forms of market control. Business firms under contemporary managed capitalism do not merely or essentially respond passively to the impersonal social process of the price system. Though influenced by market forces, including the actual or prospective reactions of their rivals, they actively endeavor to control or influence market exchange. And the variables or dimensions of control, as seen by recent contributors to the theory of managed capitalism, include product and sales promotion as well as prices.

Competition as a Dynamic Process

Recognition of competition as a dynamic process for economic change, and not merely a structure for promoting efficient allocation of resources under given static conditions, tempers somewhat, if not entirely, the traditional indictment of the market power exercised by large-scale business firms. With given similar demand and cost conditions, the long-run profit-maximizing monopolist (and oligopolist, in the absence of price war) would produce a smaller output at a higher price than purely (or even monopolistically) competitive sellers. Under changing and/or dissimilar demand and cost conditions, this need not be true. Alternatively, even if price-output combinations of firms with high degrees of market power are, at a given time, generally inferior to those that would tend to be reached under atomistic competition after all long-run adjustments to given technological and cost conditions have been made, *this* disadvantage might be offset or more than offset by a greater proclivity to engage in a dynamic process of cost-reducing and/or output creating technical invention and product innovation over the passage of time.

Pure monopoly *may* be more progressive in the introduction of new production techniques, the discovery of new sources of supply, the exploitation of new markets, the creation of new products, and so forth than the purely or monopolistically competitive firm; but, if so, it is more progressive at its own discretion and not (in view of the absence of rivals) because the existence of competitors entices or forces it to be. Indeed, because the introduction of new techniques or products may require the scrapping of existing plant and equipment before it has physically depreciated or may entice the entry of new firms, monopolists, especially old, established firms, may slow down technological progress by postponing or avoiding innovation.

Similarly, purely (or at least atomistically, though monopolistically) competitive firms *may* be more progressive in these dimensions of economic activity than purely or highly monopolistic firms. The introduction of a cost-reducing new technique or a new demand-creating product by one or some firms compels remaining firms to follow suit or risk being undersold by, or experiencing a large-scale loss of customers to, their innovating competitors. Under mildly monopolistic competition, with large numbers of firms selling slightly differentiated products, the introduction of new techniques and products is especially attractive as a device to generate a large-scale increase in sales and profits without retaliation by one's rivals. Furthermore, with small-scale plants, the possible loss from scrapping equipment made obsolete by technical and product innovations plausibly might be expected to be small relative to that of monopoly and to the gains in profits through cost reduction and expansion in sales. Lastly, pure or mildly monopolistic competition is more likely to be accompanied by freedom of entry, with the distinct possibility of technical and product innovation by new firms, than are other forms of market structure.

Yet, monopolistically (and especially, purely) competitive firms may also have certain built-in barriers to technological progress. First, their small size may inhibit or prevent them from conducting large-scale, costly, prolonged, and complex research or from maintaining R and D (research and development) laboratories or programs. Second, they may lack the capacity to do so, partly because of the lack or relative lack of pure economic profits as an easy source of funds to finance costly R and D activities and partly because (in pure competition) product homogeneity and the absence of sales promotion makes them mere "quantity adjustors," unfamiliar with or unused to the exercise of original and creative discretionary judgment. Third, because of the rapid and simple imitation by competitors of technical and product innovations, the innovator stands to lose much if unsuccessful in a major innovation and to gain little (because of the diffusion of innovatory gains, at least after a temporary head-start, throughout a large field of competitors) even if successful. Thus, the incentive to innovate—the prospect of obtaining large-scale innovatory profits—is dampened if not eliminated.

The reverse of barriers to technological progress in markets characterized by competition among many are the stimuli to such progress in markets characterized by competition among few. First, oligopolists may have the size to permit large-scale, costly, and prolonged research programs and the maintenance of research laboratories. Second, they may have the capacity to do so, partly in the form of pure economic profits as an easy source of funds to finance R and D programs and partly in the form of entrepreneurial talent familiar, through aggressive sales, product, and price policies, with the exercise of creative discretionary judgment. Third, the absence of large numbers of competitors and easy entry decreases the likelihood of rapid and diffused imitation of innovations. This permits greater and longer protection for the innovating firm and greater likelihood of innovatory profits, thus providing a powerful incentive to innovate. In addition, the special features of oligopoly —the small number of mutually interdependent rivals and the indisposition to engage in price competition—may spur technical and product innovation, especially when competition takes the form of non-price outlets. "Like advertising and salesmanship—and unlike price competition, which is unique in this respect—technical development is a safe rather than reciprocally destructive method by which any one firm can advance itself against its few powerful rivals." [3: 89–90]

Even this limited case for moderate oligopoly power needs to be tempered somewhat. As noted several times, absolute and relative size need to be distinguished. If the size of the market is large, then it is possible for a firm to be absolutely large (presumably large enough to engage even in costly R and D) without being so large relative to the market as to create oligopoly. Furthermore, large size (absolute or relative) does not appear to be either a necessary or sufficient condition for research or for technical or product innovation. It is true that most research these days is conducted in large firms. But it is also true that: (1) technical and product research and development is not the exclusive domain of large firms; and (2) large size (certainly not largest size) is no guarantee of technological progressiveness.

Many inventions and innovations still are made by small firms and/or individuals.[3] In industries characterized by large and small firms or established firms and newcomers, it is often the smaller firms (as for example in steel in the United States) or the newcomers (as, for example, in aluminum) that are more technologically progressive. Though some competitive industries (such as bituminous coal) are technologically unprogressive, some oligopolistic industries (such as cigarettes) also are notably lacking in this dimension. In several cases of oligopolistic progressiveness, the argument needs to be tempered by the recognition that much of the R and D is sponsored or financed by government (as, for example, in the aircraft, electronics, and communications industries) or is heavily in the form of costly style changes (such as automobiles). The prospects of large-scale innovatory profits may spur innovation under oligopoly; but the threat of losses through failure to innovate when competitors do may serve as a powerful substitute under monopolistic competition. Pure economic profits may provide funds for innovation under oligopoly. But alternative sources of funds (such as the Small Business Administration) and ideas (for example, the independent

---

[3] About two-thirds (40 out of 61) of important selected inventions since 1900 have come from individuals or small firms, according to John Jewkes, David Sawers, and Richard Stelliman, *The Sources of Invention* (New York City: St. Martin's Press, Inc., 1958).

profit-seeking or non-profit research institute) may be available for relatively small firms.

In short, controversy continues on the question of whether oligopoly is likely to be more technologically progressive than monopolistic competition. But from the standpoint of a broader perspective, either or both of these intermediate market structures is likely to be more technologically progressive than the extremes of either pure competition or pure monopoly. And the blend of monopolistic competition and oligopoly in the market structures of contemporary managed capitalism, with its accompanying discretionary market power by business firms, should not blind us to the prospectively or actually powerful capacity or incentive for technological progressiveness, for competition as a dynamic process.

Price System Controls over Business Firms

Corporate and managerial revolutions have expanded or created opportunities for control by business firms. The organizational revolution has expanded or created opportunities for control *of or over* business firms. In their review of contemporary social processes, Dahl and Lindblom classify three major forms of price system control over business firms as: (1) bargaining price systems; (2) hierarchial price systems; (3) autonomous price systems. [1: 183–93]

BARGAINING PRICE SYSTEMS

In (1), the power of business firms to control prices and markets is blunted by an opposing position of power on the opposite side of the market (as in Galbraith's theory of countervailing power). Thus, a buyer controls a business firm from which he buys; a seller controls a business firm to which he sells. In the first case, buyers (typically) threaten to engage or actually engage in substitution, as when an automobile producer bargains with a steel producer by threatening to enter steel production itself, thereby reducing the monopoly power of the seller. In the second case, sellers (typically) oppose the monopsony power of a business firm with a countervailing monopoly position of their own, as, for example, in labor unions and agricultural producer and marketing cooperatives.

In either event, countervailing power creates a bargaining situation, and, thereby, a negotiated redistribution of monopoly-monopsony gains, the extent of such redistribution depending on the respective bargaining skill and strength of the negotiators, the outer limits being the price the monopolist (or oligopolists) could or would obtain in the absence of countervailing monopsony (or oligopsony) power and the price the monopsonist (or oligopsonists) could or would obtain in the absence of countervailing monopoly (or oligopoly) power. In *bilateral oligopoly* (the confrontation of oligopolists with oligopsonists), the outer limits to the price remain the same, but the negotiated price (or prices) depends upon the mutual interdependencies among sellers and among buyers, as well as the bargaining skill and strength of buyers in relation to sellers.

In some cases, the establishment of countervailing power, by offsetting positions of original power, may create results very similar to those of pure competition. This is illustrated in Figs. 13.5 and 13.6. In the former, $PmQm$ represents the profit-maximizing, price-output combination of a firm with monopoly power selling to a large number of unorganized and relatively powerless consumers. Now, suppose that consumers unite and form a cooperative consumers' buying organization to countervail the monopoly power of the seller(s) and are successful in pushing price below the monopoly level. As long as the new, given, negotiated price lies above the seller's MC, it will pay him to expand output. For example, if the negotiated price is set at OPc, it will pay the seller, given the new price, to expand output to OQc, the competitive level.

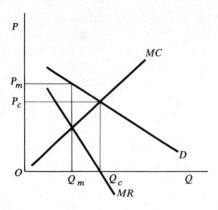

Fig. 13.5. Offsetting monopoly power

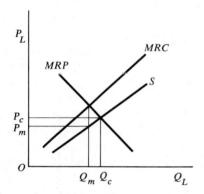

Fig. 13.6. Offsetting monopsony power

In the latter diagram, $PmQm$ represents the profit-maximizing price/employment combination of a firm with monopsony power purchasing the labor services of large numbers of unorganized, relatively powerless workers. Now, suppose workers unite and form a labor union to countervail the monopsony power of the buyer(s), and are successful in raising the wage rate above the monopsony level. As long as the new, given negotiated price lies below the buyer's MRP at the initial employment level, OQm, it will pay him to expand employment to or toward the competitive level. For example, if the negotiated price is set at OPc, it will pay the buyer, given the new price, to expand employment to OQc, the competitive level.

In some instances, however, as noted earlier, especially during periods of high and rising aggregate demand, countervailing power may evaporate as a regulatory mechanism, as wielders of original and countervailing power collaborate to promote their joint gain at the expense of unorganized groups. For example, suppose labor unions are successful in raising wage rates generally throughout selected strategic sectors of the economy (such as steel, aluminum, automobile production). Particularly if business firms (1) associate higher money wages with higher levels of aggregate demand (supported, for example, by expansionary monetary and fiscal policies) and (2) expect their rivals to respond to increased wage costs by raising prices, the result could or would be a general upward shift in expected demand curves and increase in price with no change in output or employment. There are, of course, other possibilities. If the economy is near, but below, full employment, for example, increased aggregate demand combined with increased pressure by labor unions to raise wage rates may be accompanied by increases in wages, prices, and employment. Then, too, in a dynamic setting characterized by increases in labor productivity, it is possible for wages to rise (with upward shifts in productivity) with no or little increase in prices.

GOVERNMENT PRICE CONTROLS

In (2), the market power of business firms is offset or blunted by the operation of government hierarchy. Two prominent cases are "mandatory" hierarchical price systems, where governments set prices (or price limits or price guidelines) as, for example, in agricultural price supports, minimum wage laws, price and wage "controls," and so on; and "manipulated" hierarchical price systems, where governments, through their market purchases and/or sales, affect prices, as, for example, in the manipulation of interest rates via Federal Reserve System "open-market" purchases and sales of government securities.

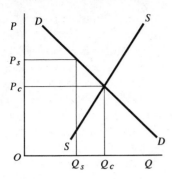

Fig. 13.7. Price controls—minimum prices

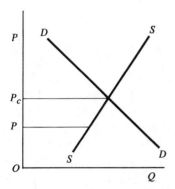

Fig. 13.8. Price controls—maximum prices

Figs. 13.7 and 13.8 illustrate *mandatory* government price controls. In both instances, a competitive market is presumed, with traditionally-shaped demand and supply functions. Fig. 13.7 depicts the endeavor (as in agricultural price supports) to establish a price (*OPs*) through government control higher than the competitive level (*OPc*), while Fig. 13.8 depicts the opposite endeavor (as in government maximum price-controls during wartime) to establish a price (*OPm*) lower than the competitive level (*OPc*).

In both instances, the endeavor to establish a mandatory price different from the competitive level creates a divergence between market supply and demand, with attendant need for further adjustment. In Fig. 13.7, supply exceeds demand at the supported price. If the price is to be maintained, supply must be decreased (as in acreage or crop restriction programs), demand must be increased or supplemented (as in government purchase and storage programs), or both. In Fig. 13.8, demand exceeds supply at the mandatory maximum price *OPm*. Accordingly, demand must be decreased ("Is this trip necessary?"), supply must be increased, or—an additional option—the smaller output (*OPs*) must be rationed among buyers on some basis other than pure market purchase. (Another possibility, of course, is the emergence of "black markets," because of the temptation among buyers to offer higher prices.) In both of these examples, government price-controls encounter obstacles emanating from the divergence between the desired price and that which would tend to emerge on competitive markets. By contrast, in markets characterized by monopoly or monopsony power, mandatory government price-controls may function as a countervailing mechanism in the manner depicted in Figs. 13.5 and 13.6.

Manipulated price systems are "indirect" rather than "direct." A classic and important example is the open-market sales and purchases of government securities by the Federal Reserve System. Manipulated price-controls operate via *shifts* in the position of demand or supply functions, thus circumventing the problems emanating from divergence between desired and free market prices. An easy money policy, for example, would entail an increase in the demand for government securities by the Federal Reserve System. This would tend to push securities prices up, which is equivalent to a decrease in interest rates. A tight-money policy would entail a downward shift in Federal Reserve System purchases of government securities.

AUTONOMOUS PRICE SYSTEMS

In (3), business firms sell to and buy from themselves. In consumer cooperatives, for example, buyers control sellers by virtue of the fact that they are also the sellers. In an agricultural marketing cooperative, sellers may control buyers by virtue of the fact that they are also the buyers. Autonomous price systems play a relatively small role in the United States, but a relatively large role in some other contemporary economies, notably those of Scandinavia.

NON-MARKET PROCESSES: BUREAUCRACY, BARGAINING, AND DEMOCRACY

Classically, the price system was regarded as the dominant, if not exclusive, social process for economic coordination and control in capitalist economies. While recognizing the continued role and relevance of price systems, managed capitalists emphasize the shift to a new blend of social processes in which bureaucracy, bargaining, and democracy play relatively larger roles than in the theory and practice of old-style capitalism.

Bureaucracy

CONCEPTIONS AND MISCONCEPTIONS

Emphasis on bureaucracy is an understandable accompaniment to increased recognition of the corporate-managerial-organizational revolutions. Bureaucracy "is the ubiquitous modern organization within which hierarchical processes are most commonly encountered; bureaucracy is also one of the most widely used and portentous social instruments for economizing found in contemporary societies." [1: 233–34] That the ubiquity of bureaucracy is not universally recognized is probably due in large part to two common misunderstandings: first, that bureaucracy is unique to governmental organizations (and thus, that the choice is between government bureaucracy and private non-bureaucracy); and second, that bureaucracy is undesirable *per se*.

In regard to the first misunderstanding, it would be more accurate to say that bureaucracy is common to all large-scale organizations in contemporary managed capitalist economies, private as well as governmental.

This means the choice often is between different bureaucracies (such as government and business) rather than between bureaucracy and non-bureaucracy. Indeed, in terms of origins and historic patterns of development in the United States, it was the private sector of the economy via the emergence and development of the large-scale, hierarchically structured, bureaucratically organized corporation which led the transformation to contemporary managed capitalism, with military, governmental, labor, and agricultural organizations following the corporation's historic lead.

In regard to the second misunderstanding, most contemporary managed capitalists define *bureaucracy* in terms of structural criteria which are neither desirable nor undesirable *per se*. Dahl and Lindblom, for example, identify the major properties of *bureaucracy* as: conscious adaptation of means to ends; hierarchical chains of command; prescribed and limited discretion for members of the bureaucracy; specialization of skill and function within the organization; separation of ownership and management of the tools or industrial capital of the organization. [1: 235–36]

LIMITATIONS AND ADVANTAGES

Organizations characterized by these structural features and embodying hierarchical social processes may, indeed, have limitations and disadvantages for economic coordination and control. In addition to such classically suggested dilemmas of large-scale organization as "red tape," "passing the buck," "inflexibility," "impersonality," and so on, bureaucracies have no intrinsic, built-in process or specialized techniques for calculating either consumer preferences or costs, as do price systems. In addition, bureaucracies are plagued (as price systems are not) by the fundamental and perhaps insoluble dilemma of centralization versus decentralization. To obtain an "overview," and to control an organization or economy in terms of that overview, the organization or economy must be centralized. To take advantage of the specialized knowledge of and problems and needs related to the particularized, concretized circumstances of time and place, an organization or economy must be decentralized. As noted earlier, (competitive) price systems need no centralized organization because the collective behavior of the system results from the market interaction of decentralized individual units of economic decision.

At the same time, bureaucracy has a number of distinct advantages for economic coordination and control. It is an important, indeed, at times, indispensable, means "by which a small number of people can coordinate the actions of a large number." [1: 239] It is an important means for coordination and control because of the increase in the size and complexity of organizations, which makes more informal and spontaneous methods of personal contact difficult if not impossible. It is at times indispensable because, given large-scale, complex organizations, there may be no practicable alternative. More specifically, the price system, as a major alternative to bureaucracy, functions at its best in the social or external coordination of units of economic decision, including bureaucratic organizations. It is cumbersome and/or inapplicable to some of the major internal problems of coordination and control within organizations, problems for which bureaucracy appears as an "obvious" and "natural" solution, especially when organizations are large and complex. In addition, the price system is not universally applicable to the resolution of all economic problems, but is limited to certain kinds of uses, namely, to the provision of marketable products and services. For the provision of non-marketable services and/or the enforcement of non-marketable values, societies turn elsewhere; and, because of its advantages, they often turn to bureaucracy.

Perhaps the major defects of bureaucracy —the tremendous inequality in economic power and control, income, and other factors actually or potentially generated within hierarchically structured, bureaucratic organizations; the inequality in political control emanating from economic inequality; the extreme difficulties which those outside the hierarchy (citizens, stockholders, workers) often have in exerting effective control over those within (political leaders, corporate managers, labor union officials); the "dehumanization" and "alienation" of humans caught up in vast, impersonal, seemingly overwhelming bureaucratic organizations— are non- or extra-economic in character. In any event, managed capitalists suggest that bureaucracy (1) is "here to stay," and (2) though pervasive and ubiquitous, is coexistent with and, to an extent, contained and countervailed by other social processes, that is, price systems, bargaining, and democracy.

PRIVATE VERSUS PUBLIC BUREAUCRACY: SIMILARITIES

Private and public bureaucracies have many features in common. Corporations, governments, and labor unions, for example, are characterized to varying extents by such similar properties as hierarchical chains of command, internal competition within the organization, conscious adaptation of means to ends, and separation of ownership and management. The last feature carries within it another similarity. In contemporary large-scale corporate enterprises, salary maximization (and other goals) have supplemented, if not superseded, profit maximization in managerial motivation, thus significantly reducing the differences between the motivational criteria of governmental and corporate managers.

In addition, the typical pattern in managed capitalist economies has been for government bureaucracies to purchase output and services from private businesses and individuals, so as to provide collective goods to the community at large, rather than to own enterprises and produce and sell marketable output. Thus, government bureaucracies purchase output as well as labor services from the private sector of the economy, and many private corporations sell significant amounts of output to governments rather than to other private businesses or consumers.

Insofar as the structure and organization of the economy affects its behavior and performance, the apparent (and apparently growing) similarities in the structure of large-scale corporate and governmental organizations diminish the likelihood that different combinations of corporate and government action will yield radically different economic results. At the least, the similarities between bureaucratic organizations, whether in public or private sectors of the economy, heighten the difficulties in drawing the clear-cut distinctions between varieties of managed capitalism that traditionally were drawn between atomistically competitive (and thereby, non-bureaucratic) capitalism and governmentally-dominated (and thereby, bureaucratic) socialism.

DIFFERENCES BETWEEN PRIVATE AND
PUBLIC BUREAUCRACIES

Despite these similarities, private and public bureaucracies (more accurately, business and governmental organizations) still retain an important difference, emanating from the institutional structure of managed capitalism and the typical division of labor between governmental and private sectors of the economy. In managed capitalism, corporate bureaucracies function primarily, if not exclusively, to produce and sell marketable output. By contrast, governmental bureaucracies function primarily, if not exclusively, to provide collective, non-marketable services. By virtue of this difference, corporate bureaucracies, even under monopolistic competition and oligopoly, are subject to (some degree of) *external* market control. By contrast, government bureaucracies do not typically face the test of marketability, but are controlled instead

by other hierarchical superiors and, indirectly, by the citizenry at the polls.

For this reason, it is probably true the incentives and pressures for efficiency and cost reduction are greater in corporate enterprises than in government agencies and departments. This is heightened by the fact that, though *internal* competition characteristically is found within both corporate and governmental bureaucracies, *external* competition among different independent organizations plausibly is greater within the private than the public sector of the economy. Further, its very penchant for marketability provides the corporate enterprise with a clearer test of efficient performance than is found within government.

It does not necessarily follow, however, that private (corporate) bureaucracy is inherently superior to public bureaucracy in the efficient use of resources. First, though probably more efficient in the reduction of private costs, the corporate bureaucracy, by virtue of its market orientation, plausibly is less sensitive to the reduction of external or social costs. Second, while more attuned to the pursuit of private revenues and benefits than government bodies, corporate enterprises also are plausibly less sensitive to the promotion of social benefits. The test for business performance is clearer precisely because it is narrower; the criterion for evaluating governmental performance is less clear precisely because the demands placed upon it and the functions which it performs are broader (and non-marketable). For these reasons, comparisons between the efficiency of governmental and corporate bureaucracy are typically inconclusive, and it is "usually not appropriate to use the performance standards of the private sector" (public sector) when evaluating the efficiency of government (private enterprise).[4]

---

[4]Campbell R. McConnell, *Economics*, Third Edition (New York: McGraw-Hill Book Company, 1966), p. 107.

The public utility is more or less unique to the American variant of managed capitalism, since such industries in Western Europe, the United Kingdom, and Scandinavia typically are government-owned. Government regulation of public utilities in the United States is a blend of private and public ownership and control. Ownership and management are private and profit-seeking, and output is produced or provided for the marketplace. But several strategic variables, notably prices or rates, are supervised and regulated by a government agency, typically a federal or state public utility commission.

The traditional rationale for this special organizational structure lies in the assumption that the economic characteristics of the regulated industries distinguish them sharply and clearly from the rest of the economy and require special treatment. The characteristics typically noted are economies of large-scale production, local boundaries (for example, the local telephone company) and inconveniences of competition (such as multiple street car tracks), and the dependence and disadvantage of buyers because of the essentiality of the product and low substitutability of competing products. Because of these factors, public utilities often have been regarded as "natural monopolies," that is, as incapable of functioning efficiently under competitive conditions.

As monopolies, however, they would be in a position to exploit the consumer and behave in ways detrimental to the public interest. Thus, they were felt to be affected "with a public interest" and, thereby, suitable for special treatment. At the same time, the political unpopularity of government ownership in the United States more or less precluded widespread application of the dominant European pattern of organization. Thus, the regulation of public utilities by government commissions emerged in the United States as a political compromise which, ideally, would avoid the defects of both private monopoly and government ownership and would combine the benefits of private managerial expertise and initiative with government regulation in the public interest.

The argument still contains a kernel of truth. But time, changing technologies, and growing substitutability of alternatives (gas for electricity, airlines for railroads, and so on) have reduced the applicability of the underlying assumption, and experience with public utility rate-regulation has revealed both theoretical and practical problems of economic organization.

The main theoretical problem has been the criteria for pricing policy. The dominant position of economists has been that of marginal cost pricing. (Recall the Lange rules for price determination by public enterprises cited in Chapter 10.) In practice, this creates a problem, since many public utilities, because of economies of large-scale production combined with limited market demand, operate under conditions of decreasing *average* cost, where *marginal* cost lies *below* average cost. Insistence on marginal cost pricing under these circumstances, as illustrated in Fig. 13.9, would entail a price lower than average cost (up to an output level at the minimum point of the average cost curve), with resulting losses. Such losses could be subsidized from the profits of other

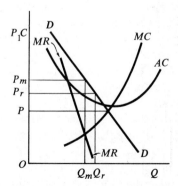

Fig. 13.9. The regulated enterprise

firms or industries with a gain in social welfare and economic efficiency through the promotion of the equality of marginal cost and price throughout the economic system. But criteria of political acceptability and administrative feasibility argue against such a procedure.

Instead, public utility commissions typically have been charged with setting "fair" prices, thus substituting the criterion of equity for the economist's penchant for allocational efficiency. Equity or fairness, in turn, has been interpreted to mean some sort of "balance" or reasonable compromise between the contending claims of public utility companies and other business and consumer users of their services. Essentially, prices are set by a negotiational process at levels low enough to avoid the excesses of complete monopolistic exploitation, but high enough to cover "full" average cost plus, or including, a "fair" rate of return on investment for stockholders, that is, a dividend rate sufficient to enable public utility companies to compete for capital expansion funds from external financing. For example, in Fig. 13.9, price is not set at the monopoly level (OPm), with its resulting restricted output (OQm). Nor is it set to yield the highest output level consistent with equality between price and marginal cost (OPc). Instead, it is set at some negotiated level (say, OPr), with its associated demand and output level (OQr).

The main practical problem has been the determination of what is "fair" through the negotiational process between the public utility company and the regulatory commission—with strong assistance from the courts. In the view of its defenders (for one, American institutionalist John R. Commons, who praised the process as a vehicle for establishing "reasonable values"), the regulatory process (1) strikes a workable and equitable balance between the interests of consumers and producers/investors; (2) blunts monopoly power and creates results significantly closer to those of competition;

and (3) by stabilizing prices, provides incentives to raise profits by reducing costs.[5]

According to its critics, the process has had two complementary defects. On the one hand, knowledge, expertise, power, and privileged monopoly position lie within the regulated enterprises. The regulatory commission, lacking knowledge (and, typically, a sufficient legal and economic staff) and required by the courts to set "fair" rates, may well (and has often) become subverted, and, in effect, function as an agent or promoter of the interests of the "regulated" enterprise. On the other hand, insofar as the regulatory commission is successful, it may well subvert managerial initiative and enterprise: first, because of the institutional costs of negotiation and general endeavors to circumvent regulation; second, because "effective regulation threatens not only the profits of monopoly pricing, but also profits that are the consequence of expanded sales or lower costs. It threatens, that is, the motivation to efficiency or progress." [67: 236]

Bargaining

In a sense, bargaining is an element in all economic activity, including that which does or would occur in an atomistically competitive economic society. But, *bargaining* in the more specialized sense of "reciprocal control among leaders" is a distinct alternative economizing process in its own right; and emphasis on it, as on bureaucracy, is an understandable accompaniment of increased recognition of the managerial-organizational revolutions.

SOURCES OF BARGAINING

Bargaining is intimately related to bureaucracy, for, if we ask, who are the bargainers, the most immediate answer is that the major bargainers in contemporary managed capi-

---

[5]See, for example, Donald S. Watson, *Price Theory and Its Uses* (Boston: Houghton Mifflin Company, 1963), p. 309.

talist economies are the leaders of large-scale bureaucratic organizations in government, business, labor, agriculture, and so forth. Bargaining arises, first, because bureaucracy is pluralistic rather than monistic (that is, because the number of more or less independent and autonomous bureaucratic organizations is several); second, because these organizations are mutually interdependent (that is, because the power and welfare of one group is intertwined with and affected by the actions and reactions of other groups); and third, because of initial disagreements among groups, with at least the potentiality of agreement or reduction of conflict through negotiation. The acceptance and institutionalization of large-scale organization, coupled with initial divergences within the framework of the art and practice of negotiation, has increased significantly the importance for economic organization and behavior of the reciprocity of control among leaders of large-scale groups.

In the United States, political pluralism supplements social pluralism as a factor conducive to bargaining. The framework of government itself—the separation and division of powers between federal and state governments, between executive and legislature, and between two houses of Congress; the absence of a centralized party system; the existence of semi-autonomous government agencies (such as the Federal Reserve System); and so forth—has built-in bargaining to the basic structure of government, and thus, to the formulation and execution of government economic plans and policies, as well as into the private sector of the economy and the relations between government and organized groups.

CRITIQUE OF BARGAINING

Opinion among students of managed capitalism is sharply divided on the subject of the social efficacy and desirability of bargaining within and between private and public sectors of the economy. We have already encountered a defense of bargaining in the context of managed capitalism in Galbraith's theory of countervailing power. Given large-scale organization as a "fact of life," bargaining appears to Galbraith as an alternative to a monistic concentration of economic and/or political power in one private and/or public organization. To such American institutionalists as John R. Commons and John M. Clark, participation in large-scale organizations enhances, rather than diminishes, freedom and power, through the attainment of aspirations beyond the scope of individual action, while the adjudication of conflicts through the judicial system and the provision of "balance," or, at least, reduction of immoderate and socially-politically divisive "imbalance" between organized groups emerges as a central goal of public policy.

Whereas a defense of bargaining emphasizes its role as a countervailing weight to monistic bureaucracy, its contemporary criticism focuses on its possibly deleterious effects upon the price system and democracy. The former is essentially related to collective bargaining within the private sector, the latter to political bargaining within government and to "national bargaining" between government and private groups.

Impact on the Price System. The general critique of collective bargaining between private economic groups, notably between labor union leaders and corporate managements, is that it functions as an alternative to price systems: The larger the relative role for collective bargaining, the smaller the relative role for the price system in determining prices and wages, and thus, the smaller the extent to which contemporary managed capitalist economies can benefit from the agility of price systems as allocational and coordinative social processes. The rejoinder of its defenders is that bargaining functions primarily as an alternative to monistic bureaucracy (notably the dominance of the large-scale corporation) rather than (atomistically competitive) price systems, and thus, that the alternative posed by critics of collective bargaining is artificial and anachronistic.

The most prominent criticism of bargaining in relation to the price system is the supply-push inflation argument. This view contends there is great temptation and pressure, especially as the economic system approaches full employment under conditions of high aggregate demand, to establish negotiated inflationary settlements between organized groups at the expense of the un- or under-organized—for example, labor and corporate management at the expense of consumers or fixed-income groups. But increases in price and wage levels, at least where wage increases exceed productivity, and in the absence of increases in aggregate demand, may generate unemployment and lower real output. Governments thus are pressured by organized groups to "ratify" the inflation by expansionary monetary and fiscal policies—such as tax cuts, government spending increases, or increases in the supply of money. This creates a Hobson's choice for government policy-makers: They can either avoid unemployment by expansionary monetary and fiscal policies, but only at the cost of inflation; or they can resist the pressure for expansionary monetary and fiscal policy (or perhaps engage in counter-inflationary policies), but only at the cost of creating greater unemployment. As a *coup de grace*, if they select the former, pressures mount to contain or curb inflation by government controls over prices and wages, leading to the substitution of government hierarchy for the price system.

Proposed remedies for inflation generated by the market power of large-scale groups within the framework of bargaining range all the way from the elimination of bargaining via the elimination of large-scale bureaucracies (through, for example, a vigorous antitrust program) to the elimination of bargaining via the substitution of comprehensive government hierarchical controls over price-wage settlements. Most defenders of bargaining emphasize economic growth as a saving grace—that is, growth of productive capacity and real output may permit simultaneous attainment of the claims and "reasonable" aspirations of organized groups with perhaps even a modest improvement in the economic position of the unorganized without "serious" inflation (say, no more than a two to three percent annual increase in the price level). They note, further, a variety of subtle and sophisticated devices whereby governments may entice organized groups to behave "responsibly" without the imposition of comprehensive direct controls. These include, for example, the formulation of a wage-price "condominium" or more or less formal agreement for a national wage-price settlement, as in the Scandinavian countries, as well as the somewhat gentler, more informal "guidelines" proposed by the Council of Economic Advisers in the United States in the mid-1960s backed by Presidential sanction, suggesting (1) wage increases be no greater than the national annual average increase in labor productivity; (2) price increases be avoided if wage increases are kept within the framework of the productivity guidelines; and (3) prices be selectively increased (decreased) when increases in productivity in particular industries lie below (above) the national average.

Impact on Democracy. The critique of bargaining in relation to democracy is twofold: First, within government, bargaining places a strategic limit upon rational economic plans and policies in the public or general interest.

This criticism has been focused particularly upon the United States, which has superimposed a rather special form of *political* pluralism (governmental separation of powers, and so on) upon the more general *social* pluralism of independent and autonomous economic groups. The traditional defense of political pluralism has been as a vehicle to curb or prevent the concentration of governmental power and the tyranny of political leaders over the citizenry. The essential ingredient of the more recent critique is that bargaining, built into the constitutional governmental system, prevents or may prevent the establishment of unified, cohesive political leadership and thus, a unified, cohesive system of government economic planning and policy. The result, in general, is inconsistency and sluggishness in action and thus, failure to formulate coherent programs to attain social goals, as, for example, when Congress supports an expansionary fiscal program while the Federal Reserve System is engaging in actions which tighten the money supply. More specific consequences are: blocked leadership, that is, the blocking of proposals of one group of government leaders by another group; the consequent need for widespread agreement among political leaders, with resulting inaction through failure to obtain agreement or irrational agreement through "log-rolling"; strategically placed representatives of minority, but highly organized, groups, which means, in effect, control of government policies by producers at the expense of consumers; and failure to control government bureaucracies by elected leaders. [1: 336–44]

Second, bargaining, when extended to relations between government and private groups and to the organization of the economy as a whole, violates or may violate the principles of political equality and citizen control by making government policy, and economic organization in general, unduly reflective of the interest of one or more powerful organized groups. If government is to be responsive to the interests of the general citizenry, and if the role of government in managed capitalist economies is to correspond, however roughly, to the principle of "one man, one vote," then government action cannot be restricted to functioning merely as "referee" between the contending organized groups, particularly when the actions of such groups may profoundly affect the welfare of the unorganized outside their precincts and where the results of unlimited bargaining would be to impose upon the majority of citizens or consumers the purposes and policies of highly organized, but minority, groups. If large-scale private organizations are "here to stay," then the maintenance of responsible, democratic government requires some sort of government supervision of or participation in the bargaining process.

Democracy

In the theory of competitive market capitalism, democracy, as a social process for the control of political leaders by the citizenry, need play no major role. On the one hand, government and economy are conceived as more or less separate sectors. On the other hand, the economic role of government is limited. Under systems of centralized political direction of the national economy, such as centralized socialism, the economic role of government is so large and comprehensive that the major issue has not been so much how democracy functions but whether and to what extent it is feasible to combine democracy and socialism.

Democracy is strategic to the economic theory and practice of managed capitalism. First, in contrast to competitive market capitalism, the size and economic role of government is extensive enough to give a distinctly economic flavor to governmental functioning. This, in turn, injects an economic content into citizen control over the political leadership and, thereby, the national economy. Second, in contrast to centralized socialism and other forms of centralized political direction of the economic system, the size of government is small enough and the extent of pluralism and autonomy in the constituent private economic organizations is great enough to make the likelihood of control of political leaders more plausible. Consequently, discussion has focused less on whether democracy and managed capitalism (as in the case of democracy and socialism) are compatible and more on how democracy does or may function as an economizing process.

Already considered (Chapter 9) have been the broader questions of the relations between freedom and government planning and between democracy and alternative forms or systems of economic organization. Suffice it to say here that democracy is basic to the theory and practice of managed capitalism in at least three major ways, namely, as a process, first, for economic reform; second, for social choice; third, for economic control.

DEMOCRACY AS A PROCESS FOR ECONOMIC REFORM

Democracy functions as a process for economic reform. It was the historic process whereby much of the transformation from old-style capitalism to contemporary managed capitalism took place. Examples of governmental response to popular pressure have included such reforms as antitrust legislation, encouragement of labor unions as agents of countervailing power, income redistributive measures, social security programs, and full employment policies. With the extension of majority rule and the democratization of the political process, it was predictable that democratic government would be used as an agency for economic reform. And it "was easy to foresee that, as ever larger strata of the population were given their full share of political power and became ever more aware of having this power and the possibilities to use it in their own interest, they would press for redistributional state intervention. . . ." [6: 37]

At the same time, democracy has limitations as an agency for economic reform. On the one hand, like other social processes, it functions imperfectly. As previously noted, democracy in practice is not characterized by the literal or perfect equality of the "one man, one vote" formula. Strategically placed minorities may block or otherwise postpone reforms desired by the majority. On the other hand, majoritarian/equalitarian democracy at its best will not function as an agent of economic reform if the majority does not want to reform. The actual functioning of democratic government in regard to economic reform thus depends on such factors as the level of economic development and past programs of reform. For example, at a low level of economic development and prior to democratically-inspired economic reform (say, the latter nineteenth century in the United States), the majority of the society is poor. By contrast, at a high level of economic development and after a period of democratically-inspired reform (as during the early 1970s in the United States), the majority is not poor, and most people already have benefited from past reforms. In the absence of a major national emergency (such as a large-scale depression), the consensus for significant economic reform thus may easily be lacking.

DEMOCRACY AS A PROCESS FOR SOCIAL CHOICE

Traditionally, the discipline of economics focused upon individual market choices and responses to these choices by enterprises. With the expansion of democratic government, and the size and economic role of government, it has become increasingly clear that democracy is itself a process for social choice and economizing.

As a process for social choice, democracy is both similar to and different from the market. The familial relationship between them has long been recognized, as illustrated, for example, by such phrases as "dollar ballots" and "consumer sovereignty." One of the more imaginative forms of interdisciplinary study in recent years has been the application of economic theory to the interpretation of democratic politics. An "economic theory of democracy" postulates, for example, that (1) citizens (like consumers) endeavor to maximize their utility/income, including that from government action;

(2) political parties (somewhat in the manner of business firms seeking profits or sales) endeavor to maximize votes.[6] From these basic propositions, or variants thereof, it is possible to construct models of the behavior and functioning of democracy in a manner analogous to the theory of the market as a process for economic coordination and social control.

The analogy, of course, is not perfect, for there are differences between democracy and the market. The market deals more clearly with marketable goods, democracy, with collective goods. The market ideally functions on the basis of one dollar, one vote; democracy, ideally according to the formula of one man, one vote. The market is biased toward the rich (since they have more ballots), while democracy is biased toward the majority. Democracy probably functions so as to correspond more closely to producer interests (relative to consumer interests) than the market. Market choice is more individualized and personalized, while voting (in representative democracy) typically occurs around a cluster of related and interdependent issues, often of national or global significance. In market choice, benefits are probably more intimately connected to payments than in voting—and even in the functioning of legislative bodies, which often delegate (as in the U. S. Congress) tax legislation to one committee and expenditures programs to another.

From these differences (and other problems connected with the logic of voting),[7] some contemporary defenders of the market system have endeavored to build a case for the rationality of market choice relative to voting and democracy. The case would be much stronger were the market and democracy alternative social processes for making the *same* kinds of choices. But, in actuality, the choices are often *different*. The rationality of the marketplace for choosing between raspberries and strawberries therefore does not demonstrate that the process for choosing a system of national defense or a program of public education ought not to be collectivized through the ballotbox. Many products and services are not effectively marketable. Even when they are, divergences between private and social costs and benefits, private monopoly power, and/or large-scale inequalities in wealth or income may make the marketplace an imperfect instrument for registering choices. "The relevant comparison is not between perfect markets and imperfect governments, nor between faulty markets and all-knowing, rational, benevolent governments, but between inevitably imperfect institutions."[8]

DEMOCRACY AS A PROCESS FOR ECONOMIC CONTROL

Lastly, democracy functions as a process for economic control, both of the economy as a whole and of private economic organizations. Under the theory of competitive market capitalism, the automatic and spontaneous functioning of the price system negates the need for the former, while the atomistic character of the economic system negates the need for the latter. Under managed capitalism, large-scale private organizations exercise significant control over the economy. Although typically producing for the market and, in part, countervailing one another's power, they are still to a significant degree autonomous and independent of traditional market controls. At the same time, they lack the comprehensivity or scope of economic power or purpose to function viably as agencies for economic stabilization and full employment. In effect, democracy, by extend-

---

[6]Cf. Anthony Downs, *An Economic Theory of Democracy* (New York: Harper & Row, Publishers, 1957). See also James M. Buchanan and Gordon Tullock, *The Calculus of Consent* (Ann Arbor: University of Michigan Press, 1962).

[7]Cf., for example, Kenneth J. Arrow, *Social Choice and Individual Values* (New York: John Wiley & Sons, Inc., 1951).

[8]Otto Eckstein, *Public Finance* (Englewood Cliffs, New Jersey: Prentice-Hall, Inc., 1964), p. 19.

ing control by the citizenry over its political leaders, provides thereby a mechanism for their (indirect) control over the functioning of the economy as a whole and its constituent private organizations. Thus, democracy supplements and complements bargaining and the market as a process for the control of private bureaucracy.

MANAGED CAPITALISM AND SOCIAL GOALS

Let us now relate the model of managed capitalism to such social goals as efficiency, equity/equality, full employment/stability, and economic growth. Because managed capitalism to some extent lies between (as well as beyond) market capitalism on the one hand and socialism on the other, it will help to review earlier comments on these systems, as well.

Efficiency in the Allocation of Resources

As discussed earlier (especially Chapters 4 and 10), "efficiency" in resource allocation has at least two major dimensions: (1) minimizing the cost of producing any level of output (and thus maximizing output for any level of cost); (2) producing that composition of output most correspondent to society's preferences.

In a market-directed economy (whether market capitalism or market socialism), economic self-interest plus (actual or simulated) competition are the processes relied upon to yield these desired results. Under centralized socialism or other systems of centralized political direction, the dedication/dynamism of the political elite, coupled with a comprehensive national plan, are expected to serve the same function. (Centralized socialists, however, as already noted, place a distinctly lower priority upon the sanctity of consumer sovereignty and the importance of static allocational efficiency than do most advocates of the market principle.)

Both market-directed and centrally planned economic systems have problems in achieving efficient resource allocation. The size of the decision-making unit in market systems necessary to make prices truly beyond individual control may well be too small in many instances (1) to yield substantial economies of large-scale production, much less to function at the technically optimum scale of plant; (2) to meaningfully consider, much less incorporate in individual calculations, social costs and benefits external to those individual units.

By contrast, the size of the decision-making unit in a centrally planned economic system is or may be so large as to (1) generate diseconomies of large-scale, with attendant costs, and (2) exclude or gloss over cost and benefit relations requiring intimate knowledge of the concretized circumstances of time and place. Market systems may be highly sensitive to consumer preferences and market values, but insensitive to social costs and benefits and non-market values. Centrally planned systems, by contrast, are relatively insensitive to consumer preferences and concrete and localized costs and benefits susceptible to incorporation by market processes. In addition, centrally planned systems depend upon the dynamic thrust of the dedicated motivation of a political elite. If that motivation should falter—or if the political leadership fails to instill a similar, though lower-level, dedication in its followers—the underpinnings of the entire system may collapse.

Managed capitalism lies between and beyond old-style competitive market capitalism and centrally planned economies. Thus, it incorporates advantages and disadvantages from each. Relative to competitive market capitalism, the size of the decision-making unit is more likely to be large enough to capture economies of large-scale production and function at or near the technically optimum scale of plant. At the same time, the pluralistic character of the basic organizational structure of managed capitalism makes it less likely to suffer from diseconomies of large-scale, than centrally planned systems. The intermediate size and scope of power and purpose of its decision-making units plausibly makes it easier to calculate social costs and benefits than under competitive market capitalism and harder to do so than in more centrally planned systems. Because of its collectivist character and positions of concentrated market power, managed capitalism plausibly is less sensitive to localized and concretized circumstances, market values, and consumer preferences than market-directed economies. But because of its pluralistic structure and production for the market, it is more sensitive to these dimensions of economic life than centrally planned systems. Because of its plurality of more or less autonomous private organizations, managed capitalism is less equipped to mobilize and allocate resources for large-scale, rapid change than a centrally planned economy, but better equipped to do so than a more market-oriented economic system.

While managed capitalism may lack (or have lower levels of) costs associated with market exchange and central planning, it has other costs of its own (and thus, in a manner of speaking, lies "beyond" both old-style capitalism and socialism). Sales promotion, for example, is likely to be substantially higher in managed capitalism, especially under conditions of differentiated oligopoly and monopolistic competition, than under either a decentralized market economy or a centrally planned one. Though some sales promotion provides useful information pertinent to more efficient and rational consumer choice, much advertising (1) simply offsets other advertising and thus is socially wasteful or of little value; (2) molds or biases consumer preferences and thereby distorts market choice in the direction of producer interests. In addition, managed capitalism, precisely because of its pluralistic organizational structure, is more likely to incur costs of bargaining (and explosive breakdowns associated with the bargaining process, such as a nationwide strike) and

regulation (for example, parallel private and public organizations, as in the public utilities).

Lastly, managed capitalism has no clear built-in mechanism for rendering economic power publicly responsible. Under competitive market capitalism, economic power is dispersed so widely that no decision-maker is in a position to rig the market or diverge from its control processes. Under centrally planned systems, economic power is highly concentrated in the hands of public authorities, but, at the same time, is in principle answerable through the political process to the citizenry or the political leadership. Under managed capitalism, economic power is highly concentrated, but in large-scale private organizations. Thus, decision-makers neither merely adapt to impersonal market forces beyond their control nor stand directly accountable to the citizenry/political leadership. In practice, the arbitrary and discretionary economic power of large-scale private organizations has been limited or countervailed by (1) some degree of market control, (2) bargaining with other organizations, (3) regulation by governmental authority, and/or (4) the emergence of a "corporate conscience." Still, managed capitalism is characterized by a large degree of arbitrary and discretionary private economic power and thus lacks a clear and unequivocal process for bringing together private and public interest.

Managed Capitalism and Other Social Goals

FULL EMPLOYMENT AND ECONOMIC STABILIZATION

No economic system is likely to be entirely free from economic fluctuations or instability. Market capitalism, even at its purely/perfectly competitive best, plausibly is characterized by some price and wage instability. Indeed, the maintenance of stability in output and employment may *require* flexibility, that is, instability, in prices and wages. In effect, deflation is the price that a competitive market economy, functioning at its best, pays to prevent or cure depressions. Further, market capitalism does not always function at its best and may under certain conditions flounder in unemployment and depression or, alternatively, inflation. Decentralization in decision-making maximizes the likelihood of macroeconomic divergence between such variables as aggregate desired saving and aggregate desired investment, and compounds and supplements the uncertainties which, in any economic system, are generated by dynamic changes (or expectations of changes) in such exogenous factors as technology, weather, population, and so on. Consequently, the price system does not necessarily function automatically to establish or restore full employment equilibrium.

Further, even if the direction of impact of the price system in a market-directed economy were toward full employment equilibrium, the magnitude and rapidity of flexibility in price and wage levels might on occasion be so great as to be politically unacceptable, or the process of market adjustment too slow.

By contrast, the sources of instability in centrally planned economic systems may lie in the political rather than the economic system (insofar as it is possible to make such a distinction). In a centrally planned economy, savers and investors (the CPB) are the same persons and are saving and investing for the same reasons. Changes in population, weather, technology, and so forth will generate unpredicted change in centrally planned systems, too. But the additional uncertainty and instability emanating from decentralization of saving and investment would be absent. Further, since unemployment is obviously a social cost, it would not be to the economic advantage of a centrally planned economy to permit involuntary unemployment.

At the same time, the power to mobilize and direct resources concentrated in the hands of the political leadership is itself a source of instability if the leadership displays instability. Large-scale industrialization programs, "great leaps" forward or "cultural revolutions," radical institutional change (such as collectivization of agriculture), or shifts in policy or organization accompanying shifts in political power among leaders, may generate profound instability in the economy.

Managed capitalism lies between these two classic alternatives. Large-scale private organizations have some degree of control over aggregate demand and supply and may, on occasion, behave countercyclically. (For example, in the 1954 recession in the United States, General Motors increased investment, thereby functioning, in effect, like a little government.) Essentially, however, the extent of control is far less than economy-wide, and managed capitalism, like competitive market capitalism, is characterized by potential instability in the level of aggregate demand because of the (essentially) decentralized character of decisions regarding consumption, saving, and investment.

By contrast to competitive market capitalism, however, the monopoly and oligopoly power of large-scale corporations and labor unions makes them price-makers rather than price-takers, and eliminates or significantly reduces the (downward) price flexibility characteristic of the decentralized market economy. But greater stability in prices and wages is acquired at the cost of potential instability in output and employment because the typical response of business enterprises under managed capitalism to decreases in demand is to lay off workers and cut back production.

On the other side of the coin, prices, though relatively inflexible downward, are by no means inflexible in the upward direction. In competitive market capitalism, inflation typically is caused by the "pull" of rising demand at or near full employment utilization of resources. In managed capitalism, the market power of sellers generates additional and supplementary inflationary pressures from the side of cost and supply.

Managed capitalism concentrates a considerable degree of economic power to control economic instability and aggregate economic activity in the hands of government authority. Governments of managed capitalist societies have at their disposal a battery of measures (notably monetary and fiscal policy) potentially capable of promoting economic stability and full employment. In practice, managed capitalist economies have been reasonably successful since the end of World War II in applying these measures.

Still, there are important potential sources of instability or departures from full employment inherent in the functioning of managed capitalist economies. Like the centrally planned economy (though to a lesser degree), managed capitalism establishes centralized political direction of the aggregate behavior of the economic system. Political instabilities may thus be a cause of economic instability. On the other hand, like competitive market capitalism (though to a lesser degree), managed capitalism is characterized by a dispersion of economic power among millions of more or less independent decision-making units. This economic decentralization may cause instability. In effect, managed capitalism lies between market-directed and central plan-directed systems, incorporating some of the advantages and limitations of each.

In addition, managed capitalism goes beyond the classic alternatives and has problems of its own. One such problem is that it has evolved out of old-style capitalism. Consequently, many ideas about the proper functioning of the economic system (for example, the annually balanced budget) which emerged and found their rationale in an earlier and different economic system tend to linger and, thereby, to constrain the application of policies to promote full employment and economic stability under managed capitalism.

Further, managed capitalism contains built-in processes for instability, especially in the direction of inflation. A crucial ingredient of the managed capitalist economic system is the existence of large-scale private economic organizations which (1) exert tremendous market power and, thereby, influence on the economy; and (2) have great influence on the political system and the choice of public policies. The commitment by government to full employment, combined with the resistance of corporations and labor unions to price and wage deflation, indeed, proclivity toward price and wage inflation, can raise a Hobson's choice for government policy-makers: curb inflation, and thereby cause recession and unemployment; or promote full employment, and thereby "ratify" inflation. The joint attainment of full employment, price stability, and equilibrium in the balance of payments may well require some involvement of government, in "condominium" with labor unions and corporations, in the formulation of wages and prices.

EQUITY AND EQUALITY IN THE DISTRIBUTION OF INCOME

Of the various models of economic systems explored herein, competitive market capitalism has the smallest degree of freedom to engage in discretionary action in the pursuit of equity/equality in the distribution of income. Competitive market capitalism at its best limits the extent of inequality (for example, inequalities caused by monopoly or political privilege) and yields a form of equity (from each according to his ability and property, to each according to his productivity and that of his property). But first, market capitalism does not always function at its best, thereby generating inequities in terms of its own normative criterion as well as inequality. Second, even at its best, competitive market capitalism plausibly generates substantial inequalities and inequities (for example, though inheritance, luck and chance). These factors, heightened by the concentration of ownership and control of industry even under competitive conditions, place strategic limitations upon the conscious pursuit of equity and equality as social goals. Though the last of these factors would be eliminated in a decentralized market socialist economy (cf. Chapter 10), reliance on the market, and its evaluation of labor productivity in terms of consumer preferences, would limit the pursuit of equality/equity there, as well.

Centralized socialism, characterized by the absence of both private property and reliance upon the marketplace for the valuation of productivities, plausibly would have the highest degree of discretionary power in the pursuit of equity and equality. The distribution of income under centralized socialism is more clearly a "policy variable" than in other systems. Gains in distributive justice through greater income equality could be more clearly compared with gains in productivity of tighter control over the use and allocation of resources in accordance with planners' preferences than in other systems. At the same time, the concentration of economic power and its combination with political power gives the centrally planned and directed economy greater potential for the pursuit of inequity and inequality (even in its own terms) than other systems.

Managed capitalism lies between these relatively extreme positions. Its greater concentration of economic power, larger role for government and non-market values and processes, separation of ownership and managerial control, and increased democratization of political life contribute to greater scope for the exercise of discretionary judgments in the distribution of income. On the other hand, its maintenance of private property, greater reliance upon markets as an allocational process, and pluralistic structure render its scope of discretionary power lower than in decentralized or centralized socialism. Further, while its tendency toward inequality in income distribution is blunted by democracy and countervailing power, it is augmented by large-scale concentrations of private economic power. Thus, managed capitalism occupies an intermediary position between more decentralized and more centralized forms of economic organization.

ECONOMIC GROWTH

The rate of economic growth depends upon both (1) the proportion of an economy's resources directed toward growth and (2) the dynamic efficiency with which these resources are employed. Given efficiency in resource utilization, the growth rate may be increased by directing a larger proportion of income to saving and investment and/or by increasing the ratio of work to leisure.

A major advantage (for the promotion of high growth rates) of a centrally and comprehensively planned economy lies in its high degree of discretionary control over saving, investment, work, and leisure. A political leadership willing to impose sacrifices upon a present generation through higher saving/ income ratios, forced labor, and longer working hours may thereby generate rapid economic growth, even with or despite inefficiencies in resource allocation.

By contrast, in competitive market capitalism, the rate of economic growth is not a policy variable of central planners, but instead emerges from and tends toward consistency with individual preferences and market choices of consumers, resource owners, and business firms. Consequently, again given resource efficiency, the rate of economic growth, though more consistent with individual preferences (of the present generation), is likely to be lower than that attainable through larger saving and investing and working longer and harder.

Managed capitalism lies between a decentralized market economy and one characterized by comprehensive central planning. Like the former, saving, investment, work, and leisure depend significantly upon individual preferences and market choices. But like the latter, managed capitalism incorporates a major role for collective, central control and influence over the growth process. First, as already noted, managed capitalism, through monetary and fiscal policies, tends to promote full employment utilization of resources, or at least to minimize depression and unemployment. While not necessarily increasing the ratio of work to leisure at full employment, this does increase the ratio of employment to unemployment; and, while not necessarily increasing the ratio of saving and investment to income at full employment, it does increase the likelihood that saving will not go to waste in unemployment and recession. In addition, the maintenance of full employment prosperity entices people into the labor force and/or longer working hours (for example, housewives, students, moonlighters, and retirees who return to work). Second, the rate of economic growth is a policy variable under managed capitalism (though less so than under centralized socialism). In the public sector, governments can and do act to increase saving and investment relative to consumption—for example, through easy monetary policies to keep interest rates low and stimulate private investment, and through tax credits, liberal depreciation and depletion allowances, and public investment programs. In the private sector, the corporate revolution and dominance of internal financing, combined with the sales and growth orientation of oligopolistic enterprises, tends to increase the profit-investment-technology-profit sequence and, thereby, promote higher growth rates. In short, through its new blend of private and public decision-making, a managed capitalist economy (for example, West Germany, Japan) may have ratios of saving and investment to national income as high or higher than those of centrally planned economies and consequently, again abstracting from efficiency in resource use, growth rates which rival or surpass those of more centrally directed economic systems.

Given the proportion of an economy's resources directed toward growth, growth rates depend upon the dynamic efficiency with which resources are employed. Here, again, as in the earlier discussion of general allocational efficiency, managed capitalism lies between more decentralized and more centralized forms of economic organization.

The motivational and institutional structure of a decentralized, market-directed economy contains a powerful thrust toward allocational efficiency in a dynamic as well as a static setting. The absence of monopoly and monopsony power means the absence of barriers to invention, innovation, and new investment. As a corollary, competition spurs technical progress, since profits cannot be generated by rigging the market, restricting output, and raising prices, but only by raising productivity and reducing costs. Under competitive conditions, the drive for individual economic gain thus is harnessed to greater efficiency and higher output. In addition, the decentralized character of the economic system provides an opportunity for experimentation and invention on a small scale, for easily drawing in new blood through conditions of easy entry, and for spontaneous responses to local conditions and circumstances which promise greater productivity.

At the same time, competitive market capitalism is least responsive to external and uncertain benefits and least likely to benefit from large-scale economies. Scientific research, research and development programs, and large-scale innovations are least likely to emerge in a decentralized, market-directed economy.

By contrast, a centrally-directed economic system lacks spontaneity, opportunity for individual creativity and experimentation, responsiveness to concrete and local circumstances, and clear motivation for technical progress among the general body of the population. But it has the offsetting advantages of large scale and centralization: Since all benefits and costs are internal, the rationale for investment in science, research and development, and education are clearer under a centrally-directed economy. Wastes from duplication in research and uncertainties emanating from dispersion of investment are lower, and large-scale, rapid technological transformations easier to execute.

Lying between a market-directed and centrally-planned economy, managed capitalism contains some of the advantages and disadvantages of each. On the one hand, economic power is dispersed widely enough and decision-making units are small enough to avoid the potentially stultifying impact upon motivation and individual experimentation of the centrally-planned economic system. On the other hand, economic power is often sufficiently concentrated and of sufficient scale to support costly but productive technical research and development. In addition, managed capitalism goes beyond the classic models of decentralized and centralized economic organization by incorporating a new feature, that is, competition among autonomous R and D organizations and research departments of large-scale corporations, thereby stimulating research and technical progress.

At the same time, exclusive or near-exclusive reliance on the private sector for promoting dynamic efficiency under managed capitalism is unlikely and, in fact, has not occurred. First, the results of technical progress by private corporations are private, rather than public, property. This, combined with oligopoly and monopoly power, may act as a barrier to dynamic efficiency and, thereby, the rate of economic growth. Second, managed capitalism, despite large-scale concentrations of private economic power, still is characterized by a considerable degree of externality and uncertainty in science, education, and basic research. For these reasons, basic science and general education are largely provided by government (or non-profit organizations) rather than by private corporations, and, in a variety of ways, governments in managed capitalist economies have encouraged and fostered research, invention, and innovation.

SUMMARY TO CHAPTER 13

1. A theoretical description of the behavior and functioning of contemporary managed capitalism differs both from the theory of old-style, decentralized, competitive market capitalism and from theories and strategies of socialism, partly as a result of lying between them and incorporating elements from both, and partly by incorporating features not clearly found in either.

2. The typical market structure of managed capitalist economies and the form of price system(s) in which the theory of managed capitalism has made its most prominent contribution, is a variant of monopolistic competition or oligopoly. Both involve a blend of monopolistic and competitive elements. Like monopoly, they are characterized by control over the market; but like competition, this control is limited by the existence of competitors.

3. In oligopoly, the interdependencies of firms preclude certain and determinate predictions of rational economic behavior. However, prominent forms of oligopoly behavior have been identified, depending upon the degree and form of collusion, including (a) independent and non-collusive oligopoly; (b) perfectly-collusive oligopoly; (c) imperfectly-collusive oligopoly.

4. The monopoly power of business firms under managed capitalism is countervailed or supplemented in several ways. In addition to traditional price competition among existing firms, businesses may compete (a) through the entry of new firms, (b) non-price competition (such as product differentiation, quality, sales promotion), and (c) dynamic development (for example, new products, technical progress). The power of business firms to control markets also may be blunted or countervailed by opposing systems of price controls, as, for example, bargaining price systems or government price controls.

5. Beyond the price system, the theory and practice of managed capitalism has been characterized by an emergence of an increased role for non-market processes. These have included private and public bureaucracy, bargaining, and democracy. Each of these

processes supplements or modifies the functioning of the price system and has both advantages and disadvantages for the promotion of such social goals as efficiency, equity, stability/full-employment, and growth.

6. Managed capitalism lies both between and beyond models of more decentralized and centralized forms of economic organization and incorporates advantages and limitations of each. The extent of collective, centralized control in managed capitalism appears to be large enough to offset some of the externalities and uncertainties of the purely market-directed economy, most notably those of depressions, unemployment, and economic instability. At the same time, the pluralistic structure of managed capitalism, its dispersion of economic power, and its greater proclivity toward the marketplace enable it to incorporate some of the major advantages for efficient resource allocation of market choice and economic decentralization. Its blend of public and private decision-making gives it greater discretionary control over the process of economic growth and the promotion of income equality than old-style market capitalism, but, at the same time, makes it more responsive to individual preferences and market choices than a centrally directed economy.

14

Democratic Socialism

Examined in Chapter 12 and 13 were recent contributions to the theory of managed capitalism with particular reference to the United States, noting how certain elements or dimensions of the socialist critique of capitalism have been incorporated, at least in part, into that body of thought. This chapter will explore recent contributions to the economic theory and social philosophy of democratic socialism with particular reference to the United Kingdom. It will examine the hypothesis that democratic socialists are becoming indistinguishable, for all practicable purposes, from liberal social reformers, and that "democratic socialism" is evaporating as a distinctive form or system of economic organization as its programs and proposals merge with and dissolve into strategies for the democratic reform and modification of capitalism. This theme will be illustrated by selective and interpretative references to recent democratic socialist literature on the following issues: ends and means; the democratic socialist critique; democratic socialist programs and proposals; and the possible transition from managed capitalism to democratic socialism.

WHAT IS DEMOCRATIC SOCIALISM? ENDS AND MEANS

Introduction

As emphasized earlier, the phrase "economic theory of decentralized (or centralized) socialism" chiefly connotes four things: economic problems, issues, and characteristics; theoretical model-building of economic systems; socialist, as distinguished from non-socialist, forms of economic organization; the decentralized (or centralized) character of economic decision-making and control.

To a limited extent, the economic theory of democratic socialism follows this pattern. Democratic socialists are concerned with economic problems. They have, on occasion, constructed more or less formal models of socialist economic organization. They do have conceptions and/or visions of a distinctively socialist economic system, distinguished from classic capitalism, modified or managed capitalism, fascism, and contemporary Communism. They are and have been concerned with decentralization and centralization in economic decision-making and control—some, like the Fabian socialists, such as Sidney and Beatrice Webb and George Bernard Shaw, favoring greater centralization and collective, governmental guidance and planning of the national economy; others, like G.D.H. Cole (who complicated matters by becoming a prominent member and president of the Fabian Society), favoring greater decentralization, industrial democracy, and worker control of industry.

At the same time, democratic socialism, especially the British variety, is distinctive. Democratic socialism is a movement for economic change and social reform as well as, indeed, more than, a body of economic theory.

This has implications for each of these four identifying dimensions of the problem.

(1) Democratic socialists often are more concerned with the ethics, philosophy, politics, and social psychology of socialism than with economics.

(2) The literature of democratic socialism does include more or less formal economic models of the socialist economy analogous to that presented, for example, by Oskar Lange. But most of what might be called the "theory of democratic socialism" is programmatic and applied in character, concerned more with a theoretical critique of capitalism and descriptions of programs and proposals intended to move the economic system *toward* socialism than with formal economic models of the behavior of a socialist economy itself.

(3) The crucial adjective in the literature of democratic socialism is neither "decentralized" nor "centralized," but *democratic*. The movement and literature of democratic socialism is an amalgam of ideas on *both* decentralized and centralized forms of economic decision-making and control, and many democratic socialists would regard the distinction between the two as artificial. Democratic socialists may reasonably be described as *economic collectivists*, that is, people who favor the utilization of collective institutions, including government, in the resolution of economic problems. But they (certainly the British democratic socialists) are not *statists*, that is, people who glorify or espouse the interests and purposes of the state as distinguished from those of individuals, and who wish to concentrate the power to make and enforce economic decisions more or less monistically in the hands of a central government as distinguished from other social-collective organizations, including cooperatives, labor unions, local governments, and (governmentally controlled or guided) private businesses and business associations.

In any event, democracy is featured and heavily emphasized in the literature of democratic socialism. First, the route to a socialist economic society must be democratic in character. As identified by Sidney Webb in 1889 [Cf., 65: 30] this entails four requirements: Social change and reform must be (a) peaceful and non-violent, involving no overthrow of the constitution; (b) relatively gradual and small-scale, or "piecemeal," generating no dislocation; (c) psychologically and morally acceptable to the people; (d) politically acceptable by a majority of the electorate. Second, both in the process of movement toward and at the time of attainment of socialism, society must be organized democratically. This involves both political and economic democracy. By *political democracy*, democratic socialists generally mean both popular control over governments by the citizenry and protection of individual freedoms of the citizenry (such as free speech, freedom of association, and legal protections in criminal suits) from arbitrary action by the state. But democratic socialists insist that true or full democracy will come only when democracy is extended to non-political dimensions of life and society, for example, to industrial democracy in the form of worker control of industry, to social democracy with the widening of educational opportunities, and to general economic democracy with government control of the national economy in the pursuit of social goals supported by the majority of the democratic electorate.

(4) It is true that democratic socialism shares certain characteristics in common with a variety of other visions, models, and proposals within the socialist family. But, in contrast with the economic theory of decentralized socialism, which is essentially a model of a prospective, future economic system, and centralized socialism, which is partly the latter and partly a general theoretical description of economic organization and development in the Communist economies, democratic socialism is essentially a movement and a theory of movement toward socialism. This means the substantive content of democratic socialist literature is often more

concerned with the economic reform of capitalism than with socialism *per se*. This raises the question of the relationship and the problem of distinguishing between socialism and economic reform of capitalism.

Both democratic socialists and right-wing anti-socialists tend to gloss over the distinction between the economic reform of capitalism and socialism. This is understandable on psychological and political grounds. Democratic socialists probably are no more immune than others from the desire to feel their actions are yielding desired results. If the economic reform of capitalism is leading, bit by bit, to the establishment of a socialist economic society, then democratic socialist efforts are not in vain. In addition, it may be politically expedient for socialists to label as "socialist" the specific reforms of particular "socialist governments," either because of their popularity or as a device to lull a conservative electorate's fears of more radical change until a more propitious moment. For anti-socialists, the temptation is equally great: If the economic reforms of capitalism lead necessarily and inevitably to "socialism," and if "socialism" is undesirable, then we must prevent and/or oppose those economic reforms.

It is, of course, *conceivable* that the economic reform of capitalism *may* lead to socialism. But there is no guarantee this will occur. It is at least equally conceivable that, by reforming, stabilizing, modifying, and/or humanizing capitalism, it will create an economic system qualitatively different both from old-style capitalism and traditional democratic socialist visions of the ideally organized and functioning socialist economic society. It is also possible that democratic socialists are becoming or may become bewitched by the reforms for which they are, in part, responsible and may come to accept a reformed and governmentally managed capitalism as a reasonable substitute for, if not facsimile of, socialism. In any event, if socialism means essentially a movement for gradual social reform and economic change

rather than a formal economic model of either an existing or prospective radically different economic system, the traditional dichotomy between capitalism and socialism becomes increasingly less meaningful.

Democratic Socialist Goals and the Structure of Democratic Socialist Economic Organization

In general, contemporary democratic socialist views on means and ends may be summarized around four central propositions: first, (democratic) socialism is concerned essentially with ends rather than means; second, among the various ends or goals of economic organization, equality and freedom head the list; third, collective or social means, not merely the individualistic methods of economic organization embodied in the theory and practice of old-style capitalism, are necessary for the attainment of these goals; but, fourth, the means suitable for their attainment are multiple and changing, not monistic and fixed.

THE PRIMACY OF SOCIALIST ENDS

In contrast to many anti-socialists (for example, Schumpeter and the neo-Austrians) and some socialists (especially the neo-Marxists) who focus upon institutional methods in their conceptions of socialism, most contemporary democratic socialists insist their primary concern is with ends. The only common element to the "bewildering variety" of democratic socialist visions and proposals is "certain moral values and aspirations," that is, "a certain kind of society," *not* particular policies or means to establish such a society or to realize such ends. [53:65] This is not nullified, democratic socialists argue, by the fact that socialist ends (such as equality) have in the past been associated in socialist literature with particular institutions or means (for example, public ownership).

But what if socialist means are used to attain non-socialist ends (such as the aggrandizement of the income and power of a party or managerial elite)? According to Hayek, this would demonstrate a socialist economic society cannot guarantee to pursue its lofty aspirations. According to Schumpeter [8: 170], this would show that socialism is "culturally indeterminate," that is, that the politics or ethics of socialism are not logically derived from its economic base. Democratic socialists insist on an opposing interpretation, as emphasized by Henry Smith, namely, that if traditionally socialist means are used in a society to pursue non-socialist ends, then "it is not a socialist society." [66: 93$_n$] (The converse may also be true: If socialist ends have been achieved by non-socialist means, the primary substance of socialism will have been realized.)

In part, of course, this is merely a semantic issue. If democratic socialists want to define *socialism* in terms of ends rather than means, there is no reason they should not do so—though it should be noted this makes their "socialism" substantially different from the "socialism" of, say, the neo-Marxists, who insist that more or less comprehensive public ownership and central governmental economic planning constitute the essence of a socialist economy. In part, however, it is a substantive issue of considerable significance, for just as it is true the same means may be used to promote a variety of ends, it is also true the same ends conceivably may be attained through a variety of means. It is precisely this flexibility of spirit on the question of appropriate means which removes democratic socialists from socialist orthodoxy and makes them difficult to distinguish at times from supporters and proponents of a managed and socially reformed capitalism.

EQUALITY AND FREEDOM

For neo-Marxists, the central goal is industrialization and economic growth. For Keynesians, it is full employment-stability. For neo-Austrians, it is efficient resource allocation and individual economic freedoms. And so on. But democratic socialists have a passionate and idealistic concern, unequaled in any of the other theories and philosophies of economic systems, for the pursuit of *equality*. "The goal of equality is both an affirmation and a reaction. It is socialism's link with social protest in the past and its idealized picture of the future. It is the heart of the socialist's struggle against class privileges and against the great inequalities of income and wealth that occur under unbridled capitalism."[1]

Thus, Henry Smith defines *socialism* as a "demand for the minimization of conflict arising out of economic relations," specifically through the elimination of poverty and injustice. [66: 9] G. D. H. Cole identifies *socialism* as a society characterized by the terminus of division "into opposing economic classes" and the existence of "conditions of approximate social and economic equality," of "a human fellowship which denies and expels distinctions of class, and a social system in which no one is so much richer or poorer than his neighbours as to be unable to mix with them on equal terms." [Cited in 55: 61] W. Arthur Lewis states it succinctly: "Socialism is about equality." [60: 10] "It is a demand for equality and social justice." [60: 11] And: "The first aim of socialists, prized above all others, is equality of income." [60: 30]

"Let us start," suggests Jay, by "clearly distinguishing between ends and means. Socialists believe in equality as an end . . . . Socialism means the belief that every human being has an *equal* right to happiness and whatever else gives value to life . . . . This belief in equality rests not on dubious statements of fact such as 'Men are born equal.' It rests on moral judgment. Every human being has as much right as anyone else to whatever gives value to human life." [59: 4, 2] *Socialism* also means that "a world society enshrining this right can best be achieved, or

---

[1] Nathaniel Stone Preston, *Politics, Economics, and Power* (New York: The Macmillan Company, Publishers, 1967), p. 102.

approached, by collective, 'social,' and not just individualist, methods. There are thus two convictions that are fundamental to Socialism. The first concerns the ultimate aim: certain equal rights for all; and the second, the basic means by which that can be attained, whether politically or economically." [59: 2]

By *equality*, democratic socialists hasten to add, they do not mean literal or complete equality of wealth or income. Even if such a goal were desirable, its attainment would conflict with other important social goals, namely, efficiency in production and resource allocation and economic growth, all of which require "*some* differential rewards for talent and ability." Short of Utopia, "justice must here be tempered with efficiency." [54: 29] The "basic economic aim for Socialists" is thus the "minimum practicable inequality" consistent with the active use of "the productive abilities of the community." [59: 9, 8]

The democratic socialist rationale for the promotion of equality (more accurately, the reduction of inequality) is a blend of economic argument with political and ethical value judgments. Inequality—in income, wealth, position, power, and authority in society—(1) is often caused by market imperfections and inequalities in bargaining power inconsistent with competitive markets, and thus, indefensible even within the context of classical liberalism; (2) even if or when consistent with competitive market-determined differentials in quality/productivity of resources, is unjust, since it ignores the needs and value of families and non-workers "outside" the marketplace; (3) denies and is inconsistent with the value and criterion of "community" which, in a democratic society, must supplement that of (market-determined) merit; (4) fosters divisiveness and feelings of class-consciousness; (5) promotes/perpetuates inequalities in opportunity; (6) promotes inequality in political power and influence and, thereby, decreases the democratic character of government and contributes to social tensions and

potential political instability; (7) promotes allocations of resources, which, however "efficient" or consistent with consumer preferences based upon given income distributions, constitute *mis*allocations in terms of generally accepted values of the democratic community (for example, the rich man's dogs getting steak before the poor man's children get milk); (8) by concentrating incomes among the rich, with their high propensity to save, tends to restrict consumption demand and thereby (in the absence of sufficiently high levels of investment to offset saving), may contribute to recession or depression.

Though not unique to socialist value systems (because it is shared by non-socialist liberalism), individual freedom or "liberty" is equivalent in importance with equality. Indeed, the two, suggests Jay, are necessarily interdependent: Equality requires equal political and economic rights for all, that is, freedom; real freedom for an entire society requires that inequality be restricted to "minimum practicable" limits. Thus, liberalism "is not enough" because it fails to recognize the necessity of equality for the attainment of equal freedom for all, while "Communism is also not enough, because, in the ostensible pursuit of economic equality, it denies political liberty to a large part of the society it rules. If the leaders of the Communist State have more political freedom than others, that State is unequal as well as unfree. The principle of equality requires that people should have equal political, as well as economic, rights. To deprive them of the one for the sake of the other is to destroy equality in its own name." [59: 6] In addition, and again not unique to socialist value systems, are the goals of full-employment stability, economic growth, and efficiency in the allocation of resources—probably (though not explicitly) in that order of priority.

The methods or means of socialism are essentially those of social and/or governmental *control* of the "production and distribution of wealth." This does *not* mean the

Table 14-1.

THE STRUCTURE OF DEMOCRATIC SOCIALISM

1. Level of development	Developed economy
2. Resource base	Capitalistic
3. Ownership-control of industry	Mixed—including a significant but limited role for "state monopolies": state ownership or control of basic industries
4. Locus of economic power	Dispersed; but conscious social control of private economic power
5. Motivational system	Individual gain, modified by the principle of cooperation and pursuit of social goals
6. Organization of economic power	Mixture of decentralization and centralization
7. Social processes for making and coordinating economic decisions	Mixture of (competitive) price system, (economic and political) democracy, (regulated and limited) bureaucracy, and bargaining; conscious regulation of the market by government planning
8. Distribution of income and wealth	Market determination—modified by large-scale government measures to reduce inequality in income, wealth, and opportunity

elimination of the market mechanism as a social process for economic calculation and coordination. Nor does it mean exclusive or even primary reliance upon government ownership. Although a democratic socialist program "consciously uses the means of public ownership, in a supple, flexible, and relevant manner, to achieve certain definite socialist ends," [54: 49] *it is not itself an end.* Indeed, as a means, it never was *the* essential ingredient of the (non-Marxist) vision of the ideally functioning socialist economic society. "The notion of public ownership (rather than public control) as in some sense a 'fundamental' means to the Socialist aim, instead of one important means among others, was a narrowing of the original conception . . . ." [59: 3] Further, for reasons to be presented later, it has declined in significance as a method for attaining socialist ends, and "would by no means constitute the most important part of [a radical democratic socialist party's] total programme . . . ." [54: 49]

THE STRUCTURE OF DEMOCRATIC SOCIALISM

The structure of democratic socialism as an economic system, as described by recent contributors, is identified more specifically in Table 14-1.

It is clear that democratic socialists conceive their proposed system as evolving out of a capitalist past, in economically developed, if not necessarily affluent, economic societies. This does not preclude the possible adaptation of democratic socialist ideas and proposals to underdeveloped economies (as, for example, in India). But it does help us to better understand the context in which democratic socialists typically, if not exclusively, write, and it makes more understandable the democratic-socialist priority system in regard to goals (that is, the primacy of emphasis upon equality in a democratic framework).

While retaining a case for social ownership or control of basic industries (such as transportation, communications, banking, fuel and power, iron and steel), contemporary demo-raticc socialists have modified earlier and more traditional views: (1) Ownership is not the key to economic power; (2) private owner-ship is not the basic cause of inequality; (3) government ownership is merely one of several possible means whereby governments affect economic life and endeavor to attain socialist aims; (4) social-collective ownership may come in a variety of forms, not merely that of state monopolies.

It should be emphasized that, in democratic socialist programs and proposals perhaps even more than in the case of the economic theory of decentralized socialism, the freedom and power to formulate economic decisions is dispersed widely among a variety of eco-nomic decision-making units, including con-sumers, businesses, business managers of government-owned enterprises, cooperatives, and so on. Democratic socialists recognize, perhaps more explicitly than any other sub-group in the socialist family, the existence and desirability of a *plurality* of groups and organizations in economic decision-making. At the same time, democratic socialists emphasize the need for conscious social control of private economic power.

Democratic socialists face a basic dilemma of combining and integrating two quite distinguishable themes: centralization in government planning for the national eco-nomy and decentralization-participation of workers in the economic life of the com-munity. This was a question raised, but never resolved, in the Marxian literature, largely ignored in the more formal model of decen-tralized socialism by Oskar Lange, and superseded by an espousal of an extreme centralization in the neo-Marxist models of centralized socialism.

Democratic socialists retain the traditional socialist hope that, in the process of demo-cratization and participation by workers in economic decision-making, more cooperative aspirations will supplement (though by no means eliminate) the calculus of individual economic gain. Recently, this hopeful expecta-tion has been accompanied and largely over-shadowed by emphasis upon the conscious social-collective pursuit of social goals for the national economy.

Recent proposals of democratic socialists incorporate a mixture or interblending of all four social processes for economic deci-sion-making and coordination: price systems, democracy, bureaucracy, and bargaining.

THE DEMOCRATIC SOCIALIST CRITIQUE

Contemporary democratic socialists are agile social-intellectual critics. Discussion of their critique is organized around three central headings: *laissez-faire* capitalism, Marxism, and modified or managed capita-lism.

The Democratic Socialist Critique of Competitive Market, *Laissez-Faire* Capitalism

The democratic socialist indictment of competitive market, *laissez-faire* capitalism contains three essential elements: first, its tendency toward instability, unemployment, and depression; second, its generation of excessive inequality in the distribution of income and wealth; third, its generation of excessive inequality in power, responsibility, and participation in industry. All three involve, in the democratic socialist view, a form of relative poverty: Instability and depression create poverty in relation to potential output or income and demonstrate a basic inefficiency of the capitalist system. Inequality in the distribution of income and wealth creates a poverty of the poor in rela-tion to the rich and demonstrates capitalism's basic inequity and injustice. Inequality in the distribution of power and responsibility in industry creates a poverty of workers-employees in relation to employers, capitalists, and stockholders, and demonstrates capitalism's failure to extend liberty and democracy from the political into the industrial realm of society.

INSTABILITY AND DEPRESSION

The contemporary democratic socialist analysis of instability under *laissez-faire* capitalism is essentially Keynesian rather than Marxian in character. During the 1930s, suggests Douglas Jay, "the essential causes of the disease came for the first time to be clearly understood." Although "many economists and writers were on the track," this "great advance is now almost universally associated with the name of J. M. Keynes; and he, of course, made by far the greatest single contribution." [59: 117n]

An essentially Keynesian analysis of the causes of capitalist instability, unemployment, and depression is characteristic of much of contemporary democratic socialist writing and may be summarized around seven central themes. First, the level of employment (and whether the economy operates at or below full employment) is determined by the flow of aggregate monetary demand. Given the size of the labor force, plant capacity, and existing technology, there is some optimum flow of spending which will be sufficient to cover costs and normal profit at full employment utilization of plant and labor. If the actual level of demand is at this optimum level, full employment without (or without substantial) inflation will ensue. If demand lies below this level, the result will be depression and unemployment. If demand lies above this level, the result will be inflation.

Second, capitalism is not self-regulating "in its global aspects." [54: 50] There "is no automatic mechanism by which this flow generates itself of its own accord." [59: 122] This arises essentially from the fact that saving and investment decisions are separate ones, made in significant measure by different people, and that "no automatic process links them together." [59: 119] The "crux of the problem," suggested elder statesman English Laborite John Strachey in his critical review

of capitalism, "is that under capitalism investment . . . is independently determined" and "by no means always or automatically follows the diversion of resources from consumption." [68: 246] The "mainspring" of capitalism is investment. But in *laissez-faire* capitalism, investment decisions are dependent upon uncertain and fluctuating profit expectations of large numbers of capitalist entrepreneurs and are largely independent of full employment saving. The rate of interest, expected in classical economic theory to bring the two together, is an exceptionally weak reed on which to depend, especially in view of large-scale shifts in profit expectations. In any event, saving need not necessarily be accompanied automatically by the creation of new capital goods. If it is not, the result is unemployment. Alternatively, because investment decisions largely are independent of the inclination of consumers and businesses to save, investors may attempt to invest at levels above full-employment saving, that is, above the proportion of total resources being withdrawn from consumption, with resulting inflation. "This has proved to be by far the most serious defect in the capitalist system. It was not the inequity, it was the *instability*, of capitalism which went far to wreck the world in the first half of the twentieth century. Great, advanced, highly developed, wealthy societies simply cannot live with a system the mainspring of which is subject to sudden and arbitrary stoppages, to stoppages which bring ruin to hundreds of millions of human beings." [68: 249]

Third, though subject apparently to countervailing forces which *eventually* correct them (and thus explain the turning points of the cycle), divergences between demand and full-employment supply tend to be cumulative, since falling (rising) spending causes falling (rising) money incomes.

Fourth, no one form of spending (consumption, investment, government, or subdivisions thereof) is uniquely responsible for these problems and relationships. A deficiency (or excess) of spending in one sector of the economy (say, private consumption or investment) can be offset by an expansion (contraction) of spending in some other sector (say, government spending). A cutback in one form of government spending (say, defense) may be offset by an increase in another (say, social welfare) or by an increase in private spending (encouraged, say, by decreased taxation).

Fifth, in the absence of a self-regulatory mechanism built into the internal workings of the capitalist system which automatically guarantees full employment or quickly and easily redirects the economy toward full employment positions if and when it departs from them, some conscious social or collective control mechanism is required. "These issues," suggests W. Arthur Lewis, "are too important to be left to the control of private enterprise." [60: 41] Prior to 1939, aggregate demand repeatedly got "out of hand, because nobody was trying to stop it." [59: 125] The basic reason for periodic under-utilization of productive resources, and thus, unemployment and low output in the midst of potential plenty was "the failure of anybody to control the flow of total demand and adjust it to productive capacity." [59: 126]

Sixth, this failure to formulate rational systems of collective control of aggregate monetary demand was, at least in part, caused by lack of knowledge, by inadequate and faulty economic analysis. "Nobody controlled it," (that is, cyclical economic fluctuations), suggests Jay, "because nobody thought of controlling it, and few were even particularly aware of its existence. Enormous loss and inefficiency were inflicted on the world in unemployment and lost production of wealth ... because the economic system was suffering from a disease which nobody understood." [59: 125–26]

Seventh, from the viewpoint of economic analysis, the depressions and inflations of old-style capitalism were *unnecessary* as well as socially wasteful. Clearly, "all sorts of levers existed which were capable, if intelligently used, of regulating and possibly ironing out altogether these oscillations . . . ." [59: 127] In any event, we now know that cyclical economic fluctuations may be brought under effective social control by methods that are "perfectly capable of curing the disease." [59: 127]

INEQUALITY AND INJUSTICE

Already noted have been the democratic socialist emphasis upon equality as a central goal of economic organization and policy, and that democratic socialists defend their position on the basis of explicit moral value judgments, rather than upon pure economic analysis. We have also noted that the contemporary democratic socialist criterion of justice in the distribution of income is not "perfect equality," but that "minimum practical inequality . . . necessary to ensure that the productive availabilities of the community are reasonably fully used." [59: 8]

The fundamental democratic socialist critique of competitive market capitalism is that it generates inequalities in income and wealth which are larger than both the "minimum practicable inequality" and than that which "should be tolerated in a democracy." [54: 28] "The highest rewards are inordinately high—far higher than any civilized person should want or need; and the lowest are inhumanly low—far lower than any civilized person should have to endure." [54: 28]

The basic cause of these unjust inequalities in industrialized capitalist economic societies, suggest many contemporary democratic socialists, is *not* private ownership of the means of production, but the process of free market exchange. Of course, actual *laissez-faire* economic systems have not typically been purely-perfectly competitive; nor have they been characterized by true equality of opportunity. These factors reinforce and supplement the tendency toward inequality in a capitalist economic society. Thus, the classical liberal and the democratic socialist may concur in the social desirability of eliminating monopolies and restrictive practices which restrict equality of opportunity, and democratic socialists can concur with nineteenth-century liberals that a competitive market economic system "is better for society than a chaos of outdated and sectional restrictions and monopolies." [59: 17] But in the democratic socialist view, equality of opportunity "is not enough" [59: 16] because of the tendencies toward inequality generated by the process of free market exchange.

Even under conditions of pure and perfect competition and equality of opportunity, excessive inequality would still exist: "The free market will almost always, immediately and cumulatively, produce greater inequality than the minimum necessary to get human capacities exercised." Why does the free market process have this result? First, the logic of the case: "Even if all started equal, the differences of ability, cunning and tenacity are so profound between man and man, and luck is so potent, that the clever and fortunate ones would very soon be earning a far higher reward than the minimum required to induce them to exercise their socially useful talents." [59: 16] Second, actual experiences with *laissez-faire* systems has demonstrated that "wherever there has been no conscious collective effort to redistribute incomes, the spectacle of poverty alongside great private wealth has immediately appeared. Where a community is quickly advancing economically, the unbalance takes the form of rapidly emerging enormous fortunes, simultaneously with a great deal of human wreckage." [59: 13–14] Third, economic systems in the last three decades, which have established collective programs for the equalitarian redistribution of income have not experienced lessened effort, production, productivity, or capital formation.

An important cause of inequality, in the democratic socialist view, is private inheritance. The inequalitarian effects of unlimited private inheritance cannot be blamed on free market exchange, for the two processes are quite distinguishable. But if inheritance is uncontrolled in a *laissez-faire* system, "it will immediately and automatically reduplicate the excessive inequality caused by free exchange itself." [59: 16]

Furthermore, in the absence of "built-in equalizers," the pressures for inequality in an affluent and growing economy are likely to be greater rather than less, and in any case, would prove "irresistible." The higher the level of total national income, "the greater the opportunities of amassing high personal fortunes," [59: 29] and thus, the greater the opportunities for acquiring property and supplementing wage or salary with property income. In addition, and somewhat ironically, the full-employment economy generates "the growingly important phenomenon of steady long-term capital gains and rising dividend incomes in the hands of the minority who hold equity shares." [59: 30] "Left to themselves, uncorrected by deliberate social decisions, natural economic forces in a *laissez-faire* regime would, today and in the future, as in the past, generate ever greater inequality." [59: 30]

Even if the distribution of income to wage-earners generated by free market exchange were morally justifiable, insist democratic socialists, a fundamental injustice would still exist. The principle that wage income should vary according to the skill, diligence, or responsibility of the worker does not, therefore, provide a case for determining *family* incomes on the basis of the earning power of the breadwinner. Nor does it support the view that non-workers (the aged, children, unemployed, and so on) should receive no incomes.

A corollary to the inequalitarian character of free market exchange is its effects upon the allocation of resources. The price system, reflecting market demands, biases the allocation of resources toward meeting the "less urgent" needs of the rich while often ignoring the "more urgent demands of the poor." [54: 51] The price system is amoral since it has no basis for weighing the intensity of need of different consumers or the intensity of sacrifice of different producers. "This is not," however, "an argument against the price-mechanism as such, but against the distribution of wealth produced by market forces; and the answer is to be found primarily in a direct attack on this unequal distribution." [54: 51]

In sum, the democratic socialist view is that a *laissez-faire* economy generates "a system of rewards and penalties which are more unequal than is necessary to make the economic machine work, and therefore have no moral validity. These rewards must in turn generate a tendency to growing inequality over time, in both property and income, if private inheritance is also unlimited. Therefore, collective intervention by the democratic State is necessary if social justice is to be achieved . . . . This is the fundamental Socialist criticism of *laissez-faire*, the kernel of the economic case for Socialism." [59: 31, 11]

INDUSTRIAL INEQUALITY AND
AUTOCRACY

But income poverty and income inequality, suggest some democratic socialists, "is merely one outward expression . . . of the power over the lives of mankind which modern industrialism confers upon those who direct industry and control the material equipment upon which both industry and social life depend." The "fundamental grievance" is not income inequality and income poverty. It is that "the government of industry and the utilization both of capital and land are autocratic." [69: 102]

The conditions of economic freedom, insisted late British democratic socialist R. H. Tawney, include not merely the freedom of individuals *from* the oppression of the state or other social bodies, but also the freedom "to associate with others in building up a social organization with a consciousness and corporate life of its own. Economic freedom must develop, in short, through the applications of representative institutions to industry." [69: 103] True industrial freedom must recognize that all workers in an industry constitute a political community and that "in that community, industrial sovereignty,

subject (inevitable contradiction) to the larger sovereignty of the community, resides. Their freedom is simply their corporate power to control the conditions upon which their livelihood depends." [69: 103]

In a capitalist economy, workers do not have that freedom, and lacking it, lack "a proper respect for their dignity as human beings." [69: 141] The worker under capitalism is a "hired hand." He is hired or fired, rewarded or punished, manipulated and controlled as a means to attain the ends of an organization into which he looks, in effect, from outside, and over which he exerts no participatory, democratic control. The relation between "capitalist employer and hired wage-worker . . . is a vicious one . . . because it classifies human beings as a part, and a subordinate one, of the mechanism of production, instead of treating that mechanism merely as an auxiliary to the labour of human beings." [69: 109] In sum:

The revolt against capitalism has its source, not merely in material miseries, but in resentment against an economic system which dehumanizes existence by treating the mass of mankind, not as responsible partners in the cooperative enterprise of subduing nature to the service of man, but as instruments to be manipulated for the pecuniary advantage of a minority of property-owners, who, themselves, in proportion as their aims are achieved, are too often degraded by the attainment of them. The problem now confronting us must be approached on that plane. It is moral, and political, even more than economic. It is a question, not only of the failures of the existing order, but of its standards of success. [69: 139–40]

The Democratic Socialist
Critique of Marxism

Though democratic socialism has never been essentially Marxian in inspiration or content, the postwar years have been characterized by intense development of a democratic socialist critique of both the Marxian analysis of capitalism and the Marxian vision of socialism. This critique has five main dimensions: first, the labor theory of value; second, the surplus value theory of income distribution; third, the theory of crisis, unemployment, and depression; fourth, the theory of transformation of capitalism; fifth, the organization of socialist economy.

LABOR THEORY OF VALUE

Marx's labor theory of value (at least in Volume I of *Capital*), argues Henry Smith in his recent reconsideration of the economics of socialism, "is not a theory of prices at all," for it explains neither why price equals embodied socially necessary labor nor how and why positions of equilibrium will be restored, if initially disturbed. [66: 59, 61] It both ignores the role of non-labor factors and consumer demands in the determination of prices and confuses factual with moral judgments, suggests Douglas Jay. [59: 38]

INCOME DISTRIBUTION

For Marx and Marxists, "it is the *source*, not the size, of incomes that matters. They . . . are and were perfectly prepared to tolerate large *inequalities* of income if they are all derived from work—if they are all earned incomes . . . . But they are not . . . willing to tolerate the existence of any property-derived, *unearned*, income, however small." [68: 99] Many contemporary democratic socialists would say just the opposite. For them, it is (excessive) *inequality* in the size distribution of income, and *not* the *source* of income, which is the basis for a moral critique of capitalism. On the one hand: "If all productive property were publically-owned, but all incomes were allowed to be determined by market forces, and all goods were distributed by the pull of consumers in a free market based on their incomes so received; most of the main forces . . . making for social injustice would operate as powerfully as ever." [59: 21] On the other hand, it is possible through democratic reform to bring substantial decreases in inequality without establishing a comprehensive system of public ownership. It is inequality in the ownership of productive capital, not private ownership *per se*, that constitutes social injustice. For democratic socialists, excessive inequality in wage income is as morally unjust as that in personal income in general. Profits, on the other hand, are neither desirable nor undesirable *per se*. Their justification depends upon the "value of the services rendered" by profit receivers and "the scale of the reward. They are not something to be abolished, but to be brought under social control and tapped for social purposes." [59: 44]

Had Marx based his critique of capitalist income distribution on the moral injustices of its excessive income inequality, generated in part by its excessive inequality in the distribution of property, his case would have been "impregnable." As it was, the Marxian critique confuses logical-factual questions with moral ones and endeavors to support unnecessary moral conclusions with faulty economic analysis. The endeavor to use the labor theory of value both to support the theory of surplus value *and* as as a theory of prices, notes Henry Smith, involved Marx in a basic logical error. If prices equal marginal, variable labor costs, then "wages must equal the value of the marginal product of labor," and surplus and the rate of surplus value (s and s/v) must be zero. If surplus values exist, then prices must exceed marginal, variable labor costs. [66: 66] In Volume I of *Capital*, Marx confused the economic question of the contribution of capital to the creation of valuable output with the quite different social-moral-political question of how capitalists ought to share in the division of national income. In Volume III, Marx abandoned the labor theory of value as a theory explaining the determination of relative prices and the creation of surplus value: "Surplus value . . . arises equally out of the fixed and circulating components of the invested capital. The total capital serves substantially as the creator of values, the instruments of labour as well as the materials of production and labor . . . .

Surplus value arises simultaneously from all portions of invested capital." [Marx, *Capital*, III, p. 48; cited in 66:70] What Marx demonstrates is that capitalism creates surpluses (of income over consumption), *not surplus values.*

But once the labor theory of value is abandoned as an explanation of the determination of surplus values, and the idea of capital (and, perhaps, capitalists) as productive or contributive to the creation of valuable output is accepted, the Marxian critique of property income *per se* must also be recognized as defective. And once this is recognized, the logical basis for the idea that a transformation from a system of private to public ownership is a "*fundamental* part of Socialism" also must be abandoned. If property income is socially unjustified *per se*, then the elimination of private ownership must be, *in itself*, a fundamental aim of Socialism. But if it is inequality in the size distribution of income, and not private ownership *per se*, which is the basis of the Socialist critique, "it follows that public ownership is not some mystic symbol or revolutionary banner, but just one practical means among various others of achieving greater social justice, productive efficiency or social advance" and "must be examined, like other instruments of Socialism such as public control, not on doctrinal grounds, but as contributors to these intelligible ends." [59:45]

INSTABILITY, UNEMPLOYMENT, AND
DEPRESSION

Though Marx correctly identified the possibility and actuality of periodic capitalist crises and depressions and correctly related them to profit rates and deficient levels of purchasing power, Marxian analysis was in error, argues Jay, at three main points: first, in assuming that saving automatically generates corresponding investment; second, in failing to recognize that, as long as investment equals full employment saving (the difference between full employment income and consumption), aggregate demand will be

sufficient to match full employment supply; third, (and most important) in attributing crises, depressions, and unemployment to private ownership of industrial capital rather than to the market system and in failing to recognize the prospective counter-cyclical compensatory role of government. [59: 49–52, 118–20]

THE TRANSFORMATION OF CAPITALISM

Even those democratic socialists who, like John Strachey, look more charitably on Marx's economic analysis, are sharply critical of Marxist political theory, especially Marx's failure to perceive the possibility of the democratic social reform of capitalism. Despite his faulty economic technique, argues Strachey, Marx formulated a more or less systematic and consistent vision of how an industrializing capitalist economy generates economic surpluses of income above consumption, how these surpluses are distributed in the main to a relatively small group of capitalist entrepreneurs, how this group then allocates these surpluses to investment projects in plant and equipment, and how capital investment, in conjunction with capitalist institutions (private ownership, the price system, competition), generate cyclical economic fluctuations, including periodic crises, unemployment, and depression. Marx's prognostications (worker immiserization, increasing monopolization, increasing intensity of cyclical fluctuations), insists Strachey, might well have come true in "*the political and social conditions with which Marx was ... familiar.*" [68: 111] Marx's predictions have, in fact, been overcome or superseded, but only in new-style, "latest-stage" capitalism, "operating in a democratic political environment." [68: 110]

Political democracy in economically developed capitalist economies, contrary to Marx's expectations, have, in fact, been used to reform and modify capitalism in two distinct ways: first, by social legislation to benefit workers and low-income groups at the expense of capitalist-high-income groups;

second, by a variety of measures supporting workers' rights to organize collectively in labor unions and bargain with employers. Somewhat paradoxically, "it has been, precisely, the struggle of the democratic forces *against* capitalism which has saved the system." [68: 185] The Marxist (and especially, Leninist) failure to understand or recognize the power of democratic governments to reform capitalism constitutes a fundamental error—but, in political perception, not necessarily in economic vision, given the political and social conditions of the nineteenth century.

The defects of the Marxian analysis of political democracy in a capitalist economic society reflect a general failure to perceive latter-stage capitalism and its prospective transition to new or different systems of economic organization. Even if capitalism cannot survive, argues Crosland in a Schumpeter-like statement, "any other than a tautological definition of socialism as the system which succeeds capitalism must allow the possibility of the disappearance of the one without the advent of the other." There is "no reason in logic or history why the succession should inevitably pass to socialism . . . ." [55: 45, 46] It conceivably could pass to Communism; it has, in fact, at times passed to fascism; and, in fact, it is currently passing to modified or managed capitalism.

SOCIALISM

Democratic socialists object to a number of features in the Marxist and neo-Marxist vision(s) of the road to and organization of socialism. Three general points merit mention. First, democratic socialists are advocates, as well as analysts. They have long advocated the desirability and pointed to the distinct possibility of peaceful, democratic routes to or toward socialism. Second, "socialism," as envisaged by contemporary neo-Marxist centralized socialists, is essentially a system for organizing and planning the industrialization of economically underdeveloped, and often non- or pre-democratic nations.

"Socialism," as envisaged by democratic socialists, is essentially a system for social reform and promotion of equality and social justice in economically developed and democratic economic societies. Thus, although inspired in part by certain elements in the Marxian vision (such as worker control of industry), contemporary democratic socialists take a radically non-Marxian view of public versus private ownership and a radically non-neo-Marxian view on the role of the price or market system versus and in relation to comprehensive government economic planning and controls.

The Democratic Socialist Critique of Modified, Managed Capitalism

Contemporary democratic socialists view modified or managed capitalism as a new system of economic organization distinctly different from the old-style capitalism which it succeeded. Capitalism, suggests C. A. R. Crosland [55: 38], is currently in the "process of metamorphosis into a qualitatively different kind of society." Modified or managed capitalism " . . . represents a major social revolution. With its arrival, the most characteristic features of capitalism have all disappeared: the absolute rule of private property, the subjection of the whole of economic life to market influences, the domination of the profit motive, the neutrality of government, the typical *laissez-faire* division of income, and the ideology of individual rights. This is no minor modification: it is major historical change." [55: 43]

This revolutionary transformation, which has taken place to a greater extent in some countries (such as the United Kingdom, Sweden) and a lesser extent in others (such as the United States, West Germany), *seems* less revolutionary than the transition to capitalism because of the "sensational change in economic technique" [55: 46] and associated social disruptions which *that* transformation entailed. Similarly, a transition from modified capitalism to socialism, were it to occur, would not seem revolutionary because of the surface continuity of economic technique in a modern industrialized society.

Causal factors in this transformation to managed capitalism have been essentially three: first, the political pressures for democratic social reform brought to bear during the last half century by labor and socialist and/or social reform movements and parties; second, the nature of capitalist development itself, especially the transformation of ownership from a system of owner-management to one of essentially non-owner-management; third, the impact of war, which stimulated growth in the size and roles of government in the economy, in government economic planning and regulation of business, and in left-wing governments, making it impossible for post-war economic societies to recapture the relative pre-war purity. [55: 37]

Crosland cites eight features of the "new society" which distinguish it from old-style capitalism [55: 38–42]:

1. The transformation of property: In new-style capitalism, property relations no longer "determine the distribution of economic power."

2. The creation of a new, non-owning, salaried managerial class, less tender in its concern for stockholders and more cooperative with government.

3. The elimination of "the absolute autonomy of economic life" by a large-scale increase in the economic role of government— through limited government ownership, direct controls over and regulation of business, and general budgetary policy to affect the level and distribution of income.

4. The creation of the modern welfare state through a large-scale increase in social security and public welfare expenditures, with the attendant consequences of: reduction of economic insecurity and, thereby, social discontent; generation of greater equality through accompanying taxation of upper-income brackets; and

extension of government intervention in the economy.

5. The substantial elimination of chronic depression and large-scale unemployment through the application of essentially Keynesian methods of public control, accompanied by the stabilizing effects of social reforms, such as the extension of social security systems, redistributive taxation, and expansion in the size of government demand itself.

6. The maintenance of more or less steady, continuous economic growth and accompanying increasing living standards.

7. The creation of greater pluralism in the structure of social classes, partly through increased living standards, partly through a decrease in the size of the "strict factory working class" and an increase in the size of the technical, professional, and managerial class, and partly through the permeation of "middle-class psychology" throughout society.

8. An ideological shift from emphasis upon property rights, profits, private initiative, and competition toward emphasis upon security, cooperative action, and government responsibilities.

These changes represent "an impressive advance as judged by socialist standards." [55: 44] "It is a major victory for the Left" that these changes have been accepted, in the main, by conservatives and liberals as well as socialists and that a general consensus exists in modified capitalism that government has the responsibility to promote or control "(1) the level of employment, (2) the protection of the foreign balance . . . , (3) the level of investment and the rate of growth, (4) the maintenance of a welfare minimum, and (5) the conditions under which monopolies should be allowed to operate." [53: 342]

Furthermore, these changes, coupled with the greater diffusion of economic power (among old capitalists, new managers, government, and labor unions), by reducing economic strains and social tensions, have undoubtedly contributed to the political and social stability of new-style capitalism. Given an equilibrium in the socio-political balance of power among pluralistic economic groups, the decreased pressures for radical change, and the reestablishment of the "normal historical pattern ... of conscious control over social and economic life, the new society may prove to be a very enduring one." [55: 44–45]

Thus, in the contemporary democratic socialist view, modified or managed capitalism does not face imminent collapse and has largely brought the most dramatic problem of old-style capitalism—large-scale depression and unemployment—under public control. By expanding employment and social security and partially reducing excessive inequalities in wealth and income, "the new society is infinitely more humane and decent than the old." [55: 44] But these accomplishments, laudable though they are, suggest democratic socialists, fall short of the ideal of the democratic-participatory-equalitarian-classless society of democratic socialism.

Despite the accomplishments of democratic social reform, suggests Crosland [55: 62], Great Britain does not "begin to approach the ideal of a classless society." The question, maintains English Laborite Roy Jenkins [55: 72], is "whether the society which is growing out of capitalism is to be a participant, democratic socialist society, or whether it is to be a managerial society, controlled by a privileged elite enjoying a standard of living substantially different from that of the mass of the population." However technically or economically successful the reforms of modified or managed capitalism, especially in the area of government ownership, argues Austen Albu [55: 121], they have "not satisfied the desire for a wider and more democratic distribution of authority nor built up any real measure of participation (by workers in nationalized industries) in managerial decisions and their execution." If democratic socialist ideals of equality, social justice, and democracy are to be realized, further and extensive modification and social reform of managed capitalism is necessary, leading, finally, to a transition to a new form of economic organization, qualitatively different not only from old-style capitalism but from new-style, managed capitalism as well.

RECENT DEMOCRATIC SOCIALIST
PROGRAMS AND PROPOSALS

For comparative purposes, recent democratic socialist programs and proposals will be examined in terms of major dimensions of economic behavior and performance: (1) allocation of resources; (2) distribution of income and wealth; (3) economic stabilization and growth. Illustrations will be drawn chiefly from the writings of Douglas Jay and C. A. R. Crosland, prominent British contributors to the critical reinterpretation of democratic socialism.

Jay, one of England's leading socialist economists, seeks "to restate the case for democratic Socialism in the world of the 1960s, and in the light of the 1940s and 1950s." [59: Author's Note.] Crosland, at various times in his career a member of Parliament, economics professor, and a Minister of Education in Harold Wilson's Labour Party government, has provided a scholarly re-evaluation and revision of socialist economics [53] and has outlined a "program of radical Left-wing reform" of managed capitalism. [54] Though primarily concerned with the British case, both make frequent cross-references to the United States.

Both present the case for and the content of what they believe to be a distinctively "democratic socialist" program for the latter third of the twentieth century, distinguishable not only from old-style pre-1929 capitalism and contemporary conservative economic nostrums, but from the New Deal–Fair Deal, liberal–labor democratic social reforms of the last 40 years as well. In doing so, however, they also demonstrate, perhaps unwittingly, how much the democratic socialist viewpoint has been absorbed by nonsocialist reform of capitalism and how difficult it is to retain the traditional dichotomy of capitalism versus socialism and the traditional vision of a distinctively "socialist" economic society.

Allocation of Resources

Crosland distinguishes neatly between two distinct types of allocational decisions: "first, what proportion of total resources is to be allocated to collective public spending . . . secondly, how the remaining resources, which are available for spending by individuals or enterprises (whether public or private) are to be allocated between different uses . . . ." [54: 14]

ALLOCATION OF RESOURCES BETWEEN PUBLIC AND PRIVATE SPENDING

Democratic socialists contend that the level of public spending for collective purposes, especially for "overcoming poverty, distress, and social squalor," is too low in contemporary mixed economies like the United States and the United Kingdom and that "exceptional priority" should be given to these in relation to other claims on resources. [54: 11] "The main case for devoting more ample resources to the public services rests on the unchallengeable judgment that a human being's need for a decent home, medical care, contentment in old age, and the protection of the law are more important than the need for a radio set in his car or an ornamental cigarette holder, or even a second washing machine." [59: 218] Despite increases in public spending for these purposes in recent years, their provision still remains excessively low, not only in relation to real and important human needs, but also to "a proper civilized standard," [59: 222] to the growth in the affluence of private consumption, and (in the United Kingdom at least) to the levels of attainment of other countries.

Jay reaches this essentially Galbraithian conclusion at least partly on the basis of Galbraithian reasoning. [56] First, "the fantastic rise of modern advertising" demonstrates not only that consumer demands for many products marketed by the private sector of the economy are low in the order of priority, but also that advertising "itself materially, if not massively, for this very reason distorts production into serving less rather than more urgent and acute needs." [59: 218, 219] Second, the price system provides an automatic and spontaneous process for expressing consumer demands for marketable products and services which is absent in the area of public services. Third, recognizing the redistributive impact of public service expenditures, "the lucky or clever minority who benefit from a market-ridden society" support and finance propaganda campaigns denigrating improvements in public services as "national extravagance." [59: 216–17] These basic factors are complicated by the "further all-pervading weakness" of "*under-payment in the public services*," [59: 221] which draws away the ablest civil servants and contributes to the degeneration in the quality of the services provided.

Crosland contends that advertising and the price system have their greatest effects upon the allocation (or mis-allocation) of resources among particular areas *within* the private sector, and that the social imbalance *between* the private and public sectors can be explained in terms of four major factors. "The first and most decisive is political." [54: 22] Given the ceiling for public spending determined by what the democratic electorate is willing to forego from private income, the actual level will depend upon whether a left-wing or right-wing government is in power. The latter, because of its priorities and values, will allocate less for public spending than the former, and it is this conservative, anti-public sector philosophy which "is the prime cause of the present imbalance." [54: 15] Supplementing this are: the character of the tax system (are taxes closely "geared to income and spending so that their yield rises proportionately (or more) with rising national income?"); the rate of economic growth (the faster the growth, "the larger the annual increase in revenue"); and the "cultural tradition and outlook of the society" (its traditions of individualism versus concern for "collective welfare"). [54: 22–23]

Crosland's proposed solutions to the problem of social imbalance stem directly from his identification of these four causal forces: "Its solution in Britain requires, first, a considerable reform of the tax structure to make it more efficiently responsive to rising income; secondly, a sharp acceleration of the rate of growth, so that the annual increment of revenue is ample as well as automatic; thirdly, a savage and sustained offensive ... against the national vices of materialism, philistinism and social separatism; lastly, and pre-eminently, a Labour Government, which, being emotionally committed to creating a public sector of which we can be proud, will increase the proportion of income allotted to social purposes." [54: 27] Jay's solution is broader: "Nothing will cure this [social imbalance] but a complete revolution in our attitude to these services, and determination that they should be expanded as a matter of national pride, and not squeezed by petty prejudice and greed." [59: 221–22]

ALLOCATION OF RESOURCES AMONG
DIFFERENT PARTICULAR USES

Given the allocation of resources between public and private spending, both Jay and Crosland, "within defined limits," [59: 216] support the maintenance and utilization of a market pricing system as a social process for allocating resources to particular uses. The positive case for this position rests, first, "on the great practical convenience and agility of the free market" [59: 216] both in expressing consumer demands and in guiding the allocation of resources by producers to most closely meeting those demands; and, second, on the value judgments ("which every radical and social democrat must passionately endorse") that "individuals should have what

they want, and that they themselves are the best judges of what they want." [54: 37]

The validity of these conclusions is not essentially modified, insists Crosland, by the recognition of real world "imperfections" (consumer irrationality, interdependence of preferences, resource immobilities) and of the price system's failure to yield some "verifiably 'ideal' output which maximizes consumer satisfaction," [54: 53] first, because the major alternative to the price system, in a complex, industrialized society, is government fiat or centralized allocation, which restricts freedom of individual choice and lacks flexibility; second, because "ideal output" is a textbook exercise, not a practical reality. For all its imperfections, "consumer choice does roughly decide what is profitable, and profitability does roughly decide what is produced." [54: 54]

Indeed, continues Crosland, these conclusions even retain their rough-hewn validity despite the existence of large-scale advertising and the market power of corporations, which give them "wide latitude in deciding their price and production policies." [54: 53] The traditional criticisms of advertising (waste, manipulation of consumer preferences) are exaggerated,[2] while its positive functions (provision of information, introduction of new products, encouragement of mass consumption) are often overlooked by social critics. Similarly, in regard to business monopoly: "While most large firms wield a substantial amount of market power, they are subject to a substantial amount of actual and potential competition," [54: 60] including that from new entrants, interindustry competition, and from foreign firms establishing subsidiaries in the United Kingdom. Further: "As to the trend through time, we have as yet no definite evidence that the degree of concentration either in individual industries (that

[2]Crosland estimates the purely manipulative, non-informative type of sales promotion as between one-half and one percent of the national income in the United Kingdom, and thus, a minor problem compared with others discussed in this chapter. [54: 61]

is, the percentage share of employment controlled by the three largest firms in each industry), or in the economy as a whole (that is, the proportion of total assets controlled by the 100 largest firms) has altered significantly over the last 30 or 50 years." [54:59] Lastly, the corporation's social as well as market power are confined within narrow limits: first, subjectively, the new business managers and "other-directed organization men" of the mid-twentieth century are an "apologetic," "constantly nervous," and "jellyfish" lot in comparison with the "masterful" and "contemptuous" indusrial lords of the past; second, objectively, corporate power is "limited by strong Trade Unions, a seller's market for labour due to full employment, a growing consumer movement, the countervailing power of nationalized industries and large distributive organization, the fear of a Labour Government, and an intense sensitivity to their public 'image' in the light of an altered climate of opinion . . . . Above all, the corporation is confined by the actions of government. We see an irresistible trend towards increasing intervention by government in the economic life of the country; and business now operates within a web of public control which would have been unimaginable in the old days of *laissez-faire*." [54:55–56]

Still, not unsurprisingly, Crosland has a number of recommendations in the areas of sales promotion-consumer choice and corporate monopoly power. In regard to the former, he makes four proposals: "First, the Government should formulate a clear consumer policy . . ." [54:65] in relation, for example, to resale price maintenance (abolish it), imports (encourage them), monopolies (discourage them), descriptive-labeling and quality standards legislation (pass them), and consumer protection (establish a "consumer Department of State" and "an independent Consumer Council to supervise the whole field of consumer protection . . ."). Second, give vigorous support to the coopera-

tive movement, "which could and should play a vital and dynamic pro-consumer role, pioneering and pace-setting in respect of prices, quality, and design, and always leading the fight against undue producer-domination." [54:65] Third, support the expansion of voluntary consumer and civic organizations. Fourth, "impose a heavy tax on advertising" consisting of (1) a graduated excise tax assessed on the price of advertising (but exempting genuinely informative advertising, such as classified advertisements) and (2) a tax on total sales promotional outlays of business firms assessed "according to the proportion which advertising bears to the final price of the product." This would discriminate in favor of informative advertisements but "encourage price-reductions as an alternative to promotional competition." [54:63]

In regard to government policy toward business monopoly, Crosland recommends a battery of new measures, including encouragement of the growth of the consumer movement, abolition of resale price maintenance (already mentioned), the extension of restrictive practices legislation to cover informal, as well as formal, price agreements, increased investigations of monopoly, the establishment of legal power to prevent any large-scale merger which "significantly restricts the degree of competition," and the election of a government which readily "*believes* in an anti-monopoly policy . . . ." [54:30]

Distribution of Income and Wealth

PAST MEASURES

Reduction of inequality in the distribution of income and wealth to "minimum practicable limits" is the most important and distinctive element in contemporary democratic socialist thought. How do contemporary democratic socialists propose to accomplish this? Because they do not believe inequality is caused primarily by private ownership, as such, democratic socialists contend that a massive shift to a system of government ownership would provide no real solution. The necessity of compensating private owners for publicly-acquired property imposes an additional limitation upon this route as a path toward equality. The most direct route is that of public finance, that is, a redistributive fiscal policy. In the past, this has taken the form primarily of progressive income taxation coupled with the extension of public services which have often tended to make greater contributions to the living standards of lower-, than of higher-, income individuals and families. Most democratic socialists support continued progressivity in the tax structure and further extensions of public services, especially in such areas as housing, pensions, and education.

As already noted, however, the democratic socialist case for increased public services rests significantly upon the social imbalance argument rather than exclusively upon redistributional grounds. Further, both of these classic redistributive fiscal measures (progressive taxation and public services) have distinct limitations as means to attain socialist ends. First, the marginal rates of income taxation, especially in the United Kingdom, though perhaps not yet at incentives limits, are probably fairly close. Second, because of the redistribution already achieved by income taxation-public expenditures in the past, any large-scale extension of free social services would "be paid for not by the rich, whose present untaxed income would be quite insufficient, but by the broad mass of the population—in other words, by the recipients of the new services. Thus no redistributive effect between rich and poor would be achieved." Once minimum levels of income security have been established, "further advances in the national income should normally go to citizens in the form of 'free' income, to be spent as they wish, and not be taxed away and then returned in the form of some free services determined by the fiat of the state." [Crosland, in 55: 63.]

CURRENT PROPOSALS

Beyond the traditional welfare state measures of modified or managed capitalism lies the vision of democratic socialism, and to realize this aspiration, contemporary socialists make other and more imaginative proposals: First, widen the base of taxable income. In addition to new measures to curb "legal or quasi-legal avoidance" of taxes [59: 268], both Crosland and Jay recommend the establishment of a capital gains tax (which did not exist in the United Kingdom in the early 1960s, but was passed by Harold Wilson's Labour Government in 1965) and "more stringent" restrictions on allowable business expenses, such as business entertainment, company automobiles, and (as noted) advertising as devices to accomplish this. [59: 269; 54: 35; 55: 77]

Second, reform the tax structure to shift a larger share of taxation from wage and salary incomes to property incomes. Jay's recommendation here is twofold: (1) the preservation and expanded use of the business profits tax, "which has in recent years been collecting a smaller share of profits in taxation than in the United States," [59: 265] and (2) a dual rate profits tax system, which weighs more heavily upon distributed than undistributed profits. Crosland agrees with Jay on (2), suggesting government policy should attempt to separate "profit as a surplus income accruing to the rich, and deserving by every socialist canon to be squeezed; and profit as a surplus for accumulation and expansion, deserving by every (sensible) socialist canon to be enlarged," [53: 304] but has reservations in regard to (1), both because of the contributions of business profits to saving and investment, and because of the relative ease with which profits taxes are shifted to consumers in the form of higher prices anyway. Lastly, Jay eyes longingly Nicholas Kaldor's proposed "expenditure tax"[3] (a tax on income

---

[3]Cf. Nicholas Kaldor, *An Expenditures Tax*, (London: Allen and Unwin, 1955).

minus saving plus dis-saving) which would recognize that "an owner of inherited capital can live on capital gains and enjoy a much higher standard of living than an active worker" and would also encourage saving and discourage consumption from dis-saving, calling it "the ideally fair type of progressive tax on 'income'," but doubts it could be practicable in administration, "even in the enormously expert hands of the United Kingdom Inland Revenue . . . ." [59: 270]

Third are proposals to reduce barriers to entry into various occupations and thereby to "reduce the disparities in pre-tax rewards from work." [54: 35] The single most important area here is education: "Overwhelmingly the most important cause of artificial scarcity is our educational system, which still disastrously restricts the opportunities for acquiring skill, training and intelligence." [54: 37] Education is not only a great equalizer; it is also a key to rising productivity and economic growth and to the attainment of the opportunity for all human beings to live in the civilized way that economic affluence and equality in income distribution permits. The Labour Party, asserts Crosland, should "make educational spending [its] . . . overriding domestic issue." [54: 179] The Jay-Crosland proposals in regard to English education are essentially two: (1) Increase significantly the proportion of national resources allocated to education. (2) Reform the British dual educational system—state and "public" [read 'private']—which is "a barrier to equality of opportunity" and breeds "the worst sort of snobbery," [59: 248–49] and "socially devisive influence." [54: 178]

Fourth are proposals to modify "the maldistribution of property, which is really grotesque." [54: 37][4] "This distribution is far more unequal than that of work-incomes. It is also more indefensible, since property often stems from inheritance and not from personal effort; more significant for the extremes of wealth, since the higher up the income-scale, the greater the ratio of property-income to total income; more significant for the creation of new extremes . . . and more significant for real living standards inasmuch as property confers advantages far greater than are measured by the income to which it gives rise." [54: 37–38]

These proposals focus upon two major areas: taxation and saving-investment policy. The saving-investment recommendations are an integral part of proposals regarding social ownership, public investment, and government policy toward saving, and will be discussed in a later section.

Democratic socialist proposals regarding property taxation are several: (1) a capital gains tax (as alredy noted in another connection); (2) death taxes; (3) a general gift tax (the absence of which largely negates the effectiveness of the death tax); and (4) an annual property tax ("capital levy"). The first causes democratic socialists some concern. Though a form of capital taxation, and thus, a basis for attacking inequality at its roots rather than its "surface manifestations," and though eminently practicable as affirmed by past experience with it in the United States [Jenkins in 55: 77], it has distinct limitations: It "can do nothing to reduce existing stores of wealth; it can only moderate the speed at at which they can be increased"; in addition, it would probably have a greater "disincentive effect than almost any other form of property taxation" and "would hit the active capitalist as opposed to the established proprietor . . . ." [55: 78] The second has none of these objections: "They are not markedly disincentive, they hit all forms of wealth equally, and they are certainly able, over a period, substantially to deplete existing stores of wealth." [55: 78] The third functions chiefly to close a major loophole in death duties. The purpose of (4) is to recognize and incorporate into the tax

---

[4]"Less than 2% of adult persons in Britain own 50% of total personal net capital; 10% of persons own nearly 80%; while 75% of persons must be content with less than 9% of the wealth." [54: 37 Cf. Lydall and Tipping, "The Distribution of Personal Wealth in Britain," in *Bulletin of the Oxford University Institute of Statistics*, February 1961.]

system the fact that the power to spend and control, thereby, the allocation of resources is a function of wealth as well as income. Taxes based upon income, no matter how progressive, "fail completely to measure . . . true taxable capacity; consider the case of an elderly millionaire widower who keeps his money in the bank—his spending power is enormous, but his income and his tax-liability are zero." [54: 38–39]

Economic Stabilization and Growth

FULL EMPLOYMENT

Contemporary democratic socialist proposals for the promotion of full employment read like a primer on post-Keynesian macroeconomics. Because unemployment and depression, like inequality in income and wealth, are not caused primarily by private ownership, they contend, a massive shift to government ownership is unnecessary to promote high-level employment and production. A strategy for the promotion of full-employment, suggests Jay, is essentially simple: "We know that there are many methods by which an intelligent Government can control total demand; and that much the most important are public finance affecting the flow of incomes directly, and the banking and credit system affecting it more indirectly." [59: 128] Through some combination of tax cuts, government spending increases, and/or increases in the supply of money (and accompanying decreases in interest rates), a democratic government has the power to manipulate the aggregate level of monetary demand and raise it to optimum levels. "The one truth which stands out as indisputably valid about the management of a modern economy is that either a cut in taxation or rise in public spending or both can quickly and certainly restore total demand to almost any extent required. . . ." If these measures "are resolutely applied," they can "normally cure any tendency to old-fashioned cyclical depression and unemployment." [59: 130–31]

These hypotheses are supported by empirical experiences as well as by the logic of economic analysis, argues Jay. Although not entirely successful (largely because of conservative timidity in applying them), postwar monetary and fiscal policies have played a significant role in keeping the level of unemployment much lower, and the growth in output much more steady, than before World War II. "The evidence is thus pretty overwhelming that the old scourge of the trade cycle and mass unemployment has been scotched, if not killed, since 1945." And: "We can thus now see clearly that the basic trouble in the past century has been very little connected, one way or the other, with the issue of public or private ownership. It is not private ownership . . . which caused the old cycle of unemployment. It was a periodic lack of total demand, due to the absence of any collective plan for controlling it." [59: 136–37] The central remaining problem is to "have the courage and intelligence to use our knowledge" to achieve attainable goals. [59: 147]

PRICE STABILITY

Toward the goal of price stability, the essential task is, when necessary, to reverse expansionary monetary and fiscal policies; that is, to increase taxes, decrease government spending, and/or decrease the supply of money to curb excessive monetary demand at full employment. The case for maintaining price stability is essentially threefold; inflation: first, causes "social injustice" by penalizing some segments of society (such as fixed-income receivers) while rewarding other segments handsomely; second, "beyond a point," generates "secondary effects" (increases in the propensity to consume, a flight from money to goods) which add to inflation; third, causes balance of payments deficits by increasing imports and decreasing exports.

Of course, the ideal case would be full employment with no inflation. But full employment is more likely a "zone," rather than a point, and *some* inflation may occur prior to the attainment of full employment when full employment policies are followed. If and when this occurs (and the extent to which it does and/or must do so, suggests Jay, has probably been exaggerated,) a choice must be made, illustrated by the practical question: "How much risk of rising prices is worth incurring for the sake of how much expansion?" [59: 156] For "all who value social justice highly," the normal choice "must surely be" to push on toward full employment, "to take the risk of slightly rising prices rather than the risk of substantial unemployment." [59: 156] This is so for three central reasons: First, mild inflation causes minor economic hardship for many people (who can, however, be largely compensated,) while unemployment "inflicts severe and concentrated hardship on a minority." [59: 156] Second, cumulative inflation, via the "secondary effects," "do not come into play if the movement of prices is only slight." [59: 156–57] Third, output is lost from unemployment, which could contribute significantly to the reduction of world poverty and/or to increased domestic living standards. The choice thus is *not* a distributional one, between one sector of society and another, but between increasing benefits for the entire society with "a little intelligent management and planning to ensure that distribution does not go awry, and on the other hand, foregoing these general gains in order to avoid the trouble of distributing them fairly." [59: 157] "Socialists used to be accused of being so obsessed with the need for a juster distribution that they ignored the need for higher production which would benefit all. Today, paradoxically, it is the Socialists advocating expansion who champion higher incomes all round, and the deflationists and 'hard money men' who are obsessed with the distributive difficulties caused by rising prices. From the point of view of society as a whole, the wise policy must be to push expansion at least to the limit here suggested, with all the promise this holds for a vigorous, dynamic and less restrictionist economy, and to use intelligently all the available instruments of planning to ease and oil the frictions and jolts which may be caused." [59: 157]

ECONOMIC GROWTH

Economic growth involves essentially two central facets: *primarily*, the full utilization of the existing labor force and plant capacity; and *secondly*, the increase in that capacity through increased investment and technological improvements. [59: 147] Though modern democratic governments have a battery of techniques to affect the second of these two facets of growth (education, encouragement of private saving and investment, public investment, and so on), their major reliance can be on the first. "A modern industrial economy which maintains reasonably full employment and invests at a moderate rate can advance its real national income from three percent or four percent a year. This would indeed enable its people to double their standard of living in less than 25 years. If a material proportion—but not all—of this investment is steered to less developed countries, a rapid advance in the world's standards would almost certainly be possible. The discovery of the possibility of intelligently planning the flow of demand can, therefore, make all the difference between poverty and affluence for the world." [59: 139]

FROM MANAGED CAPITALISM
TO DEMOCRATIC SOCIALISM?

Granting that contemporary democratic socialists have accepted freedom, equality, full employment, growth, efficiency, and price stability as their goals and have identified a number of means to better attain them, what is the role in their analysis for such traditional socialist proposals as social ownership, government planning, and worker control of industry? Would the adoption of democratic socialist proposals in these areas establish an economic system significantly distinguishable from managed capitalism?

Or is democratic socialism evaporating as a vision of a distinctly different system of economic organization?

Social Ownership

THE TRADITIONAL DEMOCRATIC SOCIALIST CASE FOR SOCIAL OWNERSHIP

The traditional democratic socialist case for social ownership was essentially twofold. On the one hand, it was seen as a strategic means to control economic power by transferring it from the private sector to some social body (typically government) more representative of the entire community. Removing ownership from private hands would remove the ability to utilize it as a private vehicle for the creation and maintenance of inequalities in wealth and income, and thereby, class privilege and status. On the other hand, through its power to control the employment and direction of resources, social ownership would enable the community to pursue social purposes (that is, equality, stability, cooperation) more effectively.

In the years prior to World War II, this general case was supplemented by more specific arguments pertinent to particular industries. These include: (1) public utilities (because of their position of "natural monopoly"); (2) monopolies (to prevent monopolistic and monopsonistic exploitation of consumers and workers); (3) "basic industries" and financial enterprises (because of their strategic, widespread impact and importance); and (4) industries in which efficiency would improve through reorganization, economies of large-scale production, or decrease in the redundancy of competition, and/or where government planning (facilitated by social ownership) could yield a higher level and more stable flow of investment. [53: 312–15]

Because democratic socialism emerged and evolved as a movement for the economic reform of capitalism, the establishment of social ownership in these industries, taken as a unit, came to be regarded as capable of removing the major bases of private economic power and providing the community with a powerful vehicle for the pursuit of social ends. In addition, public enterprises in these sectors of the economy were expected to function both as examples and pace-setters (in price, output, and investment policy, labor-management relations, and so on) and as vehicles for the regulation of private enterprise (for example, in wage determination).

REVISION OF TRADITIONAL VIEWS ON SOCIAL OWNERSHIP

Especially since World War II, democratic socialists in Western Europe and elsewhere have revised and moderated the traditional view toward social ownership. On the one hand, democratic socialists have increasingly emphasized the need for and desirability of a mixture of private and public ownership, thereby shifting emphasis from socialization in general to socialization of basic industries. On the other hand, they have increasingly underscored the desirability of forms of social ownership other than nationalization, thereby shifting emphasis from governmental to social ownership. Democratic socialists attribute these shifts in emphasis to four major factors:

First, a key issue in any society is the locus of power to make economic decisions and control their execution to attain individual and/or social goals. In contrast to Marxist and neo-Marxist orthodoxy on this issue, the contemporary democratic socialist view is that ownership is not the key to economic power and control. Within the private sector of the economy, the "separation of ownership and control" and the rise to power of new, non-owning corporate managers has reduced the significance of ownership *per se*. In the public sector, it has been discovered that effective government control over the national economy and over particular firms does not necessarily require large-scale government ownership. Second, and also in contrast to the Marxist position, private ownership is not now considered a primary cause of capitalism's major economic problems (inequality, instability and unemployment, social imbalance between collective and marketable goods). Thus, the classic case for a large-scale substitution of government for private ownership has evaporated. Third, socialism is about ends, not means, and government ownership is merely *one* of several possible *means* to attain socialist ends. "We are all empiricists now," says Jay. *"The general advance in fact to public ownership should be empirical and various according to the needs and merits of the case . . . ."* [59: 323, 329] Fourth, because the major goals of democratic socialism—a "higher working class standard of living, more effective joint consultation, better labour relations, a proper use of economic resources, a wider diffusion of power, a greater degree of cooperation, . . . more social and economic equality"—may be attained by a variety of means and because public ownership has a number of defects and problems of its own, a large-scale shift in the locus of ownership in managed capitalist economies is neither a necessary nor a sufficient condition for the realization of socialist aspirations. None of these goals, argues Crosland, "primarily require a large-scale change in ownership for their fulfillment; still less is such a change a *sufficient* condition of their fulfillment." [53: 323]

Beyond these general observations, the contemporary re-evaluation of the democratic socialist position on social ownership includes both a critique of state monopoly as the most suitable form of social ownership and a series of proposals and guidelines in regard to the role of social ownership in the process of movement from managed capitalism to socialism.

THE DEMOCRATIC SOCIALIST CRITIQUE
OF STATE MONOPOLY

The recent programmatic literature of democratic socialism contains repeated references to the need to reconsider the traditional socialist commitment to nationalization of entire industries, or "state monop-

oly," as a suitable form of social ownership. A case may be made for state monopoly in select, strategic, and limited areas of national economy: as in "natural monopoly" (public utilities); where some service is "an essential instrument of public policy" (such as the Bank of England); where an industry "dominates an entire community or district, and large-scale operation is necessary at the same time" (such as coal); or where it is "the only practicable instrument" for mobilizing and investing large-scale capital for modernization and expansion (for example, atomic energy, coal, railroads). [59: 296–97] But beyond these special and limited instances, there is *no general case* for an expansion of state monopoly; and these areas are precisely the ones which already have been nationalized in countries like Great Britain.

As a corollary to this, once a limited number of selected, strategic industries have been nationalized, as in Great Britain, remaining industries are and tend to become increasingly less suitable for nationalization. In reference to Britain, for example, Crosland suggests that with relatively minor exceptions, there "are no more public utilities," no more "basic industries," and no more pure or near-pure monopolies. Remaining non-nationalized industries are generally "unsuitable for old-model nationalization." They are (often) competitive, large-scale oligopolies, not monopolies; and it is by no means clear that government monopoly and/or an increase in the scale of plants or firms would increase efficiency. Non-nationalized industries have "indistinct boundaries," produce a heterogeneous and "diversified range of output," and face a relatively unstable final demand. In addition to these structural characteristics, firms in non-nationalized industries are not clearly inefficient or unprogressive, at least not sufficiently to justify large-scale shifts in ownership. [53: 321]

In addition, socialists need to overcome their illusions and grandiloquent expectations in regard to state monopoly. It is not effective to immediately redistribute income from owners to workers. (Because of the necessity of compensation, government ownership cannot do this; because of its direct impact upon the income stream, public finance can.) It does not automatically transfer power from private owners and/or managers to workers or by itself establish industrial democracy or worker control of industry. (So long as firms are to be managed in the interest of the community, much of the traditional relation between managers and workers is bound to remain.) It does not automatically create or guarantee increased efficiency. ("Efficiency has little to do with ownership because in the modern corporation, ownership has little to do with control. Thus, a change in ownership, by itself, makes little difference." 53: 325) The problems faced by, and the economic behavior of, large-scale corporations are essentially similar, regardless of the form of ownership. Corporate efficiency depends essentially upon managerial quality and structural and technical organization of firms. An extension of government ownership will increase efficiency only if (1) it injects better managers and/or (2) it fosters better structural or technical adaptation within industries. If these things are not done, corporate efficiency may easily prove to be lower under governmental than under private ownership. In sum: "An economic improvement may follow from public ownership where the existing industry is clearly performing poorly, where competition either cannot or is not permitted to enforce an improvement, where physical or fiscal controls are incapable of curing the situation, and where public ownership will not bring attendant disadvantages of its own."[5] The number of cases meeting these conditions in a managed capitalist economy characterized by limited government ownership is not likely to be large.

Lastly, the state monopoly has a number of distinct disadvantages. One of its fundamental defects in relation to other forms of social ownership is "it inevitably involves some restriction on personal freedom," [59: 298] since it forbids the production of the product or service in question by private individuals. This is an academic matter in, say, the production of coal, gas, or electricity. But any extension of state monopoly beyond the traditional areas of public utilities and "natural monopolies" into manufacturing and the distributive trades would entail increasing restrictions upon individual economic freedom. Supplementing this fundamental disadvantage are a number of more practical defects, including "inflexibility of movement, due partly to statutory limitations and partly to fear of public opinion" and the "acute difficulty" of defining and demarcating the boundaries of the industry to be nationalized. If state monopoly is substituted for private competition, the traditional advantages of competition in promoting efficiency and providing alternative choices for consumers is or may be lost. Possible technical economies of scale through an increase in the size of plants may be more than offset by worker and managerial diseconomies because of the increased complexity and excessive centralization generated by the increase in the size of the enterprise to encompass entire industries. In conclusion: "Socialists will thus be wise to recognize that the State monopoly form was devised to suit an earlier age which British manufacture and commerce have now largely outgrown . . . . In the future there may be few manufacturing 'industries' left which can be compressed into the traditional mould. If socialists stick to the one rigid pattern, they will find that less and less of a modern economy conforms with it." [59: 299, 300, 301]

[5]C. A. R. Crosland, *The Future of Socialism* (New York: The Macmillan Company, 1957), Chapter XXII. Cited in William D. Grampp and Emanuel T. Weiler, *Economic Policy: Readings in Political Economy*, third edition (Homewood, Illinois: Richard D. Irwin, Inc., 1961), p. 369.

DEMOCRATIC SOCIALIST PROPOSALS
FOR SOCIAL OWNERSHIP

In addition to their general critique of state monopoly, contemporary democratic socialists offer several proposals and guidelines for more flexible utilization of social ownership in the transition from managed capitalism to democratic socialism.

Government Acquisition of Corporate Stock. If one of the central purposes of public ownership is to promote greater equality in income, and if one of the major sources of inequality is the growing capital gains in a full-employment, sustained-growth economy, then a simple and effective device *"is for the state itself steadily to acquire, as an investment, the equity shares—the 'growth stocks'—which generate both the capital gains and rising dividend income."* [59: 276] This device has many advantages: "It is painless" and avoids compulsion; it in no way restricts freedom to produce in particular areas of the economy; it utilizes existing industrial organization; it automatically hitches the financial and industrial machinery of the nation to community purposes; it provides a simple basis for increasing public services and/or reducing the general level of taxation; it avoids the practical problems of parliamentary opposition to state monopoly and the need to define and demarcate industries for purposes of nationalization. But perhaps most important of all, *"this method of extending public ownership enriches the community as years go by, whereas the formation of State monopolies by compulsory purchase in most cases makes no net transfer of wealth and income from private interests to the State."* [59: 277–78]

Decentralization and Social Ownership. "In every field of social ownership," suggests Crosland, "the more decentralization the better. We do not want everything to be owned in Whitehall. The ultimate aim, which alone will guarantee personal liberty and the fragmentation of power, is a thoroughly mixed-up, variegated pattern of ownership, with the state, the nationalized industries, the Co-operatives, municipalities, Trade Unions, pension funds, and millions of private families all participating." [54: 48–49] "The aim of Democratic Socialism," notes Giles Radice, "is a flexible pattern of ownership, with public ownership of basic industries, selective nationalisation, mixed ownership, and municipal, co-operative, trade union and socially responsible private ownership as well."[6]

Mixed Ownership. A strong case may be made for *mixed* ownership in particular industries. One illustration of this is the "competitive public enterprise" approach, in which the government purchases one or more firms or builds one or more plants within an industry and uses them "by the force of example and competition, to galvanize the whole industry into raising its standards of research, efficiency, and innovation." [54: 42–43] Another illustration of a prospectively useful mixture: In areas of low or declining employment, government could build factories and lease them to private enterprise. This device "has enormous advantages and possibilities for the future . . . . It is public ownership without monopoly, bureaucracy or restriction. It is a partnership between private enterprise as manager and public enterprise as owner and planner, which reaps the advantages of both . . . ." [59: 174–75]

Democratization of Ownership. Wide distribution of private ownership of personal and industrial property and the creation thereby of a private property-owning democracy should be one of the main aims of democratic socialism, Jay suggests, both because widespread private ownership is "a condition of equality" and because "the absence of private property is also a denial of freedom." [59: 290] Emphasizing this, Jay then proposes government encourage the increase of personal savings, specifically through a *"national unit trust for the small saver through the Post Office and Trustee Savings Banks."* [59: 292] Savings deposited at these banks would give the depositor "units in a nationally-run trust invested partly, but not necessarily wholly, in equities."

---

[6]Cf. *Democratic Socialism* (New York: Praeger Publishers, Inc., 1966), p. 49.

[59: 293] Given a minimum reserve (since the value of the units would fluctuate with market prices), individuals could purchase or sell "national trust units" in very small magnitudes, which would be a boon to the small saver. Then, as the holdings of the "National Unit Trust" rose, "the cost of management would be extremely small . . . ." For these two reasons, the N. U. T. would have distinct advantages over a private investment trust. By this device, it should be possible to spread out equity gains "all over the community through the medium of actual individual savings." [59: 293]

Economic Planning

If a large-scale shift to government ownership and/or primary reliance upon nationalization or state monopoly as a form of social ownership are, in the democratic socialist view, neither necessary nor sufficient conditions for the transition from managed capitalism to socialism, what about government economic planning? What is its role? The following discussion will focus upon, first, the traditional democratic socialist case for government economic planning; second, the post-war re-evaluation of the democratic socialist position on economic planning; and third, proposals and guidelines for the agenda, methodology, and machinery of government planning.

THE DEMOCRATIC SOCIALIST CASE FOR GOVERNMENT ECONOMIC PLANNING

The democratic socialist case for government economic planning goes beyond that of the various philosophies and strategies for the economic reform of managed capitalism, especially those at, and to the right of, center. It involves two major dimensions: first, a defense of government relative to private economic power; second, a support of economizing through the social processes of political decision-making relative to the market.

Public and Private Economic Power. The corollary to the democratic socialist critique of private economic power is a defense of government decision-making. Private economic power is not only exploitative, socially divisive and disruptive, and inegalitarian in its intent and impact, but autocratic and undemocratic as well. Plural voting through income inequality makes a sham of consumer sovereignty and dollar balloting. The autocracy of the employer-employee/manager-worker relation belies freedom of exchange on the labor market. Economic inequality carries over into politics and society at large, giving the rich and economically powerful greater weight in government decisions and bolstering class privileges and status.

By contrast, the intense commitment of of democratic socialists to egalitarian aspirations, coupled with their deep and persevering faith in the democractic method, yields a firm and clear support for extension of government economic power beyond that of the theory and practice of contemporary managed capitalism. The point about government in the democratic socialist view is not that it is necessarily efficient, that is, that it does things right, but that it is (or can be) effective, that is, that it does (or can do) the "right" things. Democratic government, via the formula of one man, one vote, is responsive to the interests of the citizenry and is the primary agency whereby the values of the democratic community (equality, social justice, cooperation, and harmony) are realized.

Beyond the Market. The democratic socialist case for government economic planning is a corrollary of its critique of the market. In managed capitalism, as already seen, political decision-making and non-market processes (democracy, bureaucracy, bargaining) play significant roles in providing non-marketable services (for example, education, national defense), improving the functioning of the market system (for example, stabilization policy), correcting specific defects of the market (for example, air pollution), and promoting a "balance of power" in relations among the major organized economic groups.

The democratic socialist concept of government economic planning goes beyond the correction and supplementation of the market and its defects. Democratic socialists believe that, unless the needs of the community are considered through the democratic political process "in the making of fundamental economic decisions, a cooperative and harmonious society," characterized by the "widest possible sharing of the material benefits of the economy . . . cannot be achieved, and fundamental social purposes will be neglected or ignored altogether."[7]

Essentially, the purpose of government economic planning under democratic socialism is to provide for a "relative evaluation of potential use of resources . . . made by men acting *as a community*, judging the community's needs, and seeking to fulfill them." A democratic socialist plan substitutes an "ethical standard of values" for market values, and, through the collective processes of political decision-making, determines social priorities and imposes controls on and through the market to yield results for resource allocation and income distribution different from those that would have emerged from individual decisions and market coordination.[8]

REVISION OF TRADITIONAL VIEWS ON
GOVERNMENT ECONOMIC PLANNING

At the same time, the democratic socialist case for government economic planning does not constitute support for a comprehensive governmentally-planned economy or a rejection of the market system as a social process for resource allocation and economic coordination. Democratic socialist enthusiasm for government planning reached a

peak during the 1930s and the early post-World War II years—though for different reasons.

In the depressed 1930s, the democratic socialist espousal of government economic planning reflected primarily a deep critique of the glaring inequalities, large-scale unemployment, and economic breakdown of the capitalist system. In the early post-war period, government economic planning consisted essentially of a continuation of wartime regulations and direct controls; and proposals for economic planning reflected the "dollar shortage," balance of payments deficits, and needs for controls over resources, especially foreign exchange, in acutely short supply. Clearly, the former was a holdover from the critique of old-style capitalism, while the latter represented a special case of wartime-like emergency.

With continued economic growth, the successful application of Keynesian-type strategies for managing aggregate demand, and welfare-state measures to redistribute income, as well as actual planning experiences since 1945, the traditional democratic socialist case for government economic planning and critique of the market has been tempered and moderated. While continuing to underscore a case for government planning, contemporary democratic socialists eschew comprehensive planning and explicitly recognize a strategic role for the price system in an effectively functioning socialist economy.

DEFENSE OF THE MARKET SYSTEM

A central element in democratic socialist proposals for economic planning is a defense of the competitive price or market system within a framework of private enterprise. This defense rests upon four major points: First, the price or market system *is* a process for economic order and social control which, second, demonstrates the advantages of "convenience," "agility," simplicity, and automaticity. Its controls, in contrast to those of conscious, visible government controls, are "invisible." This system of control

---

[7]Nathaniel S. Preston, *Politics, Economics, and Power* (New York: The Macmillan Company, Publishers, 1967), p. 106, 107.

[8]*Ibid.*, p. 107.

operates to determine market demand to guide resources to meet demands, to determine income, and to promote efficiency:

> The control exercised by the market is none the less real and powerful [emphasizes W. Arthur Lewis] because it is invisible. In a free economy, production is controlled by demand. Capitalists cannot produce what they like; self-interest drives them to produce what they can sell, and that is determined by what people demand, and by how much they demand of it. Production for profit is thus, by 'the invisible hand,' transmuted into production for use. By the same agency the distribution of income is controlled. Producers cannot charge what they like, for the forces of competition are ever driving prices down to the level of costs, and forever driving capitalists to improve their efficiency. The free market is thus a powerful instrument of social control, which directs production to the service of demand, stimulates progress, and eliminates excessive earnings.
>
> The case against the invisible control, in favour of state control, cannot proceed by way of blank denial. It is obvious that the invisible hand exists, and that its influence is beneficial. [60: 7]
>
> There can be no doubt [contends James E. Meade] that money and the pricing system are among the greatest social inventions of mankind. Properly used they should be capable of giving each individual a general command over his fair share of the community's resources; of allowing each individual to decide for himself—where private choice is appropriate—in what form he will exercise this command; of allowing initiative to individual producers and merchants—where technical conditions permit—to produce what is most wanted, in the most economical manner, in the markets where supplies are most needed; in short, of combining freedom, efficiency and equity in social affairs.[9]

Third, because the main alternative to the price system in consumer and labor markets is government controls and central allocation,

---

[9]James E. Meade, *Planning and the Price Mechanism* (New York: The Macmillan Company, Publishers, 1949), p. 9.

price systems, within the framework of private enterprise, contribute to freedom of individual choice and consumer sovereignty.

Fourth, overlapping with all of these three, though the price system within the framework of private enterprise has a number of defects (especially income inequality, instability, unemployment, misallocation of resources between public and private sectors of the economy, and inability to make and adjust to rapid, large-scale changes), it also has, within certain spheres and limits, distinct advantages:

> Private ownership of industry, for instance, is a very bad method of distributing the national income, but often quite a good method of producing goods . . . .
>
> [W]hen neither social justice nor [other non-economic] values are at stake, the price mechanism may well be a convenient and useful line-of-least resistance. If allowed to work in its proper sphere, it does it job of 'clearing the market' often quickly and effectively. Though it would be disastrously wrong to leave the price of education, health, or many other necessities, such as the rent of houses, or the use of land, mainly to market forces, these forces may work perfectly well in distributing second-hand cars, strawberries and raspberries, numerous raw materials and industrial products, taxi fares, hairdos, and many other goods and services. *It would be as foolish to believe that market forces always produce the wrong result, as to believe that they always produce the right* . . . . The price mechanism, therefore, is something which we should supersede or refashion wherever a case is made out for doing so. But elsewhere, it is something not to be ostracized as evil, but welcomed as a good servant but bad master. [59: 335–36]

CRITIQUE OF COMPREHENSIVE GOVERNMENT ECONOMIC PLANNING AND DIRECT CONTROLS

The corollary to the democratic socialist defense of the price or market system is a critique of comprehensive government economic planning within a framework of public ownership and of government planning by command or direction, that is, by methods which circumvent the price system. A proliferation of direct government controls (such as price and wage controls, exchange controls, rationing systems, physical controls over allocations of raw materials or of labor, and so on), insists Crosland, is neither a necessary nor a sufficient condition for, nor route to, the establishment of democratic socialism. "A complex mass of detailed controls is highly unpopular, bad for industrial efficiency, and distorting in its effects on production. Within the framework of overall government planning, the proper way to make the private sector responsive to the needs of the community is to make it competitive." [55: 64]

Government planning by direction or command (rather than by inducement via the price system) has a number of major defects. [Cf. 60: 15–19] First, it reduces individual freedom of choice—by consumers in the choice of products and services and control of production; by workers in the choice of occupations and employers; and by industrial managers in the choice of industrial methods, allocations of resources, and adjustment to market supply and demand.

Second, "planning without prices" involves serious inefficiencies stemming from the *complexity* of the microeconomic interrelationships of the economy (which is circumvented in a price system because no one needs to formulate a comprehensive plan for an entire economy); the *inflexibility* of central plans and planners, arising from the resistance to more or less continuous revision of plans (which occurs automatically in a price system); the "procrustean" tendencies in central planning by direction, stemming from the temptations of and pressures for simplification through standardization; and the stifling effect of direct controls on entrepreneurial initiative and enterprise and its agility in developing new products, technological processes, and marketing and organizational methods (especially important for nations relying heavily upon foreign trade).

Third, direct controls are expensive, both in the staff needed to administer and supervise them, and in the time and energy devoted to circumventing them.

Fourth, comprehensive, centralized systems of direct controls not only diminish the freedom of workers, consumers, and businessmen, but also democratic participation and control. The larger, more intricate, and more complex the "plan," the more it is established by central direction and the more its results "are embodied in thousands of administrative orders and decisions, of which parliament and ministers can have only the briefest knowledge . . . the less the control that is possible." [60: 19]

PROPOSALS FOR GOVERNMENT
ECONOMIC PLANNING: FROM IDEOLOGY
TO TECHNIQUE

Thus, democratic socialist conceptions of government economic planning assume the existence, encouraged by government policy, of a competitive price system within the framework of private enterprise. As a corollary, they criticize comprehensive systems of physical planning of outputs and inputs of particular sectors and firms within the framework of government enterprise and eschew direct controls which circumvent the price system. The ideal route for government economic planning, argue most contemporary democratic socialists, is to rely primarily upon inducement rather than command and to exercise public control of the economy through monetary and price systems.

This position reflects in part the changing role of economic planning in practice in the last quarter-century or so. Although modifying, countervailing, offsetting, or correcting the market, government economic planning in the developed democratic nations of the West has functioned with and through the market system. Much of the work of planning authorities is common to both managed capitalists and democratic socialists. "The evolution of national economic planning from an issue of recondite economic theory and bitter ideological controversy to a routine exercise of respectable economic policy is certainly one of the major intellectual themes of our time . . . . What was supposedly a matter of sharp and unbridgeable division between warring social classes has become in large degree a question of pragmatic compromise and thus a job for the technician rather than the ideologue . . . conflict resolution usually occurs within a planning framework."[10]

Within this context, democratic socialist government economic planning consists essentially of the proposals, programs, and techniques of public control of the economy described earlier in this chapter. It may be summarized as an endeavor, through control and manipulation of the monetary and pricing systems, to fulfill five "fundamental conditions": ". . . first, that the total monetary demand for goods and services is neither too great nor too small in relation to the total supply of goods and services that can be made available for purchase; secondly, that there is a tolerably equitable distribution of money income and property so that no individual can command more than his fair share of the community's resources; . . . thirdly, that no private person or body of persons should be allowed to remain uncontrolled in a sufficiently powerful position to rig the market for his own selfish ends . . . ,"[11] fourthly, that a "social balance" exists between the provision of non-marketable collective goods (distributed by government) and marketable goods (produced and distributed mainly by private enterprise), and, fifthly, that the highest rate of growth in overall economic performance consistent with the other four objectives may be achieved.

Types of Plans and Plan Formulation. In part, as emphasized by Swedish economist Gunnar Myrdal [6: 23], democratic socialist

and other recent proposals in the sphere of economic planning represent merely endeavors to coordinate existing public policies to avoid inconsistencies and thus attain goals more effectively. In part, also, democratic socialist economic planning constitutes a macroeconomic strategy for the promotion of stable full-employment growth, as illustrated most effectively in Sweden. But, as mentioned earlier, democratic socialists also regard planning as an endeavor to establish, through government action, results different from those emerging from a non-governmentally-controlled price system within the framework of private enterprise. As J. R. Sargent, in a study on the relation between nationalized industries and economic policy commissioned by the Fabian Society, asserts: "If planning is to have any real meaning, any operational content, it must involve the application of criteria for production decisions which differ from the ordinary commercial criteria of a private-enterprise economy . . . . Planning means bringing about a pattern of output, a collection of goods and services, which differs from what would have emerged from unplanned private enterprise." [Cf. 64: 249, 250]

Though lacking a more or less comprehensive "master plan" for the entire economic system, a properly organized democratic socialist economic system presumably would contain at least four types of government "plans": (1) a plan for the provision of government services—education, national defense, and so on; (2) a plan for macroeconomic strategy—that is, the planned aggregate levels of government purchases, transfer payments, taxation, deficits or surpluses, and supply of money; (3) a plan for government-owned enterprises; (4) a plan for the guidance of private enterprise. Presumably, these plans would be coordinated in the form of an overall planned strategy for national economic development.

(1) is essentially a matter of budgetary policy and is by no means unique to democratic socialism. Democratic socialist proposals would differ (if at all) from those of

---

[10]Marvin E. Rozen, *Comparative Economic Planning* (Boston: D.C. Heath & Company, 1967), p. vii.

[11]Meade, *op. cit.*, p. 11.

liberal-managed capitalism in the degree of priority placed upon rectifying "social imbalance" by expanding the provision of public services. As already noted, however, contemporary democratic socialists emphasize that "socialists would be quite wrong to think that the essence of socialism lies in the indefinite extension of free services. A point will come when, unless a specific redistribution of income is desired (for example, towards large families), the liberty of the citizen to spend his extra income as he pleases must also be regarded." [55: 33]

(2) is also essentially a matter of budgetary policy and is found, in varying degrees, in the policy proposal kit of all liberal (and some conservative) social reformers, not merely democratic socialists. Further, improvements could and should be made in the process of monetary and fiscal planning. But, argues Crosland, considerable success has already been achieved in this sphere under managed capitalism, and further improvements along this line would not constitute the essence of a transition to democratic socialism.

(3) is currently an unsettled question among democratic socialists. As for most students of public enterprise, democratic socialists are torn between keeping the managers of government-owned enterprises accountable to and controlled by central governments and consistent with the objectives and expectations of an overall plan or plans for national economic development versus giving them, within the framework of broad policy guidelines (for example, those of marginal cost pricing), the flexibility to exercise enterprising decisions on more or less commercial grounds. "A government which believes in planning is plainly justified in using its powers over nationalized industry in furtherance of a long-term economic plan . . . . On the other hand, ministerial intervention does pose grave disadvantages . . . . Management must be enterprising; it must make day-to-day decisions. It cannot do its job properly if it has to keep running to the minister for approval." [64: 29, 28]

Yet, the basic principle remains: Democratic socialist economic planning through public enterprise, as well as through other means, should strive "to achieve some pattern of output other than what would be elicited from profit-seeking entrepreneurs by the uninhibited operation of monetary demand." [64: 250] Specifically, first, quantities of output of particular products and services "should be determined by a balance of social benefits against social costs" even if this does not maximize profits in terms of private cost calculations; and, second, "some people and some purposes should enjoy more of the national product than they would be granted even by the most scrupulous balancing of social benefit and social cost." [64: 250] An example of the former might be a public parking facility agency, recognizing the social costs of traffic congestion by varying the parking charge according to the time of day. The achievement of the second requires essentially the provision by public enterprises through a "cross subsidization system" of services (such as frequent, reguarly scheduled transport services), even if not commercially profitable.

Plans for (4), the guidance of private enterprise in relation to overall goals and plans, have developed in a most interesting way in France. Though by no means uniquely democratic socialist in content or inspiration, it, or something like it, could easily form part of a democratic socialist vision of a properly organized and planned economy.[12]

The crucial distinction in French planning is between the formulation of the plan and its execution. The formulation of the plan is

---

[12]Perhaps this is why some authors [such as Carl Landauer, *Contemporary Economic Systems* (New York: J. B. Lippincott Company, 1964), p. 272] identify French planning as a part of democratic socialism, while others [for example, Morris Bornstein, *Comparative Economic Systems: Models and Cases* (Homewood, Illinois: Richard D. Irwin, Inc., 1965, pp. 212–28] classify it as a form of regulated capitalism. The reference to the French case is offered as an illustration rather than a concrete description.

quite comprehensive (relative to, say, the United States or even the United Kingdom— though not to the U. S. S. R.). Somewhat like the Economic Report of the President of the United States, though in greater detail, the French Plan includes a general identification and estimate of present conditions, future prospects, alternative lines of development, and proposed policies. But it goes beyond this by incorporating a series of output-input-investment-labor-productivity-foreign trade targets (estimates) for the major industrial sectors of the economy. These targets simultaneously provide recommendations (a) for achieving overall goals for the national economy and (b) for guiding private enterprise toward fulfilling the target-estimates and thereby playing its role in meeting the objectives of the Plan. These more specific planning targets obtain prescriptive as well as prognosticative value from the fact that they are constructed by Modernization Committees whose membership includes businessmen and labor union leaders as well as government officials and professional economists.

Government Controls for Plan Execution. If democratic socialists forego comprehensive programs of physical output-input orders and directives and, in general, eschew direct controls, how are plans to be executed? In plans (1) and (2), governments directly control the execution of their own plans—for public services and for full-employment monetary and fiscal strategy. In plan (3), governments can also exert fairly tight control over the actions of government-owned enterprises— although, as noted, a democratic socialist government, like any other, must in this case seek some balance between accountability-control and managerial flexibility-discretion. Plan (4) is the difficult one—especially when the targets and plans are fairly comprehensive and detailed, and especially, as in the French and British experience, where "planners" (that is, those who formulate plans) have no direct power to control the execution of plans. First, the plan may be a gold-mine of information to private businessmen. This in itself may entice them to voluntarily act consistently with the plan. Second, the fact that planning targets have been established through the active participation and collaboration of private enterprisers themselves: (a) creates a sense of civic pride, moral obligation, and participatory comradeship—all of which contribute to voluntary acceptance; (b) reduces the uncertainties of the non-governmentally-planned economy and, thereby, generates a conviction of practicality for the plan and an expectation that, if or because others are acting on the assumption that the plan will be fulfilled, then they may safely do so, too.

Third, government commitments to a general macroeconomic strategy for maintaining stable, full-employment growth reduce the uncertainties of general recession and, thereby, contribute to general business expectations of the practicality of plan fulfillment. Fourth, in an economy in which government ownership plays a significant though limited role, the production decisions of government enterprises themselves constitute a vehicle for achieving part of the plan's targets. In addition, price and wage policies of government enterprises constitute, either as indicators or as a set of strategic variables affecting economic decisions in privately-owned industries, another means of encouraging plan fulfillment.

Fifth, governments may engage in a variety of financial inducements for particular industries or firms to entice them to move in specific directions by making it more profitable for them to do so. Lastly, by selected strategic direct controls (for example, building permits, licensing systems) governments may affect such decisions as private investment and geographic location of enterprises without directly ordering businessmen to produce specific quantities of output or to use particular combinations of inputs.

Industrial Democracy and Worker
Control of Industry

INDUSTRIAL RELATIONS

Thus, neither a massive shift toward nationalization of industry nor comprehensive government economic planning and control appear to be necessary or sufficient conditions for the transition from managed capitalism to democratic socialism. How, then, is the terminus of the division of society "into opposing economic classes" and the establishment of "conditions of approximate social and economic equality" to be achieved?

Crosland suggests three directions for democratic socialism: First, a large-scale redistribution of the ownership of wealth; second, a reformation of the educational system; third, a reorganization of industry, including privately-owned industries and enterprises. [Cf. 55: 65] The first two have already been discussed in connection with democratic socialist proposals for achieving greater income equality. The third, Crosland emphasizes, is not essentially a problem of social control; this has been largely achieved through existing processes and techniques of government economic planning. Nor is it essentially a problem of consumer control; this is capable of attainment through a vigorous anti-monopoly policy coupled with correct (marginal cost) pricing policies by nationalized enterprises. Nor is it essentially a problem of income distribution. This problem has been partly resolved through redistributive fiscal policy and is further resolvable through policies to decrease the inequality in ownership of industrial property.

The problem of industrial organization which needs inspired left-wing reform is, instead, essentially one of the political sociology or social psychology of industrial relations. Despite all the reforms of the democratic welfare state, all the changes incorporated into socially controlled and managed capitalist economies, and the increased bargaining strength of labor unions, the worker has not achieved "a new social status." Nor has managed capitalism "cured the basic class hostility which stems from his total exclusion from either rights or participation. Sole rights still belong to the functionless shareholder, and this knowledge still breeds frustration and annoyance among the workers." [55: 66] There is still a deep "and rather inarticulate wish for 'participation', higher 'status', greater responsibility and some sort of control over some managerial decisions." [59: 325] "We have to do everything we can," contends W. Arthur Lewis, "in public and private industry, to revolutionise the status of working people . . . ." [60: 100–101]

EARLIER VIEWS

A vision of such a revolutionary transformation was presented eloquently by R. H. Tawney in 1918:

> [The] first problem of industrial organization is to create in every industry . . . a constitution securing its members an effective voice in its government. The alternative to industrial autocracy must be found in the development of associations through which the mass of the workers, in each industry as a whole, and in the units which compose it, can take part in its policy and organization through representatives whom they choose . . . . The details of the transformation may be complex, but the principle is simple. It is that, instead of the workers being used by the owners of capital with the object of producing profits for its owners, capital should be used by the workers with the object of producing services for the community . . . . What is required is not simply to limit the power of Capital to impose terms upon Labour, but to make the workers, not the capitalist, the centre of industrial authority, subject to such limitations upon their sovereignty as may be imposed in the interests of the community as a whole. It is to employ things in the service of persons, instead of employing persons in the service of things and of the owners of things. [69: 103, 105, 109, 110]

A similar approach was advocated by G. D. H. Cole, the leading figure in "guild socialism," in the early 1920s. The major ideas of guild socialism contrast with those of the Fabian Society. The aims of the two groups—economic equality, social justice, democracy, a cooperative and harmonious society—were essentially similar; and, given the flexible and pragmatic character of British politics, there was a good deal of overlapping between the members and proposals of each.

Still, their positions in regard to appropriate means to attain socialist ends were different. The Fabians emphasized planning expertise and centralization in decision-making, government ownership, the worker as a citizen, and the democratic state as the agency for economic control and reform. By contrast, the guild socialists emphasized decentralization, democratic participation, worker control over industry, the worker as a producer, and producer guilds and associations as pluralistic agencies both to supersede old-style private enterprise and to countervail the centralizing and potentially autocratic tendencies of the state. In effect, the two approaches represented a democratic socialist bifurcation of the two leading dimensions of the classical Marxian conception of an ideally functioning socialist economy, as described earlier. "The real aim," argued Cole, "must be not merely the expropriation of the capitalist, but the supersession of his economic functions and his replacement by the workers in every sphere of his economic and social power. For it is by this capture and assumption of social and economic functions that the workers will alone make possible an equitable distribution of the national income and a reasonable reorganization of Society as a whole."[13]

In his various works on guild socialism, Cole conceived worker control in all areas of the economic and political order. Factories and other basic producing units would be administered by worker guilds, in the spirit if not precise organizational form of medieval guilds; that is, as associations of independent producers. Foremen, managers, and governing boards would be elected by the workers, who would participate, directly or through their democratically elected leaders, in wage, price, employment, output, and investment policies. In some industries (for example, building construction), workers would own the instruments of production. In others (such as coal), ownership would be nationalized, but managerial control would be exercised "in trust" for the public by the guild.

Government, too, would be reorganized on the basis of functional, rather than geographic, representation. Local, regional, and national "communes" would perform the traditional functions of government and would be elected by and representative of the citizenry in their various capacities as producers and consumers. Industries, professions, even consumers would be organized into larger guilds, culminating in a "Congress of Industrial Guilds" on the national level.

Industry-wide guilds would have the functions of coordinating industry supply with market demand, adjudicating conflicts within the industry, and representing the industry in bargaining with other guilds. Nationwide guilds would determine basic principles of guild organization, adjudicate conflicts between industry-guilds and between producer and consumer guilds, and determine overall industrial policies, such as wage levels for different classes of workers.

CURRENT PROPOSALS

For a variety of reasons, contemporary democratic socialists have not systematically or vigorously developed these early visions with concrete details and specific proposals.[14] For one thing, labor and voter support for worker participation in industrial management in contemporary managed capitalist economies is far from enthusiastic. It is not

---

[13]G. D. H. Cole, *Guild Socialism Restated* (London: Leonard Parsons, 1920), pp. 206–7.

[14]"Many of us feel a nagging confusion on the subject of industrial democracy and workers' control. We are emotionally in favour of the idea, but vague as to what should actually be done or even precisely why." [54: 217]

difficult to appreciate some of the key reasons for this. On the one hand, notes Crosland, "the status, power, and control over industry of the working class *have* enormously increased—but without any significant extension of workers' management. The goal has been partially achieved, but by a different route; hence the loss of interest in the old slogans." [54: 217–18] This has resulted partly from the full employment-social security policies of the contemporary democratic welfare state. But it has stemmed largely from the extension of labor union action and control from the traditional variables of wages and hours into a variety of additional dimensions of industrial decision-making (such as hiring, firing, and promotions; pay differentials; working conditions and the organization of the work process) which, in the past, were the "prerogatives" of management. This has proceeded quite far in the United States, for example, with little concerted support for "industrial democracy."

On the other hand, labor union leadership understandably and rationally is reluctant, even apathetic, to jeopardizing its independence and position of bargaining opposition by cooperating with management in the construction of "joint determination" of managerial policy. In addition, the "alienation" of labor from the work process "cannot be ascribed, as it was by Marx, to the system of property relations, nor yet to the absence of workers' management. It is surely rooted in the technological processes of large-scale industry, and, above all, in the atomization of work—the breakdown of the production process into the maximum number of repetitive low-skilled tasks." [54: 227]

One recommendation for promoting greater worker participation and control in industry, however, which has received fairly wide support among contemporary democratic socialists, is a change in the structure of the boards of directors of large corporations, both governmentally and privately owned. In privately-owned corporations, suggests Austen Albu in an essay prepared for the Fabian Society, a change in corporation law should be made, permitting workers to elect a minority of the board of directors. [Cf. 55: 136] There is no reason, concurs Douglas Jay, why 100 percent of the members of boards of directors must be appointed by stockholders. In government-owned enterprises, too, the same principle could apply, with the government appointing a majority, and employees a minority, of board members. [59: 330–31]

This "simple legislative change . . . would sweepingly alter the constitution of thousands of companies . . . ." [59: 331] It would provide a basis not merely for management "consultation" with employees, but for worker representation in the highest echelons of the company. It could also provide a basis for extending joint consultation throughout all levels of firm and plant management and giving it more real content than it tends to have in the absence of worker representation in management.

CONCLUSIONS

In practice, democratic socialism (more accurately: the programs and policies of democratic socialists and democratic socialist governments) have for some time been more or less synonymous with the social democratic reform of capitalism. A recurrent theme of this chapter has been that the post-war re-evaluation of the theory and philosophy of democratic socialism has produced a similar result in the realm of ideas, proposals, and prescriptions. If democratic socialism means the flexible, pragmatic blending of the public and private sectors of the economy, and of government planning and the price system, in the pursuit of the immediate objective of the social control of the national economy and the broader social purposes of freedom, equality, full employment, price stability, growth, and efficiency, then there is little to distinguish it clearly and fundamentally from liberal social reform of capitalism. Both involve an interblending of elements traditionally associated with both capitalism and socialism, and each is more similar to the other than to the theory and practice of old-style capitalism.

Now one highly popular way of describing this phenomenon is to say, as suggested more than a half-century ago, that we (social reformers) "are all socialists now." But an equally meaningful and, perhaps, valid expression is to say that we (democratic socialists) "are all liberal social reformers now." Democratic socialism and democratic socialists will undoubtedly continue to exist and provide a valuable source of social conscience and inspiration for left-wing democratic reform. But old-style socialism is now as obsolete for democratic socialist theory and philosophy as its premises and prognostications have been for contemporary managed capitalist practice. The grandiloquent alternatives of capitalism versus socialism, private enterprise versus government ownership, government economic planning versus the price system, and so on seem as mummified and irrelevant to contemporary economic analysis, philosophy, and policy as the horse and buggy does to today's freeway systems. From this vantage point, the real contribution of postwar democratic socialist theorists and writers has been their (perhaps unwitting) challenging and provocative contribution to the philosophy of social and economic reform in the "mixed economy."

SUMMARY OF CHAPTER 14

1. In the literature and practice of economic systems, "democratic socialism" has been essentially a body of ideas and institutions for the democratic reform of the economic order rather than a rigorously formulated model of a present or future socialist economic system. Thus, the adjective "democratic" is as important as the noun "socialism."

2. The emphasis upon democracy has had two major implications for democratic socialist movements and programs. First, democracy has been perceived as a means for or route to the establishment of a socialist economy. Second, one of the prime objectives of democratic socialism has been the extension of democracy from politics into the economy, industry, and society at large.

3. As a movement and body of programs for democratic economic reform, democratic socialism has been profoundly affected by the transformation from old-style capitalism to contemporary managed capitalism. Traditionally, democratic socialism has been associated with such means as government ownership, at least of strategic or basic industries, and government planning—as a means of going "beyond the market" to values established by the democratic political community and as a basis for controlling private, by public, economic power.

4. Recently, democratic socialists have emphasized the primacy of goals in their redefinitions of the essential character of democratic socialism. This emphasis upon ends relative to means has had two main effects. First, means associated with managed capitalism (such as monetary and fiscal policies) or even old-style capitalism (such as private ownership, the price/market system) have been incorporated into democratic socialist literature and programs of democratic socialist governments insofar as they have been perceived as contributing to or at least consistent with democratic socialist ends. Second, some means traditionally associated with socialism (for example, state monopoly in the ownership and control of industry; comprehensive, hierarchical government planning) have been rejected by many contemporary democratic socialists insofar as they have been perceived as inconsistent with or detrimental to the effective pursuit of democratic socialist ends.

5. The most prominent democratic socialist end is *equality*, generally interpreted as the reduction of inequalities in income, wealth,

and position to "minimum practicable limits." In contrast to classical Marxists, whose focus is upon the source of income and wealth (that is, capital ownership versus labor power), democratic socialists focus their critique of capitalist inequality upon differences in the magnitude of income and wealth (rich and poor).

6. From the vantage point of democratic socialist values, managed capitalism, as practiced in the United States, and with variations in Great Britain and Western Europe, has had a considerable degree of success, especially in curbing large-scale economic instability, depressions, and unemployment. But managed capitalism is "not enough," for at least three reasons: first, continued misallocation of resources between public and private sectors of the economy; second, continued excessive inequalities in income and wealth; third, inequalities in power and participation in private organizations.

7. Recent democratic socialist programs and proposals reflect these perceived successes and failings of managed capitalism. Proposals for further extension of government ownership or for more or less comprehensive government planning are eschewed in favor of redistributive tax and expenditure programs, expansion of educational opportunities, increases in the relative role of the public sector and provision of collective goods, and support for positions of countervailing power within the private sector of the economy and in the formulation of public policies. Except for differences in degree, a sharper focus upon the goal of equality, and other variations plausibly attributable to special cultural/political features of different countries, it has become increasingly difficult to distinguish sharply democratic socialist ideas and programs from the more liberal democratic variants of the programmatic literature of managed capitalism.

SOURCES CITED IN PART IV

Several works cited earlier, notably Dahl and Lindblom (1), Galbraith (3), Hayek (4), Hoover (5), Myrdal (6), Schumpeter (8), and Johr and Singer (38) are also pertinent to managed capitalism and democratic socialism. In addition, the following sources are especially useful:

48. BERLE, ADOLPH A., JR., *The Twentieth Century Capitalist Revolution* (New York: Harcourt Brace & World, Inc., 1954).

49. BERLE, ADOLPH A., JR., *Power Without Property* (New York: Harcourt, Brace & World, Inc., 1959).

50. BERLE, ADOLPH A., JR., and MEANS, GARDINER C., *The Modern Corporation and Private Property* (New York: Commerce Clearing House, 1932).

51. BORNSTEIN, MORRIS, editor, *Comparative Economic Systems* (Homewood, Illinois: Richard D. Irwin, Inc., 1965).

52. BOULDING, KENNETH E., *The Organizational Revolution* (New York: Simon and Schuster, Inc., 1961).

53. CROSLAND, C. A. R., *The Future of Socialism* (New York: The Macmillan Company, Publishers, 1957).

54. CROSLAND, C. A. R., *The Conservative Enemy* (New York: Schocken, 1962).

55. CROSSMAN, R. H. S., editor, *New Fabian Essays* (London: Turnstile, 1952).

56. GALBRAITH, JOHN KENNETH, *The Affluent Society* (Boston: Houghton Mifflin Company, 1958).

57. GALBRAITH, JOHN KENNETH, "Countervailing Power," *American Economic Review*, May 1954.

58. GALBRAITH, JOHN KENNETH, *The New Industrial State* (Boston: Houghton Mifflin Company, 1971).

59. JAY, DOUGLAS, *Socialism in the New Society* (New York: St. Martin's Press, Inc., 1963).

60. LEWIS, W. ARTHUR, *The Principles of Economic Planning* (London: Allan and Unwin, 1956).

61. MACHLUP, FRITZ, *The Economics of Seller's Competition* (Baltimore: Johns Hopkins Press, 1952).

62. MILLS, C. WRIGHT, *The Power Elite* (New York: Oxford University Press, Inc., 1957).

63. REAGAN, MICHAEL D., *The Managed Economy* (New York: Oxford University Press, Inc., 1963).

64. SHANKS, MICHAEL, editor, *The Lessons of Public Enterprise* (London: Jonathan Cape, 1963).

65. SHAW, GEORGE BERNARD, editor, *Fabian Essays* (London: 1889).

66. SMITH, HENRY, *The Economics of Socialism Reconsidered* (London: Oxford University Press, Inc., 1962).

67. SOLO, ROBERT A., *Economic Organizations and Social Systems* (New York: The Bobbs-Merrill Company, Inc., 1968).

68. STRACHEY, JOHN, *Contemporary Capitalism* (New York: Random House, Inc., 1956).

69. TAWNEY, R. H., *The Radical Tradition* (New York: Random House, Inc., 1964).

V

CONTEMPORARY COMMUNISM

One of the fascinating aspects of the contemporary Communist world is its role as a laboratory for the testing and reinterpretation of theories and doctrines of all streams of socialist thought. Outsiders of all persuasions have often found in the experience and performance of these societies a vindication of their own views (pro or con) of socialism. These economies have also been a laboratory for the fashioning of new economic concepts and doctrines. As avowed Marxists, the founders of Communist nations professed Marxian economics as the basis of their economic policies; but as they set out to build socialism, they often failed to find in Marx answers to some of the most important problems they encountered. It was often necessary to create institutions *de novo* and to work out *ad hoc* strategies drawing on their evolving experience. In the process, Communist planners have had to create a body of theory and analysis to help interpret this experience and to guide them in carrying out economic policy. Part V (Chapters 15–17) describes these strategies and theories, especially in reference to economic development, planning, pricing, and resource allocation. Given what has already been said about practice as one of the sources of these ideas, these chapters will also examine the actual practice of planning and development in the Communist countries.

The description herein draws primarily on the experience of the USSR and Eastern European Communist countries. To some degree, it applies to the whole Communist world, including Cuba and the Asian Communist countries. All the countries of the Soviet camp of socialism have endeavored to follow the Stalinist approach described in Chapter 15, though we are now beginning to see that the degree to which some countries committed themselves to it was rather limited. Most countries today have moved considerably away from Stalinist strategies and institutions in a revisionist direction that will be described in Chapter 16. Some, like Cuba, have had relatively short-lived commitments to it before starting on a revisionist course. China claims to be still true to the original goals of the Communist revolution, though Chinese institutions and strategies were always sufficiently different from the

Stalinist model to make any reference to the Chinese experience as "Stalinist" a misnomer. Much of China's experience has been conditioned by the problem of completing the revolution and making a transition to a new system rather than with operating the system. Chinese developmental strategy has fluctuated between an agricultural emphasis and an industrial one, and the Great Proletarian Cultural Revolution makes one increasingly suspect that the Soviet model was always a rather fragile scaffolding supporting a distinctive Chinese revolution, ideology, and economic strategy. Not enough research has been done on the smaller Asian Communist countries to enable evaluation of how well they have followed the Stalinist pattern; thus, they are considered only briefly. Yugoslavia is a case sufficiently different to merit separate consideration, in Chapter 17.

Having evolved through experience, Communist theories of development, planning, pricing, and allocation have changed over time. The death of Stalin in 1953 marked a dramatic historical turning-point in this evolution, and treatment herein is divided accordingly. The basic Soviet-style approach to economic development was determined in the late 1920s and continued with little change until the post-Stalin leadership decided a new approach was needed. The Stalinist concept also was slavishly imitated in the countries which became Communist after World War II. In the last several years, however, there has been a real revolution in the theory, philosophy, and strategy of economic planning in the Soviet Union and its eastern European emulators. Chapter 15 treats the Stalinist version of Communist economic theory and policy, and Chapter 16 describes the changes in this model that have taken place in the last few years. One special case is Yugoslavia, which broke away from the tutelage of the USSR quite early (in 1948). The Yugoslavs consider themselves Marxists; but in their experience with the Russians, they came to see in Stalinist society hypocrisy and perversion of true Marxism. Determined to be faithful to Marx and, at the same time, to escape the pitfalls into which the Russians had stumbled, the Yugoslavs consciously set out to build their own "road to socialism." They pioneered the development of the revisionist form of (Communist) socialism that today is coming to be accepted in varying degrees by all the Communist countries (with China the major exception). The Yugoslav form of Communist revisionism is explored in Chapter 17.

15

Contemporary Communism:
The Stalinist Model

THE BOLSHEVIK REVOLUTION AND PRECONDITIONS FOR MARXIAN SOCIALISM

The first thoroughgoing, large-scale effort to sweep away capitalist institutions and to build Socialism took place in the Soviet Union as a result of the Great October Revolution of 1917. The Bolsheviks who came to power through this revolution had long claimed to be inspired by Marxian doctrine. Considered as a Marx-inspired program, the Soviet experience with economic development is filled with paradox. The Bolshevik revolution took place in a country that hardly had fulfilled the prerequisites Marx had assumed necessary for socialist revolution. As described in Chapter 5, in the Marxian theory of a historical succession of economic systems, each stage not only prepares the way for its own termination but also develops the necessary groundwork for the creation of the next stage. According to Marx, the capitalist mode of production plays a progressive role in the historical development of a society. It develops industry at the expense of agriculture and creates an urbanized and class-conscious proletariat. Under a process of competition combined with increasingly severe crises and depressions, small capitalists (including the important class of peasants) are gradually eliminated. The resulting concentration and centralization of production in very large firms creates the machinery for socialized control of the economy. The destruction of all the traditional hindrances to the mobilization of productive forces, and the obsession of the capitalist class with accumulation of capital, creates a high level of productive capacity and establishes the basis for an era of abundance.

None of these conditions had been fulfilled when the Bolsheviks seized power in Russia in 1917. Capitalism had come late to Russia, and despite considerable growth and modernization in the three decades preceding the revolution, Russia had not yet been transformed from a backward agricultural country into a modern urban industrial one. Most of the population was still agricultural, and the typical producer in agriculture was the peasant cultivator. The proletariat was an insignificant force, the process of capital accumulation had not proceeded very far, technology still was backward, and much of the population still was illiterate. Russia in 1917 had a better start on modernization and economic development than many of the countries regarded as underdeveloped today, but she scarcely fit the Marxian image of a developed country where capitalism had already prepared the way for the creation of a socialist society.

These circumstances suggest two important

background factors important for understanding the Soviet form of applied Marxism: First, the Soviet leaders found their central concern had to be the problem of economic development. Second, they found little in Marx directly relevant to this main concern.

Of course, a variety of factors, including traditional nationalist ambitions, a desire to protect the revolution and to "build socialism," a fear bordering on obsession of "hostile and encircling capitalist powers," and the character of and struggles for political leadership within the Communist party, combined with the relatively underdeveloped economy to make industrialization and economic development the focus of concern for Communist strategy.

Even without these additional factors, however, the mere fact that the Communists came to power in a relatively underdeveloped economy where the prerequisites for Marxian socialism simply did not exist had profound significance. The problems and circumstances facing Communist leaders in post-revolutionary Russia were radically divergent from those envisaged by Marx. It is not surprising, then, that the institutions, strategies, and methods that evolved and developed in relation to these problems and circumstances also came to diverge in significant ways from at least several dimensions of the classic Marxian vision of the ideally functioning socialist economy. At the least, Stalinist Communism represents a very special variation of Marxian socialism, embodying a combination of applied Marxism, economic underdevelopment, and Russian politics. In economic terms, Stalinist Communism was *not* a successor to capitalism in the economically developed countries; it is better described as a substitute for industrializing capitalism in certain relatively underdeveloped countries.

One of the difficulties in describing the true character of the evolving Communist economic system(s) as an exercise in Marxism stems from the content of Marx's thought itself. As observed earlier, Marxian economic thought was essentially an analysis of the institutions, behavior, and development and prospective transformation of *capitalism*. The very concepts and categories of this analysis—wages, prices, profits, markets, competition, crises and depressions, and so on—had (or appeared to have) their immediate and obvious applications to a capitalist economy. In any event, it was not readily apparent how many of them could be applied to the Communist experiences and problems of centrally planned development. Remember also (Chapter 8) that Marx carefully avoided predictions about the precise form that socialism would take, dismissing such attempts as utopian speculation.

If Marx was vague about the structure or organization of the prospective socialist system, he was even more chary of providing a systematic analysis of how the system was supposed to function, that is, how central planning was supposed to work. As already noted, Marx was more of an analyst than a planner. It is an open question as to the extent to which his deterministic "laws" of social evolution and development are applicable to the fundamental idea of planning, which is the normative one of consciously and voluntaristically designing strategies and policies to attain goals. In the Soviet case, the relevance of Marxian ideas to the problem of operating the economy was still more unclear because of its relative underdevelopment.

It should be noted that this introductory assessment of the role of Marxism in Communist development is a Western interpretation and not shared by official Communist doctrine. The ideological response of Communist leaders to their anomalous situation, as will be explored later in the chapter, was to reinterpret and recast Marxism in the light of their situation, to place strategic emphasis on those dimensions of Marxian thought which seemed most applicable to their experiences, denigrating other aspects and interpretations as "deviationism" and presenting their own interpretations as "true" Marxism. The reformulation of a classic social philosophy to fit different or altered economic conditions is not unique, of course, to Communist experience. As noted in Chapter 4, something similar occurred in the transition from classical liberalism to *laissez-faire* conservatism in the United States. What is special in the (Stalinist) Communist situation is the intense degree to which the official ideology monopolized and pervaded all public discussion, and the extent to which all divergences from the classic Marxian vision were reconstituted as illustrations of the true Marxian position.

This chapter is chiefly devoted to expounding the theory and strategy which the Soviet leaders developed as ways to cope with the problem of economic development. A number of obviously related problems also require consideration, such as how this alleged application of Marxian thought has worked out in practice, what useful ideas and concepts Soviet planners found in Marxian writing and the extent to which these inspired them to new theorizing about the problem of economic development, and the impact of the "imperative of industrialization" and the Stalinist growth strategy on the institutional structure and behavior of the Soviet economic system. In conclusion, this chapter also will consider how Soviet thought and strategy concerning economic development have influenced their approach to the problem of value, pricing, and allocation. These two sets of problems interact in many ways, and it will be useful to consider how, in their concern with the problem of economic development, Soviet economic thinkers failed to appreciate some fundamental ideas about value, price, and allocation.

The Leninist Variation of Applied Marxism

The variation on the theme of applied Marxism developed by Lenin (Vladimir Ilyich Ulyanov) (1870–1924) is a classic illustration of a subtle interblending of strategically selected dimensions of Marxism with the exigencies of Russian problems and circumstances. Lenin was much less a painstaking economic scholar than Marx, but much more the professional revolutionary and (after the Bolshevik Revolution) the political leader of a regime actually in power. As the leader of the Russian Bolsheviks in the early years of the twentieth century prior to 1917 and as the leader of the Russian government and Communist party in the first half-decade after the Bolshevik Revolution, Lenin was the single most important transition figure in Russian Marxism between Marx and Stalin.

PRE-REVOLUTIONARY LENINIST THEORY AND STRATEGY

Prior to the Bolshevik Revolution, Lenin developed three major sets of ideas concerning the application of Marxism to Russian conditions directly relevant to this discussion. In *What Is To Be Done?* (1902), Lenin contended that, left to themselves, workers in the process of industrialization spontaneously tend to develop only a "trade union consciousness," that is, tend to focus upon: the organization of labor unions; bargaining with capitalists for such traditional "bourgeois" goals as higher pay, shorter hours, and better working conditions, in short, for improving their position and increasing their share of national income within the capitalist framework; and securing favorable legislation. If, by contrast, the working class is to develop a true "socialist consciousness" and support the establishment of a socialist economic system, it must be implanted from without, by a centralized, tightly organized, highly disciplined group of professional revolutionaries. In addition, in an autocratic state, such as Russia, revolutionary organizations must be secret so as to better combat repressive governmental measures and to prepare for the necessarily violent overthrow of existing governmental authority.

In *Imperialism—The Highest Stage of Capitalism* (1916) and elsewhere, Lenin presented the "law of uneven development." This "law" turned Marxism virtually upside down. Its central application to applied Marxism is the proposition that Communist revolution is more likely to occur first in a developing but relatively underdeveloped economy experiencing some of the tensions and conflicts of capitalist development in the early stages of industrialization, but lacking the wealth and economic success to bribe or buy off the upper strata of skilled workers, and, thereby, blunt or emasculate a revolutionary working-class movement. Such a society is also more likely to be characterized by a weak, autocratic, and repressive government, whose unpopularity plausibly will increase during periods of capitalist territorial wars. In short, socialism will more likely emerge by a Communist *political revolution* in an *underdeveloped economy* (like Russia) than in the economically developed and more politically stable Western democracies. The prospective success of such a premature revolution was held to depend upon two crucial conditions: first, the expectation that revolution in Russia would trigger or inspire Communist revolutions in industrially advanced countries, such as Germany, who would then come to Russia's aid with necessary economic and military assistance; second, the support of the poorer classes of rural peasantry, who, combined with the (smaller) urban proletariat, would rise against the wealthier classes in rural as well as urban areas. As seen in Chapter 8, Lenin's "law of uneven development" was combined with the "law of combined development" (that is, the idea that the "bourgeois" revolutionary transition from feudalism to capitalism can be combined with or "telescoped" into the "proletarian" revolutionary transition from capitalism to socialism) to become the orthodox Communist rationale explaining the possibility and legitimacy of a socialist revolution in a society like Russia.

In *The State and Revolution* (1917), Lenin clarified and sharpened the distinction between the "lower" stage of *socialism* and the "higher" stage of *communism*. His description of the economic and governmental organization of socialism follows that of Marx and Engels closely and is perhaps more representative of surviving idealistic Marxian anarchist-syndicalist sentiments and less of the centralized-bureaucratic dimension of Leninism than any of Lenin's other works.

His emphasis on elimination of private ownership of the means of production combined with a rationale for continued inequality of wage-income based upon differences in ability and work; the recognition that workers could not receive the "full value of their product" because of the need for investment, collective goods, provision for unemployables, and so on; the focus upon a radical increase in productivity combined with a similarly radical shift in human motivation as key prerequisites for the transition to communism; and the specification of government as a "dictatorship of the proletariat" designed to repress anti-socialist activity by capitalist reactionaries; all are there. So, too, is the basic Marxian dualism. On the one hand, efficient organization of economic activity requires tight, strict government coordination and control (the centralized, authoritarian, inequalitarian dimension); on the other hand, both the formation and execution of basic policy decisions of "accounting and control" (as distinguished from the functions of scientists and technical specialists) can be performed by the general body of "armed workers" themselves or their elected representatives (the decentralized, democratic, egalitarian dimension).

The Leninist variation incorporated some subtle shifts of emphasis, however. First, whereas Marx and Engels apparently conceived the lower stage as a temporary or transition period between a highly industrialized capitalism and a super-affluent communism, Lenin explicitly designated the socialist phase as having more or less indefinite length. Second, the emphasis on the imperative and strategic importance of centralized governmental and party authority—to plan and coordinate economic decisions, to repress possible counter-revolutionary activity, to serve as a "vanguard" in instilling and developing "socialist consciousness," and, through capital accumulation and technological improvement, to create the vast development of productive forces which would (eventually) lead to the possible transition to a communist economic society—is stronger.

POST-REVOLUTIONARY LENINIST
STRATEGY AND PRACTICE:
WAR COMMUNISM AND THE
NEW ECONOMIC POLICY

The logic of Marxism as applied to Russia may be characterized as a progressive abandonment of the anarchist-decentralized-democratic dimension of the classic Marxian dualism and the increasing, intensified dominance of the centralized and authoritarian component. The unifying theme of Communism in practice has turned out to be the rapid industrialization of a relatively underdeveloped economy. Rapid, large-scale industralization under Russian conditions required or appeared to require strong, centralized government authority and direction of the national economy. Strong, centralized governmental control over the organization and development of the economy conflicted with the anarchist, decentralized, democratic, and egalitarian dimensions of the classic revolutionary Marxian vision.

The process of strategic and selective adaptation, modification, and application of Marxism to Russian conditions, already begun prior to the Bolshevik revolution, proceeded after 1917 through several stages and incorporated numerous inconsistencies generated in part by the exigencies of war and civil war, the international response to the revolution, the need to consolidate political power, the struggles for political power among Communist leaders, and the need to retain a revolutionary élan while adapting to a post-revolutionary environment.

In the first half-decade after 1917, the major thrust in the transition from a revolutionary to a post-revolutionary version of applied Marxism was in the consolidation and development of a centralized, hierarchically-structured, tightly organized Communist party and the extension of its control over the economy and society. In effect, the Communist party became the state, and government control over the economic system came to be exercised through the apparatus of the Party.

War Communism. The consolidation and extension of centralized government-party control over the economic system was neither automatic nor smooth. Convinced by their Marxian heritage that the establishment of socialism required an urban, fully industrialized society, and obviously lacking such a base within Russia, Communist leaders hopefully anticipated their revolution would inspire Communist revolutions in industrially advanced countries, which would then come to their aid. Sustained by this expectation, the Bolsheviks turned enthusiastically to the tasks of organizing the economy and, within limits, with definite efforts to incorporate certain of the more idealistic dimensions of the pre-revolutionary Marxist-Leninist visions of the ideally functioning socialist economic society, including worker control of industry, reduction of inequality in income, and decentralization in government and economic administration. Even if Lenin himself was becoming increasingly disenchanted and embarrassed by the more decentralized aspects of his pre-revolutionary vision, their complete abandonment at an early stage could have destroyed the revolutionary élan within the Party and created internecine warfare.

Within the Communist Party, disputes arose over the desirable organizational form of the economic system (indeed, over the very possibility of the survival of the revolution). Alternative views included the Leninist position, which became increasingly characterized by a centralized and bureaucratic stance, but ranged from Trotsky's position (as leader of the Red Army during the civil war) that the economy should be organized like a vast army, with strict discipline and control over workers from above by a centralized elite, to that of the "workers' opposition," which criticized the emergence of state-party bureaucratic machinery and employment of former Czarist officials and managers, and called for control over production decisions by a cooperative association of workers, democratic election of all government officials and managers, and the promotion of equality in wage income.

In the countryside, the peasantry interpreted Lenin's revolutionary slogans ("peace, land, and bread") literally and simply took over the landed estates of the aristocrats and the Czarist family and government. Lacking government machinery to integrate and coordinate production in the argicultural sector, the Communists relied upon stringent emergency measures, including forced requisitions of grain. Nationalization of industry was not accompanied by any real planful coordination or integration of production decisions. Urban workers, responding to the egalitarian and syndicalist tone of revolutionary sentiments, often ejected former managers, extended labor union control over much of industry, and tried to run "their" own factories, typically with little thought to coordination with other parts of the economy. Salaries of managers, technicians, and government officials were sharply reduced in an effort to promote greater wage equality. Relative to the later development of the economic system under Stalin, this early period of *war communism*, as it came to be called, was in some ways an almost idyllic egalitarian anarchy.

When the Bolshevik revolution did not trigger other (successful) revolutions in Europe, Communist leaders in Russia found themselves isolated, surrounded by unfriendly powers abroad and confronted with discord and civil war at home. Faced with the absence and increasing unlikelihood of foreign assistance, the exigencies of civil war and foreign intervention, and an increasing recognition of the need to industrialize through their own efforts, the Bolsheviks shifted more and more away from the more decentralized, democratic, and egalitarian dimensions of the Marxian vision that had been established in the early months following the revolution. Worker control over industry was increasingly replaced by centralized and hierarchical government direction. Labor unions increasingly lost any semblance of independence and autonomy and became "armbands of the state," that is, part of the apparatus of government-party control. The government bureaucracy expanded and became more centralized. Former Czarist managers, technicians, specialists, and government officials were drawn back into the management of industry and government with steadily increasing salaries relative to the general body of industrial workers.

This entire period of *war communism* was one of confusion and dislocation. By 1921, the economy was in a state of virtual collapse. Output was lower than pre-World War I levels, trade was almost completely disrupted, and inflation was rampant. The peasantry, scattered throughout the countryside and beyond effective party-government control, became increasingly restive and uncooperative in response to food requisitions. With food supplies uncertain and tightening, the regime could no longer even count upon the tenuous, continued support of the small but favored urban proletariat. With increasing disenchantment and growing worker-peasant opposition, symbolized by the Kronstad revolt of 1921, the very survival of the regime came into question. Beyond the immediate issues was a more fundamental problem. Without assistance from friendly, economically developed countries, industrialization in Russia, regarded as an imperative precondition to the establishment of socialism, would have to proceed by internal efforts, which plausibly would impose burdens and sacrifices upon the general worker and peasant population. But the burdens of civil war, the increasing hostility of the peasantry to forced requisition of grain, the lack of a developed, sophisticated system of governmental and industrial administration, and the general disruption and dislocation of the economy made immediate frontal assault upon the industrialization process impracticable if not impossible.

The New Economic Policy. Lenin's response to those problems was to beat a strategic retreat. In the *New Economic Policy*, commencing in 1921, a series of measures were passed designed to create a Communist version of the "mixed economy" by a partial restoration of capitalism. Retaining government control over the "commanding heights" —heavy industry, banking and finance, transportation, and communication—Lenin released agriculture, wholesale and retail trade, and light industry to private enterprise, relying upon market motivations and processes to coordinate supplies and demands. The rationale was to save the revolution by a strategic retreat which would give the economy an opportunity to rebuild, reconstruct, and settle down, and the Communist party leadership a breathing space in which to determine its strategy for the future.

The NEP was highly successful on both counts. The limited restoration of private enterprise and market processes, combined with maintained government control over the strategically important levers and areas of economic power, constituted an environment conducive to economic recovery. By the mid-twenties, the economic losses and dislocations of war and civil war had been overcome, and the government-party apparatus of control had become more organized, centralized, disciplined, and sophisticated. During this same period, the logic of their position became increasingly clear to Communist leaders. Protection of the revolution from hostile powers abroad, maintenance and extension of political support at home, and creation of the preconditions for an effectively and efficiently functioning socialist economic system all combined to make industrialization a strategic imperative. The major debate within the Communist party became that of the character, magnitude, rapidity, and institutional form of the industrialization process.

The Great Industrial Debate

Once hope was abandoned that the Bolshevik revolution would be quickly followed by Communist revolutions in the advanced industrial countries of Western Europe, and the Stalinist conclusion accepted that the revolution could be protected only by building "socialism in one country," *how* to do so became an urgent question. Conflicting schools of thought developed on this issue. Though key individuals shifted positions at different times and in response to the political struggles among various personalities, it is a useful, simplifying device to distinguish two major positions. (For detailed analysis of this controversy and the roles of some of the most important protagonists, see 88).

THE RIGHTISTS: IN DEFENSE OF GRADUALISM

One group (including Communist theoretician N.N. Bukharin, M. P. Tomsky, head of the labor unions, and many party bureaucrats responsible for government policy during the NEP period) was generally associated with the right wing of the party. It began with a frank recognition of the government's weakness relative to the peasants, and, to a lesser degree, the workers, and thus, the strategic need to make popular accommodations and concessions as a basis for continued political support. The institutional form of economy envisaged by this group consisted essentially of a continuation of the NEP, that is, a combination of a socialized public sector, and a governmentally-controlled private sector, private enterprise coupled with free agricultural markets for the peasantry and NEP tradesmen, and liberal wage policies, shorter hours, improved working conditions, and support of labor unions and their demands for some degree of worker control over industry. As a corollary, suggested Bukharin, the excessive centralization, officious government bureaucracy, and tendency toward autocracy inherent under Russian conditions in the urge to rapid, large-scale industrialization could be avoided, or, at least, blunted.

The right-wing group recognized the need for economic growth and the strategic role played by capital accumulation in the growth process. Their growth strategy rested upon urging the necessity of relying upon a "natural" mechanism emanating from the joint and mutually supportive evolution of argiculture and industry. The expansion of industry was expected to provide industrial goods in exchange for food and raw materials from the agricultural sector. Technological improvements in industry would lower costs, raise profits, and, thereby, provide funds for investment in industry. As agricultural output and income expanded, peasant saving would spontaneously and voluntarily rise, augmenting saving-investment within the industrial sector.

Representatives of this group generally supported a deterministic interpretation of Marx and insisted "economic laws" could not be circumvented or necessary stages of historical development avoided. Economic development, even with or through the expansion of private enterprise in extension of a NEP-like mixed economy, was held necessary for the eventual transition to socialism. The growth of the agricultural sector was expected to be accompanied by an increase in the scale of production as the more enterprising rural capitalists, or *kulaks*, bought up more land and made technological improvements and capital investments. Less successful peasants would leave agriculture and contribute to an increasing urban labor force. The eventual transformation to socialism thus would deal with a relatively small number of large-scale agricultural units and capitalists rather than with millions of small-scale, inefficient, scattered peasant households.

In the process of development, according to the Rightists, the economy would expand, the alliance between workers and peasants would grow, the Party, maintaining control over the commanding heights of the economy, would demonstrate the efficiency and effectiveness of socialist organization, democracy would spread, and consciousness and understanding of the necessity and wisdom of a socialist economic system would grow. In short, gradual industrialization could and would provide, by a natural mechanism, the economic, political, social, and psychological preconditions for socialism. By contrast, rapid and large-scale industrialization would require the imposition of intolerable burdens and sacrifices upon the peasantry and workers, destroy the social and political bases for support of the revolution, increase the tendencies toward centralization and government hierarchy, conflict with laws of natural evolution, and threaten the viability and survival of the system.

THE LEFTISTS: IN DEFENSE OF SPEED

The left-wing opposition was generally associated with such party leaders as Trotsky, Zinoviev, and Kamenev. Its theoretical ideas were provided largely by an economist, Eugene Preobrazhensky. [See 74, 85, 88] Whereas the right-wing group commenced with what it regarded as a realistic assessment of existing conditions and prospective trends in accordance with a natural mechanism of evolution, the party's left wing began with the statement of an aspiration and the revolutionary transformation necessary to attain it. Socialism, they argued, requires a modern industrialized society; and rapid, large-scale industrialization is thus the central task of a post-revolutionary Communist strategy.

In the traditional Marxian view, the transition from feudalism to capitalism required a "primitive" (or pre-capitalist) accumulation of capital—through conquest, piracy, colonies, expropriation of church lands, enclosures, and the like. By analogy, a Communist revolutionary movement in a relatively underdeveloped economy requires, for its survival and growth, argued the

Leftists, a primitive socialist accumulation of capital.

The left-wing analysis of the role of capital accumulation in the industrialization process, as developed by Preobrazhensky, had two central dimensions. The first emphasized the need for a large-scale accumulation program—larger than that urged by the Rightists. The imperative need for a large magnitude of investment and, thereby, a rapid rate of increase in capital accumulation rested upon such factors as:

1. the need for incorporating the latest technologies and utilizing very capital-intensive methods of production to promote efficiency and productivity;
2. the need for massive investment in many different areas of the economy simultaneously to maximize the effectiveness of the capital accumulation programs through investment interdependencies and thereby catapult the economy out of the lethargy of underdevelopment;
3. the need to replace capital stock which had become obsolete and depreciated during the twenties;
4. the requirement of higher ratios of capital to labor in investment than in consumption goods industries and higher ratios of increments of capital to increments of output now that more or less full utilization of existing capital stocks had been achieved during the NEP period.

The second part of the left-wing argument was a pessimism about the likelihood of obtaining such large magnitudes of savings from the peasants. In brief, "the position of the Leftists was that industrialization would require tremendous savings, that these would have to come mostly from the peasantry, but that the peasants would never voluntarily make this sacrifice if the government continued to follow a policy of encouraging peasant agriculture." [71: 18–19] Therefore, the government would have to use harsh measures to push through a rate of capital accumulation significantly beyond that which would be voluntarily and spontaneously forthcoming from peasant saving.

By contrast, argued the Leftists, a gradualist policy of compromise and accommodation to the peasantry would encourage (as the Rightists admitted) the growth of the rich agricultural capitalists, or *kulaks*. With greater wealth and economic power, the *kulaks* could demand even greater concessions from the regime; by withholding grain, they could blackmail the government into meeting those demands or threaten the industrialization program with economic sabotage, perhaps even breakdown. (In the late twenties, the Leftists argued that Russian *kulaks* were behaving in precisely this manner.) In addition, with growing economic power and independence, why would the richer peasants (and their urban private-enterprise businessmen-NEP counterparts) be content simply with greater wealth and income? Would it not be more plausible to expect them to demand political power and influence as well, thus threatening to overwhelm the Communist revolution?

In their desire to develop a rationale for rapid, large-scale industrialization and "primitive socialist accumulation," the Leftists were more concerned with the need for industrialization than with the precise character of the institutions and processes to accomplish it. But they warned their Party colleagues that achievement of rapid industrialization would require harsh and dictatorial measures, the termination of concessions to the peasantry, the further development of a centralized, hierarchically structured party as the main instrument of government control, the subordination of the labor unions and worker control to the Party, and a planned centralized direction and coordination of the economic system. Presumably, an economic system with these properties would be neither communism *nor* (developed) socialism, but a necessary *transition* stage to socialism, having the same function (that is, primitive capital accumulation) as that served in the process of transition from feudalism to capitalism in Western Europe.[1]

In sum, by the late twenties, the Communist party had presented itself with the position that too rapid a rate of capital accumulation could yield extreme disorder and dislocation and, thereby, the breakdown of the system, and too slow a rate of growth could leave Russia in the quagmire of backwardness, inefficiency, and underdevelopment, with an increasingly powerful, independent, and potentially hostile counter-revolutionary force in the countryside, thereby threatening the very survival of the system. The party was caught on the horns of a dilemma.

The Stalinist Solution

The Stalinist solution to the dilemma posed by the great industrialization debate was eventually adopted in the late twenties after more than half a decade of skillful political maneuver in which Stalin disposed, first, of Trotsky and his other left-wing

opponents, and, finally, of his right-wing opposition. It constituted a *third Russian revolution* beyond the revolutions of 1917. Stalinist Communism may be described essentially as the application of totalitarian methods of political control to the process of industrialization. It rested upon the conviction, bordering on obsession, that extremely rapid and large-scale industrialization, incorporating vast magnitudes of saving and investment (even larger than those envisaged by the Leftist participants in the great industrialization debate) squeezed from an uncooperative peasantry, was the essential historic mission of Russian Communism.

The implementation of this conviction required important institutional innovations, notably, collectivization of agriculture, described more fully later. These innovations constituted the establishment and extension of total and comprehensive government control throughout the entire economic system. Their impact, coupled with the massive Stalinist program of capital accumulation, though eventually successful in accomplishing industrialization, created extreme dislocation and disruption and nearly threatened, as the Rightists had predicted, the very survival of the system.

Once the regime had started down this road, serious theoretical discussions of economics waned. The Soviet five-year plans embodied victory for the idea that the crucial variable was the rate of capital accumulation and that it had to be set very high. The implications of this were so adverse for the population that the subject could not really bear open discussion, and the next quarter-century of Soviet literature on development strategy became an exercise in obfuscation. The function of Soviet discussions of growth processes was to conceal, rather than to flaunt, the real secret of success, namely, the draconian sacrifice of current consumption enforced by the planners in order to invest in the development of industry to provide the basis for potential future consumption.

[1] In addition to these two major groups, there was a third group in the Party's extreme left wing. It consisted of idealistic old-line Bolsheviks heavily influenced by the anarcho-syndicalist strains in the pre-revolutionary Marxist-Leninist vision. For them, the NEP policy and position of the Rightists was a sham and constituted essentially a combination of free enterprise and centralized economic dictatorship by the government and party elite, each equally defective and neither expressing true socialist revolutionary aspirations. The policies and recommendations of the Leftists were regarded, if anything, as even more anti-socialist than those of the Rightists. In sum, this group held steadfast to the anarcho-syndicalist dimension of the classic Marxian dualism, claimed that the revolution had been betrayed (as in the French revolution) by a "Thermidorian reaction," and proposed a true proletarian revolution to overthrow the increasingly centralized economic dictatorship of the party and establish its vision of true socialism, characterized by democracy, equality, and decentralized worker control of industry.

THE STALINIST APPROACH TO
ECONOMIC DEVELOPMENT

Soviet Growth Strategy

Any discussion of the Soviet strategy and theory of economic development must operate on two levels: One involves simply reporting the doctrines and theories which the Communist leaders profess; another attempts to infer their theories and strategies from their actions and the behavior of the system.

As to the first of these two levels, Soviet leaders have done some articulate theorizing about their approach to economic growth and have propounded explicit principles and methods, which they have claimed guide their actions. There have been periods of controversy, when alternative theories and strategies have been proposed, especially in the twenties, before the industrialization drive actually began. Some of the ideas advanced in that debate later formed the substance of Soviet development strategy. But this debate was terminated with the inauguration of the Five-Year Plans, and it is much more difficult to find in Soviet economic literature after 1928 any interesting theoretical analysis of growth or any explicit statements about growth strategy. The outcome of the industrialization debate of the twenties was a decision by the leaders that the key to rapid growth was very high rates of capital accumulation and a concentration of resources on the capital-goods producing industries. As a corollary, the branches of the economy serving consumer wants, such as agriculture and light industry, were to be slighted. To enforce this set of priorities and to suppress mechanisms by which this decision could be influenced by the population, the Russians gave their economic system a distinct organizational form, sometimes called a "command economy." Embodying as it did the imposition of an outside purpose and urgency on the population, this strategy has been a source of tremendous tension in Soviet society. Because the emphasis on a high rate of capital

accumulation and its corollary of low consumption was such a divisive issue in the society, this decision could not well be discussed openly, and the leadership, therefore, has always framed its explicit statements about the theory of development in euphemistic terms which have had little relevance to real life.

If, therefore, the twenties generated a rich harvest of theories and ideas about the problem of economic development, Soviet discussions in later years offer much less to draw upon in trying to reconstruct a Soviet theory and strategy of development. For this part of the history, therefore, we must seek to understand their strategy through a second approach: by focusing not so much on what they say as on what they do, and by trying to induce from their actions the theoretical and strategic notions that inspired them.

Theoretical Foundations

MARXIAN REPRODUCTION SCHEMES

The central issue in the industrialization debate of the twenties was the problem of capital accumulation—how ambitious a level of investment should be attempted, how this rate of investment might be attained, and where this investment should be directed. Most of the disputants argued within a Marxian framework of concepts, which they were able to manipulate in a fruitful way. The main Marxian idea with which they started was the "reproduction scheme."

THE TWO DEPARTMENTS

In the following scheme, Department I represents the branches producing the means of production, Department II—the branches producing the means of consumption. The symbols c, v, and s have the same meanings as in Marx's theory of value, but they now refer to aggregates in a kind of national income accounting scheme. O_1 and O_2 refer to the aggregate values of output in the two main sectors of the economy.

Department I: $c_1 + v_1 + s_1 = O_1$
Department II: $c_2 + v_2 + s_2 = O_2$

Thus, for example, v_1 is aggregate wage payments in the branches of the economy producing the means of production, O_2 is the aggregate output of the consumer goods industries. The scheme is designed to show certain interrelations between the two departments in the process of production. There are two cases—"simple reproduction" and "expanded reproduction." Simple reproduction might be illustrated by the following numerical version of the scheme:

Department I
$4,000c + 1,000v + 1,000s = 6,000$

Department II
$2,000c + 500v + 500s = 3,000$

Total national economy
$6,000c + 1,500v + 1,500s = 9,000$

These numbers have been chosen to satisfy certain equilibrium requirements under conditions of no growth. The 6,000 units worth of output of Department I, (that is, the means of production, or the goods which are consumed as "constant capital" to make other goods) is just equal to the sum of constant capital used in both sectors $(c_1 + c_2)$. The output of Department II (3,000) is just equal to the sum of the incomes of the working class and of the capitalists. (We are assuming no growth, which implies that the capitalists consume all their income from surplus values and save none.) Supply and demand for each of the two kinds of output thus are equal. We can also think of the two departments as two separate groups of people, who exchange output. Retaining 4,000 out of their output of 6,000 to cover consumption of constant capital within Department I itself, the producers of Department I have left 2,000 units of output available to exchange with the producers of Department II. Fortunately, the firms of Department II need just 2,000 units worth of the means of production to cover their needs for constant capital and have available for sale 2,000 units worth of consumer goods not consumed by the capitalists and workers employed in their own sector. When exchanged for 2,000 units worth of constant capital, this 2,000 units worth of consumer goods just matches the 1,000 units worth of demand from the workers of Department I spending their wages and the 1,000 from the Department I capitalists spending their profits for consumption.

REPRODUCTION WITH GROWTH

With growth, there are some differences. Rather than consuming all the income they have received as surplus value, the capitalists save a large share of it to be invested in the expansion of production. We can illustrate what happens in this process, starting with the following numerical values for the scheme at an initial period.

Department I
$4,400c + 1,100v + 1,100s = 6,600$

Department II
$1,600c + 800v + 800s = 3,200$

Total national economy
$6,000c + 1,900v + 1,900s = 9,800$

Now, suppose the capitalists consume only 1,110 from their income of 1,900 and save 790, and then use the latter to expand each category of their capital outlays in the following period by an equal percentage in accordance with the following division:

Increase	Dept. I	Dept. II	Total
in c	440	160	600
in v	110	80	190
Total	550	240	790

In the second period, with the rate of exploitation unchanged, the account will look as follows:

Department I
$4,840c + 1,210v + 1,210s = 7,260$

Department II
$1,760c + 880v + 880s = 3,520$

Total
$6,600c + 2,090v + 2,090s = 10,780$

This procedure can be continued for as many steps as desired (an interesting exercise to carry out on your own). Doing so, we would find that, with the numbers and proportions shown, the equilibrium conditions already described for simple reproduction will also be met. In the first period, the output of Department I is large enough to reproduce the constant capital used in producing that period's output (6,000) and to provide 600 for expansion in the next period. Similarly, Department II output is just enough to cover the consumption of workers (1,900) and capitalists (1,110), and to provide an inventory of wage goods large enough to permit hiring the additional amount of labor shown for the next period.

To meet the second condition, that is, that the capitalists of the two sectors have equal amounts to exchange with each other, we have to make some special assumptions about the saving and consuming behavior of the separate groups of capitalists. Suppose the total saving (790) is composed of 550 saved by the capitalists of Department I (that is, they save 50 percent of their income) and 560 saved by the capitalists of Department II (that is, they save 70 percent of their income.) Then, the capitalists of Department I, after making good the 4,400 of constant capital they have used up in this period and adding to it 440 to expand output in the second period, have output worth 1,760 to exchange with the capitalists of Department II. This is just what the capitalists of Department II need to carry on production in the second period at an expanded level. The 1,760 worth of consumer goods which the capitalists of Department I receive in exchange for these producer goods are used up as 550 of their own consumption: 1,100 to cover the consumption of the workers in their factories in the first period, and the accumulation of an inventory of 110 of consumer goods to support the larger consumption of Department I workers in the succeeding period.

EVALUATION

If instinct tells you something is not quite right in all this, that is understandable. Things work out neatly in this example only because the numbers have been chosen to meet very stringent requirements, which make the example rather uninteresting as a representation of reality. To make the model work out like this, the division of new investment among the four possible uses must be in proportion to capital outlays of the previous period. For the quantities of output exchanged between the sectors to be in equilibrium, the division of surplus value between investment and consumption in each sector must be in a certain ratio, determined by other ratios in the system. In short, it requires constancy of all the basic proportions, as well as uniform growth.

There are many other problems apparent in this model but we are less interested in discrediting it than in noting its implications about growth. First, it suggests that growth is essentially a matter of capital accumulation. Since the output of each sector is in a fixed ratio to the capital employed, the growth of capital is the crucial variable, and this, in turn, is dependent on the rate of saving. It also shows, however, that the possibilities of expanding output by expanding outlays of c and v are limited by the output of the preceding period. Note, however, that it ignores the problem that an expansion of output requires the availability of more laborers as well as more goods. In the general structure of Marxian argument, that problem is solved by the theory of "the reserve army of the unemployed." Second, it focuses attention on the production of producers' goods as a special kind of bottleneck. The basic bottleneck in expanding output is the capacity of Department I, which sets a limit to the supply of constant capital on which expansion of both sectors depends. Third, it brings out clearly the problem of proportionality in the process of growth.

The scheme is more suggestive than

definitive in considering these problems because it does not consider explicitly the distinction between flows and stocks of goods. This general deficiency in Marxian theory has been allowed for in later modifications of Marxian theory by interpreting constant capital as *depreciation* of capital goods plus outlays on current material inputs. Many Marxian ideas are preserved under this transformation, but the neat equilibria found in the preceding numerical example are destroyed. The output of Department I clearly is a flow of goods, including capital goods, but if *c* shows only the depreciation on capital goods (the portion that consists of current material inputs poses no problem, of course), then we cannot treat increases in *c* from one period to the next as equivalent to the excess of the output of Department I over the part used up in that same period. But the ingredients are there, and deficiencies like this spur the theoretician to reformulate the model to eliminate them.

The Growth Model of G. A. Fel'dman

CAPITAL GOODS VERSUS CONSUMPTION GOODS

The most famous creative modification of the Marxian reproduction scheme and one that is truly helpful in understanding the Soviet decisions about development is that of G. A. Fel'dman. Fel'dman modified Marx's scheme slightly in accordance with the idea that the really important distinction is between activities that add to capacity (that is, create new capital goods) and those which only sustain or utilize it, rather than between the production of the means of production and the means of consumption. (The means of production is a much broader concept than the production of capital goods, since it also takes in the production of materials.) Thus, Fel'dman makes Department I the production of capital goods and Department II the production of consumption goods.

A corollary modification was to consider explicitly the *stock* of capital goods in each sector rather than the Marxian *c*. By postulating a certain proportion between the stock of capital and output, Fel'dman then sought to investigate the effect on growth when one plays with the division of the output of the redefined Department I (that is, capital goods) between adding to the capital stock in Department I and adding to the stock of capital in Department II.

AN ILLUSTRATIVE ANALOGY

It may be easier to visualize the problem via the following analogy. Imagine that, in Fig. 15.1, tank *A* holds a micro-organism that reproduces itself like yeast or algae. The mass of this organism will increase at some rate over time through cell division. Suppose that the increment over the course of a month is equal to 10 percent of the stock at the beginning of the month. This increment is the "output" of tank *A*. If this increment is left in the tank, then the increment that comes in the second month will again be 10 percent of the larger mass with which we started the second month, and so on. But imagine that it is possible to drain off whatever share of this increment is desired into a second tank, and that, in the transfer, the nature of the organism is somehow modified, so that, in reproducing itself in tank *B*, the *new* cells (produced at a fixed rate from those in the tank) are incapable of further reproduction and are somehow segregated and "harvested" from the tank. This is the "output" of tank *B*.

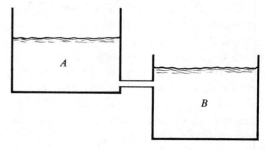

Fig. 15.1. An illustrative analogy of the Fel'dman model

Consider two ways of treating the output of A. (1) If it is all left in A, then the output of the *system* in any given period will be the increment in tank A plus the harvest from tank B (the latter remaining constant over time since the stock in B does not change.) The rate at which this output grows will be a weighted average of the rate of growth of the harvest from B (that is, zero) and the rate of growth of A. As A comes to be larger and larger relative to the mass in B, its growth rate will come to be the most important influence on the rate of growth of the total system, and the rate of growth of total output will approach the rate of growth of the stock and output of A. (2) If the increments in A are wholly transferred to B, the stock in B will grow, and since the output from B is proportional to this stock, the output from B will grow at the same rate. But as the stock in B grows relative to that in A, the flow from A (which is constant since it is in a constant ratio to the unchanging stock in A) will become smaller and smaller in relation to the growing stock in B, so that the rate of growth of the stock (and, therefore, of the output) in B declines. Again, considering the output of the system as the sum of the output of A and B, it is an average of the rate of growth of output from A, (that is, zero) and from B, but gradually approaches that of B. And since increments to the stock in B are getting smaller and smaller in relation to the stock in B, the rate of growth of output from B is continuously falling, as is also the rate of growth of the total output.

Fel'dman's model is formally identical with this kind of system. His Department I produces an output that can be devoted to increasing the capital stock of either department, and his Department II produces an output that can only be consumed. The output of each Department is proportional to the stock of capital it possesses, and the crucial variable that one can manipulate to control the growth of the system as a whole is the division of the output of the first department between additions to its own stock and additions to the stock of the second department.

Strategies intermediate between those described herein are possible—that is, the share of the output of Department I retained to increase the capital stock of Department I can vary anywhere between 0 and 100 percent. The behavior of the system then becomes very complicated, and the path of growth will depend importantly also on the initial ratio between the two stocks and the respective production rates or capital-output ratios. But the important trade-off is the following: As we move toward strategy (1), we are foregoing potential growth in B (that is, consumption) in the near term, since we are not adding to its capital stock as much as we might. But this sacrifice will be more than repaid in the long term. The retention of capital in the capital goods-producing industry will make its output grow, and a fixed share, however small, of this growing output devoted to expansion of the consumer goods industry eventually will mean large absolute increments to the capital stock of the consumer goods industry, and therefore, large increments in its output. As we move to strategy (2), the reverse is true, with large early increments in consumption bought at the expense of stultifying the growth of Department I, the output capacity of which is the ultimate bottleneck constraining the growth of the system. Still further variations are possible if the investment split is regarded not as a constant, but subject to change over time. There are still more complicated growth patterns for total output, consumption, and investment. For instance, by following strategy (1) for a while, then switching to strategy (2), we would get no growth at all in consumption in the first period, and then, very rapid growth of consumption for a while after the switch.

THE ROLE AND RELEVANCE OF THE FEL'DMAN MODEL

It is important to emphasize there are many things wrong with this model—especially its assumption that capital is the only limitational factor. Any biologist would criticize the analogy on the point that the continued growth of micro-organisms in tank *A* depends on a constantly growing food supply; and analogously, in Fel'dman's model, unless the labor force and the resources supplied by nature grow fast enough to man and sustain the new capacities, the assumed growth cannot take place. The relevance of this model is: first, it reveals clearly what the Soviet leaders saw as the strategic variable on which to concentrate; second, it provides insight into the kind of alternatives they were weighing. It is plausible to interpret what they actually did as an application of this basic idea. This does not mean they thought consistently in the theoretical terms that Fel'dman had defined, or that they regarded their actions as practical applications of Fel'dman's model. Ironically, Fel'dman probably had little direct influence on economic policy and strategy. He originally presented his theory while working in the planning apparatus; but when his model was discussed, he was subjected to heavy criticism, and like most of the other economists of the twenties, he became a casualty of the political upheavals in which Stalin destroyed his rivals. Fel'dman has only recently been restored to Soviet memory and his contribution recognized by Soviet economists. But he has his real memorial in 30 years of policy. The idea that the first task is to build the "material technical base of communism," that is, to allocate most of the output of the capital goods-producing industry to augmenting its own production base, is the fruit of his demonstration. The model also provides the justification that Soviet leaders have always offered for keeping small the share of investment goods allocated to the consumer goods industries: namely that, eventually, when the capacity of the capital goods sector becomes sufficiently large, the allocation of even a small fixed share of the output of I to II also will result in very rapid growth of consumption.

Soviet Doctrine on Economic Growth

To comprehend how the theory and strategy of growth is presented to the Soviet citizen, it will be useful to review a standard Soviet interpretation of their growth strategy, as expounded in a typical Soviet economics textbook such as *Political Economy* [83].

Growth strategy usually is treated in Soviet sources in the context of the "economic laws of socialism." The character of the economic laws of socialism has long been debated by Soviet ideologists and economists. This is a very fuzzy discussion. The usual interpretation of an *economic law* would be as some kind of empirical regularity over which man has no control. But this is not what the Soviet economists have in mind—in their view, economic laws are, in effect, normative principles that need to be discovered and consciously adhered to by Communist leaders.

For example, the "basic law of socialist economics" is said to be "an ever fuller satisfaction of the material and cultural requirements of all of society and satisfaction of the many-sided development of its members by uninterrupted growth and improvement of social production." Obviously, this is more the statement of a goal than a description of some inescapable constraint. A second example is the "law of planned proportional development of the national economy," that is, the idea that it is necessary in planning to ensure that all branches of the economy develop in a proper relationship to each other—industry and agriculture, consumption and capital accumulation, wages and productivity. Again, what is being heralded as a law is actually only an objective that may or may not be achieved in practice.

Neither of these laws is satisfactory as an empirical economic law or a theory of economic growth. The basic law presents only the goal of growth, saying nothing about how it is to be attained nor offering any assurance it will be attained. It does have a corollary:

that the power over the use of the resources is to be in the hands of the state and the planners. The law of planned proportional development is more like a statement about means—it suggests that the growth described as a goal in the first law is to be attained by proper attention to the relationship between growth rates among sectors and components. Though the law is very vague as to what these crucial relationships are, there is a large body of commentary about what Russian theorists think are the proper proportions.

The most celebrated of these is the proposition that the output of industry A must grow faster than that of industry B. Industry A and industry B represent, in the industrial sector of the economy, the distinction between the "means of production" and the "means of consumption" already cited in the discussion of Marx's reproduction scheme. What the law is supposed to mean operationally is that the output of those branches of industry producing producers' goods (such as steel or machinery) is supposed to grow faster than the output of the branches producing consumer goods (such as food and clothing.) The idea behind this assertion derives partly from the kind of strategy that Fel'dman proposed; namely that, if you want to grow, you must increase the rate of investment, and it is sector I that produces investment goods. But it also owes something to other Marxian ideas. In most presentations, the idea is explained as a consequence of the fact that the organic composition of capital (see Chapter 5) is constantly shifting in a progressive economy toward a greater emphasis on c compared to v. This is the result of more specialization in production, more machine-intensive methods of production, and so on. Thus, c is rising in relation to the total value of goods in the economy as a whole. Since the producer goods that c represents in the equation are produced by sector I, the output of sector I has to grow faster than the output of sector II. The law about industry A versus B is just the ap-

plication of this idea to the industrial part of the economy. It is not possible to take this law very seriously. As has often been pointed out, Marxian dynamics, along with the increasing mechanization of production and improvements in the techniques of production, involves a cheapening of wage goods— that is, a reduction in the socially-necessary labor required to produce a bushel of wheat, for instance. Thus, while c is rising in relation to v, the rate of exploitation is also rising, (that is, s is rising in relation to v) so that the ratio of c to the value of output need not rise at all. Also, technical progress might take place at a more rapid rate in the producer goods industries than in the consumer goods industries, so that even if the physical amount of producers' goods used in relation to a man-hour of labor increases, the labor embodied in producer goods (which is what determines relative values) need not increase in relation to the living labor being used in a given industry. In short, the "faster growth of industry A" is no more than a conjecture, demonstrable in the Marxian scheme of things only by the introduction of a number of special unsubstantiated assumptions.

Secondly, and the important point for the relationship between Soviet theory and policy, this is not an "operational" theory. Its concepts are not identifiable in the real world, and it is impossible to do in the real world the things that the theory suggests be done. The implication of the theory is that the secret of growth is to plan for the output of producer goods to grow faster than output of consumer goods. But when we try to determine what producer goods and consumer goods are, we run into trouble. Ordinarily, we think of coal as a producer's good, but, obviously, much coal is consumed for personal use by households. Or textiles may be thought of as consumer goods, but most textiles are not sold to households at all, but to the apparel industry as raw materials. Moreover, much textile output is clearly a producer good in the form of such items as tire cord and belting and materials for bags and many other technical uses. The problem is that it is only possible to determine whether a given good is a producer good or a consumer good by asking how, in fact, it is to be used, not by the inherent nature of the good itself nor the nature of the branch of industry that produced it. The Russians have required that their statistical system and their plans distinguish industry *A* and industry *B*, but, in practice, these measures have little relationship to the theory which inspired them.

From the point of view of economic development, the crucial question is the share of the national income going to investment rather than for current consumption. In any kind of theory or growth model one uses to perform mental experiments concerning the process of growth, this is the crucial choice variable. And once this is set, there is nothing more to say about the rate of growth of producers' goods versus consumers' goods. Those things are *consequences* of the basic decision about the rate of investment and about technical choices. Increasing the rate of investment means certain increases in the output of the industries producing capital goods, but that is a derivative idea, not the secret of the strategy itself.

Soviet Strategy as Interpreted by Others

Despite the extensive Soviet literature on planning for growth and the numerous interesting ideas Soviet planners have proposed on how to make the economy grow, it is difficult to find in any Soviet source a statement of their strategy or theory of how they see the process of growth that is both coherent and in accord with the actual policies Soviet planners have followed. Rather than trying to summarize the standard kind of pronouncements that one finds in Soviet discussions, it may be more to the point to combine insights found in these pronouncements with the observations of outside observers into a coherent strategy of growth. In constructing this statement of strategy, it would also be valuable to relate Soviet policies and actions to some of the traditional problems and issues in economic development. One of the reasons for interest in the Soviet approach to growth is that it is seen by others and is advertised by the Russians as a model for other underdeveloped countries. By examining how the Russians have coped with certain characteristic problems of economic development, we can ascertain whether the strategy, in fact, has universal applicability.

One of the important features of the Soviet approach to development is that it truly is a "strategic" approach. The job of planning resource allocation for an entire national economy turned out to be a Herculean job, and the Soviet and East European leaders found they could manage it only if they could concentrate their attention primarily on a limited number of large issues. When you are trying to make the whole economic mechanism move in the direction desired by a small elite at the top, it is necessary to "think big" rather than concentrate on details.

FROM PEASANT LABOR TO INDUSTRIAL CAPITAL

In contrast to industrially advanced economies, where microeconomic efficiency in the combination and allocation of resources is very important, the central focus of the Stalinist strategy for accelerating growth was on manipulating certain macroeconomic proportions, especially the rate of saving and investment. This strategy had two major facets: first, the transfer of peasant labor to the cities and factories and their transformation there into a disciplined force of industrial labor; second, the transformation of the industrial labor force thus created into capital goods. For the system as a whole, the central strategic principle was simply the maximization of the output of capital goods (and thus, within strategic limits, the minimization of the output of consumption goods). For the two major sectors of the economy, the strategy involved the maximization of the transfer of labor, food, and raw materials from the agricultural to the industrial sector, combined with the minimization of the investment of human and capital resources in agriculture and the minimization of the provision of food and other consumer goods to the peasantry.

The institutional corollary of this development strategy had several leading dimensions. First, the collectivization of agriculture provided the basic institutional mechanism for eliminating the economic power and independence of the peasantry, for ejecting peasant labor from agriculture, and for organizing production and distribution within the agricultural sector to keep peasant consumption at minimum levels. Second, government ownership of the means of production, a monopolistic relationship to the population, centralized physical allocations of resources to plant and industry managers in accordance with plans for industrial development, and a variety of controls over labor and management provided the institutional mechanism for disciplining workers and managers and inducing concentration of emphasis on the production of investment goods and the utilization of those investment goods primarily within the industrial sector. Third, control over the monetary, fiscal, and pricing systems enabled Russian planners during (and since) the Stalinist era to establish a financial mechanism to supplement and complement their physical and human allocations. This financial mechanism combined low wage levels with high prices for consumption goods (including a hidden turnover tax added to the prices of commodities), the difference between the two constituting an economic surplus that could be mobilized for and allocated to investment.

In brief, the system of central planning followed by the Communist countries was designed to take saving-investment decisions out of the hands of the population. The institutional structure of the system contributed to the ability of the regime to raise the rate of saving far above that which the people would choose had they any say in the matter. Unfortunately, the institutional features cited earlier which have contributed to this effectiveness in mobilizing resources are probably rather dysfunctional with respect to the ability of the system to utilize flexibly and efficiently the resources so mobilized. For example, the huge capital stock accumulated by the system is poorly adapted to its task and is used very unproductively. The command system that has been effective in raising the rate of investment is not conducive to the kind of microeconomic decision-making that would ensure effective utilization of this capital.

RESEARCH AND TECHNOLOGY

Another illustration of the broad macroeconomic strategy of Stalinist Communism is found in the strategic emphasis by Soviet leaders on education and scientific research. It is true these are powerful sources of growth and higher productivity, and it is a wise strategic decision to seek growth by devoting large resources to these functions, but the Russians have been more spectacularly successful in producing a great number of scientists and engineers and in creating a research and development establishment than in using these resources effectively to achieve technical progress. The incentive system that motivates lower level decision-makers to adhere to the gross priorities communicated to them from above does little to encourage them to gamble on technological improvements or to evaluate sensitively the costs and gains from possible technical changes. It is instructive that the detailed statistical study of Soviet economic development in recent years by economists outside the USSR has shown that the very impressive increase in the output of the Soviet economy is attributable more to the growth in the amount of *inputs into production* than to any extraordinary gains in the *productivity* of these inputs.

INCENTIVES AND CONTROLS

The same kind of strategic oversimplification is seen in the system of orders and incentives used to control those charged with actual execution of the plan. Both in setting planned targets for enterprises and in measuring "success" in performance, Soviet-style planning has concentrated on a limited number of measures, such as the gross value of output in constant prices or certain basic technological ratios, such as fuel input per *KWH* of electricity produced. This approach has been quite successful in focusing the attention of management on the aspects of performance that are being measured, but desiderata that may compete with the goals emphasized, as, say, quality competes with quantity, are ignored, since the system of "success indicators" cannot cover all the detailed aspects of performance. Any administrative system that tried to cover *all* aspects of performance would be too cumbersome to operate. It has been argued that, given the level of development, the level of skills, and sophistication of products, it may in the past have been rational to prefer quantity to quality, so that this strategic approach was a wise one. But in modern conditions, such strategic oversimplification may no longer be appropriate.

LEADING LINKS AND ROUTINIZATION

Another illustration of the strategic approach to getting results is in the characteristic designation of "leading links." Soviet planners have usually concentrated their efforts in some areas of the economy and let the rest hobble along as best they could. For example, the machinery and electric power industries have always enjoyed special favor as leading links and have been relatively lavishly provided with resources, while other branches have had to make do with much less resources and attention from the central authorities. Every Soviet plan ever promulgated has begun by defining a limited number of "basic tasks in the coming plan period." Soviet planners have tried to cope with large, complex problems by finding some standard formula that would settle everything, a magical system of crop rotation in agriculture or a single uniform technical choice or policy in some industry. These measures have often been seen as panaceas capable of solving the problem in every situation and suitable for enterprises in any part of the country. The history of Soviet planning is full of slogans embodying this idea—as in Lenin's adage that communism is "Soviet power plus electrification" or Stalin's (1934) pronouncement that "cadres are all important" or in Khrushchev's adulation of corn as "the queen of the fields."

One observer has characterized the Soviet method of development as "growth through routinization." Organization and routine have been adopted as a substitute for conscientious concern with growth on the part of the individual. The architects of the Soviet system have tried to design a kind of structure in which each participant, simply by going through the motions and following the orders and routines laid down from above, will do what growth calls for, without having to himself be much concerned with growth. Certainly, Soviet planning is full of routine. In technological design, for instance, standard plans for production facilities such as a power station or a refinery have been characteristic—once a basic design has been settled on, it may not be changed for 10 or 15 years. Technological progress has been sought by the routine application of selected crucial innovations rather than by innovation across the whole spectrum of possibilities.

This kind of approach is well suited to coping with some of the characteristic problems of underdeveloped countries. Development and modernization always entail changing peoples' values and routine patterns of life. The population is likely to feel disorganized by these changes and resist them. Modernization also means the adoption of some new vision of life—an inculcation of a belief in progress and a forward-looking attitude. The centralized Soviet approach, with its monopoly of the means of education and communication, has provided an effective way of imposing this new vision and these new values from above.

METHODS OF PRODUCTION

Another issue commonly confronted by development programs is whether preference should be given in technological decisions to "capital-intensive" or "capital-saving" solutions. The advanced countries from which underdeveloped countries hope to borrow technology generally have a scarcity of labor and a plentiful supply of capital. Their technology accordingly is usually capital-intensive, that is, designed to save labor by the substitution of capital. Since underdeveloped countries have abundant labor and a shortage of capital, there is an issue as to whether the foreign technology they could borrow relatively easily is efficient for them. The Russian solution is an interesting one. In their borrowing of technology (and they have done so on a large scale) the Soviet planners have tended to adopt foreign technology in its capital-intensive version in the central processes of some technology such as a blast furnace or modern oil-well drilling rigs. The less important auxiliary processes, however, such as materials handling, intraplant transport, and so on, have been left unmodernized and unmechanized so that the overall process is not especially capital-intensive.

POPULATION

Finally, one of the most important obstacles to economic development is the population problem. Most underdeveloped countries have relatively low rates of population growth as the net result of a high birth rate and a high death rate. As economic development begins, better nutrition and public health measures lead to a rapid decline in the death rate, but the birth rate remains high. The resulting acceleration of population growth prevents increases in per capita income, even if aggregate national income does grow.

The experience of the Communist countries with this dimension of the problem is complex. Generally, though most of them started with the combination of high birth rates and high death rates that are the genesis of the population explosion, they have not had high rates of population growth. The population of the USSR, for example, has grown since 1928 at a rate only slightly over one-half of one percent per year—a very low rate compared to those of other countries. Mortality, as measured by such indicators as infant mortality and the death rate from natural causes (that is, ignoring such calamities as war and mass starvation), declined, as is normal in the course of development. The factors that prevented the emergence of a population explosion have varied from situation to situation. In those countries and periods in which the government followed policies favorable to family limitation (as in making abortion free and legal), fertility declined very rapidly, though it is difficult to determine how much of this was attributable to a change in fundamental attitudes about family size and to what extent it was the result of all the other pressures on normal family life that Soviet-type societies have generated—easy divorce laws, appallingly bad housing, and the economic compulsion for wives to add to the family income by work. But in the Soviet case, the most important part of the explanation for low population growth was a series of unintended demographic disasters—emigration, famine, war casualties, both military and civilian, and very large birth deficits stemming from the disruption of family life during the purges and the war, and an extremely unbalanced sex ratio. In short, the Russians coped with the population explosion not by some special strategy or feature of their planning, but by a series of accidents, which other countries would scarcely want to imitate. There can be no doubt, however, that this fortuitious result has played an important role in their growth performance. If the population had grown at a rate of one percent per year rather than one-half percent, the Soviet population in the early seventies would have been not 245,000,000, but 275,000,000. The diversion of resources into agriculture and housing to sustain this extra 30,000,000 persons would have made impossible the rate and pattern of allocation of investment on which their actual growth has depended.

STALINIST COMMUNISM AS AN ECONOMIC SYSTEM

Our interpretation of Stalinist Communism as a strategy for economic growth and modernization raises many questions about the character of the Communist economic system and fails to deal explicitly with many questions that need to be answered with respect to any economic system. There is an implication in our treatment of it as a system for the revolutionary transformation and modernization of society that it ought to be considered not as an isolated system self-sufficient and coherent in itself, but as one stage in a historical evolution of systems. Much of what has been noted about it suggests its rationale has been the need to perform some functions that Marx assigned to capitalism in his succession of economic and social systems. It becomes interesting, therefore, to think about Communism as a kind of substitute for capitalism and to try to give a Marxian interpretation of its role in the evolving succession of social systems. It might also be located in the spectrum of possible economic systems by characterizing it in terms of the criteria used for distinguishing and evaluating economic systems, cited in Chapter 2. Finally, in the same spirit, we need to consider how it handles the central problem common to all economic systems of making decisions about resource use. We will take these up in turn.

Stalinist Communism as
Marxian Capitalism?

Parallels have often been drawn between nineteenth-century capitalism and twentieth-century Communism as processes for capital accumulation and industrialization. Though Marxian economics was essentially an analysis of capitalist industrialization, it may be interesting to consider whether the Stalinist system for accomplishing these goals could be fruitfully interpreted as a kind of Marxian capitalism. It is customary to ask how the Marxian vision of socialism has influenced decisions and policies of Communist leaders, but the interpretation of Stalinist Communism as a form of Marxian capitalism proposed here focuses upon parallels between the Marxian analysis of capitalist industrialization and the theory, strategy, and practice of industrialization in Soviet Russia.

Certainly, interesting parallels can be drawn. Perhaps the most fundamental parallel lies in the relations between the economic structure of society (its forces of production and social relations of production and exchange, in Marxian language) and its surrounding political and ideological superstructure. Nineteenth-century technology, capital accumulation, and industrialization provided the forces of production which, in turn, encouraged the development of such social relations as the factory and wage systems, private property, competition, and market exchange. In the Marxian view, the bourgeois democratic state and *laissez-faire* were the natural political and ideological corollaries in the development of a surrounding superstructure compatible with and conducive to the prosperity and power of the capitalist class.

But the technologies of the twentieth century, especially revolutions in transportation and communication, coupled with the more massive and rapid industrialization and capital accumulation policies of Communist leaders, have enabled and/or required new, tighter forms of control over human behavior and new class relations consistent with the new technologies and forces of production. In the Marxian interpretation of nineteenth-century capitalism, capitalists control workers through private ownership of the means of production. A Marxian analysis of twentieth-century Stalinist Communism might point to the emergence of a new class relation between the Communist party and the masses of workers and peasants, and the ownership and/or control of the means of production by the Party as a central vehicle for social control.

More concretely, the Marxian theory of capitalism focuses upon institutional processes for capital accumulation. An interpretation of Stalinist Communism as a variant of Marxian capitalism would do the same. In this view, the Communist party, collectivization of agriculture, government ownership and control of the means of production, the turnover tax, the emasculation of labor unions, and so on may be described essentially as institutional processes and vehicles for the mobilization and allocation of an economic surplus for capital investment.

Similarly, the Stalinist view of the Communist party as the "vanguard" of the workers (and the Communist party leadership as the vanguard of the party), might be said to provide an ideological function parallel to that provided, in the Marxist view, by classical democratic theory and the operation of the bourgeois democratic state, namely, to mask or disguise the true nature of class conflict and to thereby provide a rationale for class exploitation of the masses.

Needless to say, this application of Marxian analysis to the interpretation of Stalinist Communism diverges radically from the official Soviet interpretation. Undoubtedly, it contains an element of truth, for Stalinist Communism *is* a set of institutions designed to perform the same functions as nineteenth-century capitalism, and the parallels described earlier are too striking to ignore.

Stalinist Communism in Terms of Standard Criteria

It is interesting to reflect on the Stalinist strategy for economic growth and development in terms of some of the criteria mentioned in Chapter 2 for distinguishing and evaluating economic systems. A synopsis of the major features of Stalinist Communism in terms of these criteria is provided in Table 15-1. Most of the features itemized in the table are self-explanatory; several have already been discussed in the examination of

Table 15-1.

MAJOR FEATURES OF STALINIST COMMUNISM

Criteria	Stalinist Communism
1. Level of economic development	Underdeveloped, in process of development
2. Resource base	Landistic, in process of transformation to capitalistic
3. Ownership and control of industrial capital	Government ownership and control
4. Locus of economic power	Government
5. Motivational system	Social goals (official ideology): revolutionary transformation of society
6. Organization of economic power	Centralized
7. Social processes	Hierarchy
8. Distribution of income and wealth	Government-determined contributions to social goals; inequality

the Stalinist approach to economic development. At this juncture, it will be useful to select two or three to illustrate more fully both the institutional character of Stalinist Communism and the impact of the Stalinist development strategy upon it.

LOCUS AND ORGANIZATION OF ECONOMIC POWER

One conclusion stands out very clearly—the Stalinist strategy attempts an extreme concentration of decision-making power over resource use in the hands of the leaders. Though Soviet Communism proclaims ownership of the means of production by the working class, it has divorced ownership from control and put the latter effectively in the hands of the Party. Such institutions that might enable workers as producers to share with management in decisions about their activities—perhaps labor unions or workers councils on the Yugoslav model—have either been eliminated or made ineffective. From the other side, the worker as a consumer has been deprived of any influence in the choice of how society's resources are to be used through the command system that makes producers responsive to the wishes of higher authorities and indifferent to the desires of their customers, and by the fiscal instruments that buttress the regime's position as monopolist-monopsonist in its dealings with households.

This concentration of control over the whole spectrum of economic decisions has been strengthened by the fusion of the economic and political structure and by the substitution of the Communist party machinery for more traditional political processes. This has had two interesting effects. First, there is little in the way of a political process through which individuals or groups can work to alter the outcome of economic processes. Any idea of redistributing income or economic power as these might emerge from the operation of economic processes, or of reaching and imposing through political negotiation some social consensus about over-

all priorities in the use of resources, is largely ruled out. Second, questions of economic efficiency often fall victim to political and ideological prejudice, as when the Marxian notion that only labor is productive was taken as sufficient reason to rule out interest charges as an economic category, or when Stalin's faith in steel prejudged the question of whether some other material might not be more economical. The Chinese remain the most strongly committed adherents to this notion of fusing the two structures in their slogan that "politics takes command," though it has been generally characteristic of the Stalinist strategy wherever followed. It is significant that the Yugoslavs, in their reaction against the Stalinist model (of which more will be said in Chapter 17) have adopted as a kind of counter-slogan—"depoliticalization of the economy."

This aggrandizement of all the processes that influence economic outcomes into the jurisdiction of the Party constitutes one of the distinguishing features of the Stalinist strategy and is an important element in the concept of totalitarianism. Its genesis probably lies in the fact that Stalinist totalitarianism was, above all, a strategy for modernization—for social change. There was a big gap between what the regime saw as the goals and what the population wanted. Given the urgency felt by the regime in its self-appointed task of transforming society and its impatience with the recalcitrance of society in acceding to these demands, it was persuaded that it had to build a machine for imposing mobilization and allocation of resources (such as the division of GNP into consumption and investment), and that the economic institutions had to share the totalitarian feature. This may not have been the only possible way to modernize, but those who controlled power thought it was.

INCOME DISTRIBUTION

One of the important features that differentiates economic systems is the institutions and criteria they employ in the process of income distribution among individuals and groups. The Stalinist model had a remarkably slight interest in the traditional socialist preoccupation with issues of redistributive justice. The attitude taken by its designers was that, in eliminating property incomes and in proclaiming the criterion "to each according to his productive contribution," it had pretty well disposed of the issue of equity in income distribution. To each according to his productive contribution is clear enough as a general notion, but a couple of comments are in order concerning its implementation. The first is that, even in the area where it has been most consistently pursued, that is, in relation to urban households, the mechanism used to attain income distribution according to this principle does so very imperfectly. Official wage scales and pay systems are intended to provide substantial premiums for special skills and effort, but the labor market has always been beset by sufficient administrative interference to cause it to do an ineffective job of making money wages proportional to productivity. The distribution of real income is also perturbed from the other side by the tax system. Taxes are collected mainly through the turnover tax, that is, through large markups in the prices of consumer goods over their real resource cost, and students of the matter have generally concluded that the overall burden of the tax system has been regressive. The government has frequently used this side of the relation to distribute increments in consumption among the population, as when, in the fifties, it once each year reduced the prices of consumer goods selectively and differentially. One would think this would be a very unpredictable instrument for passing out increases in income, one hardly likely to satisfy the criterion of making incomes proportional to productive contributions.

Secondly, special arrangements outside the labor market mechanism often have been added to accord special treatment to individual groups. Military officers, for example, have been an extraordinarily favored group, while peasants have suffered particularly low income levels enforced through the adverse terms of trade which their immobility permits the regime to impose on them. In other words, their profession of this traditional socialist slogan was belied by their willingness to ignore it when it conflicted with the goal of rapid growth.

There has been major concern for what might be called "the social security aspects" of the distribution problem, though there are many obvious gaps. Those aspects closely related to production considerations or other governmental goals have generally been dominant—for example, support payments for children, free medical care, and generally free education through all levels. There is also a pension system. Most of these programs usually have been frankly discriminatory toward the urban population and against the peasants.

Beyond these elements of imperfection and/or special treatment lies a broader issue. The Stalinist strategy for economic growth and development has frankly inequalitarian implications for income distribution at variance with those of the classic Marxian vision of socialism. The Marxian vision accepts wage differentials according to differences in labor contribution in the early stages, though these were expected to decrease in the process of movement from socialism toward communism. Finally, under communism, the wage system would disappear entirely, and each person would contribute according to his ability and receive goods according to his needs.

By contrast, the central problem for Stalinist Communism was rapid and large-scale industrialization. The process of industrialization requires specialists, managers, and government officials whose talents and contributions surpass those of the general body of peasants and industrial labor and whose support and loyalty is necessary for the maintenance of the regime. It also requires incentives to entice workers to work longer and harder, to encourage movement of labor to those sectors or areas of the economy given a high priority by the central planners, to stimulate the development of skills, and so forth. The Stalinist conclusion from this argument was not simply to abandon the pre-revolutionary Marxian sentiments regarding equality, but to frankly and vividly castigate them and accompanying notions about worker control of industry as "petty bourgeois" and inimical to industrialization and economic development.

The Stalinist emphasis upon incentives and the necessity and desirability of considerable inequality in wage income, position, and power has often been interpreted by Western observers as a "capitalist" element in Soviet Communism. In a manner of speaking, this is true, though one significant difference should be emphasized. In competitive market capitalism, income differences depend significantly on the institution of private property and on the *market*-determined value of marginal productivity, resting ultimately upon *consumer* choices. Under Stalinist Communism, property ownership as a source of income is virtually extinct, and income differences are determined by *government* planners and managers in terms of their evaluations of priorities and contributions. Inequalities in competitive market capitalism have their rationale as a basis for allocating resources in the direction of consumer preferences. In Stalinist Communism, the rationale for inequalities lies in their contributions to inducing resource allocations and development in directions determined by political leaders and government planners.

THE STALINIST INTERPRETATION OF
STALINIST COMMUNISM

In some ways, the Stalinist interpretation of the totalitarian system of economy which developed as an integral part of the strategy for and process of industrialization was frank and candid. Stalin frankly and explicitly accepted and acknowledged criteria one, two, and eight (Table 15-1), that is, the imperative urge to extremely rapid industrialization, the strategic requirement of massive capital accumulation, and the motivational-institutional corollary of utilizing inequalities in income, status, and power to achieve Party aspirations for economic development.

As to the remaining criteria, the official interpretation by Communist leaders and propagandists was an effort to mask the totalitarian character of the system by its identification with "socialism." The Leftists of the twenties considered the harsh and dictatorial measures prospectively necessary for "primitive socialist accumulation" and rapid industrialization as a necessary transition stage to prepare the way for socialism. By contrast, the official Soviet view during the Stalinist era was that Stalinist Communism, as the organizational and institutional form of the Soviet industrialization process, *is* socialism, and socialism *is* Stalinist Communism. Needless to say, Stalinist Communism is *one* variant of applied Marxism and/or socialism, but by no means the only one. This is clear from reviewing the theory and practice of the democratic socialist welfare state as it has developed in West Europe (cf. Chapter 14). It will become clearer as revisionist and Yugoslav contributions to socialist thought and practice are examined in succeeding chapters.

Stalinist Views on Allocation and
Value

In focusing primarily on the Stalinist approach to running the economy as a strategy for growth we have spoken mostly in terms of what might be called "macroal-locational" questions; that is, we have interpreted the concept of a growth strategy as a problem in achieving a high rate of investment, identifying key industries and priority projects, selective emphasis on key technological changes that will raise productivity, and effecting gross allocations and reallocations of resources between major uses (the division of investment between tangible assets and investment in human beings, farm versus nonfarm employment, and so on.) But it would be a mistake to consider the Stalinist approach to running the economy only in terms of how it dealt with strategic priorities. This kind of grand strategic planning is only a part of the problem of resource allocation. Even when aggregative priorities have been fixed, there are still hundreds of decisions to be made about resource use. To extend the military analogy implied by the term *strategy*, strategic decision-making must rest on an infrastructure of lower-level command and tactical decision-making. Strategic decisions are, in a sense, no decisions at all, since they mean nothing until they are implemented in the day to day actions of the people appointed to carry them out. Effective translation of the macroeconomic allocations decided at the top into results has required, in the Soviet-type economy, a distinctive kind of approach to the microallocation problem. We will now examine this aspect of the Stalinist strategy, noting the kind of theories Soviet planners had about it and how these were influenced by the Marxian heritage. In the process, much will be said about how microallocational decisions have been made in the Stalinist command economy, with fuller exposition contained in the following chapter.

Having posed the question this pointedly, it is perhaps anticlimactic to answer it by saying that Soviet and East European economists in the Stalinist era never developed a theory of value and allocation capable of offering real guidance in attaining efficient allocation of resources. Soviet economists never busied themselves seriously or usefully with this problem. As for the ready-made body of theory which they do profess, that is, the Marxian theory of value, this has not been applied in Soviet-type economies in any operational way. It is true that practical planners in these economies have always shown great concern for such issues as pricing, controlling the actions of management, and enhancing the "effectiveness" with which resources are used. If judged by thematic content, the economic literature of the socialist countries usually has been as concerned with these problems as is our own. But the substantive contribution of the economic literature of the Stalinist era to the clarification of these problems was very slight. Lacking analytical understanding of how value and allocational efficiency are interrelated, Soviet economists, and subsequently, their confreres in Eastern Europe, were condemned to pick at any given problem year after year, without making much progress. Anyone searching Stalinist economic literature for some coherent descriptive explanation of how the Soviet system solves the basic allocational questions of what to produce, how to produce, for whom to produce, how much to save, and so on, is doomed to disappointment—there is simply no analogue in Soviet-type economies of the economic principles text used in American universities. Similarly absent is any normative analysis of how all these issues *ought* to be decided to maximize the output from given resources. On the microallocational level, policy-makers needed to know how to deal with obsolescence, how to choose between alternative technologies, and at what level the price of wheat should be set relative to the price of cotton. But Soviet economists never succeeded in enunciating any unambiguous principles for analyzing and settling these problems.

This situation resulted from two circumstances: (1) The question of microallocational efficiency does not occupy in Marxian economic thought the central place it does in the world mainstream of economics. It is not even posed in the courses on "political economy" that hold the place of honor in the socialist economics curriculum. [83] It has been said "there is no Marxian microeconomics," and this is basically true, as observed in Chapter 5, in the sense that Marx never systematically concerned himself with the question of the allocation of resources or clearly understood (or, at least, adequately explained) its relation to the theory of value. (2) The institutional system which the Soviet leaders had designed and the Eastern Europeans copied made it very difficult to devise or apply any very subtle notions of value and microallocation. Since prices did not, in fact, play much of a role in the allocation of resources, there was little pressure to improve on the Marxian theory of value as a guide to pricing. The whole rationale of Soviet style planning was to *transform* the scarcity relationships characteristic of an underdeveloped economy, rather than to accommodate to them. In this light, it is easier not to accept prices and costs as decisive or to worry about the corollary that they should therefore be "correct." Since the planners sought growth through massive reallocations of resources, the goal of short-run equilibrium also lost some of the importance it has in more sophisticated theories of value. Increments in output could be expected from strategic manipulation of macroeconomic variables, so that there was less concern with improving productivity through microallocational adjustments. It is also relevant that Soviet planners were basically unconcerned with catering to the multifarious desires of the population, but were instead trying to manipulate resources to satisfy a few relatively simple and narrowly defined goals, such as increasing the output of steel and creating a heavy machinery industry. When objectives and priorities are relatively stark and simple, they can be sensed and communicated to producers without much reliance on a price system.

In doctrine, at least, obeisance was paid to the Marxian idea that, since capital *per se* did not create value, there was no need for a capital charge in the determination of prices, and similarly, no need for rent charges for natural resources. In fact, the practical requirements of planning eventually led Soviet planners to introduce an interest charge for decision-making purposes and ultimately, for pricing purposes as well, and, in numerous instances, they juggled prices to extract a rent arising from some natural or artificial scarcity. But in the eyes of most of the theoreticians, all these practical pricing maneuvers were seen as aberrations from the true Marxian precepts about value. It was the situation common in human affairs, in which bad theory is helpless to inform practice, but worse, refuses to be reformed by the insights gained from experience.

In the one part of the economy where market forces played an important allocational and mobilizing role, that is, in the relationship with households, experience quickly illuminated the fundamentals of pricing, without any need to rely on the Marxian theoreticians. The general price level on consumer goods sold to households had to be set high enough in relation to the wages paid to workers to assure financial equilibrium, lest work incentives be eroded. Almost equally obvious was the lesson that, unless wage rates and consumer goods prices were differentiated more or less in accordance with people's preferences, there would be great shortages and deficits in these markets. But the Soviet planners never received the full instructional payoff this experience might have provided, for they had a kind of instinctive proclivity to patch up any difficulties caused by poor pricing by means of administrative interventions, such as freezing people to jobs, imposing obligatory requisitions on the agricultural population, and coping with black markets by applying criminal sanctions to speculative activity.

Thus, there is considerable justification for saying that, basically, the theorists read the situation objectively when they held that prices and money had distinctly limited functions in Soviet society. It was a basic doctrine that prices were important only in "commodity" production, involving exchanges between the state sector and the population. In the planned state production sector, they performed only accounting and fiscal functions, and no allocational functions. Indeed, it was held for a long time that the "law of value" which Marx had described as the regulator of production in capitalist society was completely replaced in socialist society by the "principle of planning." Ultimately, when experience revealed the importance of prices in the relationships with households, this dogma was revised to state that the law of value operated, but "in a transformed manner," or that, "in the socialist economy, the law of value operates but does not regulate."

CONCLUSION

Soviet growth strategy is an *ad hoc* creation developed on the basis of evolving experience and probably owes little to Marxism. It is designed to cope with some of the basic problems of an underdeveloped country. Though it usually is described in Marxian jargon and some of its main elements, like concentration on investment or producer's goods, can be described and rationalized in terms of Marxian concepts, this essentially is a homemade strategy, developed in response to the practical exigencies of stimulating economic development common to all developing countries.

It is interesting that Communist theoreticians and policy-makers seem to have implicitly evaluated their system this same way. In both their theoretical writings and international policies, they demonstrate a belief that the most likely application of their system would be in backward countries. The Russians have claimed that other countries wanting to grow fast should simply copy their experience. Indeed, when the Eastern European countries became Communist, their local leaders, trained and led from Moscow, set out to copy the Stalinist institutional model and strategy in all its details. They gave priority to the same leading links, collectivized agriculture, attempted the same mobilization of capital and shifts of population from the countryside to the planned urban industrial sector, and favored autarky in foreign trade. On balance, this strategy was probably less well suited to their special conditions. They never had quite the success with it that the Russians had, and it took a shorter span of experience for them to become disenchanted with it. Also, they were exploited by the Russians and were too small for the strategy to work as well. They needed more trade and more rational trade compared to the USSR, with its greater size and diversity of resources. The inherent deficiency of the Stalinist economic model in providing the microeconomic flexibility to take advantage of the economizing options offered by foreign trade was a much more serious drawback to these countries than it had been for the Soviet Union. In retrospect, we should probably conclude that the Stalinist model met some of the problems of economic development well enough, and in the early years, it fit the particular conditions of the country which invented it. But it was never as well adapted to the conditions of the Eastern European countries, and with the passage of time, has become less well adapted to the conditions of the Soviet Union. Three decades of industrialization have not merely increased output, but have also transformed the nature of the Soviet economy. In the new situation, the strengths of this strategy became less useful and its attendant weaknesses more costly. In recent years, there has been a growing pressure to revise both the strategy and the institutions that go with it. In the process, the economists of the Communist countries have made great progress toward a satisfactory theory of value and allocation. This revisionist trend will be examined in the next chapter.

SUMMARY OF CHAPTER 15

1. The Stalinist model of socialism, ostensibly inspired by Marxian theory, is more appropriately interpreted as an industrialization strategy. Its ideological justification is Marxian, and its economic ideas often are cast in Marxian terminology, but its policies and institutions have been decisively shaped by the goal of accelerating growth in an underdeveloped country.

2. Economic recovery in the twenties and realization that socialism would have to be

built without outside help engendered a great debate as to how this was to be done, foreshadowing all the issues familiar from contemporary concern with development, especially how to achieve the capital accumulation necessary to raise the rate of growth. The distinctive feature of Stalinism was the creation of a social-political-economic order which vested control over the rate of savings in the leadership and suppressed all forces that could challenge its decisions on this point.

3. The leadership used this power to carry out a "mobilization" strategy for growth—not only in raising the rate of savings, but also in transferring labor, designating leading links, enforcing simple priorities, such as heavy industry rather than light industry, and so on.

4. When possible, these actions were explained in Marxian terms, as in the credo that output of the means of production should grow faster than the means of consumption; but any conflicts between traditional socialist ideas, such as egalitarianism in wage structure and the imperatives of development strategy, were resolved in favor of the latter.

5. As a corollary, little attention was given to considerations of efficiency in short-run microallocation, that is, the creation of rational incentives for decision-makers or a price system for guiding decisions. Indeed, there was little appreciation of the *need* for a theory of microallocation and value to illuminate these issues and guide decision-making.

16

Contemporary Communism:
Recent Revisionist Thought

THE OBSOLESCENCE OF
STALINIST COMMUNISM

Much of the Stalinist approach to economic theory and policy died along with Stalin. Since his death, there has been a revolution in economic thought in all the Soviet-type economies. The ideas presented in the preceding chapter have given way to incomparably greater sophistication today in the USSR and the countries of Eastern Europe. In part, the increasing emancipation of economic thought in Communist countries from Stalinist orthodoxy is attributable to Stalin's death and the lessening fear of Party-government reprisals, especially in the light of denunciations by Khrushchev and his successors of the "excesses" of the Stalinist era. In addition, economic development has led to shifts in the goals of the leaders and to new theories of the economic problem and new approaches to running the economy. This is true both in regard to the strategy of stimulating growth and in the approach to allocation and decision-making about economic resources.

In particular, the leaders of Soviet-type societies have now committed themselves more and more concretely to the idea that the goal of growth is to raise the standard of living. Also, they have concluded that both growth and allocative performance of the economy can be improved by decentralzation of decision-making and by releasing initiatives at the lower levels of their system, rather than by giving orders, routinizing decision-making into rigid procedures, and trying to settle all the issues of allocation by sweeping, strategic-style decisions.

Altered Conditions

It has already been observed that post-revolutionary conditions in Eastern Europe after World War II differed from those in Soviet Russia in the twenties. Some East European countries (for example, Czechoslovakia) had a much higher level of economic development. Most of them have relied more heavily upon foreign trade and have had closer ties and relations with Western economies. The pressures and bases for reform have been eloquently summarized by many East European economists, most notably in the post-war writings of Oscar Lange, whose critique of centralized planning was described in Chapter 10.

As for Soviet Russia, the very success of the Stalinist strategy for economic development altered key conditions, which contributed to the growing obsolescence of the strategy. Some of the highlights of these altered conditions are summarized in Table 16-1. All have been interpreted by Com-

Table 16-1.

SYNOPSIS OF ALTERED CONDITIONS IN SOVIET
COMMUNISM

	Prevalent Conditions at Outset of Stalinist Era	Prevalent Conditions by Mid-1950s
1. Level and character of economic developemnt	Relatively underdeveloped; dominantly agricultural	Relatively developed, second largest industrial power in the world
2. Size and complexity of the economy	Small industrial sector; "leading links" and simple planning goals	Complex modern economy with growing interdependencies of inputs and outputs
3. Consumption and investment	Low level of economic development made high investment and low consumption strategy imperative; simplicity in magnitude and variety of consumer goods	Higher level of economic development plus consumer pressures for higher living standards make greater emphasis upon consumption both possible and necessary; growing complexity in magnitude and variety of consumer goods
4. Management	Lack of skilled managers and technicians	Development of a managerial and technical elite
5. Labor	Primarily peasant; small urban labor force	Collectivization of peasant labor; large-scale transfer of peasants to cities and factories; disciplined and skilled labor force
6. Political and social conditions	Relatively unstable (war, civil war, institutional revolution and transformation, internal political struggles)	Relatively stable (acceptance of revolution and institutional transformation)

munist revisionists as being inconsistent with the highly centralized processes and institutions for economic planning and decision-making of the Stalinist era along the following lines:

1. Whatever the suitability of Stalinist methods for transformation from an underdeveloped, dominantly agricultural society to a significantly higher level of economic development, that task now has been largely accomplished.

2. The greater size and complexity of the present economic organization requires more sophisticated and finely tuned instruments and methods.

3. The draconian sacrifices of consumption in favor of investment, and the accompanying institutional processes to enforce them, had a logic and rationale in the twenties and thirties which no longer exist. Increased emphasis upon consumption and an increased quality and variety of consumer goods accelerates the obsolescence of the Stalinist method of planning from the center and increases the need for institutional mechanisms to relate production decisions more closely to consumer preferences.

4. The lack of a skilled and loyal managerial corps and the need to create a disciplined

labor force can no longer be credibly used as rationales for concentrating and centralizing power and authority for planning and administrative decisions, for these needs have been largely attained.

5. Similarly, revolution, war, civil war, radical institutional transformation, and the danger of counter-revolution no longer credibly justify the maintenance of highly centralized planning structures in Soviet Russia. With the passage of time, new generations have emerged for whom "revolution" is but history, who more or less accept the basic institutional structure of the society, but who are willing to support reforms or changes in it.

Diminishing Returns to Stalinist Strategies

As long as the Stalinist system delivered the goods in terms of economic growth, criticism of its microeconomic crudities and inefficiencies was relatively muted. Acknowledgement of the altered conditions previously described and a willingness to consider possible revisions of the Stalinist model have been prompted most immediately and directly by a deceleration of growth. The rate of growth in all the Soviet-type economies has dropped markedly since the late fifties. In the Soviet Union, it has been estimated that, during most of the postwar period, GNP grew at a rate of about seven percent per year; but since 1958, it has been more nearly at about five percent per year. In Czechoslovakia, industrial output not only ceased to grow in the first years of the sixties; it actually declined. Indeed, such fluctuations occurred in other countries as well: for example, when industrial output declined in Hungary in 1954. The explanation for this deceleration of growth is that the Stalinist strategy has run into diminishing returns. Because of the growth in the size and complexity of the economy, the effectiveness of the old system in spurring growth has simply diminished. As noted in Chapter 15, the

Stalinist strategy for economic development involved essentially the manipulation of a few select macroeconomic variables and proportions. But this strategy has increasingly been characterized by diminishing returns. First, productivity gains from transferring peasant labor to the factories in the cities are now much reduced. Labor is now a scarce factor and needs to be economized. Second, agriculture has been shorn of economic surpluses. Further surpluses must come from elsewhere. Indeed, large-scale investments in agriculture are needed to maintain and expand food production. Third, capital is characterized by diminishing marginal productivity. Opportunities for substantial economic growth merely by expanding the capital stock are distinctly limited. Growth now increasingly requires technological improvements and careful choice among alternative investments. The crude investment policy of the past (neglect of investment in agriculture, transportation, and housing, and neglect of obsolescence) needs overhaul. Fourth, the Stalinist policy of autarky and "socialism in one country" denied the Soviet development process the advantages of international specialization and division of labor. This policy was never as applicable to the smaller and less self-sufficient East European countries as it was to Russia and is increasingly being abandoned, as demonstrated by burgeoning East-West trade.

With increasing size and complexity of the Soviet economy, the informational problem of merely accounting for production plans and performance has mounted steadily. One Soviet economist semi-seriously suggested that, in the absence of a radical reform in planning methodology, the informational requirements of plan formulation would become so great by 1980 that the entire population would be employed in recording and processing data, thus creating a bureaucratic Frankenstein that would drown its masters in a sea of facts and figures. The number of firms, commodities, resources, resource and commodity combinations, and technological possibilities has increased markedly with industrialization and economic development, which means that much more information has to be gathered and considered in making choices among alternatives. These problems are further heightened by the obvious fact that *interactions* among economic units tend to grow more rapidly than their number. An increase in the number of enterprises, commodities, or resources from, say, one to ten is accompanied by an increase in mutual interactions substantially greater than tenfold.

But the increased burden of processing the traditional kind of information as the economy grows is only part of the problem. There is an increased awareness of the need for better economic calculation, and this implies a need for new kinds of and better information. "Drowning in an ocean of data," Soviet planners and managers still complain about the lack of relevant information for day-to-day or month-to-month operations. The emphasis upon *quantities* in the economic plans of the Stalinist era and the inadequacies and inaccuracies of the Soviet price system compound the problems of economic calculation and coordination by excluding, for all practical purposes, comparisons of the *values* of alternatives foregone in production and/or consumption. In part, this is derivative from the Stalinist failure to understand and appreciate the need for and usefulness of price systems as calculational and coordinative processes.

During the Stalinist era, when economic decisions were made at the center, the magnitude of decisions was large, the scope of any decision was relatively wide and more or less indiscriminate, and revisions or modifications of such big, strategic, centralized decisions were apt to be infrequent. With increasing size and complexity and increasing problems of coordination and efficiency, each of these dimensions of the Stalinist planning methodology has been increasingly questioned or criticized. The centralization of decisions tends to overlook the concretized knowledge of the "particular circumstances of time and place" of local administrators or managers. Big, overall decisions applied more or less indiscriminately to wide areas of the economy tend to neglect both the special features of particular cases and the need for recognition of microeconomic interdependencies. Infrequent revision of strategic decisions creates an institutional mechanism insufficiently flexible and adaptable to changing circumstances.

The Stalinist economy, with its hierarchically structured vertical information channels and chains of command, tended to maximize the responsiveness of lower-level (regional, industry, and enterprise) administrators and managers to the directives and preferences of political leaders and central planners and to minimize their responsiveness to and concern for laterally related enterprises, sectors, or regions and/or consumers. Rational as this structure may have been at an earlier stage of economic development, with simpler production relations and heavy investment at the expense of consumption, it has been increasingly characterized by bottlenecks and inefficiencies with the increasing size and complexity of production and the increasing importance of consumption.

Beyond plan formulation is plan execution and control. These dimensions of Stalinist Communism have also been subject to considerable recent criticism in Communist countries. The "success indicators" of the Stalinist system have been increasingly criticized for their bizarre results and distorted impact on incentives. If the planning target for nails is in terms of weight, big, heavy nails will be produced. If it is in terms of number, large numbers of small nails will be forthcoming. If it is in terms of quantity, quality will be neglected. And so forth. In general, Stalinist Communism had no integrating, synthesizing success indicator (such as profitability) to enable planners and administrators to evaluate economic performance in a balanced and comprehensive way that would not distort local decision-making.

In addition, excessive centralization has been criticized for its inability to maintain control. With increasing size and complexity of economic organization, it has been increasingly difficult for central planners to know what commands they ought to issue or how to ensure that they will be obeyed. The very centralization of the Stalinist planning methodology, under conditions of increasing size and complexity, has probably decreased the power to inject the preferences of political leaders and made it easier for managers and government bureaucrats to incorporate theirs.

The fact that the increasingly unwieldy character of the Communist planning apparatus makes commands and directives of central planners increasingly difficult to enforce strengthens the urge to find decentralized incentive systems in which managers, workers, and peasants, seeking their own interests, are more or less automatically enticed to behave in socially beneficial ways. As will be seen later in the chapter, proposals by the revisionists regarding incentives constitute essentially a Communist version of the "invisible hand."

Changing Priorities

Another changing element in the situation today is that Communist leaders seem to be reordering their priorities somewhat and are coming to attach a greater importance to improving the standard of living. This stems partly from the fact that the level of per capita output has advanced to a point where it is possible both to satisfy the goals for investment and military expenditure that the leaders see as necessary and, at the same time, undertake to provide higher consumption levels. Even without any change in the relative shares of consumption in total output, growth creates a rising level of *per capita* consumption, so that the task of satisfying consumer demand today takes on new dimensions. When levels of per capita consumption were extremely low, it was enough to turn out the standard necessities; but today, it has become necessary to think more about quality and variety and about providing more service and convenience along with the physical goods. These new desiderata require a much more subtle and flexible system of allocating resources and making production decisions. There is thus an urgent need to reform the motivation and control system that governs production decisions so that the consumers' share of total resources can be turned into consumer goods in a way more subtly responsive to the wishes of consumers.

Whatever the reasons, Soviet economists today are clearly acknowledging much more openly than ever before that the goal of production is satisfaction of consumer wants. It is now stated explicitly that it is necessary to raise the share of consumption in the national income and to attune the production and distribution systems more sensitively to consumer preferences. Brezhnev said in his speech to the 24th Party Congress in 1971 that "the chief task of the [Ninth] Five Year Plan is to guarantee a significant rise in the material and cultural levels in the life of the people." Such sentiments are echoed in the other East European countries, as well.

A NEW LOOK AT GROWTH STRATEGY

The multifarious changes in circumstances and goals within which the leaders of the contemporary Communist world operate have called for corollary changes in the strategy of growth and in the approach to running the economy. The rationale for many characteristics of the command economy—limitations on the power of money, persistent neglect of agriculture, the system of physical allocation of resources, an incentive system which makes enterprise management sensitive to the demands of their hierarchical superiors rather than of customers—was to insulate production decisions against the various ways by which consumers might hamper the allocation of resources to investment. With that motive attenuated, there remains little reason to suffer the irrationalities of misallocation and inefficiency that seem inherent in that system. Rather, if the promise of catering to consumer preferences is to be fulfilled, it becomes urgent to introduce some new kind of system that will free producers from the system of plans and controls from above and redirect their attentions to what consumers want.

These changes also suggest that any new strategy must rest on getting better use of the capacity already built up, better allocation of resources, and more rapid and flexible adaptation to the changing opportunities for increments in output that are individually small, but large in the aggregate. Growth today cannot mean just an increased volume of output of the standard mix of commodities characteristic of the past—that will neither offer the opportunity for improvements in productive efficiency through more finesse in allocation nor provide the kind of increments in final product that can be equated with increases in "welfare." One might say that the time has passed when it makes much sense to think of a "strategy" of growth distinct from the more general goal of allocative efficiency. Today, the best way to get more output is to improve the way resources are used. In this chapter, therefore, the issue of revisionist thinking about value and allocation will overshadow the discussion of revisionist ideas about growth *per se*. But there are, in the new economic literature, some interesting themes touching specifically on growth theory, and it is to these we now turn.

Revisionist Theory Concerning Growth

Paralleling these new interpretations of both the ends and the means of economic policy, there have also been revisions in theory and ideology to conform to the new situation. Some of this adaptation of doctrine to new decisions is in the familiar tradition of the past—the Marxian theorists just find new quotes in Marx or Lenin to justify the change in line. There is a kind of creative intellectual artist in Communist societies, whose forte is to work within the Marxian intellectual system, but to take advantage of the many ambiguities in Marx to give old concepts or theories new interpretations. Since much of the economic ideology of Communist countries has not been very operational or precise, it is relatively easy to bend it to new demands.

Soviet and Marxian ideology is vague and protean and can be made to mean almost anything one wants it to. If the law of planned proportional development and its various corollaries were employed in the past as justifications for a high rate of investment, for instance, they now can be employed as a shield for raising the question of the proper proportions between investment and consumption. Similarly, the former assertion that industry A had to grow faster than industry B now can be reinterpreted to explain that this need not *always* be so, or to question *how much faster* it need be. It is now an official doctrine in the Soviet Union that the gap between the two rates of growth can be reduced at the present stage in the construction of communism and in the Five-Year Plan for 1971–1975, the rate set for industry B is slightly *above* the rate planned for industry A. The theorists are busily at work explaining how this reconciliation of the two rates (which, in the past, would have been condemned as a heresy) can now take place. The standard approach in such articles is generally to go back to Marx and find some quote or numerical manipulation of his reproduction scheme that will support the assertion that the higher rate of growth of A compared to B, does, indeed, hold in general, but not necessarily for every short period of time or not at all stages or not under certain special conditions.

At the same time, the strategy of growth is also being explored in a much more sophisticated way by the new mathematical economists. In the late fifties and the sixties, a great revival of economics took place in the countries of the Soviet bloc under the guise of an introduction of mathematical economics. (Much more will be said about this "new economics" in the forthcoming examination of new theories of value, pricing and allocation.) In exploring mathematical models of the economy, the new school of economic theorists inevitably has devised models to simulate the growth process. In manipulating their economic models, the new theoreticians have both exposed the issue of what the goals of growth should be and focused attention on the crucial policy issue, that is, what share of total output should be invested rather than consumed. What a mathematical economic model does, in essence, is to show how economic variables of interest to the planners (such as total output, its rate of growth, and the rates of growth of its various components) depend on various exogenous factors beyond the control of the planners (such as the capital-output ratio or the rate of growth of the labor force) and on certain "choice variables" which the planners *can* manipulate (such as the division of total output between consumption and investment or, say, the rate of taxation). The purpose of such a model is to help planners determine how they should manipulate the chosen variables to make the variables they want to influence behave as desired. It is interesting, in this regard, to see the new vogue enjoyed today by the Marxian reproduction scheme. Many of the new economists have started out with the basic features of this model, though, as with Fel'dman, they usually have had to make some creative modifications of it.

The attempt to express how the economy works in the form of a mathematical model naturally requires precision in the definition of relationships and in the kinds of questions that are asked. The mathematical approach thus has required these economists to think much more clearly than earlier Soviet economists about what the goals are, what variables they control, how different economic magnitudes influence each other, and so on. Growth models reveal unequivocally that choices can be made about the rate of growth of GNP, consumption, investment, and other magnitudes. Typically, one finds, as in the Fel'dman model, that it is possible to increase the rate of growth of GNP by increasing the share invested. This requires a relative, if not absolute, decrease in current consumption, though this cut eventually may be recouped through the accelerated growth of total output. In order to choose the proper rate of investment and the associated rate of growth, it is necessary, therefore, to appeal to some criterion of optimality, some index for deciding which of the many possible time streams of potential future output is best.

Growth models, therefore, inevitably focus attention on the issue that has always been obscured before, namely, how to balance or trade off sacrifices in consumption today (incurred in order to stimulate growth) against the larger but postponed amounts of consumption they will enable in the future. This question is discussed in terms of the concept of a "criterion of optimality for dynamic models." Mathematical economists in Communist countries have been wrestling with the issue of what this criterion ought to be. The controversies are too technical to permit detailed examination here; but almost inevitably, the new economists are led to the common sense idea that the most logical criterion is how the population in general feels about this postponement of consumption, or, to use the customary technical term, the population's time preference between present and future consumption [cf. 75]. This conclusion is fairly well masked by the mysterious mathematical symbolism in which the new economists speak to their colleagues, and some Soviet leaders would probably be somewhat shocked to find this is the kind of conclusion they have nurtured by permitting the new economics to flourish. But the interesting fact is that, at this technical and professional level of discourse, the desirability of referring the investment-consumption decision to the desires of the population has been mooted and approved.

REVISIONIST THEORIES OF
VALUE, PRICE, AND ALLOCATION

The sphere in which the new economics has most thoroughly and radically over-turned traditional Marxian ideas is in the theory of value and allocation. The move-ment toward reform has been prompted and guided in varying degrees in different coun-tries by a new vision of the economic process and by new insights into the theory of re-source allocation that the older generation of economists never had. There are several streams of thought in this revisionist tendency. We shall take particular note of two. These are (1) the contribution of the economic theorists inspired by mathematical approaches and (2) the practical ideas and proposals for improving economic planning. The latter have often been described as "Libermanism," after the engineer-economist who has been one of their main champions in the USSR; but there are also analogous movements, often more advanced, in the other Com-munist countries. [Cf. 72, 75, 87, 89]

The Interrelationship of
Planning, Value, and Allocation

These revisionist ideas will be easier to understand if we clearly grasp how planning, value, and allocation are related to one another. The crucial realization is that *value and allocation are simply different aspects of a single integral problem, seen from two different points of view*. Both are consequences of the fact of scarcity. Since resources do not suffice to permit full satisfaction of the unlimited wants of a society, choices must be made between alternative uses of resources. In the process of comparing alternatives, each scarce good—whether a primary re-source, an intermediate product, or a final output—may be seen to have a value. Com-parisons of alternatives disclose that a given good can be traded off in a definite proportion against others in terms of its power to con-tribute to human wants. Its value relative to other goods is revealed in terms of "oppor-tunity cost," that is, how much of other goods would have to be devoted to achieving a given objective were a unit of this good not avail-able. Thus, the fact of scarcity and the necessity for allocation implies a set of indexes telling how valuable one good is relative to others. At the same time, value is an instrument which makes it possible to identify and pursue an efficient allocation of resources. If one can establish a set of indexes showing the value of any resource or good, it is then possible to determine whether any act of production or consumption is really worth its cost by comparing the value of the resources used with the value of the output produced. These indexes make it possible to measure the gain from using a given resource one way against another and to find the cheapest among several possible ways of doing something.

This interrelatedness of value and alloca-tion is illustrated in the elementary supply and demand diagram. The intersection of the supply and demand curves shows simul-taneously the price of a commodity and the amount that will be produced. The principle is also demonstrated in linear programming. Any linear programming problem about the allocation of resources is accompanied by a "dual" problem posing the task of imputing values to whatever resources constitute the constraints.

Value, as previously described, is a theo-retical construct, an index inherent in the logic of the situation of choice. The counter-part of value in actual economic systems is price. It is not fully possible, of course, to equate the prices of an actual market system with the theoretical values of a logical model of allocation in a situation of scarcity. Real economies do not attain perfect allocation, and the price system of a real economy may represent a considerable departure from true values. Prices out of line with true values both reflect and encourage actions inconsistent with efficient allocation. In the market economy, for example, monopoly power may permit a producer to restrict the output of some commodity to less than consumers would like to have. This departure from optimum allocation is also reflected in the monopoly price, which is greater than the real sacrifices required to produce more of the commodity. In a centrally planned economy, prices distorted from true measures of value will also induce irrational actions on the part of decision-makers. For example, if coal is priced below its true value, producers are tempted to use coal in instances where some other energy source would place a smaller drain on the nation's resources.

Planning is related to value and allocation in an intimate but complicated way. Planning entails organization to achieve some set of goals. It includes both the ordering of those goals into a preference system and the use of instruments to mobilize and allocate resources to achieve those goals. The theory of value and allocation thus may serve as a kind of normative standard against which the effectiveness of any planning system can be evaluated. There is also a second, more subtle relationship. *Planning may take advantage of the interrelationship between the allocation aspect of scarcity and the value aspect.* If the real value of each good or resource can be determined, then the leaders of the system may simply announce these prices as guides to choices and let most choices about resource use be made in a decentralized way by reference to these prices (as, for example, in the economic theory of decentralized socialism described in Chapter 10). The sum of these separate actions would represent maximum attain-

ment of the goals which the planners had chosen since the prices on which decisions are based embody, in part, the priorities of the leaders.

An additional comment is warranted about *economic decision-making*. The problem of allocation may be approached by focusing on individual actors in an economic system who are engaged in making decisions about how to use resources. The decision-maker in the Soviet-type economy typically is trying to decide how much capital should be used in a given project, whether commodity *A* or commodity *B* should be produced, whether commodity *A* or commodity *B* should be exported, or where a new plant should be built and what technology it should employ. A centrally planned economy of the Soviet type can be viewed as a congeries of separate decision-making spheres and procedures. The sum of all these decisions will yield an overall outcome concerning the allocation of resources in society as a whole, and the outcome will also constitute a certain level of attainment of the planners' goals. Decision-making implies appeal to some criterion, and obviously, the ultimate test ought always to be the degree to which the given decision will further the achievement of the planner's goals. The key to effective planning, therefore, is to offer each decision-maker a set of guidelines embodying the criteria and appropriate information that will enable him to judge the impact of his actions on the attainment of overall goals and a set of incentives that will induce him to so behave. An accurate price system and an interest in economizing—that is, in maximizing the spread between cost and benefits in any decision—will do the job.

Soviet Planning "Principles"

Before examining the revisionist conclusions about value and allocation now advocated by contemporary economists in Russia and Eastern Europe, it will be useful to consider more explicitly the issues of allocation and value posed by their economic practice and with which they have struggled.

The preceding chapter noted that, apart from ritual obeisance to the labor theory of value, Stalinist thought paid little attention to theorizing in a productive way about allocation. But, of course, resources *did* get allocated; the strategic decisions made at the center were ultimately translated into a set of microallocational decisions at lower levels. Since these decisions were made in the context of the problem of administering the supercorporation that encompasses the entire economy in a Soviet-type society, one wonders whether the elusive theory of value and allocation might not be revealed if we looked for it not under that label, but in the guise of a theory of administration or decision-making. When we approach the problem from this angle, it appears that the Russians and their emulators did develop some theoretical ideas about how administrators at various levels made and really ought to make decisions, and how these decisions could be controlled. Many of these ideas are essentially the familiar principles one finds in the standard literature on administration. For example, they put a lot of emphasis on "unity of command"—the idea that, within any jurisdiction, there should be only one boss. Much is made of the notion of *khozraschet*, that is, that an enterprise will be given certain resources and, within those resources, is to fulfill certain goals. They have always argued about just how *khozraschet* ought to work, but the fundamental principle to which disputants appeal as a standard is the cliché of administration that responsibility should be commensurate with authority. They are always well aware that administration requires reasonably clear division of responsibilities between jurisdictions and that, unless any given function is explicitly assigned to someone, it will not get performed. For instance, one specific feature of Soviet plans that is treated as a special virtue is their *adresnost'*, that is, the fact that targets are addressed explicitly to some unit which is to accomplish them.

In short, the Russians and their Eastern European followers do have a good grasp of the general lore and art of administration —experience has given them that. Unfortunately, administrative thought by itself is not very specific with respect to the allocative problem as it arises on the scale of a national economy. It is traditional in the literature on administration, for example, to say that one of the functions of management is coordination and that another is control, but administrative thought *per se* does not offer much concrete guidance on the specific problem of coordination on a national economic scale, or about how best to control decisions that involve the allocation of a nation's resources. To unearth from socialist administrative thought some implicit theory of value and allocation, we have to see how the socialist planners have conceived specific problems of economic coordination and control over economic decisions. Let us examine some illustrative cases.

BALANCING SUPPLY AND DEMAND

One of the fundamental aspects of coordination is to equate supply and demand. The institutional device offered by the administrators of the Stalinist system as a socialist solution to their problem has been the "material balance." But the material balance is just an accounting statement for an administrative rationing system, showing the sources of supply and the allocation for a given commodity. The real job, of course, is to get the material balance for each commodity to balance, since the proper levels of output for different commodities are interdependent. It is impossible to say how much electricity should be produced, for example, or to allocate the total among the *users* of electric power until *their* output levels have been set, since the amount of electric power they need depends on how much they are going to produce of the items that require electric power as an input. But one cannot determine output-levels for the users without first knowing, among other things, how much of their output they will have to furnish to the electric power industry so that it can achieve its assigned goal. There are two remarkable gaps in the thought which economic administrators in Communist countries have given to this problem. First, the planners failed to develop any theoretical conception of how to take account of all these interactions simultaneously and sought the answer in simple trial-and-error bureaucratic bargaining. The theoretical conception that offers this solution is input-output analysis, but the development of input-output theory and practice—a practical accounting scheme, the mathematical formulation of the balancing problem and its actual solution by computers—was worked out by Western rather than by Soviet economists. Second, the material balancers never developed any clear conception of optimization in the balancing process. That is, they had no clear idea of how to judge whether a deficit in the first elaboration of the material balance for electric power, say, might best be resolved by expanding electricity output, by cutting the allocation to all users proportionately, or to some selectively, and so on. Until the new economists came to prominence with their general equilibrium and optimizing approach, this allocative aspect of the balancing problem was simply not understood.

TECHNOLOGICAL DESIGN

Many of the decisions to be made in an economy concern the choice of a technology for producing a predetermined output. One well-known example is the choice of capital intensity, where engineers charged with designing some technology must choose between alternatives that require little capital but sizeable expenditures each year to operate the facility, and those in which additional initial investment makes it possible to save

on operating costs each year thereafter. For instance, agriculture could be supplied with a given tractive power in the form of either gasoline or diesel tractors. Total investment in a stock of tractors of a given aggregate horsepower will be less if gasoline tractors are chosen, but the fuel requirements for operating the tractors each year thereafter will be greater for gasoline than for diesel tractors. An economist of Marxian persuasion is not inclined to regard capital as either costly or productive, and so, is likely to feel the more capital-intensive method is preferable. But if we permit all project makers throughout the economy to substitute capital wherever possible to achieve some reduction in future operating costs, the aggregate demand for capital will far exceed the supply. To cope with this practical reality, Soviet project makers eventually developed some criteria to help them choose the proper capital intensity for any given project—in particular, the so-called "pay-out" period. The notion of the pay-out period is that one should look at the number of years required to compensate for the extra capital investments through the operating cost savings it generates and refer each case to some standard pay-out period. The pay-out period approach is an ingenious surrogate for the productivity calculations that a capitalist firm would make—that is, a payout period of 20 years is just another way of expressing a rate of return of 5 percent on the incremental investment. But it is characteristic that only as an exception were some Soviet thinkers able to see this decision as part of a general equilibrium allocation problem, and thus, to get an inkling of how to determine the standard payout period, how to relate the capital-intensity decision to the price system, and so on. [Cf. 81]

PRICING DECISIONS

There are numerous cases in which administrative experience has led Soviet planners to stumble upon pricing principles more consistent with Western value theory than with Marxian ideas. It is observed, for example, that a given energy demand can be met by coal at one cost or much more cheaply by natural gas. Western value theory holds that, even if the amount of inputs used in producing a given amount of energy in the form of gas is less than for coal, equivalent energy contents are equal in value, as is also the *cost*, a conclusion rationalized by including rent as one of the costs of the more advantageous fuel. Marxian value theory repudiates rent as a real cost or an element of value; but, in practice, Soviet price-setters have found it necessary to set the price for both fuels at the level of the cost of the more expensive. Otherwise, it is difficult to persuade consumers to employ both fuels, and project makers will make decisions raising the demand for the cheaper one, though, in fact, it may be impossible to expand its supply. Analogous cases abound. Soviet pricing practice has, in the past, extracted the rent in the form of a turnover tax rather than as an explicit rent charge, and, indeed, Soviet economists thought that, in inserting this tax in the price of the more advantageous fuel, they were distorting price away from "true" value. Ideologically, they were properly embarrassed and apologetic. This contradiction between theory and practice has today been seen in its proper perspective and resolved by the new economists as one element in their general theory of value and allocation.

THE PARTIALIZATION OF DECISION CRITERIA

The Communist administrators also developed out of their experience with the control aspects of the administrative approach to resource allocation many ideas that point toward a rational theory of value and allocation. For instance, they sense fairly well the general requirements to be met if the success indicators used to measure performance and distribute rewards are to elicit the right answers from enterprise decision-makers. For example, the scope of the indicator must be coterminous with authority and responsibility. Granted that it is part of the responsibility of an enterprise to produce goods satisfactory to its customers, it is pernicious to measure "output" rather than "sales." In deciding how to use his resources, a manager, under these circumstances, will ignore a part of his responsibility. If an enterprise manager has no authority to decide whether to repair or replace machinery, it is no use punishing him for continually repairing and keeping in operation obsolete equipment. Long experience of error in fulfilling these and other requirements has taught Communist planners the correct principles. The crowning achievement in this discovery of the prerequisites for "perfect administration" is the famous dictum of Liberman that what is advantageous for society ought, in principle, also to be advantageous for the decision-makers in the firm. But lacking a sophisticated view of prices as indices of cost and benefit to society, Liberman and his followers have shown marked confusion in trying to explain how success criteria could be defined so that what is advantageous for society will, in fact, be advantageous also for the firm.

All these illustrations of the economic interpretation of administrative practices lead to the same general conclusion. The numerous glimpses of truth gained through administrative experience were never integrated into a general theory of value and allocation or a general theory of organization and administration. And such a theory, of course, is what is important in economics, since all the variables of an economic system are interrelated. Whether it is better to use diesel than gasoline engines in the problem previously cited can be answered only by determining whether or not there is some more productive use for that extra investment elsewhere in the economy. In the problem of coal and gas pricing cited earlier, it is pointless to try to establish relative prices for gas and coal without simultaneously considering whether the mix of these two energy sources currently being produced is the optimal one. This is precisely what is missing in the Marxian legacy of economic theory. As noted in Chapter 5, Marx did not have a general equilibrium concept, and he did not clearly or effectively integrate the problems of value and allocation.

Before the revisionists gained respectability, there were no writings by the economists of the Soviet bloc that could be regarded a general theory of planning or of economic administration. For example, there was apparently no Soviet or East European analogue for the work of, say, Chester Barnard or Herbert Simon. Outsiders, such as the American and West European economists who have made study of the Soviet-type economy their specialty, have done more to build these bits and pieces into a general theory of the administrative economy than have Soviet economists themselves.

The reasons for this are understandable. The nature of the economy and the pressure under which planners and administrators worked did not lead to abstract reflection on the nature of the system. The Marxian background and Stalinist dogma constituted a very unpropitious environment for the revelation and preaching of any new gospel. The existence of a body of orthodox thought and propositions in Marxism made it ideologically risky for anyone to concern himself with trying to derive an overall view of how the process worked in the Soviet Union. There were too many gaps between practice and theory, and it was much safer to deal with each separately. The result, of course, was tremendous tension and a pervasive sense of unreality. In the Soviet-type economy, the allocation of all society's resources among alternative uses is a highly visible process, and the practitioners felt an acute need for some sort of theoretical conceptions to clarify and inform the manipulation of it. The Russians are now actively engaged at the microeconomic level in a quest for what they call "effectiveness," but their past efforts to calculate effectiveness always foundered on the inadequacy of their understanding of value and how it is related to the problem of choice in its allocation aspects.

New Theories of Value and Allocation

This was clearly an unstable situation, and given the homeostatic nature of social processes, it was very likely that the economic thinkers of Communist societies would eventually abandon their exclusive allegiance to Marxism and adopt or reinvent the essence of the kind of value and allocation theory developed by Western economists. Actually, a new vision resolving many of these perplexities and pointing the way to a viable solution was already proclaimed in 1939 by L. V. Kantorovich in his pioneer work on linear programming. [76, 77] For the first decade or two, an understanding of the new gospel was shared by only a small group, but by the late fifties, it began to sweep all before it. In every one of the Communist countries, the new economics has become solidly established, though it often has to compete with remnants of older ideas. But in each, there is today a considerable group of economists who share fully the basic ideas of the science of economics as it is understood everywhere. They still pay lip-service to Marx and the labor theory of value, but they have rejected Marxian economics in essence and have adopted the concept of opportunity cost, the idea of productivity of capital and other resources which are in limited supply, the whole complex of marginalist concepts, the notion of an optimum allocation of resources, rent, and all the rest. It would be going too far to say that today this is the standard economics of contemporary Communism. But the new economists now generally have a strong influence on economic policy and a potent role in determining the direction of teaching and research in economics.

Given the essential similarity of the new

economics of value and allocation to that in the rest of the world, there is little point in describing its concepts in detail. More useful will be a couple of observations about its origin and implications. First, the circumstances of its discovery and the method of its propagation are fascinating. In the Soviet Union, the essential first step was the discovery of linear programming by L. V. Kantorovich, who began as a mathematician rather than as an economist. The original studies which led him to formulate and seek a solution to linear programming problems and, through this, to stumble on the interrelationship of the problems of allocation and value rose from some straightforward production scheduling problems. His discovery owes a great deal to the fact that, in dealing with these problems, he was guided by the unassailable corpus of mathematical thought and not burdened with Marxian preconceptions. The new economics has often been attacked by Marxian traditionalists, and the really telling defense that Kantorovich has always made is that he never smuggled any new interpretation of value into the analysis —the allocation problems on which he first worked were presented by "life," and all he did was to discover through mathematical reasoning the indexes of value for scarce resources implicit in the problems.

It would be wrong to imply that Kantorovich alone was responsible for the rediscovery of modern value and allocation theory in Communist countries. Other economists, among whom V. V. Novozhilov deserves special mention, also made important contributions; but Novozhilov's principle contribution was also originally presented in mathematical form. [80, 81] Many of the recruits to the new profession have been well trained in mathematics, and the new ideas are usually advanced first in mathematical form. In the countries of Eastern Europe, bourgeois economics was never so fully eradicated as in the Soviet Union. More people had a background that included training in economics not limited to Marx-

ism and an acquaintance with the mainstream of world economics so that the task of rediscovery was not so great. But even there, the advocacy and propagation of the new ideas often took place under a protective armor of mathematics. Indeed, the phrase "mathematical methods of economic analysis" came to be a kind of euphemism for the new non-Marxian, institutionally neutral theory of value and allocation.

Secondly, the implications of the new, improved brand of economic theory now being accepted by Russian and East European economists is ambiguous in its implications as to how the economy ought to be organized and administered. Some of the new economists have seen the new allocation ideas as a basis for rescuing administrative centralism. The new economics has been presented in mathematical terms and in conjunction with an appeal to the magic of computers. Some have thought it would be possible to construct some kind of optimizing model on the scale of the national economy and, thereby, determine a set of commands about resource allocation that would be thoroughly rational and feasible. The computers would provide the data processing capacity and the models the conceptual organization for rationalizing the command economy. Now that the concept of an optimal allocation of resources has been grasped, the idea has occurred to some Soviet economists that it might be possible simply to calculate the most advantageous output of each commodity, the best solution to every choice that confronts decision-makers, and so on, and then tell the administrators of the system to carry out these decisions.

Others have been struck with the beauty and seeming magical power of the value indicators that accompany any solution of an optimizing allocation model. As explained earlier, value and allocation are inseparable parts of the same problem, and the calculation of an optimal solution would simultaneously generate indexes for the real worth of every resource, intermediate output, and final product. With these indicators known, it is then conceivable to abandon central decisions and controls altogether and leave all decision-making to lower-level people. Anyone could then calculate for himself the real cost and real benefits to society of any action and need only be told to act so as to always be guided by the goal of maximizing the spread between these two magnitudes.

Still others have proposed various hybrid systems, in which price and market relationships could be used to handle certain parts of the problem of allocating resources, such as in determining the composition of the portion of national resources devoted to satisfying consumer wants, while leaving other decisions, such as investment allocation or equating supply and demand of producer goods, to basically administrative methods.

APPLIED REVISIONISM

With this revolution in the abstract theory of value and allocation underway, there has also been parallel agitation for reform of the planning system on a more practical and concrete level. There are many people in any one of these economies who may not have grasped the fundamental ideas of value and allocation, but whose experience tells them that egregious errors of allocation are being made, that tremendous wastes exist, and that the system generates perverse forms of behavior. In the relatively free period of criticism of the economic mechanism that has been allowed in most of the Communist countries since the late fifties, the economic press has been filled with a tremendous variety of objections and complaints. All have a common theme: a critique of overcentralization. Too few decisions are allowed at the local level, and too many regulations stultify any efforts at innovation or any interest on the part of producers in the needs of their clients. To the extent that there is room for local action and decision-making, the infor-

mation conveyed by a deranged price system and the pressures of a distorted incentive system encourage decisions and actions that are undesirable from an overall social point of view. So much effort goes into reporting to higher levels and getting permission from an essentially parasitic structure of supervising agencies that managers have no time to manage. Commentators who can detach themselves from interlevel arguments and survey the system from the outside see the higher-level planners trying so hard to control every action of the lower-level administrator that they lose real control over his actions and unwittingly motivate him to various actions neither useful nor desirable from a social point of view—for example, hoarding materials, concealing capacity, lowering quality, and rejecting innovations.

These kinds of complaints have always been made, but what is new in recent years is that this point of view has at last found coherent expression, generalization, and a kind of ideology pointing the way to substantial reform. The best known is the Soviet version—usually known as "Libermanism" after Evsey Liberman, Professor at the Kharkov Engineering and Economics Institute. In fact, there are other articulate spokesmen for the new ideology, such as the Soviet airplane designer A. N. Antonov and Professor I. Birman of the Moscow Institute of National Economy. The essence of this vision is that enterprises should be free to make their own decisions, to work out their own relationships with each other, and that the main test which superior agencies should apply to them is that of profitability. What has been added to the instinctive urge in this direction is a kind of rationalization of how this, in the end, will be beneficial to all— a kind of Communist version of the invisible hand. This vision is less elaborated than the Smithian invisible hand and not very well integrated with what the new theorists of value and allocation have discovered about the kind of price system required to make profit an accurate measure of social gain.

But, even if less elegant than the achievement of the value theorists, the vision of the Antonovs, Libermans, and Birmans is in some ways more meaningful because it clearly states recommendations and programs that can both harness the sympathy of influential people, and be connected with and employ fruitfully the insights offered by the new theory of value and allocation.

Liberman's Proposals

Though Liberman is the liberal reformer most often cited in Western publications, his proposals actually occupy a moderate midway mark among those of Russian and East European economists. His model for reform lies somewhere between those of the conservatives, who wish to improve centralized administrative decision-making through input-output analysis, linear programming, and the increased use of computers, and those of the more radical reformers, whose ideas constitute, or tend in the direction of, some variant of market socialism. [Cf. 87]

Liberman's proposals contain three major dimensions: the role of the central authorities (the centralized dimension); the freedom and flexibility of individual enterprises (the decentralized dimension); and the role of profitability (within the framework of a central plan) as a generalizing and unifying "success indicator" and incentive system. As conceived by Liberman, central authorities would continue to make the basic macroeconomic decisions affecting the character and pace of economic growth and would retain control of "all of the basic levers of central planning," that is, money, finance, prices, overall levels of saving and investment, and allocations of large capital investments. In addition, at the microeconomic or enterprise level, central planners would specify targets for output, assortment of products, and delivery dates. Within this framework and given these centrally fixed targets, however, enterprises would have

flexibility in a number of subordinate areas that have been subject to centralized specification in the past. Liberman specifically designates seven areas for the discretion of individual enterprises: labor productivity, the number of workers, wages, production costs, accumulations (savings), capital investment, and new technology.

For the complicated success-incentives of the past, Liberman proposes a dualistic procedure: First, enterprises would be expected to fulfill the three centrally determined targets. Failure to do so would forfeit bonuses or incentive pay funds, regardless of the profitability of the enterprise. Second, given fulfillment of the centrally determined targets, enterprise managers would be instructed to maximize their "profitability rate" (the total profits relative to the stock of fixed and working capital). Bonuses (from profits) would be awarded exclusively on the basis of profitability, varying directly with the relation between the actual rate of profit and "profitability norms" established for different industries and firms. Profitability norms would be established several years in advance, to avoid possible upward revision in the event of an unusually profitable year, and would be lower in the event of an introduction of a larger number of new products to encourage product innovation and technological improvement. If the actual rate of profit were lower than the profitability norm, enterprises would not be penalized, but would receive bonuses based on the profits actually created. If the actual rate of profit were higher than the profitability norm (presumably through setting an unrealistically low norm), bonuses would be based on an average figure midway between the actual and norm rates.

Like most midway measures, Liberman's proposals have raised tantalizing possibilities and have been criticized by both conservatives and more radical reformers. To conservative defenders of central planning, Liberman's proposed reforms suggest a prospectively dangerous tampering with the basic fabric of the Communist system, a substitution of profit maximization and consumer-oriented production for centrally planned directives and emphasis on investment and heavy industry, and an excessive decentralization of economic power. Liberman has taken great pains to emphasize the essentially moderate character of his proposed reforms and their contributions to improving the efficiency of central planning within the framework of "socialism" (contemporary Russian Communism), especially after the appearance of a cover story in *Time* magazine (February 12, 1965) which described his concerns for efficiency, profits, and incentives as "borrowing from capitalism." At the same time, it is the very moderate, midway character of his proposals that has been questioned by other, less conservative critics within the Soviet bloc. Central authorities would still have the power to specify output, product assortment, and delivery dates, the three most strategic decisions of individual enterprises. In addition, no bonuses would be paid unless these three targets were attained, regardless of the rate of profit. An economy embodying the Liberman proposals (in the mid-sixties, tentative experiments with some of them were made in Soviet Russia) would be characterized by conflicts and inconsistencies of motivational criteria and by a significantly retained role for centralized direction.

Present Status of Reform

In the Soviet Union, some steps have been taken toward the kinds of measures Liberman and other practical reformers have advocated. [Cf. 72] Beginning in 1965, a "new system" was established in industry, to which enterprises gradually have been shifted. By the end of the sixties, nearly all industrial enterprises were on the new system, and analogous changes had been instituted for other non-agricultural sectors of the economy, as well. Under the new system, the number of fixed indicators in the enterprise plan has been reduced somewhat, and enterprise attention has been focused on sales, total profit, and profit in relation to capital stock of the enterprise by tying incentive payments to these indicators. Incentive payments are now made from a pair of funds, the allocations to which are based on a complex formula, which need not be examined here. The important point is that successes in expanding sales or increasing total profits and the rate of profits will increase the amounts available to the management and employees of the enterprise for incentive payments.

Some of the most restrictive barriers to management's "right to manage" have been removed, such as detailed norms for different kinds of inventory, specification of the proportion between different categories of laborers, and so on. An experiment in which the management of a chemical combine was permitted to reduce the work force and raise the wages of the remaining workers above standard rates has been officially judged a success and is being extended to other firms. Enterprises have slightly increased autonomy in making investments. There is a third fund under enterprise control, formed like the incentive funds previously described, which can be used to finance enterprise-chosen investments, and funds for this purpose now also can be obtained from banks.

In 1967, an important price and fiscal reform was made. Most enterprises now pay the treasury a kind of interest charge at the rate of six percent per year on the book value of their fixed and circulating capital. Rent charges have been introduced in some branches of the extractive industries so that enterprises enjoying advantageous production situations will not have profits that exaggerate what they have accomplished. To make possible these various funds and to accommodate the interest and rent charges, prices were revised to generally eliminate losses and to achieve the necessary margin of profit.

All of these are important improvements, but they fall far short of decentralization or a transition to the market principle. The autonomy of firms is still restricted in two crucial ways. Decisions about output mix and input mix (that is, what to produce and how to produce) still are basically subject to the material balances system, which has remained virtually unchanged, and prices still are poor guides or incentives to good decision-making because they are set administratively and are based on the traditional cost of production approach. They cannot be negotiated between firms in a way to reconcile the buyer's and seller's interests, now that both are interested in profit. For instance, if a new and more productive machine is to be introduced into the economy, its price must be set high enough to make it worthwhile for the producer to undertake its production and low enough to be advantageous for the buyer to use it. A price established from above is much less likely to meet this criterion than one set in bargaining between the two parties.

Other Proposals for Reform

As might be expected, this kind of outcome results from the conservatism of the leadership and caution based on inability to accept the conclusions of an abstract theory. There is also the obstacle of vested interests—all the planners and officials whose roles are clear under the present system, but would be radically changed by real reform. The experience of the more extensive reforms with which Czechoslovakia was experimenting before the Soviet invasion cut them short bears out the importance of this consideration.[1] The deficiencies of the moderate

midway courses are clear to the new economists and to some practical men of affairs; many would like to decentralize much further and move the price system still closer to what the modern theory of value and allocation would suggest. It seems likely that all socialist countries will gradually evolve in this direction. We can probably expect this to be a slow process in which the new economists will educate the others, and individual experiments in increased enterprise autonomy will be undertaken and then more generally adopted. Perhaps the best analogue for understanding this kind of process is our 30-year history in the United States of adopting the basic ideas of the Keynesian theory of employment discovered in the thirties as a guide for actual policy-making.

CONCLUSION

In conclusion, it must be emphasized that neither of the two basic revolutions in Communist countries—the revolution in the theory of value and allocation and the more concrete pressure for institutional change—provides a fully operational new doctrine

---

by excessive centralization, the rate of growth decelerated and, finally, became negative (in 1963). Criticism of central planning and proposals for reform became widespread. These proposals came to have three major dimensions in common: first, identification of profits as the single unifying measure of economic performance and basis to coordinate the interests of workers, managers, and consumers; second, delegation and decentralization of many economic decisions—what and how much to produce, what resource inputs and combinations to use in production, sources of supply and of markets (including foreign trade), wages and employment, distribution of profit among employees and investment, purchase of equipment, determination of sources of financing for investment—to individual enterprises; third, restriction of the role of central authorities in economic coordination to broad, overall plans and policies (for example, overall macroeconomic proportions, basic character of investment, big development programs, prices of key products, money, interest, and financial conditions, and so on) and expansion of the role of market demand and supply forces. [Cf. 89]

---

[1] Outside of Yugoslavia, which has had the longest period of experimentation with decentralization of economic management, some of the most liberal proposals for reform have been developed in Czechoslovakia. As the most industrialized of the East European countries, Czechoslovakia was probably the least suitable candidate for the forced draft application of Stalinist planning methodologies in the fifties. In the early sixties, apparently encumbered

about the allocation problem. Both are like intermediate inputs into a final resolution. Several outcomes are possible, and we already can see distinct differences in different countries. [Cf. 84]

In the incipient Czech reforms (now more or less abandoned), there seems to have been a real meeting of minds between the concrete reform advocates and the new theorists of price. The Czech reforms put real reliance on market forces and the price system to guide economic decision-making.

In other cases, theory and practice seem jarringly at odds with each other. Poland combines some of the best theoretical work in economic theory now being done in the Communist countries, together with little perceptible movement toward economic reform. In Rumania, a kind of nationalist rejection of Soviet leadership in most matters combines with considerable loyalty to the centralizing and intellectually retrograde features of the Stalinist economic model, and the climate for the new economics there is very unhospitable.

The East Germans, in their reforms, have been the most consistent implementers of an idea common to many of the reforms, that is, to move decision-making power down from the center, but to an intermediate level agency, the branch industrial association, a kind of cartel, rather than to the enterprise. Such a system could hardly permit these decision-making combines to take decisions based only on the criterion of maximizing profit and leave them free to determine price and output on their own.

Also, as will be seen in the following chapter, the experience of the Yugoslavs, who have tried to implement a kind of decentralized system controlled to a large extent by market forces, suggests some serious transitional difficulties—monopoly power, inflationary pressures, and resource misallocations. Many Western economists suspect there is great potential for these same difficulties in the kind of reforms the Hungarians have introduced and the Czechs intended.

The process of decentralization will work by adjusting the overall degree of centralization through trial and error.

As already observed, the extent and pace of trends toward decentralization in economic organization depend significantly upon political conditions. Especially when changes in economic institutions are accompanied by political reforms (for example, increasing freedom of speech, of the press, of the right to dissent from and criticize government policy), as in Czechoslovakia in 1968, economic decentralization may challenge the political status quo, indeed, the long-run survival of Communist rule itself. In these circumstances, the economic pressures for decentralization may be tempered by fears of their political consequences. The constraint which the political "superstructure" places upon economic reform is further heightened by the tendency of the Russian Communists to regard their East European neighbors as buffers between them and the West, and thus, to regard the proposals and programs of such "reform Communists" as Alexander Dubcek and his colleagues as potential threats to Russian national security.

But the movement toward more decentralization and some form of market socialism seems irreversible. There are too many forces favoring it, and too many costs and difficulties in the way of successfully implementing the main rival answer to improving resource allocation, that is, the centralized-computerized utopia. The creation of computers with sufficient capacity to handle the mass of information involved is perhaps feasible, but computers need to be told what to do with this information, and the problem of communicating with the computers and formulating programs for economic decision-making on an economy-wide scale is a formidable one. Finally, one senses that the doctrinal way is being prepared. In the mid-sixties, the East European economists increasingly came to refer to the idea that socialist planning cannot be decentralized and regulated by the market as an "ideological prejudice."

The Russian ideologues have begun to talk about the "dialectical unity of plan and market"—a formula which suggests that, for some people at least, a transition to market methods of running the economic administration is bound to come.

SUMMARY OF CHAPTER 16

1. Stalinist developmental strategies and the economic institutions supporting them have been made obsolete by the growth of the Soviet economy. With greater complexity in production possibilities and multiplication of goals and choices engendered by growth, the old ways of making choices and enforcing decisions create waste, stifle initiative, and hinder growth and efficient allocation. The Stalinist model was probably never as suited to East European conditions as it was to post-revolutionary Soviet Russia, and these countries, too, have concluded that its main features must be abandoned.

2. The resulting search for a new approach has meant a new life for economics and a willingness to consider unorthodox ideas about value and allocation. Stalinism never really had a theory that considered the system as a whole or related its operation to a normative model of allocation. Some such vision was a necessary prerequisite for practicable critiques and proposals.

3. As Soviet economists struggled to develop a general concept of effectiveness to guide decision-making, they gradually discovered the main ideas of Western microeconomics—general equilibrium, value, opportunity costs, rent, the marginal calculus, and so forth. A large number of economists in socialist countries now accept the technical elements of modern economic theory, though rejecting its institutional presuppositions.

4. The renaissance in economics also involved theorizing about growth, and in doing so opened to public discussion for the first time since the late 1920s the issue of what considerations ought to govern the choice of growth goals and the rate of investment.

5. Along with the revolution in theory came a strong pressure for institutional change and proposals for change ranging from very moderate partial reforms such as greater enterprise autonomy and decentralization to outright adoption of the market principle, though under socialist ownership. Such revisionist proposals have been adopted in varying degrees in different countries, though caution and conservatism on the part of the leaders has kept all such reforms (except in Yugoslavia, to be discussed in the next chapter) well short of the market socialism model.

17

Contemporary Communism:
The Yugoslav Version of Socialism

As mentioned in Chapter 16, the Yugoslavs were pioneers in the revision of the Stalinist model of economic organization and development. They now have had two decades of experience in trying to develop a distinctive "road to socialism," and their experience is instructive for understanding contemporary Communist attitudes about economic planning. Indeed, the Yugoslav experiment has been an inspiration (though only partly acknowledged) for revisionist policies and ideas throughout the Communist world. Even today, the degree of Yugoslav decentralization far exceeds that which has been attempted elsewhere, and the Yugoslavs now are grappling with some problems of decentralized socialism that are likely to be equally important in other versions of revisionist planning.

Before 1948, the Yugoslav leaders were the most enthusiastic emulators of the Stalinist model, both in economics and in politics, of any country in Eastern Europe. In 1948, however, the Yugoslavs successfully resisted Stalin's effort to make them totally subservient to Moscow, and, as a consequence, were read out of the international Communist movement. There is no need to summarize the issues and incidents of that conflict; the important point here is that this shattering experience forced the Yugoslavs into a fundamental reconsideration of what

socialism and socialist economic planning mean. They re-evaluated their understanding of the Soviet version of socialism and ultimately differentiated their political and economic system from what they considered to be the Soviet betrayal of a true Marxian conception of socialism. The history of the two decades since the break has been strongly influenced by the political realignment and trade reallocation necessitated by the explusion and by a subsequent partial reconciliation with the Soviet Union. It is an interesting history, and these political vacillations are important in understanding the development of the Yugoslav model. Rather than recounting them here, however, let us examine the kind of economic system the Yugoslavs profess to see as the version of socialism they have tried to institute so as to avoid the mistakes of the Soviet Union and be true to the spirit of Marxism. Because not all of this vision has been coherently implemented at one time, what will be examined in the following section will be what the Yugoslavs see at the end of their road to socialism rather than a clear, exact description of how the economy operates at each step along the way. We then will review how they have moved toward it and some of the major problems in the theory and practice of the Yugoslav economic system.

THE YUGOSLAV MODEL OF SOCIALISM

The Yugoslav vision of the ideally functioning socialist economic system contains three major ingredients: (1) social ownership of the means of production; (2) a blend of the market and central planning, with primary emphasis on the former, as a process for social coordination and control; (3) workers' self-management and control over production. Dimensions (1) and (2) are the distinguishing features of the economic theory of decentralized-market socialism, a classic version of which was described in Chapter 10. Thus, the Yugoslav version of socialism may be described as a blend of *workers' self-management* and *market socialism*. [82]

Ownership and Control of the Means of Production: Workers' Self-Management and Enterprise Autonomy

For Yugoslavs, as for all Marxist socialists, socialism means, above all, the abolition of the capitalist class and transfer of ownership of productive assets to the working class. They convinced themselves that what had gone wrong in the Soviet version of this formula was that the Russians merely had substituted the state for the capitalist class, creating thereby a centralized, bureaucratic "state capitalism," and that state ownership did not devolve any more control to the working class than did capitalism. The alternative proposed by the Yugoslavs as an answer to the problem of giving the workers real command over the means of production was to put the control of productive enterprises directly into the hands of the workers in each enterprise. Each such group of workers takes on the role of trustees, responsible for the management of their particular property on behalf of the whole working class.

The workers' stewardship is institutionalized within the enterprise through a hierarchical representation system. The members of the enterprise elect a workers' council (which may have from 15 to several hundred members) as a representative body responsible for basic issues of policy such as pricing, hiring management, disposing of the income of the enterprise, and so on. The council is too large a body for effective operation of the enterprise, however, and it delegates authority to a management board of 3 to 11 people drawn from the workers' council, much as the stockholders of a capitalist corporation delegate authority to a Board of Directors. The management board, in turn, selects the top management of the enterprise in cooperation with local government authorities and the trade association for their industry. This trusteeship is to be enforced by self-interest, and one of the most important features of worker self-management is that the workers share in the income of the enterprise as a kind of residual claimant. The enterprise must make contributions to society in the form of taxes, pay for its drain on society's resources through such returns as interest payments, set aside reserves, and so on; but the net income after all these deductions is to be shared among the workers. There is an established wage scale for the enterprises at which wages are paid during the fiscal period; this is supplemented by bonuses paid out of the net income earned by the enterprise. There also exist minimum wage scales which must be met, even if enterprise revenue is insufficient, either by drawing on enterprise reserves or from funds provided by the local government unit.

In its emphasis on workers' self-management, the Yugoslav model incorporates one important dimension of the Marxian vision of the ideally functioning socialist economy, namely the decentralized, anarcho-syndicalist theme of worker control over industry. In doing so, it is at or near the opposite end of the continuum from the Leninist variant of Marxist socialism brought to fruition under Stalin. It also incorporates what has come to be a leading dimension of revisionist Communism in general, namely, a high degree of decentralized freedom and autonomy of individual enterprises, that is, the Communist version of "free enterprise." As in the proposals of the more liberal-radical Communist reformers, enterprises are to have, within limits, the freedom and discretion to determine the levels and assortment of output, the levels and composition of resource inputs, the magnitude and form of their investment, the degrees of borrowing and lending, and the allocation of net profits. In addition (and, in this, the Yugoslav model goes beyond even the Western decentralized socialist models of the thirties), enterprises are to be free, within the constraints of market forces and some government controls, to negotiate prices, as well, for producer as well as consumer goods.

One of the principal infringements on the autonomy of individual enterprises has been a complicated fiscal system, which sets down rules allocating the revenue of each enterprise. After the payment of production expenses, the income of the firm is allocated according to a very complicated system of taxes or, in the euphemism the Yugoslavs prefer, contributions. In the early years, the amount of income so diverted was very substantial. There were large contributions for an elaborate social security program, taxes to support governmental functions, and very substantial diversions into "social investment funds"—this was, in fact, the main device used to assure a high rate of saving and investment. After these deductions were made, the remaining income was to be disposed of in accordance with the decisions of the workers. Not all of it necessarily was to be paid out as income to the workers; there were also reserves, self-investment, and social-cultural programs within the firm to be covered.

Market Socialism: The Basic
Coordinative and Regulatory
Mechanism

Briefly, the rationale of workers' self-management can be stated as a device to give workers both the opportunity and the incentive to cooperate in maximizing the income of the production collective of which they are a part. By itself, however, it provides no assurance that this incentive to maximize the income of the enterprise will not take anti-social forms of exploiting others through the transactions the firm conducts with other firms and social groups.

At this point, the question of a stimulating and regulatory mechanism arises. This is where the other pillar of the system—market socialism—enters.

THE ROLE OF THE MARKET

Subject to constraints (which, at various times, have included taxes, depreciation policy, wage-level policies, minimum-wage laws, import duties and foreign exchange controls, farm price supports, controls over interest rates, and so on), prices are to be determined by the interaction of market supply and demand forces. The role of the market is to guide the production decisions of the firm and to ensure the interest of the workers in maximizing their income is coordinated with the general social interest. Any temptation to an individual group to enrich itself at the expense of society or to use its stewardship of the property of the whole working class in an anti-social way will supposedly be controlled by the market in the same way competition is taken to be society's defense against uncoordinated and selfish decision-making on the part of individuals within a capitalist economy.

THE ROLE OF CENTRAL PLANNING

A certain amount of decision-making power is reserved to the central government to be used to correct the distortions of private decisions in this kind of coordinative process, but mostly in the form of macroeconomic measures and power to change the rules, especially about the distribution of the income of the enterprise. One important corollary of the Yugoslav model is more or less complete abandonment of central microeconomic plans and a centralized administrative machinery to see to their execution. The idea of a hierarchical administrative structure which fixes a definite plan and passes down to individual units at the bottom of the hierarchy a complex of commands to be carried out has been scrapped in the Yugoslav economy. The government still promulgates a Social Plan, and Yugoslav economists speak of their economy as a "planned economy." Their concept of planning, however, resembles more what the French call "indicative economic planning" than it does Soviet-style planning. The function of the central planners is seen as one of forecasting and guiding the development process through controls over investment and other broad, aggregate relations and variables.

In effect, the role of central planning in the Yugoslav model is to provide overall coordinative and regulatory functions. These include such decisions as the overall rate of growth, the overall levels of investment versus consumption, geographic and sectoral allocation of investment, patterns of income distribution, the general extent of foreign trade, and so forth. The instruments and institutions to be used by the central authorities to ensure compliance with their plans include monetary and fiscal controls, profits taxes, collective investment by government, price and output policies in the public utilities sector, wage arbitration, and anti-monopoly laws.

Although restricted in function, scope, and degree relative to many other contemporary variants of socialism and Communism, central planning and control in the Yugoslav model still remain powerful instruments for the pursuit of macroeconomic objectives. The combination of high taxes, expansionary monetary and credit policies, fairly tight rules governing the distribution of income by enterprises, and a high propensity to invest by enterprises themselves has maintained, indeed, extended the Titoist policy of heavy investment and industrialization. Between the mid-fifties and the early sixties, personal consumption decreased from about 54 percent to less than 50 (around 47) percent of the GNP, while gross investment exclusive of inventories increased from about 22 to 30 percent of the GNP. This would appear to demonstrate that microeconomic decentralization and workers' self-management combined with markets and central planning of a macroeconomic variety are not necessarily bars to exceptionally heavy investment.

AGRICULTURE

The Yugoslavs have also followed a distinctive policy in the agricultural sector of the economy. After the break with the Russians (though with some delay), it was decided to permit the dissolution of the collective farms, and most Yugoslav peasants simply withdrew from them. Some state farms were preserved, and there also exist various kinds of agricultural cooperatives. Today, for the most part, however, the Yugoslav agricultural sector is organized on a private peasant basis, though a restriction exists on the size of an individual holding (10 hectares). The agricultural economy, therefore, is, for the most part, not really covered by the full-blown workers' management scheme, though the peasant agricultural unit really amounts to about the same thing, except that there is no workers' council, and property is private rather than social. But the mechanism of the producer's self-interest and regulation by the market are common to both.

THE GOVERNMENTAL AND POLITICAL SYSTEM

Yugoslav ideology takes issue with the Stalinist model of Communism in regard to government and politics as well as economics, though these areas are intertwined. As seen in Chapter 15, Stalin argued that the role of the state and governmental apparatus should increase in the early stage of socialist industrialization and that the state should begin to "wither away" only when "socialism" was firmly established. According to Yugoslav

Communists, the powers and functions of the state should decrease at all stages in the process of socialist development, to be increasingly replaced by "social self-management" in factories, social and cultural organizations, trade associations, local governing bodies, and so forth.

In the governmental structure, the counterpart of the general Yugoslav economic model is local autonomy and federalism, which envisage a decentralized system of local governing units ("communes") with a high degree of local autonomy, combined into a tiered federal structure of district, Republic, and Federal units with appropriate governing functions alloted to each. At each level of government, from communes to the national assembly, the popularly elected legislative body is bicameral, one part representing the voters at large, the other, workers in "socially"-owned enterprises.

The role of the Party (Yugoslavia remains a one-party political system) in this kind of society is ambiguous, and there is often a gap between what it is supposed to do and what it actually does. But the current official conception is that the League of Communists (successor to the Communist Party) should act as an ideological force to mold "socialist consciousness," to intervene at all levels in both the political and economic spheres so as to secure the principle of socialism and assure implementation of the general idea of federalism and workers' self-management, and to hold all important administrative positions in the government and the majority of the legislative seats. The League (Party) is thus the ultimate definer and defender of socialist principles and the real power behind and within the government.

Synopsis of the Yugoslav Model: Intent and Reality

A synopsis of the Yugoslav model in terms of the definitional criteria first presented in Chapter 2 and used throughout our comparisons of economic systems is provided in Table 17-1. The various dimensions of the model, previously mentioned in one connection or another earlier in this chapter, are essentially self-explanatory.

It is fascinating to note the extent to which the Yugoslav model of the ideally functioning socialist economy incorporates, explicitly or implicitly, dimensions from several diverse economic systems. Like Stalinist Communism, the Yugoslav model is a system for heavy investment, rapid industrialization, and economic development in a relatively underdeveloped economy. Like revisionist Communism, it incorporates important elements of decentralization, enterprise autonomy, and market exchange. Like market capitalism and market socialism, it relies heavily on markets as social processes for economic coordination and social control. Like individualistic-atomistic capitalism, it incorporates private property in the agricultural sector and the pursuit of economic gain by economic units in both agriculture and industry. Like managed capitalism, it supplements market exchange by various centralizing social processes and institutions with power to control the market and/or consciously pursue social goals. Like Marxian socialism, it includes social ownership of the instruments of production (in industry), and, like the anarcho-syndicalist strain in Marxian socialism, it places heavy emphasis on workers' self-management, including cooperative-worker control of the distribution of the output created by labor. But in its combination of ingredients, related to its own political, economic, and social conditions, the Yugoslav "road to socialism" is distinct. It should be emphasized, however, that what has been described thus far is more a statement of intent than a description of how the Yugoslav economy has actually worked in practice. During the fifties and well into the sixties, the principle of enterprise autonomy and effective control by workers was not realized, in fact, nor was wholehearted reliance on market forces as a mechanism for allocation and control fully implemented.

Table 17-1.

SYNOPSIS OF THE YUGOSLAV MODEL

Definitional Criteria	Properties of the Yugoslav Model
1. Level of economic development	Developing, but relatively underdeveloped
2. Resource base	Heavily agricultural, but an exceptionally heavy investment policy
3. Ownership and control of the means of production	Dominantly "social" (government-owned, with workers' self-management) in industry, private in agriculture
4. Locus of economic power	Pluralistic: League (Party), government, Central Planning Board, managers, worker councils
5. Motivational system	Mixture of social goals (as interpreted and defined by the League) and maximization of economic gain by decentralized social and private units
6. Organization of economic power	Basically decentralized, with a limited but important (essentially macroeconomic) role for central authorities
7. Social processes	Blend of market processes, worker-democracy, bargaining, and bureaucracy
8. Distribution of income and wealth	Private property income in small-scale peasant agricultural sector; worker-determined distribution of enterprise income, subject to market valuations, government regulations of rules governing distribution of enterprise income, and government macroeconomic policies

For example, freedom of market action was much constrained by extensive price-control measures, covering a very large share of all transactions. Accompanying price control was considerable reliance on subsidies, special differential taxes, and other fiscal devices to modify the distribution of income that flowed from an irrational price system. Similarly, in foreign trade, the Yugoslavs clung to an elaborate system of controls, including licensing, differential exchange rates, foreign exchange controls, and other such interferences with free decision-making in the foreign-trade sector.

The possibility of workers' councils exercising real control over management was restricted by their inexperience and apathy, by the inherent inability of a large group to effect control via indirect means, and by the direct intervention of the League, the government, and the trade associations to which most firms belonged. The disclosures of 1966 suggest that the secret police also sometimes had an authoritative voice in enterprise decision-making. Reliance on the market to guide the allocation of resources was considerably undercut by the fact that investment resources were, to a large extent, centralized through the fiscal system, to be allocated among regions and sectors by an essentially political process and on the basis of non-economic criteria that would not have stood the market test. The political goal of developing backward regions often overrode the efficiency goal of locating factories and choosing among investment projects to achieve the maximum possible productivity. Yugoslavia is characterized by sharp differences on the level of economic development between its constituent federal republics, and one part of the political compromise holding the country together has been regional redistributions of investment resources to help the more underdeveloped areas to catch up.

These failures to fully implement workers' self-management and market socialism are the results of several forces. One factor was lack of experience and inability to achieve a fully coherent view of the economy as an integrated system. The reforms were built piecemeal, and the pieces did not always fit together. A second factor was the lack of real consensus as to the desirability of this kind of system. Yugoslavia emerged from the Stalinist period with power effectively lodged in the hands of political leaders who often were unsympathetic to this conception of socialism or who did not understand it and who had a vested interest in thwarting any transfer of decision-making power to worker groups and to market forces. Management officials often held their positions by virtue of past service rendered in the revolution rather than of having the abilities needed in the market socialism setting, and it was not easy to dislodge them. There were also strong differences of interest and opinion between regions: some wanted to retain various restrictions on the power of market forces to gain favorable treatment for their area, while others chafed under these restrictions or were damaged by them. And, in the background, there was continual vacillation in international political orientation, with resulting uncertainties and changes in the direction of trade, the volume of foreign aid, and so on.

PROGRESS TOWARD THE
FULLY DECENTRALIZED MODEL

Overall, however, there was a continuing, if sporadic, movement in the direction of the model. The chronology can be briefly summarized as follows: The law on workers' councils was passed in 1950, and, by 1952, workers' management was more or less in operation throughout the non-agricultural economy. Decollectivization came a bit later —in 1953. The intended autonomy for workers' councils was never fully realized. When the principle of workers' control was first put into force, the workers strongly tended to use it to raise their wages and to raise prices; this drew an understandable response from the government in the form of extensive price controls and elaborate rules for disposing of the income of the enterprise. Until the end of the fifties, workers' management existed, but the main features of Yugoslav economic development in this period were greatly influenced by the fact that a large share of the GNP was centralized through taxation and was employed by the central planners or central administrative agencies to maintain a high rate of investment to carry out regional development schemes. The performance of this hybrid system was fairly impressive. Given the high rate of investment, which was enabled in part by a significant volume of foreign aid from Western countries, it is not surprising that a high rate of growth was maintained, with national income growing, according to Yugoslav official figures, at something like eight to nine percent per year.

In 1960 and 1961, difficulties plagued this system. One was a poor harvest, which caused internal bottlenecks and a balance of payments problem. Secondly, emboldened by past successes, the regime relaxed somewhat the kind of controls it had employed during the fifties and took a few steps toward the decentralized economy that was its goal. The year 1961 was one of "economic reform" in which controls over the balance of payments, wages, and investments were relaxed. The reform effort of 1961 might thus be described as an attempt to withdraw somewhat the tutelage to which enterprises had been subjected and to give greater play to market forces.

The result of these developments was a

very serious inflation, which, in retrospect, is seen as the consequence of an extremely high rate of investment and of a system which permitted household money incomes to rise very rapidly. That experience quickly prompted the reinstitution of price controls and more limitations on the freedom of communal governments and enterprises to make independent investment decisions.

The debacle led to great controversy as to the cause of the problem. One group claimed the renewed push toward real autonomy for local decision-making without central direction and control naturally led to this kind of chaos. Another school of opinion maintained that the difficulty was the retention of too much control and failure to fully implement the decentralized vision. The argument of this group was that market socialism could work only if consistently put into practice and that the partial reform of 1961 left enough interference with market forces so that it could not be expected to achieve the advertised results.

The outcome of this controversy was ultimately a victory for the "liberals" and the introduction of a new round of reform measures in 1965. The proponents of market socialism were able to persuade the leaders that the only possible solution was a bold move that would go all the way in eliminating central control and making market forces really decisive. The fiscal system was radically reformed to diminish the role of government bodies as collectors of funds and ultimate authorities on investment decisions. Most investment was now to be made instead by enterprises out of their own earnings or out of borrowed resources, which they were to obtain from a reformed banking system. The banking system had previously been a centralizing device for pooling funds to be disbursed within a set of political pressures that often overrode economic considerations, but it now became much more strictly accountable for the economic viability of the projects it financed and was required to attract investment funds from enterprises and other

investors interested in returns on their investments. Whereas banks previously had often been creatures of the communal governments, they were rechartered as entities responsible to the shareholders (mostly enterprises) which established them, but with rights to operate in the whole territory of Yugoslavia. The system of subsidies, artificial price supports, and differential taxes and levies which had been necessary to keep afloat the enterprises created by ill-considered investments and decisions in the past was heavily trimmed.

Of similar and equal importance in a country as small as Yugoslavia, reforms in the foreign trade sector subjected internal firms, through the competition of foreign trade, to the efficiency standards of world industry. The *dinar* was devalued to relieve the balance of payments problem, and the ramshackle structure of interferences with foreign trade was partially dismantled. The goal was to achieve a freely convertible currency within a few years—a goal which, if reached, would make Yugoslavia unique in the socialist camp.

This short sketch can give only an overall impression of the fitful movement toward the full establishment of the market socialist model. In the mid-sixties, the reform movement had not yet won a clear victory. Effective implementation of the reforms was for some time blocked by a group associated with the secret police. An alliance of the secret police under Aleksandr Rankovic with others opposing the reform was fairly effective in slowing its progress. This group was discredited in the sensational disclosures at the Party meetings in July 1966, and the outcome of that confrontation was the purging of the Rankovic group, but it is not yet clear whether even that decisive action has cleared the way for the final movement to real autonomy for firms and full reliance on the market.

Enough has been said to make clear that it is difficult to decide conclusively the effectiveness and performance of decentralized socialism on the basis of Yugoslav experience.

The concepts of workers' self-management and market socialism have until now been more slogans than working realities. Moreover, constant tinkering makes it extremely difficult to evaluate it as a special kind of economic system. The Yugoslavs have not yet established an institutionally stable model whose performance we can evaluate. The performance of the Yugoslav economy at any given time has been as much a function of hold-over features from the previous period as of the current rules and practices. Each new wave of changes has had insufficient time to achieve any stable results before it was again changed in important ways. Nevertheless, there has been sufficient experience with a substantial degree of decentralization for some characteristic problems to have emerged and to suggest some kinds of problems that flow naturally from efforts at decentralizing a centrally planned Communist economy. It seems useful, therefore, to examine in the following section some important problems which this experience has created and which seem to be related to certain features of the Yugoslav model or, perhaps, of any decentralized socialist system.

THE YUGOSLAV MODEL AS A PROTOTYPE OF DECENTRALIZED SOCIALISM

For this purpose, let us turn to a somewhat more abstract description of the essential features of this kind of planning and this form of socialism. It will be useful to have a model of Yugoslav socialism sufficiently abstract and simple to permit comparison with other models so we can see in what essential ways it differs from such systems as the capitalist market economy or central planning. This will also serve to raise some issues which may be very important in appraising the further evolution of the revisionist systems now being established in other East European countries. If we can abstract from the Yugoslav model a kind of

logical end-point to which decentralizing reforms may be carrying these countries, this effort may foreshadow and pinpoint what are likely to be serious problems in any form of decentralized socialism. In the process, we should also attempt to compare Yugoslav socialism with the one other rather general and sophisticated theory of socialism already developed, namely, the market socialism model which emerged from the debate on the economics of socialism in the 1930s, which we earlier associated primarily with the writings of Oscar Lange. It will be interesting to see to what extent that theory can illuminate problems which the Yugoslavs are having. At the same time, the Yugoslav experiment in applied market socialism may help to settle some of the controversies that developed concerning the validity of the Lange model.

Perhaps the best way to start is to recall one of the contentions that was never quite settled: the point made by critics (such as Friedrich Hayek) that the theorists of the economics of socialism brought economic efficiency into their system at the sacrifice of much of what was considered to be socialism. The debating point was that, once socialists had agreed to depend on the market and prices to control behavior, and made profit the criterion of efficiency, there was little to distinguish market socialism from capitalism. The argument was that socialism became a kind of capitalism without the capitalists, but that, given the reliance on the market, there was no reason to expect that the performance in terms of resource allocation or social justice would be any different under this mechanism from one in which market discipline and incentives were used to enforce a stewardship role on capitalists or a class of paid managers. Both the environment and the behavior of the firm seem to be nearly the same in both situations. This debating point was never properly answered by the socialists, though it is clearly an important one. It is no doubt difficult to answer *a priori*, since the Lange model was quite schematic and did not specify all the processes by which resource allocations would be made to permit one to judge just how the outcome might differ from the market capitalist system. The Yugoslav case does offer a concrete embodiment of decentralized socialism in institutions, and the impending decentralizations in other East European countries offer concrete variant forms. It will be useful, therefore, to relate our evaluation of the Yugoslav model to this larger question.

Worker Self-Management and Decision-Making

First, let us consider whether the most distinctive feature of the Yugoslav system—workers' self-management—would alter the decision-making environment in any way that would make managers responsible to workers so that decisions about resource use would differ from those made by the managers of capitalist firms representing the owners of capital. Is their situation structured differently in any way? At first, the situations seem the same. The guiding principle of worker autonomy is to give the workers a material interest in maximizing the net revenue of the firm. When confronted with most choices, they ought to reach the same decisions as capitalist managers, since both want to choose the alternative that will maximize the revenue of the firm. There is, however, one subtle difference between the two situations, in that the capitalists are interested in maximizing the net income *after payment of wages*, whereas the workers are interested in maximizing an income concept which *includes* the remuneration for their own labor. This may have important consequences. [For a further discussion, see 90.]

In the capitalist firm, all decisions are referred to the criterion of whether a given action increases the net income (profit) of the firm. On any issue—Should a few more laborers be hired? Should more capital be employed? Should one input be substituted for another? Should the output mix or the level of output be altered?—the criterion is always whether or how much the action adds to profit. This criterion also extends to such decisions as whether part of the firm's property is to be sold off or leased, whether additonal property is to be rented, or whether new assets are to be created by borrowing.

In many ways, the workers of the worker-management model should direct their appointed managerial representatives to follow the same criterion. In deciding whether to use one input mix or another, whether to alter the output mix, change the level of output, change marketing procedures, or redesign a product, their interests will be best served by the same decision that serves the interests of capitalist owners. On one range of decisions, however—those relating to the volume of labor employed—the worker-managers will refer decisions to a different criterion if they are true to their own self-interest. It is easy to imagine situations where the workers' interest in total remuneration will lead them to reject an action that would add to the net revenue or profit of the firm.

Suppose we start with a disequilibrium situation, such that Firm *A* is producing a good that is in short supply and Firm *B* is producing a good that is in surplus. In respect to decisions about capital, the mechanism under worker self-management will act just like the capitalist mechanism. Firm *A* will try to expand its output by adding to its capacity, and, in any sort of properly functioning capital market, the marginal productivity of investment in Firm *A* will be made equal to the marginal productivity of investment in Firm *B*. In the capitalist environment, the output of Firm *A* can also be expanded by hiring workers away from Firm *B*, of course. Presumably the difference in profitability of the two firms will mean high incomes for workers in Firm *A* and low incomes for workers in Firm *B*. The workers of Firm *B* would therefore be very happy to make a move and, in that way, better their earnings. In moving toward an equilibrium, if it is to be optimal, some such shift of labor should take place along with the reallocation of capital at the margin until the marginal productivity of labor applied in Firm A is just the same as that in Firm B. This is one of the well-known conditions of Pareto optimality, as described in Chapter 4. Unless an economic system can achieve this result, it will be producing less output than its capacity.

If we now ask whether the worker-managers of Firm A, as decision-makers in the socialist context, would agree to this and make the decision to hire more laborers away from Firm B, clearly the answer is going to be "no." As long as the voting rule in the disposition of the income of the firm is that all workers will share alike in the gains, then hiring an additional worker whose marginal productivity is below the average for workers already employed and giving him the same wage as everyone else will reduce the incomes of those workers now employed in the enterprise. In refusing to expand employment, they will be doing what the ideology says they should do, namely, maximizing their incomes.

An analogous result for capital in a capitalist organized market would not occur. If the marginal productivity of capital is higher in Firm A than Firm B, the owners will attract capital from Firm B. If we ask how this paradox could exist, it comes down to the kinds of contracts involved in the two situations. The managers of capitalist Firm A can contract for additional capital at a market rate of interest and can preserve for themselves whatever return is already accruing to the capital they own. Even if they decide to obtain additional financing through the flotation of new equity instruments, such as common stock, they still can preserve the portion of their income that consists of a quasi rent. The opening of the opportunity to buy an equity share in the firm will bid up the prices of stocks, and this appreciation in the values of their old shares will capitalize whatever rents they are now earning. In the worker-management system, however, the decision rules imply no such flexibility in contractual relationships. In a sense, the

contract of the worker with his firm through membership in its workers' council is analogous to a property right. That is, his position as a present worker in the firm gives him a claim against its net earning. But the only way he can exercise this claim is by sticking with the firm and refusing to let his share of the residual be diluted by admitting outsiders.

Another way of viewing this problem is to recall Lange's idea about the parametric function of prices under market socialism. In the model of competitive capitalism, the prices of capital and labor are parametric. With regard to these alternative inputs, the firm is a price-taker rather than a price-maker, and, as noted in our discussion of Lange's model, this is essential for rational decision-making. This is not true, however, in the case of the worker-managed firm. In their most recent reforms, the Yugoslavs have moved quite close to making the price of capital a parametric price. That is, firms are going to compete against one another for loans through the banking system, and there will even be the possibility of one firm investing its income not internally, but in other firms, if the resulting return is above the internal rate of return. In its actions affecting the employment of labor, however, the worker-managed firm is a price-maker rather than a price-taker. That is, the worker-managers of the firm have an opportunity to choose the price to be placed on labor and do not have to accept it as given. As is well known, whenever the firm in the capitalist economy is cast in the role of price-maker rather than price-taker (as in the case of a monopoly), there will be an infringement of Pareto optimality.

There is nothing fundamentally insoluble in this problem; the solution obviously lies in contractual innovations. The Yugoslavs need only alter the decision rules and the voting rules for the worker-managed enterprise so that the worker can exercise his claim against the earnings of the firm and preserve any special privileges that association with that firm has in the past created for him independently of any future or current decisions about the hiring of labor. If the firm's existing workers had the kind of contracts which would enable them to retain any rents now accruing to them from special situations in the firm, they would then have every incentive to add workers in the example described earlier. As long as there is any difference between the marginal productivity of the worker in Firm *A* and the wage at which he would be willing to transfer from Firm *B*, the worker would have a motivation to move, and the total output of the economy would be increased; there would be an increment of income which could be captured by the existing workers of the enterprise.

This conception of a worker having property rights protected by contract is no doubt repugnant to socialists. On reflection, however, it seems a logical enough extension of other ideas that form the ideology of worker-managed market socialism. After all, the basic premise of the total concept is that the workers own the property, rather than letting it be held by a capitalist class; and most of the other features of Yugoslav socialism are intended to put the workers in effective and direct trusteeship of this property. Certainly, it would be better to provide a mechanism by which these property rights which may have accrued through technological change, obsolescence, and so on could be captured and enjoyed without interference with the optimal allocation of resources in the current period, rather than making the enjoyment of these property rights depend on continued frustration of Pareto optimality. It is ironic to find that a socialist-inspired economic system has gone much farther in setting up institutions to provide for mobility of capital than it has in providing for the mobility of labor, which, after all, in Marxist ideology, is deemed the sole source of value.

Monopoly Power and Price Control

A second problem that has continually arisen in Yugoslav socialism is that of the market power of a firm—monopolistic and oligopolistic behavior. This is interesting in itself, but merits careful analysis because it represents a whole class of problems in the decentralization of socialist systems. Let us begin by recalling another facet of the debate on the economics of socialism. One counter to the charge that market socialism offered no advantages over market capitalism was that market socialism would make it possible to solve the problem of monopoly. In the Lange model, one of the functions of the Central Planning Board is to set prices. It is supposed to follow basically the market rule of moving prices up or down to make supply equal to demand, but it is important that the board fixes these prices rather than leaving them to be negotiated directly between buyers and sellers. The outcome would be the same as under a market regime where competition prevails, but for cases where there are few enough firms to imply some monopoly power, the procedure would make a real difference. By making price parametric for the monopolist, this procedure removes his power to take advantage of society through raising prices. Monopolists and oligopolists become price-takers rather than price-makers, so that the allocational distortions of monopoly power are avoided. The validity of this assertion is an interesting issue, one to which we will return, but the point at hand is that the Yugoslav system does not work this way. The Yugoslav version of socialism seems to have envisaged market-negotiated prices rather than administered prices; and though there has been in practice a great deal of government price-fixing, the "progressive" attitude has always favored eliminating this feature in favor of free prices.

It is interesting to ask why. The main reason is probably that the Lange conception is not really feasible. The Yugoslav experience seems to confirm that constant price-fixing and juggling by a central planning board (CPB) is too slow and cumbersome. However, the decision in favor of market-negotiated prices unfortunately leaves the economy vulnerable to the danger of monopoly and oligopoly distortions. In following the legitimate aim of maximizing their incomes, the workers of a firm that enjoys a strong market position will be able to exploit weaker groups in society through high prices and distort the allocation of resources. How prevalent monopoly power is in the Yugoslav economy is a sensitive subject, one that is not much talked about by the Yugoslavs. There is clearly a very high degree of industrial concentration in the Yugoslav economy and numerous examples of the use of monopoly power. It has been reported, for instance, that, though there are a number of companies engaged in the retail distribution of petroleum products, they are organized as regional monopolies that agree not to interfere in each other's territories. This suggests the communal autonomy that characterizes the political and social system may serve to buttress monopoly, since political power may be used to protect "local" producers from outside competition. Also, Yugoslavia is a small country. When the technical characteristics of an industry require production on a large scale to be economical, there can

hardly be enough firms to make competition effective. It is hard to say what the most recent changes will do; in many ways they seem destined to strengthen monopolistic tendencies, since they involve consolidating the small plants that have grown up in the hothouse atmosphere of subsidized political factories and are too small to be efficient into larger combines. On the other hand, the effect of more foreign competition through a freer foreign trade system should work in the opposite direction. [86]

As to whether such anti-social use of market power might not be controlled by central price-fixing, the answer is not encouraging. Consider more closely the Lange argument outlined earlier. In that scheme, the CPB would set the price for the product, and the instruction to the manager of the monopolistic firm would be the standard "given that price, produce the amount that will maximize your profit." The possible outcome where a given product is produced by a monopolist is shown in Fig. 17.1a.

If the CPB set the price above or below P_3, there would be a difference between supply

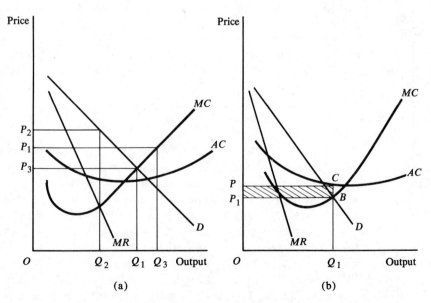

Fig. 17.1. (a) Monopoly, (b) marginal cost pricing and losses

and demand. At P_1, for example, the firm, following the rule of producing the amount that would maximize profit at that price, would supply O_3—more than consumers were willing to buy; and at a price below P_3, it would produce less than the amount consumers wanted. The argument here is along the familiar lines that profit is a maximum where marginal revenue equals marginal cost. In manipulating the price to eliminate such disequilibria, the CPB would finally settle on P_3. This is a superior outcome to what would occur in the usual model of the market capitalist economy, since it satisfies the Pareto rule that *price* $= MC$. In a market system, where the monopolist could manipulate the price at will, his interest in maximizing profit would lead him to set the price at P_2 and restrict his output to O_2. (This again is by the familiar logic of maximizing revenue by making $MC = MR$.) The argument is somewhat different in the situation represented in Figure 17.1b, since at Q_1, which is the output that CPB wants produced, where $P = MC$ and supply equals demand, the firm would be taking a loss (equal to area $PCBP_1$). The answer in the Lange proposal is that the CPB could assure such firms that, if they incurred a loss in following the rule to produce where $MC = price$, the CPB would reimburse the loss. This outcome would again be superior to the results of a purely competitive model, as noted in Chapter 10.

Some reflection, however, indicates this view overlooks some difficulties in achieving these desirable results. If the monopolist is aware that the rule followed by the CPB in its price juggling is to raise the price for any commodity in short supply and lower it for those in excess supply, he can beat the system by violating the rule that he has been told to follow. If, for instance, in Figure 17.1a, the CPB sets a price of P_1, the firm can cut its output (say, to Q_2) rather than producing the Q_3 amount the rule prescribes for that price. Its production will therefore be less than the amount people wish to buy at P_1, and the CPB, according to its rule, will raise the price.

Proceeding in this way, the monopolist can force the CPB to set the price at P_2, which is the same price a monopoly would set in a market capitalist economy. The price will maximize the income of the firm and so, presumably, the income of the firm's managers (or workers, if this is a firm with Yugoslav-style worker management).

The same general line of argument can be developed for any situation where there are few enough firms to have some degree of market power, though it would be a bit more complex than in the monopoly case just described. The situation would involve a bargaining problem, and the exact outcome would depend on the kind of bargaining strategy we might expect the firms to follow.

The conclusion is that market socialism seems to offer no special ways of eliminating monopoly problems. We should expect that all Soviet-type economies will encounter some form of this problem as they move toward decentralization and use of market methods. If the central authorities try to control this form of power through price-fixing at the center, they may find they have not really eliminated much of the burden of centralized supervision that they bore under more centralized planning. Central authorities will have to meddle in the affairs of the enterprise, and in order to do so, will need much more information about the internal affairs of the company than decentralizers realize.

Central Rules and Decentralized Decisions

This problem of compliance with the behavior rules proclaimed by the CPB is an important one and merits closer examination. Some have asked whether it is reasonable to expect that, under a decentralized form of socialism, the manager-bureaucrats (or worker-managers) would meekly follow the rules of behavior which the CPB announces. Certainly, in the centralized, Soviet-type versions of socialist planning, managers have been far from simple automata relentlessly pursuing the goals authorities have set for them. Rather, they are continually trying to deceive the superiors as to their real potential, hoping for easier plans. Once plans have been assigned them, they try to fulfill them by "simulation." They are also careful not to overfulfill plans too much, even though that would mean bonuses, since it might invite greater pressures in the next planning period.

This characteristic of enterprise managers working at cross-purposes with the central planners who are trying to maximize the national income has been a major deficiency of the command economy. The desire to eliminate it has been one of the main motivations for economic decentralization. A major notion of the newly emerging ideology of decentralized socialism is the slogan made famous by Liberman that "in principle, under socialism, what is advantageous for society should also be advantageous for the enterprise." The basic argument of the decentralizing ideology is that this principle can be validated by setting rational prices for all commodities and then releasing enterprises from detailed supervision from above and telling them to maximize their profits. Since the reward system for management would be tied to profit performance, it presumably would be in their interest to run their firms to maximize profits. Sober second thoughts suggest this idea may be hard to implement, especially regarding "rational prices." There is conjecture that, in fact, the goal of perfectly coordinating the two interests may not always be achievable. To understand the reasoning behind this conjecture, we need to examine how it is proposed that decentralized socialism might work.

In one form of the decentralized scheme, the "rational prices" are to be generated by a process like the following: The CPB would instruct enterprises to propose for themselves a plan that would maximize profits at existing prices. These plans would indicate the levels of current output they expected to achieve and the kinds of inputs they would require to carry on production at this level. When the CPB reviewed these plans, it would no doubt find many instances where the proposed output of some commodity did not match the amount demanded. Using some kind of optimizing procedure (say, a linear programming approach), the CPB would estimate a proposed adjustment of outputs and inputs that would eliminate these imbalances and would also be optimal. A key feature of the various methods for calculating this optimum plan is that they also produce a set of "shadow prices," that is estimates of true opportunity cost prices implied by the inconsistencies in the enterprise proposals and by the goals of the CPB. The CPB would then communicate these shadow prices to the enterprises and ask them to revise their plans, seeing what adjustments in inputs and outputs they would now make in the light of the new prices so as to maximize profits. Because this would be a new set of prices, the new plans would differ from the original ones but would still involve some inconsistencies in supply and demand. The CPB would then have to conduct a new round of its optimizing calculation. It is presumed that several iterations of this process would bring the enterprise plans into consistency, and into such a form that, taken altogether, they constituted an optimum economic plan for the economy as a whole. The last round of the process would have generated a final set of shadow prices, and these would be the rational prices people have in mind when they talk about letting enterprises make their own decisions. An important characteristic of this process is that the final shadow prices are such that each firm, in making all its decisions according to the criterion of which alternative is more profitable, would find itself just breaking even, making neither a profit nor a loss. The importance of this point will become obvious shortly.

The plan then would be *executed in a decentralized manner*, with the CPB announcing only the shadow prices that emerged from the process and telling the firms they should make all their own decisions with the aim of maximizing their profits at these prices. Such an economy would still be socialist, clearly enough, and also planned. In this latter respect, it would not quite fit the Yugoslav notion of a fully market-controlled economy, since prices would be set from the center. But, equally important, this would be something other than the traditional Stalinist-type command economy, in which the superior organs give the enterprise explicit and detailed instructions as to how they are to operate.

Let us now ask whether it is reasonable to expect that those in charge of the firm would be willing to play the game according to the rules specified. It is obvious that the prices which the CPB finally calculates and promulgates depend on the information which the firms have released in their proposals during the planning process. Each time the enterprise proposed a plan, it revealed something about its production possibilities. If a manager has any inkling of the whole drama in which he is playing a part, then he should recognize it may not be in his interest to propose a plan that would maximize his profits at the given prices. He will have an interest in dissimulation. It may be possible to deceive the CPB in a way that will lead it, in playing its part in the game, to generate a set of prices under which the firm can make large profits without strain. The likelihood that an enterprise will be successful in such an effort depends significantly on how important a role it plays in the production and consumption of individual commodities. In effect, this is another aspect of the monopoly problem previously described.

There is thus a real conflict between the interests of the firm trying to maximize profits and that of the CPB, which is trying to maximize some more ultimate goal on behalf of society. The implication is that it would probably take a major policing effort on the part of the CPB to ensure compliance, and that might be only partly successful. It is important to add that this situation may be no worse than that of the free market

economy of capitalism, but that is just the point. Market socialism, whether in the market-negotiated price form or the centrally fixed price form, seems to have no advantages in terms of its self-policing properties over the capitalist market system. And, indeed, it seems important that socialist economists in the Communist countries are not yet well aware that they are going to have to deal with this problem. They seem to believe a bit too naively in the virtues, which they have only recently discovered, of the market as a method of organizing the economy. Similarly, their faith in "optimal prices" as guides to rational decentralized decision-making is not supported by a fully convincing conception of how optimal prices can be generated.

Problems of Macroeconomic Balance

One of the most important problems that has plagued the Yugoslav economy is inflation. This raises the question whether economies based on decentralized models of socialism are not likely to have serious problems of macroeconomic balance. We might reasonably expect this just on *a priori* grounds. Once the power of money is restored and price movements permitted to influence allocation, there arises the possibility of inflation, balance of payments problems, and redistribution of income between groups or between consumption and investment in ways the leadership may not desire.

Under the Stalinist form of Communism described earlier, this kind of problem was not of much concern. The command system was an effective way of keeping sufficient pressure on resources so that there was no overt unemployment of resources. Resources were often used very unproductively, but everyone who wanted a job could find one, and enterprises worked as close to capacity as they desired. Actually, the problem was largely of the opposite nature—excess demand—but, though poor financial planning often meant a problem of repressed inflation, the system of physical controls made it possible even in this situation to control the allocation of real output between investment and consumption, between population groups, and so on. And the foreign trade monopoly, though it may have served poorly in optimizing the volume and composition of foreign trade, permitted Soviet planners to insulate the internal economy from world market influences. (East European countries were less successful in this regard.)

The Yugoslavs have had a persistent problem of inflation. Much of the time, it has been repressed by means of price controls, as already indicated. But whenever any attempt was made to move toward the free market model as it is supposed to work, and to loosen price controls, the result has been a new round of price rises.

This inflation can best be understood in the traditional terms of excessive aggregate demand used to explain inflationary processes in any market economy. With prices more or less free to respond to demand, then excessive aggregate demand will cause inflation. The simplest explanation of how this excessive demand arose is that the fiscal and banking system permitted too much money to flow into the hands of people willing to spend it. If we think of the usual circular flow diagram, the flow of money incomes that was generated in the production sector and flowed through the hands of various kinds of spenders to return as demand for goods was somehow augmented along the way to make it exceed the value of current output at existing prices, flowing in the opposite direction. Any leakages from this flow, as through savings, were more than balanced by other additions, as, for example, the creation of new credits. All major spending groups had very strong pressures to spend. Households, as one might expect in a low-income economy, had a very high propensity to consume. Investment spending was under the control of institutions, the motivations of which made them want to invest to the limit of the resources available to

them with no particular concern for the economic viability of the projects involved. The investment funds available to enterprises were the least important component here, but they spent all they could get because they really had nothing else they could do with it. The bulk of these funds was under the control of communal units of government, which had a more or less insatiable appetite for various kinds of social investment, such as housing and schools, and centralized investment funds, subject to intense political pressures to make resources available so that each region could fulfill its ambitious plans for development. And, finally, the government spent beyond its income. For most of these kinds of expenditure it was possible to exceed the incomes of the group involved through the creation of credit. There was a large growth of consumer credit, the banks financed deficits in government budgets, and investment expenditures were augmented out of reserves and by bank credit, often obtained under the pretense of short-term credit granted to cover working capital needs.

In addition, the composition of demand was not well matched to sectoral output capacities, so that there was great pressure on particular sectors (such as the production of investment goods and agriculture). This led to price rises in these sectors, which then spread to others through a cost-push mechanism. In addition to causing inflation domestically, this pressure also meant persistent difficulties with the balance of payments. During all this time, people would have liked to import at given prices more foreign goods than the system could pay for through its exports, and this discrepancy then had to be constrained by foreign exchange controls and a system of import licensing.

In all this, there is nothing very distinctive about the Yugoslav model. We can interpret and understand this episode in economic history in the same way we think about any market economy faced with excessive demand. Similarly, in considering how these problems could be handled, we would conclude that the remedies are essentially the same macroeconomic policy instruments as are used in our own economy—monetary policy, fiscal policy, debt management, and so forth. There are two distinctive things about the Yugoslav case, however. First, it is intriguing to see how imperfectly they apparently understood the nature of the problem and how ill prepared they were to cope with the problem because of their lack of experience. For example, the policy-makers seem to subscribe to the so-called "real-bills" doctrine— the notion that the creation of bank credit cannot generate inflationary pressure as long as loans are made only on the security of existing goods. This is a venerable, but thoroughly fallacious, doctrine, and monetary policy based on it is not going to be very helpful against inflation. An increase in the supply of money through an expansion of bank credit can (though it need not necessarily) cause an excess demand for goods at or near full employment, regardless of the "security" of the goods which "back" the loan. Similar inexperience and absence of theoretical awareness of the problems of macroeconomic balance seem to exist in all the countries now considering decentralization. This insouciance is no doubt connected with the ideological and political aspects of the matter. As socialists, the economic planners in Soviet-type countries have always thought they had little to learn from the economic theories and policies developed in the capitalist countries for dealing with problems of macroeconomic balance. That attitude has not helped them learn very quickly from their own experience. This is not surprising, considering how long it took the capitalist countries to develop and accept the theory and principles of public policy for macroeconomic stabilization. Moreover, socialists have always had a distrust of money and a distaste for financial manipulation. To the extent that they ever took much account of theoretical economic developments in the West, the thing that most struck them was precisely the growth of this kind of theory and

policy, which they always excoriated under the label of "Keynesianism" and which they have interpreted as a desperation measure to stave off the inevitable collapse of capitalism.

The second problem— the adequacy of the instruments available to the Yugoslavs and other socialist decentralizers to attain macroeconomic balance—is more an institutional one. The instruments used for macroeconomic stabilization in market economies—primarily the monetary policy of the central bank and the fiscal policy of the government—are usually strongly dependent on highly developed financial markets. Central bank policy ordinarily works through some kind of securities market, such as the government bond market. Fiscal policy involves manipulating not only the flow of state revenues and expenditures through the budget, but also the debt management activities that accompany it. The mechanisms for balancing foreign trade may involve interest rate manipulations effected through the money market. The effect of public policy in these areas is conveyed and reinforced through changes in interest rates, changes in the prices of different kinds of assets, and so on. Socialist economies thus far have not developed financial markets of this type, since, under socialism and planning, the kind of debt and equity instruments traded in such markets do not exist.

Our interest in Yugoslav policy and experience is not only for itself, but also because it may constitute some kind of blueprint for what will happen in other Communist countries as they decentralize. Certainly, one of the notable omissions in the proposed reforms is any intention to create innovations in fiscal and monetary instruments and financial markets that would give them something to manipulate in handling these macroeconomic problems.

CONCLUSION

This chapter began with the suggestion that Yugoslav ideas, to some extent, had been an inspiration for the revisionist trend in most Communist countries. The Yugoslavs have been groping somewhat in advance of the rest along a path that others now are also following. It is unlikely that we can use the Yugoslav experience as a model for a definitive assessment of the decentralized form of socialism. There are enough distinctive features in the Yugoslav situation to have led them to structure their economic institutions somewhat differently from what others will do, and the Yugoslav experience has been perturbed by enough variation and indecision in the policies followed that it probably does not constitute a test of the performance of the revisionist form of socialism now beginning to emerge. But, despite all the differences, the Yugoslav "road to socialism" marks out the general route that others will follow, and we can abstract from it certain things that seem inherent in any effort to construct a decentralized socialist economic system.

The really distinctive feature of the Yugoslav experiment—workers' management —has not been copied. It is probably the political implications of workers' management that have made other Communist countries reluctant to adopt it, but we have also shown that it has some economic drawbacks. It may veer economic decision-making away from efficient outcomes unless the contractual relationship of workers with society is permitted to become more complicated than under the simple form of workers' management set up by the Yugoslavs. These new contractual relationships can be regarded as a new kind of property right. This reminds us that the concept of property is quite a subtle one, and the socialist reluctance to accept any kind of private property claims makes the functioning of the system more clumsy than it needs to be.

Assuming decentralized forms of socialism must involve control through price and value mechanisms rather than through direct commands about resource use, the Yugoslav experience draws our attention to the dilemma in choosing between administered prices and market generated prices. To really let prices be determined by market forces confronts planners with the problem of market power and with the attendant problems of equity and efficient resource allocation found in capitalist market economies. On the other hand, it may be impossible to avoid these problems through administration of prices without imposing grave administrative interference on the system.

It will probably take some time for any decentralized socialist system to learn how to resolve the problem of macroeconomic equilibrium. When the power of money is restored and decisions are made independently by many separate groups and individuals, the danger of macroeconomic imbalance becomes real. The instruments for the attainment of macroeconomic balance are close at hand in the experience of the United States and other managed capitalist economies. If the Yugoslav economists are adaptable and flexible in building their own road to socialism in the future, as they have been in departing from the centralized Stalinist model in the past, the problems of macroeconomic imbalance generated in the process of decentralization are, in principle, soluble. Somewhat ironically, the solution lies in taking lessons on central planning from the modern, managed form of capitalism.

Finally, it is interesting to speculate on what impact revisionist modifications of the economic system may have on political and other institutions. There has been a great deal of dispute among students of the Communist societies as to whether economic liberalization necessarily also promotes the growth of political freedom and an erosion of totalitarianism. This is an unsettled question, but it is interesting that, as the most advanced of the revisionist countries, Yugoslavia seems to have experienced both simultaneously. One scholar who has followed this issue closely in Yugoslavia concludes that this is not a fortuitous combination. The issues have always been packaged in such a way that victories for economic decentralization have usually been won in coalitions with groups with an interest in promoting political change. [91]

SUMMARY OF CHAPTER 17

1. Although the Yugoslav Communists began as faithful emulators of the Stalinist model, a political conflict with the Russians led them to develop a distinctive "road to socialism." The central elements of this Yugoslav version of socialism are social ownership of the means of production, workers' self-management, and considerable reliance on the market as a coordinating mechanism.

2. In practice, Yugoslavia moved rather slowly toward this model between the early fifties and the early seventies. The experience of the Yugoslav economy in this period is useful in forecasting some of the transitional and permanent problems that socialist decentralizing reforms are likely to face.

3. In particular, the relaxation of price controls and the enhancement of the power of money caused serious inflationary problems in Yugoslavia. The failure to control inflation is explained mostly by a lack of understanding of the nature of the problem. But even with such an understanding, the Yugoslav economy did not have the instruments and institutions required to operate a macroeconomic stabilization policy; nor do other socialist societies.

4. Workers' management has succeeded but poorly in putting effective control over the operation of "their" enterprises in the hands of the workers. As in capitalist firms, real control almost inevitably ends up in the hands of the technical managerial class. But to the extent that workers' control does substitute the goal of maximizing income per worker for that of maximizing total enterprise income, the outcome of the system will be non-optimal from the point of view of allocative efficiency. This deficiency can be remedied, but only if socialist ideologues are willing to entertain more sophisticated notions of property than they have in the recent past.

5. Yugoslav experience with monopoly problems directs our attention to one of the unsettled issues of the market socialism concept we use in thinking about decentralized socialist models. No thoroughly convincing rationale has ever been offered to affirm that a central planning board in a market socialist system can eliminate monopoly behavior. There is a real motivation for enterprise management to violate the rules of the game and act in anti-social ways. The monopolizing tendencies of Yugoslav firms will no doubt appear in other decentralized socialist systems, and there seems to be no easier way for a socialist system to counter such behavior than those available in a capitalist market system.

SOURCES CITED IN PART V

70. BERGSON, ABRAM, and SIMON KUZNETS, *Economic Trends in the Soviet Union* (Cambridge: Harvard University Press, 1963).

71. CAMPBELL, ROBERT W., *Soviet Economic Power*, 2nd ed. (Boston: Houghton Mifflin Company, 1966).

72. CAMPBELL, ROBERT W., "Economic Reform in the USSR," *American Economic Review*, May 1968.

73. DOMAR, EVSEY, *Essays in the Theory of Economic Growth* (New York: Oxford University Press, 1967), Chapter 9.

74. ERLICH, ALEXANDER, *The Soviet Industrialization Debate*, 1924–1928 (Cambridge: Harvard University Press, 1960).

75. FEIWEL, GEORGE R., *New Currents in Soviet-Type Economics: A Reader* (Scranton, Pennsylvania: International Textbook Company, 1968).

76. KANTOROVICH, L. V., *The Best Use of Economic Resources* (Cambridge: Harvard University Press, 1965).

77. KANTOROVICH, L. V., *Matematicheskie Metody Organizatsii Proizvodstva*, Leningrad, 1939, available in English as "Mathematical Methods of Organizing and Planning Production," *Management Science*, July 1960.

78. KORNAI, J., "Mathematical Programming as a Tool in Drawing up the Five-Year Economic Plan," *Economics of Planning*, 1965, No. 3.

79. KYN, O., et al., "A Model for the Planning of Prices," in C. H. Feinstein, (ed.) *Socialism, Capitalism, and Economic Growth* (Cambridge: Cambridge University Press, 1967).

80. NOVOZHILOV, V. V., "Measurement of Expenditures and their Results in a Socialist Economy," in Nemchinov, V. S., *The Use of Mathematics in Economics* (Oliver and Boyd, Edinburgh and London, 1964).

81. NOVOZHILOV, V. V., "On Choosing Between Investment Projects," *International Economic Papers*, No. 6.

82. PEJOVICH, SVETOZAR, *The Market-Planned Economy of Yugoslavia* (Minneapolis: University of Minnesota Press, 1966).

83. *Political Economy: A Textbook* (Lawrence and Wishart, London, 1957).

84. PRYBYLA, JAN S., *Comparative Economic Systems* (New York: Appleton-Century-Crofts, 1969).

85. PREOBRAZHENSKY, E., *The New Economics* (Oxford: Oxford University Press, 1965).

86. RUSINOW, DENNISON, *Yugoslavia's Problems with Market Socialism*, American Universities Field Staff Reports, Southeast Europe Series, Vol. XI, No. 4, May 1965.

87. SHARPE, MYRON E. (ed.), *Planning, Profit and Incentives in the USSR*, Vol. 1, The Liberman Discussion, International Arts and Sciences Press, 1966.

88. SPULBER, NICOLAS, *Soviet Strategy for Economic Growth* (Bloomington: Indiana University Press, 1964), and a companion volume which contains translations from some of the major participants in the controversy, *Foundations of Soviet Strategy for Economic Growth*.

89. STALLER, GEORGE, "The Czechoslovak Economic Reform," *American Economic Review*, May 1968.

90. WARD, BENJAMIN, *The Socialist Economy* (New York: Random House, Inc., 1967).

91. WARD, BENJAMIN, "Economic Reform and Political Change in Yugoslavia," *American Economic Review*, May 1968.

Index

private vs. social, 95-96
social
  in capitalism, 95-96
  in decentralized socialism, 284
Countervailing power, 363-64
Creative destruction, in Schumpeterian 156, 163, 272
Creativity, human, in Marxian philosophy, 228
Credit, role of in Schumpeterian analysis, 156
Critique of the Gotha Programme (Marx), 229, 347
Crosland, C.A.R., on managed capitalism, 431-38 *passim*, 452
Cyclical economic fluctuations
  centralized socialism and, 345-46
  Keynesian theory of, 191-94
  Marxian analysis of, 122, 128, 130-32
    mature capitalism and, 140-41
  Schumpeterian analysis of, 157-61
Czarist officials, 466
Czechoslovakia
  economic reforms in, 508
  industrial output of, 493

Dahl, Robert A., 20-21, 261-63
Darwin, Charles, 104
Darwinism, social, 104
Decentralization vs. centralization, of economic power, 19-20, 506-8
Decentralized socialism
  competitive market capitalism and, 270-72
  economic decisions
    CPB vs. enterprise, 524-26
    social coordination of, 270
  Lange model of
    critique of, 290-308
    defense of, 283-90
    economic behavior under, 273-83
    organization of, 267-73
    rules in, 274-76, 300
    macroeconomic balance in, 526-28
    market equilibrium, trial and error process, 274, 277-78, 283
  as a mixed economy, 291-92
  practicability of, 293-96
  prices in, 283-84
  in Yugoslavia, 517-28
Decisions, economic, 4, 9-10, 13
  bureaucratic systems for, 21-22
  competitive market capitalism and, 61-63
  decentralized socialism and, 268-70
  democratic socialism and, 418-19
  laissez-faire capitalism and, 99

neo-Austrian view on, 238-39
power of, 17-19
resource allocation and, 499
social coordination of, 238-41
social processes and, 20-21
Stalinist communism and, 484
worker self-management and, 520-22
Democracy
  collective bargaining and, 406-7
  competitive market capitalism and, 245-46
  economic control and, 409-10
  economic planning and, 22, 250-51, 261-63
  Keynesian analysis and, 200
  managed capitalism and, 407-10
  Marxian social reform and, 149-50
  monopoly and, 91
  prospective impact on socialism, 245-63
Democratic socialism
  defined, 418-20
  income distribution in, 436-38
  laissez-faire capitalism and, 424-28
  managed capitalism and, 431-33
  Marxism and, 428-31
  social goals of, 420-24
  social ownership and, 441-45
  structure of, 423-24
Depression(s)
  in Keynesian theory, 172-73, 189, 191, 209-10
  in *laissez-faire* capitalism, 425-26
  in Marxian analysis, 131-32, 140-41, 145
  in Schumpeterian analysis, 159-60, 162
  in U.S.A. (1930s), 162, 208
Dictatorship, economic
  neo-Austrian view on, 247-48, 249-50
  socialist planning and, 251-52
Dobb, Maurice
  critique of Lange model, 290, 292, 295
  views on centralized socialism, 310, 315, 316, 320-21
    on coefficients of production, 323-25
    on plan execution, 338-39
"Dollar ballots," 45, 109-10, 408
Domar, Evsey, 182
Drewnowski, Jan, 266-67
  definition of socialism, 313
  Lange model and, 293
"Dynamic models, criterion of optimality for," 497
Dynamics, economic, in Marxian theory, 108
  in Schumpeterian theory, 153-55, 163

Economic and Philosophical Manuscripts (Marx), 218, 230
Economic development, 14-15
  in managed capitalism, 355-57
  Marxian vision of, 217-20
    Bolshevik revolution and, 461-63
Economic power, organization of, 19-20
  in managed capitalism, 361-76
  in Stalinist communism, 484
Economic reform, 10, 13
  democracy and, 255-57, 408
Economic stability. See Equilibrium, economic; Full employment equilibrium
Economic systems, 3-40
  criteria for classification, 14-23
  major types of, 23-40
Economics, as a discipline, 12-13
Education
  in democratic socialism, 438
  Soviet economic growth and, 481
Employment
  in Marxian analysis, 128
  production and, 8-9
  See also Full employment; Unemployment
Employment Act (1946), 198, 371-72, 375
Engels, Friedrich, 55, 107, 111, 150
England. See Great Britain
Enterprise(s)
  free, 50-51
  private, 86-91
    classical liberalism and, 106
    government planning and, 259
    managed capitalism and, 357
  types of, 16-17
  in Yugoslavia, 512-13, 522, 524-26
Entrepreneur, in Schumpeterian theory
  as the innovator, 156-57
  obsolescence of, 166-67
  temporary monopoly and, 163-64
Environmental pollution, 47, 96
Equality, as goal in democratic socialism, 421-23
  See also Income equality
"Equation of exchange," 6, 49
Equilibrium, economic, 5-6
  in Keynesian theory, 183-88
  in Lange model
    individual, 273-77
    market, 274, 277-81
  in managed capitalism, 411-13
  in Schumpeterian theory, 153-55, 160
Europe, Eastern
  allocational efficiency and, 487
  contemporary communism in, 491

National Unit Trust, 444-45
Nazis, fascism of, 33-34
Neo-Austrian critique of socialism, 232-63
  competitive price system and, 237-39
  democracy and, 247-63
  economic organization and, 235-36
  goals of economic planning and, 235
  political structure and, 234
  rational economic calculation and, 236-41
  responses to, 241-43
  social coordination and, 238-39
New Deal, 103, 153, 168, 173, 208
New economic policy, in U.S.S.R., 467
Novozhilov, V.V., 504

Occupations, and freedom of choice, 259-60
Oligopoly, 383-89
  in actual capitalism, 289
  corporate power and, 363
  exit and entry of business firms, 392-93
  imperfectly collusive, 389
  independent, 384-87
  perfectly collusive, 387-89
Oligopsony, 389-91
Organizational economy, 17, 18
  managed capitalism and, 364-65
Orthodox economic theory, 272, 314-15
Output
  national, 5-7, 47, 112-13
  real, 161, 164
Owen, Robert, 218, 219
Ownership
  governmental
    in centralized socialism, 313, 315
    in decentralized socialism, 268
  private vs. public, 11-12
  of property, Marxian view, 110-11, 138
  social, democratic socialist view on, 441-45

Pareto, Vilfredo, 241
Pareto optimality, 521-22
Paris commune, 223
Pay-out period, in Soviet economic planning, 501
Peasants, Russian, 466
  income distribution and, 485
  industrialization and, 468, 469, 479
Pigou, Arthur C., 188, 285
Pigou effect, 188
Plan, "physical vs. financial," 331

Plan formation, in centralized socialism
  consistency and efficiency of, 331-34
  problems of, 334-38
  revision of, 338-39
  social control and, 339-43
Planning, economic, 9
  competitive market capitalism and, 63-66
  concept of, 41-42, 49-51
  execution of, 51-53
  by government
    in democracy, 261-63
    in democratic socialism, 445-51
    individual freedoms and, 257-61
  ideal vs. actual, 42-43, 46
  indivisibilities of, 323-25
  neo-Austrian view of, 235
  Soviet principles of, 499-500
  in Stalinist communism, 479-82, 493-95
  value and allocation in, 498-99
Plant manager(s)
  in centralized socialism, 333-34
  in decentralized socialism, 298-301
  in Lange model, 275-76, 278-81
Plato, 101
Pluralism, social, and government economic planning, 263
Polanyi, Karl, 98-99
Population growth rate
  decreases in, 165
  secular stagnation and, 197-98
  Stalinist economic growth and, 481-82
Poverty, amidst "plenty," 186
Power, economic, 17-19
  See also Decisions, economic
"Power elite," 363
Power state, 102
Preobrazhensky, Eugene, 468, 469
Price(s)
  "accounting," 243, 321
  allocation of resources and, 66-69
  flexibility of, 79, 81
  Keynesian analysis of, 181-82, 187-91
  labor theory of value and, 115-16
  market system and, 21
  in oligopoly, 384-87
  parametric function of, 277-78, 298, 521
  "rational," 525
  "shadow," 525
  Soviet economic planning and, 501-2
  trial-and-error process for, 242, 243, 277-78, 283-84
  values and, 118-21, 498-99

Price control
  CPB vs. competitive market capitalism, 296-99
  in Yugoslavian socialism, 522-24
Price deflation, full employment prosperity and, 188
Price stability
  in democratic socialism, 439-40
  Keynesian analysis of, 199
Price system(s)
  autonomous, 399-400
  bargaining, 397-98, 405-7
  in centralized socialism, 314, 337-38
  governmental hierarchy, 398-99
  variety of, 380-81
Pricing decisions, in revisionist communism, 501-2
Private enterprise. See Enterprise(s), private
Product quality, competition in, 393-94
Production
  fixed coefficients of, 323-25
  Marxian historical development theory and, 135-38
  possibility frontier and, 8-9
  rules for in decentralized socialism, 275-77
  socialization of, 143-44
  See also Means of production
Profit, expected rate of
  interest rate and, 191-92
  Marxian ratios and, 113-14, 120, 130
Profit maximization
  allocational efficiency and, 71-72
  in decentralized socialism, 275-77, 281-82
  in Marxian capitalism, 115
  in monopoly, 88, 382
  in oligopoly, 388
  in Schumpeterian analysis, 163
  in Yugoslavian socialism, 520, 524-26
  See also "Rule of maximization"
Profit-investment-technology model, of capitalist growth, 127-28
Proletariat, 138-39
Proletariat revolution, 221, 222
Property
  class structure and, 138
  private, 28, 167
  See also Ownership
Prosperity, recession and, 158-59
Public services, in democratic socialism, 434-35, 437
Public utilities
  in democratic socialism, 442
  in managed capitalism, 403-4
Pump priming, government spending and, 207

Radice, Giles, 444

Railroadization, 156, 157, 160
Rankovic, Aleksandr, 518
Rational economic calculation
competitive market capitalism and, 245
neo-Austrian critique of, 236-40
Ratios. *See* Marxian ratios
"Real balance effect." *See* Pigou effect
Recession, 158-59
Research, scientific, and Soviet economic growth, 479
Resource allocation, 4-9, 44
in competitive market capitalism, 66-72, 94-96
in decentralized socialism, 275-77, 281, 283-85
in democratic socialism, 434-36
in Keynesian analysis, 173-74, 201-2
in managed capitalism, 410-11
in Marxian analysis, 114-15, 121, 224-25
monopoly and, 87-88, 142
in revisionist communism, 498-506
in Schumpeterian economics, 153-55
in Stalinist communism, 486-89
See also Allocational efficiency
Resource market, in competitive market capitalism, 62, 67-70
Resources, scarcity of, 3-7 *passim*, 237, 498-99
Revenue, as an economic variable, 47
Revolution, 43
in communist countries, 464, 465, 466, 467
in Leninist theory, 221, 463-64
in Marxism, 107-8, 150, 221-22
in U.S.S.R., 461-67
Ricardo, David, 197
Road to Reaction (Finer), 256
Road to Serfdom (Hayek), 211
Robbins, Lionel, 237, 240
Roosevelt, Franklin D., 173
Rostow, W.W., 14
Routinization, in Stalinist economic growth, 480-81
"Rule of maximization," 64, 72
Russia. *See* Bolshevik revolution; Union of Soviet Socialist Republics

Saint Simon, 218, 219
Sales promotion, 393-94
Sales tax, 53
Samuelson, Paul A., 174
Sargent, J.R., 449
Saving vs. consumption, in competitive market capitalism, 85-86
Saving-investment market, 77-79

Keynesian analysis of, 177, 179-80, 185-86
capital accumulation and, 182-83
Soviet economic growth and, 479-80
Say's Law, 345
Scandinavia
changes in capitalism, 353
economists of, 42
Schumpeter, Joseph A., 50, 152, 233
views on
Keynesian economics, 194
Lange model, 290-91, 293-94, 295
Marxian philosophy, 134
socialism and democracy, 253-55
Schumpeterian analysis of capitalism, 20, 54
cyclical fluctuations in, 157-61
approximations in, 157-60
defined, 152-53
economic development in, 155-61
economic growth in, 155, 161
entrepreneur in, 156-57, 166
future of, 162, 165-66, 169-70
innovation in, 155-61
past performance of, 161-65
Second Treatise on Government (Locke), 28
Secular stagnation, capitalist
Keynesian views on, 194-97
Keynesian vs. Schumpeterian theories of, 164-65
Sherman Act (1890), 376
Simons, Henry, 50-51
Slogans, and Soviet economic planning, 480
Smith, Adam, 174
views on
businessmen, 104, 106
consumption, 63
division of labor, 84
laissez-faire, 102
state government, 99, 105
See also "Invisible hand theory"
Smith, Henry, 421
Smithies, Arthur, 50
Social control, 20-21, 51-53, 64-66
Social costs, 47
in capitalism, 95-96
in decentralized socialism, 284
Social processes
in decentralized socialism, 270-71
in managed capitalism
bargaining, 404-7
bureaucracy, 400-404
democracy, 407-10
price systems, 380-400
Social reform
Marxian theory of, 149-50

Schumpeterian analysis of, 161-62
U.S. microeconomic strategy and, 374
Socialism
centralized vs. decentralized, 264-67, 300-304, 314-17
compared to
capitalism, 23-28, 353-54
decentralized socialism, 315-16
democracy, 253-57
Stalinist communism, 486
economic laws of, 476-77
Keynesian views on, 209-11
Marxian version of
basic concept in, 222-24, 315
full employment stability and, 227-28
income distribution and, 225-27
perfection of, 218-19
resource allocation in, 224-25
means and ends of, 248-49
mixed economies and, 246-47
planning in, 55
dictatorship and, 251-52
individual economic freedoms and, 247-51
transformation of
from capitalism, 139, 146-47, 169, 220-22, 430-31
to communism, 463-67
See also Centralized socialism; Decentralized socialism; Democratic socialism; Marxism; Neo-Austrian critique of socialism; Yugoslavian socialism
Socio-capitalism, 31, 55-56
South America, 7
Spencer, Herbert, 100, 104
Stabilization, economic, in competitive market capitalism, 76-83
See also Full employment equilibrium
Stalin
death of, 491
slogan of, 480
steel and, 484
See also Communism, Stalinist
State, "withering away of," 27, 228
State and Revolution, The, (Lenin), 464
State monopoly, democratic socialist view of, 442-43
Statists, 419
Steel, in Soviet economic planning, 484, 488
Strachey, John, 425, 430
Strakhovka, 342
Streeten, Paul, 210n
Success indicators
in Libermanism, 506-7

in Soviet economic planning, 502
in Stalinist communism, 580, 494-95
Sumner, William Graham, 104
Supply and demand, 6
in competitive market capitalism, 65-70
saving-investment market and, 77-79
inflation and, 189-91
Marxian analysis and, 117-18
material balance and, 500-501
monopoly and, 87-90
value and, 498-99
Surplus, economic
in centralized socialism, 325-30
economic fluctuations and, 130-32
in Middle Ages, 101
surplus value and, 347-48
Surplus value
Marxian theory of, 117-18, 119, 122, 125-26, 429-30
Schumpeterian analysis of, 154
Sweden, full employment in, 449
Sweezy, Paul, 215, 290, 292, 310, 315, 316, 317, 338
Switzerland, 20

Tariff(s), American, 50
Tawney, R.H., 428
on industrial organization, 452
Taxation
in democratic socialism, 437-39
of non-marketable goods, 95
See also Sales tax
Taylor, Fred M., 242
Technology
economic growth and, 198
in capitalism, 84, 86
in Stalinist communism, 479
future of capitalism, and, 165
in managed capitalism, 355-57
in Soviet economic planning, 501
in underdeveloped countries, 481
Television market, allocation of resources and, 69-70, 73
Theory of Economic Development (Schumpeter), 153
Tinbergen, Jan, 42, 45n
Tomsky, M.P., 467
Totalitarianism, 31-35, 252
Trotsky, Leon, 221, 465, 468
Tuna, American tariff on, 50

Ulyanov, Vladimir I. See Lenin, V.I.

Underdeveloped countries, modernization of, 480-81

Underdeveloped economies, 35, 221, 311-14
Unemployment
in centralized socialism, 345
inflation and, 189-90
Keynesian analysis of, 183-203
Marxian vs. Schumpeterian theories on, 162
"open" vs. "disguised," 5
production and, 8-9
Union of Soviet Socialist Republics, 234
Bolshevik revolution in, 220, 256, 461-67
economic growth in, 7, 11
gross national product of, 493
industrialization in, 311
population in, 481
reforms in enterprises of, 507-8
See also Administration
United Kingdom, democratic socialism in, 434-35
See also Great Britain
United States, 56, 61, 100, 353
future of capitalism and, 162
labor unions in, 454
managed capitalism and, 353-417
Marxian monopoly theory and, 143
"new economics" of the 1960s, 373
private vs. public ownership in, 11-12, 16, 18, 20
Utopia, in Marxian ideal communism, 228-30
Utopian socialism, 218-19

Value
allocation and in revisionist communism, 498-505
converted into prices via Marxian ratios, 118-20
of the marginal product (VMP), 72-73, 74n, 122
See also Labor theory of value
"Variable capital," 112
Variables, economic, 46-47
continuity vs. discontinuity of, 323-24
endogenous, 48
Viner, Jacob, 105

Wage(s)
in centralized socialism, 348
differentials, in decentralized socialism, 285-86, 303-4
flexibility vs. fiscal policy, 188
Keynesian analysis of, 175, 176, 181-82, 187-89

Marxian theory of, 122-25, 128
in mature capitalism, 146
price rigidity and, 174
"Wage-slave," 110, 145, 218
Walras, Leon, 153
War communism, in Russia, 465-67
Wealth, in ideal communism, 228-30
Wealth effect, in competitive market capitalism, 83
Wealth of Nations (Smith), 106
Webb, Beatrice, 418
Webb, Sydney, 418, 419
Weimar government, 190
Welfare economics (theoretical), 50
Welfare state, 11, 102
managed capitalism and, 377
Western economies, value theory of, 502, 503
What is to be done? (Lenin), 463
Wooton, Barbara, economic planning and, 257-61
Work vs. leisure, 85
Worker self-management, 512-13, 517, 520-22
Worker(s)
alienation of, 217-18, 223, 228
in ideal communism, 230
in market capitalism, 428-29
in mature capitalism, 144-47
in Stalinist communism, 484
See also Exploitation; Labor
Workers' councils, in Yugoslavia, 512, 516, 517
Workers' Party, German, 225
Worker-state ownership, 222-23, 225, 230
Working day, Marxian, 125-26
World War I, 164
World War II, 208

Yugoslavia
Communist revisionism in, 460
"depoliticalization of the economy" in, 484
Yugoslavian socialism
central planning and, 513-14, 520-22, 524-26
compared to other economies, 515-16
decentralization in, 517-27
Lange model and, 519-20, 522-23
macroeconomic balance and, 526-28
market socialism and, 513, 517, 522-24, 526
monopoly and, 522-24
price control and, 522-24
worker self-management in, 512-13, 517, 520-22